D1719535

The European Commission's Jurisdiction to Scrutinise Mergers

EUROPEAN MONOGRAPHS

Editor-in-Chief Prof. Dr. K.J.M. Mortelmans

In this series *European Monographs*, this book *The European Commission's Jurisdiction to Scrutinise Mergers* is the updated sixteenth title.

The titles published in this series are listed at the end of this volume.

EUROPEAN MONOGRAPHS

The European Commission's Jurisdiction to Scrutinise Mergers

Second edition

Morten P. Broberg

KLUWER LAW INTERNATIONAL

THE HAGUE / LONDON / NEW YORK

Published by:
Kluwer Law International
P.O. Box 85889, 2508 CN The Hague, The Netherlands
sales@kluwerlaw.com
http://www.kluwerlaw.com

Sold and Distributed in North, Central and South America by:
Aspen Publishers, Inc.
7201 McKinney Circle
Frederick, MD 21704
USA

Sold and Distributed in Scandinavia by:
Djøf Publishing
Lyngbyvej 17
DK 2100 Copenhagen
Denmark

Sold and Distributed in all other countries by:
Turpin Distribution Services Limited
Blackhorse Road
Letchworth
Herts SG6 1HN
United Kingdom

A CIP Catalogue record for this book is available from the Library of Congress

Printed on acid-free paper.

Typeset by *Steve Lambley Information Design*, The Hague.

ISBN 90-411-1804-7
© 2003 Kluwer Law International

PREFACE TO THE SECOND EDITION

The first edition of this work was finished in the autumn of 1997 and published in April 1998, meaning that it was possible to take into account the first revision of the Merger Regulation. Much to my joy the work sold very well and therefore early in 2000 I agreed with Kluwer Law International to prepare a second edition. This has proved to be a much more extensive task than I had imagined and so I have more than once had to ask Kluwer to extend the submission deadline. Fortunately Kluwer proved to be very obliging to my tedious requests. Final completion of the second edition awaited the Commission's publication of its proposal for a revised Merger Regulation. The proposal was published on 11 December 2002 and – much to my surprise – both the turnover thresholds defining Community dimension and the rules on calculating the relevant turnover have been left almost untouched. With regard to jurisdiction the Commission instead proposes to amend (or 'fine-tune' as they put it) the referral mechanisms between the Commission and the Member States. I have been assured that I may now safely rule out the possibility that the definition of Community dimension will be changed as part of this revision. As it is moreover likely that the revised Regulation will not be adopted until the end of 2003 (and apply as of 1 May 2004) and as I cannot continue to postpone completion of the second edition for all eternity, I have decided to complete the work on the second edition now. I will, however, outline the extent to which any foreseeable amendments may have an impact on my examination. According to the Commission's proposal, the original Merger Regulation (Regulation 4064/89) and the amending regulation (Regulation 1310/97) will be recast into a new EC Merger Regulation. This together with the amendments now proposed by the Commission will mean that the numbering of the subarticles (and possibly also of some articles) will change. Since the numbering in the finally adopted version is likely to differ from the numbering found in the Commission's proposal, this work will be based on references made to the regulations presently in force (i.e. Regulations 4064/89 and 1310/97).

The second edition is first of all an updated version of the first edition. Apart from taking into account the revised notices, I have gone through the excessive number of cases issued since the first edition. Moreover, as far as possible I have updated the references to the legal doctrine and references to the EURO have replaced references to the ECU.[1] In addition to this 'normal revision', I have also tried to orient the second edition more towards the needs of practitioners. One reason for this is simply that since publishing the first edition I have gained practical experience, *inter alia* from work in private practice. This experience has given me a better understanding of the problems that a practitioner is faced with. For instance, I am now much more appreciative of the great advantages of the one-stop-shop principle.

Also during my work on the second edition I have drawn on the assistance of a number of people. In particular I should like to mention *Ms Anny Tubbs* and *Mr Niels Fenger*, both of the EFTA Surveillance Authority, *Dr Søren Schønberg*, formerly in the cabinet of Advocate General Francis Jacobs at the European Court of Justice and now an official of the European Commission and *Dr Ole Spiermann* of the University of Copenhagen. The views expressed, as well as all errors and omissions, remain my own.

This work was originally written as a Ph.D. thesis under the supervision of *Professor, dr.jur. Mogens Koktvedgaard*. Working with a true master has been a great privilege which I continue to cherish and benefit from. To him I dedicate this work with great affection and thanks.

Copenhagen March 2003
Morten P. Broberg

---

[1] For the sake of convenience all references to ECU have been changed to references to EURO (converted on a one-to-one basis).

PREFACE TO THE FIRST EDITION

This book is based on my Ph.D. thesis on the European Commission's jurisdiction to control mergers. Writing this thesis has been far from a solitary process. On the contrary, throughout the writing I have been in contact with legal practitioners, academics, government officials and many others. The help which many of them provided me with has been essential for the successful completion of my thesis.

I would have liked to have mentioned each and every of those who so unselfishly helped me in my work, but the number of people who helped me is so large that this is simply impossible. I must therefore limit myself to simply expressing my sincere thanks to them all. Some have, however, helped me to such an extent that failing to mention them here would be truly unjust.

The first person whom I must mention is my old friend, good colleague and fierce critic, *Mr. Niels Fenger* who read every piece of my thesis at the drafting stage. Many of my ideas have been tested on him. And many ideas have not passed this test.

It will be no surprise that several functionnaires in the European Commission provided essential help and support in my work. Special mention must go to the former director of DG IV's library, *Mr. Hans Witt*. Also, I must mention *Mr. Luc Norro* who was a perfect conseiller while I was a stagiaire in DG IV in 1992-93. Many people from the Commission's Merger Task Force have helped me on numerous occasions. Particular mention must go to *Mr. José Chantre* who on several occasions took time to provide me with comments and advice.

I spent the first year working on the thesis as a visiting research scholar at Université Robert Schuman, Centre d'Etudes Internationales et Européennes, in Strasbourg, where *Professor Vlad Constantinesco* was my hospitable and generous host. In Strasbourg, *Professor Robert Kovar* kindly took time to read and discuss drafts of my work. I am most grateful for this.

Following my year in Strasbourg, I spent my second year at the Max-Planck-Institut für ausländisches und internationales Patent-, Urheber und Wettbewerbsrecht in Munich where *Dr. Annette Kur* was my hospitable and generous host.

In Munich, I had numerous interesting discussions which greatly benefited my work with other scholars at the Institute. Particular mention must, however, go to *Dr. Andreas Heinemann* of both the Max-Planck-Institute and the University of Munich.

The third and last year, I spent at the University of Copenhagen. Throughout the work on my thesis, I have benefited from the enduring support and excellent advice provided by my supervisor, *Professor, dr.jur. Mogens Koktvedgaard*. From the very beginning until the very end of my work, Professor Koktvedgaard has provided an unbelievable number of comments and insights. Moreover, Professor Koktvedgaard has continuously provided me with invaluable support in my work. It will be no surprise to learn that I enjoyed my work under his supervision enormously, and I feel very grateful to him for the generous help which I received throughout my three years as a research fellow at the University of Copenhagen. And which I continue to receive.

The thesis will be examined by a distinguished Committee of Examiners consisting of the committee chairman, *Adj. Professor, Former President of the European Court of Justice, jur.dr. h.c. Ole Due*, University of Copenhagen together with *Professor, dr.jur. Jens Fejø*, Copenhagen Business School and *Professor, jur.dr. Ulf Bernitz*, Stockholm University. I am of course both honoured and delighted that these highly distinguished authorities have agreed to examine my thesis.

Lastly, I am indebted to *Det Finneske Legat* for sponsoring parts of the costs associated with the publication of the thesis and to Kluwer Law International which agreed to publish the thesis in their European Monographs Series.

Needless to say, I alone shall be held responsible for any remaining errors and inadequacies in the work.

Copenhagen, October 1997
Morten P. Broberg

CONTENTS

Preface to the Second Edition v

Preface to the First Edition vii

1. INTRODUCTION 1

1. Control of Concentrations and the World of Politics 1

2. The Scope of the Merger Regulation 3

3. One-Stop-Shop 6
   3.1. The main rule 6
   3.2. The exceptions 8
   3.3. The relationship between the one-stop-shop and the Community
        dimension 13

4. The Thresholds 14

5. Basic Overview of the Merger Regulation Procedure 19

6. This Work 20
   6.1. The subject matter 20
   6.2. Structure 21
   6.3. Cut-off date for the work 21

2. THE UNDERTAKINGS CONCERNED 22

1. Introduction 22

2. The General Definition 24
   2.1. 'The direct participants' 24
   2.2. The two-thirds threshold and the undertakings concerned 26
   2.3. Individuals and families as undertakings concerned 28

3. Joint Bidding and Full-Function Joint Ventures 30
   3.1. Introduction 30
   3.2. Setting up a full-function joint venture 31
   3.3. Joint Acquisition of Control 34
        3.3.1. Introduction 34
        3.3.2. Direct and indirect joint acquisition of control 34
        3.3.3. Acquisition of control by an independent joint venture 37

3.3.4. Consequences of the distinction between bid vehicles and
    independent joint ventures 38
3.4. Acquisition of joint control in order to split assets immediately 40

4. Taking Over a Part Only 42
4.1. Introduction 42
4.2. Definition of a 'part' 44
4.3. Going from joint to sole control 46
4.4. Reductions or increases in the number of parents of a joint venture 48
4.5. Replacing one shareholder with another in a joint venture 50
4.6. Dividing jointly controlled assets 52
4.7. Asset swaps 54
4.8. Demergers 55
4.9. Applying Article 5(2) to the creation of a joint venture 57
4.10. The *British Airways/Dan Air* case 58
    4.10.1. Introduction 58
    4.10.2. Background 59
    4.10.3. The judgment of the Court of First Instance 60
    4.10.4. Article 5(2) and Dan Air 61
    4.10.5. Minimising the damage 63
4.11. Staggered transactions 65
    4.11.1. Introduction 65
    4.11.2. What transactions are covered? 68
    4.11.3. When are the parties to a transaction 'the same' ? 71
    4.11.4. Creeping acquisitions 73
    4.11.5. How is the two-year time limit calculated? 74
    4.11.6. When must the Commission examine the transactions? 75

3. THE GROUP **77**

1. Introduction 77
2. The Notion of Control 79
2.1. Introduction 79
2.2. Actual versus formal control 80
2.3. Direct and indirect control 83
2.4. The point in time when control must exist 84
2.5. The four criteria in Article 5(4)(b) 88
    2.5.1. Introduction 88
    2.5.2. Owns more than half the capital or business assets 88
    2.5.3. Has the power to exercise more than half the voting rights 89

2.5.4. Has the power to appoint the majority of the board (etc.) of the undertaking 99

2.5.5. Has the right to manage the undertakings' affairs. 103

2.6. Networks of undertakings 106

3. The Related Undertakings 110

3.1. Introduction 110

3.2. Subsidiaries 110

3.3. Parent undertakings 111

3.4. Sister-undertakings 114

3.5. Group-members have joint control over an undertaking 115

3.6. Undertakings concerned have joint control over a third undertaking ... 117

3.7. The Commission's approach to joint control 120

3.7.1. Introduction 120

3.7.2. The undertaking concerned is under joint control 120

3.7.3. The undertakings concerned have joint control within the meaning of Article 3(3) 122

3.7.4. The undertaking concerned has joint control together with a third undertaking 124

3.7.5. Final comment 126

3.8. Agents 127

3.9. Public undertakings 128

4. THE BASIC RULES 135

1. Introduction 135

2. Preceding Financial Year 135

2.1. The main rule 135

2.2. Taking new but unaudited figures into account 136

2.3. Acquisitions and divestitures completed since the preceding financial year 138

2.4. Financial year of more/less than 12 months duration 142

2.5. Accounts which do not follow the EC standards 144

2.6. No reliable accounts available 145

3. Ordinary Activities 146

3.1. The main rule 146

3.2. Extraordinary items 147

3.3. State aid 149

4. Taxes and Sales Rebates 151

5. Conversion into Euros 154

6. Intragroup Sales 156
    6.1. Introduction 156
    6.2. Sales between the undertakings concerned 156
    6.3. Joint ventures and intra-group sales 159
        6.3.1. Joint venture is not part of the group 159
        6.3.2. Joint venture is part of the group 159
        6.3.3. Joint control only together with a third party 161
    6.4. Selling off a part and intra-group sales 163

5. GEOGRAPHIC ALLOCATION OF TURNOVER 165

1. Introduction 165
2. The Relevant Sale 167
    2.1. Sale out of the group 167
    2.2. Sales through agents 168
3. Tangible Products 169
    3.1. Place of purchaser, place of delivery 169
    3.2. Place where the product is used 171
    3.3. Three guiding rules 172
    3.4. Sale of rights to tangible products 174
4. Services 175
    4.1. The main rule 175
    4.2. Transport and courier services 177
        4.2.1. Transport of goods 177
        4.2.2. Transport of persons 179
    4.3. Telecoms 183
    4.4. Banking and insurance 186
    4.5. Radio and television 186
    4.6. The Internet 187
5. Changes in the Community Territory 189

6. THE FINANCIAL SECTOR 192

1. Introduction 192
2. Credit Institutions and Other Financial Institutions 193
    2.1. Background 193
    2.2. The definition of 'credit institutions and other financial institutions' ... 196
    2.3. Banking income under the Merger Regulation 199
    2.4. Geographic allocation of banking income 200

3. Insurance Undertakings 201
   3.1. Introduction 201
   3.2. Definition of an insurance undertaking 202
   3.3. Gross premiums written 204
       3.3.1. Introduction 204
       3.3.2. Amounts received and receivable 204
       3.3.3. Contracts issued by or on behalf of the insurance undertakings ... 205
       3.3.4. Outgoing reinsurance premiums 205
       3.3.5. Taxes and parafiscal contributions or levies 206
       3.3.6. Premiums from the reserves for reimbursement in life
              insurance 207
   3.4. The definition of 'residence' in Article 5(3)(b) 209
       3.4.1. Introduction 209
       3.4.2. Residence explained 210
       3.4.3. Applying the residence criterion 211

4. Mixed Groups 213
   4.1. Introduction 213
   4.2. Article 5 and mixed groups 213
   4.3. Holding securities on a temporary basis (Article 3(5)(a) of the
        Merger Regulation) 215
   4.4. The Commission's approach 217
       4.4.1. The *AG/Amev* case 217
       4.4.2. The *Midland Bank* case 219
   4.5. Evaluating the mixed groups rule 221

7. THE EEA AGREEMENT **223**

1. Background 223

2. The Basic Rules in the EEA Competition-enforcing System 225
   2.1. Two enforcement bodies 225
   2.2. Co-operation between the European Commission and the ESA 227
   2.3. Judicial review 227

3. Jurisdiction 229
   3.1. Introduction 229
   3.2. EEA dimension? 231
   3.3. EFTA dimension 232
   3.4. Allocation of jurisdiction 234
       3.4.1. The main rule 234
       3.4.2. Referral from the Commission to a Member State 235

3.4.3. Referral from a Member State to the Commission 238
3.4.4. Consequences of splitting the EEA into two separate areas 239
3.5. Co-operation in the field of concentrations 241

4. Final Comment 243

8. FORUM SHOPPING UNDER THE MERGER REGULATION 245

1. Introduction 245
2. A Brief Outline of the Jurisdictional Rules 246
3. Giving the Concentration a Community Dimension 248
3.1. Introduction 248
3.2. Making an acquisition through a joint venture................................ 249
3.3. Escaping the two-thirds rule by including an extra undertaking
concerned 253
3.4. Acquisition of sole control over previously reduced or enlarged
companies 254
3.5. Splitting one transaction or joining more transactions 256
3.6. Other possibilities.. 258

9. THE REAL COMMUNITY DIMENSION 260

1. Introduction 260
2. The Turnover Thresholds and Real Community Dimension 260
2.1. 'Real Community dimension' 260
2.2. The external limit of the Merger Regulation 261
2.2.1. Before the Gencor judgment 261
2.2.2. The Gencor judgment by the Court of First Instance 266
2.2.3. Has the Commission duly observed the Regulation's limits?....... 271
2.2.4. Conclusion on the extraterritorial reach 275
2.3. The internal limit of the Merger Regulation 276
2.3.1. Member State control or Community control? 276
2.4. Concentrations with a real Community dimension that escape the
thresholds 282
2.5. Conclusion on whether the turnover thresholds provide a suitable
definition of 'real Community dimension'?...................................... 283
3. Is it Possible to Improve The Regulation's Definition of Community
Dimension? 285
3.1. Introduction 285
3.2. The problem in the present definition 285

3.3. Solutions 287
    3.3.1. Introduction 287
    3.3.2. Market shares 288
    3.3.3. Size of transaction 291
    3.3.4. Refining the present system 293
3.4. Recommendations for improving the delimitation of jurisdiction 295
4. Final Comments 296

Annex 1. Council Regulation (EEC) No 4064/89 of 21 December 1989
    on the control of concentrations between undertakings with subsequent
    amendments 299
Annex 2. Commission Regulation (EC) No 447/98 of 1 March 1998
    on the notifications, time limits and hearings provided for in Council
    Regulation (EEC) No 4064/89 on the control of concentrations
    between undertakings 327
Annex 3. Commission Notice on calculation of turnover under Council
    Regulation (EEC) No 4064/89 on the control of concentrations
    between undertakings 351
Annex 4. Commission Notice on the concept of undertakings concerned
    under Council Regulation (EEC) No 4064/89 on the control of
    concentrations between undertakings 373
Bibliography 393
Table of Cases 413
    Commission decisions in merger cases 413
    Commission decisions in antitrust cases 430
    Decisions by the European Court of Justice and by the Court of
    First Instance 430
    Judgments and decisions by national courts and authorities and by the
    Permanent Court of International Justice 432
Index 435

1. INTRODUCTION

1. CONTROL OF CONCENTRATIONS AND THE WORLD OF POLITICS

The present work is about jurisdiction over concentrations in the European Community. To be more precise, it is about the European Commission's jurisdiction to vet concentrations under the EC Merger Regulation. Before embarking on an examination of the legal technicalities of this matter, I will, however, briefly account for the place which concentration control occupies in the world of politics.

It is often said that an efficient economy presupposes efficient competition. Efficient competition, it is said, presupposes that competition law is not entangled in the mesh of industrial policy. While these views probably hold a lot of truth, they are at the same time much too simplistic. Hence, in my view, competition policy forms a part of industrial policy. To undo the connection between the two would be an impossible task.

Among the different fields of competition policy, control of mergers is probably the most politically sensitive one. Massive lay-offs, substantial new investments and national pride are only a few of those politically important buttons which large mergers may easily hit. Politicians are well aware of this and even the strongest advocates of competition may be swayed by the political prospects of the creation of a national champion. Seeing the American antitrust enforcers blocking the merger between Boeing and McDonnel Douglas in the United States seemed an extremely remote possibility even if it had been clear that the concentration would lead to a significant decrease in competition in the aeroplane market.[1]

The power to allow or prohibit concentrations is something that politicians value. To surrender this power to someone else is, therefore, not an easy task. The EC Treaty does not vest in the Commission the power to vet mergers, but in the early

---

[1] *See* Guy de Jonquières, 'Storm over the Atlantic – The challenge by the EU competition commissioner to Boeing's merger plans may spark a row with the US', *Financial Times*, Thursday 22 May 1997, p. 13 and Michael Skapinker, 'Boeing merger: EU sets out objections', *Financial Times*, Friday 23 May 1997, p. 6.

seventies the Commission asked the Member States to provide it with specific powers to control concentrations.[2] Considering the political importance attached to such control it was not surprising that the Member States did not exactly jump at this offer. Instead, the negotiations soon developed into a protracted trench warfare in which both sides bitterly fought to capture or keep as much jurisdiction as possible. This situation could have persisted until today had the Court of Justice not issued its decision in the *Philip Morris/Rothmans case*[3] in 1987 which extended the Commission's powers to vet mergers under the Treaty's antitrust provisions. The judgment caused a change in the Member States' attitude, and, in 1989, the Council finally adopted the Merger Regulation.[4] Even after the adoption of the Regulation, however, the political sensitivity surrounding the subject became apparent when the Regulation was to be revised. Thus, the 1993 revision, provided for in the Regulation itself, had to be suspended, but eventually in April 1997 the Commission was successful in getting a revision through the Council.[5] The second

---

[2] This was *inter alia* caused by the so-called *Continental Can judgment*; Case 6/72, *Europemballage and Continental Can Co.* v. *Commission*, [1973] ECR 215.

[3] Cases 142 and 156/84, *B.A.T. and R.J. Reynolds* v. *Commission*, [1987] ECR 4487.

[4] Council Regulation (EEC) No. 4064/89 of 21 December 1989 on the control of concentrations between undertakings, published in OJ L 395, 30.12.1989, corrigendum OJ L 257, 21.9.1990. The Merger Regulation has been called 'the single most important addition to European competition law since its inception', cf. David J. Gerber, *Law and Competition in Twentieth Century Europe – Protecting Prometheus*, Clarendon Press, Oxford 1998. Fine historical expositions of the birth of the Regulation are provided in Stephen Woolcock, *European Mergers: National or Community Controls?*, Royal Institute of International Affairs, Discussion Paper No. 15, London 1989, at pp. 2-3 and 12-13, D.G. Goyder, *EC Competition Law*, 3rd ed., Oxford University Press, Oxford 1998, pp. 379-385 and in Pierre Bos, Jules Stuyck, and Peter Wytinck, *Concentration Control in the European Economic Community*, Graham & Trotman Ltd., London 1992, pp. 119-122.

[5] At the time of the adoption, it was the general view that the 1997 amendment would only lead to a very limited expansion of the Commission's jurisdiction, cf. for instance *Butterworths Merger Control Review*, Vol. 6, No. 3, June 1997, p. 9. Even the Commission was aware of this as is clear from its XXVIIIth Report on Competition Policy 1998, Luxembourg 1999, where at p. 63 it explains that '[t]he supplementary turnover thresholds … appear to be having the expected effect. Fourteen cases in all of this type were notified in the year, amounting to six per cent of all cases notified. This is broadly in line with the Commission's estimates'. Nevertheless, in the *2001 Green Paper on the review of Council Regulation (EEC) 4064/89*, COM(2001) 745 final of 11.12.2001, at para. 24, the Commission observes that in 2000 only 20 cases were notified under the additional set of thresholds in Art. 1(3). This made up only some 5% of all notifications made. In Annex 1 to the *2001 Green Paper on the*

revision, that is going on at the time of writing, proves that the division of jurisdiction remains high on the agenda. This time the Commission's attempts to broaden its powers were stunted by the efforts of the Member States reinforced by the Commission's remarkable defeats in three merger cases before the Court of First Instance.[6] Nevertheless, in the longer term it is probably reasonable to expect that the Commission will resume its pressure for an expansion of its jurisdiction until the point where virtually all major mergers must be notified in Brussels.[7]

2. THE SCOPE OF THE MERGER REGULATION

The long gestation period of the Regulation was in particular due to diverging views on the scope of the Merger Regulation. Some Member States, among whom France figured most prominently, feared that to give the Commission powers to investigate and possibly prohibit (or significantly modify) concentrations on competition grounds could run counter to their industrial policy. At the same time, Germany in particular feared that the Commission would evaluate concentrations on the basis of broad industrial policy criteria as opposed to narrow competition-based criteria. The conclusion for both France and Germany (and other Member States) was that it would not be wise to surrender jurisdiction to vet concentrations; if jurisdiction had to be surrendered they would try to limit this as much as possible. The consequence was that the definition of the Regulation's scope

---

review of the Merger Regulation the Commission at para. 61 concludes that 'Article 1(3) in its current form has not been effective in removing the multiple filing problem'. As is clear from the preceding example, at the time of the adoption of the supplementary thresholds both the Commission and external observers were acutely aware of their limited scope. The conclusion in the Green Paper should therefore not come as a surprise.

6   Case T-5/02 (and Case T-80/02) *Tetra Laval* v. *Commission*, judgment of 25 October 2002, Case T-310/01 (and Case T-77/02), *Schneider Electric* v. *Commission*, judgment of 22 October 2002 and Case T-342/99, *Airtours* v. *Commission*, judgment of 6 June 2002.

7   *See* likewise Werner Kleinmann, 'Die Umsatzschwellen für Zusammenschlüsse von gemeinschaftsweiter Bedeutung in der Europäischen Fusionskontrolle und ihre Revision', *Wirtschaftsrecht und Wirtschaftspolitik*, vol. 150, Wettbewerbspolitik im Spannungsfeld nationaler und internationaler Kartellrechtsordnungen, 1997, pp. 131-141 at pp. 140-141.

became instrumental in obtaining the necessary unanimous support in the Council of Ministers.[8]

It is rather obvious that Community legislation on concentrations must be based on two distinct tests. Firstly, the operation to be examined must bring about a structural change (*i.e.* it must constitute a concentration)[9] and secondly, this change must have such characteristics that it should be handled by the Community (*i.e.* it must produce effects at Community level). This two-step test is apparent from the very first proposal for a Merger Regulation, but even though the concept of 'concentration' underwent changes between the first proposal and the finally adopted Regulation,[10] these changes are insignificant when compared with the changes simultaneously made to the concept of 'Community dimension'. One may reasonably assume that this is a clear reflection of the considerable importance which has been attached to the scope of the Regulation.

The first Merger Regulation proposal copied the qualitative definition of Community dimension applied in Articles 81 and 82, *i.e.* the operation had to 'affect trade between Member States', but this requirement was combined with a fairly low turnover threshold and a market share threshold.[11] In contrast, the eventual definition was based on three turnover thresholds relating to the size of the parties

---

[8]   P. Bos *et al*, *supra* note 4 at pp 18-26, and S. Woolcock, *supra* note 4 at pp. 20-31 show the differing views of the Member States regarding the relationship between competition policy and industrial policy. *See* also Sir Leon Brittan, speech to the Friedrich-Ebert-Stiftung, entitled *European Policy on Competition*, Bonn, 25 June 1992, at pp. 7-9 and Claus-Dieter Ehlermann, 'In Brüssel gibt es keine industripolitischen Intrigen, sondern nur andere Auffassungen vom Wettbewerb', *Handelsblatt* 25 November 1992.

[9]   The term 'concentration' covers a range of structural changes. Acquisitions and joint ventures are the most common forms of concentrations whereas true mergers are much more rare. Nevertheless, the terms 'merger' and 'concentration' are frequently used interchangeably *vis-à-vis* the Merger Regulation. This is also the case in this work.

[10]   Compare, for example, Art. 3 of the Merger Regulation with Art. 2 of Proposal for a Regulation (EEC) of the Council on the control of concentrations between undertakings, OJ 1973 C92/1.

[11]   *See* Proposal for a Regulation, *supra* note 10, Art. 1(1)(1) ('... in so far as the concentration may affect trade between Member States.') and Art. 1(2) (the aggregate turnover of the participating undertakings had to exceed 200 million units of account and the goods and services concerned by the concentration had to account for at least 25% of the market in at least one Member State).

and was thus purely quantitative. In the 1997 revision of the Regulation, an extra set of thresholds was added, but these new thresholds, too, are purely quantitative.[12] The quantitative thresholds were chosen in order to provide a clear and easily applicable dividing line between Community jurisdiction and Member State jurisdiction.[13] Thus, Sir Leon Brittan, Commissioner for competition at the time the Regulation was adopted, characterised the turnover thresholds as 'in some ways a blunt and even arbitrary instrument' which 'has the great merit of clarity'. He added that the thresholds bring about a 'clear division of tasks' which means that 'there will be no scope for argument about jurisdiction between the Commission and Member States'.[14] It is clear that the thresholds constitute a compromise between two objectives. On the one hand they are intended to reflect effects on a Community level which essentially means cross-border effects in the Community.[15] On the other hand they are also intended to be readily understandable and easy to apply in the real world.[16] In other words, when applying a teleological

---

12 Essentially, Ernst Niederleithinger's prognosis that the original thresholds would not survive until the end of this decade, therefore, was correct, *see* 'Vier Prognosen zur europäischen Fusionskontrolle' in *Festschrift für Karlheinz Quack sum 65. Geburtstag am 3. Januar 1991*, (Harm Peter Westermann and Wolfgang Rosener, eds.), Walter de Gruyter, Berlin 1991 at p. 647.

13 Based upon a survey amongst undertakings that have been engaged in multiple filings, the Commission has observed that: 'Advantage of the turnover-based test was seen in the fact that turnover figures are mostly readily available or can be compiled with reasonable effort from accounting material', cf. *2001 Green Paper on the review of the Merger Regulation*, *supra* note 5, Annex 1, para. 185.

14 Sir Leon, *Competition Policy and Merger Control in the Single European Market*, Grotius Publications Ltd., Cambridge 1991, p. 53 and the same in his speech *European Policy on Competition*, *supra* note 6, p. 11. *See* also Sir Leon's speech *The Future of EC Competition Policy* given to the Centre of European Policy Studies in Brussels on 7 December 1992, at pp. 2-3. (A summary of the last-mentioned speech may be found in press release IP(92)1009 of 8 December 1992. This press release has been reproduced in [1993] 4 C.M.L.R. 7 pp. Sir Leon Brittan in 2000, when looking back at the events leading up to the adoption of the Merger Regulation, has described the decision on the actual size of the thresholds as 'horse trading', cf. Sir Leon Brittan, 'The Early Days of EC Merger Control' in *EC Merger Control: Ten Years On*, International Bar Association, London 2000, p. 2.

15 *See* for instance, Commission Notice on calculation of turnover under Council Regulation (EEC) No 4064/89 of 21 December 1989 on the control of concentrations between undertakings, OJ C66/25 of 2.3.1998, at para. 3.

16 *See* for instance para. 5 of the Commission Notice on calculation of turnover, *supra* note 15. Bill Allan and Christopher Bright, 'Restrictive Agreements and Dominant Positions: Opening New Markets' in *Business Law in the European Economic Area* (Christopher Bright, ed.),

interpretation to the Regulation, it is necessary at one and the same time to aim at legal certainty and clarity as well as at catching concentrations with cross-border effects in the Community.[17]

3. ONE-STOP-SHOP

3.1. The main rule

The importance attached to the definition of the scope of the Merger Regulation was enhanced by the fact that the Regulation was intended to institute a so-called one-stop-shop principle in the Community.[18] The idea was that *either* a concentration's effects on competition would be examined at the Community level, *i.e.* by the Commission, *or* they would be examined at the Member State level, *i.e.* by the national competition authorities. In other words, the Regulation was to institute a system of mutually exclusive jurisdictions.[19]

Before the Merger Regulation entered into force, a concentration could be examined under two different sets of competition rules in the Community: The Commission could examine some concentrations under Articles 81 and 82 of the EC

Clarendon Press, Oxford 1994 at p. 103 find that '[u]nder the EC Merger Control Regulation jurisdictional analysis has assumed a degree of importance that few could have anticipated' and add that the Commission's case law in respect of jurisdiction 'has the hallmarks of an inefficient law: one which leads to repeated calls for decisions to clarify or interpret'.

[17] See also John Bridgeman, 'Commission and National Competence – a Debate', *International Business Lawyer*, March 1998, vol. 26, No. 3, pp. 102-103 at 103.

[18] As will be shown below in chapter 7, this principle has since been extended to include those EFTA States which are parties to the EEA Agreement.

[19] Indeed, Frédéric Jenny, 'Competition and Competition Policy', in *Singular Europe – Economy and Polity of the European Community after 1992*, (Willam James Adams, ed.), The University of Michigan Press, Ann Arbor 1992 at p. 89 notes that '[a] similar system could be used in the future for anti-competitive practices and, thereby, solve some of the problems [relating to] Articles [81] and [82].' For the same view, *see* Claus-Dieter Ehlermann, 'Anwendung des Gemeinschaftsrechts durch Behörden und Gerichte der Mitgliedstaaten' in *Gedächtnisschrift für Eberhard Grabitz*, (Albrecht Randelzhofer, Rupert Scholz and Dieter Wilke, eds.), C.H. Beck'sche Verlagsbuchhandlung, München 1995, pp. 45-55 at p. 49 and Pierre-Vincent Bos, 'Towards a Clear Distribution of Competence between EC and National Competition Authorities', *European Competition Law Review*, Vol. 16, No. 7, 1995, pp. 410-416.

Treaty and in addition some of the Member States had introduced concentration control giving their national competition authorities the power to vet concentrations. In other words, a concentration could be scrutinised both under the antitrust provisions in the EC Treaty and under Member State competition laws.

As noted above, the introduction of the Merger Regulation meant that a system of reciprocal exclusivity was introduced. Thus, in principle, if a transaction comes within the scope of the Regulation, neither Articles 81 and 82 nor Member State competition rules apply.

The basic workings of this system is that where an operation constitutes a 'concentration' and where this concentration has a 'Community dimension' the Regulation applies. If an operation does not constitute a concentration it might come within the scope of Articles 81-82 and/or the Member States' competition rules. As a clear main rule, an operation which does constitute a concentration will not be examined under Articles 81-82 regardless of whether it has a Community dimension.[20] Thus, in principle, a concentration without a Community dimension will not be examined under Articles 81-82 nor can it be examined under the Merger Regulation. Such an operation, therefore, falls within the exclusive ambit of the Member State competition authorities. A table may illustrate the main principles regarding the division of jurisdiction:

Table 1: The Division of Jurisdiction

	+ Concentration	– Concentration
+ Community dimension	Merger Regulation	Articles 81 + 82 National Competition Authorities
– Community dimension	National Competition Authorities	Articles 81 + 82 National Competition Authorities

---

[20] Cf. Comments to Art. 22 in 'Notes on Council Regulation (EEC) 4064/89' published in Supplement 2/90 of the Bulletin of the European Communities at pp 23-26 and Sir Leon Brittan, *European Competition Policy – Keeping the Playing-Field Level*, Brassey London and CEPS Brussels, 1992 at p. 94. Apparently neither Art. 81 nor Art. 82 has been applied to a concentration since the Merger Regulation entered into force. A number of cases have, however, included both co-operative and concentrative aspects meaning that the Regulation applied to the concentrative aspects and Art. 81 to the co-operative.

Table 1 shows that – as a main rule – a concentration will either be examined only at the national or only at the Community level. In contrast, operations which do not qualify as concentrations, may be examined at both levels.

3.2. The exceptions

The tough negotiations leading up to the introduction of the Merger Regulation, however, necessitated compromises *vis-à-vis* the one-stop-shop principle. In the first place, the Germans insisted that concentrations meeting the thresholds should be referable to the national authorities and such provision was included in Article 9 which is often referred to as the German clause.[21] Equally, the high thresholds

---

[21] The number of Art. 9 referrals has become very substantial. A complete list of referrals may be found on the Commission's homepage at www.europa.eu.int/comm/competition/mergers/cases/index/by_dec_type_art_9.html. Examples of the application of Art. 9 are *Steetley/Tarmac*, Case IV/M180, decision of 12 February 1992, *Holdercim/Cedest*, Case IV/M460, decision of 6 July 1994, *McCormick/CPC/Rabobank/Ostmann*, Case IV/M330, decision of 29 October 1993, *Gehe/Lloyds Chemists*, Case IV/M716, decision of 22 March 1996, *RWE/Thyssengas*, Case IV/M713, decision of 25 November 1996, *Bayernwerk/Isarwerk*, Case IV/M808, decision of 25 November 1996, *Rheinmetall/British Aerospace/STN Atlas*, Case IV/M894, decision of 24 April 1997 (together with IP/97/353), *Sehb/Viag/PE/BEWAG*, Case IV/M932, decision of 25 July 1997 (together with IP/97/693), *Promodes/Casino*, Case IV/M991, decision of 30 October 1997, *Compagnie Nationale de Navigation/Sogelfa-CIM*, Case IV/M1021, decision of 1 December 1997, *Lafarge/Redland*, Case IV/M1030, decision of 16 December 1997, *Promodes/S21/Gruppo GS*, Case IV/M1086, decision of 10 March 1998, *Vendex/KBB*, Case IV/M1060, decision of 26 May 1998, *Krauss-Maffei/Wegmann*, Case IV/M1153, decision of 19 June 1998, *Alliance Unichem/Unifarma*, Case IV/M1220, decision of 23 July 1998, *Rabobank/Beeck/Homann*, Case IV/M1461, 6 April 1999 (*see* press release IP/99/220 of 9 April 1999), *CSME/MSCA/ROCK*, Case IV/M1522, decision of 11 June 1999 (*see* press release IP/99/391 of 14 June 1999), *Cruzcampo/Heineken*, Case IV/M1555, decision of 17 August 1999 (*see* press release IP/99/632), *Totalfina/Elf Aquitaine*, Case IV/M1628, decision of 5 October 1999, *Anglo American/Tarmac*, Case COMP/M1779, decision of 13 January 2000 (*see* press release IP/00/32 of 13 January 2000), *Interbrew/Bass*, Case COMP/M2044, decision of 22 August 2000, *Enel/FT/Wind/Infostrada*, Case COMP/M2216, decision of 19 January 2001, *Metsäliitto Osuuskunta/Vapo Oy/JV*, Case COMP/M2234, decision of 8 February 2001 (*see* also IP/01/183), *Govia/Connex South Central*, Case COMP/M2446, decision of 20 July 2001, *Shell/DEA*, Case COMP/M2389, decision of 23 August 2001, *BP/E.ON*, Case COMP/M2533, decision of 6 September 2001, *Haniel/Fels*, Case COMP/M2495, decision of 17 October 2001, *Haniel/Ytong*, Case COMP/M2568, decision of 30 November 2001, *SEB/Moulinex*, Case COMP/M2621, decision of 8 January 2002, *see* also Case T-119/02, *Royal Philips Electronics* v. *Commission*, judgment

led other Member States to argue that the national authorities should be able to refer concentrations without a Community dimension to the Commission for examination. The main proponent was the Netherlands, which in 1989, like the other smaller Member States, lacked concentration control schemes. The rule in Article 22(3) was, therefore originally, referred to as the Dutch clause.[22] Over the years

---

of 3 April 2003), *Nehlsen/Rethmann/SWB/Bremerhavener Entsorgungsgesellschaft*, Case COMP/M2760, decision of 30 May 2002, *Sogecable/Canalsatélite Digital/Via Digital*, Case COMP/M2845, decision of 14 August 2002 (the last-mentioned case is the subject of annulment proceedings before the Court of First Instance, cf. Case T-346/02, *Cableuropa and others* v. *Commission* and Case T-347/02, *Aunacable and others* v. *Commission*). In *Leroy Merlin/Brico*, Case COMP/M2898, decisions of 11, 12 and 13 December 2002 (together with IP/02/1881) the Commission for the first time decided to refer a case to the competition authorities in three Member States. It is within the Commission's discretion, however, to decide whether or not to make a referral, and in a number of cases it has refused to refer, *see Varta/Bosch* Case IV/M012, decision of 31 July 1991 published in [1991] OJ L320/26, *Alcatel/ AEG Kabel* Case IV/M165, decision of 18 December 1991, *Mannesmann/Hoesch*, Case IV/ M222, decision of 12 November 1992, published in [1993] OJ L114/34, *Siemens/Philips Kabel*, Case IV/M238, decision of 8 January 1993 (the parties decided to withdraw the case after it had been referred to a second phase investigation), *MSG Media Service*, Case IV/ M469, decision of 9 November 1994, [1994] OJ L364/1, *ABB/Daimler-Benz*, Case IV/M580, decision of 17 October 1995, [1997] OJ L11/1, *Bertelsmann/Kirch/Premiere*, Case IV/M993, decision of 27 May 1998, [1999] OJ L53/1, *Deutsche Telekom/BetaResearch*, Case IV/M1027, decision of 27 May 1998, [1999] OJ L53/31, *Exxon/Mobil*, Case IV/M1383, decision of 29 September 1999, *Carnival Corporation/P&O Princess*, Case COMP/M2706, decision of 24 July 2002, *EDF/London Electricity*, Case IV/M1346, decision of 27 January 1999 and *Nabisco/United Biscuits*, Case COMP/M1920, decision of 5 May 2000. A substantial number of these refusals concern requests from the German authorities. *See* also Simon Hirsbrunner, 'Referral of Mergers in E.C. Merger Control', *European Competition Law Review*, 1999, pp. 372-378 (with further references). To complete the picture, it may be added that the Commission in the 'Proposal for a Council Regulation on the control of concentrations between undertakings', COM(2002) 711 final, OJ C20/4 of 28.1.2003, proposes a number of amendments to the workings of Art. 9.

22   The Dutch clause was amended in 1997 in order to allow for two or more Member States to make a joint referral to the Commission. Art. 22(4) provides that the referral to the Commission 'must be made within one month at most of the date on which the concentration was made known to the Member State or to all Member States making a joint request or effected.' Moreover, only concentrations which affect trade between Member States may be reviewed by the Commission and the Commission is only entitled to ascertain whether the concentration 'creates or strengthens a dominant position as a result of which effective competition would be significantly impeded within the territory of the Member State or States making the joint request' (Art. 22(3)). *See* for example *British Airways/Dan Air*, Case IV/

the German clause has gained in importance whereas the fact that virtually all Member States now have their own merger control schemes has meant that the importance of the Dutch clause has faded considerably. The two provisions, however, play central roles in the Commission's 2002 proposal for an amended Merger Regulation.[23] The idea basically is that merger cases shall be referred more extensively than at present thereby leading to a better allocation of cases than that which is achieved by the turnover thresholds.[24] One of the novelties is that the notifying parties shall be given an exclusive right of initiative (to request a referral of their case) at the pre-notification stage whilst the Commission and the Member States may only request the referral after the concentration has been notified.[25]

M278, decision of 17 February 1993, *RTL/Veronica/Endemol*, Case IV/M553, decision of 20 September 1995, [1996] OJ L134/32, *Kesko/Tuko*, Case IV/M784, decision of 20 November 1996 (*see* Commission press release IP/96/1044), [1997] OJ L110/53, *Toys R Us/ Blokker*, Case IV/M890, decision of 26 June 1997 (*see* Commission press release IP/97/ 570), [1998] OJ L316/1, *Promatech/Sulzer Textil*, Case COMP/M2698, decision of 24 July 2002 and *GEES/Unison*, Case COMP/M2738, decision of 17 April 2002.

23 *2002 proposal for a new regulation, supra* note 21.

24 The intention is that '[c]oncentrations with a significant cross-border effect' shall be examined by the Commission, cf. recital 13 of the *2002 proposal for a new regulation, supra* note 21. This concept arouses associations to that of the effects on trade between Member States contained in Arts 81 and 82 of the Treaty, although the Commission in the just quoted recital 13 is careful to emphasise that the two concepts are distinct.

25 Fine-tuning of the referral system is in line with the ideas put forward by Ulf Böge, president of the German Bundeskartellamt, cf. 'Dovetailing Cooperation, Dividing Competence – a Member State's View of Merger Control in Europe' in *EC Merger Control: Ten Years On*, International Bar Association, London 2000. The Commission's proposal however includes features which are likely to give rise to controversy. This is not least so with regard to the idea that a request for referral to the Commission by a minimum of three Member States shall give the former exclusive jurisdiction to vet the concentration irrespective of whether other Member States do not wish to relinquish their jurisdiction. Another problem that may give rise to second thoughts amongst the Member States is that the proposal may mean that a large part of the cases referred from the Commission to the Member States will concern harmless (non-controversial) but time consuming joint ventures. In contrast a large proportion of the cases referred to the Commission is likely to concern cases that cannot be classified as harmless. in other words, streamlining the referral system may mean that the Member States are exchanging important cases for unimportant ones.

Other factors than the referral possibilities contribute to the undermining of the one-stop-shop principle.[26] Thus, Article 296(1)(b) of the Treaty provides that '[a]ny Member State may take such measures as it considers necessary for the protection of the essential interests of its security which are connected with the production of or trade in arms, munitions and war material'.[27] This essentially means that mergers in the armament industry may be fully or partly exempted from the application of the Merger Regulation.[28] Moreover, the Merger Regulation in Article 5(2)(2)

---

26 Until the expiration of the ECSC-Treaty on 23 July 2002, the most important exception to the one-stop-shop principle was that concentrations, which were partly covered by the provisions in the ECSC-Treaty, might have to undergo examinations both under the EC Merger Regulation and under Article 66 of the ECSC-Treaty. *See* as examples *Usinor/ASD*, Case IV/M073, decision of 29 April 1991, *PowerGen/NRG Energy/Morrison Knudsen/Mibrag*, Case IV/M402, decision of 27 June 1994, *British Steel/Svensk Stål/NSD*, Case IV/M503, decision of 7 November 1994, *Mannesmann/Vallourec*, Case IV/M906, decision of 3 June 1997, *ELG Haniel/Jewometaal*, Case IV/M849, decision of 25 November 1996, *Klöckner/ODS*, Case IV/M918, decision of 5 August 1997, *Krupp Hoesch/Thyssen*, Case IV/M925, decision of 11 August 1997, *Klöckner/Comercial de Laminados*, Case IV/M971, decision of 26 August 1997, *Thyssen/Krupp*, Case IV/M1080, decision of 2 June 1998, *USINOR/FINARVEDI*, Case IV/M1203, decision of 29 September 1998, *Usinor/Cockerill Sambre*, Case IV/M1329, decision of 4 February 1999, *British Steel/Hoogovens*, Case IV/M1595, decision of 15 July 1999, *Balli/Klockner*, Case COMP/M2481, decision of 31 September 2001, *BHF/Billiton*, Case COMP/M2413, decision of 14 June 2001, *Salzgitter/Mannesmann-Röhrenwerke*, Case COMP/M2045, decision of 5 September 2000, *Endesa/CDF/SNET*, Case COMP/M2281, decision of 17 April 2001 and *Usinor/Arbed/Aceralia*, Case COMP/M2382, decision of 19 July 2001. But note also *Krupp (II)*, Case IV/M740, decision of 2 May 1996, para. 4, which shows the difference between the two schemes in respect of the notion of a concentration. However following the expiry of the ECSC Treaty, concentrations in the coal and steel sector are now subject to the normal rules on allocation of competencies between the Commission and Member States (*i.e.* Merger Regulation vs. national rules).

27 The provision continues: 'such measures shall not adversely affect the conditions of competition in the common market regarding products which are not intended for specifically military purposes.' *See* also Art. 298 of the Treaty.

28 *See* recital 28 of the Regulation and *British Aerospace/VSEL*, Case IV/M528, decision of 24 November 1994, *GEC/VSEL*, Case IV/M529, decision of 7 December 1994, *GEC/Thomson-CSF (II)*, Case IV/M724, decision of 15 May 1996, *British Aerospace/Lagardère*, Case IV/M820, decision of 23 September 1996, *GEC Marconi/Alenia*, Case IV/M1258, decision of 28 August 1998, *Matra/Aérospatiale*, Case IV/M1309, decision of 28 April 1999, *British Aerospace/GEC Marconi*, Case IV/M1438, decision of 25 June 1999, *Saab/Celsius,* Case COMP/M1797, decision of 4 February 2000, European Commission, *XXIIIrd Report on Competition Policy 1993*, Luxembourg 1994 at paras. 324-326 and the same in *XXIVth Report on Competition Policy 1994*, Luxembourg 1995 at para. 336.

provides a special rule to prevent circumvention. Essentially, this rule provides that transactions between the same purchaser and seller within a period of two years must be viewed together. The consequence is that the transactions may have a Community dimension when viewed together even though they do not have such a dimension when viewed separately. In some cases, this may mean that the parties must first notify a transaction with Member State authorities, but later a second transaction between the same parties brings both the first and the second transaction within the scope of the Merger Regulation so that they must be notified with the Commission.[29] Somewhat similarly, an operation may include two or more concentrations some of which possess a Community dimension and some which do not possess such a dimension. This may particularly be the case where the parent companies decide to break up a joint venture.[30] Likewise, it may be that an operation includes both concentrative aspects which must be vetted under the Merger Regulation and co-operative aspects which must be vetted under Article 81.[31] In order to complete the picture, one must also note that Article 21(3) of the Regulation permits the Member States to 'protect the legitimate interests other than those taken into consideration by this Regulation'. This is, however, not an exception to the one-stop-shop principle since it is only meant to apply outside the field of competition.[32]

---

[29] *See* further chapter 2 at section 4.11 concerning Art. 5(2)(2). In the *2002 proposal for a new regulation, supra* note 21, the Commission proposes a minor change of Art. 5(2)(2).

[30] *Solvay-Laporte/Interox*, Case IV/M197, decision of 30 April 1992 is an example of this.

[31] *See* in particular Commission Notice on the concept of full-function joint ventures under Council Regulation (EEC) 4064/89 on the control of concentrations between undertakings, OJ C66/1 of 02.03.1998 at para. 16. Following the 1997 amendment such cases are entirely dealt with within the Merger Regulation's procedural framework, *see* further C.J. Cook and C.S. Kerse, *E.C. Merger Control*, 3rd ed., Sweet & Maxwell, London 2000, pp. 48-52.

[32] *See IBM France/CGI*, Case IV/M336, decision of 19 May 1993, *Newspaper Publishing*, Case IV/M423, decision of 14 March 1994, *Lyonnaise des Eaux/Northumbrian Water*, Case IV/M567, decision of 21 December 1995 (regarding the last-mentioned case, *see* also Commission decision of 29 March 1995 entitled: 'Regulation (EEC) 4064/89: Application by the United Kingdom of 6.3.95 for the recognition of a legitimate interest under Article 21(3) re certain provisions of the Water Industry Act 1991 (as amended by the Competition and Services (Utilities) Act 1992)'), *Sun Alliance/Royal Insurance*, Case IV/M759, decision of 18 June 1996, *EDF/South Western Electricity*, Case IV/M1606, decision of 19 July 1999, *Electrabel/Epon*, Case IV/M1803, decision of 7 February 2000, European Commission, *XXIIIrd Report on Competition Policy 1993, supra* note 28 at para. 321, the same in *XXIVth Report on Competition Policy 1994, supra* note 28 at para. 335 and the same in *XXVth*

3.3. The relationship between the one-stop-shop and the Community dimension

The Merger Regulation's one-stop-shop principle and its notion of a Community dimension form two important and closely related pillars of the Regulation. In this work, I will focus on the notion of a Community dimension, but my findings will clearly also be important *vis-à-vis* the one-stop-shop principle. This is not least due to the fact that the Regulation has achieved such popularity in the business community that undertakings are often prepared to go to great length in order to come within the Regulation's scope (*i.e.* to make the transaction a 'concentration' with a 'Community dimension') and thereby escape the scope of the national merger control schemes, due to the one-stop-shop principle. One reason probably is that having to go through only one examination rather than several means a significant reduction of uncertainty.

Report on Competition Policy 1995, Luxembourg 1996 at para. 145. According to Barry E. Hawk and Henry L. Huser, *European Community Merger Control: A Practitioner's Guide*, Kluwer Law International, the Hague 1996 at p. 114 Member States may apply their foreign investments regulations without needing to seek the Commission's approval that the case comes within Art. 21(3) of the Regulation, provided, of course, that the application thereof is made with due regard to other parts of Community law, including the principle of non-discrimination between Community nationals. *See* also Stephen Weatherill, 'The Changing Law and Practice of UK and EEC Merger Control', *Oxford Journal of Legal Studies*, Vol. 11, Winter 1991, pp. 520-544 at p. 532 with note 72 and Sideek Mohamed, 'National Interests Limiting E.U. Cross-Border Bank Mergers', *European Competition Law Review*, 2000 pp. 248-257. In *EDF/London Electricity*, *supra* note 21 (*see* also *XXIXth Report on Competition Policy 1999*, Brussels 2000, p. 76), *Secil/Holderbank/Cimpor(Art. 21)*, Case COMP/ M2171, decision of 22 November 2000 (*see* also IP/00/1338) and *BSCH/A. Champalimaud*, Case IV/M1616, decisions of 20 July 1999 and 20 October 1999, the Commission opposed a British (*EDF/London Electricity*) respectively two Portuguese (*Secil/Holderbank/Cimpor (Art. 21)* and *BSCH/A. Champalimaud*) wishes to apply Art. 21(3). In particular the last mentioned case attracted extensive press coverage. It concerned the Spanish undertaking BSCH's bid for the Portuguese Champalimaud financial group. The Portuguese authorities attempted to block the bid on *inter alia* prudential grounds. However, they failed to prove this and the Commission declared the blocking decision to be in breach of the Merger Regulation. Only after the Commission had opened an accelerated infringement procedure against Portugal, did the Portuguese authorities eliminate their veto and allow the acquisition. In case C-42/01, *Portugal* v. *Commission* (pending), the Portuguese Government has challenged the Commission's interpretation of Art. 21 as laid down in the *Secil/Holderbank/Cimpor* case.

4. THE THRESHOLDS

As noted above, the Merger Regulation's scope is defined by a number of turnover thresholds. A concentration which meets these thresholds is said to have a Community dimension. In 1997, the Regulation's original set of turnover thresholds in Article 1(2) was supplemented by a second one in Article 1(3), which entered into force on 1 March 1998, so that Community dimension within the meaning of the Regulation is defined in the following way:

Article 1

Scope

1. Without prejudice to Article 22, this Regulation shall apply to all concentrations with a Community dimension as defined in paragraphs 2 and 3.

2. For the purposes of this Regulation, a concentration has a Community dimension where;
   (a) the aggregate worldwide turnover of all the undertakings concerned is more than [€] 5 000 million, and
   (b) the aggregate Community-wide turnover of each of at least two of the undertakings concerned is more than [€] 250 million,

   unless each of the undertakings concerned achieves more than two-thirds of its aggregate Community-wide turnover within one and the same Member State.

3. For the purposes of this Regulation, a concentration within the meaning of Article 3 that does not meet the thresholds laid down in paragraph 2 has a Community dimension where:
   (a) the combined aggregate worldwide turnover of all the undertakings concerned is more than [€] 2 500 million;
   (b) in each of at least three Member States, the combined aggregate turnover of all the undertakings concerned is more than [€] 100 million;
   (c) in each of the three Member States included for the purpose of (b), the aggregate turnover of each of at least two of the undertakings concerned is more than [€] 25 million; and
   (d) the aggregate Community-wide turnover of each of at least two of the undertakings concerned is more than [€] 100 million;

unless each of the undertakings concerned achieves more than two-thirds of its aggregate Community-wide turnover within one and the same Member State.

4. …

A Community dimension is thus found on the basis of two alternative sets of turnover thresholds, both of which relate to the size of the parties. According to the first set of thresholds, all the undertakings concerned must generate a joint worldwide turnover of at least € 5000 million, at least two undertakings concerned must generate minimum € 250 million in the Community and not all the undertakings concerned may generate more than two-thirds of their individual Community-wide turnover in one and the same Member State. According to the second set of thresholds, all the undertakings concerned must generate a joint worldwide turnover of at least € 2500 million, at least two of the undertakings concerned must generate minimum € 100 million in the Community, in each of at least three Member States, the combined aggregate turnover of all the undertakings concerned must be more than € 100 million and in a minimum of three of the Member States where the combined aggregate turnover exceeds € 100 million, the aggregate turnover of each of at least two of the undertakings concerned must exceed € 25 million. Finally, all the undertakings concerned may not generate more than two-thirds of their individual Community-wide turnover in one and the same Member State.[33]

At first glance, this two-set definition of a Community dimension appears to be very complicated and difficult to apply. Not least the addition of the second set of thresholds in the 1997 revision has contributed to this impression.[34] A figure might, therefore, prove beneficial to help understand the system.

---

[33] In reality the thresholds have been 'lowered' due to the expansion of the Community and to the inflation. According to the Commission in its *2001 Green Paper on the review of the Merger Regulation*, *supra* note 5, Annex 1, para. 33, based upon the assumption of an annual inflation of 2%, the € 5 billion threshold correspond to approximately € 6.1 billion in the year 2000. Likewise the € 250 million threshold would correspond to approximately € 305 million. The envisaged enlargement to 25 Member States will mean a further lowering of the thresholds in real terms.

[34] Indeed, at times it seems that the Commission itself has difficulties in applying the second set of thresholds. *See* for example the two decisions *Reckitt & Colman plc/Benckiser NV.*, Case IV/M1632, decision of 3 September 1999 and *WPP/Young Rubicam*, Case COMP/M2000, decision of 24 August 2000 where the Commission appears to have found that the thresholds in Art. 1(3) have been met where the undertakings have a combined aggregate

The workings of the definition of Community dimension

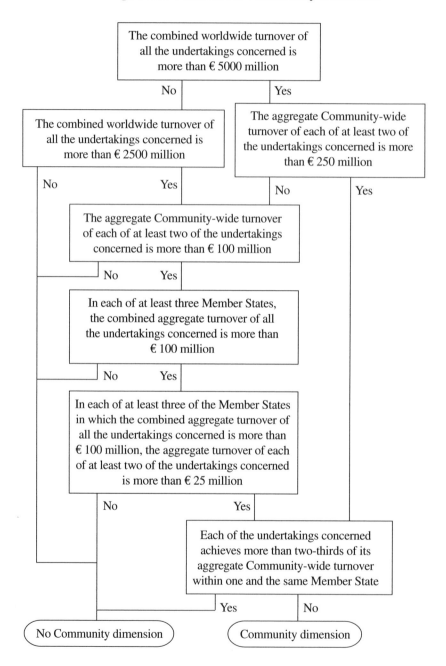

Even though the thresholds provided in Article 1(2) may appear confusing, they have been very carefully designed. Regarding the first set, the € 5 billion world-wide turnover threshold (Article 1(2)(a)) 'reflects the general economic and financial power of the undertakings', the € 250 million Community-wide turnover (Article 1(2)(b)) for each of at least two of the undertakings concerned 'demonstrates significant activity in the Community by two or more parties' and the two-thirds threshold (Article 1(2) *in fine*) 'is designed to exclude operations which are primarily of a national nature'.[35]

The second set of thresholds, laid down in Article 1(3), to a fair extent mirrors the first set. This is true with respect to the € 2.5 billion worldwide turnover threshold (Article 1(3)(a)) and with respect to the € 100 million Community-wide turnover (Article 1(3)(d)) as well as with respect to the two-thirds rule (Article 1(3) *in fine*). In addition, the second set requires a minimum turnover in at least three Member States (Article 1(3)(b) and (c)). This last requirement is a vague reminder of the original amendment-proposal that the Commission should have jurisdiction where a concentration was notifiable with a minimum number of national competition authorities.[36]

---

worldwide turnover of more than € 2500 million, at least two have an aggregate Community-wide turnover of more than € 250 million and not all achieve more than two-thirds of their Community-wide turnover in one and the same Member State. Dominique Berlin, 'Concentrations – (1er janvier 1998 – 31 décembre 1998)', *Revue trimestrielle de droit européen*, No. 1 2000, pp. 139-237 at p. 176 in a slight understatement observes 'qu'il est parfois bien difficile d'expliquer aux entreprises cette hypothèse (*i.e.* the second set of thresholds) de competence communautaire' (*i.e.* that at times it is rather difficult to explain this hypothesis of Community competence to the undertakings). In the same article, Berlin moreover characterises the additional set of thresholds as the 'fruits d'un savant compromis entre Etats membres au sein du Conseil' (*i.e.* the fruits of a wise compromise between the Member States within the Council). Personally I do not agree with Berlin that the second set of thresholds constitute a wise compromise.

35 All quotations from Claus-Dieter Ehlermann, *Submission of Mr. Claus Dieter Ehlermann to the House of Lords Select Committee on the European Communities*, given on 16 June 1993 in London (available in DG COMP's library) at p. 22. *See* equally European Commission *Review of the Application of Council Regulation (EEC) No. 4064/89 of 21 December 1989 on the Control of Concentrations between Undertakings*, Working Paper of the Services of the Commission, Revised version of 17 May 1993 (B), at p. 3.

36 Indeed Council Regulation (EC) No 1310/97 of 30 June 1997 amending Regulation (EEC) No 4064/89 on the control of concentrations between undertakings in recital 1 still refers to 'multiple notification'. Frederic Jenny, 'National Authorities and the Commission', *International Business Lawyer*, Vol. 26, No. 3, 1998, pp. 105-111 at 106 find that the additional

Even though turnover was chosen because it is a reasonably unambiguous standard for deciding whether an operation has a Community dimension, the drafters were still aware that turnover may give rise to ambiguities.[37] In Article 5, they, therefore, included a number of guidelines for the calculation of the Community dimension. Still, the notion of a Community dimension has given rise to a significant number of problems, as will be apparent from the examination provided in this work.

---

thresholds 'will certainly alleviate some of the problems of multiple filings but not all of them'. Eleanor J. Morgan, 'Subsidiarity and the division of jurisdiction in EU merger control', *The Antitrust Bulletin*, Spring 2000, pp. 153-193 at pp. 173 and 192 rightly observes that the additional thresholds were rather arbitrary and that it was likely that they would be able to catch only a minority of all multiple notification cases. The original proposal may be found in *Communication from the Commission to the Council and to the European Parliament Regarding the Revision of the Merger Regulation*, COM (96) 313 final, Brussels 12.9.1996. For critical comments on the original multiple filings proposal, *see* my article 'The EC Commission's Green Paper on the Review of the Merger Regulation', *European Competition Law Review*, 1996, no. 5, pp. 289-294 and B.E. Hawk and H.L. Huser, *supra* note 32 at p. 75. In the *2001 Green Paper on the review of the Merger Regulation*, *supra* note 5, the Commission again tabled the idea that it should have jurisdiction where a concentration is notifiable in more Member States. And again this proposal had to be abandoned.

[37] There are several examples of concentrations where it has not been immediately clear whether the thresholds were met. One such example is the concentration between the brewing interests of Orkla, a Norwegian conglomerate, and the Danish brewer Carlsberg. Thus, shortly after the announcement of the concentration, two out of three analysts quoted in the Danish financial newspaper Børsen expressed fears that the transaction would be prohibited by the Commission (RB-Børsen 31 May 2000, 'Frygt for EU-stop for Carlsberg-fusion'). The following day Financial Times quoted Carlsberg's CEO for saying that 'he did not expect any problem with the European Union authorities, as the total size of the deal fell below the monopoly threshold' (Clare MacCarthy, 'Carlsberg in Dkr 10bn deal with Orkla', Financial Times, 1 June 2000). On 5 June 2000 the Danish Competition Agency was quoted for saying that the concentration fell to be examined by the European Commission (Peter Suppli Benson, 'EU lurer videre på Carlsberg', Politiken 5 June 2000). Five days later the Danish Competition Agency had changed its mind and found that the transaction did not meet the thresholds (Charlotte Harder and Bent Højgaard Sørensen, 'Ølgigant slipper for fusionskontrol', Berlingske Tidende 10 June 2000). Nevertheless, in its issue covering 15-21 June 2000, European Voice was able to quote Commission sources for saying that the Commission 'had not yet determined whether the deal exceeded the sales thresholds required to trigger an EU investigation ...'. In the end it turned out that the transaction did not have a Community dimension.

5. BASIC OVERVIEW OF THE MERGER REGULATION PROCEDURE

The question of which authority is to have jurisdiction necessarily arises at a very early point in the notification procedure. Indeed, it is probably more correct to say that it arises before the procedure is opened. Nevertheless, a brief explanation of the Merger Regulation's procedural mechanics may be beneficial in aiding the reader during the voyage through the legal subtleties of the notion of 'Community dimension'.

It is a common experience that to require a concentration to be unwound after completion is much more problematic than prohibiting it before it has been completed. The Merger Regulation, therefore, requires that the Commission is notified of concentrations before they are completed, provided of course that it has a Community dimension.[38] Following notification, the Commission must carry out a preliminary investigation which may last up to one month.[39] During this investigation, the Commission must first ascertain that the Regulation falls within the scope of the Merger Regulation,[40] and if the answer is affirmative, it must examine whether the concentration 'raises serious doubts as to its compatibility with the common market'.[41] The vast majority of all cases are cleared upon this preliminary first stage examination, but a small number are found to give rise to serious doubts and are, therefore, referred to a second phase in-depth examination. This examination may last up to four months.[42]

As will be clear from this brief overview, the question of whether a concentration meets the thresholds and thus falls within the scope of the Merger Regulation, is one which the parties must consider even before they notify the Commission. Moreover, the Commission must consider this issue before entering a more substantive examination of the notified transaction.

The burden which the Regulation (and the Commission) imposes on the parties to a concentration must somehow be proportionally linked to the potential adverse

---

[38] Cf. Art. 4.

[39] Art. 8(1).

[40] It has often happened that the parties to the concentration have contacted the Commission in advance in order to discuss the different aspects of the concentration on a confidential basis. The question of whether the transaction falls within the scope of the Regulation will normally be clarified already at this stage.

[41] Art. 6(1)(c).

[42] Art. 8(3).

effects on competition in the Community which may flow from the transaction. Thus, the burden which the Regulation imposes on the parties during the second phase, *i.e.* at a stage where there is a strong presumption that the concentration may be anti-competitive, may be significantly heavier than the burden which may be imposed during the first phase where there is no such presumption. Along the same line, it seems that the burden imposed on the parties in order to ascertain whether their transaction is notifiable, *i.e.* even before it is clear whether it has a Community dimension, must be even lower. Put differently, there must be limits to how extensive an examination the parties may be required to carry out only in order to decide whether or not their transaction is notifiable.

6. THIS WORK

6.1. The subject matter

The subject matter of this work is the Merger Regulation's notion of Community dimension. One does not need to spend much time working with the cases decided under the Merger Regulation before the question arises of whether the Commission's interpretation of the Regulation's definition of Community dimension is correct.[43] The notion of Community dimension defines the Commission's jurisdiction under the Merger Regulation. If the Commission applies a wrong definition, this is likely to mean that the Commission acquires too wide (or too narrow) a jurisdiction. It follows that an analysis of whether the Commission follows the 'correct interpretation' is of considerable interest. This was the primary issue I set out to examine in the first edition of this work and I found that the interpretation applied by the Commission was incorrect on a number of important points.

In this second edition I have shifted my focus somewhat. Hence, my primary focus now is on providing a careful and critical examination of the construction of the Merger Regulation's notion of Community dimension. In this respect I will

---

[43] Regrettably the Commission in the public versions of its decisions increasingly omits information about its definition of Community dimension. *See* for example *Publicis/BCOM3*, Case COMP/M2785, decision of 18 June 2002 and *Metronet/Infraco*, Case COMP/M2694, decision of 21 June 2002.

primarily draw upon the case law of the Commission and of the Community courts in Luxembourg.

6.2. Structure

The structure of this work is straightforward. Thus, following this introduction, in chapter two I examine the definition of the Regulation's concept of *undertaking concerned*. Chapter three is an examination of the *group*, a term which is not used in the Regulation although the concept plays an important role. In chapter four I go through what I have termed the *basic rules* (such as how to make the conversion of turnover figures into EUROs). The majority of the thresholds require that the turnover be allocated to the Community or to one or more Member States. I look at this *geographical allocation* in chapter five. A special calculation of the Community dimension applies in the *financial sector* and this I examine in chapter six. In chapter seven I examine the *EEA Agreement's* effects on the allocation of jurisdiction in merger cases and in chapter eight I look at the possibilities of *forum shopping* under the Regulation.

In the last chapter I consider the turnover thresholds' suitability as a means for defining 'real Community dimension' as well as the possibility of improving the current jurisdictional delimitation.

6.3. Cut-off date for the work

I have endeavoured to take into account all sources available to me as at 1 January 2003. Conversions into EUROs have been made on the basis of the rates on 31 December 2002.

2. THE UNDERTAKINGS CONCERNED

1. INTRODUCTION

The Community dimension is calculated on the basis of the turnover of 'the undertakings concerned', but even though the Merger Regulation applies this notion several times,[1] no definition of it is provided in the Regulation.[2] During the first years after the Regulation entered into force, merging parties' only basis for identifying the 'undertaking concerned' was the Commission's practice which provided a somewhat blurry picture.[3] On 31 December, 1994, however, the Commission published a notice on the notion of undertakings concerned.[4] This Notice was revised in 1998.[5] The Notice basically summarises the Commission's previous practice, but on points where this practice is contradictory or otherwise ambiguous, the Notice typically provides a clarification.

---

[1] *See* Arts. 1(2)(a), 1(2)(b), 1(2) *in fine*, 1(3)(a), 1(3)(b), 1(3)(c), 1(3)(d), 1(3) *in fine*, 2(1)(b), 2(4), 5(1), 5(4), 5(4)(a), 5(4)(b), 5(4)(c), 5(5), 5(5)(a), 5(5)(b), 6(2)(1), 6(2)(2), 6(3)(b), 6(5), 7(3), 8(2)(1), 8(2)(2), 8(5)(a), 8(5)(b), 9(1), 9(2), 9(7), 10(1)(2), 10(2), 14(2), 15(1), 18(1), 18(2), 18(4), 19(5), 19(7), Recitals 10, 11, 12, 15, 19, 23, 25 and 31.

[2] Arts. 81 and 82 both apply the term 'undertakings' which has been given a broad definition in the Commission's and the Court's practice. A fine exposition of this practice is given in Richard Whish, *Competition Law*, 4th edition, Butterworths, London 2001, pp. 66-76. It seems doubtful, however, whether today the interpretation of this term may provide guidance in the interpretation of the notion of 'undertaking concerned'.

[3] *See* in this regard my article, 'The European Commission's Jurisdiction under the Merger Control Regulation', *Nordic Journal of International Law*, Vol. 63, 1994, pp. 17-108.

[4] Commission Notice on the notion of undertakings concerned under Council Regulation (EEC) No 4064/89 of 21 December, 1989 on the control of concentrations between undertakings, published in OJ C385/12 of 31.12.1994.

[5] Commission Notice on the concept of undertakings concerned under Council Regulation (EEC) No. 4064/89 on the control of concentrations between undertakings, published in OJ C66/14 of 2.3.1998. Hereinafter Undertaking Concerned Notice.

The correct definition of the undertaking concerned is important when ascertaining whether an operation has a Community dimension.[6] The Community dimension is based on group turnover, as will be explained further in chapter 3 below. Whether the parent or the subsidiary is identified as the undertaking concerned is, therefore, not important as long as they belong to the same group.[7] If the subsidiary has more than one parent (*i.e.* a joint venture) or if the concentration concerns the acquisition of a part of an undertaking, however, the correct identification of the undertaking concerned may be crucial for the finding of a Community dimension. For example, if undertakings A and B set up a joint venture to make a bid for undertaking C, then undertaking C is an undertaking concerned. But is the joint venture also an undertaking concerned or are A and B individually? The answer will be crucial to the finding of a Community dimension if A and B each have a Community-wide turnover of € 4 billion but C only has a Community-wide turnover of € 50 million since only if both A and B are undertakings concerned is it possible that the concentration will meet the thresholds.

In this chapter I will examine the notion of undertaking concerned as provided in the Regulation and I will compare this with the interpretation provided by the Commission in the decisions and in the Undertaking Concerned Notice. In so doing, I will attempt to focus on the general principles. An alternative would have been to follow the casuistic structure of the Undertaking Concerned Notice. I do not consider such a structure suitable for the purposes of this work, however. In other words, where the Notice primarily sets out to identify the undertaking concerned in each of the many different forms of transactions which may constitute concentrations, I will start from the general definition of the 'undertaking concerned' and examine its different aspects in order to make it possible to apply this principle to all concentrations. This approach, I believe, makes a coherent interpretation more likely.

---

[6]   On the other hand, the notion is only relevant with respect to determining jurisdiction and is of importance neither regarding who has the duty to notify nor regarding the substantive appraisal of the concentration. *See* also Undertaking Concerned Notice at paras. 3 and 11.

[7]   Likewise Mario Siragusa and Romano Subiotto, 'The EEC merger control regulation: The Commission's evolving case law', *Common Market Law Review*, vol. 28, 1991, pp. 877-934 at p. 896 who at the same time point out that 'the Commission's decisions appear inconsistent as to its use in the context of acquisitions made by subsidiaries, in a number of cases using it to designate the parent company and in others the subsidiary making the acquisition'.

Accordingly, in part 2, I will examine the general definition of the undertaking concerned. In part 3, I will look at how this definition may be applied to cases of joint bidding and full-function joint ventures and finally, in part 4, I will look at the application of the definition to situations of acquisitions of only 'a part'. Frequently, the rules set out in parts 3 and 4 will apply simultaneously, as, for example, where undertakings A and B make a joint bid for the subsidiary of undertaking X.

2. THE GENERAL DEFINITION

2.1. 'The direct participants'

In the Undertaking Concerned Notice, the Commission defines the undertakings concerned as 'the direct participants in a merger or acquisition of control.'[8] At first glance, this definition might appear simultaneously imprecise and so self-evident that it is almost without meaning. Nevertheless, in most cases it is sufficient to identify the undertakings concerned.[9]

Hence, in order to identify the undertakings concerned, it is first necessary to make an exact delimitation of the concentration in question. Difficulties in this regard may arise in particular where the transaction involves more than one concentration.[10] When the individual concentration has been delimited, those

---

8 The Undertaking Concerned Notice at para. 5. *See* also Commission Notice on the definition of the relevant market for the purposes of Community competition law, OJ C372/5 of 9.12.1997, which in note 2 explains: 'For the purposes of this notice, the undertakings involved will be, in the case of a concentration, the parties to the concentration.'

9 The definition is significantly more developed than the one originally put forward by the European Commission in its *XXIst Report on Competition Policy 1991*, Luxembourg 1992, at point 7.1 in Annex III (p. 351).

10 Frequently the Commission is confronted with complex configurations of transactions making it difficult to decide whether the case concerns one or more concentrations, cf. Francisco Enrique González-Díaz, 'Tenth Anniversary of the Merger Regulation: the Way Forward', *EC Merger Control: Ten Years On*, International Bar Association, London 2000, pp. 405-425 at p. 407. For examples *see McCormick/CPC/Rabobank/Ostmann*, Case IV/M330, decision of 29 October, 1993, *Scandinavian Project*, Case IV/M522, decision of 28 November, 1994, *Du Pont/ICI*, Case IV/M214, decision of 30 September, 1992, [1993] OJ L7/13, *L'Oréal/Procasa/Cosmétique Iberica/Albesa*, Case IV/M957, decision of 19 September 1997, *Alcan/Alusuisse*, Case COMP/M1663, decision of 14 March 2000 together

undertakings which are directly participating in it are normally easy to identify. For instance, if the concentration concerns A's acquisition of a subsidiary or of a license, this subsidiary or licence is a 'direct participant' in the concentration and so is A.[11] Likewise, if A and B decide to merge, they are both direct participants. If A and B decide to jointly acquire C, all three are direct participants. Thus, it is not necessary to be in a position to take the relevant decisions with respect to the concentration in question in order to qualify as an undertaking concerned.[12] More- over, in principle, a group as defined in Article 5(4) and (5) of the Regulation can only have one undertaking concerned as a member.[13] In some situations, it is, how-

---

with *Alcan/Pechiney*, Case COMP/M1715, aborted and Undertaking Concerned Notice at paras. 49-50. In a decision of 22 June 2000 in *Canal+/Lagardère*, Case COMP/JV47 and *Canal+/ Lagardère/Liberty Media*, Case COMP/JV40 the Commission treated two closely related concentrations together. The Commission – correctly it is submitted – calculated the Commu- nity dimension separately for both concentrations so that the decision contains two different calculations of turnover. In 'Proposal for a Council Regulation on the control of concentra- tions between undertakings', COM(2002) 711 final, OJ C20/4 of 28.1.2003, the Commis- sion proposes to amend Arts. 3(4) and 5(2)(2) to be better able to catch this type of transaction.

[11] *See* as examples *Unilever/Diversey*, Case IV/M704, decision of 20 March 1996 and *Bosch/ Allied Signal*, Case IV/M726, decision of 9 April 1996 (business areas constituted undertak- ings concerned). Where a third undertaking is involved in a concentration by providing financing or simply acting as an intermediary, but without being the part acquired or without being the part obtaining control, this third undertaking is not an undertaking concerned. The Commission in *Rhodia/Donau Chemie/Albright & Wilson*, Case IV/M1517, decision of 13 July 1999, appears to have taken a different position. *See* also *McCormick/CPC/Rabobank/ Ostmann*, *supra* note 10.

[12] Contrast with Enrique González Díaz, 'Case Note: TNT/GD Net', *EC Merger Control Re- porter*, Kluwer Law International, The Hague 1991 and later (looseleaf), p. 516. Neither in the Undertaking Concerned Notice, nor in its decisions does the Commission require the undertaking concerned to be in such position.

[13] This has been implicitly acknowledged by the Commission in the Undertaking Concerned Notice at para. 19. *See* also *Frantschach/Bischof+Klein/F+B Verpackungen*, Case IV/M961, decision of 26 September 1997 (concerning the question whether the transaction took place *between* two independent groups or *within* one group). In practice situations may arise where, technically, two undertakings concerned belong to the same group. This is particularly likely to be the case where an undertaking acquires sole control over an undertaking that used to be under joint control (as defined in Art. 3(3)). *See* for example *CNH/FHE*, Case COMP/M2369, decision of 26 June 2001. Also, it must be noted that it is possible to have one undertaking which belongs to the group of more than one of the undertakings concerned, as is recognised by Art. 5(5) of the Merger Regulation. Indeed, this appears to have been the situation in *Danish Crown/Vestjyske Slagterier*, Case IV/M1313, decision of 9 March 1999, [2000] OJ

ever, difficult to identify the direct participants in the concentration or it may be difficult to precisely delimit the size of these partîcipants as will be shown in this chapter.

Two further issues must be addressed here. First, it is necessary to examine whether the undertakings concerned in a concentration *vis-à-vis* the € 5 billion or the € 2.5 billion thresholds and the € 250 million or the € 100 million thresholds are the same as the undertakings concerned *vis-à-vis* the two-thirds threshold. The second question is whether a person or a family may be an undertaking concerned.

2.2. The two-thirds threshold and the undertakings concerned

The two-thirds threshold provides that where all the undertakings concerned generate more than two-thirds of their Community-wide turnover in one and the same Member State, the concentration does not have a Community dimension. This leads to the question of whether this threshold must be viewed individually so that it applies to all undertakings concerned, or whether it is linked to the thresholds requiring at least two of the undertakings to generate at least € 250 million respectively € 100 million in the Community. In the latter case, the two-thirds threshold will only apply to those undertakings which meet the Community-wide turnover thresholds.

It is difficult to simply reject either of the two possible interpretations and, indeed, one may claim that both readings are literal. The Commission's notices do not provide an answer, but the decision in *Prudential/HSBC/Finnish Chemicals*[14]

L20/1, where the two merging undertakings jointly controlled four other undertakings. The Commission, considered the transaction to constitute one single concentration consisting of both a merger and an acquisition of joint control. Hence, both the two merging parties and the four joint ventures were considered to be undertakings concerned for the purposes of calculating turnover. The correct approach, it is submitted, would have been to consider only the two merging parties to be undertakings concerned.

Nevertheless, in some cases one wonders whether or not the Commission has established a Community dimension on the basis of more than one undertaking concerned belonging to one and the same group. *See* for example *Granaria/Ûltje/Intersnack/May-Holding*, Case COMP/JV32, decision of 28 February 2000 (on the face of it, the undertakings concerned 'Intersnack' and 'Felix' appear to belong to the same group).

[14] Case IV/M883, decision of 13 February 1997.

apparently provides a clear answer.[15] In that case, Prudential and HSBC jointly acquired Finnish Chemicals. Only Prudential and HSBC generated € 250 million in the Community and both of these undertakings generated more than 2/3 of their Community-wide turnover in United Kingdom. In contrast, Finnish Chemicals did not generate more than 2/3 of its Community-wide turnover in the United Kingdom. The Commission, therefore, concluded that the transaction had Community dimension. In other words, the 2/3 rule must have been applied to all undertakings concerned regardless of whether they generate more than € 250 million in the Community.[16]

I fully agree with this interpretation. The Merger Regulation in Article 1(2) and (3) respectively provides thresholds which are defined in positive terms together

---

[15] In particular the Commission's earlier case law is, however, somewhat unclear on this point. Thus *Avesta/British Steel/NCC*, Case IV/M239, decision of 4 September 1992, *ABC/Générale des Eaux/Canal+/W.H.Smith TV*, Case IV/M110, decision of 10 September 1991, *Sextant/ BGT-VDO*, Case IV/M290, decision of 21 December 1992, *Sidmar/Klöckner Stahl*, Case IV/M444, decision of 30 May 1994, *Scandinavian Project*, *supra* note 10, *NAW/SALTANO/ CONTRAC*, Case IV/M698, decision of 26 February 1996, *Go-Ahead/Via/Thameslink*, Case IV/M901, decision of 24 April 1997, *DIA/VEBA Immobilien/Deutschbau*, Case IV/M929, decision of 23 June 1997, *Bain/Hoechst-Dade Behring*, Case IV/M954, decision of 2 September 1997, *@Home Benelux B.V.*, Case IV/JV11, decision of 15 September 1998 and *Asahi Glass/Mitsubishi/F2 Chemicals*, Case COMP/JV42, decision of 21 March 2000 indicate that the Commission has applied the two-thirds rule to each and every participant in the concentration including those with a Community-wide turnover of less than € 250 million. *Eureko*, Case IV/M207, decision of 27 April 1992, *Fletcher Challenge/Methanex*, Case IV/ M331, decision of 31 March 1993, *Krupp/Thyssen/Riva/Falck/Tadfin/AST*, Case IV/M484, decision of 21 December 1994, [1995] OJ L251/18, *Montedison/Groupe Vernes/SCI*, Case IV/M639, decision of 8 December 1995, *Enderly/S.B.E.*, Case IV/M789, decision of 15 July 1996, *Saint Gobain/Wacker-Chemie/NOM*, Case IV/M774, decision of 4 December 1996, *Castle Tower/TDF/Candover/Berkshire*, Case IV/M887, decision of 27 February 1997, *Médéric/ORRPIMMEC/CRI/Munich Re*, Case IV/M949, decision of 2 July 1997 and *Hochtief/ Aer Rianta/Düsseldorf Airport*, Case IV/M1035, decision of 22 December 1997 indicate the opposite.

[16] *See* equally *WSI/Webseek*, Case IV/JV8, decision of 28 September 1998 and H. Colin Overbury, 'Politics or Policy? The Demystification of EC Merger Control', *1992 Fordham Corp. L. Inst.* 557-589 (B. Hawk, ed. 1993) at p. 575. Likewise Ivo Van Bael and Jean-François Bellis, *Competition Law of the European Community*, 3rd ed., CCH Europe, Bicester (UK) 1994, at p. 377, Dorothy Livingston, *Competition Law and Practice*, FT Law & Tax, London 1995, at p. 727 and Hartmut Krause, 'E.C. Merger Control: An Outside View from Inside the Merger Taskforce', *Journal of Business Law*, November 1995, pp. 627-637 at p. 633.

with one threshold (the two-thirds) defined in negative terms. All of the thresholds include the term 'undertaking concerned'. To include all undertakings concerned when calculating the worldwide turnover thresholds and the Community-wide turnover thresholds, but to exclude some of these when calculating the two-thirds thresholds, amounts to applying two different interpretations of the term without any clear indications from the drafters that they had this intention. Accordingly, even though the wording of the Regulation is not unequivocal on this point, I consider the Commission's interpretation to be the better one.

2.3. Individuals and families as undertakings concerned

The term 'undertaking concerned' seems to refer to companies and other legal entities, but not to natural persons. Under Articles 81 and 82, however, an individual has been held to qualify as an undertaking on numerous occasions.[17] In its application of the Merger Regulation, the Commission has also counted individuals as undertakings concerned where the individuals 'carry out economic activities of their own.'[18]

This interpretation must be correct as the opposite interpretation would simply lead to clear inconsistencies such as where Mr X personally acquires a major industrial company to add to his large number of companies, while Mr Y does the same, but through his 100% owned holding company, Ypsilon-holding. If Ypsilon-holding is an undertaking concerned (together with the target) but Mr X is not an undertaking concerned, this may induce Mr Y to make the acquisition in his personal capacity to avoid having to obtain a clearance under the Merger Regu-

---

[17] *See* for example case 35/83 *BAT Cigaretten Fabriken GmbH* v. *Commission of the European Communities* ECR [1985] 363, *RAI/Unitel*, [1978] OJ, L157/39 and *Reuter/BASF*, [1976] OJ L254/40.

[18] Undertaking Concerned Notice at para. 51. *See* for example *ASKO/Jacobs/Adia*, Case IV/M082, decision of 16 May 1991 and *Hicks/Bear Stearns/Johns Manville*, Case COMP/M2133, decision of 25 September 2000. In contrast, if the individual does not carry out any economic activity on its own, it is simply disregarded for the purpose of calculating the Community dimension. *See* for example *Carlyle/Gruppo Riello*, Case COMP/M2003, decision of 27 June 2000.

lation. Thus, it is submitted that individuals, too, may qualify as undertakings concerned.[19]

The real problems arise where more than one individual is involved, for instance where Mr Y owns a wide range of companies, but a major acquisition is made by his wife. If the acquisition is made at Mr Y's request and out of his funds it seems right to 'pierce the veil' and consider Mr Y to be the undertaking concerned since the acquisition is in reality made on his behalf. In contrast, if Mr Y and his wife each makes acquisitions out of their respective funds, and if they do not run their respective companies together, but as separate groups, they must be treated individually when calculating turnover.[20] This necessarily means that even where Mr Y acquires a company from Mrs Y, this may amount to a concentration with a Community dimension.

It is submitted that the dividing line should be drawn between those situations where the individuals act independently and those where they act either on behalf of someone else or jointly. If a person, Z, in his individual capacity, acquires a company, he must be considered to be the undertaking concerned, and turnover generated by companies and entities belonging to him within the meaning of Article 5(4) and (5)[21] must be included when calculating the Community dimension. Mr Z may be part of the family Q that jointly, for instance on the basis of a shareholders' agreement, owns and controls a group of companies. These companies may only be included in Mr Z's turnover to the extent that they fulfil the preconditions laid down in Article 5(4) and (5). Likewise, where the family Q jointly acquires a new company, the family should be considered an undertaking concerned, and companies which belong to the group as defined in the Regulation must be

---

[19] Contrast this with the view of Pierre Bos, Jules Stuyck and Peter Wytinck, *Concentration Control in the European Economic Community*, Graham & Trotman, London 1992, p. 149 who finds that 'the turnover of undertakings controlled by an individual acquiring control of another undertaking should not be taken into account.' These authors continue by noting that '[t]he resulting imbalance in the treatment of undertakings and persons should, and probably will be redressed when the Regulation is revised.'

[20] In Germany shareholders in market dominant and financially powerful undertakings have evaded the merger control laws by having members of the family to acquire shares in other companies, cf. Monopolkommission, *Die Wettbewerbsordnung erweitern: Hauptgutachten 1986/87*, Monopolkommission, Nomos Verlagsgesellschaft, Baden-Baden 1988 at pp. 170-171 (*see* also p. 330 in the English Summary).

[21] *See* further chapter 3 below.

included when calculating the Community dimension.[22] The present high thresholds mean that cases involving individuals or families rarely arise.

It may be argued that the above distinction does not duly take the possibilities of control and co-ordination between family members (for instance Mr and Mrs Y) into account. The definition of the undertaking concerned is, however, only concerned with the allocation of jurisdiction while it does not affect the substantive appraisal.[23] In other words, if the case has a Community dimension, the above distinction does not preclude the Commission from taking the personal links into account when carrying out its substantive appraisal. Equally, if the concentration falls below the thresholds, national competition authorities may consider such links in their substantive appraisal.

3. JOINT BIDDING AND FULL-FUNCTION JOINT VENTURES

3.1. Introduction

Regarding the identification of the undertaking concerned, joint bidding and joint ventures have a lot in common. This is not least clear where two companies join together to submit a bid for a third company, but do this through a joint venture set up for the purpose. In this situation, one may ask whether the undertaking concerned is the joint venture or the two bidders?

---

[22] *See* for examples, *Lyonnaise des Eaux Dumez/Brochier*, Case IV/M076, decision of 11 July 1991, *Saudi Aramco/MOH*, Case IV/M574, decision of 23 May 1995 and *Northern Telecom/ Matra*, Case IV/M249, decision of 10 August 1992. In the last-mentioned decision the Commission at para. 13 explains that it has based the calculation of turnover on 'the Lagadère family group of companies'. *See* also *Mondi/Frantscach*, Case IV/M210, decision of 12 May 1992, *Auchan/Leroy Merlin/IFIL/La Rinascente*, Case IV/M934, decision of 16 June 1997, *Accor/Ebertz/Dorint*, Case COMP/M2997, decision of 23 December 2002 and (apparently) *Ispat/Unimetal*, Case IV/M1509, decision of 22 June 1999. In *A.P. Møller*, Case IV/M969, decision of 10 February 1999, [1999] OJ L183/29, the Commission at para. 6 notes that it has based the calculation of turnover on the shareholdings of Mr 'Maersk McKinney Møller and several family foundations …'.

[23] Likewise, Undertaking Concerned Notice, para. 11.

Below, I will discuss the different aspects of joint bids and full-function joint ventures in order to ascertain to what degree the general definition of undertaking concerned may be applied to them.

3.2. Setting up a full-function joint venture

Setting up a full-function joint venture necessarily constitutes a concentration within the meaning of the Merger Regulation. Thus, if two independent undertakings agree to set up a full-function joint venture, they agree to carry out a concentration.[24] The outcome of the concentration is the joint venture.

It is only logical that since the joint venture is the outcome (it is only created when the concentration is completed) it cannot be one of the participants in the operation. Consequently, only the parties setting up the joint venture – the 'parents to be' – are undertakings concerned.[25]

Only undertakings participating in the concentration can be undertakings concerned. This means that if five undertakings set up a joint venture, but only two of them hold joint control (*i.e.* they are the parties in the concentration), only the two controlling undertakings will be considered to be undertakings concerned.[26]

The alternative to this understanding would be to hold the joint venture to be the undertaking concerned. Apart from the fact that this would constitute a rather illogical solution as shown above, the consequence would be that there would only be one undertaking concerned and therefore it would be impossible to have the minimum two undertakings concerned to meet the € 250 million threshold (*i.e.* the first threshold set) or the minimum € 100 million threshold (*i.e.* the second threshold set). There can be no doubt that the Merger Regulation was intended to also cover the creation of joint ventures.[27] This is well founded

---

24 In *Hoechst/Wacker*, Case IV/M284, decision of 10 May 1993 a joint venture between Hoechst and Wacker set up a new joint venture with Hoechst. The Commission found that this constituted a concentration. *See* my comments on this case in 'Fusionskontrolforordningens kontrolbegreb' in *Festskrift til Mogens Koktvedgaard*, (Mads Bryde Andersen, Caroline Heide-Jørgensen and Jens Schovsbo, eds.), Jurist- og Økonomforbundets Forlag, Copenhagen 2003.

25 Likewise, Undertaking Concerned Notice, para. 21.

26 Likewise, Undertaking Concerned Notice, para. 21 and from the Commission's practice *Dresdner Bank/Banque Nationale de Paris*, Case IV/M021, decision of 4 February 1991.

27 *See* Art. 3(2) of the Merger Regulation.

since many mergers are technically made in the form of joint ventures where the joint venture takes over all activities and the parents become mere holding companies.[28]

Where the joint venture is created by turning a subsidiary under sole control into a joint venture between the former parent and a third party, the Commission considers the third party (the new parent) and the original sole parent to be undertakings concerned.[29] The subsidiary is thus not considered to be an undertaking concerned.[30] In contrast, where an extra parent is added to an already existing joint venture, the Commission considers all parents and the joint venture to be undertakings concerned.[31] An example may illustrate this approach.

Example

At first glance, the case *Avesta/British Steel/NCC*[32] appears rather problematic. Here, NCC and Axel Johnson jointly controlled Avesta. The concentration arose when British Steel and AGA were included as parents (joint control).

---

[28] *See* for an example *AG/Amev*, Case IV/M018, decision of 21 November 1990.

[29] Likewise, if a non-full function joint venture is turned into a full function joint venture, the Commission appears to consider only the (controlling) parents to be undertakings concerned, whereas the joint venture is not considered an undertaking concerned, *cf. Bayer/Röhm/ Makroform*, Case COMP/M1814, decision of 17 April 2000.

[30] *See* Undertaking Concerned Notice, para. 23 and *Credit Suisse/Nikko/MSA*, Case IV/M1273, decision of 14 August 1998, para. 13. It is worthy of note that the Commission originally took the view that not only the original and the new parent undertakings, but also the subsidiary were undertakings concerned. *See* further the 1994-edition of the Undertaking Concerned Notice, *supra* note 4, at para. 23 and *Bain/Hoechst – Dade Behring*, *supra* note 15, para. 9 with footnote 3 as well as the first edition of this book at pp. 26-27. *See* also the decision of 3 March 1999 in Case IV/M1420, *BASF/Svalöf Weibull*, in which the Commission apparently returned to its original interpretation. In *Matra/Aérospatiale*, Case IV/M1309, decision of 28 April 1999, the Commission seems to have considered the incoming parent and the subsidiary to have been the undertakings concerned. Perhaps the reason is that the other parent was the French State. Likewise, where the former parent is an individual or a family, the Commission appears to consider the incoming parent and the subsidiary to be the undertakings concerned. *See* for instance *Kohlberg Kravis Roberts/Wassall/Zumtobel*, Case COMP/M1876, decision of 13 April 2000 and *Accor/Ebertz/Dorint*, *supra* note 22 (where, however, not only the incoming parent and the subsidiary but also the Ebertz family – the former sole parent – were considered to be undertaking concerned).

[31] *See* Undertaking Concerned Notice, para. 44.

[32] *Supra* note 15.

Only the four parents should have been held to be undertakings concerned according to the above interpretation (Avesta's turnover should have been allocated to NCC and/or Axel Johnson in accordance with Art. 5(4) and (5)). The Commission apparently held the joint venture Avesta and each of the four parents to be undertakings concerned, however.[33]

I find the Commission's interpretation in *Avesta/British Steel/NCC* somewhat dubious. Firstly, I consider the existing parents of the joint venture – together with the incoming parent – to be parties to the concentration whereas I do not consider the joint venture to be a direct participant as such to the concentration. Secondly, I find it somewhat difficult to understand why the target must be counted as an undertaking concerned if it is under joint control whereas it shall not be so counted if it is under sole control. In my view, whether or not the target is under joint or sole control before the entry of the extra parent, the direct participants are the parents only.

It must be acknowledged that the interpretation that the parents to a joint venture are the undertakings concerned creates a major problem since setting up even the most insignificant full-function joint venture may be notifiable if the parents meet the thresholds. Thus, if minor subsidiaries of General Motors and IBM, sharing some offices, together decide to set up a small staff restaurant, this may well constitute a full-function joint venture. As the Community dimension is calculated on the basis of group turnover, the concentration will meet all the turnover thresholds and consequently be notifiable. Indeed, it does not matter whether the staff restaurant is set up inside or outside the Community.[34]

---

33 *See* likewise *Kirch/Richemont/Multichoice/Telepiù*, Case IV/M584, decision of 5 May 1995. *See* also below section 4.5 concerning replacing one joint controlling parent in a joint venture with another.

34 A real life example is *Saab Ericsson Space*, Case No. IV/M178, decision of 13 January 1992 where Saab Scania and Ericsson, both of Sweden (which at the material time was not part of the Community) set up a joint venture in Sweden with an annual turnover of € 30 million. The concentration fell within the scope of the Merger Regulation and was notifiable.

3.3. Joint Acquisition of Control

3.3.1. Introduction

In some situations, it may be difficult to identify the 'direct participants' in a concentration. This is not least the case where two undertakings acquire a third undertaking, but do so through a joint venture. Are the parents the direct participants or is it the joint venture (in either case together with the target)?

The only way of clarifying this matter is by looking more closely into the actual concentration to ascertain whether the joint venture is acting on its own, or whether it is the parents that are making the acquisition through the joint venture. Obviously, this distinction may be difficult to draw and it, therefore, hampers the aim that the Community dimension should be straightforward and easy to apply. The present definition of Community dimension leaves no room for a simpler system, however, since a more formalistic and easy-to-apply approach would make forum shopping extremely easy.[35]

Below, I shall first examine the situations where the parents are the acquirers, either because they make the acquisition directly or because they make it indirectly through a joint venture. Thereafter, I will look at the situation where the joint venture is the real acquirer.

3.3.2. Direct and indirect joint acquisition of control

If two (or more) undertakings make a joint acquisition by which they acquire joint control, these undertakings (together with the acquired entity) are the undertakings concerned. As noted in section 2.1 above, the essential question is who the direct participants are, and it, therefore, does not matter whether the acquisition (for technical or other reasons) has been made indirectly via a joint venture.[36] It is,

---

[35] Cf. European Commission, *supra* note 9 at point 7.1 in annex III (page 351), F.E. González Díaz, *supra* note 12 at p. 516 and I. Van Bael and J.-F. Bellis, *supra* note 16 at p. 377. Nevertheless, Heinz F. Löffler in *Langen/Bunte – Kommentar zum deutschen und europäischen Kartellrecht*, 9th ed., Luchterhand, Neuwied 2001 at pp. 2405-2407 takes a very sceptical stance to the lifting of the veil. Moreover at p. 2407 he puts forward the view that the veil shall only be lifted in respect of undertakings which are set up solely to make the acquisition and which do not undertake any other functions or where there is an intention of circumvention.

[36] Likewise, the Undertaking Concerned Notice, para. 28.

however, important to emphasise that it is either the joint venture or the parents that may be undertakings concerned.[37]

Example

A fine illustration of how the veil may be lifted is provided in *TNT/GD Net*.[38] In this case, five large undertakings set up a joint venture named GD Net. The purpose of this was to be able to set up a joint venture (named JVC) between, on the one hand, the five undertakings' joint venture (*i.e.* GD Net), and, on the other hand, the company TNT. This may be illustrated in the following way:

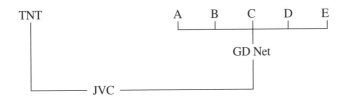

JVC is the joint venture set up as a consequence of the concentration so this is obviously not an undertaking concerned. Equally, TNT is one of the parents having control over JVC so it must be an undertaking concerned. The question is, however, whether GD Net or each of its five parents must be considered to be undertakings concerned with respect to the setting up of JVC. Upon examination of the case, the Commission concluded that GD Net was 'simply a vehicle set up to enable the [five parents of GD Net] to participate in JVC in order to facilitate decision-making amongst themselves and to ensure that they speak and act as one.'[39] In other words, GD Net was not a direct participant in the concentration, but only a vehicle. When piercing the veil, the Commission found that the five parents were

---

37 Likewise, Undertaking Concerned Notice, para. 28. Contrast, however, with *Warner Bros./ Lusomundo/Sogecable*, Case IV/M902, decision of 12 May 1997 at para. 10 where the Commission held both the joint venture (Sogecable) and its parents (Prisa and Canal+) to be undertakings concerned.

38 Case IV/M102, decision of 2 December 1991.

39 Para. 10 of the decision. *See* likewise *GTS Hermes Inc./HIT Rail BV*, Case IV/M683, decision of 5 March 1996, para. 8. It seems to follow from the wording of the Commission's decision that the Commission does not require the parents of the bid vehicle to have control (veto rights over the important decisions) of the bid vehicle. This equally means that the parents do not have such control *vis-à-vis* the full function joint venture itself.

the direct participants and consequently they would have to be considered to be undertakings concerned. A, B, C, D, E and TNT were, therefore, considered to be undertakings concerned.[40]

While it may be easy to apply the general principle in the above example, in practice, the dividing line is often somewhat more difficult to draw. In order to aid the undertakings, the Commission has provided some guidelines as to how to draw this line.[41]

The following are indicators of a full-function joint venture, strongly indicating that it is not a bid vehicle:[42]

- The joint venture operates on the market and performs the functions normally carried out by other undertakings operating on the same market.

- Thus, the joint venture must have a management dedicated to its day-to-day operations and access to sufficient resources including finance, staff and assets (tangible and intangible) enabling it to operate a business activity on a lasting basis.

The following indicators point towards considering the joint venture to be only a bid vehicle:[43]

---

[40]   Another example of the Commission's lifting the veil is provided in *Eucom/Digital*, Case IV/M218, decision of 18 May 1992; *see* in particular para. 12. I. Van Bael and J.-F. Bellis, *supra* note 16 at p. 381 with note 77 finds that the Commission was wrong in lifting the veil in this case. In contrast, in *France Telecom/EDITEL/LINCE*, Case IV/M1553, decision of 30 July 1999, (where the set up was very similar to the one in *TNT/GD Net*) the Commission chose not to lift the veil irrespective of the fact that Editel was 'created under Spanish law to facilitate the participation of its shareholders in the Lince joint venture'. Hence, Editel was considered to be one of the undertakings concerned. It appears that the Commission would have had jurisdiction irrespective of what interpretation it had chosen.

[41]   Barry E. Hawk and Henry L. Huser, *European Community Merger Control: A Practitioner's Guide*, Kluwer Law International, the Hague 1996, at pp. 95-96 observe that the Commission originally applied a clear dividing line for determining whether the joint venture or the parents are the undertakings concerned. The guidelines that have been introduced in the Undertaking Concerned Notice have obscured this 'for no readily apparent enforcement purpose or benefit.' The two authors in note 68 on p. 96 indicate that the aim of the dividing line was 'to further expand the jurisdictional scope of the Merger Regulation.'

[42]   *See* further 'Commission Notice on the concept of full-function joint ventures under Council Regulation (EEC) No 4064/89 of 21 December 1989 on the control of concentrations between undertakings', OJ C66/1, 2.3.1998, at para. 12.

[43]   *See* further, Undertaking Concerned Notice at paras. 27-28 and 'Commission Notice on the concept of full-function joint ventures', *supra* note 42 at paras. 13-15.

– The joint venture is set up especially for the purpose of acquiring the target company.
– The joint venture has not yet started to operate.
– An existing joint venture is used, but this has no legal personality or full-function character.
– The joint venture is an association of undertakings.
– There is a significant involvement by the parent companies themselves in the initiative, organisation and financing of the operation.
– The acquisition leads to a substantial diversification in the nature of the joint venture's activities (*i.e.* the target company operates on a different market than does the joint venture).
– The joint venture has taken over only one specific function within the parent companies' business activities (*e.g.* R&D or distribution).
– The joint venture is dependent on the parent companies as sellers or purchasers for more than just an initial start-up period.
– The joint venture has been established for a short finite duration only.

Most of these indicators are well founded, but it is obvious that they are very broad. This means that the Commission has a large margin of discretion (subject to review by the Court of Justice) when deciding whether an acquisition is made by a joint venture or its parents. It has been pointed out that the Commission's practice does not fully comply with these indicators so that, in some cases, a Community dimension has been found where this appears to be at least doubtful.[44] In addition, more than a decade after the Merger Regulation entered into force, one wonders whether it is not now possible to provide some narrower and more specific guidelines.

3.3.3. Acquisition of control by an independent joint venture

If the acquisition is made by a full-function joint venture and this joint venture carries out the acquisition itself and intends to run the acquired entity independently of its parents, the direct participants are the joint venture and the

---

44 *See* I. Van Bael and J.-F. Bellis, *supra* note 16 at p. 381 with note 77.

acquired entity. Consequently, these must be considered to be the undertakings concerned.[45]

Joint ventures must be categorised as either a 'vehicle' or as a 'full-function' joint venture. In order to establish whether the joint venture is 'full-function' (*i.e.* it is an undertaking concerned) or a 'vehicle' (*i.e.* the parents are the undertakings concerned), the guidelines set out just above in section 3.3.2 apply.

3.3.4. Consequences of the distinction between bid vehicles and independent joint ventures

An important purpose of lifting the veil is to prevent forum shopping. Nevertheless, even though it is obvious that the present regime does result in this prevention, it still allows a fair amount of forum shopping as will be shown below in chapter 8.

---

[45] Likewise, Undertaking Concerned Notice, para. 27. From the Commission's case law, *see* for example *Fortis/La Caixa*, Case IV/M254, decision of 5 November 1992, (Fortis is a joint venture between AG and Amev, but the Commission rightly treated Fortis as the undertaking concerned) and *GEC Alsthom NV/AEG*, Case IV/M706, decision of 3 September 1996, (GEC Alsthom NV is a joint venture between General Electric Company plc and Alcatel Alsthom CGE). Another fine example is provided in *Ford/Jardine*, Case IV/M1435, decision of 23 February 1999, concerning the acquisition of the undertaking Dagenham by the undertaking Polar, the latter a joint venture between Ford and Jardine. In this case the Commission explains that '… Polar is … not a full-function joint venture within the meaning of Article 3(2) of the Merger Regulation. The undertakings concerned are therefore Dagenham, Ford and Jardine.' In some cases the Commission has diverted from the interpretation set out here, however. Thus, in *Elenac/Hoechst*, Case IV/M1287, decision of 24 November 1998, two full-function joint ventures (jointly referred to as Elenac and earlier examined and cleared by the Commission in *BASF/Shell*, Case IV/M1041, decision of 23 December 1997) acquired sole control over another business. Even though it appears from the Commission's decision that Elenac was the undertaking concerned the Commission considered Elenac's two parents to be the undertakings concerned for the purpose of calculating Community dimension. A rather remarkable example of a diversion from the interpretation set out above may be found in *Wacker/Air Products*, Case IV/M1097, decision of 4 August 1998. This case concerned a concentration involving Wacker (a full-function joint venture of Hoechst and the Wacker family) and Air Products. There can hardly be any doubt that the undertakings concerned were Wacker and Air Products. The Commission however considered Wacker, Air Products and Hoechst to be the undertakings concerned. *See* also *Thomson-CSF/Eurocopter*, Case IV/M1516, decision of 10 June 1999 (concerning the creation of a joint venture between Thomson-CSF and Eurocopter, but the Commission considered Thomson-CSF and Eurocopter's two parents to be the undertakings concerned).

Lifting the veil also has significant consequences for the calculation of Community dimension. Indeed all the thresholds may be affected.

It is submitted that the thresholds based on combined aggregate turnover (€ 5 billion or € 2.5 billion worldwide turnover and € 100 million Member State-wide turnover) may be affected since not all parents of the joint venture may fulfil the requirements for being counted as part of the joint venture's group, even though they would be counted as undertakings concerned if the veil were lifted. This is so because the Regulation applies one concept of control in Article 3 concerning the notion of concentration and another in Article 5 concerning the notion of Community dimension. This difference and the Commission's view thereon is further discussed below in chapter 3.

Example

A and B jointly own JV. A owns 60% of all shares, holds 60% of all voting rights and appoints the majority of the board. B holds the outstanding 40% of JV. Neither A nor B manages JV's affairs. A shareholders' agreement, however, gives A and B joint control within the meaning of Article 3 of the Merger Regulation. If JV makes an acquisition and is considered to be the undertaking concerned, only the turnover of A may be included in accordance with Article 5(4) of the Regulation. In contrast, if A and B are considered to be the undertakings concerned, the full B-group must be included when calculating the combined aggregate turnover thresholds.[46]

Also, the Community-wide and the Member State-wide thresholds (€ 250 million or € 100 million Community-wide turnover and € 25 million Member State-wide turnover) may be affected. Thus, if a JV acquires a target having a turnover of less than € 100 million in the Community, it is only possible to meet the second threshold set's € 100 million Community-wide turnover threshold if the veil is lifted. Otherwise, there will only be two undertakings concerned (the JV and the target) and since one of these does not achieve a Community-wide turnover of more than € 100 million, the threshold cannot be reached. Just as in the above example relating to the combined aggregate turnover thresholds, lifting the veil may mean that a concentration is given a Community dimension. Lifting the veil may, however, also mean that a concentration no longer has a Community dimension.

---

[46] Likewise, H.F. Löffler, *supra* note 35 at p. 1954.

Example

The Japanese undertakings A and B decide to acquire the German undertaking Z through a joint venture, JV. Though both A and B have worldwide turnovers exceeding € 5 billion, they only generate € 75 million each in the Community. Z has a Community-wide turnover of € 300 million. Only if the veil is not lifted will the operation have Community dimension.

Finally, lifting the veil may also influence on the two-thirds rule and again this may mean that the operation either gains or loses a Community dimension.

Example

A, B and C jointly own a joint venture, JV, on a 60/20/20 basis. JV acquires X which has a Community-wide turnover of € 300 million, all of which is achieved in France. A, B and C each have worldwide turnovers of € 6 billion. While A and B each achieve all of their turnover in France, C achieves only 60% of its Community-wide turnover in this country. If the veil is not lifted, therefore, only X and JV are undertakings concerned and the operation does not have a Community dimension, but if the veil is lifted, A, B, C and X are undertakings concerned and since C generates less than two-thirds of its Community-wide turnover in France, the operation has a Community dimension.

3.4. Acquisition of joint control in order to split assets immediately

Recital 24 of the Merger Regulation provides that acquisitions of joint control with the object of sharing the assets of the target are notifiable under the Regulation.[47] If the acquirers share the target's assets immediately after the acquisition, however, there is no concentration of economic power between all of the acquirers and the full target.[48] Rather each acquirer enters into a concentration with the

---

[47] For the background to the inclusion of this provision, *see* T. Antony Downes and Julian Ellison, *The Legal Control of Mergers in the EC*, Blackstone Press Ltd., London 1991 at pp. 39-40.

[48] Along the same line, the Commission has found that if two undertakings decide to acquire joint control over a third undertaking, but as part of this acquisition one of the acquirers will hold sole control for a short term, this will be viewed as only one single concentration (joint control), *cf. Deutsche Bank/Commerzbank/J.M. Voith*, Case IV/M891, decision of 23 April 1997.

assets acquired. Thus, the operation constitutes more concentrations, and it is, therefore, necessary to calculate the Community dimension for each of these.[49]

Example

This may be illustrated by the following example where A and B jointly acquire T in order to split T's assets:

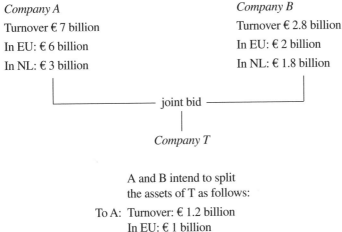

Company A	*Company B*
Turnover € 7 billion	Turnover € 2.8 billion
In EU: € 6 billion	In EU: € 2 billion
In NL: € 3 billion	In NL: € 1.8 billion

— joint bid —

Company T

A and B intend to split
the assets of T as follows:

To A: Turnover: € 1.2 billion
In EU: € 1 billion
In NL: € 0.7 billion

To B: Turnover: € 1 billion
In EU: € 1 billion
In NL: € 1 billion

If the acquisition is seen as one concentration, the worldwide turnover will be € 12 billion, the Community-wide turnover will in all three cases exceed

---

49 *See* also Undertaking Concerned Notice, paras. 24-25, *Norsk Hydro/Saga*, Case IV/M1573, decision of 5 July 1999, *Siemens/Dematic/Sachs/VDO*, Case COMP/M2059, decision of 29 August 2000 but contrast with *Bosch/Rexroth*, Case COMP/M2060, decision of 4 December 2000 and *Avnet/Veba Electronics*, Case COMP/M2134, decision of 18 October 2000. In the *2001 Green Paper on the Review of Council Regulation (EEC) No 4064/89*, COM(2001) 745 final, Brussels 11.12.2001, para. 130 with note 25 the Commission confirms the interpretation set out here but adds that 'to the extent that there is any uncertainty concerning this future disposition of the jointly acquired assets, the joint bid will be considered, in its totality, as a single concentration, the assessment of which will include any known dispositions to break up the acquired assets.'

€ 250 million and only B and T achieve more than two-thirds of their Community-wide turnover in one and the same Member State. In other words, the operation has a Community dimension.

If the acquisition is considered to constitute two concentrations, only Company A's acquisition of parts of T will be notifiable since B itself as well as as the assets that B acquire of T generate more than two-thirds of the Community-wide turnover in the Netherlands. Hence the two-thirds rule has not been met.

The above rule is not likely to provide the business community with a possibility of circumvention or forum shopping. This is so since such circumvention necessarily implies that the acquirers either do not split the target's assets (if they had claimed that they so intended) or they do split the assets (if they have not claimed so). Often, this will be very easy to verify. Thus, the acquirers run the risk that either the Commission or one or more Member State competition authorities will decide to examine the operation if it becomes apparent that the original outcome regarding the Community dimension examination was wrong. Put differently, rather than avoiding having the operation vetted by a certain competition authority, the acquirers run the risk of having to go through more than one examination.

4. TAKING OVER A PART ONLY

4.1. Introduction

The basic idea underlying the calculation of the Community dimension is that concentrations between large undertakings are more likely to have effects at Community level than are concentrations between small undertakings. After all, merger control is meant to prevent a damaging accumulation of market power.

Where one large undertaking acquires sole control over a subsidiary, a production unit or the like from another large undertaking, this constitutes a concentration. The selling party cedes control over the part sold, however, and it follows from the basic principle underlying the notion of Community dimension that the seller should not be included when making the necessary calculations.[50]

---

[50] Likewise, 'Commission Notice on calculation of turnover under Council Regulation (EEC) No 4064/89 of 21 December 1989 on the control of concentrations between undertakings', OJ C66/25 of 2.3.1998, at para. 31; (Turnover Calculation Notice).

Article 5(2) of the Merger Regulation, therefore, provides that where only a part of an undertaking is acquired, this part – and not the seller – is taken into account for the purposes of calculating the Community dimension.

Example

In 1991, the British computer company ICL aquired Nokia Data from the Finnish company Nokia OY. In addition to the full turnover of the group of companies, to which ICL belonged (€ 18.437 billion), only the small turnover of Nokia Data was taken into account (€ 318 million) rather than the much larger turnover of Nokia OY.[51]

The crucial point is that the seller cedes control over the part sold. This means that the seller may remain financially involved (*i.e.* keep a minority interest) and still be excluded when calculating the Community dimension.[52]

Below, I will examine how the general definition of 'undertaking concerned' fits with the notion of a part as provided in Article 5(2)(1). The first question, of course, is how one defines a part. Following this, I will examine the application in a number of difficult situations, after which I will turn to the judgment by the Court of First Instance in the *British Airways/Dan Air case*.[53] To a fair extent, this judgment ruined what was otherwise a fairly coherent system. Finally, I shall examine the provision laid down in Article 5(2)(2), a provision which has been created to prevent circumvention of Article 5(2)(1).

---

51 *ICL/Nokia Data*, Case IV/M105, decision of 17 July 1991.

52 *See* as examples *Digital/Kienzle*, Case IV/M057, decision of 22 February 1991, *Alcatel/ Telettra*, Case IV/M042, decision of 12 April 1991, OJ [1991] L122/48 and *Magnetti Marelli/ CEAC*, Case IV/M043, decision of 24 May 1991, OJ [1991] L222/38. Contrast with *Cereol/ Aceprosa*, Case IV/M720, decision of 7 June 1996, where Cereol acquired 'sole control' of Aceprosa's 'assets in the oleaginous seed crushing and oil refining business', but the Commission nevertheless considered Aceprosa (the seller) to be an undertaking concerned together with Cereol (the acquirer). The same mistake appears to have been committed in *Hitachi/IBM Harddisk Business*, Case COMP/M2821, decision of 2 August 2002.

53 Case T-3/93, *Société Anonyme à Participation Ouvrière Compagnie Nationale Air France* v. *Commission of the European Communities*, [1994] ECR II-121.

4.2. Definition of a 'part'

The Merger Regulation nowhere provides a definition of a 'part'. One characteristic is, however, certain: the part must be able to generate turnover since otherwise it cannot be used for calculating the Community dimension. For example, a business logo will not in itself constitute a 'part' while the licensing rights to attach a logo or name (such as Mickey Mouse or Christian Dior) to a product may constitute a 'part'.

The Commission has attempted to define a part in the following way:

> 'The concept of 'parts' is to be understood as one or more separate legal entities (such as subsidiaries), internal subdivisions within the seller (such as a division or unit), or specific assets which in themselves could constitute a business (e.g. in certain cases brands or licenses) to which a market turnover can be clearly attributed.'[54]

This definition essentially provides that any unit or asset to which a turnover in the market can clearly be attributed may constitute a part.[55] The definition seems to hit the nail on the head, although, admittedly, it is extremely vague. Nevertheless, it is fair to presume that it will not create significant problems:[56] Where there is only

---

[54] Undertaking Concerned Notice, para. 14.

[55] For a somewhat conflicting view, *see* Ulrich Immenga, 'Zur Umsatzberechnung öffentlicher Unternehmen im Rahmen der europäischen Fusionskontrolle' in *Festschrift für Ulrich Everling* (Ole Due, Marcus Lutter and Jürgen Schwarze, eds.), Nomos Verlagsgesellschaft, Baden-Baden 1995, pp. 541-550 at p. 550. *See* also T.A. Downes and J. Ellison, *supra* note 47 at p. 59 who write: 'A part of an undertaking, although nowhere defined, must be assumed to be either a subsidiary or a discrete business, and not merely assets, since it must have a turnover attributed to it'. It might be interesting to know that under Hungarian merger control law the term 'part of an undertaking' has been defined in the following way: '… those assets and/or rights – including the client base of an undertaking – shall qualify as a part of an undertaking, the acquisition of which – individually or together with the assets and rights at the disposal of the acquiring undertaking – is sufficient for conducting market activities', cf. Baker & McKenzie, *European Legal Developments Bulletin*, January 2002, Vol. 14, issue 1, p. 46.

[56] In cases where one undertaking straightforwardly acquires a part of another undertaking, the rule appears to present no problems, although an exception is perhaps provided in *Zürich/ MMI*, Case IV/M286, decision of 2 April 1993, in which the insurance company Zürich acquired a right to renew a part (but not all) of the insurance company MMI's portfolio. Nevertheless, according to the wording of the decision, MMI (and not only the parts of MMI acquired by Zürich) were considered to be an undertaking concerned. Apparently the part

one acquirer, the turnover generated by the part must amount to minimum € 100 million (or € 250 million) if the operation is to have a Community dimension. Parts generating turnover of this size are so large that only large production units, licenses and trademarks etc. will be covered. If a trademark generates a turnover of more than € 100 million in the Community, it is probably fair to accept that, to a certain degree, it constitutes a business in its own right.[57] In contrast, where there is more than one acquirer, these may by themselves fulfil the Community dimension requirements.[58] In such case, the problem is not, however, whether the

---

acquired from MMI generated more than € 250 million in the Community (meaning that the concentration had a Community dimension in any case) so one should probably not attach too much significance to the decision.

[57] In *Delta Air Lines/Pan Am*, Case IV/M130, decision of 13 September 1991 Delta Air Lines acquired Pan Am's North Atlantic air transport business (*i.e.* the North Atlantic routes) and related interests. *See* also *Blokker/Toys 'R' Us*, Case IV/M890, decision of 26 June 1997, [1998] OJ L316/1, paras. 15 and 17, in which the Commission observes: 'In this operation Blokker takes over all the assets (leases, fixtures and inventory, personnel, use of brand name) which make up the business of Toys 'R' Us in the Netherlands. To this business a turnover can clearly be attributed'. Nevertheless, the € 5000 million turnover was not met so the concentration did not have a Community dimension. In *AT&T/IBM Global Network*, Case IV/M1396, decision of 22 April 1999, AT&T acquired some physical and logical infrastructure together with certain related assets. This acquisition met the thresholds. In *EDF/ South Western Electricity*, Case IV/M1606, decision of 19 July 1999, EdF (through a subsidiary) purchased 'the goodwill and certain assets of South Western Electricity plc's supply activities and [entered] into an Agency Agreement with South Western Electricity plc …'. This constituted a notifiable concentration. Other examples include *Celestica/IBM (EMS)*, Case COMP/M1841, decision of 25 February 2000, *Solectron/Ericsson*, Case COMP/M1849, decision of 29 February 2000, *Michel Mineralölhandel/Thyssen-Elf Oil*, Case COMP/M2335, decision of 28 February 2001 and *Sanmina-SCI/Hewlett Packard*, Case COMP/M2815, decision of 28 May 2002. *See* also *Saint-Gobain/Wacker-Chemie/NOM*, *supra* note 15, concerning the acquisition of certain tangible and intangible assets and *Enron/MG*, Case COMP/ M2006, decision of 4 July 2000 concerning the aquisition of certain client lists, warrants and physical inventory. In neither of these two cases the assets were included as an undertaking concerned for the purposes of calculating the Community dimension, however. It may be added that for practical reasons, the assets to be sold will often be placed in a company set up for that specific purpose (so that formally the transaction concerns a company and not only assets). *See* for example *Flextronics/Italdata*, Case COMP/M2116, decision of 25 September 2000.

[58] *See e.g. Kelt/American Express*, Case IV/M116, decision of 20 August 1991. M. Siragusa and R. Subiotto, *supra* note 7 at p. 902 with note 45 indicate that this case constitutes 'a questionable application of Art. 5(2)'. Support for this view cannot be found in the decision

acquisition concerns a part (as this is only relevant *vis-à-vis* the calculation of the Community dimension), but whether the acquisition constitutes a concentration within the meaning of Article 3 of the Regulation. The problem is, therefore, not one of Community dimension, but one of the definition of a concentration in Article 3, a problem which falls outside the scope of this work.

Example

A fashion designer builds up a number of clothing brands in the Community. Each brand name and related intellectual property rights are owned by a company, but all production and all services are subcontracted so that the different companies own nothing but these intellectual property rights. If the designer sells one of the companies, it will clearly be a sale of a part (of the designer's holdings). The same is true, however, if the designer retains the company, but sells the intellectual property rights therein.

4.3. Going from joint to sole control

The Merger Regulation applies to 'concentrations' with 'a Community dimension'. The Commission has interpreted the notion of concentration to cover also passages from joint to sole control. For instance, where two parents of a joint venture decide that the one parent shall sell its stake to the other. The purchaser remains in control over the joint venture (which ceases to be a joint venture), but this control changes from being joint to being sole.

The problem to be dealt with here is how to calculate the Community dimension. It is obvious that the seller, ceding control, shall not be included. It is equally obvious that the purchaser, acquiring sole control, must be included. But how do we calculate the turnover of the part sold? An example based on the first set of thresholds may illustrate the problem.

Example

A and B jointly control JV, with A holding 40% of the shares in JV while B holds the remaining 60%. A and B agree that A shall acquire all of B's shares, thereby giving A sole control over JV. If A has a turnover of € 5.5 billion in the

---

itself, neither does Gerwin Van Gerven, 'Case Note: Kelt/American Express', *EC Merger Control Reporter*, Kluwer Law International, The Hague 1991 and later (looseleaf), pp. 345-346 at p. 345 support the view of Siragusa and Subiotto.

Community and does not achieve more than two-thirds thereof in any Member State, the operation has a Community dimension if JV generates more than € 250 million in the Community.

Three calculation methods may be considered.

First, we may consider A's acquisition to constitute the 60% of JV acquired from B. Hence, the 60% must amount to at least € 250 million (*i.e.* JV must have a Community-wide turnover of at least € 417.7 million). According to this view, the calculation must reflect the size of the part of the joint venture acquired by the purchaser.

Second, we may apply the principle provided in Article 5(5) of the Merger Regulation. This principle provides that if two (or more) undertakings concerned jointly control a joint venture, the turnover of this joint venture must be allocated equally between the undertakings concerned, regardless of the actual holding in it, when calculating the Community dimension. Applying this principle to the above example means that one must count half of JV's turnover for the purpose of calculating the Community dimension. (*i.e.* JV must have a Community-wide turnover of at least € 500 million).

The third option is to emphasise that the parents (A and B) formerly had joint control over all of the joint venture (JV) and the sale means that one parent (A) will obtain sole control over the whole joint venture. In other words, the situation does not concern the sale of only a part of the joint venture, it concerns the joint venture as a whole.

In the Undertaking Concerned Notice, the Commission has submitted to the third option.[59] I do not agree with this view.

---

[59] *See* para. 30 of the Notice. Examples from practice include *ICI/Tioxide*, Case IV/M023, decision of 28 November 1990, *Eridania/ISI*, Case IV/M062, decision of 20 July 1991, *Grand Metropolitan/Cinzano*, Case IV/M184, decision of 7 February 1992, *ABB/BREL*, Case IV/M221, decision of 26 May 1992, *Volkswagen/VAG (UK)*, Case IV/M304, decision of 4 February 1993, *Sanofi/Kodak*, Case IV/M480, decision of 12 July 1994, *Volvo/VME*, Case IV/M575, decision of 11 April 1995, *GE/Power Controls B.V.*, Case IV/M577, decision of 28 April 1995, *Ferruzi Finanziaria/Fondiaria*, Case IV/M576, decision of 9 June 1995, *Metallgesellschaft/Safic-Alcan (II)*, Case IV/M834, decision of 21 November 1996, *Klöckner/ODS*, Case IV/M918, decision of 5 August 1997, *AXA-UAP/Royale Belge*, Case IV/M1193, decision of 12 June 1998, *MAN Roland/Omnigraph (II)*, Case IV/M1448, decision of 5 May 1999 and *INA/LuK*, Case COMP/M1789, decision of 22 December 1999. In *ABB/BREL*, *Eridania/ISI*, *Grand Metropolitan/Cinzano*, *Klöckner/ODS* and *MAN Roland/Omnigraph (II)* the € 250 million threshold would not have been met if the Commission had applied

The idea underlying the Community dimension is to measure the concentration of economic power as only major concentrations going across the Member State borders are considered to have effects at Community level.[60] Taking the above example, A and B have held joint control over JV. Thus, previous to the passage to sole control, A has held joint control over JV. Acquiring sole control over JV does not mean that A's economic power increases to an extent which corresponds to the full economic power of JV. Nevertheless, this is what the third solution, adopted by the Commission, reflects. In other words, the Commission treats the passage from joint to sole control in exactly the same way as going from no control to sole control.

In my view, applying the principle provided in Article 5(5) of the Regulation provides a better solution since it more accurately reflects the actual change of economic power. Applying the principle in Article 5(5) means that we divide the joint venture equally between the parents having joint control, irrespective of their actual holding. In the above example, this will mean that A must only apportion half of JV's full turnover to JV when calculating the Community dimension. If, instead, we have four parents holding joint control over a joint venture, but one acquires the holdings of the three others thereby taking sole control, three-quarters or 75% of the joint venture's turnover must be counted as the 'part' acquired for the purpose of the Community dimension.

It is submitted that the Commission's interpretation implies an overstatement of the importance of this kind of transaction, whereby more transactions are likely to be given a Community dimension than would otherwise be the case. In other words, the Commission's interpretation implies an expansion of the Commission's jurisdiction.

4.4. Reductions or increases in the number of parents of a joint venture

Where the number of controlling parents of a joint venture is changed, but the joint venture remains under joint control (instead of coming under sole control), the

---

the interpretation I advocate here. Note also that *Klöckner/ODS* concerned Klöckner's acquisition of sole control of a co-operative joint venture.

[60] *See* recitals 9, 10 and 11 to the Merger Regulation.

Commission takes the view that this may amount to a concentration, though it also states that this is not normally the case.[61]

Example

In *Avesta (II)*,[62] the four largest shareholders held joint control over Avesta through a shareholders' agreement. Part of the shareholders' agreement was that prior written consent from the two largest shareholders and at least one of the two remaining large shareholders (but not necessarily both) was required regarding certain major decisions. When one of the two last mentioned shareholders sold its stake to third parties, the shareholders' agreement remained in force so that it was now necessary to obtain written consent from all three (remaining) parties to the agreement. The Commission found that this constituted a qualitative change of control since one of the (now) three large shareholders thereby acquired a negative veto right.

In reality, *Avesta (II)* concerns a situation where the number of controlling parents rose from two to three. An increase in the number of parents jointly controlling a joint venture is generally considered to constitute a concentration.[63]

In my view, the principle set out in Article 5(5) and explained above in section 4.3 should be applied. In *Avesta (II),* this would have meant that the exiting parent will not be an undertaking concerned. The concentration directly concerns the remaining three parents, however, so they should be considered to be undertakings concerned. Moreover, Article 5(5) explicitly provides that where the undertakings concerned jointly control an undertaking (in this case Avesta), the turnover of the latter should be apportioned equally to these parents. Thus, the turnover of Avesta must be divided equally between the three remaining parents.

The Commission chose a different approach where it considered Avesta and each of the parents to be undertakings concerned. This approach follows the principle applied by the Commission *vis-à-vis* changes from joint to sole control. The Commission's justification in the case of changes from joint to sole control cannot,

---

61 Cf. Undertaking Concerned Notice, para. 38.

62 Case IV/M452, decision of 9 June 1994.

63 *See* as examples *CEA Industrie/France Telecom/Finmeccanica/SGS-Thomson*, Case IV/M216, decision of 21 January 1993 and *Particitel International/Cableuropa*, Case IV/M1251, decision of 30 July 1998. In *Norske Skog/ABITIBI/PAPCO*, Case COMP/M2493, decision of 3 July 2001 and in *Vodafone/BT/Airtel JV*, Case COMP/M1863, decision of 18 December 2000 the Commission considered a decrease from three to two controlling parents to constitute a notifiable concentration. Hopefully, these were just unfortunate mistakes.

however, be applied to cases of reductions or increases in the number of parents of a joint venture (without being adapted at least).[64] Moreover, it is respectfully submitted that the Commission's approach does not harmonise with Article 5(5) of the Merger Regulation.[65]

Again, it is noteworthy that the Commission's approach leads to a broader scope than the interpretation which I subscribe to.

4.5. Replacing one shareholder with another in a joint venture

If the number of controlling parents in a joint venture remains the same, though one parent is replaced by another, the Commission finds that this amounts to a concentration.[66]

Example

A and B jointly control JV. A sells its share to C meaning that C and B now jointly control JV.

In my view, this situation differs from the one where the number of parents is reduced or increased, as the latter change necessarily affects the control of all the parents. (If the number of controlling parents changes, there will be either more or fewer with whom to share control). Simply substituting one parent with another does not really affect the quality of control of the remaining parent or parents.

The Commission has, however, taken the opposite view. It, therefore, finds that substituting one parent with another 'implies a change in the nature and quality of control of the whole joint venture, even when both before and after the operation, joint control is exercised by a given number of shareholders. ... The Commission therefore considers that the undertakings concerned in cases where there are changes in the shareholding are the shareholders (both existing and new) who exercise joint

---

[64] *See* Undertaking Concerned Notice, paras. 38-39.

[65] *See* likewise *PTT Post/TNT-GD Net*, Case IV/M787, decision of 22 July 1996, where PTT, TNT and four other undertakings had joint control of GD Express. When the four last-mentioned undertakings gave up their joint control over GD Express TNT and PTT were left as the only (jointly) controlling undertakings. Like in *Avesta (II)*, the Commission considered not only TNT and PTT but also GD Express to be undertakings concerned.

[66] Undertaking Concerned Notice, para. 43.

control and the joint venture itself.'[67] It has been pointed out that this interpretation may 'open the floodgates to an enormous number of concentrations' (many of which would be notifiable) if it were to cover also indirect changes of control, such as where X and Y jointly control JV, and X is acquired by Z, indirectly giving Z joint control over JV.[68] In order to avoid being flooded with notifications, the Commission will normally only investigate the transaction if the acquisition of joint control over the joint venture is the principal transaction. Obviously, this does not contribute to the coherence of the Commission's interpretation.[69]

In my opinion, a better interpretation is to view the incoming parent's acquisition of a shareholding in the joint venture as an acquisition of a part of the control over this joint venture. In the above example, this would mean that C (the incoming parent) would be an undertaking concerned and that the part sold by A would be the other undertaking concerned. Following the principle in Article 5(5), this amounts to half of JV's turnover regardless of the actual size of the shareholding sold.

It is obviously true that the acquisition of sole control over a part (such as a subsidiary) and the acquisition of joint control, (by substituting one parent in a joint venture), are two rather different transactions leading to different kinds of control. In my view, however, this solution is the one which best reflects the economic concentration of power brought about by the transaction. An example may illustrate this.

Example

Ten undertakings jointly control JV. One of these controlling parent undertakings is substituted by another, but this does not affect the rights and obligations of the other controlling parents, nor of the joint venture.

Is the best reflection of the economic importance of this transaction to take:

    i) the full group turnover of the nine remaining parent undertakings,

---

67   Undertaking Concerned Notice, paras. 43 and 44. *See* also *Synthomer/Yule Catto*, Case IV/ M376, decision of 22 October 1993, *James River/Rayne*, Case IV/M162, decision of 13 February 1992, *RVI/VBC/HEULIEZ*, Case IV/M092, decision of 3 June 1991 and *Knorr-Bremse/Robert Bosch*, Case IV/M1342, decision of 14 December 1998.

68   D. Livingston, *supra* note 16, at p. 745.

69   *See* also the *2001 Green Paper on the review of the Merger Regulation*, *supra* note 49, paras. 131-132 and the example provided in chapter 8, section 3.5 concerning the possibilities of circumventing the jurisdictional rules which this interpretation lays open.

   ii) the full group turnover of the new parent undertaking, and

   iii) the full group turnover of the joint venture, but excluding turnover generated by the parents if they are included in the group.

Or should one take:

   i) the full group turnover of the new parent, and

   ii) the full group turnover of the joint venture.

Or should one take:

   i) the full group turnover of the new parent, and

   ii) one-tenth of the full group turnover of the joint venture.

Admittedly, where ten undertakings have joint control over a joint venture, each
parent undertaking does not simply hold control over one-tenth of this joint venture. On the other hand, I believe that the higher the number of undertakings sharing control over a joint venture, the less real control each of these parents has. I
find it difficult, therefore, to accept the Commission's interpretation according
to which a transaction in which undertaking Q has two parents holding joint control and one is substituted with another is less likely to have a Community dimension than if undertaking Q had fifty parents holding joint control and one is
substituted with another. In my view, the solution which I adhere to better reflects
the economic significance of a concentration and thus is the better reflection of a
Community dimension. As in the situations dealt with in sections 4.3 and 4.4,
the Commission's interpretation leads to a much broader scope of the Merger Regulation than does my interpretation.

4.6. Dividing jointly controlled assets

For a variety of reasons, the parents of a joint venture may decide to break it up and
divide the assets. Thus, there is a change from joint control over the joint venture
to sole control over the acquired assets. The Commission finds that each parent's
acquisition of a part of the joint venture constitutes a concentration, though this
concentration will normally be dependent on the other parent's or parents' acquisition of sole control of their part(s) of the joint venture.[70]

---

[70] It seems that the Commission's practice concerning whether mutually interdependent transactions form one or more concentrations is rather inconsistent. Hence, in *Kingfisher/*

It is not too difficult to identify the undertakings concerned in this situation. On the one hand, we have the acquiring parent and, on the other hand, we have the part acquired.

Example

A and B jointly own and control JV which has two divisions, X and Y. Deciding to break up JV, A and B agree that A shall acquire X and B shall acquire Y. This constitutes two concentrations in which respectively A + X and B + Y are the undertakings concerned.

Other interpretations are hard to conceive. Thus, to argue that the total assets of the joint venture should be included would be wrong since this would clearly overstate the economic size of the concentration. To include all the parent undertakings as undertakings concerned would be even more wrong as this presupposes that the break-up is considered to constitute only one concentration and that the transaction should lead to an aggregation of economic power between the undertakings concerned (where in fact it concerns a segregation). Even though the Commission uses the term 'concentration' rather extensively, a construction as broad as this would be difficult to conceive.

The Undertaking Concerned Notice[71] shows that the Commission unambiguously supports the interpretation submitted here. To some extent, this is surprising as the case law from before the issuing of the Notice does not fully support this. Indeed, in *Campsa*,[72] the first case concerning a break-up of a joint venture, the Commission viewed the operation as one single concentration so that all the major shareholders that acquired parts of the joint venture's assets were considered to be undertakings concerned. Subsequently, in *Solvay-Laporte/Interox*,[73] the Commission was again faced with a break-up of a joint venture, and, this time, it applied the interpretation submitted here. In this decision, the Commission went to great lengths to distinguish the case from that in *Campsa*, making it clear that the inter-

---

Grosslabor, Case IV/M1482, decision of 12 April 1999, the Commission regarded a number of transactions as one single concentration 'since the different elements were mutually interdependent'.

[71] Para. 48 of the Notice.

[72] Case IV/M138, decision of 19 December 1991.

[73] Case IV/M197, decision of 30 April 1992.

pretation provided in the latter should be considered to be only an exception.[74] The Undertaking Concerned Notice apparently definitively reverses the interpretation applied in *Campsa*.[75]

4.7. Asset swaps

Where two undertakings agree to swap assets, this essentially amounts to two sales transactions.

Example

The brewer A and the mineral water producer B agree that A shall acquire B's brewery-subsidiary and that B shall acquire A's mineral water-subsidiary.

The Commission views an asset swap as two (mutually interdependent)[76] concentrations so that for each concentration, the acquirer and the part acquired are considered to be the undertakings concerned.[77] This interpretation is in full conformity

---

[74] *See* paras. 14-19, in particular para. 19, in *Solvay-Laporte/Interox, supra* note 73. *See* also Colin Overbury, 'Case Note: Solvay-Laporte/Interox', *EC Merger Control Reporter*, Kluwer Law International, The Hague 1991 and later (looseleaf), at pp. 772.1-772.2.

[75] The interpretation applied in *Solvay-Laporte/Interox* has since been followed in *McDermott/ ETPM (Deconcentration)*, Case IV/M1154, decision of 4 June 1998, *Philips/Lucent Technologies (II)*, Case IV/M1358, decision of 6 January 1999, *Siemens/Italtel,* Case IV/M1717, decision of 15 December 1999, *BP/JV Dissolution,* Case COMP/M1820, decision of 2 February 2000, *Mobil/JV Dissolution*, Case IV/M1822, decision of 2 February 2000 and *BT/ Concert*, Case COMP/M2642, decision of 17 December 2001. Concerning the divergences between the interpretations applied in *Campsa* and *Solvay-Laporte/Interox, see* my article, *supra* note 3 at pp. 33-35.

[76] Concerning this aspect, *see Campsa, supra* note 72, *Solvay-Laporte/Interox, supra* note 73, *VIAG/EB BRÜHL*, Case IV/M139, decision of 19 December 1991, *CCIE/GTE*, Case IV/ M258, decision of 25 September 1992, *Du Pont/ICI, supra* note 10, *Royal & Sun Alliance/ Trygg Hansa*, Case IV/M1617, decision of 26 August 1999, Undertaking Concerned Notice, para. 49 and my article, *supra* note 3 at p. 34.

[77] Undertaking Concerned Notice, paras. 49-50, *Du Pont/ICI, supra* note 10, *Stinnes/BTL*, Case IV/M1056, decision of 4 February 1998 and *BP Chemicals/Solvay (PP)*, Case COMP/M2297, decision of 29 October 2001. The Commission in its *2001 Green Paper on the review of the Merger Regulation, supra* note 49, at para. 133 and in the *2002 proposal for a new regulation, supra* note 10, at para. 42, in recital 16 and in Art. 3(4), proposes that the interpretation is changed so that an asset swap is considered to constitute one single concentration. This

with the general principle and it seems not to create any substantive problems.[78]

It is worth noting that some legal writers have argued that the rule provided in Article 5(2) is not applicable to asset swaps since each party is seller *and* buyer and Article 5(2) refers only to sellers.[79] An asset swap, however, consists of two (mutually dependent) concentrations, each having only one buyer and one seller. I, therefore, do not submit to the view that Article 5(2)(2) is not applicable to asset swaps.[80]

4.8. Demergers

A demerger on many points resembles a break-up of a joint venture or an asset swap. While in these two latter situations, however, there will always be more than one independent undertaking involved in each concentration (the parents to the joint venture or the parties swapping assets), in a demerger this need not be the case.

Example

Conglomerate X, having four divisions, A, B, C and D each covering a distinct market, decides to demerge so that each division is turned into an undertaking which is completely independent of the three other undertakings/divisions. All shareholders in X will instead be given shareholdings in A, B, C and D exactly mirroring the holdings they previously had in X.

In the above example, one may argue that the management of X let go of their previous control over A, B, C and D. On the other hand, one may also argue that the control is in the hands of the shareholders, at least when it comes to the more important issues. In my opinion, the better view is not to consider this as a concen-

---

will mean that the thresholds are much more easily met. It is submitted that the arguments advanced by the Commission in support of this new interpretation do not appear so very convincing.

[78] An interesting example of several mutually dependent transactions that were viewed as individual concentrations is made up by the decisions in *AGF/Royal*, Case IV/M1131, decision of 23 April 1998, *Generali/AMB/Athena*, Case IV/M1098, decision of 23 April 1998 and *Allianz/AGF*, Case IV/M1082, decision of 8 May 1998.

[79] Lennart Ritter, W. David Braun and Francis Rawlinson, *EEC Competition Law – A Practitioner's Guide*, 2nd edition, Kluwer Law International, The Hague 2000 at p. 435.

[80] *See* further my article, *supra* note 3 at pp. 35-36.

tration, as I find it difficult to see that such demerger constitutes an accumulation of economic power. Whether the Commission would reach the same conclusion *vis-à-vis* the above example is not clear.

The Commission, however, in the Undertaking Concerned Notice,[81] provides a different example where it does find that a demerger constitutes a concentration. The Commission presupposes that first two undertakings merge and then subsequently they demerge 'with a new asset configuration.'[82]

Example

X and Y merge bringing with them the subsidiaries A + B + C and D + E + F, respectively. Subsequently, they decide to demerge taking with them A + B + F and D + E + C respectively.

According to the Commission, this constitutes two concentrations. One where X acquires various assets and one where Y does the same. The undertakings concerned are the acquirers (X and Y) and the assets they acquire (F and C). Apparently, the Commission finds that X and Y must be viewed in their original configuration. Thus, calculating Community dimension in the case of X means that one must aggregate the turnovers of A, B and C (the original configuration of X) as one undertaking concerned and of F (for the assets acquired by X) as the other undertaking concerned.

To the extent that the demerger amounts to little more than an asset swap, it is submitted that this interpretation is correct. If the demerger is not an asset swap in disguise, however, this interpretation may be impossible to apply. For instance, if Royal Dutch Shell (made up of Royal Dutch and Shell) or Carlsberg (made up of Carlsberg and Tuborg) decide to demerge, it is probably impossible to decide which assets were brought in by one party and which by the other. Indeed, most assets may have been acquired subsequent to the original merger.[83]

In my view, a true demerger (*i.e.* a demerger which is not simply an asset swap in disguise) does not constitute a concentration.[84] After all, it is difficult to accept

---

[81] Paras. 47-48 of the Notice.

[82] Undertaking Concerned Notice, para. 47.

[83] The Commission has put forward similar considerations in its decision in *Worms/Saint-Louis*, Case IV/M909, decision of 4 June 1997, (which concerned a change from joint to sole control).

[84] Likewise B.E. Hawk and H.L. Huser, *supra* note 41 at p. 99.

that a true demerger may lead to a concentration of market power. If it does, I find it difficult to see how one may calculate the Community dimension. Hence, if we view the demerger as more concentrations (one for each new undertaking, rising from the ashes of the original), there will only be one undertaking concerned for each concentration, making it impossible to find a Community dimension. In order to find a Community dimension the Commission will probably have to view the demerger as one single concentration so that each of the new undertakings may be considered an undertaking concerned. It is respectfully submitted that such interpretation should not be applied.

4.9. Applying Article 5(2) to the creation of a joint venture

Article 5(2) provides that in the case of a sale of a part of an undertaking, only the turnover generated by this part shall be taken into account on the side of the seller. Above, in part 3, it is argued that the undertakings creating a full-function joint venture and holding joint control are undertakings concerned. In some situations, these two rules may appear to clash.

Example

A and B agree to set up a joint venture and to transfer certain assets to it. Does Article 5(2) apply in this case so that only the turnover related to these assets shall be taken into account rather than the full turnover of A and B?

Example

A and B agree that B shall acquire 50% of A's subsidiary X so that this subsidiary is transformed into a joint venture under joint control. Are A and B undertakings concerned or are X (instead of the 'seller' A) and B undertakings concerned?

Article 5(2) concerns the acquisition of a part where the seller cedes control over this part. Ceding control over the part, the seller will play no role in the future running of it, and does not contribute to the concentration of economic power.[85] In the case of a full-function joint venture, there is no seller within the meaning of the term in Article 5(2) since the 'seller' remains in control (albeit joint rather than sole control) and the 'seller', therefore, clearly plays a role in the future running of the part.

---

[85]   Likewise, Turnover Calculation Notice, para. 31.

In contrast, if the seller cedes control over the part sold, Article 5(2) applies.

Example

A, B and C agree to transfer all of their activities in a given market into a new company, X. As part of the agreement, A and B will have joint control while C will only have a minority interest which does not carry with it any joint control. Thus, Article 5(2) will apply to the part provided by C, so that this part together with A and B are the undertakings concerned.

Consequently, there is no real clash on this point and Article 5(2) should not be applied to the creation of joint ventures.[86]

4.10. The *British Airways/Dan Air* case

4.10.1. Introduction

While there is an abundant number of Commission decisions that explicitly deal with the interpretation of Community dimension, there is only one judgment by the Community courts in the field,[87] namely the *Dan Air* case.[88] In 1992, British Airways (BA) acquired the British airline company Dan Air, an operation which clearly constituted a concentration. The Commission declined to vet the acquisition, finding that it did not have a Community dimension. This prompted Air France to sue the Commission before the Court of First Instance.

In *Dan Air,* the Court of First Instance accepted the Commission's interpretation of the term 'part' in Article 5(2). As I will explain below, I do not agree with this interpretation. Furthermore, in chapter 8, below I will show that the judgment has opened, if not a Pandora's box then at least a possibility of forum shopping.

---

[86] Likewise, Undertaking Concerned Notice, paras. 21 and 23, but contrast with P. Bos *et al, supra* note 19 at p. 135. *See* also M. Siragusa and R. Subiotto, *supra* note 7 at pp. 902-903, Jacques H.J. Bourgeois, 'Case Note: Aerospatiale/MBB', *EC Merger Control Reporter,* Kluwer Law International, The Hague 1991 and later (looseleaf), pp. 100.1-100.3 at 100.2 and D. Livingstone, *supra* note 16 at p. 735.

[87] In addition to this judgment, on 12 July 1996 the President of the Court of First Instance has issued an order concerning a dispute relating to the finding of Community dimension in Case T-52/96, *Sogecable v Commission.* The main case was subsequently withdrawn.

[88] *Supra* note 53.

4.10.2. Background

In 1992, Dan Air encountered severe problems and, on 23 October of that year, BA agreed to acquire Dan Air by paying £ 1 in consideration to the owner to the point of the acquisition; Davies and Newman Holdings plc.

BA's acquisition on 23 October was, however, conditional. BA did not want to acquire Dan Air's charter activities, so only if Dan Air could divest itself of these activities would BA complete the acquisition. During talks with the Commission, BA renounced the possibility of waiving this condition even though this had been left open in the agreement of 23 October. Eventually, on 8 November, 1992 the acquisition was brought about.

During the negotiations, the question arose as to whether the takeover would have to be approved by the European Commission or by the British Mergers and Monopolies Commission. It was clear that the acquisition constituted a concentration within the meaning of the Regulation, but there were doubts as to whether the concentration had Community dimension. The question was whether Dan Air generated more than € 250 million in the Community as only then would the concentration have a Community dimension.[89]

Dan Air's accounts for the preceding financial year showed a Community-wide turnover of more than € 250 million. This figure included Dan Air's charter activities, however. If the charter activities were not included, the € 250 million threshold would not be met and the question, therefore, was whether or not the turnover of these activities should be excluded.

Article 5(1) of the Regulation provides that when examining whether a concentration has a Community dimension the turnover 'in the preceding financial year' of each of the undertakings concerned must be used.[90] Hence, since in the preceding financial year Dan Air had a turnover of more than € 250 million, the starting point was that the concentration had a Community dimension.

The central question was whether the 'part-rule' in Article 5(2) meant that the charter activities of Dan Air would have to be deducted so that the concentration did not have a Community dimension? In order to solve this problem, the lawyers advising on the concentration asked the Commission for advice.

On 30 October, 1992, a spokesman for Sir Leon Brittan, then Commissioner for Competition, declared that the concentration did not have a Community dimen-

---

[89] At the time of the concentration the Regulation only had one set of thresholds, namely € 5 billion worldwide, € 250 million Community-wide and the two-thirds rule.

[90] *See* further below, chapter 4.

sion because the € 250 million threshold had not been met by Dan Air which meant that the Commission could not intervene. This statement was reported by Agence Europe on 31 October, 1992.[91]

On 2 November, 1992, the concentration was cleared by the British authorities and, on 8 November, the transfer of the securities was brought about.

The next day, on 9 November, Air France sent a letter to the Commission challenging the latter's interpretation. The Commission remained firm on its interpretation and on 5 January, 1993, Air France sued the Commission before the Court of First Instance requesting that the Commission's decision not to take jurisdiction should be annulled.

4.10.3. The judgment of the Court of First Instance

The Court first established that since BA's acquisition had been conditional upon Dan Air divesting itself of its charter activities and since BA had renounced waiving this condition, BA had only acquired those of Dan Air's activities which did not include the charter activities.[92]

Thereupon, in paragraph 102, the Court went on to establish that the general scheme of Article 5 of the Regulation shows that the Community legislature intended that the Commission should only intervene in a concentration 'where the proposed operation is of a certain economic size, that is to say, where it has a "Community dimension".' It furthermore established that '[t]he objective of Article 5(2) of the Regulation is thus to determine the real dimension of the concentration for the purposes of examining whether, having regard to the parts of the undertaking which are actually acquired, whether or not constituted as legal entities, the proposed operation has a "Community dimension"...'

Despite the fact that Article 5(2) does not contain an express reference to the discontinuance of activities, the Court established that a 'partial transfer' and a 'partial discontinuance of activities' are comparable since 'they both allow a precise appraisal to be made of the exact subject-matter, composition and extent of the proposed concentration.' The Court, therefore, laid down the following interpretation of Article 5(2): 'It follows that only the turnover relating to those parts of the undertaking which are actually acquired are to be taken into account for the

---

[91]   Agence Europe, 'CE/Concurrence: La prise de contrôle de Dan Air par la British Airways ne relève pas des compétences de la Commission en matière de fusions', 31 October 1992.

[92]   Para. 100 of the judgment.

purposes of appraising the dimension of the proposed operation. Consequently, reference should only be made to the turnover for the last financial year of those parts of the undertaking which are actually acquired.'[93]

Applying this principle to the case in question led the Court of First Instance to the conclusion that the charter activities of Dan Air were not to be taken into account and, accordingly, that the concentration did not possess a Community dimension.[94]

4.10.4. Article 5(2) and Dan Air

It is commonly accepted that the notion of Community dimension is intended to achieve two aims. Firstly, the thresholds are intended to reflect the economic size of the undertakings concerned by the concentration and secondly, the thresholds are purely quantitative criteria providing clarity and leaving no scope for argument at the cost of being very arbitrary. In its judgment, the Court emphasises these two aims in its interpretation of Article 5(2).

Since BA only acquired Dan Air, which formed only one business unit in the Davies & Newman Holdings group, Article 5(2) was applicable to the transaction. Hence, only the turnover generated by Dan Air would have to be taken into account, not the full group turnover of Davies & Newman Holdings. By holding that discontinued activities should also be excluded from the calculation, the Commission and the Court, however, went one step further in their interpretation of Article 5(2).

Where the closure of an activity has been effected so long ago that it is reflected in the accounts for the preceding financial year, there is no problem regarding calculating the Community dimension. Where this is not the case, the problem is that it is difficult, if not impossible, to state when a closure must be considered to be decisive:

Is an interim closure of a production facility enough or must the closure be of a more permanent kind? Must the production facilities have been sold and what if the production facilities can easily be acquired again? Must the intellectual property rights have been abandoned? Must (all) the liabilities and rights relating to this production have been finally settled? and so forth.

---

93 Para. 103 of the judgment.

94 Since Air France was not successful in its three other pleas either, the application for annulment was dismissed.

The Court restricts itself to stating that a partial discontinuance of activities 'allow a precise appraisal to be made of the exact subject-matter, composition and extent of the proposed concentration.'[95] It is, of course, true that in the *Dan Air* case, BA was required to renounce its right to waive the condition that Dan Air divested itself of its charter activities. This seems to show that some degree of certainty must be required. For instance, a proposed interim closure of a production facility will probably not suffice, while an actual interim closure of a production facility before an acquisition does not seem to conflict with the judgment.

Hence, there is a stark contrast between the situation concerning a discontinuance of activities and the situation where a part has been sold by a seller which remains active. Moreover, almost all markets change from year to year: In one year, demand increases so that the employees must work in shifts or an extra production line must be opened. The following year, there is a decrease in demand so that a production line is closed down. Meanwhile, the undertaking might close down in some geographic or product markets while starting in other geographic or product markets. The Court's ruling in the *Dan Air* case appears to cover all of these situations.

Matters may be complicated even more: If discontinuance of activities must be taken into account under Article 5(2), logic requires that the start of new activities should be taken into account as well. It is easy to see that this would make the calculation of turnover extremely complex and bring about a high degree of uncertainty. This would not accord very well with the aim that the thresholds should provide a clear division of jurisdiction so that there will be no scope for argument and the thresholds should be easy to apply in the real world. Luckily, the Court's judgment only explicitly covers discontinuance of activities. It is, therefore, possible to construe the judgment restrictively so that the start of new activities since the end of the preceding financial year shall not be taken into account.

A further important observation is that where, for instance, an undertaking sells a subsidiary, the seller presumably remains active in the market and the parts which have not been sold, therefore, still constitute economic power. Thus, it seems logical to make a distinction between the economic power acquired (the subsidiary) and the economic power which remains in the market (the seller). In the case of a discontinuance, the situation is different. Thus, in the *Dan Air* case, the seller, Davies & Newman, remained in the market and clearly should not be taken into account. While Dan Air returned all its slots relating to its charter flights, disposed

---

[95] Para. 103 of the judgment.

of all its aircraft providing charter flights, terminated its charter contracts and reduced its flight staff, however, none of these facts – viewed independently or together – necessarily means that a new economic power equal to the discontinued activities is created. Put differently, there seems to be a very strong argument that all of the economic activities which could be 'labelled' Dan Air were acquired by BA. In this way, the *Dan Air* case differs fundamentally from the situation where one undertaking acquires a part of another undertaking.

On the basis of the above examination, the Court's interpretation appears a little surprising to me.[96]

4.10.5. Minimising the damage

As will be shown below in chapter 8, the Court of First Instance's judgment in *Dan Air*, has created some interesting possibilities of forum shopping. This has been recognised by the Commission.

The Commission has, therefore, issued guidelines in which it attempts to restrict the application of the *Dan Air* ruling. Hence the Commission states that 'if a company disposes of part of its business at any time before the signature of the final agreement or the announcement of the public bid or the acquisition of a controlling interest bringing about a concentration, or where such divestment or closure is a pre-condition for the operation the part of the turnover to be attributed to that part of the business must be subtracted from the turnover of the notifying party as shown in its last audited accounts.'[97]

Even though a 'disposal' or a 'closure' appears to be slightly more final (*i.e.* difficult to undo) than a mere 'transfer' or 'discontinuance', the Commission's choice of terms does not in itself seem to indicate a real deviation from the Court's judgment. The Commission goes on, however, to explain that:

---

[96] It might be added that if Davies & Newman Holding, Dan Air's parent-company, had separated the charter activities and the non-charter activities into independent subsidiaries and if BA thereupon had acquired only the activities and liabilities relating to the non-charter activities the case would appear to fall squarely within Art. 5(2). Likewise if BA had acquired both the charter and non-charter activities from Davies & Newman Holding and thereupon had closed down the charter activities it seems equally clear that the charter activities would not be deductible on the basis of Art. 5(2).

[97] Turnover Calculation Notice, para. 27. *See* also Undertaking Concerned Notice at para. 17.

'Other factors that may affect turnover on a temporary basis such as a decrease of the orders of the product or a slow-down in the production process
within the period prior to the transaction will be ignored for the purposes of
calculating turnover. No adjustment to the definitive accounts will be made to
incorporate them.'[98]

The latter interpretation clearly is not founded on the Court's ruling in the *Dan Air*
case. Nevertheless, it seems that, at least to a limited extent, it re-establishes some
of the structure and logic which the notion of Community dimension was intended
to provide and, presumably, the Commission has thereby managed to get the best
out of an awkward situation.

Apparently, the rule has only been considered a few times since *Dan Air*. In
Deutsche Bank/Banco de Madrid,[99] in *Ingersoll-Rand/Clark Equipment*[100] and in
Allianz/Vereinte,[101] the Commission applied the rule. In the second case, this meant
that the transaction did not have a Community dimension, so the Commission had
to decline jurisdiction while it appears that the Commission only had jurisdiction
in the last of the three cases due to this rule. In contrast, in *Rhône Poulenc Rorer/
Fisons,*[102] concerning a public offer by Rhône Poulenc Rorer to acquire control of
Fisons, the parties argued that the transaction did not have a Community dimension because Fisons had signed an agreement prior to the bid to sell two of its
divisions bringing its Community-wide turnover below € 250 million. The Commission refused to accept this argument holding that both of these two sales were
conditional upon regulatory approval and one also remained subject to the approval of the company's shareholders. At least, the sale which remained subject to
both shareholder and regulatory approval would, therefore, have to be included
bringing Fison's turnover in the Community above € 250 million. It has, however,
rightly been pointed out 'that the Commission normally considers sale and purchase agreements that remain subject to regulatory and shareholder approval

---

[98] Turnover Calculation Notice, para. 28.

[99] Case IV/M341, decision of 28 May 1993. *See* also Edurne Navarro Varona, 'Case Note:
Deutsche Bank/Banco de Madrid', *EC Merger Control Reporter*, Kluwer Law International,
The Hague 1992 and later (looseleaf), p. 1102.7.

[100] Case IV/M588, decision of 15 May 1995.

[101] Case IV/M812, decision of 11 November 1996. *See* in connection to this case also *Allianz/
Hermes*, Case IV/M813, decision of 27 September 1996.

[102] Case IV/M632, decision of 21 September 1995.

sufficiently binding to be notified and reviewed.'[103] Thus, apparently the Commission has engaged in a rather narrow interpretation of the *Dan Air* ruling.[104]

4.11. Staggered transactions

4.11.1. Introduction

The part-rule in Article 5(2) is well-founded. It may be used for circumventing the Merger Regulation, however, where two undertakings agree to split a transaction into pieces so that one or more of these fall beneath the thresholds and thereby escape the Commission's scrutiny. The drafters of the Regulation foresaw this and, therefore, inserted Article 5(2)(2) to make it easier for the Commission to catch these cases. Article 5(2)(2) provides that where two (or more) transactions concerning parts as defined in Article 5(2)(1) take place between the same persons or undertakings within a two-year period, these shall be treated 'as one and the same concentration arising on the date of the last transaction.' This provision thus catches situations where the parties intend to make one concentration appear as more separate ones.[105] Where one concentration is made in stages (with no intent to circum-

---

103 Robbert Snelders, 'Developments in E.C. Merger Control in 1995', *European Law Review, Competition Law Survey 1996*, pp. CC66-CC88 at p. CC72 with note 22. As noted below in chapter 3, section 2.4, the agreement to sell one of the two divisions was only signed after the concentration had been notified to the Commission. This in itself may justify that the Commission excluded that division when calculating the Community dimension.

104 *British Airways/Air Liberté*, case IV/M857, decision of 28 February 1997 in footnote 1 also indicates that the Commission took the *Dan Air* rule into account.

105 Examples of the application of the provision are *Volvo/Lex (2)*, Case IV/M261, decision of 3 September 1992, *Alcatel/STC*, Case IV/M366, decision of 13 September 1993, *Akzo/Nobel Industrier*, Case IV/M390, decision of 10 January 1994, *Scandinavian Project, supra* note 10, *Winterthur/Schweizer Rück*, Case IV/M518, decision of 14 March 1995, *Allianz/Elvia/ Lloyd Adriatico*, Case IV/M539, decision of 3 April 1995, *Norsk Hydro/Enichem Agricoltura-Terni (II)*, Case IV/M832, decision of 25 October 1996, *CGEA/South Eastern Train Company Limited*, Case IV/M816, decision of 7 October 1996, *Volkswagen/Rolls-Royce/Cosworth*, Case IV/M1283, decision of 24 August 1998 and *Kingfisher/Grosslabor*, Case IV/M1482, decision of 12 April 1999. *See also Pepsico/KAS*, Case IV/M289, decision of 21 December 1992 in which the reference to Art. 5(2)(2) apparently is a mistake, cf. Götz Drauz and Dirk Schroeder, *Praxis der europäischen Fusionskontrolle*, 3rd ed., RWS Verlag, Köln 1995, at pp. 20-21. (Presumably G. Drauz and D. Schroeder's comment on *Pepsico/Kas* equally applies to *Scandinavian Project, Winterthur/Schweizer Rück* and *Allianz/Elvia/Lloyd Adriatico*).

vent the Merger Regulation) the concentration must, in my opinion, be viewed as a whole when calculating the Community dimension and it is not necessary (or correct) to refer to Article 5(2)(2) to view the different transactions making up the concentration together.[106] In contrast, where one undertaking sells parts (*e.g.* subsidiaries) to another several times over a two year-period[107] with no intention of circumventing the Regulation[108] and not as part of an overall scheme (*i.e.* as more concentrations, not just as one), Article 5(2)(2) still applies.[109]

Example

A of the US and B of France are the two only undertakings with the necessary intellectual property rights to produce a medicine against infectious hepatitis. Producing the medicine requires a special production unit which is extremely

---

According to B.E. Hawk and H.L. Huser, *supra* note 41 at p. 82 'both the Commission and merging parties have invoked this exception on an opportunistic basis in situations beyond those contemplated by the Regulation's drafters.' Unfortunately the two authors do not really elaborate on this view.

[106] This also seems to be the normal approach of the Commission, *cf.* e.g. *Anglo American Corporation/Lonrho*, Case IV/M754, decision of 23 April 1997, [1998] OJ L149/21. *See* also the somewhat peculiar situation in *Bell Cable Media/Cable & Wireless/Videotron*, Case IV/M853, decision of 11 December 1996. A few exceptions appear, however. *See* for example *Allianz/Elvia/Lloyd Adriatico, supra* note 105.

[107] Neither the wording nor the purpose of Art. 5(2)(2) seem to require that the transactions take place at different points in time. Thus, if two simultaneous transactions between the same parties cannot be considered as one single concentration they may instead be caught by Art. 5(2)(2). Perhaps *Rhône-Poulenc/Novalis/Nyltech*, Case IV/M1083, decision of 15 April 1998, is an example of this. *See* also *Siemens/Dematic/Sachs/VDO, supra* note 49, at note 2.

[108] Note, however, that the Commission in its *2001 Green Paper on the review of the Merger Regulation, supra* note 49, at para. 127 and the *2002 proposal for a new regulation, supra* note 10, at para. 45 finds that '[t]he Merger Regulation has established a legal presumption that all transactions meeting the requirements of Article 5(2)(2) are to be considered as one concentration'. By referring to 'a legal presumption' the Commission indicates that the application of Art. 5(2)(2) may be avoided if the presumption is rebutted.

[109] *See* also Turnover Calculation Notice, para. 32 and G. Drauz and D. Schroeder, *supra* note 105, at p. 19. Note, though, that the Commission in its *2001 Green Paper on the review of the Merger Regulation, supra* note 49, at paras. 127-128 implicitly seem to indicate that hitherto it has been of the opinion that only transactions that are 'equivalent to a single concentration' are covered by the rule in Art. 5(2)(2). This implicit view does not find support in the Commission's case law, however, cf. for example *Alcoa/British Aluminium*, Case COMP/M2111, decision of 27 October 2000.

costly and which cannot be set up within a period of less than six years. Moreover, the medicine must be injected into the patient within six hours after it is produced. A has production units in North America, Japan, Australia and Saudi Arabia and, two years ago, it began setting up a new unit in Belgium. In contrast, B has only two production units, both situated in Northern France. This means that A holds a monopoly position outside Europe while B holds a monopoly position in Europe. If A acquires only one of B's two production units this will introduce competition in the European market, at least four years earlier than if A would have to wait for its Belgian unit to become operational. Thus, it would be pro-competitive. In contrast, if A acquires both of B's production units, this would mean that only A would remain in the market and no new entrants are likely. Thus this would clearly be anti-competitive.

Imagine that A and B do not have a combined aggregate turnover of more than € 100 million in any single Member State (so that the second threshold set is not met), but that A generates a worldwide turnover of more than € 5 billion, a Community-wide turnover of more than € 250 million (of which not more than two-thirds is generated within one and the same Member State) and if B's two production units each generate a Community-wide turnover of € 200 million, the part-rule in Article 5(2) may make it very tempting to try to avoid the Commission's scrutiny by dividing the acquisition into two, so that each of these would fall below the thresholds.[110] If A and B are prepared to allow more than two years to pass from the first to the second transaction, Article 5(2)(2) would not apply, but the Commission may instead be able to prove that the case concerns actual circumvention so that the transactions really make up only one concentration giving the Commission jurisdiction to vet it.

Article 5(2)(2) gives rise to four questions: What transactions are covered? When is a transaction made 'between the same persons or undertakings'? How is the two-year time limit calculated? And, lastly, at what point in time must the Commission examine the transactions?

---

[110] If the transaction does not meet the thresholds, it may come within one or more Member State merger control schemes. The fact that a transaction originally has been duly cleared by a Member State competition authority does not mean that it may not later be examined by the Commission if the conditions set out in Art. 5(2)(2) are later met. *See* for example *Bravida/ Semco/Prenad/Totalinstallatören/Backlunds*, Case COMP/M3004, decision of 13 December 2002 at para. 5.

4.11.2. What transactions are covered?

According to its wording, Article 5(2)(2) covers situations where 'two or more transactions within the meaning of the first subparagraph' take place between the same parties within a two-year period. Hence, there is no requirement that both transactions must lack a Community dimension. Indeed, there is no requirement according to the wording of the provision that at least one of the transactions must lack a Community dimension.[111] Moreover, where two parties divide one transaction into two in order to circumvent the Merger Regulation, this may be done by designing only the first, or only the second, or both transactions so that they lack Community dimension.

Example

In the above example concerning a French and an American producer of a medicine against infectious hepatitis, either transaction of a production unit from B to A (viewed individually) lack Community dimension. If, however, the first transaction had had Community dimension, this is unlikely to change the situation as the anti-competitive effects are only brought about by the second transaction (which lacks Community dimension).[112]

Example

The Widget producer A agrees to acquire P from B. P has a small production of widgets and a large production of gadgets. Only the widgets production creates competition problems. A and B, therefore, agree that first P's widget business shall be transferred to A as this lacks Community dimension. Later B shall transfer the gadget business of P to A. The latter transaction does not create any competition problems, but does possess Community dimension.

Thus, both a teleological and a literal interpretation lend support to the construction that where two (or more) transactions covered by the part-rule in Article 5(2) take place between the same parties within a two-year period, this triggers Article

---

[111] If neither of the transactions lack Community dimension there is obviously no circumvention and, moreover, when evaluating the subsequent transaction the Commission (if it has jurisdiction) may always take the consequences of the earlier transaction into account, making it both unnecessary and questionable to apply Article 5(2)(2) in these cases. *See* in this respect also *Wacker/Air Products*, *supra* note 45, para. 8.

[112] In *Volvo/Lex (2)*, *supra* note 105, only the second transaction lacked Community dimension.

5(2)(2) regardless of whether one (or more) of these does possess Community dimension.

Article 5(2)(2) refers to transactions between 'the same persons or undertakings'. One may, therefore, ask whether this also covers situations where in the first transaction one party is a seller and the other a buyer, but in the second transaction they take the opposite roles. Article 5(2)(2) is intended to prevent that Article 5(2)(1) is used to circumvent the Merger Regulation. This happens where a sales-transaction is divided into parts. Consequently, it is intended for situations where the parties take the same roles (as either seller or buyer) in all transactions. This means that if, for instance, A and B agree to swap assets, this must be viewed as two distinct transactions, each having only one buyer and one seller.[113] If A purchases a subsidiary from B one year later, however, this transaction may have to be vetted together with the part of the asset swap where A acquired a part from B, depending upon whether the thresholds have been met, of course.[114]

Article 5(2)(2) explicitly provides that it concerns 'two or more transactions within the meaning of the first subparagraph', *i.e.* acquisitions of a part of another undertaking. But what if one of the transactions does not concern an acquisition of a part?

Example

A and B intend to merge. They each generate more than € 5 billion worldwide, but while A generates € 4 billion in the Community, B only generates € 400 million there and all of this turnover is generated in the UK and Ireland.[115] If the merger has this configuration, it will have a Community dimension and be notifiable. In order to escape the scope of the Merger Regulation, A acquires a part of B generating € 200 million in the Community. This transaction does not have a Community dimension and when the two parties later merge, B only generates € 200 million in the Community and this latter transaction does not constitute an acquisition of a part within the meaning of Article 5(2).

---

[113] *See* likewise Turnover Calculation Notice, para. 15, but note that the Commission is contemplating changing this rule, cf. *2001 Green Paper on the review of the Merger Regulation, supra* note 49, para. 133.

[114] *See* for example *Akzo/Nobel Industrier, supra* note 105.

[115] This means that the second set of thresholds has not been met, cf. Art. 1(2)(c) which requires that 'in each of [minimum three Member States] the aggregate turnover of each of at least two of the undertakings concerned is more than € 25 million'.

A literal reading of Article 5(2)(2) shows that only the acquisition of a part is covered. It is equally clear that Article 5(2)(2) is included to prevent circumvention. In the above example, a circumvention of the Regulation's scope (including the rule in Article 5(2)(2)) necessarily implies that first one party acquires a part of the other and thereafter all of the seller of the part (and not just a part of the seller) is included in a concentration with the acquirer of the part,[116] leaving no seller (not even an 'empty' holding company) in the market.[117] Since the wording of Article 5(2)(2) so very clearly does not cover this situation, it is difficult to argue that it should nevertheless be covered.[118] The same line of argument must apply where one of the concentrations concerns setting up a full-function joint venture since this is not an acquisition of a part.[119] If, however, the transactions constitute one single concentration and if this concentration has a Community dimension it still

---

[116] It is not possible first to acquire all of/merge with an undertaking and thereupon to acquire a part thereof. The order must necessarily be the other way round.

[117] Turnover Calculation Notice, para. 34 provides an example where the buyer acquires all of the target's market activities. However, the seller remains in the market, though having no activities. *See* likewise *Akzo/Nobel Industrier, supra* note 105 where Akzo acquired Nobel, but the majority shareholder Securum AB, which apparently held control over Nobel, remained in the market and even kept one of Nobel's subsidiaries.

[118] The Commission may, however, claim that the two transactions in reality constitute only one concentration. If the Commission is right, it will have jurisdiction.

[119] Likewise the Commission in *ABB/Renault Automation*, Case IV/M409, decision of 9 March 1994, *Ingersoll-Rand/MAN*, Case IV/M479, decision of 28 July 1994, *Mannesmann Demag/ Delaval Stork*, Case IV/M535, decision of 21 December 1994 and apparently also *Fortis/ CGER*, Case IV/M342, decision of 15 November 1993. In *Scandinavian Project, supra* note 10 the Commission at first glance seems to apply Article 5(2)(2) to four transactions creating four joint ventures which the Commission treats as two concentrations. This interpretation of Article 5(2)(2) seems to be neither correct nor to accord with the Commission's earlier case law. A closer look, however, seems to reveal that the transactions did in fact constitute two concentrations so that the finding of jurisdiction is correct. *See* also *Bank of New York/Royal Bank of Scotland Trust Bank*, Case IV/M1618, decision of 25 August 1999 together with *Bank of New York/Royal Bank of Scotland/RBSI Security Services*, Case IV/ M1660, decision of 26 August 1999. In the former of these two cases Bank of New York acquired a subsidiary of Royal Bank of Scotland whilst in the latter Bank of New York and Royal Bank of Scotland set up a full-function joint venture. The two transactions were not viewed as one under Art. 5(2)(2).

comes within the scope of the Merger Regulation.[120] Consequently the Commission must take jurisdiction. If the transactions are not caught by Article 5(2)(2), the onus of proving that they make up only one concentration will, however, be on the Commission.

Article 5(2)(2) was inserted to prevent circumvention of the Merger Regulation by separating one concentration into more transactions. One may therefore reasonably ask whether the provision also catches transactions that are linked merely by the time criterion and the identity of the parties, but concern unrelated economic sectors. Under the present wording of the provision, the answer must be that such transactions are covered.[121] However, in its 2002 proposal for a new regulation[122] the Commission proposes to change the wording so that such cases will no longer fall within Article 5(2)(2).

4.11.3. When are the parties to a transaction 'the same'?

Deciding whether the parties to two transactions are the same may be very difficult.

---

[120] Likewise the Commission in *Mannesmann/Hoesch*, Case IV/M222, decision of 12 November 1992, [1993] OJ L114/34. In *EDF/TXU Europe/West Burton Power Station*, Case COMP/M2675, decision of 20 December 2001 and *EDF/TXU Europe/24 Seven*, Case COMP/M2679, decision of 20 December 2001, the Commission found that two notified transactions constituted 'a single operation', but nevertheless issued a decision for each of the two transactions. *See* also Joachim Rudo, 'Die Behandlung mehrerer Erwerbsvorgänge als einheitlicher Zusammenschluß im Rahmen der Umsatzberechnung nach Art. 5 Abs. 2 Fusionskontrollverordnung', *Recht der Internationalen Wirtschaft – Betriebs-Berater International*, Vol. 43, August 1997, pp. 641-648 at p. 642.

It is worth of note that the Commission has made it very clear that in principle one concentration cannot be made up of two operations involving different natures of control (*i.e.* joint control and sole control), cf. *Dana/GKN*, Case COMP/M1587, decision of 4 November 1999, para. 6 and 'Commission Notice on the concept of concentration', OJ C66/5 of 2.3.1998, para. 16. *See* also *A&C/Grossfarma*, Case COMP/M2573, decision of 30 August 2001 and *BP Chemicals/Solvay/HDPE JV*, Case COMP/M2299, decision of 29 October 2001 together with *BP Chemicals/Solvay (PP)*, *supra* note 77.

[121] This equally is apparent from the wording of para. 51 of the *2002 proposal for a new regulation*, *supra* note 10.

[122] *Supra* note 10.

Example

A sells a subsidiary to B. A subsequently experiences difficulties and is acquired by C which then sells its subsidiary D to B. Now B has acquired a part from the group to which A belongs twice, but is this situation covered by Article 5(2)(2)?

Example

A and B each almost simultaneously sell a subsidiary to X. One year later A and B merge and thereupon the merged entity AB sells another subsidiary to X. Must all these three transactions be viewed together according to Article 5(2)(2)?

Article 5(2) has been drafted with the situation in mind where A sells subsidiary X to B and, within two years, A sells subsidiary Y to B. Also where the first sale from A is to a subsidiary of B and the second sale to another subsidiary of B, however, the transactions are covered by Article 5(2)(2).[123] Only if this group approach is applied is it possible to achieve the aim of preventing Article 5(2)(1) being used in order to circumvent the Regulation. The question, thus, is which group approach should apply? Apparently, Article 5(2)(2) has been drafted with reference to the group definition laid down in Article 3(4) as indicated by the reference in Article 5(2)(2) to 'persons or undertakings'.[124] This group-definition is rather difficult to apply in practice since it is not based on a formal definition of control, as is Article 5(4), but on a material definition of control provided in Article 3(3).

Moreover, where the configuration of the buyer or the seller is altered subsequently to the first transaction, the construction of Article 5(2)(2) may become extremely confusing.

Example

The conglomerate A has four divisions (A_1, A_2, A_3 and A_4) while conglomerate B has five (B_1, B_2, B_3, B_4 and B_5). A_1 sells a subsidiary to B_1. Subsequently, A_4 is acquired by C and conglomerate B undergoes a demerger where each division becomes a fully independent entity. A number of situations may be imagined, a few of which will be outlined here:

---

[123] *See* for example *Volvo/Lex (2)*, *supra* note 105, *Alcatel/STC*, *supra* note 105 and *Sara Lee/BP Food Division*, Case IV/M299, decision of 8 February 1993.

[124] Contrast with J. Rudo, *supra* note 120 at p. 643.

(1) C sells a subsidiary to B_1.

(2) A_4 sells a subsidiary to B_1.

(3) A_2 sells a subsidiary to B_1.

(4) A_1 sells a subsidiary to B_2.

Which of these situations (if any) are covered by Article 5(2)(2)?[125]

It appears that Article 5(2)(2) does not provide a clear and unambiguous dividing rule.[126] In most situations, however, it is probably very easy to ascertain who the seller is and who the buyer is. Where this is not easy to ascertain, I submit to the view that Article 5(2)(2) should be applied with caution with the primary guideline being to prevent circumvention of Article 5(2)(1). This means that where it is doubtful whether the seller and the buyer are identical, the Commission shall only take jurisdiction in accordance with Article 5(2)(2) if it may reasonably suspect that the transactions constitute an attempt to circumvent the Regulation. I believe that this approach allows the undertakings a fair amount of legal certainty while not bringing the achievement of the purpose behind Article 5(2)(2) into jeopardy.

4.11.4. Creeping acquisitions

'Creeping acquisitions' via the stock exchange constitute a particular problem *vis-à-vis* Article 5(2)(2). Hence, one may imagine that an undertaking makes a hostile bid for a publicly listed target. The bidder acquires a number of both small and large holdings and at one point it gains control as defined in Article 3 of the Merger Regulation. The undertakings concerned obviously are the acquirer and the target. Under the current rules, however, only one of the acquirer's (perhaps many) share acquisitions is viewed as constituting the concentration, namely the one whereby the acquirer has gained control over the target. The Commission in its *2001 Green*

---

125 Note that in this example it is immaterial to the answer whether Article 5(2)(2) is based on the group definition in Article 3 or the one in Article 5(4).

126 Cf. Angus K. Maciver, 'The First Year of Enforcement under the EEC Merger Regulation – A View from the Trenches', *1991 Fordham Corp. L. Inst.*, (B. Hawk, ed. 1992), pp. 751-765 at p. 758 concerning the proposed (but abandoned) railroad merger between GEC Alsthom and Fiat Ferroviaria.

Paper on the review of the Merger Regulation,[127] paras. 134-135, proposed to change Article 5(2)(2) in such a way that all the acquirer's acquisitions of shares in the target would be viewed together. In the *2002 proposal for a new regulation*[128] these proposed changes have been abandoned. Instead the Commission simply proposes to interpret Article 5(2)(2) in such a way so as to cover this type of acquisitions.[129]

4.11.5. How is the two-year time limit calculated?

Where one undertaking acquires parts of another undertaking's business activities two or more times within a two-year period, Article 5(2)(2) provides that these transactions shall be treated as one and the same concentration arising on the date of the last transaction. Under the present scheme, the question is how this two-year time limit is calculated. The time limit must begin running with the first transaction. The Merger Regulation in Article 4(1) provides that the requirement to notify is triggered by 'the conclusion of the agreement, or the announcement of the public bid, or the acquisition of a controlling interest', whichever occurs first. For practical reasons, the undertakings are allowed one week from this time before they must submit the notification, but in order to obtain a clear-cut rule (and, thus, legal certainty) it must be the actual time when the triggering event occurs for the purposes of calculating the two-year time limit. Along the same lines, a second transaction between the same parties must be caught by Article 5(2)(2) if the triggering event occurs within two years from the triggering event of the first transaction. This is so even if the 'one-week respite' granted in Article 4(1) means that the parties are not obliged to notify the transaction until after the two-year time limit has expired.

One may also ask whether any sale triggers a new two-year time limit to start running.

Example

A sells three subsidiaries to B at intervals of one-and-a-half years. Only if the parts acquired by A have a turnover exceeding € 250 million will the trans-

---

[127] *Supra* note 49.

[128] *Supra* note 10.

[129] Cf. recital 16 of the *2002 proposal for a new regulation, supra* note 10.

action have a Community dimension. The first sale obviously triggers the two-year time limit to start running, but does the second sale also do this? Only if the answer is yes will the third sale come within the scope of the Regulation.

In my opinion, each transaction must trigger the time limit to start running since, otherwise, Article 5(2)(2)'s prevention against circumvention will have a lacunae, as the following two examples may illustrate.

Example

A agrees to sell a division, generating € 250 million, to B. The sale may give rise to competition concerns regarding a part of the division generating € 90 million in turnover. A has sold another division to B almost two years earlier, however, so the parties agree that only the part of A's division which does not give rise to competition concerns shall be transferred to B before the two-year time limit expires. This transaction is caught by Article 5(2)(2) and cleared under the Regulation. The remaining (and problematic) part is only transferred after the two-year time limit has expired. Only if the second transaction, too, triggers the time limit, will it be caught by Article 5(2)(2).

Example

In May, 1990, A acquires an insignificant subsidiary from B. In April, 1992, A acquires a large subsidiary from B, but even when viewed together, the two acquisitions do not have a Community dimension. In August, 1992, A acquires a third (large) subsidiary from B. Only if this acquisition is viewed together with the April acquisition of the same year will it have a Community dimension.

Lastly, as mentioned earlier, Article 5(2)(2) is intended to prevent circumvention. If the Commission can actually prove circumvention, however, it is not necessary to rely on Article 5(2)(2). Instead, the Commission may simply hold the different transactions to constitute one concentration, but in such a situation, the burden of proof is on the Commission.

4.11.6. When must the Commission examine the transactions?

Article 5(2)(2) expressly provides that the transactions 'shall be treated as one and the same concentration arising on the day of the last transaction.' While the calculation of turnover must be made according to the figures applying at the time of the individual transaction, the substantive examination must be made with regard to the circumstances at the time of the last transaction.[130] This means, for instance, that if the first acquisition has been sold to a third party or closed, the Commission must take this into account when making the substantive appraisal.

In its 24th Report on Competition Policy, the Commission appears to take a more liberal view on this, however, since it states that Article 5(2)(2) 'applies in principle with retroactive effect, but in practice the Commission considers that a prospective application is also conceivable.'[131] Though it is not fully clear what situations the Commission is aiming at, it seems that this interpretation infringes the wording of Article 5(2)(2). The quotation even indicates that the Commission is aware of this.

---

[130] Both Undertaking Concerned Notice, para. 15 and Turnover Calculation Notice, para. 33 appear to support this. As will be shown below in chapter 4, the Commission must rely on the figures for the last financial year for which audited accounts are available. It may, of course, be that newer audited accounts (giving the turnover figures of the first transaction at the time of this transaction) have become available at the time of the second transaction. If so, the Commission must base its calculation of the Community dimension on these figures rather than on the (older and inaccurate) figures available at the time of the first transaction.

[131] European Commission, *XXIVth Report on Competition Policy 1994*, Brussels 1995, para. 269.

3. THE GROUP

1. INTRODUCTION

The two sets of turnover thresholds (the Community dimension) that define the scope of the Merger Regulation are based on aggregate turnover. This means that the calculation of the Community dimension is not based on the turnover of the individual undertaking concerned but instead on the turnover of the full group to which the undertaking concerned belongs.[1] This is well-founded since the Community dimension is intended to reflect the economic power of the undertakings concerned,[2] the intention being to catch only those situations where significant economic powers are accumulated. Nevertheless, even though the Community dimension is calculated on group turnover, the term 'group' appears nowhere in the Merger Regulation.[3]

---

[1] As shown above in chapter 2, an acquired part constitutes an undertaking concerned and in this case only the turnover of the part, not of the group from which it is sold, is taken into account, cf. Art. 5(2). In some cases the Commission appears to have based the calculation of turnover *vis-à-vis* some of the thresholds on only the undertaking concerned and not on the full group. *See* for example *Klöckner/ODS*, Case IV/M918, decision of 5 August 1997, para. 6 and *Klöckner/Comercial de Laminados*, Case IV/M971, decision of 26 August 1997 at para. 6. In both decisions the Commission refers to the full Viag-group (to which Klöckner belong) in respect of the € 5 billion threshold, but to Klöckner (the undertaking concerned) in respect of the € 250 million threshold. That the Commission thereby has understated the total Community-wide group turnover of Klöckner seems to be apparent from the turnover figures for the Viag-group set out in *Viag/Bayernwerk*, Case IV/M417, decision of 5 May 1994 and *Watt AG II*, Case IV/M958, decision of 4 December 1997. The mistake did not have any material consequences in the two first-mentioned decisions.

[2] Likewise, para. 36 of Commission notice on calculation of turnover under Council Regulation (EEC) No 4064/89 of 21 December 1989 on the control of concentrations between undertakings, OJ C66/25 of 2.3.1998. (Turnover Calculation Notice).

[3] In contrast, Form CO, annexed to Commission Regulation (EC) No 447/98 of 1 March 1998 on the notification, time limits and hearings provided for in Council Regulation (EEC) No 4064/89 on the control of concentrations between undertakings, OJ L61/1 of 2.3.1998 (The Implementing Regulation), applies this term several times.

Community law does not provide any standard definition of a 'group',[4] but, under Community antitrust law, a group definition focusing on actual control[5] has evolved[6] which may be both cumbersome and difficult to ascertain. The Community dimension is intended to provide a clear-cut dividing line which is easy to apply. For the purposes of calculating the aggregate turnover of the undertakings concerned, Article 5(4)(b) therefore introduces a simple definition of the group based on a formal notion of control. As a result, according to this provision, control exists where an undertaking directly or indirectly meets at least one of the following four conditions:

- owns more than half the capital or business assets, or

- has the power to exercise more than half the voting rights, or

- has the power to appoint more than half the members of the supervisory board, the administrative board or bodies legally representing the undertakings, or

- has the right to manage the undertakings' affairs;

Obviously, however, a formal notion of control is not well-suited to the purpose of making a substantive appraisal, so for this reason Article 3 endows the Regulation with a second and more sophisticated definition of control. Article 3(3) thus provides that 'control shall be constituted by rights, contracts or any other means which, either separately or jointly and having regard to the considerations

---

4   A draft for a Group Directive (the 9th Company Directive) has been discussed for years, but as Vanessa Edwards, *EC Company Law*, Clarendon Press, Oxford 1999 observes at p. 391 in respect of this draft '[s]ince the 1984 version, no further work has been undertaken on the draft proposal, which at least for the foreseeable future seems to have sunk without trace'. Likewise Søren Friis Hansen, 'The "Takeover" of Corporate Group Law – Examples from a Scandinavian Perspective', in *The Internationalisation of Companies and Company Law* (Mette Neville and Karsten Engsig Sørensen, eds.), DJØF Publishing, Copenhagen 2001, pp. 31-51 at p. 38 notes that the draft was 'taken off the agenda during the late 1980s, and any further initiatives in the area from the Commission are not expected in any foreseeable future.'

5   Compare this with Art. 3 of the Merger Regulation.

6   *See* for example Case 22/71 *Béguelin Import Co.* v. *S.A.G.L. Import Export*, ECR 1971, p. 949 and Case 170/83 *Hydrotherm Gerätebau GmbH* v. *Firma Compact del dott. Ing. Mario Andreoli & C. sas*, ECR 1984 p. 2999.

of fact or law involved, confer the possibility of exercising decisive influence on an undertaking'.[7]

Two aspects are important when delimiting the group. The first is the applicable notion of control, the second is the identification of which undertakings must be included in case control has been established. Below, I first examine the Regulation's notion of control for the purposes of finding the Community dimension (part 2), whereupon I will identify the related undertakings (part 3).

2. THE NOTION OF CONTROL

2.1. Introduction

Article 5(4)(b), indents 1-4 set out four alternative ways in which control may be brought about for the purpose of defining the group in Article 5. I will examine these four possibilities below. Before doing this, however, I will first look at three questions of a preliminary nature.

As noted above, the Merger Regulation provides two different notions of control; one in Article 3(3) based on actual control and a more legalistic one in Article 5(4). I shall, therefore, first examine the differences between these two approaches.

Secondly, Article 5(4) refers to direct and indirect control and one may, therefore, ask what exactly these two terms cover. I shall examine this question next.

Thirdly, one may reasonably ask at what point in time the control (as defined in Article 5(4)) must exist. For instance, one may imagine a situation where an undertaking concerned has control over a subsidiary at the event triggering notification (e.g. announcement of a public bid for a target undertaking) but has ceased to have

---

[7] In the *2001 Green Paper on the review of Council Regulation (EEC) No 4064/89*, COM(2001) 745 final, Brussels 11.12.2001, paras. 105 and 145-152, the Commission proposed that the definition of control set out in Art. 5(4) was replaced by the one set out in Art. 3. However, in the 'Proposal for a Council Regulation on the control of concentrations between undertakings', COM(2002) 711 final, OJ C20/4 of 28.1.2003, the Commission abandoned this idea again. In my article 'Muddying the Clear Waters: On the Commission's Proposal for a New Delimitation of Jurisdiction in the Field of Merger Control', *European Competition Law Review* Vol. 23, no. 9, 2002, pp. 429-433, I have explained why in my opinion it was a very bad idea to replace the present notion of control found in Art. 5(4) with that provided in Art. 3.

control over the subsidiary when the actual transaction (acquisition of control of the target) is to occur.

2.2. Actual versus formal control

Merger control is concerned with situations where control over business powers is accumulated, thereby threatening the competition in the marketplace. Accordingly, in order to make a substantive appraisal, a sophisticated definition of control is required. The Merger Regulation provides this in Article 3.[8]

Calculating the Community dimension does not require a sophisticated concept of control. Indeed, a sophisticated concept of control would run counter to some of the essential aims of the Regulation's notion of Community dimension; that the rule must be easy to apply and provide a clearcut dividing line. As noted above, Article 5(4)(b) provides an exhaustive list of four ways in which control may be brought about. Whether only one criterion or all four criteria have been met is immaterial; in either case there will be control within the meaning of Article 5(4)(b). The legalistic concept applied in Article 5(4)(b) may, however, cause problems. This is particularly the case where one (or more) of the four criteria has been fulfilled but the case does not concern actual control.

> *Example*
>
> Company A holds more than 50% of the share capital in Company B, but the shares carry no voting rights, and Company A does not have actual control over Company B.

Likewise, one can easily imagine situations where there is actual control but none of the four criteria in Article 5(4)(b) has been met. This may, for example, be due to personal links between two undertakings: where, for instance, several of

---

8   For an analysis of the notion of control provided in Art. 3, *see* my article 'Fusionskontrolforord-ningens kontrolbegreb' in *Festskrift til Mogens Koktvedgaard*, (Mads Bryde Andersen, Caroline Heide-Jørgensen and Jens Schovsbo, eds.), Jurist- og Økonomforbundets Forlag, Copenhagen 2003. Even though the notion of control provided in Art. 3 is very wide, it has been argued that '[t]he notion of control cannot reach far enough in order to cover all anti-competitive minority acquisitions' cf. Robin A. Struijlaart, 'Minority Share Acquisitions Below the Control Thresholds of the EC Merger Control Regulation: An Economic and Legal Analysis', *World Competition* 2002 pp. 173-204 at p. 173.

the board members in one company are also members of the board of another company.

In either case, the solution is rather straightforward. In my opinion, the very fact that the drafters of the Merger Regulation included one notion of control based on actual and another based on formal control in itself shows that different notions apply. The fact that Article 5(4)(b) does catch certain situations which do not concern actual control and does not catch certain situations which do concern actual control is the inevitable result of this. If Article 5(4)(b) were to cover all cases of actual control and leave out all cases which do not concern actual control, the provision should have been drafted along the lines of Article 3 and there would thus be no reason to include two differing notions in the Regulation. Consequently, the notion of control provided in Article 5(4)(b) may cover situations which will not be caught by Article 3(3) and it may leave out situations which would have been caught by Article 3(3). This is simply a reflection of the differing purposes of Articles 3 and 5.

Example

In late 1990, Volvo and Renault agreed to put their respective bus divisions under their joint control.[9] The following year the two bus divisions agreed to take joint control over a third bus producer, Heuliez.[10] Irrespective of the finding of joint control over the Volvo and the Renault bus divisions (within the meaning of Article 3(3)) it appears that within the definition of control provided in Article 5(4)(b) the two bus divisions were still under sole control of Volvo and Renault respectively. Consequently, for the purpose of calculating the Community dimension in *RVI/VBC/Heuliez*, the Commission had to calculate the turnovers of Volvo and Renault separately.[11]

---

[9]   *Renault/Volvo*, Case IV/M004, decision of 7 November 1990.

[10]   *RVI/VBC/Heuliez*, Case IV/M092, decision of 3 June 1991. Before this transaction Renault held joint control over Heuliez together with a third party.

[11]   *See* also Gerwin Van Gerven, 'Case Note: RVI/VBC/Heuliez', *EC Merger Control Reporter*, Kluwer Law International, The Hague 1991 and later (looseleaf), pp. 176.1-176.2. In *La Redoute/Empire*, Case IV/M080, decision of 25 April 1991 the Commission in para. 7 wrongly refers to Article 3 (though this has no bearing on the outcome). *See* also *Jefferson Smurfit Group Plc/Munksjo AB*, Case IV/M613, decision of 31 July 1995, para. 6 and *Gencor/Shell*, Case IV/M470, decision of 29 August 1994, para. 1, and below section 3.7.

In other words, the two notions of control must be viewed as being distinct.[12] It is also noteworthy that Article 3(3) concerns the relationship between the undertakings concerned whereas Article 5(4)(b) concerns the relationship within the group of the individual undertaking concerned. It follows that the two notions will not apply to the same relationship simultaneously.[13]

The difference between Articles 3(3) and 5(4)(b) has been explicitly acknowledged by the Commission in paragraph 42 of the Turnover Calculation Notice which provides that Article 5(4) 'is simpler and easier to prove on the basis of factual evidence, [whereas Article 3(3)] is more demanding …'. Presumably, what is meant is that Article 5(4)(b)'s simpler concept makes it easier to establish whether one or more of the criteria provided in this provision have been met. Consequently, in order to establish whether there is control as defined in Article 5(4)(b), it is not necessary to enter a substantive analysis. This clearly contrasts with Article 3(3).[14] Form CO provides support to the view that the Commission does not consider that Articles 3(3) and 5(4)(b) provide identical notions of control. In the present Form CO, the Commission, in Section 3, footnote 4, refers to '… Articles 3(3) to (5) and 5(4)' for the definition of control. In the original Form CO, the Commission only referred to '… Article 3(3) to (5)' for the definition of control. If the Commission considered the two definitions to be identical there would be no need to make this amendment to Form CO.[15]

---

[12] Likewise Götz Drauz, 'EEC Merger Control – The First Year' in *Papers of Antitrust Keynote Speakers – Section on Business Law, 10th Biennal Conference, Hong Kong, Committee C, Antitrust and Trade Law, October 1991* at p. 22.

[13] The difference may however be clearly exhibited if undertaking A gains *de facto* control over undertaking B through a minority holding whereupon undertaking B enters into a concentration (e.g. setting up a JV) with undertaking C. When calculating the Community dimension in the latter case only the turnover of B and C may be taken into account. Hence, one may imagine that the exclusion of A means that the transaction involving B and C is not notifiable.

[14] Barry E. Hawk and Henry L. Huser, *European Community Merger Control: A Practitioner's Guide*, Kluwer Law International, The Hague 1996, pp. 105-106, do not agree with the above interpretation of para. 42 of the Turnover Calculation Notice. They interpret para. 42 as a Commission statement holding that Art. 5(4) control standards are 'more easily satisfied with a lower quantum of control rights' than Art. 3(3)'s standards. This statement they vigorously criticise. When the Notice was revised in 1998, para. 42 in reality remained untouched.

[15] The significance which one may pay to the fact that the former Form CO only referred to Art. 3 is discussed in Mario Siragusa and Romano Subiotto, 'The EEC merger control regulation: The Commission's evolving case law', *Common Market Law Review*, vol. 28, 1991,

In conclusion, in my view, Articles 3 and 5 provide two distinct notions of control which must be interpreted independently of each other. This means that the interpretation of Article 5 is not bound by the interpretation of Article 3 or *vice versa*.[16]

2.3. Direct and indirect control

According to Article 5(4)(b) an undertaking may be either 'directly or indirectly' controlled. Thus, it may also be possible to fulfil the criteria set out in Article 5(4)(b) through an intermediary. The question is whether a personal link may constitute such intermediary?

Example

Company A enters into a concentration with company B. By coincidence, three of the nine members of A's supervisory board are shareholders in company C, in which they jointly hold 60% of the voting rights. Must A include C in its group for the purpose of calculating the Community dimension?

No doubt, the personal link between A and C might be important in evaluating the concentration between A and B. This, however, concerns the substantive appraisal, whereas Article 5(4)(b) only concerns establishing jurisdiction. Including personal or other such links under Article 5(4)(b) does not harmonise well with the intention that the Community dimension shall provide a clearcut and easy to apply delimitation of jurisdiction. Moreover, there is no indication in Article 5(4)(b), indents 1-4 that such links shall be covered.[17] It is thus submitted that personal

---

pp. 877-934 at p. 900 and in my article, 'The European Commission's Jurisdiction under the Merger Control Regulation', *Nordic Journal of International Law*, Vol. 63, 1994, pp. 17-108 at p. 85 with note 11.

[16] B.E. Hawk and H.L. Huser, *supra* note 14 at pp. 99-100 observe that 'the Commission (primarily through its Turnover Calculation Notice) has effectively replaced the bright line standards of Articles 5(4) and (5) with ambiguous standards, which resemble Article 3(3)'s lower 'control' standard.' In my opinion, the two authors are right that the Commission has obscured the original clear dividing line, as I will show below. The Commission, however, still does not consider the two kinds of control to be interchangeable.

[17] Note though that in *IFINT/EXOR*, Case IV/M187, decision of 2 March 1992, the Commission appears to have taken into account a personal link between two undertakings in order to establish control within the meaning of Art. 5(4)(b). *See* also *Valinox/Timet*, Case IV/M917, decision of 12 June 1997. The two cases are discussed further below in section 2.5.3.

links shall not be taken into account for the purpose of establishing jurisdiction under the Regulation.

In my view, the terms 'directly' and 'indirectly' simply cover those situations where control is exercised either directly or through a subsidiary. This interpretation harmonises well with the wording of Article 5(4)(b), indents 1-4, it harmonises well with the idea that the Community dimension shall be easy to ascertain, and it harmonises well with the common understanding of the two terms. The Commission's decisions clearly support this interpretation.[18]

Article 5(4)(b) only concerns subsidiaries. In section 3.3, below, I shall discuss whether direct and indirect parents are included in the group.

2.4. The point in time when control must exist

It may reasonably be asked at what point in time the control relationship must exist between on the one hand the undertaking concerned and on the other hand the other members of the group. Article 5(4) applies the present tense clearly indicating that the control relationship must be a present (rather than a prior or future) one.[19] The three most obvious cutoff dates would seem to be (1) the event triggering notification, or (2) the date of notification or (3) the date when the actual transaction (acquisition of control) is to occur.[20]

---

[18] *See* for example *Elf/Occidental*, Case IV/M085, decision of 13 June 1991 (refers to 'indirect subsidiary' in para. 1), *BP/PETROMED*, Case IV/M111, decision of 29 July 1991 (refers to 'indirect subsidiary' in para. 1), *Spar/Dansk Supermarked*, Case IV/M179, decision of 3 February 1992, (refers to 'unmittelbar beteiligten Tochtergesellschaften' in para. 4), *IFINT/ EXOR*, *supra* note 17 (refers to 'La société EXOR détient directement ou indirectement par l'intermédiaire des filiales …' in para. 10), *BANESTO/TOTTA*, Case IV/M192, decision of 14 April 1992 (refers to 'directamente, e indiractemente a través de …' in para. 1).

[19] Arguing that the reference to the 'preceding financial year' in Art. 5(1) means that the control relationship should exist at that time is therefore not persuasive, it is submitted. *See* also *Paribas/MTH/MBH*, Case IV/M122, decision of 17 October 1991 together with my comments thereon in chapter 5, section 5, below.

[20] In some cases the Commission appears to use the 'last annual general meeting' as the cutoff date, cf. for example *Arjomari-Prioux/Wiggins Teape Appleton*, Case IV/M025, decision of 10 December 1990, paras. 6-7 and *Elkem/Sapa*, Case COMP/M2404, decision of 26 June 2001, para. 3. Under the German merger control scheme it appears that the calculation of turnover is made on the basis of the members of the group at the time when the competition authorities issue their decision on the legality of the merger, cf. Hans-Jürgen Ruppelt, *Kommentar zum deutschen und europäischen Kartellrecht*, 9th edition, Luchterhand, Berlin 2001, p. 995.

Solid arguments may be put forward in favour of all three possibilities. However, in the *Dan Air* case[21] the Court of First Instance rather unambiguously pointed to 'the event triggering notification' as the decisive point in time for establishing which parts may be included in the group of the undertaking concerned in order to establish jurisdiction.[22]

In its case law the Commission has, nonetheless, opted for the second solution and the third solution in addition to the first one.[23]

---

[21] Case T-3/93, *Air France* v. *Commission*, 1994 ECR II-121.

[22] The Court of First Instance equally found that if a divestiture or closure of existing operations is a precondition for the notified transaction, it is appropriate to deduct the turnover attributable to such operations. In conformity with the *Dan Air* judgment, *see* likewise the Undertaking Concerned Notice, para. 17, the Turnover Calculation Notice, para. 27, Jonathan Faull & Ali Nikpay, *The EC Law of Competition*, Oxford University Press, Oxford 1999, at p. 232 and *Bellamy & Child – European Community Law of Competition*, 5th ed., (P.M. Roth, ed.), Sweet & Maxwell, London 2001 at p. 381 and 383. The last-mentioned at p. 381 explains that turnover of a part of one of the undertakings concerned will only be excluded where 'the divestiture [is] effected either between the closing of the relevant accounts and the time of signature of the merger agreement or as part of the notified concentration by means of an irrevocable condition precedent'. Dominique Berlin and Hugues Calvet, 'Concentrations – 1er janvier 1995 – 31 décembre 1996', *Revue trimestrielle de droit européen*, 1997, pp. 521-627 at pp. 558-559 observe that the decision to divest or close an existing operation must be final on the date of the notification at the latest. Thus in *Rhône-Poulenc Rorer/Fisons*, Case IV/M632, decision of 21 September 1995, Fisons claimed that the concentration did not meet the thresholds as certain operations had been divested before the concentration were to be put into effect. One of these divestitures was signed on 29 August 1995 while the concentration was notified on 18 August 1995. The Commission was therefore right in including the turnover derived from this operation when calculating turnover.

[23] *See* for example *Cereol/Sofiproteol-Saipol*, Case IV/M1125, decision of 10 March 1998, para. 17, for an example of the explicit application of the first solution. In some cases it is very difficult to see which of the three options – if any – the Commission has opted for. Hence, in *Preussag/Babcock Borsig*, Case IV/M1594, decision of 17 August 1999, the Commission when calculating Babcock Borsig's turnover explicitly excludes that of AE Energietechnik Beteiligungs AG. The latter undertaking had been acquired by Babcock shortly before the *Preussag/Babcock Borsig* concentration was notified, cf. *Babcock Borsig/AE Energietechnik*, Case IV/M1552, decision of 30 June 1999. The two decisions do not reveal why the Commission excluded the turnover of AE Energietechnik. Equally, in *Unilever France/Amora-Maille*, Case COMP/M1802, decision of 8 March 2000, the acquirer and the target agreed that the latter should sell off certain activities before the acquirer gained control. It is not clear from the decision whether these activities were included or excluded when calculating the Community dimension. In *Enron/MG*, Case COMP/M2006, decision of

In *Valinox/Timet*[24] the Commission in respect of Vallourec – one of the two undertakings concerned – explicitly points out that '[f]or the purposes of jurisdiction Vallourec was controlled by Usinor Sacilor' and that this control was present '*[a]t the time of the notification*'.[25] The reference to the time of the notification is important since the Commission in its earlier decision *Mannesmann/Vallourec*[26] cleared Usinor Sacilor's transfer of control over Vallourec to Mannesmann. This transfer had not been completed, however, at the time when *Valinox/Timet* was notified with the Commission.[27]

In contrast, in *Cargill/Vandemoortele – JV*[28] (read in conjunction with the Commission's decision in *Cargill/Vandemoortele*[29]) the two undertakings, Cargill and Vandemoortele, agreed on a number of operations as part of a wider transaction. One of these operations concerned Cargill's acquisition of sole control over a part of Vandemoortele's business while another operation concerned the creation of a joint venture. These operations were notified and examined simultaneously. However, when calculating Vandemoortele's Community-wide turnover, the Commission explicitly excluded the turnover generated by the business to be sold to Cargill (although Vandemoortele presumably had control over this business until operations were going to take place).[30] Likewise, in the Turnover Calculation Notice the

---

4 July 2000, the Commission at para. 6 declined to take a position because 'it has no incidence on the community dimension'.

[24] *Supra* note 17. *See* also *MCI WorldCom/Sprint*, Case IV/M1741, decision of 28 June 2000.

[25] Para. 3 of the decision, emphasis added

[26] Case IV/M906, decision of 3 June 1997.

[27] In *Torras/Sarrio*, Case IV/M166, decision of 24 February 1992, the concentration was notified almost one year too late. Unofficially it has been claimed that for the purposes of calculating the Community dimension, the Commission included turnover of Torras' subsidiary Ebro although Torras had ceased to control Ebro (within the meaning laid down in Art. 5(4)) in the time period between the operation and the notification. In its decision the Commission at para. 7 explicitly refers to 'the financial year *preceding the operation*' (emphasis added). Hence, the time of the notification was not considered to be the decisive point in time.

[28] Case IV/M1227, decision of 20 July 1998.

[29] Case IV/M1126, decision of 20 July 1998.

[30] The decision does not say whether the business in question was instead calculated towards Cargill's turnover.

Commission explicitly points out that 'Article 5(4) refers only to the groups that already exist *at the time of the transaction ...*'[31]

The conclusion must be on the one hand that 'the event triggering notification' should be considered the decisive point in time for establishing which parts may be included in the group of the undertaking concerned in order to establish jurisdiction. On the other hand, it must also be concluded that the Commission's practice does not unambiguously support this conclusion.[32]

---

[31] Para. 41, emphasis added.

[32] If a merger decision is annulled by the Court of Justice or the Court of First Instance the Commission may be required to re-examine the case. Due to the considerable delays at the two courts in Luxembourg, this re-examination is likely to take place several years after the merger was originally notified. The Community dimension must however be calculated on the basis of the original turnover figures. *See* for example *Kali+Salz/Mdk/Treuhand*, Case IV/M308, decision of 9 July 1998.

In the German *Eon/Ruhrgas* case, Eon's intended acquisition of Ruhrgas did not meet the turnover thresholds and was therefore notified to the German Bundeskartellamt which prohibited the transaction. Eon, however, applied to the Finance Minister to override the prohibition and the undertaking was successful in that the merger was conditionally allowed. Third parties challenged this permission in court. In its ruling the German court expressed doubts over whether, as a consequence of the application to the Finance Minister to set aside the decision of the Bundeskartellamt, the Community dimension should have been re-assessed. Whereas the Court did not reach a conclusion on this point, it did observe that at the time of the application to the Finance Minister, the transaction would have had a Community dimension due to certain structural changes that had occurred between the notification to the Bundeskartellamt and the application to the Minister. *See* further *Lovells – EU and Competition Newsletter*, August/September 2002, Issue no. 44, pp. 3-4. In my opinion the question put by the German court is rather misplaced. Whether or not a transaction does or does not possess a Community dimension is established at the time of the event triggering notification only. The fact that the decision of the authorities is challenged (before an administrative body or before the courts) does not affect the question of Community dimension. This is true with regard to both transactions with a Community dimension and transactions without such a dimension.

2.5. The four criteria in Article 5(4)(b)

2.5.1. Introduction

In what follows, I will analyse the construction of each of the four criteria provided in Article 5(4)(b), indents 1-4. Before doing this, it is probably worth noting that Article 5(4)(b) has been construed so that where the criterion provided in the first indent (to own more than half the capital or business assets) has been met, the three following criteria will normally also have been met. Where the first criterion has not been met, the second (to have the power to exercise more than half the voting rights) may still be met. If so, the last two criteria (to have the power to appoint more than half the members of the body legally representing the undertaking, and to have the right to manage the undertaking's affairs) are also likely to have been met. And so on. In other words, there is a kind of in-built hierarchy between the four criteria.

2.5.2. Owns more than half the capital or business assets

Article 5(4)(b), first indent establishes that where an undertaking concerned 'owns more than half the capital or business assets' in another undertaking, the latter must be included in the group of the undertaking concerned for the purposes of calculating the Community dimension.[33]

This criterion is straightforward. Problems may arise, however, where uncertainty surrounds the ownership. For instance, where a seller of a company later claims the sales agreement to be void. Or where the actual size of the capital or the business assets is not clear, as when, for instance, one undertaking acquires a part of some assets, the final price (and thus the final share) of which will be decided at a later stage (*e.g.* on the basis of the performance during the first two years after the acquisition).

This kind of problem is rare and the solution very clearly depends on the specific facts in the individual case. Consequently, the solution must be found on a case by case basis when (or if) such cases arise.

---

[33] In *KNP/BT/VRG*, Case IV/M291, decision of 4 May 1993, [1993] OJ L217/35, paras. 5 and 6, KNP held a 50.6% stake in VRG but still the Commission chose to consider not only KNP and BT but also VRG as undertakings concerned. *See* also *supra* chapter 2, note 13.

As noted above in chapter 2, section 2.3, individuals and families may also constitute an undertaking concerned. Likewise, if an individual (or a family) has control (as defined in Article 5) of more undertakings, these undertakings may be considered to be part of the same group for the purpose of calculating turnover. Indeed, the Commission has gone one step further since it has taken the view that it is possible to accumulate the holdings (capital or voting rights) of an individual with the holdings of a number of family foundations that are related to that individual.[34]

2.5.3. Has the power to exercise more than half the voting rights

According to Article 5(4)(b), second indent, where an undertaking concerned 'has the power to exercise more than half the voting rights' in another undertaking, this latter undertaking must be included for the purposes of calculating the Community dimension.

An undertaking may hold more than half of the capital in another undertaking without being able to exercise more than half the voting rights and *vice versa*. In particular, where the shares in a company carry different voting rights, it may be possible to hold more or less than half of the capital without this necessarily meaning that one holds more or less than half of all the voting rights in the company. Likewise, the articles of association or an agreement between two shareholders may have the same effect.[35]

---

34 *See A.P. Møller*, Case IV/M969, decision of 10 February 1999, [1998] OJ L183/29. Hitherto the A.P. Møller group has been made up of two parent companies that are both listed on the Copenhagen Stock Exchange. Amongst the major shareholders of these two companies are Mr. Mærsk McKinney-Møller and three foundations that are all closely connected to the Møller family. Together Mr. McKinney-Møller and the three foundations hold more than 50% of both the capital and the voting rights in either company. By accumulating the holdings of Mr. Mc-Kinney Møller and the three family foundations the Commission managed to bring several unnotified transactions within the scope of the Regulation. Whilst there seems to be no reason to doubt that the two A.P. Møller parent companies are under the control of Mr. McKinney-Møller as defined in Art. 3 of the Regulation, it seems to be equally clear that Mr. McKinney-Møller does not have control as defined in Art. 5(4) of the Regulation. The Commission decided to impose a fine on the A.P. Møller group of companies for failing to notify the concentrations. It is respectfully submitted that the decision imposing the fine was based on a misinterpretation of the Merger Regulation.

35 C.J. Cook and C.S. Kerse, *E.C. Merger Control*, 3rd ed., Sweet & Maxwell, London 2000, p. 74 with note 41 put up the presumption that *La Redoute/Empire*, *supra* note 11 provides

Example

A holds 60% of the voting rights in X whereas B and C each hold 20%. According to the articles of X, however, no shareholder may exercise voting rights equivalent to more than 20% of all voting rights. In other words, A, B and C may exercise excactly the same voting rights.[36]

A question of great importance is whether Article 5(4)(b), second indent only covers situations where an undertaking has the power *de jure* to exercise more than half of all the voting rights, or whether it also covers situations where the undertaking has this power *de facto*. In the Commission's view, cases of *de facto* control are also covered as shown in for example *Eurocom/RSCG*.[37]

Example

In *Eurocom/RSCG*, Eurocom and RSCG had agreed to merge. Eurocom was 44.25% owned by the group Havas, and only if Havas' turnover was included in Eurocom's group turnover, would the concentration have a Community dimension. The Commission therefore looked closely into this matter and found that Havas did control Eurocom within the meaning of Article 5(4)(b), second indent since Havas had been able 'to exercise, during the last three general shareholders' meeting … respectively, 69.5%, 68% and 77.5% of the voting rights present or represented.' In other words, the fact that Havas had been able to exercise more than half of the voting rights at the three latest annual general meetings was considered to constitute the necessary proof that

---

an example of a parent company holding more than 50% of the voting rights but less than 50% of the sharecapital. Thus, this appears to be a good case for applying Art. 5(4)(b), second indent. Another example is *@Home Benelux B.V.*, Case IV/JV11, decision of 15 September 1998. *See* also *Valinox/Timet, supra* note 17 where Usinor Sacilor held 27.63% of the shares in Vallourec, but under Vallourec's Articles of Association these shares carried double voting rights so that Usinor Sacilor had *de facto* control over Vallourec.

[36] Contrast this with Article 1(1)(a) of the Seventh Council Directive of 13 June 1983 on Consolidated Accounts, [1983] OJ L193/1 which simply requires that the company 'has a majority of the … voting rights …', thus apparently not requiring that the holder of the rights is also able to actually exercise a majority thereof. It may be added that this directive includes more detailed rules regarding the calculation of these rights. It seems doubtful, however, what value (if any) these rules may have in the interpretation of Article 5(4)(b), second indent.

[37] Case IV/M147, decision of 18 December 1991.

Havas had control within the definition set out in Article 5(4)(b), second indent.

Basing the calculation on *de facto* rather than *de jure* control clearly makes it much more difficult to ascertain whether Article 5(4)(b), second indent has been met. It, therefore, detracts from the legal certainty *vis-à-vis* calculating the Community dimension.[38] For this reason, I tend to find that a *de jure* interpretation constitutes the better solution. On the other hand, the wording of the provision lends support to the Commission's interpretation since it requires the undertaking to have 'the *power* to *exercise* more than half the voting rights' (italics added). One may argue that if the drafters of the Regulation had wanted to cover only *de jure* control, they would have made this clear by, for instance, requiring the undertaking to control more than half of *all* the voting rights. It is, therefore, difficult to argue that the Commission's interpretation is incorrect.

Accepting the Commission's interpretation, based on *de facto* control, the question is how this control is ascertained. The Commission's decisions do not provide much guidance on this point. *Arjomari-Prioux/Wiggins Teape Appleton*[39] (which refers to Article 5(4)(b), third indent concerning the power to appoint more than half of the board of another undertaking) may, however, be interpreted to mean that the decisive point is whether it has been possible to exercise more than half of the votes present at the last annual general meeting and not to consider whether this would also be the case at the time of the concentration.[40] This decision is discussed below in section 2.5.4.

---

[38] See for example *Mannesmann/Vallourec*, *supra* note 26, in which the acquisition of 21% of the capital in a target constituted *de facto* control (within the meaning of Art. 3(3)), cf. *XXVIIth Report on Competition Policy 1997*, Luxembourg 1998, p. 171. Jonathan Scott, 'Case Note: Arjomari-Prioux/Wiggins Teape Appleton', *EC Merger Control Reporter*, Kluwer Law International, The Hague 1991 and later (looseleaf), pp. 24.1-24.2 at p. 24.2 argues in favour of a *de jure* approach. However, he goes as far as to require the undertaking in question to own (not simply have the power to exercise, *e.g.* on the basis of an agreement) 50% or more of (all) the voting rights.

[39] *Supra* note 20.

[40] Thus, according to M. Siragusa and R. Subiotto, *supra* note 15 at p. 899, in *Arjomari-Prioux/Wiggins Teape Appleton*, 'the Commission was of the view that it was not appropriate to take account of changes in voting rights that had occurred since the last annual general meeting even though these changes apparently gave [another company] control over Arjomari by the time of notification.' Note, though, that with regard to precisely the question of when an owner of a minority stake may be in control because he holds a majority at the shareholders'

I subscribe to a different interpretation. Thus, in my view, the *de facto* control (for calculating the turnover thresholds) must be present at the time of the concentration.[41] The solution must be to look at the division of votes at the preceding annual general meetings. If the undertaking has been able to exercise a comfortable majority (or if it has not been able to exercise such majority) it is submitted that one may presume that this will still be the case at the time when the concentration is brought about. This does not differ from the Commission's interpretation. The difference arises, since, in my view, the presumption must be rebutted if the undertaking has only been able to secure a narrow majority and if one may reasonably assume that this majority could not have been secured had a question of importance been on the agenda at the annual general meeting (which presumably would have caused more shareholders to attend[42]). It is equally submitted that the presumption must be rebutted if an undertaking has been able to exercise a comfortable majority at the last annual general meeting, but it has since divested itself of a part of its shareholding, meaning that at the time of the concentration it is unlikely that it would be able to exercise a majority at a similar annual general meeting. Or similarly, where the undertaking was not able to exercise more than half of the votes present or represented at the last annual general meeting (meaning that it did not then possess *de facto* control), but it has since increased its shareholding to a degree which, while not giving it an absolute majority, would have given it a comfortable majority at the last annual general meeting.

The Commission's interpretation of Article 5(4)(b), second indent in *IFINT/ EXOR*,[43] deserves special mention here. In 1992, the Luxembourg company IFINT made a public bid for all the shares of the French company EXOR. In order for the concentration to have a Community dimension, it was necessary to show that IFINT

---

meetings, Jonathan Faull & Ali Nikpay, *supra* note 22, at p. 212 (concerning the notion of *de facto* control in Art. 3(3)) state that the decisive criterion is whether 'the holder of a qualified majority will be likely to achieve a majority at *future* [shareholders'] meetings' (emphasis added).

[41] *See* further section 2.4 above.

[42] One may imagine that in particular shareholders with very small holdings will only bother to attend the shareholders' meeting if important matters are on the agenda. These shareholders may, however, vote in favour of other boardmembers than those the major shareholders will vote for. For a similar view, *see* Dorothy Livingston, *Competition Law and Practice*, FT Law and Tax, London 1995 at p. 729.

[43] *Supra* note 17.

was part of the Agnelli-group (together with *inter alia* FIAT)[44] and that Perrier was part of the EXOR-group. The Commission concluded that Perrier was part of the EXOR-group in accordance with Article 5(4)(b), second indent and did so on the basis of the following observations:

(1) EXOR holds directly or indirectly through subsidiaries 28.69% of the capital and 33.29% of the voting rights in Perrier.

(2) OMINCO, a company which is owned 49% by EXOR and 51% by GENEVAL (a subsidiary of Société Général), owns 6.32% of Perrier's capital. GENEVAL owns 0.48% of Perrier's capital.

(3) EXOR, GENEVAL and OMINCO entered into a shareholders' agreement according to which the three parties will consult each other before making any decisions as shareholders (direct or indirect) in Perrier.

(4) Perrier itself controls 13.82% of its own shares.

(5) The above figures (28.69 + 6.32 + 0.48 + 13.82) amount to a total of 49.31%.

(6) The Commission des Opérations de Bourse determined that EXOR held 52.1% of the voting rights present and represented at the general meeting in June 1990.

(7) Perrier's Président Directeur Général and EXOR's Président Directeur Général is one and the same person.

(8) In official documents, IFINT introduces itself as 'belonging to the AGNELLI group'.

The above construction *vis-à-vis* holdings of shares may be illustrated in the following way:

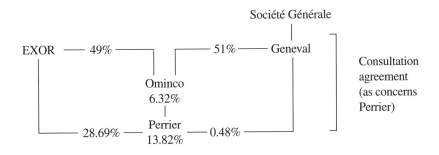

In my view, the Commission's interpretation is very creative. Indeed, I tend to think that it is almost too creative. Seven points are worthy of note in this respect.

(1) Normally, shares held by a company in the company itself do not carry voting rights. They are, so to speak, neutralised. These shares should not be attributed to any 'external' shareholder, but instead they should be excluded from the examination of whether Article 5(4)(b), second indent has been met. It is very difficult to see how the Commission can justify counting the voting rights relating to Perrier's own holding as rights which EXOR may exercise.[45]

(2) It is also surprising that the Commission bases its calculation on capital size since Article 5(4)(b), second indent explicitly refers to voting rights. It is apparent that Perrier had different share classes so it would be relevant to know if the capital size of 49.13% attributed to EXOR also carried with it 49.13% (or more/less) of the voting rights.

(3) As pointed out by Anand S. Pathak,[46] one may wonder why the Commission refers to the situation at the 1990 general shareholders' meeting. After all, the transaction was notified in 1992, so it would be far more relevant to refer to the 1991 general shareholders' meeting (provided that such meeting was held).[47] Moreover, 52.1% of the votes present or represented in a single general shareholders' meeting is not exactly a comfortable majority which may be taken as a strong indication of the power *de facto* to exercise more than half of the voting rights in Perrier on a more continuous basis.

(4) Anand S. Pathak also points out that the Commission indicates that EXOR, OMINCO and GENEVAL acted as one economic entity. The facts provided seem to indicate, however, that rather than being one economic entity, they were independent undertakings holding joint control over Perrier.

(5) Also, if the Commission intended to show that EXOR held joint control over Perrier (together with OMINCO and GENEVAL), it is important to note that, in my view, a joint venture between an undertaking concerned

---

[45] *See* also Art. 2(3) of the Seventh Council Directive of 13 June 1983 on Consolidated Accounts, *supra* note 36.

[46] 'Case Note: Ifint/Exor', *EC Merger Control Reporter*, Kluwer Law International, The Hague 1991 and later (looseleaf), pp. 702.3-702.5.

[47] Unfortunately Perrier has not been willing to provide information on this point and the company also consider their annual reports confidential.

(such as EXOR) and a third party (such as OMINCO or GENEVAL) may not be included for the purposes of calculating the Community dimension.[48] Even if one takes the opposite position, the Commission could only add one-third, or at most half, of Perrier's turnover (as it had to be split between the parents in accordance with Article 5(5)) to EXOR's turnover.[49]

(6) Moreover, as noted above in section 2.3, personal links cannot be taken into account for the purpose of establishing control under Article 5(4). One, therefore, wonders why the Commission expressly notes that the Président Directeur Général of Perrier and of EXOR was one and the same person.

(7) Lastly, it should be observed that the fact that IFINT has introduced itself as 'belonging to the AGNELLI group' neither constitutes proof of actual nor of formal control.[50]

In conclusion, the facts provided in the public version of *IFINT/EXOR* indicate that the Commission has not restricted itself to applying a creative interpretation. Rather, it is submitted that the Commission has embarked on a questionable interpretation in this case.

Unfortunately it appears that, to some extent at least, the decision in *IFINT/ EXOR* has been followed in *Valinox/Timet*.[51] In this case the two undertakings Vallourec and Timet notified the establishment of a joint venture. While there was no doubt that these two undertakings were undertakings concerned, there was considerably more uncertainty as to what undertakings were to be included in the respective groups according to Article 5(4). With regard to Timet, the Commission found that the undertakings Tremont and Contran (together with all of these two

---

48 *See* further below section 3.7.4.

49 Cf. Götz Drauz and Dirk Schroeder, *Praxis der europäischen Fusionskontrolle*, 3rd ed., RWS Verlag Kommunikationsforum GmbH, Cologne 1995, at pp. 25-26.

50 Likewise, in *Adeg/Edeka*, Case IV/M1303, decision of 9 November 1998, when establishing a Community dimension the Commission concerning one of the parties observed that 'Zum anderen lässt sich aus der gemeinsamen Nutzung der Marke EDEKA und dem Auftreten gegenüber Lieferanten und Kunden auf eine gruppenähnliche Struktur schliessen'. In the translation of the EC Merger Control Reporter: 'It is also possible to substantiate the existence of a group-like structure on the basis of the common usage of the brand EDEKA and the representation to suppliers and customers'. In my opinion this observation is utterly irrelevant *vis-à-vis* establishing a Community dimension.

51 *Supra* note 35.

undertakings' direct and indirect subsidiaries) should be included in the group according to Article 5(4).

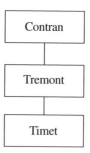

Whilst the relationship between Tremont and Contran did not pose insurmountable problems,[52] the Commission was faced with considerable difficulties in establishing that the relationship between Timet and Tremont qualified under Article 5(4).

Until shortly before the Commission was notified, the shares in Timet had been split 75/25 between Tremont and the undertaking UTSC. Hence, Tremont had held 75% of all the shares at the last general meeting. However, at the time when the concentration was notified with the Commission, the shares in Timet were split as follows:

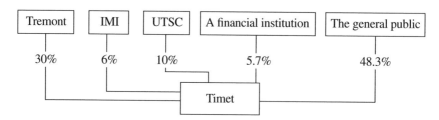

In other words, whilst Tremont had held more than half the votes cast in the last general meeting it was difficult to base jurisdiction on this fact following the very considerable dilution of Tremont's shareholding. Likewise it was very obvious that Tremont did not hold more than half of all the shares in Timet.

---

52   The Commission at para. 11 of the decision observes that Contran and its subsidiaries controlled in excess of 40% of the shares in the parent of Timet and that Contran had had a majority of the votes cast at the two latest general meetings. Contran thus had *de facto* control over Tremont.

The Commission nevertheless found that the relationship between Tremont and Timet fell within the scope of Article 5(4) and did so on the basis of the following observations:[53]

- At the last general meeting Tremont had a majority of the votes cast.
- Tremont had a call option for 4.5% of IMI's shares.[54] The Commission therefore found that Tremont 'effectively' had 34.5% of the shares in Timet. Tremont therefore had more than twice the votes of the next largest shareholders.[55]
- Tremont had nominated four of the six directors of Timet.[56]
- The Commission points out that three of the directors on Timet's board are also directors of Tremont.
- Moreover, the Commission points out that 'three senior officers are common to the two companies, which also share the same office space'.

On this basis the Commission concluded that Tremont controls Timet 'in the sense of Article 5(4)(b)'.[57]

In my opinion, the Commission's interpretation is dubious, to say the very least. Hence:

- The fact that Tremont had a majority of the votes cast at the last general meeting is irrelevant as Tremont had since decreased its holding from 75% to 30%.
- The inclusion of the optional 4.5% shares seem to conflict with the wording of Article 5(4)(b).[58] Gaining control through options may in extraordinary

---

[53] See paras. 9 and 10 of the decision.

[54] UTSC similarly had a call option for 1.5% of IMI's shares.

[55] The Commission attributed 11.5% of the shares to UTSC and 0% to IMI due to the call options on IMI's holdings.

[56] Presumably this nomination was made at the last general meeting, i.e. when Tremont held 75% of all the shares in Timet.

[57] Cf. paras. 12 and 10 of the decision.

[58] The option only provided Tremont with a possibility of acquiring the shares sometime in the future whereas Art. 5(4)(b) refers to the situation at the time of the transaction. It may be added that in my view it seems to be of minor relevance that the Commission in the decision observes that according to a shareholders' agreement IMI (the holder of 6% of the shares of which Tremont has a call option for 4.5%) was required to vote its shares in favour of directors nominated by Tremont as this presumably means that IMI was free to vote its shares as wished in all other respects.

cases constitute a concentration under Article 3,[59] but does not constitute control within the meaning set out in Article 5(4)(b). Including the optional 4.5% shares in Tremont's holding, is yet again another indication that the Commission has replaced the clear definition of control in Article 5(4) with the one found in Article 3.[60]

– The fact that Tremont had nominated four out of six directors is certainly relevant as Article 5(4)(b), third indent, provides that control exist where the undertaking in question 'has the power to appoint more than half …' of the directors. However, it seems fairly obvious that the four directors appointed by Tremont were appointed at a time when Tremont held 75% of all the shares in Timet. Hence, it seems to be immaterial for establishing control in the actual case.[61]

– Lastly, as has already been noted, personal links cannot be taken into account for the purpose of establishing control under Article 5(4).

Taking all this into account, I am of the view that the Commission's reasoning in *Valinox/Timet* is wrong.[62]

---

[59] *See* for instance *Mannesmann/Vallourec, supra* note 26, concerning Mannesmann's acquisition of a call option in Vallourec. This acquisition constituted a concentration under Art. 3 of the Regulation. *See* likewise *Banco Santander Central Hispanico/AKB*, Case COMP/M2578, decision of 12 November 2001, but compare with *Nomura/Blueslate*, Case IV/M1037, decision of 17 November 1997, para. 7. *See* also C.J. Cook and C.S. Kerse, *supra* note 35, at pp. 32-33 and Jonathan Faull & Ali Nikpay, *supra* note 22, at p. 212-213. In this connection it is worth pointing out that in *Canal+/Lagardère*, Case COMP/JV40 and *Canal+/Lagardère/ Liberty Media*, Case COMP/JV47, joined decision of 22 June 2000, the Commission took into account the future setting-up of some joint ventures. (*See* also *Vivendi Universal/Hachette (Lagardère)/Multithématique*, Case COMP/M2766, decision of 3 May 2002).

[60] *See* further section 2.2 above.

[61] The Commission implicitly seems to be of the same view since it is difficult to conceive any other explanation why it has not simply restricted itself to pointing out that Art. 5(4)(b), third indent has been fulfilled.

[62] In *Coca-Cola/Amalgamated Beverages GB*, Case IV/M794, decision of 22 January 1997, OJ L218/15 of 9.8.1997, the Commission at length discusses the relationship between the acquirer Coca-Cola Enterprises Inc. (CCE) and the Coca-Cola Company (TCCC). Amongst other things the Commission observes that while TCCC only has a 45% shareholding in CCE and has not been able to muster a majority in recent annual general meetings (49.79% in 1994; between 49.09% and 49.84% in 1995; and between 48.2% and 48.8% in 1996) the actual dependency of CCE on TCCC meant that the latter was in control within the definition provided in Art. 3(3). Indeed, with special regard to the history of TCCC's failure to muster

2.5.4. Has the power to appoint the majority of the board (etc.) of the undertaking

Article 5(4)(b), third indent provides that where an undertaking concerned 'has the power to appoint more than half the members of the supervisory board, the administrative board or bodies legally representing the undertakings' this undertaking must be included in the group of the undertaking concerned for the purposes of demonstrating the Community dimension.

It is submitted that this provision must be interpreted along the same lines as those set out regarding Article 5(4)(b), second indent. Hence, where it is obvious that the undertaking concerned holds the right to appoint the majority of the board of another undertaking the latter must be included in the group. This may, for example, be the case where the articles of association vests the powers to appoint the majority of the boardmembers in a specific undertaking. Where no such clear proof exists, it is necessary to refer to the last annual general meeting. In my opinion, if the undertaking concerned was able to appoint the majority of the board members and if this was not simply due to the fact that no important matters were on the agenda at this meeting (which presumably would have caused more shareholders to attend), it seems reasonable to put up a rebuttable presumption that the

---

an absolute majority in the annual general meetings the Commission at para. 10 observes that '[i]f TCCC had any difficulty in finding a majority, it could easily purchase a 2% shareholding on the stock exchange, thus acquiring an absolute majority. The fact that it has not found it necessary to do so is a further indication that it already enjoys practical control' (*sic*!). When it comes to the actual calculation of turnover CCE alone generated a worldwide turnover of more than € 5 billion and met the € 250 million threshold, albeit only by a narrow margin, (between € 251.23 million and € 259 million). Obviously, on the basis of the facts set out by the Commission, TCCC and CCE do not belong to the same group for the purposes of calculating the Community dimension. Rather than acknowledging this, however, the Commission simply observes that 'it is not necessary to consider the turnover of TCCC for jurisdictional purposes' (para. 21). In Joined Cases T-125/97 and 127/97, *The Coca-Cola Company and Coca-Cola Enterprises* v. *Commission,* ECR 2000 II-1733, TCCC and CCE amongst other things challenged the Commission's finding that TCCC controlled CCE. Since the Commission had not based its calculation of the Community dimension on the challenged finding it had not had any legal effects with regard to the two applicants, and the Court of First Instance therefore held the challenge to be inadmissible, cf. paras. 107-109 of the judgment.

See also the rather cryptic observations made on the relationship between Nomura International and another – unidentified – undertaking in *Nomura/Blueslate, supra* note 59 at paras. 13-14.

undertaking concerned still has this power. Conversely, if the undertaking did not have the power to appoint a majority on the board at the last annual general meeting, one may normally presume that it still does not possess this power.[63]

The Commission apparently chose a different interpretation in *Arjomari-Prioux/ Wiggins Teape Appleton*.[64] In this case, Arjomari-Prioux SA (Arjomari) and Wiggins Teape Appleton plc agreed to merge their respective businesses. The parties claimed that the concentration had a Community dimension since the company Groupe Saint Louis should be included in the Arjomari group in accordance with Article 5(4)(b), third indent (*i.e.* they claimed that Groupe Saint Louis was able to appoint more than half of the board of Arjomari).

The Commission first noted that Article 5(4)(b), third indent is met where an undertaking has a contractual right to appoint the majority of the board. It went on to note that the requirement may also be met 'where an undertaking, although not having an absolute majority of the voting rights in an undertaking, holds the largest share and the remaining voting rights are dispersed. Where it can be proved that the undertaking holding such a share has actually been able to make these appointments by controlling more than 50% of the voting rights in the general meeting due to the absence of other voting rights, it is reasonable to assume that the power referred to under Article 5(4)(b) third indent exists.'[65]

At the last annual general meeting of Arjomari, Groupe Saint Louis had only exercised 45.19% of the voting rights (it is not clear how large a shareholding this represented). The Commission also found that Groupe Saint Louis' shareholding in Arjomari had since increased to 45.12% (it is not indicated whether this also amounted to 45.12% of all voting rights). This increase was 'not sufficient itself to establish that [Groupe Saint Louis] has the power referred to in Article 5(4)(b) third indent of the Regulation.'[66] The Commission, therefore, held that the concentration did not have a Community dimension.

One may find that the Commission in *Arjomari-Prioux/Wiggins Teape Appleton* mixes the rule provided in Article 5(4)(b), second indent with the rule provided in

---

[63] As rightly pointed out by Alec Burnside and Carl Meyntjens, 'The EEC Merger Regulation and its Impact on Non-EEC Business', *Brigham Young University Law Review*, Vol. 1990, No. 4, pp. 1373-1411 at p. 1409, if Art. 5(4), third indent was based on a strict legal power only, less uncertainty would be introduced into the Regulation.

[64] *Supra*, note 20.

[65] Para. 6 of the decision.

[66] Para. 7 of the decision.

the third indent: If Groupe Saint Louis had been able to control more than 50% of the voting rights at the last annual general meeting, this would indicate that Article 5(4)(b), second indent has been met. If so, there seems to be no need to refer to the third indent. It may be argued that referring to the third indent where the second has been met does not duly observe the hierarchy built into Article 5(4)(b), as explained above in section 2.5.1. If the Commission has mixed (or confused) these two criteria, it presumably means that the decision also prejudices the interpretation of Article 5(4)(b), second indent. Another possible interpretation is, however, that the Commission decided to apply Article 5(4)(b), third indent to cases of *de facto* control of more than half the voting rights giving the undertaking the power to appoint more than half the members of the board.[67] Only where *de facto* control of more than half the voting rights does not give the undertaking this power, is it necessary to refer to Article 5(4)(b), second indent. In this way, the Commission is likely to be able to avoid the criticism of applying Article 5(4)(b), second indent to cases of *de facto* control without making any substantive changes to its interpretation.

In the Commission's Report on Competition Policy covering 1990, the Commission explains its interpretation in *Arjomari-Prioux/Wiggins Teape Appleton* in the following way: 'the condition attaching to the existence of the power to appoint more than half of the members of the board or other bodies of an undertaking within the meaning of the third indent of Article 5(4)(b), which is established only where the main shareholder has been able to make such appointments by exercising more than half the voting rights present or represented at the last general meeting of shareholders (Arjomari/Wiggins Teape)'.[68] In other words, if at the time of the concentration, the undertaking concerned does not either hold more than 50% of all the voting rights or have a contractual right to appoint more than half of the members of the board, the Commission will only accept that Article 5(4)(b), third indent has been met if, at the last annual general meeting, the undertaking concerned was able to exercise more than 50% of the voting rights present or represented. One may assume that this also applies to Article 5(4)(b), second indent.

The Commission's interpretation is easier to verify than the interpretation which I have submitted above. It seems to me, however, that an interpretation based on *de facto* control of more than 50% of the voting rights, must refer to the time of the

---

[67] *See* Götz Drauz, *supra* note 12 at p. 22.

[68] European Commission, *XXth Report on Competition Policy 1990*, Luxembourg 1991 at para. 31(d).

concentration.[69] If the Commission finds that this approach may lead to too high a degree of legal uncertainty, it should have opted for an interpretation based on *de jure* control of more than 50% of all voting rights.

Arjomari-Prioux/Wiggins Teape Appleton used to be the leading case on Article 5(4)(b), third indent.[70] Nevertheless, it seems that most subsequent cases have referred to the power to appoint the majority of the board at the last annual general meeting rather than to the power to exercise a majority of the voting rights; *see* for example *Courtaulds/SNIA*,[71] *Rhône-Poulenc/SNIA*,[72] *Eridania/ISI*[73] and *STRABAG/ Bank Austria/STUAG*[74] but contrast with *Tractebel/Synatom*.[75] Perhaps one may, therefore, hesitantly assume that Article 5(4)(b), third indent should not slavishly be interpreted in accordance with *Arjomari-Prioux/Wiggins Teape Appleton*, but rather that an interpretation placing more emphasis on the actual power to appoint members to the board and less emphasis on the relative size of the voting rights controlled may now be considered to prevail.[76]

---

[69] *See* further section 2.4 above.

[70] *See* for instance D. Livingston, *supra* note 42 at p. 729. D.G. Goyder, *EC Competition Law*, 3rd ed., Oxford University Press, Oxford 1998, p. 387 apparently takes the view that in the *Arjomari* case the Commission based itself upon Art. 5(4)(b), fourth indent. In its decision, the Commission explicitly refers to Art. 5(4)(b), third indent, however.

[71] Case IV/M113, decision of 19 December 1991.

[72] Case IV/M206, decision of 10 August 1992.

[73] Case IV/M062, decision of 20 July 1991. In this decision the Commission notes that the undertaking concerned was consolidated in the accounts of the company which had been able to appoint more than half of the board of the former. The fact that the undertaking concerned had been consolidated in the accounts of another undertaking has no bearing on the actual decision so presumably it may be disregarded as a kind of *obiter*.

[74] Case IV/M661, decision of 15 January 1996.

[75] Case IV/M466, decision of 30 June 1994. *See* likewise *Tractebel/Distrigaz II*, Case IV/ M493, decision of 1 September 1994. Other cases where Article 5(4)(b), third indent has been applied include *IFINT/EXOR*, *supra* note 17, *Rhône Poulenc/SNIA II*, Case IV/M355, decision of 8 September 1993, *Rhône Poulenc-SNIA/Nordfaser*, Case IV/M399, decision of 3 February 1994, *Jefferson Smurfit Group Plc/Munksjo AB*, *supra* note 11, *Elektrowatt/Landis & Gyr*, Case IV/M692, decision of 12 February 1996. In *Noranda Forest/Glunz*, Case IV/ M599, decision of 8 September 1995 the Commission left the question of the application of Article 5(4)(b), third (or perhaps second) indent open as it was not necessary in order to show a Community dimension.

[76] Perhaps, European Commission, *XXIst Report on Competition Policy 1991*, Luxembourg 1992, Annex III, point 7.1 (page 351) in footnote 3 indicates that the Commission also finds

2.5.5. Has the right to manage the undertakings' affairs.

Article 5(4)(b), fourth indent provides that where an undertaking 'has the right to manage' another undertaking's affairs, the latter must be included in the group of the former for the purposes of calculating the Community dimension.

One must observe that the provision only provides that the undertaking shall have a *right* to manage the other undertaking's affairs. It is not a condition that the right is actually used. Nevertheless, it is difficult to conceive a situation where the Commission will take jurisdiction on the basis that one undertaking has the right to manage another undertaking's affairs (but the relationship does not fulfil any of the criteria laid down in Article 5(4)(b), indents 1-3), but this right is not exercised.

Moreover, one may reasonably presume that it will be a rare sight that one undertaking has the right to manage the affairs of another undertaking without at the same time fulfilling at least one of the criteria provided in Article 5(4)(b), indents 1-3. In *Accor/Wagons-Lits,*[77] however, the Commission found it necessary to refer to the fourth indent in order to delimit the group of Accor. The case is probably the best illustration of how this criterion applies.

In 1991, the French catering group Accor made a bid for the Belgian catering, hotel and tourism group Wagons-lits. At first glance, the total worldwide turnover of the two undertakings amounted to only € 4.3 billion, thus falling clearly below the Merger Regulation's € 5 billion threshold.[78]

Accor operated a number of hotels under hotel management contracts, however. These hotels did not belong to Accor and neither of the first three criteria in Article 5(4)(b) were met in this regard. The question therefore was whether these management contracts fulfilled the fourth criterion. In order to answer this question, the Commission provided the following line of reasoning in paragraph 6 of the decision:

---

that *Arjomari-Prioux/Wiggins Teape Appleton* contrasts with the subsequent decisions on the point. Also, it has been held that, strictly speaking, the statement in *Arjomari* is *obiter* as it concerns a decision where the Commission lacked jurisdiction, cf. C.J. Cook and C.S. Kerse, *supra* note 35, pp. 74-75. This view must however be wrong. The Commission's decision that it lacked jurisdiction is binding on the parties as well as on the Commission and the statement is essential to this decision. Consequently the statement is not simply an *obiter dictum*, but rather it forms part of the decision's *ratio decidendi*.

77 Case IV/M126, decision of 28 April 1992, [1992] OJ L 204/1.

78 Only the first set of thresholds applied in 1991.

'– Accor runs the hotel under one of the group's established names and undertakes its management. Its terms of reference are general in scope, and it looks after the operation of the hotel, marketing, sales, accounting and financial management, management control, and legal, administrative and tax matters. The owner has the option of entrusting it with other services as well.

– Accor has full control of staffing policy; it recruits, manages, dismisses and supervises staff. It plays an important role in training. Only the negotiation of collective agreements and the secondment of members of Accor's staff to the hotel require the explicit agreement of the owner,

– the contract is long term (10 years on average, with renewal often tacit),

– if the owner sells, leases or otherwise disposes of the hotel, the buyer or new lessee must undertake to comply with and assume all the obligations incumbent on the owner *vis-à-vis* Accor. However, Accor may refuse the transaction and purchase or lease the hotel at the same price or rent and on the same terms and conditions as those set out in the owner's notification. If the buyer or new occupant refuses to assume the obligations incumbent on the owner and if Accor does not wish to purchase or lease the hotel, the contract will be terminated, and Accor will receive [...] compensation.

In conclusion, it appears that the contract allows the owner virtually only the role of providing capital and confers on Accor the role of fully fledged manager. It follows that Accor has the right to manage the relevant undertakings' affairs within the meaning of the fourth indent of Article 5(4)(b) of the Regulation. This conclusion is based on a detailed analysis of the contract, notably as regards the precise powers of the owner on budgetary matters, an analysis which has allowed the Commission to accept Accor's argument. The turnover generated by the contracts concerned is € 495 232 730.'[79]

---

[79] The Advisory Committee on Concentrations in its opinion on the case agreed with the Commission's finding of jurisdiction, cf. [1992] OJ C184/2. Note also that the approximately € 500 million generated by the management of hotels did not suffice to meet the € 5 billion threshold in the Regulation. The Commission, however, included two more items from the accounts in order to meet the threshold. This inclusion I discuss below in chapter 4 at section 3.2.

The Commission's reasoning seems to be sound.[80] It has been suggested that the case may have particular importance to franchisors as the interpretation in *Accor/Wagons-Lits* might be interpreted to mean that they have to include the turnover of independent franchisees.[81] One may, however, doubt whether a franchisor has the right to manage the franchisee's affairs. Normally, the franchisor will only provide specific guidelines as to the running of the business while the franchisee himself will be the one to carry out the day-to-day management.[82]

---

80 One may reasonably assume that the Commission has applied the same approach in *Bass Plc/Saison Holdings BV*, Case IV/M1133, decision of 23 March 1998, although this is not explicitly stated in that decision and possibly also in *BC Funds/Sanitec*, Case COMP/M2397, decision of 6 June 2001 as well as in *CD & R Fund VI Limited/Brake Bros Plc*, Case COMP/M2891, decision of 25 July 2002. Also, according to *Bellamy & Child – European Community Law of Competition*, *supra* note 22, p. 368 with note 84, in *CCIE/GTE*, Case IV/M258, decision of 25 September 1992, '[e]ffectively CCIEL had the right to manage the affairs of the company through which the acquisition was carried'. CCIEL only held 19% of the shares in the acquiring company EDIL whilst the remaining 81% were held by an investment banking firm. If the acquisition in reality was made by CCIEL the investment banking firm should not be included for the purpose of establishing a Community dimension. In contrast, if EDIL was the real acquirer, both CCIEL and the majority shareholder should be included for the purpose of calculating the Community dimension, as both would qualify as parents; the one according to Art. 5(4)(b), first and second indent, and the other according to Art. 5(4)(b), fourth indent.

81 Cf. Charles Price, 'Case Note: Accor/Wagons-Lits', *EC Merger Control Reporter*, Kluwer Law International, The Hague 1991 and later (looseleaf), pp. 752.23-752.24 at 752.24.

82 Thus, in *UBS/Mister Minit*, Case IV/M940, decision of 9 July 1997 the Commission refused to accept that a franchisor could include the turnover of the franchised businesses in its own group turnover. In its *XXVIIth Report on Competition Policy 1997*, *supra* note 38, p. 171, the Commission explains that 'the activities of a franchising network cannot always be taken into account when calculating the turnover of a franchising group, especially if the latter does not hold half the working capital and does not have the right to manage the affairs of the franchisees' and the Commission continues by pointing out that in this respect the situation in *UBS/Mister Minit* 'was different from that observed in *Accor/Wagon-Lits*'. Moreover, in *Blokker/Toys 'R' Us*, Case IV/M890, decision of 26 June 1997, [1998] OJ L316/1, para. 14, the Commission also seems to take this approach (albeit *vis-à-vis* the notion of concentration). Nevertheless, in *Kingfisher/BUT*, Case IV/M1248, decision of 21 August 1998, it appears that the Commission has not considered the fact that only a minority of the target's (BUT) stores were actually owned by BUT whilst the majority were franchised. In one other case, brought before the President of the Court of First Instance, the Commission has expressly relied on Art. 5(4)(b), fourth indent; *see* Order of the President of the Court of First Instance of 12 July 1996 in Case T-52/96R, *Sogecable SA* v. *Commission of the European Communities*, unreported, in particular para. 30. Note that the Commission argued that

2.6. Networks of undertakings

A special situation arises where an undertaking appears to the public at large as one single entity, but in reality is made up of a number of formally independent undertakings that cooperate under a single name. This situation arose in the *Price Waterhouse/Coopers & Lybrand* case.[83] Price Waterhouse and Coopers & Lybrand belonged to what was then called the Big Six audit and accounting organisations worldwide. These organisations are (were) essentially networks of national offices that cooperate under a single name. Hence, the concentration was going to be a combination of the two networks. In practical terms the Price Waterhouse firms carrying on business in any particular territory would merge with the Coopers & Lybrand firms that carried on business in the same territory. The new combined local entities would subsequently accede to a new integrated structure (a so-called 'Combination Agreement').

Given the multi-partnership structure of the parties, the Commission found it necessary to examine whether the two respective groups of firms could be regarded as two single undertakings whose combination would constitute a single concentration within the meaning of Article 3(1)(a) of the Merger Regulation. The Commission therefore first examined whether each of the two networks had 'a sufficiently high degree of concentration of decision-making and financial interest to confer on it the character of a single economic entity for the purposes of the Merger Regulation'.[84]

With regard to Price Waterhouse, the Commission observed that this network had achieved a significant degree of integration over recent years. Thus forming 'a new system under which a combination board reviews and provides guidance to the national firms essentially on all aspects of the conduct of their business'.[85] In Europe a so-called combination agreement had been adopted to 'allow the European PW firms to operate in a manner which harmonised the interests of

---

two undertakings jointly could have control under Article 5(4)(b), fourth indent. (*See* also the Commission's comments on the case in *XXVIth Report on Competition Policy (1996)*, Luxembourg 1997, part III at paras. 15-16). The Commission's approach to joint control is discussed below in section 3.7. Perhaps *Swiss Life/I.N.C.A.*, Case IV/M644, decision of 25 October 1995 has also been based on Article 5(4)(b), fourth indent. At least it is hard to find any other way of justifying the Commission's calculation of the Community dimension.

[83] Case IV/M1016, decision of 20 May 1998, OJ L50/27, 26.2.1999.

[84] Cf. para. 8 of the decision.

[85] *Id.*

proprietors of the individual PW firms and promoted their collective interests …'.[86] 'Separately, PW US entered into bilateral agreements with other PW firms around the world … under which they agreed to pool resources and coordinate their strategies to their mutual benefit. Moreover, the PW Europe combination has recently been extended in a combination contract among the PW firms operating in Europe and the USA'[87]. On this basis the Commission concluded that '[t]he combination has the effect that the constituent PW firms function collectively as a single economic unit. The combination comprises PW firms in Western Europe, the USA, Eastern Europe, the Middle East, North Africa and the Republic of South Africa'.[88]

In my view, based upon the facts put forward by the Commission, it is not obvious that the harmonisation and coordination carried out between the members of the Price Waterhouse network amounts to more than extensive cooperation between the individual firms in the network.[89] However, even if one were to accept that the Price Waterhouse network made up one single economic unit, it is rather clear that it did not fulfil any of the four criteria in Article 5(4)(b). The individual firms appear to have been owned and managed by the firm's local partners. In other words, the individual firms of the network did not make up a group as defined in Article 5(4).

Even though virtually all information about the relationship between the individual firms of the Coopers & Lybrand network has been considered confidential information and therefore deleted from the public version of the decision, it implicitly appears that the Coopers & Lybrand network was founded on significantly less coordination than the Price Waterhouse network. The Commission therefore 'left open whether the C & L firms made up a single economic entity' but added that 'the series of individual mergers between each of the national partnerships of PW and C & L have been examined as part of one single transaction between the two groups of firms'.[90]

---

86 *Id.*

87 *Id.*

88 *Id.*

89 In *Deloitte & Touche/Andersen (UK)*, Case COMP/M2810, decision of 1 July 2002, the Commission equally applied the network criterion. According to the decision a 'division of Andersen UK decided not to join [Deloitte & Touche]'. *Quare* whether it is normal that a part of a single economic unit can itself decide whether or not to be transferred as part of 'sale' to another undertaking.

90 Cf. para. 17 of the decision.

When it comes to the question of a Community dimension the Commission apparently completely overlooks the fact that the group definition in Article 5(4) of the Merger Regulation is not based on the single economic unit doctrine. Hence, the Commission simply assumes that its finding of a single economic unit implies that the Price Waterhouse network makes up one single group for the purpose of calculating the Community dimension. As regards the Coopers & Lybrand network, the Commission leaves it open as to whether the individual firms must be considered to be parts of the same group.[91]

In a decision of May 2000 in *Cap Gemini/Ernst & Young*,[92] the Commission applied the 'single economic unit' approach anew while expressly referring to its decision in *Price Waterhouse/Coopers & Lybrand*.[93] Today, the Commission has based its jurisdiction on the 'network criterion' in so many cases that this criterion

---

[91] The Commission notes that 'in at least three Member States, namely the United Kingdom, the Netherlands and Germany, the Coopers & Lybrand firms generate a Community-wide turnover in excess of € 250 million'. It thus appears that the Commission finds that if Coopers & Lybrand does not make up a single group, then at least the concentration between on the one hand the total Price Waterhouse network and on the other hand the British, Dutch and German Coopers & Lybrand firms each make up a concentration with a Community dimension (*i.e.* three distinct concentrations). In this respect the Commission appears to have overlooked the fact that the concentration between the Price Waterhouse network and the Dutch Coopers & Lybrand firm only generates a worldwide turnover of € 4929 million and thus fails to meet the € 5 billion threshold! In any event it appears from the decision that the Commission has treated the transactions as one single concentration comprising all of the two networks' firms that are present in the Community.

[92] Case COMP/M1901, decision of 17 May 2000.

[93] Just as in the *Price Waterhouse/Coopers & Lybrand* decision, the Commission in the *Cap Gemini/Ernst & Young* decision observes that even if the 'network' (*i.e.* Ernst & Young) does not make up a single group for the purpose of calculating a Community dimension, then at least the turnover of some of the network's national partnerships would suffice to meet the thresholds. Based on the information provided in the decision this clearly seems to be wrong. Hence, the Commission in paras. 1 and 5 of the decision observes that the transaction concerns Cap Gemini's acquisition of sole control over Ernst & Young's IT-activities. In other words, according to the Commission the transaction concerns Ernst & Young's sale of its IT-activities to Cap Gemini. This necessarily means that only the turnover generated by Cap Gemini on the one hand and Ernst & Young's IT-activities on the other should be taken into account for the purpose of establishing a Community dimension, not the total turnover of Ernst & Young.

is now firmly established.[94] Based upon the facts put forward by the Commission in both *Price Waterhouse/Coopers & Lybrand* and *Cap Gemini/Ernst & Young* it seems rather obvious that neither Price Waterhouse nor Coopers & Lybrand nor Ernst & Young constituted a group as defined in Article 5(4).[95] As a consequence neither of the two transactions had a Community dimension. It is therefore submitted that the Commission erred in law when taking jurisdiction over the transactions.[96]

---

[94] *See* for example *Andersen Consulting/BT/JV*, Case COMP/M1994, decision of 28 July 2000, *Deloitte & Touche/Andersen (UK)*, *supra* note 89, *Ernst & Young/Andersen Germany*, Case COMP/M2824, decision of 27 August 2002, *Ernst & Young France/Andersen France*, Case COMP/M2816, decision of 5 September 2002, *IBM/PWC Consulting*, Case COMP/M2946, decision of 23 September 2002. Likewise, the Commission appears to have applied this approach in *Schroders/Liberty International Pensions Limited*, Case COMP/M1997, decision of 28 June 2000. At least it is difficult to find any other basis upon which the Commission could include Schroders Ventures Funds when calculating the turnover of Schroders cf. para. 6 of the decision. It nevertheless appears that Schroders and Schroders Venture Funds do not even constitute a single economic unit: According to information provided to me by Schroders, at the time of the transaction the Schroders Venture Funds were not controlled by Schroders. Hence, in none of the funds does Schroders have more than a very limited share of the capital, and all the funds are run independently of Schroders. Although Schroders and the funds work closely together they do so as independent parties. According to Schroders, the largest of the funds has renamed itself Permira thereby emphasising its independence from Schroders. To complete the picture it may be added that perhaps *SLDE/NTL/MSCP/ NOOS*, Case COMP/M2137, decision of 16 October 2000 is another example of the application of the network criterion (regarding Morgan Stanley Dean Witter).

[95] Contrast this view with that of Dominique Berlin, 'Concentrations – (1er janvier 1998 – 31 décembre 1998)', *Revue trimestrielle de droit européen*, 2000, no. 1, pp. 139-237 at pp. 180. When commenting upon the *Price Waterhouse/Coopers & Lybrand* decision, Berlin has not even found it necessary to consider the possible incompatibility *vis-à-vis* Art. 5(4).

[96] In *Adeg/Edeka*, *supra* note 50, concerning the question of whether the concentration had a Community dimension, the Commission similarly observed that it was 'possible to substantiate a group-like structure on the basis of the common usage of the brand EDEKA and the representation to suppliers and customers' (quoted from the unofficial translation of the EC Merger Control Reporter at p. 4816.3). This observation, it is submitted, has no bearing on the question of whether the transaction has a Community dimension. *See also OK Ekonomisk Förening/Kuwait Petroleum Sverige AB*, Case IV/M1256, decision of 21 December 1998, where the Commission apparently – but rightly – found that seven (independent) OK-associations operating on the Swedish market did not form a group for the purpose of calculating a Community dimension.

3. THE RELATED UNDERTAKINGS

3.1. Introduction

Above, I have examined the definition of control provided in Article 5(4)(b), indents 1-4, for the purposes of calculating the Community dimension. In itself, Article 5(4)(b) only defines when an undertaking must be counted as a subsidiary. In order to delimit the group of an undertaking concerned, it will normally be necessary to decide also on the inclusion of, for example, parent undertakings and sister-undertakings. Article 5(4) and (5) explain how the delimitation must be done. I will examine this below. It is so obvious that the undertaking concerned itself must be included[97] that I shall not weary the reader by reiterating this fact. Accordingly, I shall first look at the subsidiaries (section 3.2), at parent undertakings (section 3.3) and at sister-undertakings (section 3.4). Then I shall turn to the difficulties surrounding joint ventures (sections 3.5-3.7). Lastly, I shall examine the treatment of agents (section 3.8) and of public undertakings (section 3.9).[98]

3.2. Subsidiaries

According to Article 5(4)(b), a subsidiary of the undertaking concerned must be included in the group. Article 5(4)(b) refers to 'undertakings' in the plural, thereby showing that the rule also covers situations where one undertaking concerned has more than one direct subsidiary. Moreover, it is argued in section 2.3 above that the terms 'directly or indirectly' as applied in Article 5(4)(b) cover indirect subsidiaries, *i.e.*, for example, sub-subsidiaries.

The coverage of Article 5(4)(b) may be illustrated by the following figure:

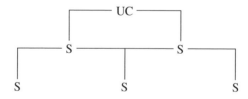

---

[97] Cf. Art. 5(4)(a).

[98] A figure setting out the principal rules for establishing the group may be found at p. 134.

3.3. Parent undertakings

According to Article 5(4)(c), the group of the undertaking concerned also covers 'those undertakings which have in the undertaking concerned the rights or powers listed in (b)'. This means that a parent to an undertaking concerned must be included for the purpose of calculating the Community dimension.

Article 5(4)(c) gives rise to two questions. Firstly, one may ask whether it is possible to have more than one parent. Secondly, one may ask whether both direct and indirect parent undertakings are included in the group of the undertaking concerned.

Article 5(4) makes it possible that an undertaking concerned has more than one parent undertaking. Article 5(4)(c) explicitly provides that where an undertaking has the powers of control listed in Article 5(4)(b), this parent undertaking must be included in the group of the undertaking concerned. Article 5(4)(c) however applies the plural: 'undertakings'. This clearly indicates that the drafters of the Merger Regulation foresaw that situations may arise where more than one undertaking controlled the undertaking concerned within the meaning of Article 5(4)(b). A standard example of such dual control may be where one parent owns more than 50% of the share-capital, but another parent owns shares carrying more than 50% of the voting rights in the undertaking concerned.[99] It is, therefore, submitted that it is possible to have more than one direct parent undertaking when calculating the Community dimension.[100] The Commission has also found that the plural refers to situations where there is more than one parent undertaking. It has, however, taken the view that this concerns situations where two or more parents jointly control the undertaking concerned. Apparently this joint control is defined in accordance with Article 3(3) rather than Article 5(4)(b).[101] I discuss this interpretation in section 3.7 below.

---

[99] Likewise, C.J. Cook and C.S. Kerse, *supra* note 35 at p. 74 and B. Hawk and H. Huser, *supra* note 14 at pp. 104-105.

[100] So far none of the published Commission decisions reflects this situation.

[101] *See* Turnover Calculation Notice, para. 38(3) and European Commission, *Review of the Application of Council Regulation (EEC) No. 4064/89 of 21 December 1989 on the Control of Concentrations between Undertakings*, Working Paper of the Commission, revised version of 17.5.1993, p. 31 and annex 6. In *Sogecable SA* v. *Commission of the European Communities*, *supra* note 82 the Commission apparently took the view that an undertaking concerned had two direct parents, but found both parents' control over the undertaking concerned to have been constituted on the basis of Article 5(4)(b), fourth indent.

The second question is more problematic. In section 2.3 above, I argue that the terms in Article 5(4)(b) 'directly' and 'indirectly' refer to direct subsidiaries and to indirect subsidiaries (sub-subsidiaries). In the English version, Article 5(4)(c) does not include the words 'directly or indirectly'. The immediate interpretation is that only direct parent undertakings may be included.

Example

A large British bank acquires a medium-sized German bank which mainly does business in Bavaria. The acquisition is made by a Luxembourg-based subsidary of the British bank. The British bank has placed all foreign banking activities in a separate subsidiary forming just one of a number of divisions (such as UK high street banking, merchant banking, insurance activities and mortgage credit lending). The Luxembourg-based subsidiary is the undertaking concerned. If only the direct parent may be included in the group, only the foreign banking activities of the British bank may be counted when calculating the Community dimension.

This interpretation is untenable. First it would lead to an inadequate measuring of the financial strength of the group of the undertaking concerned. Secondly, it would mean that very similar transactions made by the same business would be treated completely differently and it would make forum shopping very easy. An example may illustrate this.

Example

Say that a large company called JCN has set up one large subsidiary in each of the Community Member States. Each subsidiary only undertakes sales in its own Member State. For tax reasons, however, the Dutch and German subsidiaries are each owned by an intermediary holding-company. These two holding-companies have been set up in the Bahamas and they, in turn, are wholly owned by JCN Europe which is registered in France. All the other subsidiaries of JCN in the Community are directly held by JCN Europe. JCN Europe has a Community-wide turnover exceeding € 5 billion.

Imagine that JCN Spain makes an acquisition of another Spanish company. In order to calculate the turnover of JCN Spain, it is necessary to look to its direct parent, JCN Europe and to include all subsidiaries of JCN Europe.[102] JCN Spain

---

[102] The inclusion of sister-undertakings is discussed below in section 3.4.

will have a worldwide turnover of more than € 5 billion and a Community-wide turnover of more than € 250 million. Thus, if the acquired company generates more than € 250 million in the Community, the transaction will be notifiable under the first set of thresholds.

Imagine, instead, that JCN Germany makes a parallel acquisition of another German company. If only direct parents may be taken into account, then only the Bahama parent (generating no turnover in itself) must be included in the turnover of JCN Germany, and even though the transaction (*i.e.* JCN Germany and the acquired company) generates more than € 250 million in the Community, it does not meet the € 5 billion worldwide turnover threshold and the first set of thresholds has not been met. Moreover, as JCN Germany only generates sales in Germany, the requirement in the second set of thresholds (Article 1(3)(c)) that at least two of the undertakings concerned shall each generate more than € 25 million in at least three Member States is not met. The transaction is therefore not notifiable.

To require an examination of whether the direct parent is only an empty shell, and, if it is, to pierce the veil, does not provide an adequate solution to the problem since this will still lead to wholly arbitrary results, for instance, if the German acquisition was made by a subsidiary of JCN Germany.

It is submitted that it is unacceptable if indirect parents are not included in the group.[103] The Commission has taken the same view and does this by relying on the fact that the word 'undertakings' is in the plural in Article 5(4)(c). The Commission argues that the use of the plural shows that the provision not only covers the direct but also the indirect parent undertakings. Above, it is submitted that the plural of the word 'undertakings' refers to situations where more than one undertaking has control within the meaning in Article 5(4)(b). These two interpretations of the plural of 'undertakings' do not necessarily conflict so this interpretation clearly appears to be an acceptable way of solving the problem.

The better solution would of course have been if the Merger Regulation expressly applied the expression 'directly or indirectly'. Indeed the Danish version of the Regulation does include this expression. The reason for this is unknown.

---

[103] Indeed there are plenty of cases in which the Commission has included indirect parents in the group. *See* for an example *Eridania/ISI*, *supra* note 73. Also, Article 5(4) is based on a formula well-known in Community competition law. This formula includes both direct and indirect parent undertakings; *see* for example para. 12(2)(b) of Commission Notice on agreements of minor importance which do not appreciably restrict competition under Article 81(1) of the Treaty establishing the European Community *(de minimis)*, OJ C368/13 of 22.12.2001.

One may guess that the complete provision was originally taken from another piece of Community legislation, but that it was decided to exclude the expression 'directly or indirectly' during the subsequent work on the draft.[104] Only the Danish version failed to delete this expression.[105]

3.4. Sister-undertakings

According to Article 5(4)(d), a subsidiary of a parent undertaking of an undertaking concerned must be included in the group the last-mentioned undertaking is part of. In other words, when calculating the Community dimension, it is also necessary to include the turnover of sister-undertakings.

Just as in Article 5(4)(c) concerning parent undertakings, only the Danish version of Article 5(4)(d) concerning sister-undertakings apparently includes the words 'directly or indirectly'. Exactly the same line of argument applies to Article 5(4)(d) as the one which applied to Article 5(4)(c). It is thus submitted that Article 5(4)(d) also includes indirect sister-undertakings in the group. This may be illustrated in the following way:

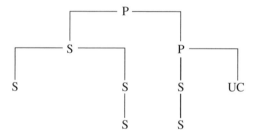

A problem arises, though, where a sister-undertaking has more than one parent undertaking.

---

[104] This is supported by the fact that Amended proposal for a council Regulation (EEC) on the control of concentrations between undertakings, OJ C130/4 of 19.5.1988 includes the terms 'directly or indirectly' in the provisions which correspond to Art. 5(4)(b)-(d) in the adopted Regulation.

[105] Concerning this point, *see* further my article *supra* note 15 at pp. 74-76.

Example

P_1, the parent undertaking of the undertaking concerned, has two subsidiaries as defined in Article 5(4): the undertaking concerned (UC) which is wholly owned, and S in which it holds 70% of the share-capital. P_2, however, holds more than half the voting rights in S so it may also be considered a parent of S within the meaning of Article 5(4). The question is whether P_2 (and related undertakings) must be included in the group of the undertaking concerned.

When calculating the Community dimension, the starting point is the undertaking concerned. Article 5(4)(b) provides that all direct and indirect subsidiaries of the undertaking concerned must be included in the group. Likewise, all direct and indirect parent undertakings to the undertaking concerned shall be included (Article 5(4)(c)) and all direct and indirect subsidiaries of an included parent undertaking must be included (Article 5(4)(d)). Article 5(4) does not, however, provide any possibility of including a parent to a sister-undertaking if this parent is not covered by Article 5(4)(c). Figuratively speaking, one may say that from the undertaking concerned it is possible to 'go straight down', to 'go straight up' and to 'go straight down from any undertaking which has been hit when going straight up', but it is not possible to 'go up' from any undertaking hit when 'going down'. This may be illustrated in the following way (where undertakings included in the group of the undertaking concerned are in **bold**):

3.5. Group-members have joint control over an undertaking

In sections 3.5 and 3.6, I provide my interpretation of how to calculate the turnover thresholds with respect to joint control. This interpretation differs significantly from that of the Commission. In section 3.7, I thereupon provide an account of the Commission's interpretation.

Article 5(4)(e) concerns the situation where different undertakings within one and the same group jointly have control, as defined in Article 5(4)(b), over another undertaking.

Example

The undertaking concerned UC has control over S_1, S_2, S_3 and S_4 as defined in Article 5(4)(b). UC holds 35% of the share-capital in JV in which S_1, S_2, S_3 and S_4 each hold 5%. This means that UC and S_1, S_2, S_3 and S_4 jointly hold 55% of the share-capital in JV. Since the undertaking concerned as well as the four subsidiaries belong to the group of the undertaking concerned and since they jointly have control over JV as defined in Article 5(4)(b), first indent, the full turnover of JV must be included for the calculation of the Community dimension according to Article 5(4)(e).

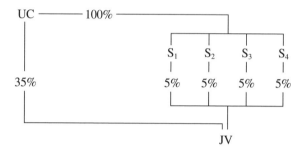

Article 5(4)(e) explicitly refers to Article 5(4)(b) concerning the notion of control. Also, it is expressly provided that the joint control must be held by undertakings defined by Article 5(4)(a) to (d), *i.e.,* those undertakings which belong to the group of the undertaking concerned.[106]

---

[106] Likewise Turnover Calculation Notice, para. 38 (*see* in particular the figure). *See* also Trevor Soames, 'The 'Community Dimension' in the EEC Merger Regulation: The Calculation of the Turnover Criteria', *European Competition Law Review*, 1990, no. 5, pp. 213-225 at p. 217, table 5, and Kurt Stockmann and Klaus-Peter Schultz, *Kartellrechtspraxis und Kartellrechtssprechung 1995/96*, 11th ed., RWS Verlag, Cologne 1996, p. 258. *Thomson/Daimler-Benz*, Case IV/M744, decision of 21 May 1996, [1996] OJ C179/3, seems to provide an example of this: In order to carry out the transaction, Daimler-Benz used the undertaking Temic; a joint venture between DASA and AEG, both of which were part of the Daimler-Benz group. In the decision Temic is classifed as a subsidiary to Daimler-Benz.

3.6. Undertakings concerned have joint control over a third undertaking

Article 5(5) provides that if the undertakings concerned jointly have control (as defined in Article 5(4)(b)) over a third undertaking, this third undertaking must be included in the groups of the undertakings concerned. There does not seem to be any basis for requiring that the undertakings concerned have actually jointly exercised this control before the concentration takes place.

Example

UC$_1$ and UC$_2$ each hold 30% of the share-capital in JV. The joint holding of 60% of JV's share-capital means that they have joint control as defined in Article 5(4)(b). JV must, therefore, be included in the groups of UC$_1$ and UC$_2$.[107]

The turnover must be apportioned equally between the undertakings concerned that have joint control,[108] *i.e.* no regard shall be taken of the actual size of the undertakings' holdings in the jointly controlled undertaking. This calculation may give rise to some problems in particular regarding the deduction of intra-group turnover, required in Article 5(1). I consider this below in chapter 4 in section 6.3.2.

Article 5(5) applies '[w]here undertakings concerned by the concentration jointly have the rights or powers ...'. This gives rise to the question whether only undertakings under joint control held (directly or indirectly) by the undertakings concerned themselves are covered by the provision, or whether also undertakings jointly controlled by, for instance, sister-undertakings to the undertakings concerned are covered by Article 5(5). An example may illustrate this problem.

---

[107] In *McDermott/ETPM*, Case IV/M648, decision of 27 November 1995 the Commission explicitly applied Article 5(5). It is, however, unclear whether the case has followed the approach set out here.

[108] Cf. Art. 5(5)(b). *See* further chapter 4, section 6.3. In *Danish Crown/Vestjyske Slagterier*, Case IV/M1313, decision of 9 March 1999, [2000] OJ L20/1, the two merging undertakings, Danish Crown and Vestjyske Slagterier, had holdings in four other undertakings which when aggregated would lead to control (as defined in both Art. 3 and Art 5(4)) over these other undertakings. The Commission, wrongly it is submitted, considered both the two merging undertakings and the four joint ventures to be undertakings concerned.

Example

UC$_1$ agrees to acquire UC$_2$. UC$_2$ and the parent undertaking of UC$_1$ jointly control JV within the meaning of Article 5(4)(b).

For the purpose of defining which undertakings that (directly or indirectly) may have joint control over a third undertaking, Article 5(5) refers to 'undertakings concerned by the concentration'. Article 5(5) also applies the expression 'undertaking concerned' indicating that the drafters intended a difference between these two definitions. The 'undertaking concerned' is a term of art designating the direct participants in the concentration. In contrast, 'undertakings concerned by the concentration' appears to have a wider meaning. It therefore seems plausible that the latter expression refers to all the undertakings concerned by the concentration within the context of Article 5(4) and (5), *i.e.* all undertakings included for the purpose of calculating turnover.

A teleological interpretation lends support to the above result. The Community dimension is found on the basis of the groups of the undertakings concerned in order to reflect the economic strength of the parties to the concentration. The drafters have taken the view that it is necessary to take account of undertakings which are under joint control. In other words, the purpose of calculating turnover is to measure the strength of the full group and the drafters have shown that they consider that joint ventures must be included when measuring this strength. The consequence is that Article 5(5) should not be restricted to situations where it is the undertakings concerned themselves which (directly or indirectly) jointly control another undertaking. This interpretation does not detract from the clear dividing line which the Community dimension is intended to provide, and it provides a better reflection of the economic strength of the undertakings concerned.

It is, therefore, submitted that Article 5(5) covers all undertakings controlled jointly (within the meaning of control laid down in Article 5(4)(b)) by members of the groups of the undertakings concerned (within the meaning of Article 5(4)).[109]

Another question caused by Article 5(5) is whether sole control must prevail over joint control?

Example

UC$_1$ and UC$_2$ hold 45% and 55% respectively of the share-capital in JV. Even though they jointly control more than 50%, UC$_2$ has sole control within the

---

[109] Likewise, K. Stockmann and K.-P. Schultz, *supra* note 106 at p. 258.

meaning of Article 5(4)(b). The question thus is whether this means that the full turnover of JV must be apportioned to UC_2.

In my opinion, logic requires that sole control takes priority over joint control. Otherwise, the conclusion would be that where one undertaking concerned holds a majority of the capital in an undertaking, any holding by another undertaking concerned in the same undertaking would lead to joint control.[110] Thus, even a 99%/1% split of the capital would lead to joint control and would therefore mean that Article 5(5) should apply.

Moreover, if sole control did not prevail, this would open the possibility of introducing the Article 3(3) notion of control through the backdoor.

Example

UC_1 and UC_2, which own 70% and 30% respectively of the share-capital in JV, have agreed to jointly manage JV. Under the notion of control in Article 5(4)(b), first indent, UC_1 must aggregate the full turnover of JV towards its own turnover. One could, however, argue that Article 5(5) refers to situations where more than one undertaking concerned jointly have the powers listed in Article 5(4)(b). In this example, UC_1 and UC_2 jointly have the right to manage JV (Article 5(4)(b), fourth indent), so, according to this construction, Article 5(5) would apply in a case like this one.

Allocating the full turnover of JV to UC_1 (Article 5(4)(b)) and 50% of the turnover to UC_2 (Article 5(5)) will amount to double counting.[111] Consequently, it is again necessary to decide whether sole control shall have priority over joint control. Following the approach taken above, and having regard to the fact that the Community dimension is intended to be easy to apply, it is submitted that sole control shall prevail over simultaneous joint control. Otherwise, the drafters' distinction between formal control (as provided in Article 5(4)(b)) and actual control (as provided in Article 3(3)) would be blurred.

In section 3.7 below, I discuss the Commission's approach to cases of joint control.

---

[110] It is recalled that we are dealing with the legalistic notion of control in Art. 5(4).

[111] This type of doublecounting is not a problem which only applies to the Merger Regulation. *See* Valentine Korah, *Exclusive Dealing Agreements in the E.E.C. – Regulation 67/67 replaced*, European Law Centre Ltd., 1984 at p. 19 with note 39.

3.7. The Commission's approach to joint control

3.7.1. Introduction

According to the Turnover Calculation Notice, paragraphs 38(3), 39 (footnote 10) and 40 and the Undertaking Concerned Notice paragraph 26, the Commission takes an approach to cases of joint control which significantly differs from the one that I have taken in three respects.

These concerns the situation where the undertaking concerned is under joint control (as defined in Article 3(3)) of two or more parent undertakings; the situation where two or more undertakings concerned have joint control (as defined in Article 3(3)) over a third undertaking; and the situation where an undertaking concerned together with a third party has joint control over an undertaking. I will examine these three situations below, whereupon I will make a few general comments on the Commission's interpretation.

3.7.2. The undertaking concerned is under joint control

'When two or more companies jointly control the undertaking concerned … in the sense that the agreement of each and all of them is needed in order to manage the undertaking's affairs, the turnover of all of them should be included.'[112] The Notice provides an example of a joint venture which is split 50/50 between two parents.[113]

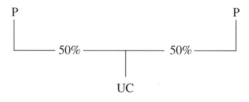

The Commission explains that '[a]lthough the Merger Regulation does not explicitly mention this rule for those cases where the undertaking concerned is in fact a joint venture, it is inferred from the text of Article 5(4)(c), which uses the plural

---

[112] Turnover Calculation Notice, para. 38(3).

[113] Turnover Calculation Notice, para. 38.

when referring to the parent companies.'[114] In other words, the Commission bases its interpretation on the plural of the word 'undertakings' in Article 5(4)(c). In section 3.3 above, it is argued that it is possible to have more than one parent undertaking, for instance, where one undertaking holds more than 50% of the share-capital and another holds more than 50% of the voting rights. One may also reasonably assume that the use of the plural in Article 5(4)(c) refers to both direct and indirect parents. These two interpretations fall squarely within the limits set up by Article 5(4). Moreover, the drafters explicitly included Article 5(4)(e) and (5) to cover situations of joint control. Why then did they not also explicitly show that Article 5(4)(c) should be applied to situations of joint control? Presumably the reason was that they did not intend the provision to cover joint control.[115]

It is noteworthy that, in support of this interpretation, the Commission claims that the interpretation 'has been consistently applied by the Commission.'[116] B.E. Hawk and H.L. Huser dryly observe that 'during the first several years of implementation of the Merger Regulation, the Commission consistently adhered to Article 5(4)(b)'s 'bright line' majority-based standards to determine when a 'parent' entity should be included in a concerned undertaking's group.'[117]

In *Sogecable SA* v. *Commission of the European Communities,*[118] the Commission applied Article 5(4)(b), fourth indent to a situation of joint control over an undertaking concerned. In this case, the Commission claimed that two parent undertakings would have to be included in the group of the undertaking concerned (which would bring the transaction within the scope of the Merger Regulation) because they had the right to jointly manage the affairs of the undertaking concerned. As shown just above, I do not find these arguments persuasive.[119]

---

[114] Turnover Calculation Notice, para. 38(3). *See* also European Commission, *supra* note 101 at p. 31 and annex 6 and Christopher Jones and Enrique González-Díaz, *The EEC Merger Regulation*, Sweet & Maxwell, London 1992, p. 21 with note 5.

[115] C.J. Cook and C.S. Kerse, *supra* note 35 at p. 81 with note 68 point out 'that Art. 5(4)(e), which does relate to joint control ... expressly uses the term 'jointly', whereas Art. 5(4)(c) does not.' These authors find that the use of the plural 'undertakings' in Art. 5(4)(c) 'appears to be merely a matter of drafting style rather than an indication that it applies to joint control.'

[116] Turnover Calculation Notice, para. 38(3).

[117] *Supra* note 14 at p. 104.

[118] *Supra* note 82.

[119] The President of the Court of First Instance held that, in the absence of exceptional circumstances, he did not have jurisdiction to suspend the Commission's decision to examine the

In my view the Commission's interpretation, above all, leaves an impression of creativity, not of convincing arguments.[120]

3.7.3. The undertakings concerned have joint control within the meaning of Article 3(3)

If two undertakings concerned have joint control (as defined in Article 3(3) rather than Article 5(4)(b))[121] over a third undertaking, the Commission takes the view that this situation is covered by Article 5(5) so that the turnover of the third undertaking must be included for the purposes of calculating turnover.[122] This may be illustrated by the following figure:

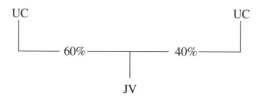

Apparently the Commission finds that this interpretation falls squarely within the wording of Article 5(5).[123] One, therefore, wonders how it is possible to overlook

---

transaction under the Merger Regulation. Another example of the Commission's application of this interpretation of Art. 5(4)(c) is *Adeg/Edeka*, *supra* note 50 and probably also *Gencor/Shell*, *supra* note 11 and *SCA/Graninge/Scaninge Timber*, Case COMP/M1996, decision of 5 July 2000.

120 Likewise B.E. Hawk and H.L. Huser, *supra* note 14 at pp. 104-105. *See* also C.J. Cook and C.S. Kerse, *supra* note 35 at p. 81.

121 Guidance Note III at point B(II)(a) explicitly states that the control must be defined in accordance with Article 3(3) and (4). *See* also B.E. Hawk and H.L. Huser, *supra* note 14 at p. 104.

122 Turnover Calculation Notice, para. 39 with footnote 10. Presumably *Ameritech/TeleDanmark*, Case IV/M1046, decision of 5 December 1997, is an example of the application of this interpretation.

123 P.F.C. Begg, *Corporate Acquisitions and Mergers – A Practical Guide to the Legal, Financial and Administrative Implications*, 3rd ed., Graham & Trotman, London 1991 at pp. 8.92-8.94 takes the same view.

Article 5(5)'s explicit reference to Article 5(4)(b)'s definition of control.[124] It is submitted that to base Article 5(5) on the definition of control provided in Article 3(3) conflicts both with the wording and the intention of Article 5(5).[125] Also, this interpretation of Article 5(5) may conflict with Article 5(4).

Example

Two undertakings concerned, UC_1 and UC_2, jointly control (within the meaning of Article 3(3)) JV. UC_1 holds 60%, however, while UC_2 only holds 40% of the share-capital in JV. According to Article 5(4)(b), first indent, UC_1 must include the full turnover of JV in its group when calculating the Community dimension. According to the Commission's innovative interpretation of Article 5(5), however, the turnover must now instead be split between UC_1 and UC_2 even though this clearly conflicts with Article 5(4).[126]

I strongly disagree with the Commission's interpretation.

---

[124] M. Siragusa and R. Subiotto, *supra* note 15 at p. 900 finds that where the parents of the undertaking concerned can only exercise control jointly, this 'means that none of them would individually satisfy the conditions contained in Article 5(4)(c)' and the turnover of these parents should therefore be excluded when calculating the Community dimension of the (jointly controlled) undertaking concerned. Presumably the authors presupposes a situation where none of Art. 5(4)(b)'s four possibilities of exercising sole control has been met.

[125] Likewise, Pierre Bos, Jules Stuyck and Peter Wytinck, *Concentration Control in the European Economic Community*, Graham & Trotman, London 1992, p. 134 and B.E. Hawk and H.L. Huser, *supra* note 14 at p. 103. According to M. Siragusa and R. Subiotto, *supra* note 15 at p. 901 in the merger between BSB and Sky, the Commission apparently excluded the turnover of the jointly controlling parents of BSB because they did not satisfy any of the four requirements in Art. 5(4)(b) individually. In other words, the Commission appears to have applied Art. 5(4) instead of Art. 3(3).

[126] In *Frantschach/B+K/Volfin*, Case IV/M733, decision of 8 May 1996, the Commission considered Frantschach and B+K to be undertakings concerned together with the target company Volfin. However, B+K was a joint venture between Frantschach (40%) and another company (60%). In this case the Commission thus surprisingly applied the interpretation I (amongst others) adhere to. Perhaps one should add that the concentration would not have met the thresholds if the Commission had applied its usual interpretation. Equally it seems likely that *Granaria/Ültje/Intersnack/May-Holding*, Case COMP/JV32, decision of 28 February 2000 is an example of the Commission applying the interpretation that I adhere to. The case concerned four undertakings' pooling of their nut snack businesses (A, B, C and D). Two (C and D) of the four undertakings already had pooled their nut snack activities in a concentrative joint venture (JV). When calculating the Community dimension one of these two undertakings (C) was considered an undertaking concerned whereas the other (D) was not. Instead the joint venture was considered an undertaking concerned. This only seems to

3.7.4. The undertaking concerned has joint control together with a third undertaking

'[I]n the case of joint ventures between undertakings concerned and third parties, the Commission's practice has been to allocate to each of the undertakings concerned the turnover shared equally by all the controlling companies in the joint venture. In all these cases, however, joint control has to be demonstrated.'[127] This situation may be illustrated as follows.

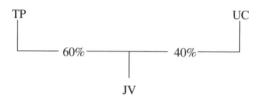

The Commission bases this interpretation on an analogy of Article 5(5)(b) which provides that where the undertakings concerned jointly have control over a third undertaking (as defined in Article 5(4)(b)), the turnover of this third undertaking 'shall be apportioned equally amongst the undertakings concerned'. The intention is that where, for example, two undertakings concerned (UC_1 and UC_2) jointly hold 80% of the share-capital in another undertaking (JV), JV's turnover shall be apportioned equally between UC_1 and UC_2. The Commission intends to apply this

---

make sense if the joint venture was under the sole control (as defined in Art. 5(4)) of undertaking D. In *PTT Post/TNT/GD Express Worldwide*, Case IV/M843, decision of 8 November 1996, PTT and TNT jointly controlled GD Express Worldwide. PTT made a public bid for TNT. If the bid had been successful PTT would not only have gained control of TNT, but would also have gone from joint to sole control of GD Express Worldwide. The Commission viewed the changes of control as one single concentration. Surprisingly, however, it considered not only TNT and PTT, but also GD Express Worldwide to be undertakings concerned.

[127] Turnover Calculation Notice, para. 40. Already in its *XXIst Report on Competition Policy 1991*, *supra* note 76 the Commission submitted to this interpretation since in Annex III, point 7.1 it stated that '[t]urnover from companies in which an undertaking exercises joint control with a third undertaking is taken into account as to 50%.' (The text refers the reader to the decision in *Accor/Wagons-Lits*, *supra* note 77, but this decision does not provide any guidance on the point).

rule by analogy to situations where UC$_1$ and a third party (TP) jointly control JV.[128] This rule cannot, however, be based on the notion of control in Article 5(4)(b), as this would lead to the inclusion in the group of the undertaking concerned of every undertaking in which the undertaking concerned, together with third parties, holds more than 50% of the share-capital (or the voting rights or the right to appoint more than half of the board).

Example

UC$_x$ and 19 third parties each hold 5% of the share-capital in X. Together with 10 of the thirdparties, UC$_x$ will hold more than 50% of the share-capital.

It is submitted that a clear minority holding, such as UC$_x$'s 5%-holding in X, shall not lead to a (partial) inclusion of X in the group of UC$_x$ for the purposes of calculating the Community dimension.[129] As in the two preceding interpretations, the Commission has therefore based its interpretation on the notion of control found in Article 3(3). It is submitted that this in itself shows that the interpretation is untenable. As pointed out by B.E. Hawk and H.L. Huser,[130] applying an Article 3(3) notion of control to Article 5(5) may result in this provision 'preempting most of the Article 5(4) 'general rule'.' These authors find that the Commission's 'claimed reasoning 'by analogy' is based on nothing more than the Commission's tacit rejection of the original intent of the Merger Regulation's drafters.'[131] In addition, one may add that the original Form CO[132] in Guidance Note III expressly provided that 'joint undertakings existing between one of the undertakings concerned and a

---

[128] Examples from the Commission's practice are *McDermott/ETPM*, *supra* note 107 and *Swissair/Allders International*, Case IV/M782, decision of 17 July 1996. At least in the latter case this calculation method was decisive for giving the Commission jurisdiction. Perhaps *IFINT/EXOR*, *supra* note 17 is one more example of the application of this interpretation. The last-mentioned decision is discussed above in section 2.5.3.

[129] C. Jones and E. González-Díaz, *supra* note 114 at pp. 31-32 discuss this problem and reach the same conclusion.

[130] *Supra*, note 14 at pp. 103-104.

[131] B.E. Hawk and H.L. Huser, *supra* note 14 at p. 105.

[132] Annexed to Commission Regulation (EEC) No 2367/90 of 25 July 1990 on the notifications, time limits and hearings provided for in Council Regulation (EEC) No 4064/89 on the control of concentrations between undertakings.

third undertaking shall … not be taken into account.'[133] Having regard to the (new) interpretation set forth in the Turnover Calculation Notice, it is not surprising that the Commission has deleted this point in the subsequent Form COs.[134] In my view, the Commission's interpretation on this point must be considered to be very doubtful.[135]

3.7.5. Final comment

If an undertaking concerned has two joint parents, exercising joint control (within the meaning of Article 3(3)), or if the undertakings concerned jointly control a third undertaking, or if an undertaking concerned has joint control (as defined in Article 3(3)) together with one or more third parties, it seems reasonable to take this into account in order to ascertain the economic strength of the group of the undertaking concerned.[136] The problem is that taking due account of such joint ventures when calculating the Community dimension presupposes that control is defined in accordance with Article 3(3), not in accordance with Article 5(4)(b). In other words, I agree that there may be valid reasons underlying the Commission's interpretation. Only, I find that this interpretation does not find support in the Regulation.[137]

---

[133] *See* point (B)(II)(e) of Guidance Note III. Only if the joint undertaking had already been consolidated in the turnover of the undertaking concerned would the Commission allow that it was taken into account.

[134] *See* what is now Guidance Note II annexed to Form CO, *supra* note 3.

[135] The Commission in the *2001 Green Paper on the review of the Merger Regulation*, *supra* note 7, para. 152, implicitly acknowledges this as it finds that it 'appears appropriate to clarify the approach in the provision itself'. *See* likewise Francisco Enrique González-Díaz, 'Tenth Anniversary of the Merger Regulation: the Way Forward' in *EC Merger Control: Ten Years On*, International Bar Association, London 2000, pp. 405-425 at p. 407.

[136] Indeed, in the Turnover Calculation Notice from 1998 the Commission at para. 40 makes it clear that in respect of turnover calculation of joint ventures, priority should always be given 'to the general principles of avoiding double counting and of reflecting as accurately as possible the economic strength of the undertakings involved in the transaction'. Put differently, the Commission proposes that the drafting fathers' intention of creating an unambiguous dividing line should not be given priority.

[137] One wonders whether the Commission's proposal in its *2001 Green Paper on the Review of the Merger Regulation*, *supra* note 7, that the definition of control found in Art. 5(4) should be replaced by the definition found in Art. 3 was an implicit acknowledgement that the present interpretation conflicts with the Regulation? The proposal was later abandoned.

When the Merger Regulation was adopted the Commission and the Council agreed that 'a special re-examination of the method of calculation of turnover of joint undertakings as referred to in Article 5(5)' was required when the Merger Regulation thresholds were to undergo a review.[138] Nevertheless, in the *1996 Green Paper on the Review of the Merger Regulation,* the Commission stated that the review of Article 5(5) 'is not considered to be necessary' since the provision has been clarified in the Turnover Calculation Notice.[139] One may say that the Commission made the review of the Council's Merger Regulation through its Turnover Calculation Notice. I find this approach very problematic.

3.8. Agents

An agent[140] is an independent undertaking which provides another undertaking with a service in the form of a sale. In contrast to an independent trader, an agent does not assume the financial risk inherent in the transaction (apart from a *del credere* guarantee). The actual (*i.e.* formal) designation of the agent is immaterial in this regard.

Under the Community's antitrust rules, agents are often considered to be merely an auxiliary organ of the principal. The principal and the agent will therefore often

---

[138] Notes on Council Regulation (EEC) 4064/89 at 're Article 1', third point. The notes were published by the Commission at the time of the publication of the Merger Regulation. Alan Dashwood, 'Control of Concentrations in the EEC: The New Council Regulation' in *Le contrôle des concentrations d'entreprises*, F.I.D.E., 14e Congrès, Madrid 1990, Vol. III, pp. 21-44 at p. 22 comments on this publication. Moreover, he points out that the minutes cannot alter the meaning of the enacted text. It is, nevertheless, submitted that the minutes may provide some guidance in understanding the drafters' intentions and in this way may play a part in the interpretation of the Regulation.

[139] European Commission, *Community Merger Control – Green Paper on the Review of the Merger Regulation*, COM(96) 19 final, Brussels 31.1.1996, at para. 147. In the *2001 Green Paper on the review of the Merger Regulation*, *supra* note 7, at para. 152 the Commission, nevertheless, proposed that Art. 5(5) was amended.

[140] References to 'agent' not only covers commercial agency but also the commissionaire structure (*i.e.* commission agent or undisclosed agency). Concerning the commissionaire structure, *see* further Marc Picat and Eric Resler, 'Between Commercial Agency and Distributorship', *International Business Lawyer*, May 2002, Vol. 30, no. 5, pp. 211-213.

be considered to form an economic unit.[141] Under the Merger Regulation, an agent will only be considered to be part of the principal's group if the principal has control as defined in Article 5(4)(b). This is not likely to be commonplace.

This means, for instance, that where an agent sells a good on behalf of a principal, the turnover must be allocated to the principal, not to the agent. The only turnover allocated to the agent is the commission paid by the principal in connection with the sale. The Commission has taken the same approach.[142]

3.9. Public undertakings

In Article 86, the EC Treaty basically provides a non-discrimination principle between public and private businesses. This principle also applies to the Merger Regulation so that concentrations involving public undertakings may be notifiable under the Regulation in the same way concentrations involving private undertakings are. In this regard, it is immaterial whether the public undertaking is owned by the State or by a regional authority such as a city council.[143]

When it comes to calculating turnover, the drafters must have found that this principle created problems and so they included recital 12 in the Regulation.[144] The recital establishes that 'in the public sector, calculation of the turnover of an undertaking concerned in a concentration needs ... to take account of undertakings making up an economic unit with an independent power of decision, irrespective of the way in which their capital is held or of the rules of administrative supervision applicable to them'. This rule provides a clear derogation from the system otherwise provided by Article 5(4) and (5) since the reference to 'an economic unit with an independent power of decision' essentially is a reference to

---

[141] *See* for example Joined Cases 40-48, 50, 54-56, 111, 113 and 114/73 *Coöperatieve vereniging 'Suiker Unie' UA and others* v. *Commission of the European Communities*, 1975 ECR 1663.

[142] Cf. Turnover Calculation Notice, para. 13. *See* also *Péchiney World Trade/Minemet*, Case IV/M473, decision of 20 July 1994.

[143] For example in *GEAL/CREA/CGE*, Case IV/M1186, decision of 18 June 1998 one of the undertakings concerned was the local council of Leicca (Italy). In this work references to 'State' covers public authorities in general – including local authorities.

[144] Indeed, the even-handed treatment of public and private undertakings was an important issue in the negotiations leading to the adoption of the Regulation, cf. A. Dashwood, *supra* note 138 at p. 28.

actual control (in contrast to Article 5(4)(b)'s formal notion of control) so that, on this point, the delimitation of the group must follow a definition of control similar to the one laid down in Article 3(3).[145]

The justification for this rule is that undertakings belonging to the State would much too easily be considered to have a Community dimension if all the turnovers of all undertakings belonging to the same State were aggregated towards the turnover of the undertaking which is party to the concentration. The rule also carries with it the rather obvious benefit that where two undertakings belonging to the same State merge, this will be considered to constitute a concentration if the two undertakings are not linked together in accordance with the notion of control provided in Article 3(3).[146] Thus, if the rule in recital 12 had not been included, one could imagine that two state-owned undertakings were considered to be independent undertakings under Article 3(3) so that they could enter into a notifiable concentration, but it would not be possible to calculate Community dimension because both undertakings were considered to belong to the same group as defined in Article 5(4).[147]

While the principle in recital 12 may seem well-founded, it is not so very easy to apply in practice. In the Turnover Calculation Notice paragraph 44, the Commission has attempted to provide a few guiding principles which may be summarised as follows:

(1) Is the State-owned undertaking part of an overall industrial holding company? If yes, this indicates that the undertaking must be viewed together with the other undertakings in the holding company.[148]

---

[145] Likewise, P. Bos, *et al*, *supra* note 125, p. 132 who at the same time take a very sceptical stance on recital 12.

[146] *See Pechiney/Usinor*, Case IV/M097, decision of 24 June 1991, *CEA Industrie/France Télécom/Finmeccanica/SGS-Thomson*, Case IV/M216, decision of 22 February 1993, *Neste/IVO*, Case IV/M931, decision of 2 June 1998, Undertaking Concerned Notice, paras. 55 and 56 and European Commission, *XXIIIrd Report on Competition Policy 1993*, Luxembourg 1994, para. 266. With particular regard to the *Neste/IVO* decision, *see* the observations made by D. Berlin, *supra* note 95 at pp. 151-152.

[147] This situation may also arise in the case of private undertakings, but it is much more likely to arise *vis-à-vis* state-owned undertakings.

[148] *See* likewise Commission Notice on the Concept of Concentration, OJ C66/5 of 2.3.1998, para. 8, *in fine*.

(2) Is the State-owned undertaking subject to coordination with other State-controlled holdings? If yes, this indicates that the undertaking concerned must be viewed together with the other undertakings subject to coordination.[149]

(3) Are there any other reasons which make it clear that the State-owned undertaking forms part of an 'economic unit with an independent power of decision'?

Principles two and three do not seem to provide any guidance *in addition* to the one provided by recital 12 itself. In contrast, the first principle may throw some light on the application of recital 12. It is, therefore, unfortunate that it is very unclear how much emphasis the Commission places on this principle as is not least apparent from its decisions involving undertakings belonging to the State-owned Italian holding company IRI SpA.[150]

Even though there are a large number of decisions involving State-owned undertakings, it is hard to see that these decisions may provide much guidance and it is certainly difficult to see that the Commission is applying a true 'single economic unit' approach to the matter.[151] In the majority of the cases involving a State-owned undertaking, it either does not explain the basis on which it identifies an undertaking's economic unit[152] or it does not mention that it applies the economic unit approach provided in recital 12.[153]

---

[149] *See EDFI/ESTAG*, Case IV/M1107, decision of 17 May 1998.

[150] *See* for example *CEA Industrie/France Télécom/Finmeccanica/SGS-Thomson*, *supra* note 95, *Marconi/Finmeccanica*, Case IV/M496, decision of 5 September 1994, *Siemens/Italtel*, Case IV/M468, decision of 17 February 1995, [1995] OJ L161/27 and *Thomson-CSF/Finmeccanica/Elettronica*, Case IV/M767, decision of 29 July 1996. Contrast with *Alcan/Inespal/Palco*, Case IV/M322, decision of 14 April 1993 and *Torras/Sarrio*, *supra* note 27. (In the last-mentioned case Torras' parent company was the Kuwait Investment Office which manages investments on behalf of the State of Kuwait. Apparently all holdings of the Kuwait Investment Office were taken into account).

[151] Likewise, C.J. Cook and C.S. Kerse, *supra* note 35 at pp. 26-27, 32 and 84-85.

[152] *See* for example *Koipe-Tabacalerea/Elosua*, Case IV/M117, decision of 28 July 1992, para. 5. In *DFO/Scandlines*, Case IV/M1045, decision of 29 January 1998 and *British Steel/Europipe*, Case IV/M1014, decision of 26 February 1998, the Commission explicitly has abstained from identifying the undertakings' economic unit, observing that this is not necessary to establish the Community dimension.

[153] *See* for example *ABB/Renault Automation*, Case IV/M409, decision of 9 March 1994, *Rhône-Poulenc/SNIA*, *supra* note 72, *Hochtief/Aer Rianta/Düsseldorf Airport*, Case IV/M1035,

In *Kali + Salz/MdK/Treuhand,*[154] the Commission considered a concentration which involved the German Treuhand Anstalt, a publicly owned trust set up to first restructure the State-owned enterprises of the former East Germany to make them competitive and then to privatise them. The Commission found that the Treuhand Anstalt itself was an undertaking with a direct interest in the operation, but, at the same time, it made it clear that 'even if it were assumed that there were within the Treuhand a number of economic units with independent power of decision within the meaning of recital 12, the lowest conceivable organizational level that would constitute such an economic unit would be a directorate' and, even at this level, the thresholds would have been met.[155] Thus, the Commission did not 'exclude the possibility of regarding the different organizational units within the Treuhand (up to the level of directorate) as economic units with independent power of decision within the meaning of the 12th Recital.'[156] The case shows that the Commission may be prepared to stretch the economic unit definition very far.

In *Swissair/Sabena,*[157] the Commission rather confusingly notes that '[t]here is no need in the present case to calculate the turnover of the Belgian State, even though it is an undertaking concerned within the meaning of Article 1 of the Merger

decision of 22 December 1997, *GEAL/CREA/CGE, supra* note 143 and *EADS*, Case COMP/ M1745, decision of 11 May 2000. In *Telecom Eireann*, Case IV/M802, decision of 18 December 1996, the Commission apparently finds that the Irish State was not an undertaking concerned although it is explicitly stated that following the transaction the Irish State will have joint control together with two other undertakings. It thus appears that the State was completely left out when calculating the Community dimension. This did not affect the actual finding of a Community dimension, however. In *RWE/Vivendi/Berliner Wasserbetriebe*, Case IV/M1633, decision of 13 September 1999, the Commission equally calculated the Community dimension while leaving out the Land Berlin. It is rather clear from the decision that the Land Berlin was an undertaking concerned, however. (On the last-mentioned case, *see* also *Bulletin Quotidien Europe*, no. 7533 of 20 August 1999 at p. 3). In *RWE/Kärtner Energie Holding*, Case COMP/M2513, decision of 2 August 2001, the Commission apparently considers the Austrian Land Kärnten to be an undertaking concerned, but does not explain why.

154 Case IV/M308, decision of 14 December 1993, [1994] OJ L186/38.

155 *See* para. 9 of the decision.

156 European Commission, *supra* note 95 para. 250.

157 Case IV/M616, decision of 20 July 1995.

Regulation'.[158] In *Air France/Sabena,*[159] however, the Commission seems to have considered Sabena alone to constitute the full group for the purposes of calculating turnover. One wonders whether this change is due to changes in the relationship between Sabena and the Belgian State or a change in the Commission's interpretation.

Nonetheless, it is possible to extract some basic guidelines from the Commission's decisions; first of all, from the cases involving the Italian holding company IRI.[160] Thus if the holding company covers a large number of undertakings in a variety of sectors, this indicates that the economic unit must be found beneath the level of the holding company.[161] In contrast, if the holding company has been set up to cover a limited number of undertakings in a clearly defined business area, this indicates that the holding company constitutes an economic unit.[162]Moreover, if a company is listed on the stock exchange (in which case the State does not hold all shares therein) this apparently indicates that the company in itself forms a single economic entity. Nevertheless, Ulrich Immenga[163] is probably right when he finds that each case must be decided on its own merits.

The reason for the blurry picture provided by the Commission in this field is not obvious. Perhaps it may be explained by the fact that the economic unit approach is not only applied in respect of the Community dimension, but also in respect of the substantive appraisal. Where a State is involved in a concentration through the ownership of an undertaking concerned, for political reasons it may be extremely

---

[158] As noted by G. Drauz and D. Schroeder, *supra* note 49 at p. 6, the State cannot be an undertaking concerned. Likewise, P. Bos, *et al*, *supra* note 125 at p. 148.

[159] Case IV/M157, decision of 5 October 1992.

[160] *See supra* note 150.

[161] The Commission's decision of 5 August 1998 in *IVO/Stockholm Energi*, Case IV/M1231, seems to contradict this, however. In that case one of the undertakings concerned was a holding company owned by the City of Stockholm. This holding company consolidated companies in a number of fields including energy and water supply, school property management, housing, harbour administration, refuse collection and recycling, parking and cultural activities. The Commission apparently included all the companies held by the public holding company when calculating the Community dimension.

[162] *See* for example *Maersk Air/LFV Holding*, Case IV/M1124, decision of 6 July 1998.

[163] 'Zur Umsatzberechnung öffentlicher Unternehmen im Rahmen der europäischen Fusionskontrolle' in *Festschrift für Ulrich Everling*, (Ole Due, Marcus Lutter and Jürgen Schwarze, eds.), Nomos Verlagsgesellschaft, Baden-Baden 1995, pp. 541-550 at pp. 548-549.

problematic for the Commission to prohibit the concentration or to require amendments to it in order to clear it. In this situation, the obscurity surrounding the economic unit doctrine may be advantageous.

Example

Member State A owns the two largest banks in the country, X (having 40% of the market) and Y (having 20% of the market). Y acquires the third-largest bank, Z (having 10% of the market) so that State A's holding-company now controls the three largest banks having a marketshare of more than 70% in State A. If it is possible to consider X and Y as distinct economic units, the merger will 'only' lead to a combined marketshare of 30%, and it may be possible to argue that the concentration must be cleared.[164]

As noted above, it is submitted that the economic unit referred to in recital 12 shall be based on actual control which means that the notion of control provided in Article 3(3) constitutes an excellent point of departure. It is also submitted that if recital 12 and Article 3(3) are interpreted along the same lines, this will provide a more coherent scheme for the working of the Merger Regulation. At present, the Commission's obscure interpretation of recital 12 does not add to such coherence.

---

[164] *See Texaco/Norsk Hydro*, Case IV/M511, decision of 9 January 1995 (para. 26), *Siemens/ Italtel, supra* note 150 (para. 13) and *Fortis/CGER*, Case IV/M342, decision of 15 November 1993 (para. 14). *See* also Adrian Brown, 'Case Note: Siemens/Italtel', *EC Merger Control Reporter*, Kluwer Law International, The Hague 1991 and later (looseleaf), pp. 1826.25-1826.27 in particular at 1826.25 (para. 4) and C.J. Cook and C.S. Kerse, *supra* note 35 at pp. 26-27.

Figure setting out the principal rules for defining the group

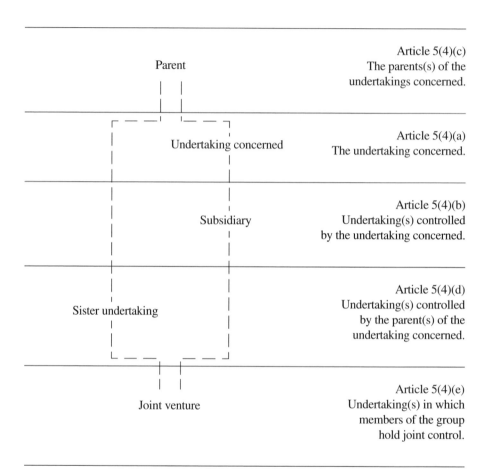

	Article 5(4)(c)
Parent	The parents(s) of the undertakings concerned.
Undertaking concerned	Article 5(4)(a) The undertaking concerned.
Subsidiary	Article 5(4)(b) Undertaking(s) controlled by the undertaking concerned.
Sister undertaking	Article 5(4)(d) Undertaking(s) controlled by the parent(s) of the undertaking concerned.
Joint venture	Article 5(4)(e) Undertaking(s) in which members of the group hold joint control.

4. THE BASIC RULES

1. INTRODUCTION

When the undertakings concerned and their respective groups have been identified, it is possible to determine their turnover. Turnover is not a completely unambiguous standard and the drafters have therefore included some basic rules on the calculation of it. These rules show that the calculation must be based on the (audited) accounts provided by the undertakings concerned, though the Regulation requires some adjustments for anomalies to be made.[1] Unfortunately, as will be shown below, in my view, the Commission's practice has unnecessarily obscured the clear principles provided in the Regulation.

In this chapter, I shall examine the basic rules by ascertaining what accounts must be used, what activities shall be included, how taxes and sales rebates are to be treated, and how the conversion into EUROs is made. Finally, I shall look into the problems related to intragroup sales.

2. PRECEDING FINANCIAL YEAR

2.1. The main rule

> '[T]he basic principle is … that for each undertaking concerned the turnover to be taken into account is the turnover of the closest financial year to the date of the transaction.'[2]

---

[1] The special rules applying to the accounts of financial institutions and insurance undertakings are examined below in chapter 6.

[2] Commission Notice on calculation of turnover under Council Regulation (EEC) No 4064/89 of 21 December 1989 on the control of concentrations between undertakings, OJ 2.3.1998 C66/25, at para. 24. Hereinafter Turnover Calculation Notice. *See* for example *Bombardier/ADtranz*, Case COMP/M2139, decision of 3 April 2001, [2002] OJ L69/50.

Referring to the preceding financial year achieves two ends. Firstly, it will make the Community dimension more reliable since it will be possible to base the calculation on audited accounts. Secondly, it eases the burden on the undertakings concerned since, in principle, they will be able to rely on their published accounts instead of having to prepare a new set.[3] Nevertheless, where the financial year of an undertaking concerned ends shortly before the transaction takes place, the accounts may not have been finalised, not to mention audited. In order to achieve the just-mentioned two ends, it will be necessary to refer to the latest financial year for which audited accounts exist.[4]

Only in a minority of situations does this main rule create problems. These problems will be examined below.

2.2. Taking new but unaudited figures into account

The above main rule is blurred by the Commission's statement in the Turnover Calculation Notice that '[w]here there is a major divergence between [the older audited and the newer unaudited accounts], and in particular, when the *final* draft figures for the most recent years are available, the Commission may decide to take those draft figures into account.'[5] On the face of it, this may appear well founded. There is, however, no particular reason why one should choose the new accounts where it is obvious that the new (unaudited) and the old (audited) accounts will lead to the same result. Accordingly, it seems to me that the Commission's statement only makes sense if it is interpreted to mean that where the unaudited and the audited accounts may lead to differing results regarding the finding of Community

---

[3] Nonetheless, according to Mario Siragusa and Romano Subiotto, 'The EEC Merger Control Regulation: The Commission's Evolving Case Law', *Common Market Law Review*, 1991, pp. 877-934 at p. 896 'the Commission has on occasion insisted that the calendar year be used, contrary to Article 5(1).' Whether the reference to 'the calendar year' in *Deutsche BP/ Erdölchemie*, Case COMP/M2345, decision of 26 April 2001, was made at the insistence of the Commission is not clear however.

[4] Likewise, the Commission in the Turnover Calculation Notice at para. 26 and *Rheinmetall/ British Aerospace/STN Atlas*, Case IV/M894, decision of 24 April 1997.

[5] Para. 26 of the Turnover Calculation Notice. The view that the Commission may take such draft figures into account is supported by C.J. Cook and C.S. Kerse, *E.C. Merger Control*, 3rd ed., Sweet & Maxwell, London 2000 at p. 66.

dimension, the unaudited accounts shall be used.[6] This understanding appears to have been confirmed in the Commission's decisions.[7] Another ambiguity in the statement is that it provides that 'the Commission *may* decide' (emphasis added). This indicates that the Commission is at liberty to decide whether to base the calculation on the audited or the unaudited accounts. Such construction essentially amounts to vesting in the Commission the powers arbitrarily to decide whether a concentration has a Community dimension (and thus falls within the scope of the Merger Regulation). It is submitted that the Regulation does not vest such power in the Commission. Consequently, it seems to me that the statement must be interpreted to mean that the Commission must (rather than may) apply the unaudited accounts, unless the audited accounts can be presumed to provide the same result.

While this rule is more (though still not fully) consistent with the basic idea that the financial strength of the undertakings concerned must be ascertained at the time of the transaction,[8] it is also possible to foresee a number of problems. For instance, how close to being finalised must the accounts be before they may be used for calculating the Community dimension, and what happens if, after the Commission has taken or ceded jurisdiction, the auditors find miscalculations which have had a material influence on the finding of a Community dimension?[9]

---

6   Contrast with Götz Drauz and Dirk Schroeder, *Praxis der europäischen Fusionskontrolle*, 3rd ed., RWS Verlag Kommunikationsforum GmbH, Cologne 1995 at p. 16 who find that where the last financial year has been ended so recently that audited accounts are not yet available the Commission will accept the preliminary figures as long as this does not affect whether the concentration has a Community dimension. *Quare*, what is the purpose of using the unaudited accounts, if they are only used where they provide the same result as do the audited accounts?

7   *See Deutsche Telekom/SAP-S*, Case IV/M705, decision of 29 March 1996, *Bank Austria/ Creditanstalt*, Case IV/M873, decision of 11 March 1997 and *Preussag/ELCO Looser*, Case IV/M714, decision of 14 March 1996. Equally Jonathan Faull & Ali Nikpay, *The EC Law of Competition*, Oxford University Press, Oxford 1999, at p. 232 find that new unaudited accounts may only be used 'if the result of using these figures would be decisive for the jurisdictional question'.

8   Cf. Case T-3/93, *Société Anonyme à Participation Ouvrière Compagnie Nationale Air France v. Commission of the European Communities*, (the *Dan Air* case) [1994] ECR II-121.

9   J. Faull & A. Nikpay, *supra* note 7, at p. 232 explain that in order to have the Commission take the new unaudited figures into account '[t]he undertakings concerned would … have to provide sufficient evidence that [these] unaudited figures may be relied on'. Unfortunately the authors do not explain what the Commission considers to be 'sufficient evidence'.

In my view, the obvious solution is to base the Community dimension exclusively on audited accounts apart from in exceptional cases such as where no such accounts are available.

2.3. Acquisitions and divestitures completed since the preceding financial year

As just noted, calculating the Community dimension on the accounts for the preceding financial year is not fully consistent with the basic idea of ascertaining the financial strength of the undertakings concerned at the time of the transaction.[10] This inconsistency is particularly clear where acquisitions and divestitures have taken place in the period between the end[11] of the preceding financial year and the transaction.[12]

In most cases, the solution is rather straightforward. The Community dimension is calculated on a 'legal entity by legal entity' basis, meaning that the turnover of the different constituents of the group are added together. This rule is particularly important with regard to groups which are formed from both financial and non-financial undertakings since different calculation methods apply, as is shown below.[13] Hence, if the group of an undertaking concerned has divested itself of five

---

[10] *See* further chapter 3 at section 2.4. Compare with *Arjomari-Prioux/Wiggins Teape Appleton*, Case IV/M025, decision of 10 December 1990, in which the Commission apparently decided whether the concentration met the thresholds on the basis of the situation prevailing at the time of the last shareholders' meeting, cf. M. Siragusa and R. Subiotto, *supra* note 3 at p. 899 and above chapter 3, section 2.5.4.

[11] In *Siebe/APV*, Case IV/M936, decision of 16 June 1997, the Commission notes that it has made 'adjustments to Siebe's turnover to reflect the full contribution of acquistions, disposals made, and new joint ventures entered into *during* Siebe's most recent financial year …' (emphasis added). Likewise in *Siebe/BTR*, Case IV/M1380, decision of 13 January 1999, the Commission notes that the turnover of BTR had been 'adjusted to reflect acquisitions and disposals made *during* the course of the relevant accounting year' (emphasis added). Presumably these acquisitions and disposals had not been reflected in the accounts of the undertakings in question.

[12] Changes in the Community territory is another kind of event, affecting the calculation of the Community dimension, which may occur subsequently to the preceding financial year. *See* below chapter 5, section 5.

[13] *See* chapter 6, section 4.

companies and acquired six, the solution is simply to deduct the turnover of the five sold companies (as it appears in their respective accounts for the preceding financial year), and in the same way to add the turnover of the six acquired companies.[14]

The situation becomes more tricky where the acquisition or divestiture does not concern a legal entity in the group which has its own audited accounts, but instead a production facility, a trademark or the like.[15] For instance, if Coca-Cola decides that the license to produce and market its soft drinks in Sweden and Norway shall be awarded to a new licensee, the change in turnover for both the former and the new licensee will be substantial. Nevertheless, audited accounts are made for the respective companies (which might be engaged in activities other than producing

---

[14] Likewise, Turnover Calculation Notice, para. 27. *See* for example *Go-Ahead/VIA/Thameslink*, Case IV/M901, decision of 24 April 1997, *WorldCom/MCI*, Case IV/M1069, decision of 8 July 1998, [1999] OJ L116/1. The same is true in respect of a merger between one or more companies, cf. *Stinnes/HCI*, Case COMP/M2202, decision of 4 December 2000 with note 5 and *Degussa/Laporte*, Case COMP/M2277, decision of 12 March 2001. However, contrast with *Preussag/Babcock Borsig*, Case IV/M1594, decision of 17 August 1999, in which the Commission in notes 3 and 4 explicitly states that the turnover of Babcock Borsig has been calculated without including the turnover of AE Energietechnik Beteiligungs AG. Babcock's acquisition of the latter undertaking had been cleared by the Commission on 30 June, *i.e.* 16 days before the notification of the *Preussag/Babcock Borsig* case. According to Jacques Zachmann, *Le contrôle communautaire des concentrations*, Librairie Générale de Droit et de Jurisprudence, Paris 1994 at p. 87, in *Accor/Wagons-Lits*, Case IV/M126, decision of 28 April 1992, [1992] OJ L204/1 the Commission did not take account of the turnover of a subsidiary of Accor since Accor had ceded control thereover before the notification date. In contrast, unofficially it has been claimed that in *Torras/Sarrio*, Case IV/M166, decision of 24 February 1992, the Commission wrongly included the turnover of Torras' subsidiary Ebro, since even though Torras controlled Ebro through a 51% holding in the preceding financial year, at the time when the Commission calculated the Community dimension, Torras no longer held control of Ebro. Even if this claim proves correct, it is important to note that *Torras/Sarrio* was notified almost one year too late. The Community dimension should therefore be calculated on the basis of the situation at the time when the concentration should have been notified, not when the actual notification took place. *See* further above chapter 3 at section 2.4, the Court of First Instance in the *Dan Air* case, *supra* note 8, at para. 99 and the European Commission, *Commission Notice on the concept of undertakings concerned under Council Regulation (EEC) No 4064/89 of 21 December 1989 on the control of concentrations between undertakings*, OJ 2.3.1998, C66/5. (Hereinafter Undertaking Concerned Notice) para. 17.

[15] *See* Undertaking Concerned Notice, at para. 14. For a decision that appears to have been founded on the same line of reasoning, *see Shell UK/Gulf Oil (Great Britain)*, Case IV/M1013, decision of 28 November 1997, at paras. 4 and 7.

and distributing Coca-Cola), not for Coca-Cola production as such. This situation, it is submitted, does not differ much from the sale/acquisition of a company. Even where the transferred activity is not specifically covered in the audited accounts of the seller, definitive accounts will normally be available since it is unusual to transfer production facilities, trademarks, etc., without the purchaser obtaining the necessary financial statements regarding, *inter alia*, the turnover generated by the transferred activity. The solution must therefore be the same as the one applicable to the transfer of companies so that the turnover generated by newly acquired activities is added to, and turnover of divested activities is subtracted from, the group turnover.[16]

The real problem arises where the change in turnover in the period between the preceding financial year (with audited accounts) and the transaction is not due to a transfer, but to a closure or start, of activities. For instance, if Lufthansa decides to cease servicing its trans-atlantic connections, the decrease in Lufthansa's turnover presumably will be the same as if it decided to transfer all of its trans-atlantic flights to, say, United Airlines. Since the Community dimension essentially is intended to reflect the economic strength of the undertakings concerned, it could be argued that it is correct to take such closure into account. While this line of argument may appear convincing at first glance, it really is rather weak. Firstly, it must be noted that the effect on the accounts in the case of a transfer is different than in the case of a closure. In the case of a transfer, the transferor is likely to receive consideration from the transferee (although this consideration is likely to be treated as extraordinary income and therefore not included for the purposes of calculating the Community dimension).[17] Where the consideration is clearly nominal, *e.g.* € 10, this indicates that the economic strength which the activity vested in the transferor is also nominal. Secondly, where an activity such as a manufacturing plant is sold, it remains an economic power in the market which contrasts with the situation where the plant is closed down. Thirdly, as rightly noted by the Commission, the aim of the turnover-based thresholds is 'to provide a simple and objective mechanism that can be easily handled by the companies involved in a merger in order to determine if their transaction has a Community dimension and is therefore notifiable.'[18] If the undertakings were required to assess effects on turnover caused by the closure and/or start of activities in the period from the preceding

---

[16] Likewise, Turnover Calculation Notice, para. 27.

[17] Cf. Art. 5(1)(1) and below section 3.2.

[18] Turnover Calculation Notice, para. 5.

financial year to the day of the transaction, it would not be possible to fulfil this aim. Consequently, in my opinion, such changes should not be included in the turnover calculation.[19]

Unfortunately, the ruling by the Court of First Instance in the *Dan Air* case[20] means that the legal situation is not as clear as just indicated. The ruling is discussed at length above in chapter 2.[21] Suffice it here to note that where an undertaking concerned either has closed down an activity before the transaction day or such closure is a precondition for the transaction, the turnover generated from this activity must be subtracted when calculating the Community dimension.[22] By the same token, it seems logical for the opposite of closing an activity, *i.e.* starting new activities, to be taken into account.[23] The Turnover Calculation Notice is strangely quiet on this point, however, indicating that only closures may be taken into account. Moreover, the *Dan Air* case concerned a closure of activities. The ruling by the Court of First Instance does not explicitly deal with the start of new activities and it seems difficult to extract any guidance from this ruling *vis-à-vis* how to treat the initiation of new activities.

At least the Commission's Notice makes clear that '[o]ther factors that may affect turnover on a temporary basis … will be ignored for the purposes of calculating turnover.'[24] As examples of such factors, the Commission gives 'a decrease in orders for the product or a slow-down in the production process'. One may argue that a decrease in orders or a slow-down in the production process may be

---

[19] Likewise, Dirk Schroeder, 'Case Note: Paribas/MTH/MBH', *EC Merger Control Reporter*, Kluwer Law International, The Hague, 1991 and later (looseleaf), at p. 460.2, but contrast with Pierre Bos, Jules Stuyck and Peter Wytinck, *Concentration Control in the European Community*, Graham & Trotman, London 1992 at p. 130.

[20] *Supra*, note 8.

[21] In *Deutsche Bank/Banco de Madrid*, Case IV/M341, decision of 28 May 1993, *Ingersoll-Rand/Clark Equipment*, Case IV/M588, decision of 15 May 1995, *Rhône Poulenc Rorer/Fisons* Case IV/M632, decision of 21 September 1995 and *Allianz/Hermes*, Case IV/M813, decision of 27 September 1996 the Commission has applied and distinguished the *Dan Air* rule.

[22] Apparently in this situation the Commission is prepared to rely on management and other forms of provisional accounts, cf. Turnover Calculation Notice, para. 26 read in conjunction with para. 27.

[23] Likewise, C.J. Cook and C.S. Kerse, *supra* note 5 at p. 67.

[24] Para. 28 of the Notice.

permanent and consequently have more than a temporary effect on turnover. The Commission would probably argue that such an occurrence *may* have only a temporary effect on turnover, whereas a closure always has a more permanent effect.[25] Nevertheless, if a European air carrier closes its trans-atlantic routes in order to be able to open new routes to Asia (using the same planes, the same European airport slots and the same staff), one may ask whether this closure has permanent effects on turnover?

In conclusion, while the Commission's interpretation regarding divestitures and acquisitions of companies and activities is sound, the special rule regarding the closure of activites seems to me to be misplaced.

2.4. Financial year of more/less than 12 months duration

When the drafters of the Regulation referred to the 'preceding financial year' they probably only envisaged financial years of 12 months' duration. Not only is it possible to decide the starting date for the financial year of a company at the time of registration, however, it is also possible subsequently to change the financial year. When such a change is made, this necessarily implies that one intermediate financial year is either longer or shorter than the usual 12 months. The question is how to deal with this when calculating the Community dimension?

Two solutions may be considered. Either the preceding financial year is used for the calculation irrespective of its length or the preceding financial year is 'adjusted' to cover a 12-month period.

In support of the former solution, one may note that the different accounting practices, not only between the Community and the rest of the world, but also within the Community, means that the Community dimension is based on a mixed bag of standards. Why then adjust the length of the financial year?

To answer this question one has to look at the scheme on which the Community dimension is based. Article 5(1) of the Regulation sets up a scheme whereby the

---

[25] Hence, the Commission in its *XXVIIth Report on Competition Policy 1997*, Luxembourg 1998 at p. 171 note that 'even if an airline has ceased operations definitively or for a long period on a particular route, the turnover attributable to the route will be preserved if the airline has kept the corresponding slots in order to pursue operations elsewhere'. *See* also *British Airways/Air Liberté*, Case IV/M857, decision of 28 February 1997, para. 8 with footnote 1 and Lennart Ritter, W. David Braun and Francis Rawlinson, *European Competition Law: A Practitioner's Guide*, 2nd edition, Kluwer Law International, The Hague 2000, at p. 434.

turnover figures are, so to speak, 'purified' for anomalies such as sales rebates, VAT and other taxes directly related to turnover. Likewise, only ordinary income is counted while an extraordinary loss or income is excluded. Clearly, it would be inconsistent if, for instance, the Commission based its calculation on the turnover generated throughout a fifteen-month financial year, while at the same it excluded an extraordinary loss from the calculation. Indeed, one is tempted to liken the additional three months to an extraordinary income.

To base the calculation of the Community dimension on a financial year of more or of less than 12 months will therefore be contrary to the scheme provided in the Regulation, and it is therefore submitted that such financial years shall be recalculated to 12 months' duration. In the case of an eight-month financial year, it is, therefore, necessary to add 50% to the figures provided by the audited accounts, and likewise in the case of a fifteen-month financial year, it is necessary to deduct an amount equalling 20% from the accounts. One counterargument may be that in the case of undertakings experiencing significant fluctuations over the year, such as toy producers up to Christmas or travel companies in the holiday seasons, this adjustment may superficially inflate (in the case of a financial year which includes the peak season to a disproportionate degree) or deflate (in the case of a financial year which disproportionately covers the off-season) the real 12-month turnover. It is acknowledged that it cannot be ruled out that adjusting the financial year to 12 months may have such effect. There are, however, only a few business areas which experience such pronounced fluctuations as those given in the examples. It is therefore submitted that on an overall basis adjusting the financial year to 12 months duration will produce the better result.[26]

In the *Ricoh/Gestetner Case*,[27] the figures for calculating the Community dimension have been based on 'the fourteen months to 31 December 1994 for Gestetner.'[28] It is not clear whether the two additional months were crucial in meeting the thresholds. In contrast, in the Turnover Calculation Notice, the Commission

---

[26] When changing the financial year it is not unusual to include figures for the twelve months leading up to the end of the 'intermediate financial year' (*i.e.* the year of more/less than twelve months duration) to make comparisons with earlier years possible. These figures are normally taken from the internal interim report and not audited. Only where these twelve-month figures have been duly audited, it is submitted, shall they replace the figures for the actual financial year.

[27] Case IV/M622, decision of 12 September 1995. Likewise *Inchcape plc/Gestetner Holding PLC*, Case IV/M583, decision of 1 June 1995.

[28] Note 1 to para. 5 of the decision.

twice explicitly refers to a 12-month year.[29] Consequently, it is not possible to provide a fair indication of which interpretation the Commission would support.

2.5. Accounts which do not follow the EC standards

In the Community, a fair amount of work has been put into harmonising the accounting rules of the Member States. The accountancy standards of non-Member States may differ significantly from those of the Community, however. This presents a problem since, on the one hand, very differing standards invariably means that the Community dimension is found on an uneven basis. On the other hand, however, a certain amount of consideration is appropriate towards undertakings in non-Member States. Accordingly, it is submitted that the Commission shall only require a restatement of the accounts in accordance with Community standards if the following three conditions are met:

(i) there are major differences between the Community's accounting standards and those applicable to the undertaking from the non-Member State,[30]

(ii) the restatement is necessary to ascertain whether the concentration has a Community dimension[31] and

(iii) the concentration must come within the Commission's jurisdiction as defined (*i.e.* limited) by public international law.[32]

In other words, it is submitted that if the concentration rather clearly falls outside the Commission's jurisdiction or if the figures are not necessary to ascertain whether the concentration has a Community dimension, it will be out of propor-

---

29 Paras. 49 and 50. It does not seem to clarify the matter that Form CO in section G explains that 'all references to the word 'year' should be read as meaning calendar year, *unless otherwise stated*' (emphasis added).

30 *See* likewise Turnover Calculation Notice, para. 26.

31 If, for instance, three undertakings concerned are involved in the concentration, and on the basis of the figures of two of these undertakings it is possible to ascertain that there is (or is not) a Community dimension, it will be disproportionate to require the third undertaking to produce corresponding figures if this presupposes a restatement of the accounts.

32 Below in chapter 9 I argue that the Merger Regulation does not apply to concentrations which are excluded from the Commission's jurisdiction under international law. In practice the effects doctrine will in most cases constitute the outer boundary to this jurisdiction.

tion to require a restatement of the accounts. Otherwise, it will be necessary to make such restatement.

2.6. No reliable accounts available

Basing the Community dimension on turnover obviously presupposes knowledge about the actual turnover figures. It appears that no case has presented this problem so far, but an example may provide an illustration:

Example

Imagine that, in 1994, a Swede comes up with an invention whereby petrol for cars may completely be replaced with soya oil. He sets up a company, and, within the first two months, he has managed to make a number of very lucrative licensing contracts. Two of the largest German industrial groups, Siemens and Daimler-Benz, join forces to acquire the new company. Assume that, while these two undertakings easily meet the € 5 billion worldwide turnover and the € 250 million Community-wide turnover (as well as the equivalent thresholds in the second set of thresholds), they both achieve more than two-thirds of their Community-wide turnover in Germany.[33] It is, therefore, crucial to ascertain whether the Swedish company, the third undertaking concerned in the concentration, also achieves more than two-thirds of its Community-wide turnover in Germany,[34] but for obvious reasons there is no 'preceding financial year' to refer to.

---

[33] In the early 1990s, this assumption was not completely far-fetched, cf. Rainer Bechtold, *1992 Fordham Corp. L. Inst.* 607 (B. Hawk ed. 1993) and Alexander Riesenkampff, 'Perspektiven und Probleme der europäischen Fusionskontrolle', *Beiträge zum Handels- und Wirtschaftsrecht – Festschrift für Fritz Rittner zum 70. Geburtstag*, (Manfred Löwisch, Christian Schmidt-Leithoff and Burkhard Schmeidel, eds.), CH. Beck, München 1991, pp. 491-507 at p. 493. *See also Siemens/Sommer Alibert*, Case IV/M800, decision of 14 August 1996 (noting that Siemens achieved more than two-thirds of its Community-wide turnover in Germany). Today Siemens achieves less than two-thirds of its Community-wide turnover in Germany, cf. *Siemens/HUF*, Case IV/M912, decision of 29 April 1997. The same is true regarding Daimler Benz (today Daimler-Chrysler), cf. *Daimler Benz/Deutsche Telekom – Telematik*, Case IV/M962, decision of 31 July 1997. A fair number of the larger German and French undertakings still, however, generate more than two-thirds of their Community-wide turnover within their respective Member States.

[34] Above in chapter 2, section 2.2 it is argued that the two-thirds threshold applies to every single of the undertakings concerned irrespective of the size of their Community-wide turnover.

Similar situations may arise where, for instance, a non-Community undertaking has applied accountancy standards which differ from the Western standards to such extent that a conversion is not possible, or where a company has run into such problems that the accounting has become a complete mess. Also, the situation may arise where the audited and certified accounts prove to be absolutely misleading or where the auditors have refused to certify the accounts.[35]

It is submitted that the problems thus presented must be solved on an *ad hoc* basis and that the solution should not go beyond the minimum requirement to establish a Community dimension. Thus, where it is clear that the concentration does/does not have a Community dimension regardless of what the accounts of the 'problem undertaking' may show, no accounts need to be prepared in this respect. In contrast, where the turnover figures of the 'problem undertaking' may be crucial for determining jurisdiction, accounts which will make it possible for the Commission to determine whether the concentration has a Community dimension are required. Proportionality probably requires that where it is fairly clear that the concentration will have no adverse effects on competition in the common market, it is not necessary to carry out a full audit. In highly contentious cases, it cannot be excluded, however, that a full audit will not be disproportionate.

3. ORDINARY ACTIVITIES

3.1. The main rule

According to the Regulation, only turnover generated by 'the sale of products and the provision of services falling within the undertakings' ordinary activities' shall be used for the purpose of finding a Community dimension.[36]

---

[35] On 5 March 1991 the Danish bedding manufacturer Nordic Feather went into bankruptcy. In its field, the undertaking was amongst the largest in the world. It soon appeared that the audited and certified accounts were one big sham. For instance, a number of sales made to what were supposed to be independent companies, proved to have been made to controlled companies set up in the English Channel Islands and the Isle of Man. The purpose was to inflate the value of the assets, but as a side effect the turnover was inflated as well.

[36] Until its expiration in July 2002, the ECSC Treaty provided an independent merger control scheme regarding the products covered by that Treaty. Nevertheless, turnover derived from

This means that the Community dimension must be based on the figures for ordinary activities provided in the undertaking concerned's accounts.[37] Still, turnover is not an unambiguous standard so, in borderline cases, it will almost always be possible to increase/decrease the turnover figure in accordance with what the parties to the concentration wish.[38] Below, I will look at the Commission's approach in two cases where it did not accept the figures which appeared in the certified accounts.

3.2. Extraordinary items

In *Accor/Wagons-Lits,*[39] the Commission found that *inter alia* 'proceeds from the sale of used cars by [a car rental subsidiary] and volume discounts granted to [the car rental subsidiary] by manufacturers on its purchases'[40] should be included in the ordinary activities. This amounted to € 422,436,636 which was instrumental in bringing the combined worldwide turnover above the € 5 billion mark[41] and thus the concentration within the Commission's jurisdiction.[42]

Admittedly, a car rental company's sale of its used cars takes place on a regular basis making it arguable that such sale forms part of the company's 'ordinary

---

the sale of these products also had to be included when calculating the Community dimension under the Merger Regulation.

[37] The definition of ordinary activities/ordinary income varies between the European countries, cf. Christopher Nobes, *Interpreting European Financial Statements*, 2nd ed., Butterworths, London 1994, at pp. 89-90.

[38] For instance, if a shipyard works on a ship in both 1996 and 1997, but is only paid upon delivery in 1997, the question arises whether this payment shall be considered to be only 1997 turnover or whether it shall be allocated to both 1996 and 1997? One may argue that the payment shall only be taken into account when it is received, or one may argue that since 3/4 of the work was carried out in 1996, 75% of the payment should be counted as 1996 turnover.

[39] *Supra* note 14.

[40] Footnote to para. 7 of the decision.

[41] In 1992 only the first set of thresholds applied.

[42] According to Eleanor J. Morgan, 'European Community Merger Control in the Service Industries', *Service Industries Journal*, Vol. 14, no. 1, 1994 at p. 69 'Accor made a number of proposals to the Commission to … bring the transaction within the Regulation, perhaps to avoid enquiry by the French authorities.'

activities'.[43] In contrast, it is more difficult to accept that proceeds arising from cash payments received as volume discounts on purchases of cars[44] may be regarded as turnover generated by an ordinary activity.[45]

Even though one may be justified in adding amounts which do not figure as an ordinary item in the calculation of the Community dimension, this approach must be used with great caution. Otherwise, the basic idea that the notion of Community dimension shall be based on a clear and easy to apply concept is undermined. With special regard to *Accor/Wagons-Lits*, the Commission's failure to add any convincing reasons for its approach makes it difficult to identify (and thereby to apply) the Commission's interpretation.[46] Undertakings striving to bring a concentration within the scope of the Regulation may find it worthwhile to look closely into their accounts in order to seek out amounts derived from regular sales of assets used in their business.[47]

---

[43] C.J. Cook and C.S. Kerse, *supra* note 5 at p. 65 rightly takes a sceptical stance to the inclusion of 'profit from sales of items where they are assets employed in the business but not products of that business'. Perhaps they are hinting at the sale of used cars by car-rental companies?

[44] In the accounts, Europcar, a car-rental subsidiary of Wagons-Lits, included the full price of the cars (which were bought at a discount) as costs and increased the turnover correspondingly.

[45] Ivo Van Bael and Jean-François Bellis, *Competition Law of the European Community*, 3rd ed., CCH Europe, Bicester (UK) 1994 at p. 382 with note 79 find that the Commission's approach 'broadly follow the accounting distinction between operating and non-operating income.' (Basically, operating income is the same as turnover derived from the ordinary activites). These two authors have identified the following as strong candidates for inclusion when calculating the ordinary turnover: intellectual property royalties, cash discounts on purchases, interest for late payment on sales, fees for sub-letting plant and production equipment, and income from the lease of property rights. In contrast, they are able to identify the following weak candidates: interest on investment of sales revenue, regional grants, dividends on minority interests, legal settlements, and lastly capital gains on the sale of operating assets, investments and securities.

[46] In its Opinion of 26 March 1992 the Advisory Committee on Concentrations agreed 'with the Commission that the concentration between Accor and the CIWLT has a Community dimension', thereby implicitly accepting the Commission's interpretation.

[47] Concerning the treatment of financial income, *see* chapter 6, in particular section 4.5.

3.3. State aid

In *Cereol/Continentale Italiana*,[48] the Commission had to decide how to deal with aid granted to undertakings by public bodies. The facts were that Cereol intended to acquire Continentale's operations relating to the grinding, refining and marketing of vegetable oil and this aquisition would constitute a concentration with a Community dimension if Continentale had a Community-wide turnover of more than € 250 million. According to Continentale's accounts, it had a Community-wide turnover of € 291 million, but this amount included Community aid. Excluding the Community aid, the figure would be less than € 250 million.[49]

The Commission found that the Community aid was paid to Continentale to compensate for the price difference between the (high) Community price and the (low) worldmarket price of oil seeds. In effect, this meant that the aid was really directed to the oil seed producers (who could sell at a higher price than the world market price) rather than at the oil grinders (who were simply compensated for having to pay a higher price). The Commission also noticed that while the aid was proportional to oil seed producers' sales, to the grinders, the aid was only proportional to the amounts of oil seeds purchased. On this basis, the Commission decided to exclude the aid from Continentale's turnover, whereby it was found that the operation lacked a Community dimension.

The *Cereol/Continentale Italiana* decision has given rise to a number of comments in the literature. Frank L. Fine[50] takes the view that the case provides that subsidies which have no relation to sales (such as investment or R&D grants) shall 'not be considered turnover because they are not 'derived from' sales.' Not only would this distinction be difficult to apply, but also its reasonableness may be questioned. After all, subsidies paid towards the development of a new product may be reflected in the price of the product when marketed. In addition, the interpretation differs from that of the Commission as shown below.

Timothy G. Portwood[51] finds that aid must be included in an undertaking's turnover if the recipient is the ultimate destination of the aid. He also finds, however,

---

[48] Case IV/M156, decision of 27 November 1991.

[49] In 1991 only the first set of thresholds applied.

[50] *Mergers and Joint Ventures in Europe – The Law and Policy of the EEC*, 2nd ed., Graham & Trotman Ltd, London 1994, at p. 175.

[51] *Mergers under EEC Competition Law*, The Athlone Press, London 1994 at pp. 35-36.

that where the aid concerns purposes outside the normal commercial activities of the undertaking concerned, the aid shall not be counted as turnover. It appears that Portwood is thinking of situations where the public is compensating rather than subsidising an undertaking. This view, it is submitted, is correct.

In the Turnover Calculation Notice, the Commission has translated the *Cereol/ Continentale Italiana* decision into the following rule:

> 'With regard to aid granted to undertakings by public bodies, any aid relating to one of the ordinary activities of an undertaking concerned is liable to be included in the calculation of turnover, if the undertaking is itself the recipient of the aid and if the aid is directly linked to the sale of products and the provision of services by the undertaking and is therefore reflected in the price ...'[52]

If a shipyard receives € 20 million in public aid for each ship it builds, it will be able to sell the ships at a discount of € 20 million while still making the same profit as if it had sold it at the 'full price' but without receiving such aid. If the aid is not included, this essentially would mean that the turnover figure is artificially deflated.[53] Equally, if steel consumers such as the automotive industry receive aid to purchase European steel, this will make it possible for the European steel producers to inflate prices above the worldmarket price without losing their market. The question is whether in reality the aid is not directed at the producers rather than at the consumers? If we want to exclude public aid from the turnover when calculating the Community dimension, it will be necessary to ascertain both the direct and the indirect public aid given. Such calculations may prove very difficult and sometimes virtually impossible to carry out, thereby making a strong argument in favour of counting public aid as turnover in accordance with the Commission's interpretation. One counterargument may be, however, that such aid more closely resembles financial income (which is not normally counted as ordinary income) than a sale. Also, if an undertaking (or an industry) receives public aid, this often is an indication of lack of competitiveness, meaning that the turnover less the public aid is more likely to adequately reflect the economic strength of this undertaking.

---

[52] Para. 16 of the Notice.

[53] Likewise, Siún O'Keeffe, 'Merger Regulation Thresholds: An Analysis of the Community-dimension Thresholds in Regulation 4064/89', *European Competition Law Review*, 1994, No. 1, pp. 21-31 at p. 29. It is acknowledged that this explanation of how state aid affects the market prices constitutes a gross simplification.

While the latter argument might hold some truth it seems likely that it will be impossible to apply consistently. In comparison, it is submitted that the Commission's interpretation is easy to apply while being economically sound. This interpretation must therefore be endorsed.

4. TAXES AND SALES REBATES

Article 5(1) provides that sales rebates, value-added tax and other taxes directly related to turnover must be deducted when calculating the Community dimension. This hardly comes as a surprise. The Commission lucidly defines 'sales rebates' as 'rebates or discounts which are granted by the undertakings during their business negotiations with their customers and which have a direct influence on the amounts of sales.'[54] Hence, for instance, liquidated damages to be paid by a contractor in case of failure to deliver on time shall not be counted as sales rebates.[55] In cases of doubt it would seem justifiable to look to the Sixth VAT directive for guidance.[56]

The exclusion of VAT is equally well founded and is unlikely to pose problems. Problems arise, however, regarding 'other taxes directly related to turnover'. The

---

[54] Turnover Calculation Notice, para. 20.

[55] Heinz F. Löffler in *Langen/Bunte – Kommentar zum deutschen und europäischen Kartellrecht*, Luchterhand, Berlin 2001 at p. 2535 writes that (the German version of the Regulation's term corresponding to) 'sales rebates' include price allowances, repayments such as cash discounts, incentive bonuses, quantity and loyalty discounts, lump sum settlements in the case of longterm debt for goods and services where this debt carries no or only insignificant interests, allowances for price, weight or quantity variances. Taking into account the problems of translating these terms with the necessary precision, the original German quotation follows here: 'Erlösschmälerungen umfassen Preisnachlässe, zurückgewährte Entgelte, wie etwa Skonto, Boni, Mengen- und Treuerrabatte, Abfindungsbeträge bei langfristigen unverzinslichen oder niedrig verzinslichen Waren- und Leistungsforderungen, Gutschriften für Preis-, Gewichts- oder Mengenunterschiede.'

[56] The 6th Council Directive on the harmonization of the laws of the Member States relating to turnover taxes – Common system of Value Added Tax: uniform basis of assessment, 77/388, OJ 1977 L 145/1, in Art. 11(A)(3)(b) provides that 'the taxable amount shall not include ... (b) price discounts and rebates allowed to the customer and accounted for at the time of the supply'. For an example of the application of this provision to a rather complicated rebate system, *see* case C-86/99, *Freemans* v. *Commissioners of Customs Excise*, ECR 2001 I-4167.

Commission finds that this 'is a clear reference to indirect taxation since it is directly linked to turnover, such as, for example, taxes on alcoholic beverages.'[57]

Article 5(1) has to a pronounced degree been based on Article 28 in the Accounting Directive[58] which reads as follows:

> 'The net turnover shall comprise the amounts derived from the sale of products and the provision of services falling within the company's ordinary activities, after deduction of sales rebates and of value added taxes directly linked to the turnover.'

Moreover, the Accounting Directive also provides that a Contact Committee be set up, *inter alia,* to facilitate a harmonised application of the directive. One of the matters that has been discussed within the Committee is the more precise meaning of the expression 'other taxes directly linked to the turnover' and the Committee has come up with the following conclusion:

> 'There is a particular need to clarify whether excise duty should be considered to be such a tax. Unlike VAT, which is levied and reimbursed at each stage in the production chain, excise duty is normally paid only once by the producer when the product first leaves the factory. Excise duty therefore forms an integral part of the price of the product and cannot be separately identified. The most logical approach would seem to be to regard excise duty as an inseparable part of the price of the product, which should therefore always be included in the net turnover.'[59]

Taking into consideration the close relation between Article 5(1) of the Regulation and Article 28 of the Accounting Directive, the views of the Contact Committee necessarily must carry weight.

---

[57] Turnover Calculation Notice, para. 21. For example, in *Toyota Motor/Toyota Denmark*, Case IV/M1592, decision of 23 July 1999, when calculating the Community dimension not only VAT but also the high Danish duties on cars were excluded from the turnover of Toyota Denmark.

[58] The Fourth Council Directive on the Annual Accounts of Certain Types of Companies, 78/660/EEC, OJ 14.8.1978, L222/11.

[59] *The Accounting Harmonization in the European Communities – Problems of applying the fourth directive on the annual accounts of limited companies,* Office for Official Publications of the European Communities, Luxembourg 1990, at p. 22.

Thus, on the one hand, there is no doubt that, particularly in the case of producers of alcoholic beverages and tobacco, the inclusion of excise duties will lead to an artificial inflation of turnover.[60] On the other hand, one may reasonably presume that the drafters of the Regulation intended Article 5(1) to be construed in accordance with Article 28 of the Accounting Directive which apparently does not provide for the exclusion of excise duties. Moreover, Community undertakings must prepare their accounts in accordance with the accounting rules, which means that (indirectly) they must apply Article 28 of the Directive. Also, it is noteworthy that Article 5(1) reads 'value added tax and other taxes directly related to turnover' indicating that 'other taxes' must be related to turnover in the same way as is VAT.[61] Excise duties are normally based on other factors than turnover, for example quantity or alcohol percentage.

Also, it must be noted that the Contact Committee points out that the producer is normally the one paying the excise duty, meaning that when the product has left the factory, the duty becomes an integral part of the price. In other words, to the distributor and the retailer, the excise duty is part of the price paid in the same way as are other taxes paid by the producer.

It is not clear whether the Commission Notice must be interpreted to exclude excise duties only from the turnover of the party actually paying the duty to the Treasury,[62] or whether it also covers subsequent links in the supply chain. There is nothing in the Notice supporting a limitation to only the party paying the duty,

---

[60] The same is true where other substantial duties are imposed on special products. For instance fragrances, petrol or duties imposed on cars in countries like Denmark and Greece.

[61] The 6th Council Directive, *supra* note 56 in Article 33 'prohibits Member States from introducing or maintaining taxes, duties or charges which can be characterized as turnover taxes.' cf. the Court of Justice in *Dansk Denkavit aps and P. Poulsen Trading aps, supported by Monsanto-Searle A/S* v. *Skatteministeriet*, Case C-200/90, [1992] ECR I-2217 at para. 10. As a general rule, therefore, turnover taxes exhibiting the essential characteristics of VAT is unlikely to be lawful under Community law. *See* further Paul Farmer and Richard Lyal, *EC Tax Law*, Clarendon Press, Oxford 1994 at pp. 132-134. The reference to 'other taxes directly related to turnover' may, however, be of considerable importance *vis-à-vis* non-Community undertakings. For the same view, *see* Dominique Berlin *Contrôle communautaire des concentrations*, Editions A. Pedone, Paris 1992 at p. 108 who also notes that it cannot be excluded that there may be other taxes than VAT in the Community which are directly related to turnover.

[62] I. Van Bael and J.-F. Bellis, *supra* note 45 at p. 382 with note 80 supports this understanding of the Commission's view.

however. Nevertheless, the Solomonic solution to the problem seems to me to be to require undertakings paying excise duties directly to the Treasury to deduct this duty when calculating the Community dimension, and to do so regardless of the actual size of the duty. This deduction should, however, not be made by undertakings further down the supply chain.[63]

Admittedly, deducting excise duty does not accord with a strict interpretation of Article 5(1).[64] Nevertheless, since the excise duty is not an integral part of the price to the undertaking that transfers the money to the Treasury, since this undertaking is likely to be the one whose turnover is most inflated due to the duty, and since the solution provides a simple and objective mechanism that can be easily handled by the undertakings involved in a concentration, it is submitted that this teleological interpretation constitutes the better solution.

5. CONVERSION INTO EUROS

It may be no surprise that the Merger Regulation states the turnover thresholds in EUROs.[65] A consequence is that the turnovers of the undertakings concerned must be converted into this currency.[66]

---

[63] Likewise Jacques Zachmann, *supra* note 14 at p. 86. *See* also Christopher Jones and Enrique González-Díaz, *The EEC Merger Regulation*, Sweet & Maxwell, London 1992 at p. 17 and Dorothy Livingston, *Competition Law and Practice*, FT Law & Tax, London 1995 at p. 731.

[64] D. Berlin, *supra* note 61 therefore apparently finds that such duties – as well as direct taxes – cannot be deducted when calculating the Community dimension.

[65] Strictly speaking the Merger Regulation itself states the thresholds in ECU. However, Council Regulation 1103/97 of 17 June 1997 on certain provisions relating to the introduction of the euro, OJ 1997 L162/1 provides that as of 1 January 1999 every reference to the ECU in a Community legal instrument shall be read as a reference to the euro at a rate of one euro to one ECU.

[66] Exchange rates may fluctuate considerably over a year so that chosing one rate rather than another may provide substantially differing results. Likewise, though on a different level, inflation may affect the thresholds. Based on an assumption of an average yearly inflation of 2% the € 5 billion threshold today corresponds to € 4.1 billion while the € 250 million threshold corresponds to € 205 million, cf. Annex I, para. 33, of the *2001 Green Paper on the review of Council Regulation (EEC) No 4064/89,* COM(2001) 745 final, Brussels 11.12.2001.

The Regulation does not provide any guidance regarding such conversion so the Commission has been relatively free to lay down rules on this point. Paragraph 49 of the Turnover Calculation Notice thus, *inter alia*, provides that:

> '[t]he annual turnover of a company should be converted at the average rate for the 12 months concerned. This average can be obtained from the Commission.'

In paragraph 50 of the Notice, the Commission continues to explain that where a company has sales in a range of currencies, the conversion shall be made from the consolidated accounts. In other words, if consolidated accounts have been prepared in a currency other than the EURO, the undertakings concerned may not make the conversion of local currency sales directly into EUROs.

Presumably, the intention is to make the conversion as easy and straightforward as possible. A positive side effect of the rule is that an obvious possibility of forum shopping is closed.[67]

As of 1 January 1999, the EURO replaced the ECU. Where it is necessary to include turnover that has been generated before 1 January 1999 this must be done on the basis of the average ECU exchange rate and converted into EUROs on a one-for-one-basis.[68]

---

[67] The rule is partly inconsistent with Article 50a in the Fourth Council Directive *supra* note 58 which opens the possibility of publishing the Annual Accounts in EUROs as well as in the currency in which they are drawn up since Article 50a explicitly requires the translation to be made 'at the exchange rate prevailing on the balance sheet date.' Special (lighter) notification requirements apply to certain *de minimis* joint ventures. In order to qualify for this short-form notification, it is necessary to meet both a turnover and an asset threshold. Strangely, the Commission has not provided any indication on the conversion of first of all the asset figure. *See* Form CO at point C(a) with note 3. Concerning the conversion of balance sheet figures under the former rules provided in Art. 5(3)(a), *see* my article 'The Commission's Jurisdiction over Mergers in the Financial Sector', *Legal Issues of European Integration*, 1996, no. 2, pp. 35-92 at p. 41 with note 24.

[68] See Council Regulation 1103/97, supra note 65, art. 2. Virtually all decisions now contain a footnote in which the conversion into EURO is briefly explained. For example note 3 (to para. 11) in *Deutsche Post/Securicor*, Case IV/M1347, decision of 23 February 1999, provides that '[t]o the extent that figures include turnover for the period before 01.01.1999, they are calculated on the basis of the average ECU exchange rates and translated into EUR on a one-for-one basis'. Information on how to make the conversion as well as how to obtain the relevant exchange rates may be found at DG COMP's homepage (www.europa.eu.int/comm/competition/mergers/others/exchange_rates.html).

6. INTRAGROUP SALES

6.1. Introduction

In order to properly reflect the economic strength of the parties to the concentration, the Community dimension thresholds are based on the aggregate group turnover of the undertakings concerned. The inclusion of turnover derived from sales between the different members of the group will amount to little more than double-counting and Article 5(1) therefore provides that '[t]he aggregate turnover of an undertaking concerned shall not include the sale of products or the provision of services between any of the undertakings' belonging to the same group'.[69]

In chapter 3, above, the different members of the group have been identified, and it is the sale between these members that Article 5(1) refers to.[70]

Three points require a few comments, however. The first is whether turnover between the undertakings concerned (and their respective groups) must be excluded. The second concerns the treatment of joint ventures' turnover. The last relates to the treatment of sales between a seller and its subsidiary or other entity which is being sold, thereby creating a concentration. These points are dealt with below.

6.2. Sales between the undertakings concerned

Article 5(1) provides that sales 'between any of the undertakings referred to in paragraph 4' shall not be included in the turnover. Article 5(4)(a) simply provides: 'the undertaking concerned'. One may therefore argue that, according to a strict literal reading, sales between the different undertakings concerned must be excluded. The consequence would be that turnover between the respective groups of the undertakings concerned must be excluded when calculating the Community dimension. In particular, in cases of vertical integration, this may be important.

---

[69] Equally the Seventh Directive on consolidated accounts, Council Directive 83/349/EEC of 13 June 1983, OJ 18.7.1983 L193/1 in Art. 26(1)(b) provides that intragroup sales must be excluded when setting up consolidated group accounts. For a good example of the application of the rule, *see Henkel/Schwarzkopf*, Case IV/M630, decision of 31 October 1995.

[70] *See* also paras. 38(4) and 22-23 of the Turnover Calculation Notice.

Example

The Japanese producer A sells only one product in the Community and does this through an independent distributor B, situated in the UK. A has a world-wide turnover of € 4.7 billion of which € 250 million is achieved in the Community through the sales to B. B has sales only in the Community, where it generates a turnover of € 350 million.

On the face of it, an acquisition of B by A will be likely to have a Community dimension since the aggregate worldwide turnover appears to be € 5.05 billion and since both undertakings concerned appear to achieve more than € 250 million in the Community. If the sales between the undertakings concerned must be deducted, however, the € 250 million EURO sales from A to B must be excluded which means that neither the € 250 million nor the € 5 billion threshold will be reached.[71]

The question now is whether this interpretation is correct. On the one hand, it must be acknowledged that it is well in line with one of the basic aims of the notion of Community dimension, namely that it must reflect the economic importance of the concentration. Taking the figures from the above example, the merged undertaking AB will have a Community-wide turnover of only € 350 million (the turnover of B) and it will have a worldwide turnover of € 4.8 billion (the turnover of A plus the turnover of B deducted the € 250 million sales which has become an intra-group transaction). It may therefore be argued that not only a literal but also a teleological interpretation may support this construction since this is the better way of reflecting the economic strength of the entity created by the concentration.

On the other hand, one may argue that Article 5(4)(a) reads 'the undertaking concerned', thus applying the singular. Furthermore, Article 5(4) simply provides guidance on which undertakings must be included in the respective groups of the undertakings concerned. In other words, the undertakings referred to in the Article all belong to one and the same group; the provision does not refer to *all* the groups of *all* the undertakings concerned.[72]

---

[71] Moreover, since A sells only to B in the UK the second set of thresholds is not met (Art. 1(3)(c)).

[72] Other pieces of Community legislation have a definition of the group which lies very close to the one in the Merger Regulation. Some of these other pieces of Community legislation seem to support the view advanced here (*see* for example Commission Regulation (EEC) No 1983/83 of 22 June 1983, art. 5(3)) whereas others seem to support the opposite view (*see* for example Commission Regulation (EEC) No 417/85 of 19 December 1984, Art. 6).

If the conclusion was only going to be reached on the above argument, I would tend to subscribe to the view that the drafters only had intra-group sales in mind when excluding sales between the undertakings referred to in Article 5(4) from the turnover. Put differently, I would have been inclined to support the view that inter-group sales shall be included when calculating the Community dimension. Nevertheless, Article 5(5) seems to point in the opposite direction. Article 5(5) concerns joint ventures which have more than one of the undertakings concerned as parents and Article 5(5)(a) explicitly provides that 'no account shall be taken of the turnover resulting from the sale ... between the joint undertakings and each of the undertakings concerned ...' Of course, it is possible that this specific exclusion of intergroup sales should be construed as an exception to a general inclusion of intergroup sales in Article 5 as such. It seems to me, however, that a more convincing interpretation of Article 5(5) is that it simply provides guidance on the treatment of joint ventures having more than one of the undertakings concerned as parents. In the latter case, the better view seems to be to assume that the drafters only intended that Article 5(5) should clarify the application of the general rules.

Certainly, the conclusion is not straightforward. I hesitantly subscribe to the view that intergroup turnover must be excluded when calculating turnover, however. This approach better reflects the economic power *after* the concentration while the other approach better reflects the economic power before the transaction. After all, merger control is concerned with an *ex post* evaluation.

In *British Airways/TAT (II)*,[73] the Commission implicitly reaches the opposite conclusion in a case where a joint venture goes from joint to sole control by simply pointing out that sales from the joint venture (the first undertaking concerned) to the acquiring parent (the second undertaking concerned) and to the selling parent are not intra-group sales. In other words, the Commission does not pay any consideration to the question of whether inter-group sales may be included for the purpose of calculating the Community dimension.[74]

---

[73] Case IV/M806, decision of 26 August 1996.

[74] The Commission has confirmed its interpretation in *MRW/MHP*, Case IV/M886, decision of 22 April 1997.

6.3. Joint ventures and intra-group sales

6.3.1. Joint venture is not part of the group

Where a joint venture is not included in the group of an undertaking concerned in accordance with Article 5(4), the sales of this joint venture shall not be aggregated towards the group turnover. Hence, if the joint venture has been consolidated in the turnover of the undertaking concerned,[75] it will be necessary to deduct this turnover when calculating the Community dimension and to add any sales from the group to this joint venture.

6.3.2. Joint venture is part of the group

Where a joint venture is included in the group of an undertaking concerned, in accordance with Article 5(4), the sales of this joint venture must be included in the group turnover.[76] This may, for instance, be the case where an undertaking holds 51% of the share capital in a joint venture since holding 'more than half the capital or business assets' means that the joint venture must be considered to be a subsidiary.[77]

If, however, the undertakings concerned jointly fulfil the criteria laid down in Article 5(4)(b), for instance, if they jointly hold more than half the capital in a joint venture, Article 5(5) provides that turnover to/from, on the one hand, the joint venture, and, on the other, the undertakings concerned, shall not be taken into account, while sales by the joint venture to third parties must be apportioned equally among the undertakings concerned.[78]

---

[75] The Seventh Council Directive on consolidated accounts, *supra* note 69, in Art. 32(1) provides the Member States with the possibility of introducing proportional consolidation. According to Christopher Nobes, *supra* note 37 at p. 100, Germany, France and the Netherlands have seized this opportunity.

[76] *See* chapter 3, section 2.5.

[77] Art. 5(4)(b), first indent.

[78] The interpretation of Article 5(5) is discussed above in chapter 3, sections 3.6 and 3.7.

Example

Assume that UC_1 and UC_2 jointly control JV, generating sales amounting to
€ 100 million per year. Of these, € 60 million are sales to UC_1, € 20 million are
sales to UC_2 and the rest is sales to third parties. In accordance with Article
5(5), the € 80 million (60 + 20), which are sales to UC_1 and UC_2, must be
disregarded and the € 20 million must be equally apportioned to UC_1 and
UC_2, meaning that € 10 million must be apportioned to each.

In Guidance Note II annexed to Form CO, the Commission sets out the following
preconditions for applying Article 5(5):

(a) The joint venture is jointly controlled by the undertakings concerned, irrespective of any third undertaking participating in the joint venture.

(b) The joint venture is not consolidated by the undertakings concerned in their
profit and loss accounts.

(c) The joint venture's turnover resulting from operations with the undertakings concerned shall not be taken into account.

(d) The joint venture's turnover resulting from operations with any third undertaking shall be apportioned equally amongst the undertakings concerned,
irrespective of their individual shareholdings in the joint venture.

In chapter 3, section 3.7, above, it has already been pointed out that under 'point
a' the Commission (wrongly, it is submitted) requires the control over the joint
venture to be defined according to Article 3(3) and 3(4) instead of according
to Article 5(4). It is equally surprising that in order to take the turnover of the joint
venture into account the Commission in 'point b' requires no consolidation to be
made in the profit and loss accounts of the undertakings concerned.

Example

Two undertakings concerned, UC_1 and UC_2 each holds 30% of the sharecapital
in JV whereby they have joint control according to Article 5(4). Only UC_1 has
consolidated the turnover of JV into its profit and loss accounts (on a proportional basis), however. According to the view of the Commission, this consolidation means that there is no basis for taking account of JV when calculating
the turnover of UC_2.

In most cases, this approach will mean that the aggregate turnover of all undertakings concerned will be less where one of the undertakings has consolidated
the turnover of a jointly controlled (within the meaning of control provided in

Article 5(4)(b)) undertaking, than would be the case if no such consolidation had been made. It is submitted that a more consistent approach would have been to disregard the turnover included due to the consolidation, and instead make the calculation provided for in Article 5(5).[79]

Points 'c' and 'd' simply reiterate the rules provided in Article 5(5)(a) and (b).

It seems fair to question the value of Guidance Note II regarding the application of Article 5(5). The Note sets out four preconditions, but two of these have been taken straight from Article 5(5) and the two others are, with respect, misplaced.

6.3.3. *Joint control only together with a third party*

In the original Form CO, Guidance Note II's predecessor included the following additional consideration: 'Any joint undertaking existing between one of the undertakings concerned and any third undertaking shall (unless already consolidated) not be taken into account.' In the new Form CO, this consideration has been deleted. Instead, the Commission has replaced it with paragraph 40 of the Turnover Calculation Notice which expresses the exact opposite, namely, that joint ventures between one undertaking concerned and third parties must be taken into account so that the joint venture's turnover must be allocated equally to all the undertakings controlling the joint venture. In my opinion, the Commission's interpretation is highly questionable.[80] As long as no-one challenges the interpretation before the Court, however, this interpretation constitutes the law and it is, therefore, necessary to explain how the rule must be applied.

The rule applies where one or more undertakings concerned do not have control over an undertaking as defined in Article 5(4)(b), but together with third parties the undertaking(s) concerned does/do possess control.[81]

---

[79] P. Bos, *et al*, *supra* note 19 at pp. 134-135 apparently subscribe to the Commission's rule on this point.

[80] *See* further above chapter 3, section 3.7.4.

[81] As noted above and in chapter 3, section 3.7 the Commission apparently applies a concept of control which is based on Art. 3 instead of Art. 5. This interpretation is more than simply surprising.

If an undertaking concerned has sales to/from a joint venture, owned (and controlled) jointly with one or more third parties, to a certain extent these sales constitute intra-group sales, but, to a certain extent they also constitute sales out of the group of this undertaking concerned.

Example

An undertaking concerned, UC, and a third party, TP, jointly control JV which generates sales of € 100 million per year. € 60 million are sales to UC, € 20 million sales to TP, and € 20 million sales to others. From the point of view of UC, the joint venture only has 'external sales' amounting to € 40 million (to TP and to others). Thus, half of this must be allocated to UC, *i.e.* € 20 million.[82]

Apparently, the Commission takes the same approach.[83] Thus, it takes the full turnover of the joint venture, deducts the turnover derived from sales to the undertaking concerned and apportions the remaining turnover equally between all undertakings which have control over the joint venture.

Example

Together with TP$_1$ and TP$_2$, UC holds joint control over JV. Each of these three parents holds 20% of the shares in JV. JV generates a turnover of € 100 million, of which sales to UC amounts to € 10 million. It is likely that the Commission will apportion € 30 million to UC on the basis of the following calculation: € ((100 – 10) : 3).

Where more than one undertaking concerned holds joint control over a joint venture together with one or more third parties, the same principle is applied.

Example

UC$_1$, UC$_2$ and TP have joint control over JV which generates sales of € 100 million. Of these, € 25 million are to TP, € 50 million are to UC$_1$ and € 5 million are to UC$_2$. It is likely that the Commission will apportion

---

[82] From the point of view of TP, JV has external sales of € 80 million, half of which must be allocated to TP, *i.e.* € 40 million. Thus, even though, formally, JV has sales of € 100 million, only € 60 million is allocated to the parents (the € 20 million to others, the € 30 million from TP to UC and the € 10 million from UC to TP). The rest is excluded as intragroup sales.

[83] Cf. para. 40 of the Turnover Calculation Notice.

€ 15 million to each of the two undertakings concerned on the basis of the following calculation: € ((100 − (50 + 5)) : 3).

When it comes to sales from the undertaking concerned to the joint venture, it seems logical to apply the same principle as the one submitted above.

Example

UC, together with three third parties, controls JV which has sales of € 800 million. UC has sales to JV of € 100 million. Assuming that JV has no sales to UC, € 200 million (€ 800 : 4) must be allocated to UC when calculating the Community dimension. Moreover, from UC's 'own' turnover, presumably we must subtract the sales from the latter to JV, *i.e.* 25% of € 100 million; € 25 million. Hence, one may view the other € 75 million as sales to 'the parts of JV owned by the other parents'.

Note, however, that, while the Commission almost certainly will apply the rule set out above regarding sales from the joint venture, there are no indications how, if at all, it will make deductions for sales to a joint venture as in the preceding example.

6.4. Selling off a part and intra-group sales

In chapter 2, above, Article 5(2), concerning the calculation of turnover where only a part is sold/acquired, is discussed. The part sold may have sales to the rest of the group of which it has been a part until the divestiture.

Example

S is the owner of the production plant P which generates sales of € 300 million. 60% of P's sales are to S and the rest to third parties. A agrees to acquire P. Will both the sales from P to S and the sales from P to third parties be attributed to P when calculating the Community dimension?

Even though intra-group sales may not have been made at arm's length prices, it is submitted that inclusion of these sales is likely to provide a better reflection of the economic strength of the part acquired than if these sales were excluded. This is particularly clear where, before the acquisition, the part has sold virtually all of its production to its parent. If one were to exclude the sales between the part (the former subsidiary) and the seller (the former parent) the part would generate no turnover. It is thus submitted that such sales shall not be counted as intra-group sales.[84]

---

[84] On this point, *see* also Andre Fiebig, 'Outsourcing under the EC Merger Control Regulation', *European Competition Law Review*, 1996, issue 2, pp. 123-133 at pp. 128-130. The Commission has considered the question in *SEB/Moulinex*, Case COMP/M2621, decisions of 8 January 2002 (Arts. 6(2) and 9(3)). However, it restricted itself to pointing out that turnover could be calculated either by simply aggregating the sales figures of the parts sold by the parts acquired or by in addition taking intragroup sales into account.

5. GEOGRAPHIC ALLOCATION OF TURNOVER

1. INTRODUCTION

Article 1(2) and (3) of the Merger Regulation, setting out the two sets of thresholds defining Community dimension, provides the following:

'2. For the purposes of this Regulation, a concentration has a Community dimension where;

(a) the aggregate worldwide turnover of all the undertakings concerned is more than [€] 5 000 million, and

(b) the aggregate *Community-wide* turnover of each of at least two of the undertakings concerned is more than [€] 250 million,

unless each of the undertakings concerned achieves more than two-thirds of its aggregate Community-wide turnover within *one and the same Member State*.

3. For the purposes of this Regulation, a concentration within the meaning of Article 3 that does not meet the thresholds laid down in paragraph 2 has a Community dimension where:

(a) the combined aggregate worldwide turnover of all the undertakings concerned is more than [€] 2 500 million;

(b) *in each of at least three Member States*, the combined aggregate turnover of all the undertakings concerned is more than [€] 100 million;

(c) *in each of the three Member States* included for the purpose of (b), the aggregate turnover of each of at least two of the undertakings concerned is more than [€] 25 million; and

(d) the aggregate *Community-wide* turnover of each of at least two of the undertakings concerned is more than [€] 100 million;

unless each of the undertakings concerned achieves more than two-thirds of its aggregate Community-wide turnover within *one and the same Member State*.' (emphasis added)

The € 5,000 million threshold in Article 1(2)(a) and the € 2,500 million threshold in Article 1(3)(a) do not require a geographic allocation. In contrast, the € 250 million threshold in Article 1(2)(b) and the € 100 million threshold in Article 1(3)(d) require an allocation of turnover to the Community. Likewise, the € 100 million and € 25 million thresholds in Article 1(3)(b) and (c), as well as the two-thirds thresholds in Article 1(2) *in fine* and (3) *in fine* require an allocation of turnover to a single Member State. In most cases, it will be clear from the audited accounts whether the concentration has a Community dimension and, for those, the Commission will simply rely on these accounts.[1] Sometimes, this is not so however. In these cases, the method applied when allocating the turnover geographically may be decisive in determining whether the concentration has a Community dimension which, in turn, may prove decisive for whether the concentration is successful.[2] In this chapter, I shall therefore examine how to make the geographic allocation, and, in particular, I shall provide solutions to those problems which the allocation most often gives rise to. In high-profile borderline cases, it may be necessary to make a detailed analysis of all sales to decide whether the Commission has jurisdiction to vet the concentration.[3] I will base this chapter on a number of examples, some of which may appear to concern trivial transactions such as the purchase of a car. The examples are intended to illustrate the principle which must be applied, not only to the one car sold in the example, but to all cars and other products sold in the Community.

It is important to emphasise that neither the Merger Regulation nor the Commission's Turnover Calculation Notice[4] provides any substantial guidance

---

[1] However, in a number of cases the company accounts are not well suited for making the calculations required under the Regulation. For instance Dorothy Livingston, *Competition Law and Practice*, FT Law & Tax, London 1995 at p. 732 note that 'many English and Scottish companies' accounts divide their woldwide turnover by reference to their activities in three or four areas, the UK, Europe and the rest (giving North America separate treatment if they have significant business there). They frequently do not distinguish between European Community and EFTA turnover. Turnover in the Republic of Ireland is often treated as if it were generated in the UK. In the case of a hostile takeover, the result may be that a bidder has no way of knowing whether to notify the Commission or national merger control authorities and has to make fail-safe notifications to both.'

[2] Successful meaning that the concentration is not fully or partly prohibited.

[3] A good example of this is provided in *Hong Kong and Shanghai Bank/Midland*, Case IV/ M213, decision of 21 May 1992.

[4] Commission Notice on calculation of turnover under Council Regulation (EEC) No 4064/

regarding the geographic allocation of turnover. Moreover, even though the Commission's merger decisions and the legal literature frequently touch upon the issue, it is often difficult to deduce any clear guidelines from these sources. Accordingly, where it is impossible to establish the law relating to the specific issue, I shall instead endeavour to identify workable solutions within the framework provided by the Merger Regulation.

It is obvious that, in order to allocate turnover geographically, it is necessary to identify the sale which is to be 'allocated geographically'. Accordingly, I will first identify this sale. Allocating turnover generated by the sale of tangible products and turnover generated by the provision of services create different problems. I will therefore first examine the allocation of turnover regarding tangible products and, following this, I will turn to the difficult problems which services create.[5] Particular problems arise where the geographic territory of the Community changes. In the final part, I will therefore explain how these problems are best solved regarding allocation of turnover.

2. THE RELEVANT SALE

2.1. Sale out of the group

Article 5 of the Merger Regulation provides detailed provisions on the calculation of the turnover-based thresholds. Since the turnover, which must be allocated geographically, must be calculated in accordance with Article 5, the logical inference must be that the relevant sale must be the one identified by Article 5.

According to Article 5, the relevant turnover of an undertaking concerned is the turnover of the full group to which this undertaking concerned belongs, not just the turnover of the undertaking itself. Article 5(1) first sub-paragraph *in fine* therefore explicitly provides that the relevant turnover 'shall not include the sale of

---

89 of 21 December 1989 on the control of concentrations between undertakings, OJ 2.3.1998, C66/25, (hereafter 'Turnover Calculation Notice').

[5]   Even though in some cases computer software may be classified as a service rather than as a product, a sale of a CD-ROM containing a computer game or a word processing program is normally more akin to the sale of a tangible product and in such case it shall be treated like a product.

products or the provision of services between any' undertakings belonging to the same group as the one which the party to the merger belongs to. This means that the relevant sale is the first sale to an undertaking which does not form part of the group as defined in Article 5(4).[6]

Example

The computer manufacturer JCN produces computer hard disks in New York State and ships all of its production to Ireland. Eighty per cent of the hard disks are send to an Irish company in the JCN group assembling computers, while the remaining 20% are sold to an Irish company which is not a member of the JCN group. Even if the hard disk manufacturer registers all sales as 'sales to Europe', under the Merger Regulation, only the 20% sold to a non-JCN group company will be calculated as a European sale. If the Irish JCN assembly plant sells all its computers to a South American distributor not part of the JCN-group, this sale must be calculated towards the JCN-sale and the turnover generated hereby will not be attributed to the Community or any Member State therein.

2.2. Sales through agents

A sale may be effected in many different ways. A company may distribute its products through sales subsidiaries (the sale to the subsidiary is an intra-group sale) or through independent distributors (the sale to the distributor is a sale out of the group). In addition, a third possibility exists, namely sale through an agent. Agents neither form part of the group nor do they purchase the products. The agent simply provides the producer with a service in that the agent assists the producer with the sale. In return, the agent will normally receive a commission.[7] Accordingly, the fact that the producer delivers a product to the agent is not a 'relevant sale'. Only the sale to a third-party (via the agent) shall be counted as a relevant sale.

Example

Matahari, a Japanese producer of widgets, channels its sales to the Scandinavian market through Sol AB, an agent based in Sweden. Of the Scandinavian sales,

---

[6] *See* chapter 3 above.

[7] *See* further chapter 3, section 3.8.

40% go to Sweden while 30% go to Norway and Denmark respectively. Even though all of Matahari's Scandinavian sales are channelled through its Swedish agent, only the 40% which are sold to Swedish customers shall be counted as Swedish sales.

3. TANGIBLE PRODUCTS

3.1. Place of purchaser, place of delivery

Article 5(1) second subparagraph provides:

'Turnover, in the Community or in a Member State, shall comprise products sold and services provided to undertakings or consumers, in the Community or in that Member State as the case may be.'

This provision shows that the geographic allocation is made with reference to the place of the purchaser of the product in question.[8]

The place of the purchaser is, however, not an unambiguous concept. A Brit may go to Italy to buy a brand new Ferrari which he thereupon drives back home.[9] Or, an Anglo-French company may take delivery of some goods in Le Havre, while the billing is made to the company's Irish subsidiary and the company's headquarters are in London.

The Commission, in its Turnover Calculation Notice, simply notes that '... turnover should be attributed to the place where the customer is located because that is, in most circumstances, where a deal was made, where the turnover for the supplier in question was generated and where competition with alternative suppliers took

---

8 According to Dominique Berlin, 'Concentrations – (1er janvier 1998 – 31 décembre 1998)', *Revue trimestrielle de droit européen*, No. 1 2000, pp. 139-237 at p. 176 it follows from Art. 5(1), second subparagraph, that the geographic allocation must be made according to the place of the purchaser at the time when the transaction took place. This might be correct although I am not sure upon what terms in the provision this reading is based. Even if it is possible to read this time requirement into Art. 5(1), second subparagraph, the question of what 'the time of the transaction' covers still remains. Is it the point in time when the contract is entered into or is it the time when delivery takes place or is it something else?

9 Example adapted from the Turnover Calculation Notice, para. 46.

place.'[10] Unfortunately, the Notice does not go on to provide any substantive guidance on how to decide the location of the customer. It therefore appears doubtful whether the quoted statement provides any real help in the allocation of turnover under the Merger Regulation.[11]

Pierre Bos, Jules Stuyck and Peter Wytinck,[12] write that '[a]s an instrument used to measure economic achievement and thereby economic power, turnover should be linked to market share, if it is to have any relevance, while market share is, of course, linked to the relevant geographic market in which the undertaking in question is competing for the preference of the consumer.' Essentially, this means the same as the Commission's statement in the Turnover Calculation Notice; namely that the relevant location is where the seller competed to make the sale. These authors go on to note that this location must be 'where the recipient of goods has acquired these and not where he will use these.' These three authors also find that the 'basic assumption is that turnover should be allocated to the territory where the underlying economic transaction has had its incidence on competition. Normally, this will be the territory where the customer has directly or indirectly elicited competition by being active on the demand side of a relevant geographic market, and not where the undertaking selling the product or providing the service is established.' While this seems to be in full conformity with the Commission's view that the relevant location is where competition with alternative suppliers took place, it also seems that it does not provide any further guidance on this.

To allocate the turnover according to the domicile of the purchaser appears to provide an inadequate reflection of the place of purchase.[13] This is quite clear in the above example concerning the purchase of a Ferrari where the car is purchased

---

[10] Turnover Calculation Notice, para. 46.

[11] D. Berlin, *supra* note 8 at p. 177 criticises that the rule advanced by the Commission is more fitting for establishing where the effects of the concentration on competition will take place than as a means for establishing jurisdiction. He also finds that this solution differs from the one provided in Art. 9(2)(c) of the sixth VAT-directive (Council Directive 77/388 of 17 May 1977 on the harmonisation of the laws of the Member States relating to turnover taxes, OJ L145/1, 15.10.1977).

[12] *Concentration Control in the European Economic Community*, Graham & Trotman ltd., London 1992 at p. 136.

[13] Contrast with Siun O'Keeffe, 'Merger Regulation Thresholds: An Analysis of the Community-dimension Thresholds in Regulation 4064/89', *European Competition Law Review*, 1994, pp. 21-31, at p. 22 who finds that 'Article 5(1) states ... that [the geographic allocation of turnover] is based on the domicile of the recipient of the goods or services.'

in Italy, but the purchaser is domiciled in Britain. Likewise, to let the place be decisive where, in legal terms, the sale of the good or the provision of the service was concluded also appears to inadequately reflect the place of purchase.[14] In my view, the better approach is to hold the place of the purchaser to be where the product is physically delivered.[15] This has the great merit of clarity regarding tangible products as, in principle, these can only be in one place at a time, making the application of the rule fairly straightforward. Thus, where the aforementioned Brit goes to Italy to buy a Ferrari, the sale should be allocated to Italy rather than Britain. And where an Anglo-French company takes delivery of some goods in Le Havre, the sale of these goods should be allocated to France.[16]

3.2. Place where the product is used

Whether the sale is to an end-user is immaterial just as it is immaterial whether the purchaser intends to use the product in the country where it has been delivered.[17]

Example

A Canadian producer of car engine warmers delivers twenty containers to a European car-parts wholesaler. The containers are delivered in Rotterdam in the Netherlands and subsequently the engine warmers are distributed to the wholesaler's European outlets; half of them go to Norway, the other half to Sweden. Even though half of the engine warmers end up in Norwegian cars, *i.e.*, outside the Community, the sale will be classified as a Community sale.

The situation would be different if, instead, the producer had delivered ten containers directly to Norway and ten containers to Sweden. In this case, only the ten containers delivered in Sweden will be counted towards the Canadian company's Community-wide turnover.

---

14 Dominique Berlin, *Contrôle Communautaire des Concentrations*, Editions A. Pedone, Paris 1992, at p. 110 appears to be in preference of this approach.

15 This is not necessarily the same place as where in legal terms delivery has taken place.

16 In Turnover Calculation Notice, para. 46 footnote 13 the Commission explicitly notes that '[i]f the place where the customer was located when purchasing the goods or service and the place where the billing was subsequently made are different, turnover should be allocated to the former.'

17 *See* also para. 47 of the Turnover Calculation Notice.

3.3. Three guiding rules

To require that the parties to a concentration examine the geographic allocation of every single sale will be wholly disproportionate in almost all cases. Firstly, because it will often be so obvious that the thresholds have or have not been met that such examination will be superfluous. Secondly, because such examination may be very costly for the parties. In order to minimise the work necessary to make the geographic allocation, it is submitted that three guiding rules or presumptions shall apply.

Firstly, where an agent or a sales subsidiary has been assigned a given geographic sales area, it seems fair to presume that all sales made by this agent or subsidiary shall be allocated to this area. Thus, if a sales subsidiary is assigned the sales to South America, it is fair to presume that none of the sales effected by this subsidiary shall be counted as Community-wide turnover. On the other hand, if a sales-subsidiary is assigned the sales to the Nordic countries, this presumption is not of much help as these countries include both Community Member States (Denmark, Finland and Sweden) and non-Community States (Iceland and Norway).[18] Hence, in this latter case, it may be necessary to make a thorough investigation into the sales-subsidiary's division of sales between Nordic Community Member States and Nordic non-Community Member States.[19]

Secondly, in the case of direct exports, the relevant country must be presumed to be the one to which the goods are shipped, even though this country may differ from the one where the purchaser is resident and from the place where the performance takes place.[20]

---

[18] A special merger control regime, closely mirroring the one provided in the Merger Regulation, has been set up under the EEA Agreement. This scheme covers the Community as well as Norway, Iceland and Liechtenstein. In chapter 7 I examine the EEA Agreement's allocation of jurisdiction in respect of concentrations.

[19] For a concordant view, *see* Christopher Jones and F. Enrique González-Díaz, *The EEC Merger Regulation*, Sweet & Maxwell, London 1992 at p. 18.

[20] Likewise, C. Jones and F. Enrique González-Díaz, *supra* note 19 at p. 18. In this regard it does not matter whether the seller itself carries out the transport to the purchaser or whether the transport is carried out by an independent shipper. For the same view, *see* Peter Stockenhuber, *Die Europäische Fusionskontrolle – Das materielle Recht*, Nomos Verlagsgesellschaft, Baden-Baden 1995 at p. 166.

Example

An Austrian-based chain of computer retailers purchases a container of laptops from an Irish producer. The container is shipped to Germany for sale in the chain's German outlets and the contract is performed when the container leaves the Irish plant. Even though the purchaser is situated in Austria, the Irish producer must allocate the turnover derived from this sale to Germany, as this is the country where the laptops are delivered.

One may ask whether the Commission takes the same stance. The Turnover Calculation Notice in paragraph 47 provides that where an undertaking 'sources all its requirements for a good or service from one location. The fact that the components are subsequently used in ten different plants in a variety of Member States does not alter the fact that the transaction with a company outside the group occurred in only one country. The subsequent distribution to other sites is purely an internal question for the company concerned.' Barry E. Hawk and Henry L. Huser have interpreted this quotation to mean that where a multi-national undertaking has one central purchasing office, but the input is delivered at the various facilities where it is to be consumed, the supplier must allocate the turnover to the place of the purchasing office. The two authors criticise this view.[21] I agree that such interpretation is open to criticism, but I do not agree that the Turnover Calculation Notice necessarily must be interpreted in this way. In particular, the last sentence of paragraph 47 providing that '[t]he subsequent distribution to other sites is purely an internal question for the company concerned' indicates that the Commission is thinking of situations where an undertaking sources all its requirements through a central office *and* delivery takes place there. The subsequent distribution to various sites is an internal matter which does not concern the supplier of the input. Consequently, in my opinion, the interpretation advanced by me here does not necessarily conflict with the Commission's interpretation set out in the Turnover Calculation Notice.

Thirdly, in the case of indirect exports, *i.e.,* where a sale is made to a purchaser situated in the same country as the seller and this purchaser re-sells the goods to someone in another country, the place of the first purchaser is decisive. This means that in the case of indirect exports the sale must be categorised as domestic.

---

[21] Barry E. Hawk and Henry L. Huser, *European Community Merger Control: A Practitioner's Guide*, Kluwer Law International, The Hague 1996 at pp. 86-87.

Example

A Spanish wine producer sells all of its production to a Spanish wine merchant. The wine merchant exports 99% of the wine so that almost all of the
producer's wine ends up outside Spain. Nevertheless, all of the producer's
turnover must be allocated to Spain.[22]

3.4. Sale of rights to tangible products

In some situations, a tangible product is sold without this meaning that the seller
will direct the goods to the purchaser.

Example

An American company owns a cargo of crude oil which is on its way from
Saudi Arabia to Rotterdam in the Netherlands. The American company sells
the cargo to a Dutch company, which in turn sells the cargo to a Swiss company. The Swiss sells the cargo to a trader in Milan, Italy, who sells it on to
another company in Milan.

While all these deals have taken place, the cargo has been on its way to the
Netherlands where delivery will take place. Nevertheless, even though the sale
from the Dutch company to the Swiss concerned a tangible product which would

---

[22] Mark Clough, *EC Merger Regulation – A practical guide to the EC merger and acquisition
rules*, Financial Times Management Report, 1994 at p. 142 notes that 'where Japanese companies sold to export houses in Japan on free on board (f.o.b.) terms even if the goods are
then exported to the EC' this situation would, presumably, be treated as a domestic sale. *See*
in support of this C. Jones and F. Enrique González-Díaz, *supra* note 19 at p. 18. The situation is, of course, different if the Japanese company sells directly to the EC on f.o.b. terms.
In this case the goods are shipped directly to the Community and must be considered to be a
sale thereto although in legal terms the goods are delivered when on board the ship and
although the purchaser pays for the freight. *See* in partial support of this, P. Bos *et al*, *supra*
note 12, p. 136 with note 36 and, more doubtful, Trevor Soames, 'The 'Community Dimension' in the EEC Merger Regulation: The Calculation of the Turnover Criteria', *European
Competition Law Review*, 1990, pp. 213-225 at p. 217. Robert Merkin (ed), *Encyclopedia of
Competition Law*, Sweet & Maxwell, London 1987 and later (looseleaf) at point 4-605D
finds that '[t]he place where products are sold may depend on the contractual arrangements,
i.e. whether they are sold *c.i.f.* or *ex works* ...' Thus, the last author's view appears to conflict
with the one advanced here.

be delivered in the Netherlands, it would be misleading to hold this to be a domestic Dutch sale. Likewise, when the Milanese trader sells the cargo to another Milanese company this cargo is to be delivered in the Netherlands, but it seems rather misleading to hold this to be a sale from Milan to the Netherlands.

Essentially, the sale concerns an intangible right to a tangible product rather than a sale of the tangible product itself. This has obvious parallels to the provision of a service. Accordingly, I find that the place of the purchaser should not be considered to be the place of delivery, but rather to be the place of residence. This means that even if the Milanese trader bought the cargo from the Swiss company over his mobile phone while driving through the Netherlands, the sale should still be allocated to Italy. This approach is similar to the one which applies when allocating turnover generated through the provision of services.

4. SERVICES

4.1. The main rule

Services create special problems because they do not move like a tangible good. If a German goes to Denmark to buy a car, he purchases the good in Denmark, and as Denmark is place of delivery, the sale must be allocated to that country. The fact that subsequently he drives his new BMW back to Munich is immaterial in this respect. But what if a Swedish company asks a London-based firm of solicitors to provide advice in a competition case before the European Commission? Part of the advice may be given in meetings in London, in Stockholm and in Brussels. Another part may be given over the phone, by fax, or by mail. And the London solicitors may also contact the Commission in Brussels directly. Nevertheless, in my view there can hardly be any doubt that the service is going from London to Sweden and accordingly the turnover should be allocated to Sweden.

We might, however, complicate the situation a bit more. Again the London-based firm of solicitors provides advice. This time it is to the London-based subsidiary of a Japanese company, which is considering acquiring a German company. Should the turnover generated in this case be allocated to Britain, to Japan or perhaps to Germany? Strong arguments may be put forward for any of them.

Hence, a workable main rule must be construed.[23] Christopher Jones and F. Enrique González-Díaz have proposed that, in the case of services, the turnover shall 'be attributed to the country in which the consumer receives the benefit of the service in question'.[24] This presumption will work well in most cases such as where the service is a stay in a hotel or the provision of office-cleaning. Regarding the examples given above (concerning legal advice), it may, however, be difficult to determine precisely where the benefit is received. Perhaps this is why the Commission in its Turnover Calculation Notice at paragraph 46 provides that '[t]he second subparagraph of Article 5(1) does not focus on where a good or service is enjoyed or the benefit of the good or service derived.'

Article 5(1) focuses on the place of the consumer of the service.[25] Regarding certain types of services, the consumer must go to the place of the seller to obtain the service. This is, for instance, the case with regard to hotels and casinos. In other situations, the service is provided at the place of the purchaser as, for instance, in the case of legal advice and office cleaning.

Generally, this means that where the purchaser obtains the service at the place of the service provider, the sale must be allocated to that place. Where the purchaser may stay at home while obtaining the service, however, the sale should be allocated to the place of the purchaser.[26] It is submitted that, for practical reasons, this should be interpreted to mean the residence of the purchaser.

Example

If a Brit buys a British Airways flight to Greece in his local travel agency and thereafter, in Greece, buys a number of stays in small Greek hotels, British Airways would have to allocate the sale of the flight in accordance with those

---

[23] In a case which has certain parallels to the present issue, albeit it concerned the interpretation of the 6th VAT Directive, *supra* note 11, the European Court of Justice held that 'since forms of transport may easily cross frontiers, it is difficult, if not impossible, to determine the place of their utilization and that in each case a practical criterion must therefore be laid down' cf. Case C-190/95, *ARO Lease* v. *Inspecteur van de Belastingdienst Grote Ondernemingen te Amsterdam*, ECR 1997 I-4383, at para. 14.

[24] *Supra* note 19 at p. 19.

[25] P. Bos *et al*, *supra* note 12 at p. 136 appear to focus more on the place where a particular service causes impact on competition than on the place of the consumer of the service but compare with *Nomura/Blueslate*, Case IV/M1037, decision of 17 November 1997, para. 15.

[26] See likewise D. Berlin, *supra* note 8 at p. 177.

rules which apply to international transport[27] while the Greek hotels would have to allocate the sales of the hotel stays to Greece. If, instead, the Brit had bought a package holiday to Greece in the local travel agency, the travel agency would be the one who had purchased the flights and the hotel rooms in order to resell them. It seems rather obvious to me that the travel agency is providing a service to Britain, not to Greece. Indeed, if the travel agency was the one to arrange the package holidays it would have purchased the hotel rooms from Greece in order to resell them to Brits and it would therefore seem illogical that the turnover derived from the Greek hotels' sales to the British agency should be allocated to Greece. Hence, it seems that the better view is to apply a residence criterion to the package holiday situation.[28]

While the above main rule is likely to solve most of the situations involving services, some types of services may still create particular problems. Below these services will be given special attention.

4.2. Transport and courier services

4.2.1. Transport of goods

International transport and courier services pose particular jurisdictional problems.[29] Regarding courier services and transport of goods, the main rule set out just above provides that the residence of the purchaser must be decisive. Thus, if a company in Munich asks a courier service to bring a parcel to Vienna, the turnover generated by providing this service must be allocated to Germany. This, however, is not likely to make a great difference as the courier service will probably bring a more or less equal number of mailings back from Austria in order to exploit as fully as possible

---

[27] *See* section 4.2.2 below.

[28] This also appears to be the position taken by the Commission *cf. Thomas Cook/Sunworld*, Case IV/M785, decision of 7 August 1996 (concerning the geographic allocation of Sunworld's turnover).

[29] *See* for instance Alan D. Neale and Mel L. Stephens, *International Business and National Jurisdiction*, Clarendon Press, Oxford 1988 at p. 102.

the transport capacity. Thus, a more or less equal amount of turnover is likely to be allocated to Austria.[30]

Where, for instance, the lorries of a Danish hauler go to Italy full of goods but return empty, all of this hauler's turnover is likely to be generated exclusively from clients resident in Denmark. Consequently, all turnover should be allocated to Denmark with the result that the international dimension of the transaction is not reflected. On the other hand, the fact that all lorries return empty indicates that the hauler is only aiming his sales at the Danish market and that he is not competing with alternative suppliers in the Italian market. Allocating all turnover to Denmark may therefore be the best reflection of the hauler's activities.[31]

The national postal monopolies present a particular case. When British residents deliver letters, bound for France, to their local post office, Royal Mail of Britain will receive the payment from the purchaser and will then forward the letter to La Poste in France, which will deliver the letter. According to the rule set out above, the turnover so generated must be allocated to Britain. While at first glance, this may not appear to be a good reflection of the obvious international dimension of the transaction, a closer look may convey a different view. Royal Mail only brings the letter to the French border where La Poste takes over. Hence, Royal Mail only provides a service in Britain. Moreover, when La Poste takes over it provides a service to Royal Mail for which Royal Mail pays and the turnover so generated by La Poste must be allocated to Britain as this is the residence of the purchaser of the service; Royal Mail. When a letter goes from France to Britain, Royal Mail will obtain payment from La Poste for delivering the letter in Britain. This turnover will be allocated to France (residence of La Poste). It therefore seems

---

[30] According to Götz Drauz and Dirk Schroeder, *Praxis der europäischen Fusionskontrolle*, 3. auflage, RWS-Skript 232, Verlag Kommunikationsforum GmbH, Köln 1995 at p. 17 in *TNT/GD Net*, Case IV/M102, decision of 2 December 1991, concerning the setting up of a joint venture in the international express delivery business between TNT, which is involved in transport services, and five national postal administrations, the Commission accepted that turnover should be allocated to the country of the respective sender because the transport service is usually paid by the sender.

[31] For a concordant view, *see* the Turnover Calculation Notice para. 46 which emphasises the place where competition with alternative suppliers takes place. Other kinds of transport of goods include transport by sea, inland waterways, by rail and air and through pipelines.

that the rule based on residence of the purchaser of the service (*i.e.* the main rule) provides an adequate solution.[32]

4.2.2. Transport of persons

Transport of persons differs from transport of goods since the purchaser is not receiving the benefit of the service at home (while the transporter does the job), but instead the person is being transported and therefore obtains the benefit in different places. According to the rule set out above in section 4.1, the turnover shall be allocated to the place where the service is provided and, on the face of it, this creates problems regarding international transport.

> *Example*
>
> In 1991, the American carrier Delta Air Lines acquired the North Atlantic air transport business of Pan Am, also of the US. In examining whether the concentration had a Community dimension, the Commission first noticed that the two undertakings had a worldwide turnover which clearly exceeded € 5 billion.[33] Regarding the geographic allocation of the turnover, however, the Commission found that 'the following three methods of allocating turnover could reasonably be considered: one possibility would be to attribute the operating revenues deriving from transatlantic air transportation services to the country of destination, this being the final destination point outside the home country of the airline (for example, in the case of a flight New York/ Paris/New York by a US carrier the turnover would be allocated to France). A second option could be to allocate the revenues in a 50%/50% ratio to the

---

[32] If the British and the French postal authorities decided to merge so that we would have to calculate the turnover of these two undertakings, the counting method set out here may lead to doublecounting since, for instance, the revenue from the letter going from Britain to France will first be counted as domestic turnover generated by Royal Mail (the first undertaking concerned), whereupon La Poste (the second undertaking concerned) will count Royal Mail's payment for delivering the letter in France as British turnover, thus partly counting the payment twice. However, above in chapter 4 I (hesitantly) submit that sales between the different business groups to which the parties to the concentration belong, must be excluded from the calculation of the turnover. This means that La Poste shall not count the turnover achieved by sales to Royal Mail and *vice versa*. As also noted in chapter 4, the Commission does not agree with this interpretation.

[33] In 1991 only the first set of thresholds applied.

country of origin and the country of final destination, so as to take into account the cross border character of the service provided. A third alternative would be to attribute the air transport revenues to the Member State where the ticket sale occured.'[34] In *Delta Air Lines/Pan Am,* the thresholds would have been met irrespective of which calculation method was chosen, and the Commission therefore left the question open.

In *Air France/Sabena,*[35] the Commission reiterated the three possible ways of allocating turnover set out in *Delta Air Lines/Pan Am.* This time, also, the Commission found that the thresholds would have been fulfilled regardless of which of the three methods was applied.[36] It went on to note, however, that the second method, according to which turnover is allocated 50%/50% between the country of origin and the country of final destination, 'seems to be closest to the spirit of Article 5, paragraph 1, since it takes into account the two points between which the air transport service is rendered, thus reflecting the cross-border character of the service provided'.[37]

F. Enrique Gonzalez-Diaz, in a case note to *Air France/Sabena,* has criticised the Commission for showing a preference for the 50%/50% method. In particular, he noted that this method 'seems unsatisfactory since the analysis of the financial strength of an airline company should be carried out on the basis of its ability to create business in a particular area, irrespective of the places visited during the journey. In the case of air transport it seems artificial to say that the service is rendered in the various countries crossed in order to reflect the economic reality underlying the commercial activity of airlines. The point of sale criterion, however, seems to reflect more accurately the ability of an airline company to create business in a particular geographical area apart from being an easier criterion to apply from an accountancy point of view.'[38]

---

[34] *Delta Air Lines/Pan Am*, Case IV/M130, decision of 13 September 1991 at para. 9.

[35] Case IV/M157, decision of 5 October 1992.

[36] Again in *British Airways/TAT*, Case IV/M259, decision of 27 November 1992 the Commission in para. 14 refers to the three possible methods of calculation and again it simply notes that the thresholds were met irrespective of which of the three methods is used.

[37] Quotation taken from paragraph 20 of the (unofficial) English translation of *Air France/ Sabena* provided in *EEC Merger Control Reporter*, Kluwer Law International, The Hague 1991 and later (looseleaf), p. 932.7.

[38] F. Enrique Gonzalez-Diaz, 'Case Note: Air France/Sabena', *EEC Merger Control Reporter*, Kluwer Law International, The Hague 1991 and later (looseleaf), p. 932.18.

This view must be endorsed.[39] For example, on the routes between Europe and Japan, a number of different carriers compete, and it would be wrong to say that the competition for customers is only carried out on the ground and not in the air. Nevertheless, it must be equally true that turnover, generated by sales of tickets in Frankfurt for flights between Frankfurt and Tokyo, is really achieved in Germany only. It is not so that only half of the turnover is achieved in Germany and the other half in Japan, or that a minor percentage is achieved in Germany, a correspondingly small percentage in Japan and the rest is achieved in those countries through whose air territory the plane flies. Along the same lines, the purchase of Lufthansa tickets in Frankfurt for flights bound for Tokyo shall not be allocated 100% percent to Japan. Regardless of whether the purchase in Germany concerns one-way or return tickets, the same arguments are valid. Thus, the point of sale criterion appears to be the better approach.

Applying the point of sale criterion does not necessarily mean that the international aspects of international air transport will not be reflected in the allocation of turnover under the Merger Regulation.[40] When Lufthansa sells tickets in Japan, the turnover so generated will, of course, be allocated to Japan. Only where an international carrier does not sell tickets abroad, but only domestically, will the international aspect not be reflected. But it seems in such case that this carrier's market is a purely domestic one, making the point of sale criterion a fine reflection of the actual situation. The Commission now apparently supports the point of sale criterion, though it appears to leave the door open for the 50/50 method.[41]

---

[39] Likewise, G. Drauz and D. Schroeder, *supra* note 30 at p. 17.

[40] Athanassios D. Chronas, *Legal Constraints in the Liberalisation of the European Air Transport Sector: With special reference to the external aviation relations of the Community and the extraterritorial application of EEC Competition Law to foreign-based airlines*, LL.M. thesis submitted at the European University Institute, Florence, 1991 at p. 115 discusses the application of the threshold criteria to the air transport sector. For an account of these views as well as a critical discussion thereof, *see* my article 'Geographic Allocation of Turnover under the Merger Regulation', *World Competition – Law and Economics Review*, Vol. 20, no. 2, December 1996, pp. 23-43 at p. 34 with note 33.

[41] Cf. Turnover Calculation Notice, para. 46 read in conjunction with footnote 7 in *Swissair/ Sabena*, Case IV/M616, decision of 20 July 1995, *British Airways/Air Liberté*, Case IV/ M857, decision of 28 February 1997 (footnote 1) and *Marine-Wendel/SAirGroup/AOM*, Case IV/M1494, decision of 3 August 1999 (footnote 2). Note also that it seems unlikely that the 50/50 method has been applied in the calculation of Lufthansa's turnover in *EDS/Lufthansa*, Case IV/M560, decision of 11 May 1995, para. 14 with footnote 3, thus supporting the view that the place of sale criterion must now be applied. *See* also B.E. Hawk and H.L. Huser,

It is submitted that the point of sale criterion should be applied to all forms of international transport of persons. Ferries,[42] trains and buses present problems very similar to the ones presented by air transport. With special regard to train transport, it must be noted that if a train goes from Germany to the Netherlands, the German and Dutch railways must co-operate much in the same way as the postal authorities co-operate.[43] Accordingly, where the German Bundesbahn sells a ticket in Hamburg, the full revenue should be allocated to Germany (as in the case of air transport). The Germans, however, must pay the Dutch a part of this revenue for the distance from the Dutch border to the final destination, and the Dutch railways must allocate the turnover so generated to Germany (as in the case of postal services).

---

supra note 21 at p. 85 and Lennart Ritter, W. David Braun and Francis Rawlinson, *European Competition Law: A Practitioner's Guide*, 2nd edition, Kluwer Law International, The Hague 2000, who at p. 434 explain that '[t]o calculate turnover in *air transport* the Commission bases the geographic allocation of turnover on the 50-50 method ... or on the point of sale method'. C. Jones and F. Enrique González-Díaz, *supra* note 19 at p. 32 propose a very different method of calculation; worldwide turnover shall be the total turnover figure of the airline. EC turnover shall be the turnover generated by all flights in which a Member State is the country of destination. Turnover within one Member State shall be the turnover generated by flights which have that country as destination. While the authors note that this method of calculation will have the advantage that it parallels the accounting practice already adopted by Community carriers, they also rightly identify a number of anomalies produced by the method. It is submitted that the point of sale criterion presents a better solution to the problem.

Moreover, it is worthy of note that 'even if an airline has ceased operations definitively or for a long period on a particular route, the turnover attributable to the route will be preserved if the airline has kept the corresponding slots in order to pursue operations elsewhere', cf. the Commission's *XXVIIth Report on Competition Policy 1997*, Luxembourg 1998, at p. 171.

[42] Cruises are similar to package holidays so that the turnover must be allocated to the point of sale. If a passenger only purchases the cruise on board the ship the turnover must be allocated to the port of embarkation. In *Carnival Corporation/P&O Princess*, Case COMP/M2706, decision of 24 July 2002, the Commission almost certainly applied the point of sale criterion.

[43] *See* above section 4.2.1. Note also that the question concerning doublecounting, which arises with respect to postal operations, also arises regarding train operations.

4.3. Telecoms

Generally speaking, the allocation of turnover generated by telecom operators is very similar to that which applies to postal undertakings and it is therefore submitted that the same method should be applied.[44] Thus, in the case of telephone calls made from Belgium to Britain, the callers will normally pay a Belgian telecom operator, but this operator must in turn pay a British telecom operator for the use of capacity on the British telephone network. Likewise, where British callers make calls to Belgium, the callers must pay a British telecom operator for the call, and the British operator must in turn pay a Belgian operator for the use of capacity on the Belgian network. The Belgian telecoms operator must count calls from Belgium to Britain as domestic while the British operator must count the payment from the Belgian operator for use of the line as turnover from Belgium. Where the calls have been made from Britain to Belgium, the Belgian operator must count the payment from the British operator as British while the British operator must count the turnover as domestic.[45]

In the case of transit calls, for instance, where the French telecoms operator provides capacity for telephone calls from Belgium to Italy, the turnover generated by the provider of transit capacity must be allocated to the country of the telecom undertaking paying for the capacity.[46]

---

[44] Note also that the question concerning doublecounting arising in the case of postal operations also arises regarding telecom operations.

[45] Earlier the Commission had been doubtful as to whether to apply a method based on a 50/50 approach or whether the turnover should be allocated to the place of the caller. Apparently, the Commission has decided in favour of the latter so that the Commission's approach is in conformity with the one proposed here. It is important to add, however, that the Commission is careful not to publicly settle on a specific solution, *cf. WorldCom/MCI*, Case IV/M1069, decision of 8 July 1998, [1999] OJ L116/1, where the Commission explicitly observed that '[t]here are various possible methods of allocating revenue earned by telephone companies providing services which generate revenue outside the country in which they are based.' However, '[o]n all variants proposed.' the two undertakings concerned would meet the thresholds.

In reality the situation is no different where the receiver (rather than the caller) is partly or fully charged for the call. Earlier, at least, the possibility of using reverse-charge and return-dial calls were only used to a minor extent, cf. Philip Lowe, *Telecommunication Services and Competition Law in Europe*, speech given at the 5th Annual Seminar on 'Telecommunication Services and Competition Law in Europe', Amsterdam 15 April 1994.

[46] Another type of transit call is where, for instance, a Danish businessman uses his American free phone card to make a call from France to Denmark. Here the call will be directed via the

Mobile telephony seems to create a particular situation. If, for instance, a subscriber to Danish TDC's Mobil's GSM system makes a call from Florence, Italy, to Rome, he will be invoiced by TDC who will count this revenue as turnover. TDC will then pay the Italian telecoms operator for the use of the Italian network. It will not be any major problem for TDC to calculate how much turnover has been derived from calls made from outside Denmark; from Community Member States and non-Member States. Thus, it is possible for TDC to allocate the turnover so generated to Italy and it seems to me that this will provide the best reflection of the actual situation. Regarding the Italian telecom operator, the transmission from Florence to Rome was provided to TDC rather than to the Danish subscriber and the payment was made by TDC. Accordingly, in my view, the Italian telecom operator shall allocate this turnover to Denmark.

Long distance cables (often submarine systems) and satellite systems are frequently constructed by a contractor who sells the capacity to a consortium of telecom operators. In the unusual case where the contractor retains ownership of the equipment, it is submitted that the turnover generated must be allocated in accordance with the geographic location of the consortium members.

Example

In *Alcatel/STC*,[47] the French company Alcatel was to acquire STC, a British telecommunications equipment supplier. According to the notifying parties, the concentration had a Community dimension, in particular, they found that STC generated a Community-wide turnover of € 272 million. The parties had found that € 244 million of the Community-wide turnover could be justified on the basis that STC generated this amount 'from contracts for submarine systems having at least one landfall in the EC, i.e. a direct physical link with the Community.'[48] The Commission rejected this approach and stated that rather than the physical link, it is the geographic location of the purchasers of the capacity in the submarine cables which is decisive. The Commission therefore found that the turnover was significantly smaller than what the parties

---

USA and the businessman will be billed as if he had made the call from the USA to Denmark. Nevertheless, it is clear that the American telecoms operator has provided a service to a customer in France and it is therefore submitted that the turnover should be allocated to this country.

47   Case IV/M366, decision of 13 September 1993.

48   Cf. para. 8 of the decision.

had stated in their notification and as a consequence the concentration did not have a Community dimension.[49]

In other words, it is submitted that turnover generated through telecom operations shall be allocated in accordance with the main rule, *i.e.,* to the residence of the purchaser.[50] The only exception to this rule is mobile telephony where the turnover is allocated to the actual place of the caller.[51]

---

[49] *See* also Christopher Jones, 'Case Note: Alcatel/STC', *EC Merger Control Reporter*, Kluwer Law International, The Hague 1991 and later (looseleaf), p. 1180.1, Jacques Zachmann, *Le contrôle communautaire des concentrations*, L.G.D.J., Paris 1994 at p. 88 and B.E. Hawk and H.L. Huser, *supra* note 21 at p. 86. The last-mentioned authors presume that 'the same allocation rule may be applied to other industries involving 'delivery' of goods or services in 'international' areas.' As examples they mention satellite manufacture and/or launch services. In my view the rule laid down in *Alcatel/STC* can only be applied in respect of the sale of transmission capacity of a satellite. In particular I find it difficult to see any reason why the manufacture of a satellite shall be treated any different than the manufacture of other goods for the purposes of calculating the Community dimension.

[50] P. Lowe, *supra* note 45 notes that the Commission has 'decided to base [its] calculation of EC turnover for the time being only on services provided to domestic subscribers (home and international), charges for international calls to other network operators and direct corporate services.' This approach seems to conform with the one set out here. Nevertheless, in the Unisource-concentration involving the Swedish, Dutch and Swiss national telecom-providers one might assume that a different approach has been taken since the Commission apparently found that the concentration did not have a Community dimension. *See* further my article 'A Comment on the Geographic Allocation of Turnover under the Merger Regulation', *European Competition Law Review*, Vol. 18, no. 2, pp. 103-109 at p. 105 with note 9.

[51] In *British Telecom/MCI(II),* Case IV/M856, decision of 14 May 1997, [1997] OJ L336/1, the question arose as to the size of the American telecom undertaking MCI's Community-wide turnover. In para. 8 of the decision the Commission observed 'MCI is a US-based company, and its revenues are treated for accounting purposes as being earned in the United States. There are various possible approaches to the question of geographical allocation of turnover earned by telephone companies on international calls. The parties have provided figures based on different calculation methodologies. On all variants proposed, MCI's Community-wide turnover in 1995 exceeded € 250 million. The parties do not achieve more than two thirds of their Community-wide turnover within one and the same Member State'. As is thus clear, this statement in no way provides any clarification of the issue.

4.4. Banking and insurance

Article 5(3) of the Merger Regulation provides special rules for calculating turn-over regarding credit institutions and other financial institutions and regarding insurance undertakings. I examine this provision, including the geographic alloca-tion of turnover *vis-à-vis* undertakings in the financial sector, in chapter 6, below.[52] I shall therefore not examine this sector here.

4.5. Radio and television

Radio and television may be produced in one country, transmitted from another, the commercials may come from a third country, and the audience may be in a fourth. The effects of a concentration may be felt in all four countries, and it seems doubtful to what degree the turnover thresholds will provide a true reflection of whether a concentration has a Community dimension.

> *Example*
>
> The Scandinavian Broadcasting Company (SBC) is a purely commercial sta-tion which broadcasts to the Scandinavian countries via satellite. The pro-grammes are mostly recorded in Scandinavia, the station broadcasts from London and most of the advertising revenue, amounting to € 200 million per year, is paid by American-based multinationals.

If a major multinational mediagroup, such as US-based AOL Time Warner, ac-quires SBC, the acquisition will not be notifiable under the Merger Regulation as less than half of SBC's turnover of € 200 million is generated from Community-based undertakings so that it will not have a Community-wide turnover of € 100 million as required in the second set of thresholds.[53]

Thus, even larger mergers in the media sector may escape the jurisdiction of the Commission under the Merger Regulation. This is not so much due to the rules on

---

[52] *See* chapter 6, section 2.4 concerning the geographic allocation of turnover regarding credit institutions and other financial institutions and section 3.4 concerning the geographic allo-cation of turnover regarding insurance companies.

[53] The first set of thresholds requires a minimum Community-wide turnover of € 250 million which is obviously not met either.

allocating turnover geographically, however, but to the basic definition of Community dimension.

Moreover, it seems doubtful whether it is really a problem that the Commission cannot vet the merger set out in the above example. Firstly, the purchasers of air time for commercials on the station in question are mostly American so the competition problems caused by a concentration presumably will be most felt in the United States. Secondly, as the concentration does not have a Community dimension, Member States may apply their own merger laws where applicable. Lastly, regardless of whether the Merger Regulation applies, Member States may intervene to protect their legitimate interests such as the plurality of the media.[54]

4.6. The Internet

Sales via the Internet were unknown at the time of the adoption of the Merger Regulation but today have reached a material size.[55] Such sales may be divided

---

[54] Cf. Art. 21(3) of the Merger Regulation. In those merger cases which have been dealt with by the Commission 'aspects of balanced information and pluralism of the media was simply not an issue', cf. Ingrid Nitsche, *Broadcasting in the European Union: The Role of Public Interest in Competition Analysis*, T.M.C. Asser Press, The Hague, 2001, p. 127. *See* also *Pluralism and Media Concentration in the Internal Market – An assessment of the need for Community action*, Commission of the European Communities, COM(92) 480 final, Brussels, 23 December 1992 at pp. 78-79 and 81-88, in particular p. 86. During the 1990s the Commission on more occasions presented a draft for a directive aimed at protecting freedom of speech and freedom of opinion by preventing the concentration of opinion-shaping media. As observed by Ingrid Nitsche (p. 125-126), so far these drafts have not been met with enthusiasm. *See* moreover Martin Schellenberg, 'Europäische Konzentrations-kontrolle im Medienbereich', *Deutsche Zeitschrift für Wirtschaftsrecht*, 1994, No. 10, pp. 410-415.

[55] When the two database service providers DataStar and DIALOG merged in 1993 a reference to the Commission was discussed. However, apparently the transaction fell outside the Commission's jurisdiction, cf. Barry Mahon, 'Barry Mahon looks at the background to the Dialog-Data-Star linkup – What did you expect?', *Information World Review*, May 1993, pp. 5-6, at p. 5. According to the legal counsel to the parent company of the merged entity (Knight Rider Information) '[t]he reason why the Commission was not competent was probably simply because the relevant turnover did not occur in the EU, but in Switzerland and in the USA, where the databases were located, where the customer access took place and where the legal owners where domiciled.' According to the main rule set out above in section 4.1 the residence of the customer should be decisive in allocating turnover in respect of sales of

into two different groups. Firstly, there are those situations where products are ordered via the net (essentially mail order shopping). Secondly, there are those situations where the service is provided on the screen, *e.g.* information from a database. This type may cause considerable problems as concerns the geographic allocation.

Example

> An American company sells information via the net. A purchaser may download the information after making a computer-transfer of money to the seller's account. This means that during a trip to Japan an English businessman may transfer money from his Swiss bank account to download this information to his laptop from the American company's Canadian database. To which country must the American company allocate the turnover so generated?

Today it is possible to make money transfers on the Internet absolutely anonymously[56] and, in such a case, the seller has no possibility of allocating the revenue on a geographic basis. At present, however, in most cases the seller will know at least from what country the money was transferred, while the seller is less likely to know to which country the information is transferred. This means that a likely way to allocate turnover will be on the basis of the location of the bank from which payment was made. As is clear from the above example, this may not be a good reflection of the actual place to which the service is delivered.[57]

The fact that transactions via the Internet may be partly or fully anonymous creates considerable problems when making the geographic allocation of turnover; problems which it appears to be very difficult to solve satisfactorily.[58]

---

information from a database. I therefore do not agree with the explanation provided by legal counsel.

[56] Cf. Bird & Bird, *Internet Law and Regulation* (G.J.H. Smith, ed.), 3rd ed., Sweet & Maxwell, London 2002, p. 512f.

[57] D. Berlin, *supra* note 8 at p. 177 equally observes that e-commerce and the provision of internet services provide considerable problems *vis-à-vis* the geographic allocation of turnover.

[58] Problems with regard to the identification of the correct jurisdiction in connection with commercial activities over the Internet also arise regarding ordinary contract law, cf. Lars Davies and Chris Reed, 'The Trouble with Bits – first steps in Internet law', *Journal of Business Law*, July 1996, pp. 416-430, at p. 424.

5. CHANGES IN THE COMMUNITY TERRITORY

Over the years, the territory of the EC has been expanded several times and it seems likely that more expansions may occur in the years to come as new Member States join the Community. Likewise, it may be that a Member State or a region leaves the Community,[59] that a non-Community State or region becomes part of a Community Member State[60] or that a region changes from being part of one Member State to being part of another, and it may happen that one Member State splits to become more Member States.

Where a change of the Community territory occurs, the question arises as to how this affects the calculation of turnover under the Merger Regulation. In my view, the starting point in answering this question can be found in the very purpose of the Merger Regulation. Hence, concentration control is concerned with the *future* competitive structure of the market.[61] This means that where the borderlines have been altered between the time when the turnover for the calculation of the thresholds was generated and the time when the concentration is made, it must be the new borderlines, not the old, which apply. Turnover generated in a state which has left the Community before the merger transaction must be calculated as non-Community turnover while turnover generated in a state which has joined the Community before the cut-off day (*i.e.* the day of the concentration) must be counted as Community turnover.[62]

---

[59] So far a withdrawal from the Community has only occurred once, namely when in 1985 Greenland, part of the Kingdom of Denmark, was excluded from the Community at its own request. Greenland is now treated as one of the overseas countries and territories under Articles 182-188 of the Treaty, cf. OJ L 29, 1985 at p. 1. *See* also Frederik Harhoff, 'Greenland's Withdrawal from the European Communities', *Common Market Law Review*, vol. 20, 1983, pp. 13-33.

[60] This happened when the then German Democratic Republic joined the then Federal Republic of Germany.

[61] In contrast, Articles 81 and 82 of the Treaty in principle concern behaviour which has occurred.

[62] *See* for example *TWD/Akzo Nobel-Kuagtextil*, Case IV/M533, decision of 10 February 1995 where turnover derived in Austria was counted as Community turnover even though at the time when it was generated, Austria was not part of the Community. Likewise *Starck/ Wienerberger*, Case IV/M702, decision of 1 March 1996.

Example

In 1991, the French company Paribas and the German company MTH notified an agreement with the Commission pursuant to which these parties jointly would acquire control over MBH Maschinenbau- und Technikhandel AG.[63] MBH Maschinenbau- und Technikhandel AG was a former state-owned East German company which had been transformed into a private company in order to be sold to private investors. Paribas achieved a turnover of more than € 250 million in the Community. MBH Maschinenbau- und Technikhandel AG also achieved a turnover of more than € 250 million. This turnover had mostly been achieved in the former Eastern Germany, but, as the transaction was to occur shortly after the German re-unification, this area had become part of the Community at the time of the concentration. The question, therefore, was whether this turnover could be aggregated towards the Community-wide turnover or whether it would have to be counted as non-Community turnover.

The Commission answered this question in the following way:

'MBH achieved most of its turnover in a territory that for part of 1990 did not belong to the European Community. As to the question of determining the size of the Community-wide activities of an undertaking for which, according to Article 1(2) of the Merger Control Regulation, the turnover is the decisive criterion, one has to look at the time when the concentration was carried out, not the financial year preceding the concentration. Article 5(1) of the Merger Control Regulation determines only the reference period for the calculation of the turnover. This provision does not contain any stipulation as to which territorial part of the European Community should be taken into account when considering the Community-wide activities of undertakings. With respect to this question, the general rules, regarding the assessment of the legal-technical characteristics of the undertakings participating in the concentration, such as whether or not they belong to the same group (Art. 5(4)) apply. According to this provision, one should look at the situation at the time of the concentration.'[64]

---

[63] *Paribas/MTH/MBH*, Case IV/M122, decision of 17 October 1991.

[64] Quotation taken from para. 9 of the translation in the EEC Merger Control Reporter, Kluwer Law International, The Hague 1991 and later (looseleaf), p. 458-459. The original decision provides: 'Allerdings erzielte MBH diesen Umsatz in wesentlichen auf einem Gebiet, das in einem Teil des Jahres 1990 noch nicht zur Europäischen Gemeinschaft gehörte. Für die

It thus appears that the Commission's answer to the question is very similar, perhaps even identical, to the answer submitted here.[65]

Frage der Bestimmung des Gewichts der gemeinschaftsbezogenen Aktivitäten eines Unternehmens, für das nach Art. 1 Abs. 2 lit.b der Fusionskontrollverordnung der Umsatz den Größenmaßstab bildet, ist jedoch auf den Zeitpunkt des Vollzuges des Zusammenschlusses abzustellen, nicht aber auf das vor dem Zusammenschluß liegende abgeschlossene Geschäftsjahr. Art. 5 Abs. 1 der Fusionskontrollverordnung legt nur die Referenzperiode für die Umsatzberechnung fest; diese Vorschrift trifft keine Bestimmung darüber auf welshes territoriale Gebiet der Europäischen Gemeinschaft bei der Frage nach den gemeinschaftsbezogenen Aktivitäten der Unternehmen abzustellen ist. Für diese Frage gelten die allgemeinen Regeln für die Bewertung von formalen Eigenschaften der am Zusammenschluß beteiligten Unternehmen, wie z.B. Konzernzugehörigkeit (Art. 5 Abs. 4). Danach ist auf die Situation zum Zeitpunkt des Zusammenschlusses abzustellen.'

65 *See* also G. Drauz and D. Schroeder, *supra* note 30, at p. 10.

6. THE FINANCIAL SECTOR

1. INTRODUCTION

In this chapter, I will examine the Merger Regulation's rules on establishing jurisdiction over companies in the financial sector. Undertakings in this sector create special problems because turnover will reflect their financial strength only to a very limited extent. This is particularly true in respect of banks.[1] In accordance with the approach taken in other areas of Community law,[2] the drafters of the Regulation therefore decided not to use ordinary turnover for defining the Regulation's scope in the financial sector. Originally, the Merger Regulation provided that, in the case of credit institutions and other financial institutions, the turnover thresholds should be calculated on the basis of a special asset test, while in the case of insurance undertakings a figure based on insurance premiums should replace the turnover figures.[3] As part of the 1997 amendment, Article 5(3)(a), concerning the calculation of the thresholds in respect of credit institutions and other financial institutions, was changed so that now the figures must be calculated on the basis of

---

[1] Cf. Sir Leon Brittan, *European Competition Policy – Keeping the Playing-Field Level*, Brassey's London and CEPS Brussels, 1992 at p. 39, but contrast with Blanche Sousi-Roubi and Jacques Zachmann, 'Le contrôle communautaire des concentrations bancaires – La spécifité en question', *Revue de Droit Bancaire et de la Bourse*, No. 36, March/April 1993, pp. 77-85 at p. 81.

[2] Thus, for example Art. 1(2) of the Fourth Council Directive (78/660/EEC) of 25 July 1978 on the annual accounts of certain types of companies, OJ[1978] L222/11 and Art. 40 of the Seventh Council Directive (83/349/EEC) of 13 June 1983 on consolidated accounts, OJ [1983] L193/1 in Art. 1(2) exempt banks and other financial institutions and insurance undertakings from their scope.

[3] Presumably the German Gesetz gegen Wettbewerbsbeschränkungen (Competition Act) provided the original inspiration for delimiting the scope of the Merger Regulation's scope *vis-à-vis* credit institutions and insurance undertakings. Curiously, it appears that the subsequent change of the Merger Regulation in this respect has since been followed by the Germans, *see* now § 38 of the Act.

so-called banking income as defined in Directive 86/635/EEC.[4] In this chapter, I will not consider the old calculation method.[5]

In part 2, below, I examine the problems related to 'credit institutions and other financial institutions' (Article 5(3)(a)) while in part 3, I examine the special provisions which apply to insurance undertakings (Article 5(3)(b)). Difficulties arise where the group of an undertaking concerned includes financial institutions and/or insurance undertakings and/or 'ordinary' undertakings (a so-called mixed group) and this I examine in part 4.

2. CREDIT INSTITUTIONS AND OTHER FINANCIAL INSTITUTIONS

2.1. Background

When the Council adopted the Merger Regulation in 1989, Article 5(3)(a) provided that, in the case of credit institutions and other financial institutions, turnover should be replaced by a special calculation based on the financial institution's assets. At the same time, the Council acknowledged that this asset test was not appropriate with respect to at least some of the financial institutions. Thus, 'Notes on Council Regulation (EEC) 4064/89'[6] – adopted simultaneously with the Merger Regulation – included the following statement:

---

4 Council Directive of 8 December 1986 on the annual accounts and consolidated accounts of banks and other financial institutions, directive 86/635/EEC, OJ L372 of 31 December 1986, pp. 1-17. Hereinafter referred to as the Bank Accounts Directive.

5 An examination of the original method may be found in my article 'The Commission's Jurisdiction over Mergers in the Financial Sector', *Legal Issues of European Integration*, 1996 no. 2, pp. 35-92. An illustrative example of the problems caused by the old calculation method may be found in *Credit Suisse First Boston/Barclays*, Case IV/M1068, decision of 19 December 1997.

6 Published in Supplement 2/90 of the Bulletin of the European Communities at pp 23-26. Concerning these Notes, *see* Alan Dashwood, 'Control of Concentrations in the EEC: The New Council Regulation' in *Le contrôle des concentrations d'entreprises*, F.I.D.E., 14th Congress, Madrid 1990, Vol. III, pp. 21-44 at p. 22.

'te Article 5(3)(a)

The Council and the Commission consider that the criterion defined as a proportion of assets should be replaced by a concept of banking income as referred to in Directive 86/635 on the annual accounts and consolidated accounts of banks and other financial institutions, either at the actual time of entry into force of the relevant provisions of that directive or at the time of the review of thresholds referred to in Article 1 of this regulation and in the light of experience acquired.'

One might wonder why the Council decided to introduce an asset test of an interim nature instead of simply introducing the banking income test right from the beginning. Presumably, the reason was that while Directive 86/635/EEC (the Bank Accounts Directive), which introduced banking income, had to be implemented by 31 December, 1990 the regulations and provisions implementing the Directive would only be applicable to annual accounts and consolidated accounts for financial years beginning during the calendar year 1993.[7] On the face of it, it would be strange to let the Merger Regulation rely on a provision in a directive before this provision were to apply.[8]

In 1993, the Commission tried to amend the Merger Regulation and, as part of this amendment, it proposed that the original asset test should be replaced by a calculation based on banking income. Due to the political climate surrounding the Merger Regulation, however, the revision was postponed. The Commission's second attempt to amend the Regulation, put forward in 1996, again included changing Article 5(3)(a) from being based on assets to being based on banking income.[9]

---

[7] Accord Art. 47(1) and (2) of the Directive.

[8] This argument I examine more closely in my article *supra* note 5 at pp. 47-48.

[9] Concerning the Commission's proposal for a revision, *see* my article 'The EC Commission's Green Paper on the Review of the Merger Regulation', *European Competition Law Review*, Vol. 17, issue 5, 1996 at pp. 289-294 and the Opinion by the Economic and Social Committee on the Review of the Merger Regulation, ECOSOC 1157/95 at point 2.4.2. The Commission's proposal for a revision of Art. 5(3)(a) attracted only limited attention, cf. European Commission, *Communication from the Commission to the Council and to the European Parliament regarding the revision of the Merger Regulation*, COM(96)313 final, Brussels 12.9.1996, p. 35. *See* also Lovell White Durrant, *EU and Competition Law Newsletter*, July 1996 at p. 12. The Commission, nevertheless, retained the change of Art. 5(3)(a) in the proposal finally submitted to the Council, *see* the aforementioned *Communication from the Commission* at para. 30 and Eric Cuziat, 'La revision du règlement sur le contrôle

When, in 1997, the Council finally agreed to amend the Regulation the amendment included a change of Article 5(3)(a) in accordance with the Commission's proposal.

Article 5(3)(a) now provides the following:

'In place of turnover the following shall be used

... for credit institutions and other financial institutions, as regards Article 1(2) and (3), the sum of the following income items as defined in Directive 86/635/EEC ... after deduction of value added tax and other taxes directly related to those items, where appropriate:

(i) interest income and similar income;

(ii) income from securities:

– income from shares and other variable yield securities;

– income from participating interests;

– income from shares in affiliated undertakings;

(iii) commissions receivable;

(iv) net profit on financial operations;

(v) other operating income.

The turnover of a credit or financial institution in the Community or in a Member State shall comprise the income items, as defined above, which are received by the branch or division of that institution established in the Community or in the Member State in question, as the case may be'.

The terms 'credit institutions and other financial institutions' cover a surprisingly wide range of undertakings. In section 2.2, I provide a definition of these. Subsequently, in section 2.3, I look into the problems which banking income may create and, in section 2.4, I look at how one makes the geographic allocation of banking income.

---

des concentrations – La proposition de la Commission', *Competition Policy Newsletter*, Vol. 2, No. 2, Summer 1996, pp. 9-11 at p. 11.

2.2. The definition of 'credit institutions and other financial institutions'

The Merger Regulation itself does not provide a definition of 'credit institutions and other financial institutions'. Similar terms have, however, been defined in Community banking law, namely in the Banking Directives, and the Commission has expressed its willingness to apply those definitions.[10] The Commission does not, however, consider these definitions to be binding.

I agree that the definitions laid down in the banking directives do not bind the interpretation of the Merger Regulation. First of all, nothing in the Merger Regulation obliges the Commission to apply the definitions laid down in the banking directives.[11] Moreover, the definition has changed over time meaning that the banking directives do not provide an unequivocal definition.[12]

---

[10] Thus, in the Commission notice on calculation of turnover under Council Regulation (EEC) No 4064/89 of 21 December 1989 on the control of concentrations between undertakings, OJ C66/25, 2.3.1998, (herinafter referred to as Turnover Calculation Notice) at paras. 51-52 the Commission expressly refers to the definitions laid down in the First Banking Directive (First Council Directive 77/780/EEC of 12 December 1977 on the coordination of laws, regulations and administrative provisions relating to the taking up and pursuit of the business of credit institutions, OJ [1977] L322 at pp. 30-37) and the Second Banking Directive (Council Directive 89/646/EEC of 15 December 1989 on the coordination of laws, regulations and administrative provisions relating to the taking up and pursuit of the business of credit institutions and amending Directive 77/780/EEC OJ [1989] L386 pp. 1-13). Also in *GECC/AVIS LEASE*, Case IV/M234, decision of 15 July 1992 the Commission explicitly made a reference to the First and the Second Banking Directives when deciding whether Avis Lease was a financial institution, cf. footnote 1 to para. 8 of the decision. *See* also Norbert Gugerbauer, *Handbuch der Fusionskontrolle – Kommentar zur Verordnung Nr. 4064/89 des Rates über die Kontrolle von Unternehmenszusammenschlüssen und zu den §§ 41ff KartG*, Verlag Orac, Wien 1995 at p. 158 who refers to the Banking Directives for a definition of the terms.

[11] Cf. B. Sousi-Roubi and J. Zachmann, *supra* note 1 at p. 79.

[12] *See* Council Directive (EEC) 83/350 of 13 June 1983 on the supervision of credit institutions on a consolidated basis, OJ [1983] 193/18 (later repealed by Council Directive 92/30/EEC of 6 April 1992 on the supervision of credit institutions on a consolidated basis, OJ [1992] L110/52) which provided a definition of 'financial institutions' that was slightly different from the one found in the Second Banking directive. In the words of Anthony Thompson, *The Second Banking Directive*, Butterworth & Co. (Publishers) Ltd., London 1991, at p. 22: 'The net has been cast more broadly' in the Second Banking Directive as compared with the 1983 Directive. *See* also B. Sousi-Roubi and J. Zachmann, *supra* note 1 at p. 79.

In practice, the Commission applies the definition found in the banking directives and I shall therefore explain this definition here.

The First Banking Directive[13] Article 1, first indent provides that:

> "'credit institution" means an undertaking whose business is to receive deposits or other repayable funds from the public and to grant credits for its own account.'[14]

In practice, this definition covers banks, savings banks and mortgage institutions. The Second Banking Directive[15] Article 1(6) provides that:

> "'financial institution" shall mean an undertaking other than a credit institution the principal activity of which is to acquire holdings or to carry on one or more of the activities listed in point 2 to 12 in the Annex;'

The Annex gives the following list of activities in point 2 to 12:

- Lending.[16]
- Financial leasing.
- Money transmission services.
- Issuing and administering means of payment.[17]
- Guarantees and commitments.

---

13 *Supra* note 11.

14 The Directive exempts certain credit institutions from falling within the definition, but these exemptions do not affect the definition of a credit institution as such, cf. the Second Banking Directive, *supra* note 11, Art. 1(1). Paolo Clarotti, 'The Harmonization of Legislation Relating to Credit Institutions', *Common Market Law Review*, no. 2, 1982, pp. 245-267, at pp. 248-253 points out certain problems flowing from the definition. *See* also Gert Uwe Lanzke, 'Umsetzung und Anwendung der europäischen Bankrichtlinien durch die Mitgliedstaaten', *Wertpapier Mitteilungen – Zeitschrift für Wirtschafts- und Bankrecht*, Vol. 48, 1994, pp. 2001-2010 in particular pp. 2002-2003 and Udo-Olaf Bader, 'Inhalt und Bedeutung der 2. Bankrechtskoordinierungsrichtlinie – ein EG-Grundgesetz für die Banken?', *Europäische Zeitschrift für Wirtschaftsrecht*, issue 4, 1990, pp. 117-122 at p. 119.

15 *Supra* note 11.

16 Including *inter alia*: consumer credit, mortgage credit, factoring, with or without recourse, financing of commercial transactions (including forfeiting).

17 *E.g.* credit cards, traveller's cheques and bankers' drafts.

- Trading on one's own behalf or on behalf of customers in:

    (a) money market instruments (cheques, bills, bills CDs, etc.);

    (b) foreign exchange;

    (c) financial futures and options;

    (d) exchange and interest rate instruments;

    (e) transferable securities.

- Participation in share issues and the provision of services related to such issues.

- Advice to undertakings on capital structure, industrial strategy and related questions and advice and services relating to mergers and the purchase of undertakings.

- Money brokering.

- Portofolio management and advice.

- Safekeeping and administration of securities.

The definition of financial institutions as laid down in the Second Banking Directive covers a broad spectrum of undertakings. Probably the most surprising is that holding companies are also covered by the definition, so that, in particular, income from shares in companies which are not controlled as defined in Article 5(4) (*i.e.* portfolio assets) must be counted as 'turnover' together with the turnover of undertakings which are under Article 5(4) control by the holding company.[18] In *Torras/ Sarrio,*[19] the Commission had to deal with a holding company. In that case, the Commission followed the same interpretation as the one set out here.[20]

---

[18] *See* further part 4 below. This approach does not differ from the one which applies to all other financial institutions. In para. 62 of the Turnover Calculation Notice the Commission advises that '[i]n practice, the turnover of the financial holding company (non-consolidated) must first be taken into account. Then the turnover of the Art. 5(4) companies must be added, whilst taking care to deduct dividends and other income distributed by those companies to the financial holdings ...'

[19] Case IV/M166, decision of 24 February 1992.

[20] Frank L. Fine, *Mergers and Joint Ventures in Europe – The Law and Policy of the EEC*, 2nd ed., Graham & Trotman, London 1994, at pp. 175-176 takes a sceptical stance to the Commission's view that the holding company in this case should be considered a credit or other financial institution. Likewise Barry E. Hawk and Henry L. Huser, *European Community Merger Control: A Practitioner's Guide*, Kluwer Law International, The Hague 1996 at pp. 89-90. *See* also my article *supra* note 5 at pp. 55-56. The Italian Anti-trust Act 287 of

2.3. Banking income under the Merger Regulation

Today, all banks in the Member States must prepare their accounts in accordance with the Bank Accounts Directive which means that the banks must now give a banking income figure in their accounts. As shown above, banking income is found by adding together the following five income items:

- Interest income and similar income;
- Income from securities;
- Commissions receivable;
- Net profit on financial operations;
- Other operating income.

Two problems in particular deserve special mention in this regard.

The first problem is that the Bank Accounts Directive provides two alternative layouts of the profit and loss account. With respect to banking income, the difference between these two layouts is that one includes only net profits on financial operations while the other also allows the banks to include net losses on such operations.[21] The problem arises if a bank suffers considerable losses on its financial operations since this may significantly decrease the size of the banking income. Indeed, in exceptional cases, the loss may exceed the total of the four other income items so that the total banking income becomes negative.

In other words, in principle, large losses on financial operations may significantly reduce the banking income figure and even lead to a negative figure. One may imagine the problem of establishing a Community dimension if three banks plan to merge and one has a banking income of € 1.5 billion, the second

---

10 October 1990 to a large extent mirrors the EC competition rules. Regarding concentrations the Act provides that the Italian competition authority has jurisdiction where a certain turnover threshold has been met and regarding banks and financial institutions turnover is replaced by one-tenth of assets. However, holding companies which do not operate directly on the market follows the general rule based on turnover and not the exception based on assets, according to Paolo Criscione, 'The Italian Anti-trust Act: Three Years Later', *European Competition Law Review*, issue 2, 1994, pp. 108-112, at p. 110.

21 The Bank Accounts Directive in Art. 27 point 6 provides the Member States with the option of requiring the banks to include: 'Net profit or net loss on financial operations' while Art. 28(B) point 4 provides the Member States with the option of requiring the banks to include only: 'Net profit on financial operations'.

has a banking income of € 1.0 billion and the last one has a banking income of
€ – 0.1 billion. Does it meet the € 2.5 billion threshold?

In order to avoid this type of problem, Article 5(3)(a) explicitly requires that
only net profit on financial operations be taken into account. Hence, where a bank
has included a net loss on financial operations for the purpose of calculating its
banking income, it will be necessary to make a minor adjustment (*i.e.* to 'neutral-
ise' this negative figure) when a Community dimension is going to be established.

The second problem is that banking income may change very significantly from
year to year. The consequence is that the definition of Community dimension will
produce an allocation of jurisdiction *vis-à-vis* credit institutions which is more
arbitrary than the allocation of jurisdiction *vis-à-vis* ordinary undertakings.[22] Put
differently, the dramatic fluctuations are likely to lead to rather haphazard results
as to which banking concentrations are to be vetted by the Commission and which
are not. It appears difficult to find a workable solution to avoid this problem which
is inherent in banking income. It seems that the only apparent solution is to base
the Community dimension figure on the average banking income for more than
just one year. This solution is, however, not available since the Merger Regulation
in Article 5(1) requires the Community dimension to be based on the figures of
'the preceding financial year'. No other workable solution seems to be apparent.

2.4. Geographic allocation of banking income

Article 5(3)(a) *in fine* provides:

> 'The turnover of a credit or financial institution in the Community or in a
> Member State shall comprise the income items, as defined above, which are
> received by the branch or division of that institution established in the Com-
> munity or in the Member State in question, as the case may be;'

Basically, banking services are not much different from other services. In chapter
5, above, I find that, regarding services which the purchaser does not have to go to
the service provider to obtain, an allocation of turnover based on the purchaser's
residence should be applied. Article 5(3)(a) provides a different rule. Thus, it

---

[22] This was one of the main reasons why the Banking Advisory Committee, set up in accordance with Art. 11 of the First Banking Directive, doubted that the banking income test would
be better than the asset test. *See* further my article, *supra* note 5 at p. 59.

requires that turnover is allocated according to the location of the bank.[23] The difference between the residence principle and the location principle is particularly clear where the 'turnover' is generated by a branch established in a different State. For instance, if a British branch of a German company pays a commission to a London-based branch of a German bank, the German bank will have to allocate this 'turnover' to Britain, even though the residence (*i.e.* the place of incorporation) of the customer is Germany.[24]

3. INSURANCE UNDERTAKINGS

3.1. Introduction

When the Merger Regulation was adopted on 21 December, 1989, the Insurance Accounts Directive[25] had not yet been adopted but only existed in the form of a proposal.[26] This fact is important to observe because Article 5(3)(b) is drafted from Articles 30 and 31 of the Proposal Directive.[27] However, in the finally adopted Insurance Accounts Directive the equivalent provisions in Articles 35 and 36 have been altered so that the wording now differs fairly significantly from that of the Proposal Directive. This means that we now have a Community definition of

---

23 The original Art. 5(3)(a) referred to the residence of the recipients of loans and advances from the bank.

24 The Commission in the Turnover Calculation Notice at para. 54 somewhat confusingly refers to 'the residence of the branch or division'. The reference to the 'residence' of a 'branch' indicates that in reality the Commission refers to the location principle, not the residence principle.

25 Council Directive of 19 December 1991 on the annual accounts and consolidated accounts of insurance undertakings (91/674/EEC), OJ [1991] L374/7. Herinafter referred to as the Insurance Accounts Directive.

26 Amended proposal for a Council Directive on the annual accounts and consolidated accounts of insurance undertakings, COM(89) 474 final – SYN 78 [Submitted by the Commission pursuant to Art. 149(3) of the EEC Treaty on 30 October 1989] (90/C 30/04) published in OJ [1990] C30/51. Hereinafter referred to as the Proposal Directive.

27 This is particularly clear regarding the English version of the Proposal Directive. *See* also Lennart Ritter, W. David Braun and Francis Rawlinson, *EEC Competition Law – a practitioner's guide*, 1st edition, Kluwer, Deventer 1991 at p. 356 with note 86.

the term 'gross premiums', but the way that this term is defined in the Merger Regulation differs, at least regarding the wording, from the definition found in the Insurance Accounts Directive.

The insurance undertakings in the Community must prepare their accounts in accordance with the provisions (as they have been implemented by the Member States) of the Insurance Accounts Directive. The question therefore arises whether it is possible simply to use these figures even though the definition of 'gross premiums' in the Merger Regulation differs from the definition in the directive, or whether it is necessary to adapt the figures for the purpose of establishing a Community dimension. Before looking at this question, however, I will provide a definition of an insurance undertaking.

3.2. Definition of an insurance undertaking

The Merger Regulation does not define what precisely is covered by the term 'insurance undertakings' in Article 5(3)(b). A guideline may be found in other Community legislation, and, in particular, reference to the Insurance Accounts Directive may be helpful in this respect. The Insurance Accounts Directive applies to all Member States[28] and works independently of the Member States's own (differing) definitions. Moreover, using the Insurance Accounts Directive as a guideline will make it easier to draw a dividing line between insurance undertakings and financial institutions, as we can simply follow the dividing line drawn between the Insurance Accounts Directive and the Bank Accounts Directive.

The Insurance Accounts Directive 'covers all insurance undertakings carrying on direct insurance, including mutuals and cooperatives and Lloyd's, with the exception only of certain small mutuals. It also covers specialist reinsurers.'[29]

---

[28]   The national measures to implement the Insurance Accounts Directive had to be adopted before 1 January 1994. The national measures were required to apply to accounts for financial years beginning during the calendar year 1995, cf. Art. 70(2) of the Directive.

[29]   Cf. Bill Pool, *The creation of the internal market in insurance*, Office for Official Publications of the European Communities, Luxembourg 1990, at p. 86. *See* also Julian Maitland-Walker, *EC Insurance Directives*, Lloyd's of London Press Ltd., 1992 at paras. 7.3-7.6. (Julian Maitland-Walker is commenting on the Proposal Directive, not on the adopted directive). In *La Roche/Syntex*, Case IV/M457, decision of 20 June 1994, the Commission in para. 5 observes that it has calculated the turnover 'in accordance with Article 5(3)(b)'. However, according to the decision the two undertakings concerned were primarily active in

In particular, it is noteworthy that both direct insurers and reinsurers are included[30] and that certain undertakings, which will normally be classified as pension funds, are also covered.[31]

Insurance underwriting is done by insurance undertakings. Insurance brokering[32] is done by an intermediary between the insurance undertaking and the policy holder. This means that the broker is providing a service, but not providing insurance cover or receiving an insurance premium. Article 5(3)(b) only concerns underwriting.[33] An insurance underwriter can also act as an insurance broker, however, for instance where life/non-life insurance is not allowed in the same company. The consequence is that where the brokering activity and the underwriting activity are carried out through one and the same legal entity, the calculation of turnover, as provided in Article 5(3)(b), will not be able to include the brokering activity.[34]

---

the development and marketing of pharmaceuticals, diagnostics and vitamins. It is therefore difficult to understand why the Commission has applied Art. 5(3)(b) in this case.

30 Regarding reinsurance *see* for instance *ERC/NRG Victory*, Case IV/M433, decision of 27 May 1994 *General Re/Kölnische Re*, Case IV/M491, decision of 24 October 1994 and *Employers Reinsurance Corporation/Aachener Rückversicherungs-Gesellschaft AG*, Case IV/M601, decision of 30 June 1995.

31 Thus for instance Margaret Jordan 'European Community', *International Financial Law Review* – Special supplement, March 1991 pp. 13-18 at p. 13 writes that 'in some Member States life insurance may be linked to savings or investments which make it more akin to a savings or pension scheme than a pure insurance policy.' Note also *AEGON/Scottish Equitable*, Case IV/M349, decision of 25 June 1993, which in para. 3 provides that Scottish Equitable Life Assurance Society's 'principal activity is the transaction of life assurance, *pension* and annuity business' (emphasis added). *See* also *Nordic Capital/Transpool*, Case IV/M625, decision of 23 August 1995.

32 *See* Council Directive of 13 December 1976 on measures to facilitate the effective exercise of freedom of establishment and freedom to provide services in respect of activities of insurance agents and brokers (ex ISIC group 630) and, in particular, transitional measures in respect of those activities (77/92/EEC) published in OJ [1977] L26/14 (validity of the directive expires in January 2005).

33 An undertaking, which is exclusively dealing in insurance brokering and which does not hold a concession to carry out insurance underwriting, does not come within the definition of an insurance undertaking.

34 The result will be different if these two activities are carried out through separate legal entities. *See* further part 4 below. *See* also *ASKO/Omni*, Case IV/M065, decision of 21 February 1991, annotated by Charles Price and Paul Maeyaert in *EC Merger Control Reporter*, Kluwer Law International, The Hague 1991 and later (looseleaf) at pp. 88.1.

3.3. Gross premiums written

3.3.1. Introduction

Article 5(3)(b) provides that:

> 'the value of gross premiums written which shall comprise all amounts re-
> ceived and receivable in respect of insurance contracts issued by or on behalf
> of the insurance undertakings, including also outgoing reinsurance premi-
> ums, and after deduction of taxes and parafiscal contributions or levies charged
> by reference to the amounts of individual premiums or the total volume of
> premiums …'

Below, I will examine each of the links in the above definition of gross premiums.

3.3.2. Amounts received and receivable

The terms 'all amounts received and receivable' in Article 5(3)(b) were taken from
Article 30(2), first subparagraph of the Proposal Directive. This formulation was
considered to be somewhat imprecise so it was changed in the adopted Insurance
Accounts Directive to 'all amounts due …'. No substantive change of the definition
in the Proposal Directive was intended. Consequently, even though the two wordings
are different, the contents are intended to be identical, so it appears reasonable not
to divert from the Insurance Accounts Directive on this point. In other words, it is
submitted that where an insurance undertaking has prepared its accounts in accordance with the Insurance Accounts Directive, no correction is required on this
point for the purposes of calculating the Community dimension.

Another question is whether the term 'premiums' covers all premiums related
to contracts in force during the accounting year being considered, or whether only
premiums relating to new insurance contracts made during this accounting
year should be taken into account. The Commission, in its Turnover Calculation
Notice,[35] notes that the former of these two approaches must be used. I agree with
this conclusion. The intention is to measure the economic strength of the undertakings concerned. The full portfolio of contracts provides a much better reflection of

---

[35] Para. 56, second indent.

this strength than if only the new contracts are considered, thereby supporting the Commission's interpretation.[36]

3.3.3. Contracts issued by or on behalf of the insurance undertakings

The terms 'in respect of insurance contracts issued by or on behalf of the insurance undertakings' have also been taken from Article 30(2), first subparagraph of the Proposal Directive. The Insurance Accounts Directive does not include an equivalent formulation, however. The meaning of the terms is that it is immaterial whether the gross premiums have been written directly by the insurance undertaking itself or through an intermediary, *i.e.* through an agent or broker.

The usual understanding of the concept of 'gross premiums' is that it covers directly written as well as indirectly written premiums. This is also how Article 35 of the Insurance Accounts Directive is interpreted. Put differently, there is no substantive difference between the Directive and the Merger Regulation on this point. It is therefore submitted that Article 5(3)(b) shall be interpreted in accordance with the Insurance Accounts Directive on this point as well.

3.3.4. Outgoing reinsurance premiums

The terms 'outgoing reinsurance premiums' come from Article 31 of the Proposal Directive. In Article 36 of the Insurance Accounts Directive the terms have been changed to 'outward reinsurance premiums'. This change in itself appears to be immaterial. The definition of 'outward reinsurance premiums' in the Insurance Accounts Directive is, however, different from that of 'outgoing reinsurance premiums' in the Proposal Directive. Article 31 of the Proposal Directive provided:

> 'Outgoing reinsurance premiums shall comprise all amounts paid and payable in respect of outgoing reinsurance contracts entered into by the insurance undertaking.'

Article 36 of the Insurance Accounts Directive provides:

---

[36] Indeed, one may imagine that in a given market a small non-dominant insurance undertaking would be able to underwrite more new insurance contracts during one year than would the old dominant insurance undertaking. If only those new insurance contracts underwritten during the last year were to be taken into account, the result would be very misleading for the purposes of establishing the economic strength of these two undertakings.

'Outward reinsurance premiums shall comprise all premiums paid or payable in respect of outward reinsurance contracts entered into by an insurance undertaking. Portfolio entries payable on the conclusion or amendment of outward reinsurance contracts shall be added; portfolio withdrawals receivable must be deducted.'

The first link of the two definitions are identical. The Insurance Accounts Directive has added an extra link to its definition, however, and the question therefore is whether this addition carries with it a material difference.

The term 'gross premiums' in itself includes 'outgoing reinsurance premiums'. Thus, by proclaiming (in Art. 5(3)(b)) that gross premiums shall also include outgoing reinsurance premiums, the provision only provides that something which has already been included in the gross premiums shall not thereafter be deducted from them. In other words, the inclusion of the formulation 'including also outgoing reinsurance premiums' in Article 5(3)(b) of the Merger Regulation does not have any material relevance regarding the definition of the term 'gross premiums'.[37]

3.3.5. *Taxes and parafiscal contributions or levies*

Article 5(3)(b) provides that 'taxes and parafiscal contributions or levies charged by reference to the amounts of individual premiums or the total volume of premiums' must be deducted from the gross premiums. Again, the wording is (almost entirely) taken from the Proposal Directive.[38] And again, the terms have been significantly altered in the Insurance Accounts Directive which provides:

'The above amounts shall not include the amounts of taxes or charges levied with premiums.'[39]

Both definitions require that taxes[40] and charges[41] levied with the premiums must

---

[37] For the same conclusion, *see* Turnover Calculation Notice, para. 56, first indent.

[38] Art. 30, *in fine* of the Proposal Directive.

[39] Cf. Art. 35, *in fine* of the Insurance Accounts Directive.

[40] An example is a German insurance tax referred to in Clifford Chance, *Insurance in the EEC – The European Community's Programme for a New Regime*, 2nd edition, Lloyd's of London Press Ltd., London 1991 at p. 61.

[41] An example of this is the annual charge on authorised insurers in Ireland, cf. Clifford Chance, *supra* note 40 at p. 65.

be deducted from the gross premiums. The term 'charges' is the equivalent of 'parafiscal contributions or levies' so to levy a tax or a charge with the premium simply means that it is levied with reference to the amounts of individual premiums or the total volume of premiums. Thus, on this point there is no material difference.

On one point, it seems, however, that the two definitions do differ in a material respect. Thus, Article 5(3)(b) provides '… charged by reference to the amounts of individual premiums or the total volume of premiums' while the Insurance Accounts Directive provides '… levied with premiums'. The latter formulation might be construed to be broader than the former so that it also covers charges and taxes which are levied with the premiums, though without such charge or tax being charged by reference to the amounts of the premiums.

On the one hand, the Insurance Accounts Directive does not bind the interpretation of Article 5(3)(b), it only provides guidance. On the other hand, the insurance undertakings in the Community must now prepare their accounts in accordance with the Directive. It seems to me that to require these undertakings to provide new accounts solely for the purpose of establishing jurisdiction should only be done if there are convincing reasons for this. In my view, this is primarily so where the preparation of new accounts is necessary to make the Merger Regulation apply evenly throughout the Community. In this case, this does not appear to be the situation, however. Accordingly, in my view, Article 5(3)(b) should be interpreted in the light of the Insurance Accounts Directive on this point also.

3.3.6. Premiums from the reserves for reimbursement in life insurance

Article 35 of the Insurance Accounts Directive provides that national legislation may require or permit that the insurance undertakings calculate the premiums from the reserves for reimbursement in life insurance as gross premiums.[42] Thus, the Member States are given a choice on this point and (at least) in Germany such calculation is admissible.

'Premiums from the reserves for reimbursement in life insurance' are not premiums paid in by the insurance taker. Rather, they cover certain changes in the

---

[42] Art. 35 provides: 'Gross premiums … shall include *inter alia* … in life assurance, single premiums resulting from bonus and rebate provisions in so far as they must be considered as premiums on the basis of contracts and where national legislation requires or permits their being shown under premiums'. The Proposal Directive included an equivalent provision in Art. 30(2)(a).

accounts. These 'premiums' might be of a significant size. Hence, to calculate them as gross premiums would mean that measuring the financial strength of life insurance undertakings in different Member States would be done on an uneven basis since, in some Member States, the gross premiums would include 'premiums from the reserves for reimbursement in life insurance' while in others they would not.

The Commission in *Allianz/DKV* held the following regarding this problem:

> 'Allianz and DKV did not achieve their respective Community-wide turn-over within one and the same Member State.[43] With regard to Allianz, the premiums from the reserves for reimbursements in life insurance, amounting to € 1 billion were not taken into account. They are a surplus from life insurance which is credited to the beneficiaries every year.
>
> In its balance sheet, Allianz adds these credits to its premium income, which is admissible under German law. However, these credits are not gross premium received within the meaning of Article 5(3)(b) of the Merger Control Regulation. The premiums from the reserves for reimbursements are already a benefit under the insurance contract. Even though they are called a premium they do not affect the obligation to pay premiums and they do not lead to the conclusion of an additional insurance contract. The gross premium income of Allianz in Germany thus is € 11.5 billion and therefore constitutes less than two-thirds of its Community-wide turnover of € 17.4 billion.
>
> ...'[44]

---

[43] Apparently there is a flaw in the Commission decision at this point. What is meant is that Allianz and DKV did not achieve *more than two-thirds of* their respective Community-wide turnover within one and the same Member State.

[44] Cf. *Allianz/DKV*, Case IV/M252, decision of 10 September 1992 at para. 5. It is worthy of note, that if the Commission had not applied this interpretation Allianz would have achieved more than two-thirds of its Community-wide turnover within Germany. The English translation has been taken from the *EC Merger Control Reporter*, Kluwer Law International, The Hague 1991 and later (looseleaf) at pp. 889-890. The original version provides the following:

> 'Allianz und DKV erzielten ihren jeweiligen gemeinschaftsweiten Umsatz nicht in einem und demselben Mitgliedstaat. Dabei bleiben bei der Allianz die Beiträge aus der Rückstellung für Rückerstattung in der Lebensversicherung in Höhe von 1 Mrd. € unberücksichtigt. Hierbei handelt es sich um Überschüsse aus der Lebensversicherung, die den Versicherungsnehmern jährlich gutgeschrieben werden.

Adding premiums from the reserves for reimbursement in life insurance to the gross premium may significantly inflate the gross premium figure. If the Merger Regulation is to apply evenly throughout the Community, it is necessary to adjust at least for the more significant differences. In my opinion, the Commission's approach in *Allianz/DKV* therefore appears to be sound.

3.4. The definition of 'residence' in Article 5(3)(b)

3.4.1. Introduction

The majority of the thresholds laid down in Article 1(2) and (3) of the Merger Regulation require a geographic allocation of the turnover. Where the turnover is calculated in accordance with Article 5(3)(b), this allocation must be made on the basis of the *residence* of the customers from whom gross premiums have been received.[45] Below, I shall first provide an explanation of the residence criterion and, next, I shall provide some guidelines for the application thereof. Then I will review the Commission's interpretation of the criterion before I end with an evaluation of it.

Die Allianz rechnet diese Gutschriften zwar in ihrer Bilanz den Beitragseinnahmen hinzu, was nach deutschem Recht zulässig ist. Doch handelt es sich hierbei um keine vereinnahmten Bruttoprämien im Sinne von Artikel 5 Absatz 3 Punkt b) der Fusionskontrollverordnung. Die Beiträge aus der Rückstellung für Rückerstattung sind bereits eine Leistung aus dem Versicherungsvertrag. Obwohl als Beitrag bezeichnet, berühren sie die Prämienzahlungspflicht nicht und bewirken auch nicht den Abschluß eines zusätzlichen Versicherungsvertrages. Die aus Deutschland stammenden Brutto-Prämien-einnahmen der Allianz belaufen sich deshalb auf 11,5 Mrd. € und machen damit weniger als zwei Drittel des gemeinschaftsweiten Umsatzes in Höhe von 17,4 Mrd. € aus.
...'

45 Residence is a commonly used concept in Community law, though no general Community definition exists. Instead the different areas of the law, where residence is a relevant concept, have developed their own definition. For examples, *see* my article, *supra* note 5 at p. 83, note 149.

3.4.2. Residence explained

The present Implementing Regulation accompanying the Merger Regulation does not contain a definition of residence.[46] Neither does the Turnover Calculation Notice include an explicit definition. The first Implementing Regulation[47] did, however, in footnote 1 to section 2 of the annexed Form CO, include such explicit definition which *inter alia* provided the following:

> 'For insurance undertakings … Community-residents and residents of a Member State are defined as natural or legal persons having their residence in a Member State, thereby following the respective national legislation. The corporate customer is to be treated as resident in the country in which it is legally incorporated.'

This definition is not perfectly clear, but there can hardly be any doubt that it provides that residence must be interpreted in accordance with national legislation.[48] Moreover, it is obvious that applying the definitions laid down in national legislation may provide a somewhat ambiguous result. For instance, under English law, a person can be resident in more than one place at the same time,[49] and frequently a Member State will have one definition for the purpose of taxation and

---

[46] Commission Regulation (EC) No 447/98 of 1 March 1998 on the notifications, time limits and hearings provided for in Council Regulation (EEC) No 4064/89 on the control of concentrations between undertakings, OJ L61/1 of 2.3.1998. The same is true as concerns the previous Implementing Regulation, Commission Regulation (EC) No 3384/94 of 21 December 1994 on the notifications, time limits and hearings provided for in Council Regulation (EEC) No 4064/89 on the control of concentrations between undertakings, OJ L377/1 of 31.12.1994.

[47] Commission Regulation (EEC) No 2367/90 of 25 July 1990 on the notifications, time limits and hearings provided for in Council Regulation (EEC) No 4064/89 on the control of concentrations between undertakings, OJ L219 of 14.8.1990.

[48] C.J. Cook and C.S. Kerse, *EEC Merger Control Regulation 4064/89*, 1st ed., Sweet & Maxwell, London 1991, at p. 57 write that '[i]n the absence of a definition of 'residents' the Commission may turn to the practice in Member States under the Capital Movements Directives, although this may produce an uneven result.' Thus, it would seem that these authors take the view that the definition of residence must be based on the exchange regulations in force in each Member State.

[49] Cf. Trevor C. Hartley, *Civil Jurisdiction and Judgments*, Sweet & Maxwell, London 1984, p. 33.

another for the purpose of naturalisation. Which definition shall apply in the case of Article 5(3)(b) of the Merger Regulation is not clear.

Perhaps due to these problems, the Commission deleted the definition of residence in the 1994 Implementing Regulation and replaced it with a different implicit definition in the 1994-Turnover Calculation Notice. In 1998 the Commission even abandoned this implicit definition.

What the original definition provided was:

 – In the case of *natural persons,* the definition of residence as laid down in the Member States' national legislations shall apply.

 – In the case of *legal persons,* the place of incorporation is decisive.

What the 1994-Implementing Regulation provided together with the 1994-Turnover Calculation Notice was:

 – In the case of *natural persons,* the allocation shall be based on residence. No definition of residence is provided.

 – In the case of *legal persons,* the allocation shall be based on residence. Residence is presumed to be the place of incorporation.[50] Nevertheless, 'branches, divisions and other undertakings operating on a lasting basis but not having a legal personality [shall] be considered as residents in the countries in which they have been established.'[51]

In the currently applicable version of the Implementing Regulation and of the Turnover Calculation Notice (both from 1998) there is no guidelines *vis-à-vis* the definition of residence in Article 5(3)(b).

3.4.3. Applying the residence criterion

In the first edition of this work I tried to show why in my view the definition of residence put forward by the Commission in the 1994 Implementing Regulation was flawed.[52] Since that definition has not been reiterated in the currently applica-

---

[50] Paras. 66 and 67 of Commission Notice on calculation of turnover under Council Regulation (EEC) No 4064/89 of 21 December 1989 on the control of concentrations between undertakings, OJ C385/21 of 31.12.1994 (1994-Turnover Calculation Notice) read in conjunction.

[51] Para. 67 of the 1994-Turnover Calculation Notice.

[52] *See* pp. 162-165.

ble Implementing Regulation, in the current edition of this work I will limit myself to explaining how, in my opinion, the notion of residence in Article 5(3)(b) should be construed.

It is obviously an almost insurmountable task to ascertain the residence of every single insurance taker when applying the residence criterion in the case of natural persons. It therefore appears justifiable to make a rebuttable presumption that the insurance taker is resident at the place of the insurer. In most cases of insurance contracts, underwritten with natural persons, the insurance taker is likely to be resident in the country where the underwriting insurer is established.[53] If, however, a UK insurance company sells a property insurance policy to a French national resident in Paris in respect of a Spanish holiday villa, the presumption is rebutted and the insurance company must treat these premiums as turnover earned in France. As Article 5(3)(b) explicitly refers to the residence of the person paying the insurance premium, the turnover cannot be considered to be earned in the UK.[54]

Where the insurance taker is a legal person, it is submitted that the place of incorporation must be considered to be the place of residence. Just as in the case of natural persons, however, one may in most cases reasonably presume that the insurance taker is incorporated at the place where the insurance provider provides the insurance thereby avoiding difficult and costly examinations only in order to establish jurisdiction.[55]

---

[53]   *See* also Gerard Dickinson, 'Insurance' in *European Economy – Market services and European integration – The challenges for the 1990s*, 1993, no. 3 (Pierre Buigues, Fabienne Ilzkovitz, J.-F. Lebrun and André Sapir, eds.), pp. 183-210 at p. 193.

[54]   Example taken from C.J. Cook and C.S. Kerse, *supra* note 48, p. 45.

[55]   For the purpose of defining 'residence' it might be worthwhile interpreting this in the light of the interpretation given to this term in Second Council Directive 88/357/EEC of 22 June 1988 on the coordination of laws, regulations and administrative provisions relating to direct insurance other than life assurance and laying down provisions to facilitate the effective exercise of freedom to provide services and amending Directive 73/239/EEC, OJ L172/1 of 4.7.1988. Hence, Art. 2(d), last indent, thereof provides: ''Member State where the risk is situated' means ... – the Member State where the policy-holder has his habitual residence or, if the policy-holder is a legal person, the Member State where the latter's establishment, to which the contract relates, is situated, in all cases not explicitly covered by the foregoing indents'. Establishment has been defined in Art. 2(c) in the following way: ''establishment' means the head office, agency or branch of an undertaking ...'. *See* also Case C-191/99, *Kvaerner plc* v. *Staatssecretaris van Financiën*, ECR 1001 I-4447 at para. 42.

4. MIXED GROUPS

4.1. Introduction

Frequently, a group of companies will include undertakings which are not all covered by either Article 5(3)(a) or by Article 5(3)(b) or by the main rule laid down in Article 5(1).[56] I will refer to these conglomerates as mixed groups. In the case of mixed groups, the question arises as to what the correct calculation method is. Imagine, for instance, that a large conglomerate, with interests in the banking sector and the industrial sector, acquires an insurance company. This will constitute a concentration. But how do we calculate whether the concentration has a Community dimension? Do we apply the calculation method applying to insurance companies now that the target is in this sector? Or do we apply the method applicable to banks, or the main rule applicable to undertakings in the industrial sector? Or do we apply a mix of all these rules? This is the question I examine below. First, in sections 4.2 and 4.3, I shall provide my own interpretation. Then, in section 4.4, I provide an account of the Commission's approach.

4.2. Article 5 and mixed groups

The idea behind the concept of Community dimension is that concentrations involving undertakings with a significant financial strength in the Community and at Community level shall be subject to scrutiny by the Commission. As explained above, in part 1, the drafters of the Merger Regulation took the view that, regarding credit institutions and other financial institutions and insurance undertakings, the Community dimension could not be calculated on the basis of ordinary turnover so a turnover substitute would have to be applied instead. Article 5(3) simply

---

[56] The Second Banking Directive in Title IV provides certain restrictions regarding the ownership of credit institutions and also provides certain ceilings for the amount of individual and cumulative shareholdings that a credit institution is permitted to hold in undertakings which do not come within the definition of a credit institution or other financial institution. *See* further A. Thompson, *supra* note 12, pp. 31-34 and George S. Zavvos, 'Banking Integration and 1992: Legal Issues and Policy Implications', *Harvard International Law Journal*, vol. 31, no. 2, 1990, pp. 463-506, at pp. 489-490. Less restrictive rules may apply to non-Community credit institutions, and concentrations involving such institutions regularly do come within the scope of the Merger Regulation.

constitutes a special way of calculating the thresholds set out in Article 1(2). It does not constitute an independent set of thresholds.

If one were to construe the Merger Regulation so as to provide that *either* the usual turnover calculation *or* Article 5(3)(a) *or* Article 5(3)(b) could apply to one and the same concentration, this would frequently create results which very clearly would counteract the basic purpose of the thresholds.

Example

An industrial conglomerate acquires an insurance undertaking. The industrial conglomerate does not have any gross premium income and the insurance undertaking does not produce any real turnover. Applying either the usual turnover calculation rule or the rule laid down in Article 5(3)(b) will therefore mean that one of the two parties will not produce any turnover within the meaning of the Merger Regulation. The consequence will be that the concentration will not be caught by the Merger Regulation.

There is no reason to assume that the drafters included the special rules in Article 5(3)(a) and (b) in addition to the main rule in Article 5(1) to let a number of concentrations 'escape' the jurisdiction of the Commission. On the contrary, the purpose of Article 5(3) presumably was to avoid large-scale Community concentrations escaping the scope of the Merger Regulation. Moreover, if the drafters had intended only one of the three different calculation methods to apply at a time, why then did they not include any guidance on how to establish which of the three methods should apply where more than one could be implicated.

On the other hand, however, the apparent conclusion that all three calculation methods may be applied regarding one and the same concentration leads to another problem, namely that of double counting.

Example

A bank, which has majority holdings in a number of industrial undertakings, enters into a concentration. If one were to calculate the turnover of these subsidiaries in accordance with Article 5(1) and (4) together with the income from these shareholdings in accordance with Article 5(3)(a), the financial strength derived from these undertakings would in reality have been counted twice.

Article 5(4) of the Merger Regulation may help solve this problem since it provides that:

'… the aggregate turnover of an undertaking concerned … shall be calculated by adding together the respective turnovers of [the different undertakings belonging to the same group as the undertaking concerned]'.

Thus, Article 5(4) states that each undertaking belonging to the same group as the undertaking concerned, *i.e.* each legal entity belonging to the group, must have its turnover calculated and added together with those of the other undertakings in order to ascertain whether the thresholds have been met.

Since Article 5(3) only provides special ways of calculating the turnover, each legal entity's turnover must be established in accordance with the type of undertaking that the legal entity constitutes, before aggregating the figure towards the group turnover.

It is worth noting that there appears to be no basis for assuming that the way in which the capital has been raised influences the outcome. Thus, for instance, whether the capital of a subsidiary has been raised out of an insurer's technical reserves is immaterial in this regard.

This means that where an undertaking falls within the definition of a credit institution or a financial institution, the turnover of this legal entity must be calculated in accordance with Article 5(3)(a) only. Where the undertaking is an insurance undertaking, the calculation must follow the one laid down in Article 5(3)(b) only. And, in all other cases, the calculation must follow the one provided in Article 5(1). This may be termed a 'legal entity by legal entity calculation approach'.[57]

4.3. Holding securities on a temporary basis (Article 3(5)(a) of the Merger Regulation)

Article 3(5)(a) of the Merger Regulation provides an exception to the definition of control as laid down in Article 3(3). This exception might be relevant regarding the

---

[57] It seems that in the legal literature there is a consensus of opinion that the interpretation advanced here is the correct one. *See* for instance *Bellamy & Child – European Community Law of Competition*, 5th ed., (P.M. Roth, ed.), Sweet & Maxwell, London 2001 at p. 382, Pierre Bos, Jules Stuyck, and Peter Wytinck, *Concentration Control in the European Economic Community*, Graham & Trotman Ltd., London 1992, at p. 131 and J. Lovergne and A. Maillé, 'Réflexions sur le fonctionnement du contrôle communautaire des concentrations', *Revue de la concurrence et de la consommation*, No. 72, March-April 1993, pp. 5-27 at p. 20.

'mixed groups rule'. According to Article 3(5)(a), where credit institutions, financial institutions or insurance undertakings hold securities on a temporary basis[58] as part of their normal activities and with a view to reselling, this holding will not be viewed as falling within the definition of control as it has been defined in Article 3(3) of the Merger Regulation.[59]

This conclusion provokes a new question, however, namely: what if a bank or other financial institution holds, say, 60% of the shares in a company, but only does this on a temporary basis? This holding must be included in the calculation of the Community dimension. But must it be included as banking income, *i.e.* the income derived from the shareholding, or will one have to aggregate the full turnover of the company on the basis that it is a subsidiary? The matter may be boiled down to a question of whether the notion of control in Article 3(3) or Article 5(4) shall apply.[60]

Article 5 provides the rules for establishing a Community dimension. Article 5(1) provides the calculation rule in respect of ordinary products and services while Article 5(3) provides special calculation rules in respect of the financial sector.

---

[58] In order to apply Art. 3(5)(a) the Commission requires that the bank or banks in question will only be in control for a maximum of a year. Hence, if the bank *may* be in control for a longer period, as a mainrule Art. 3(5)(a) will not be applicable, *cf. Deutsche Bank/ Commerzbank/J.M. Voith*, Case IV/M891, decision of 23 April 1997.

[59] The Commission in the *2001 Green Paper on the review of Council Regulation (EEC) No 4064/89*, COM(2001) 745 final, Brussels 11.12.2001 at paras. 137-144 observes that the equity market has seen a new form of financing; namely venture capital investments. At para. 140 the Commission explains that where such investments are 'made in order to provide capital for a new business during its early development phase, with the ultimate aim of floating the company on the stock exchange in the medium term … [i]t has been argued that this type of venture capital should be seen as equivalent to traditional loan facilities provided by banks. The main feature of relevance under the Merger Regulation is that VC investors will hold shares in the new business and typically have at least veto rights over its budget and business plan. Under traditional financing methods banks would normally not hold shares, but would instead retain a possibility to refuse renewal of loan facilities'. Such growth capital investments are frequently syndicated, which means that two or more venture capital investors will share the investment. Due to the construction of the merger thresholds such transactions may – even in the case of start-up-businesses with no sales – be notifiable under the Regulation. The Commission in the *2001 Green Paper on the review of the Merger Regulation*, makes it clear that it is open to enlarging the scope of Art. 3(5) of the Merger Regulation to cover these transactions to some extent.

[60] *See* further chapter 3, section 2.2.

Article 5(4) provides which undertakings must be included when establishing whether a concentration has a Community dimension. In contrast, Article 3(3) applies when establishing whether a transaction constitutes a concentration. This scheme shows that the notion of control provided in Article 5(4) is the one which must be applied *vis-à-vis* Article 5(3). The consequence of this is that where the credit institution or financial institution has control over another undertaking within the meaning of Article 5(4), the turnover of this 'subsidiary-undertaking' must be aggregated towards the group turnover of the credit institution or financial institution (counted in accordance with Article 5(1)). A typical situation will be where, on a temporary basis, the credit institution or financial institution holds more than 50% of the capital or business assets of the other undertaking. Moreover, it follows that the banking income derived from the subsidiary undertaking, whose turnover will be aggregated to that of the parent (in accordance with Article 5(1)), will not also be counted under the rule in Article 5(3)(a), since this would mean that the subsidiary was, so to speak, counted twice.[61]

4.4. The Commission's approach

4.4.1. The AG/Amev case

Already in *AG/Amev*,[62] the second case leading to a decision under the Regulation, the Commission was faced with a mixed group. The Commission took a 'legal entity by legal entity approach' to the matter in order to establish a Community dimension.[63] A brief account of the case will show this approach.

---

[61] *See* also section 4.2 *in fine*.

[62] *AG/Amev*, Case IV/M018, decision of 21 November 1990.

[63] See in this respect Turnover Calculation Notice at paras. 57-58 which explicitly refers to 'the turnover of the subsidiary or affiliated company' in explaining the rule provided in *AG/Amev*. C.J. Cook and C.S. Kerse, *supra* note 48, p. 58 in footnote 49, when commenting on *AG/Amev*, ask whether 'it would have been legitimate to add in the 'turnover' arising from the real estate investment if that had been conducted directly by the insurance company itself.' Thus, these two authors do not (necessarily) share the view that in *AG/Amev* the Commission applied an interpretation based on a calculation of the turnover company by company and *not* on an activity by activity basis. Also, K. Platteau, 'EC Merger Control in the Banking and Financial Sector', *Revue de la Banque*, No. 4, 1996, pp. 223-229 at p. 225 finds that *AG/Amev* supports a rule based on 'each activity concerned'. Most other authors,

AG and Amev were two insurance companies that intended to merge their activities. Both companies had subsidiaries which were active in the real estate sector. If the calculation of turnover were based entirely on Article 5(3)(b), the aggregate worldwide turnover of the two companies would be € 4,903 million, but if the turnover of the real estate subsidiaries were included the turnover would be € 5,053 million. The question of whether only Article 5(3)(b) should be applied was, therefore, decisive.[64]

The companies' investments in the real estate sector were made on the basis of part of the premiums received. AG and Amev argued that the real estate investments were inherent in the insurance activities. Consequently, the financial results of these investments should not be taken into account since Article 5(3)(b) applied. In addition, they pointed out that insurance companies are under a legal obligation to invest the acquired premiums and, therefore, the turnover from real estate investments should not be treated differently than other investments.

In paragraph 5, the Commission gave the following conclusion to the problem:

'Article 5(3)(b) states that for insurance undertakings the value of gross premiums shall be used in place of turnover. This provision does not constitute a special threshold for insurance companies, but only a special method of calculation of turnover and does not exempt them from the general rules stated in Article 5. Article 5(4) provides for the turnover of an undertaking to be calculated by adding together the respective turnover of the undertaking itself and the other companies belonging to the same group. If an insurance company conducts other kinds of business through a subsidiary, this business generates a turnover which has to be added to the turnover of the insurance company itself (i.e. its gross premiums income). In this case, it is irrelevant that the capital of the subsidiary is raised by the insurance company out of its technical reserves. For the purposes of the thresholds laid down in Article 1, the aims and methods of generating turnover are immaterial.'[65]

---

however, support the understanding of *AG/Amev* which has been submitted here. *See* for example Christopher Jones, 'Case Note: AG/Amev', *EC Merger Control Reporter*, Kluwer Law International, The Hague 1991 and later (looseleaf) at p. 16.1.

[64] It is recalled that in 1990 only the first set of thresholds applied.

[65] This has been labelled '[a]n expansive approach to the test of Community dimension', cf. Linklaters & Paines, *Competition Law Bulletin*, Spring 1991, at p. 7.

Following the decision in *AG/Amev,* the Commission has applied what has since been termed the *AG/Amev*-rule in several cases, though this is rarely clear from the wording of the public version of the individual case.[66]

4.4.2. *The* Midland Bank *case*

At first glance, the *Hong Kong and Shanghai Bank/Midland* case,[67] concerning Hong Kong and Shanghai Bank's acquisition of the British Midland Bank, does not appear to constitute any derogation from the *AG/Amev*-rule. Nevertheless, the public version of the decision, in paragraph 7, contains a statement which, on closer examination, might cast doubt upon such a conclusion:

> 'As holding companies both undertakings [the Hong Kong and Shanghai Bank and the Midland Bank] have interests in different economic areas such as banking, insurance, financial and other services. Calculation of the *geographic breakdown of turnover* of the various business activities under the Merger Regulation requires a split of the assets according to the *main activities.*' (emphasis added).

Apparently, the main problem in *Hong Kong and Shanghai Bank/Midland* regarding jurisdiction was whether both banks achieved more than two-thirds of their Community-wide turnover within the United Kingdom. If this were the case, the concentration would not have a Community dimension meaning that the Commission would not have jurisdiction. In order to examine this issue, the Commission had to allocate the turnover on a geographic basis.

The geographic allocation of turnover, however, must, of course, be made with regard to the calculated turnover. Above, it has been submitted that the turnover must be calculated on a 'legal entity by legal entity basis'. This means, for example, that if one and the same legal entity issues insurance contracts and provides loans, then either Article 5(3)(a) or Article 5(3)(b) must be applied. Thus, both

---

66 Another example is provided in *Banesto/Totta*, Case IV/M192, decision of 14 April 1992, *see* further my article, *supra* note 5 at p. 80 with note 139. *See* also *Torras/Sarrio, supra* note 19, *Hong Kong and Shanghai Bank/Midland*, Case IV/M213, decision of 21 May 1992, *Société Générale de Belgique/Générale de Banque*, Case IV/M343, decision of 3 August 1993, *AGF/LA UNION Y EL FENIX*, Case IV/M403, decision of 25 April 1994. Note, however, that according to Jacques Zachmann, *Le contrôle communautaire des concentrations*, L.G.D.J., Paris 1994 at p. 96 the *AG/Amev*-rule only applies to insurance companies.

67 *Supra* note 66.

provisions cannot apply at the same time. It is, therefore, puzzling that the above quotation refers to 'a split of the assets according to the main activities'. Indeed, this statement only seems to make sense if, in reality, the Commission has applied a concept different from the one based on the legal entity.[68]

It is even more puzzling that, in paragraph 6 of the decision, the Commission provides the following turnover figures:

Worldwide turnover:

For HSBC: € 12,346 million

For Midland: € 8,555 million

Community-wide turnover:

For HSBC: € 2,062 million

For Midland: € 9,814 million

The curious thing is that Midland's worldwide turnover is less than it's Community-wide turnover! Of course, this might be thought to be simply a typographical error. But it might also be that the Commission has calculated the turnover on a legal entity by legal entity basis regarding the worldwide turnover, while it has calculated the turnover on an activity by activity basis when calculating the thresholds which require a geographic allocation. The 'activity by activity' calculation method thus means that each separate activity is calculated in accordance with the special calculation rules laid down in Article 5 of the Merger Regulation, regardless of whether the activities are carried out within different legal entities or within one and the same legal entity.[69]

It therefore seems to me that one may reasonably doubt whether the Commission's decision in *Hong Kong and Shanghai Bank/Midland* conforms with the interpretation concerning mixed groups advanced in this chapter.

---

[68]   In the Turnover Calculation Notice at paras. 59-61 the Commission apparently supports the 'legal entity by legal entity approach' supported here, and does so with a reference, *inter alia*, to *Hong Kong and Shanghai Bank/Midland*.

[69]   *See* further Jonathan Scott, 'Case Note: Hong Kong and Shanghai Bank/Midland', *EC Merger Control Reporter*, Kluwer Law International, The Hague 1991 and later (looseleaf) at p. 786.1, F.L. Fine, *supra* note 20, at p. 175, European Commission, *Directorate-General for Competition – Merger Task Force, Revision of the EEC Merger Regulation, Article 5(3)(a), Turnover of credit institutions and other financial institutions*, Undated (from before March 1993, not publicly available) and my article, *supra* note 5, p. 81 with note 143.

4.5. Evaluating the mixed groups rule

It is important to be aware that although it seems to be very difficult to question the legality of the approach which has been submitted here and which is the one the Commission has taken in the *AG/Amev* case, this approach does carry with it certain problems.

Where an undertaking within the same legal entity engages in substantial activities which would be calculated under different calculation methods had these activities been split into separate legal entities, the approach laid down by the Merger Regulation may not always adequately reflect the financial strength of such an undertaking.

Example

Formerly, Spies Rejser was an independent, private Danish company whose principal activity was to provide travel services. In the early eighties, the company was not only known as the largest charter tour operator in Scandinavia, but also for having a very considerable part of its assets invested in securities. In the financial year 1982/83, the company had a turnover of just over 1.36 billion Danish Kroner and profit before taxes and extraordinary items was over 160 million Danish Kroner.[70] More than 56% of the profit before taxes and extraordinary items was derived from securities which, however, made up more than 88% of all assets in the company.[71]

Even though it is fair to say that Spies Rejser was a semi-funds management company, it did not fall within the definition of a financial institution as laid down in the Second Banking Directive.[72] Semi-funds management companies like Spies Rejser will, therefore, not fall within the scope of Article 5(3)(a). This accords with the rule laid down in *AG/Amev*.

---

[70] Due to the inflation these amounts would today be the equivalent of more than 2.54 billion Danish Kroner and of more than 299 million Danish Kroner respectively. These figures equals approximately € 342.1 million (turnover) and € 40.3 million (profit).

[71] Cf. *Published accounts for the Spies Group for the year 1 May 1982 to 30 April 1983*.

[72] Art. 1 of the Second Banking Directive defines a 'financial institution' as '… an undertaking other than a credit institution *the principal activity of which* is to acquire holdings or to carry on one or more of the activities listed in points 2 to 12 in the Annex;' (emphasis added). The principal activity of Spies Rejser was, and is, to provide travel services, not to carry out portfolio management.

Hence, the present rules may, in some cases, only inadequately reflect the actual economic strength of the undertakings concerned. Nevertheless, the problem should not be exaggerated. Firstly, the number of semi-funds management companies like Spies Rejser presumably is fairly limited. Secondly, if the company (or the Commission) count the financial income as an ordinary activity, the actual economic strength derived from the securities is, indeed, accounted for. Thus, in Spies Rejser's 1982/83 accounts, financial income is shown as an ordinary activity and would therefore be counted towards the relevant turnover under the Merger Regulation. In other words, if the Commission had had to examine Spies Rejser for the purpose of establishing a Community dimension, the calculation would take due account of Spies Rejser's financial income.

While it is acknowledged that mixed groups may cause some headache, it is submitted that the above approach keeps these problems to a minimum. Perhaps with the odd exception of *Hong Kong and Shanghai Bank/Midland* it appears, moreover, that the Commission has chosen the same approach.

7. THE EEA AGREEMENT

1. BACKGROUND

The Agreement on the European Economic Area was signed in Oporto in May, 1992 and entered into force on 1 January, 1994.[1] The parties to the Agreement were the then twelve Community Member States and the then seven EFTA States which together formed what was then the largest free trade area in the world. The Swiss electorate rejected ratification of the Agreement, however, and this rejection caused problems for Liechtenstein which had a customs arrangement with Switzerland. The Agreement therefore did not enter into force *vis-à-vis* Liechtenstein until 1 May, 1995.[2] Moreover, on 1 January, 1995, Sweden, Finland and Austria left the EFTA to join the Community. This means that the EEA today encompasses the fifteen Community Member States and three of the four remaining EFTA States.[3]

---

[1] For an overview of the political background to the creation of the EEA, *see* Auke Haagsma, 'The Competition Rules of the EEA and the Europe Agreements: Lawyer's Paradise or User's Safe Harbour', in *Procedure and Enforcement in EC and US Competition Law*, (Piet Jan Slot and Alison McDonnel, eds.), Sweet & Maxwell, London 1993, pp. 241-266 at pp. 248-250.

[2] Cf. Decision of the EEA Council No 1/95 of 10 March 1995 on the entry into force of the Agreement on the European Economic Area for the Principality of Liechtenstein, OJ 20.4.1995, L86/58 and EEA Supplement to the OJ 20.4.1995, No. 14/1.

[3] In this chapter references to EFTA States only cover Norway, Iceland and Liechtenstein. It is somewhat confusing that the contracting parties to the EEA Agreement decided not to amend the Agreement subsequent to the accession to the Community by Sweden, Finland and Austria. Consequently, Art. 2(b) EEA as adjusted by the Adjusting Protocol, Art. 2 EEA still (rather misleadingly) provides: 'The term "EFTA States" means the Republic of Austria, the Republic of Finland, the Republic of Iceland, the Kingdom of Norway, the Kingdom of Sweden and, under the conditions laid down in Article 1(2) of the Protocol Adjusting the Agreement on the European Economic Area, the Principality of Liechtenstein;' In practice, however, the Community is considered to include Austria, Finland and Sweden while the EFTA-States are considered to include Norway, Iceland and Liechtenstein.

Basically, the EEA Agreement provides that the four fundamental freedoms of the Internal Market of the Community shall apply within the EEA in the same way as within the Community.[4] Roughly speaking, therefore, one might say that the EEA Agreement extends the Internal Market beyond the borders of the Community.[5] One of the objectives of the EEA Agreement is to establish a system ensuring that competition is not distorted and that the rules on competition are equally respected.[6] Thus, Part IV of the Agreement provides a set of provisions based on the corresponding competition provisions of the EC Treaty.[7] Article 57 of the Agreement provides the following:

'1. Concentrations the control of which is foreseen in paragraph 2 and which create or strengthen a dominant position as a result of which effective competition would be significantly impeded within the territory covered by this Agreement or a substantial part of it, shall be declared incompatible with this Agreement.

2. The control of concentrations falling under paragraph 1 shall be carried out by:

(a) the EC Commission in cases falling under Regulation (EEC) No 4064/89 in accordance with that Regulation and in accordance with Protocols 21

---

4   In addition a range of accompanying policies are covered by the Agreement.

5   Accord Sven Norberg, 'The Agreement on a European Economic Area', *Common Market Law Review*, 1992, pp. 1171-1198 at p. 1172. A number of provisos must however be added. For instance that the EEA Agreement does not cover agricultural products, cf. Art. 8 of the Agreement. For references to general works on the EEA Agreement, *see* my article 'The Delimitation of Jurisdiction with regard to Concentration Control under the EEA Agreement', *European Competition Law Review*, vol. 16, no. 1, 1995, pp. 30-39 at p. 30 with note 6.

6   Cf. Art. 1(2)(e) EEA. Compare this with Art. 3(g) of the EC Treaty.

7   It is noteworthy that the competition provisions of the EEA Agreement only apply with regard to products falling within the product range of the Agreement as defined in Art. 8(3) EEA. *See* for example *Masterfoods/Royal Canin*, Case COMP/M2544, decision of 15 February 2002 and *Nestlé/Ralston Purina*, Case COMP/M2337, decision of 27 July 2001 (both cases concerned pet foods that is not covered by the EEA Agreement). Furthermore, it is noteworthy that Art. 1(1) as well as Recital 4 EEA refer to *equal conditions of competition* while Recital four of the EC Treaty provides: 'Recognising that the removal of existing obstacles calls for concerted action in order to guarantee ... *fair competition*' (emphasis added). *See* further Sven Norberg, Karin Hökborg, Martin Johansson, Dan Eliasson and Lucien Dedichen, *The European Economic Area – EEA Law – A Commentary on the EEA Agreement*, CE Fritzes AB, Stockholm 1993, pp. 396-397.

and 24 and Annex XIV. The EC Commission shall, subject to the review of the EC Court of Justice, have sole competence to take decisions on these cases;

(b) the EFTA Surveillance Authority in cases not falling under subparagraph (a) where the relevant thresholds set out in Annex XIV are fulfilled in the territory of the EFTA States in accordance with Protocols 21 and 24 and Annex XIV. This is without prejudice to the competence of EC Member States.'

In this chapter, I will examine the delimitation of jurisdiction under the EEA Agreement with regard to the control of concentrations. First, in part 2, below, I will explain the EEA competition-enforcing system. Then, in part 3, I examine the allocation of jurisdiction with regard to concentrations. Finally, in part 4, I will evaluate the system.

2. THE BASIC RULES IN THE EEA COMPETITION-ENFORCING SYSTEM

2.1. Two enforcement bodies

The EEA competition rules are enforced by the European Commission and the EFTA Surveillance Authority (ESA).[8] In order to enable the ESA to give effect to the EEA Competition rules, the Authority has been entrusted with powers and functions similar to those of the European Commission, and the ESA also applies procedural rules similar to those applied in the Community.[9] The European Commission implements the EEA competition rules on the basis of its own procedural rules.[10]

---

[8] Cf. Arts. 108 – 110 EEA.

[9] Cf. Art. 108(1) EEA, Art. 1 of Protocol 21 EEA and Protocol 4 to the ESA/EFTA Court Agreement.

[10] Cf. Protocol 21 EEA and Council Regulation (EC) No. 2894/94 of 28 November 1994 concerning arrangements for implementing the Agreement on the European Economic Area, OJ L305/6 of 30.11.1994.

In the field of concentrations, this means that both the ESA and the Commission can receive and examine notifications[11] as well as complaints,[12] they can conduct investigations[13] and they can adopt decisions.[14] The ESA is required to undertake investigations in the EFTA States at the request of the Commission during which investigations the Commission is entitled to be represented and take an active part. In contrast, the ESA cannot require the Commission to make an investigation in the Community.[15]

A notification of a concentration should be made to the authority which has jurisdiction over the concentration.[16] If a notification is made to the wrong authority, however, this will not invalidate the notification[17] although it will only be effective as of the date when it is received by the competent surveillance authority – which is not necessarily the day of notification.[18]

According to Articles 6 and 7 EEA, the Agreement is based on the *acquis communautaire*, meaning that at the time of the agreement the EFTA States accepted the relevant Community legislative framework as it was then interpreted by the Court of Justice.[19] The *acquis communautaire* does not include Commission decisions which means that the ESA and the EFTA States are not bound by the Commission's interpretation under the Merger Regulation as manifested in the

---

[11] Cf. Art. 10 of Protocol 24 EEA.

[12] Cf. Art. 10(2) of Protocol 24 EEA.

[13] Cf. Art. 8(4)-(7) of Protocol 24 EEA.

[14] Cf. Art. 57 EEA.

[15] Cf. Art. 8 of Protocol 24 EEA. Contrast this with Art. 8(3)-(5) of Protocol 23 EEA.

[16] Art. 10(1) of Protocol 24 EEA.

[17] Cf. Art. 10(2) of Protocol 24 EEA.

[18] Cf. Art. 11 of Protocol 24 EEA. Compare this with Art. 11 of Protocol 23 EEA. Note, however, that Robert Strivens, 'Competition Law under the EEA Agreement', *International Business Lawyer*, December 1993, Vol. 21, No 11, pp. 512-517 at p. 516 finds that notifying the wrong authority does not affect the effective date of the notification.

[19] Thérèse Blanchet, Risto Piipponen, Maria Westman-Clément, *The Agreement on the European Economic Area (EEA) – A Guide to the Free Movement of Goods and Competition Rules*, Clarendon Press, Oxford 1994, p. 188 with footnote 108 apparently take the view that also modifications to the Regulation made after the entry into force of the EEA Agreement 'should certainly be considered as 'relevant *acquis*' and be integrated in the Agreement following the EEA decision-making procedure.' I do not agree that such amendments are part of the *acquis* accepted by the EFTA States.

Commission decisions. The ESA, however, takes the Commission's case law into account even though it cannot rely on this case law to the same extent as can the Commission. ESA has also stated that until its own equivalent notices are produced, it 'intends to apply the principles set out in the Commission notices whenever relevant'.[20] Moreover, the Commission is of the view that its decisions should be considered as persuasive authority in the application of the EEA provisions.

2.2. Co-operation between the European Commission and the ESA

In order to develop and maintain a uniform surveillance throughout the EEA in the field of competition and to promote a homogeneous implementation, application and interpretation of the relevant rules, Article 58 of the EEA Agreement provides that the European Commission and the ESA shall co-operate.

The co-operation relates both to general policy issues and to the handling of individual cases falling under the EEA competition rules.[21] Thus, regardless of which of the surveillance authorities an individual case is attributed to, the policy followed and the way to apply the EEA competition rules to the particular case, presumably, will be the same.

2.3. Judicial review

The European Court of Justice and the Court of First Instance are competent for appeals concerning decisions by the European Commission. The EFTA Court is competent for appeals concerning decisions in the field of competition adopted by the ESA.[22]

---

[20] Cf. information provided on ESA's internet homepage at www.eftasurv.int/fieldsofwork/fieldcompetition/otherpublications/. ESA continues by observing that '[a]s it is not very likely that a merger falling within the competence of the Authority [*i.e.* ESA] will occur, the Authority has given lowest priority to the adoption of notices in the field of concentrations'.

[21] Cf. Art. 1 of Protocol 23 EEA and Art. 1 of Protocol 24 EEA. As far as co-operation is concerned, there are some differences between the policy followed and the way to apply the EEA competition rules in merger cases and in anti-trust cases.

[22] The original proposal for an EEA Agreement envisaged an EEA Court, *i.e.* a joint EFTA/EC Court. The European Court of Justice in its Opinion 1/91, [1991] ECR I-6079, however, held

Even though there are common rules throughout the EEA, the fact that these rules are interpreted by two different courts means that there is an inherent risk that they will not be applied in a uniform manner. A central objective of the EEA Agreement is to bring about 'equal conditions of competition'[23] and a heterogeneous interpretation would put the attainment of this objective in jeopardy.[24]

In order to avoid such an unfortunate situation, a system of exchange of information concerning judgments has been formed,[25] together with a system ensuring co-operation between national courts on the one hand and the European Court of Justice and the EFTA Court on the other concerning the correct interpretation and application of EEA provisions.[26] Furthermore, the EEA Agreement provides for an EEA Joint Committee to review the development of the case law of the Court of Justice of the European Communities and the EFTA Court[27] and for the possibility

---

this – among other things – to be incompatible with the Treaty. An EFTA Court running parallel to the European Court of Justice was therefore set up together with a considerable system which should ensure homogeneity in the application of the provisions of the EEA Agreement. In its Opinion 1/92, [1992] ECR I-2821, the European Court of Justice held the renegotiated Agreement to be compatible with the Treaty. Concerning the Court's two Opinions *see* further Henry G. Schermers, 'Opinion 1/91 of the Court of Justice, 14 December 1991; Opinion 1/92 of the Court of Justice, 10 April 1992', 29 *Common Market Law Review* 1992, 991-1009, Barbara Brandtner, 'The 'Drama' of the EEA – Comments on Opinions 1/91 and 1/92', *European Journal of International Law*, no. 3, 1992, pp. 300-328, Jean Boulouis, 'Les avis de la Cour de justice des Communautés sur la compatibilité avec le Traité CEE du projet d'accord créant l'Espace économique européen', *Revue trimestrielle de droit européen*, no. 3, 1992, pp. 457-463, Jacqueline Dutheil de la Rochère, 'L'Espace économique européen sous le regard des juges de la Cour de justice des Communautés européennes', *Revue du Marché et de l'Union Européenne*, July/August 1992, No 360, pp. 603-612 and Trevor C. Hartley, 'The European Court and the EEA', *International and Comparative Law Quarterly* 1992, vol. 41, pp. 841-848.

[23] Cf. Art. 1(1) EEA and recital 4 EEA.

[24] Accord S. Norberg, *supra* note 5 at p. 1172.

[25] Cf. Art. 106 EEA.

[26] Cf. Art. 107 EEA together with Protocol 34 EEA and Art. 34 of the ESA/EFTA Court Agreement.

[27] Cf. Art. 105 EEA.

of intervention before the European Court of Justice and the EFTA Court respectively by the Contracting Parties.[28]

3. JURISDICTION

3.1. Introduction

One of the most significant characteristics of the Merger Regulation is the one-stop-shop principle whereby *either* the Commission *or* the Member States' competition authorities have sole jurisdiction to vet a given concentration. For obvious reasons, it was important to the Community that the creation of the EEA did not result in a deterioration of this principle. Dr. Thinam Jakob-Siebert of the European Commission, has explained that the fact that the Merger Regulation only entered into force in September 1990, meaning that the Commission had only gained limited experience in its application, together with the fact that the Regulation lays down some very strict time limits, meant that it was considered too early to change the complicated jurisdictional provisions of the Regulation.[29] In addi-

---

[28] Cf. Arts. 20 and 37 of the Statute of the European Court of Justice and Arts. 20 and 36 of the Statute of the EFTA Court. For a further exposition of the systems set up in order to ensure a homogeneous application of the provisions throughout the EEA, *see* S. Norberg *et al*, *supra* note 7 chapter IX, Olivier Jacot-Guillarmod (ed.), *Accord EEE – Commentaires et réflexions*, Schulthess Polygraphischer Verlag, Zürich 1992, pp. 547-666, Jacques Bourgeois, *Competition Rules and their Enforcement in the Enlarged Free Trading Area*, Paper delivered at European Study Conferences' competition conference, Brussels, November 1992, and Sven Norberg, 'EES-avtalet – De institutionella lösningarna för ett dynamiskt och homogent EES', *Svensk Juristtidning*, 1992, pp. 337-348.

[29] Thinam Jakob-Siebert, 'Wettbewerbspolitik im europäischen Wirtschaftsraum (EWR) – Das Zwei-Pfeiler-System', *Wirtschaft und Wettbewerb*, Mai 1992, Heft 5, pp. 387-400 at p. 396. *See* also Christine Federlin, 'Division of Competences between the EFTA Surveillance Authority and the EC Commission in the handling of Individual Antitrust and Merger Cases' at p. 58 in *EEA Competition Law* (Vassili Christianos and Steen Treumer, eds.), European Institute of Public Administration, Maastricht 1994. Alec Burnside, 'Preventing Structural Impediments to Competition: Merger Control in the European Economic Area' in *Business Law in the European Economic Area* (Christopher Bright, ed.), Clarendon Press, Oxford 1994, p.110, is less diplomatic than Thinam Jakob-Siebert. Hence, he finds that the departure from the one-stop principle set out in Art. 57 EEA 'seems based on no better reason of policy than a lack of confidence in the effectiveness of the EFTA Surveillance Authority'.

tion, it might be added that one should not overlook the significance which the Member States as well as the Community attribute to the control of concentrations. Thus, the Commission did not want to lose competence in the area of concentration control.[30]

In other words, the Community was not prepared to give up any of its competence. The consequence was that the two competition authorities could not cooperate on an even footing in concentration cases. Article 57 of the EEA Agreement therefore provides, firstly, that either the European Commission or the ESA will have jurisdiction. There is no joint jurisdiction. Secondly, it provides that, where the Commission has jurisdiction under the Merger Regulation, both the ESA and the individual EFTA States must abstain from vetting the concentration in question.

The quantitative thresholds, on which the scope of the Regulation is based, mean that concentrations between undertakings based outside the Community may also be notifiable.

Example

Before Sweden's accession to the Community, two Swedish undertakings, Saab and Ericsson, notified a transaction whereby they proposed to combine their electronic space equipment production in a joint venture.[31] The joint venture would only generate a turnover of about € 30 million and even on the basis of the narrowest definition of the product market, it was not possible to find market shares of more than 5% in Europe for each of the products of the joint venture. Nevertheless, as the thresholds had been met, the concentration was notifiable.

The Merger Regulation thus vests in the Commission jurisdiction to vet concentrations between undertakings based in EFTA countries, provided the thresholds have been met.[32] Until the entering into force of the EEA Agreement, however, the competition authorities in the EFTA countries were not restrained from examining

---

[30] *See* Michael J. Reynolds, *Procedural Elements of the Regulation on the Control of Concentrations*, Paper delivered at European Study Conferences' competition conference, Brussels, November 1992.

[31] *Saab Ericsson Space*, Case IV/M178, decision of 13 January 1992.

[32] A few examples are *Tetra Pak/Alfa-Laval*, Case IV/M069, decision of 19 July 1991, *Volvo/Atlas*, Case IV/M152, decision of 14 January 1992, *Volvo/Procordia*, Case IV/M196, decision of 11 October 1993 and *Norsk Hydro/Saga*, Case IV/M1573, decision of 5 July 1999.

these concentrations simultaneously with the Commission. This meant that the EFTA-based undertakings did not benefit from the one-stop-shop principle to the same degree as most Community-based undertakings presumably did.

3.2. EEA dimension?

One could reasonably expect that, as a consequence of the EEA Agreement, the thresholds in the Merger Regulation were amended to include both the Community and EFTA turnovers with regard to those thresholds which presuppose a geographical allocation.[33] The effect of such an 'expansion' would, however, be equal to a lowering of the thresholds which would be unacceptable to some of the Member States.

As a result, in contrast to the EEA Agreement's objective of creating a common market with equal competition,[34] Article 57 of the Agreement does not provide for an EEA dimension, *i.e.* a concept encompassing the full territory of the EEA, but instead uses a concept according to which the Community and the EFTA states are viewed as distinct areas.[35]

---

[33] At the time of the negotiation – and subsequent adoption – of the EEA Agreement these were the € 250 million turnover threshold in Art. 1(2)(b) and the two-thirds threshold in Art. 1(2), last subparagraph, of the Merger Regulation.

[34] In *EFTA Surveillance Authority comments on the European Commission's Merger Review Green Paper*, 2002, available at www.eftasurv.int/fieldsofwork/fieldcompetition/otherpublications/ at p. 5, ESA has observed that: 'The absence of any 'catch-all' competence to cover situations where the threshold criteria are met when one considers the EEA as a whole creates a gap in competencies when it comes to assessing concentrations. The failure of Article 57 of the EEA Agreement to introduce a concept of 'EEA dimension' results in a loss of control by either authority of concentrations which possess neither a Community nor an EFTA dimension but which may still have an EEA dimension. Examples include *KLM/Braathens* (and would have included *Storebrand/Skandia* had Pohjola not become a party to the merger). The fact that only national authorities will have jurisdiction in such cases is not in keeping with the spirit of the EEA Agreement, which aims at creating a homogenous European Economic Area with equal competition (*Article 1 and Recitals to EEA Agreement*).'

[35] According to ESA, *EFTA Surveillance Authority comments on the European Commission's Merger Review Green Paper*, *supra* note 34, at p. 5, 'the question of whether an EEA dimension needs to be introduced to the merger control rules under the EEA Agreement was apparently considered by the EFTA States in 1997' and it continues by noting 'that in their comments on the Green Paper, the EFTA States have flagged a general need to discuss how to ensure equal treatment of undertakings and homogeneity within the EEA'. To complete

3.3. EFTA dimension

The EEA Agreement introduces a new concept alongside the concept of Community dimension, namely that of EFTA dimension. This concept closely mirrors the definition of Community dimension. Thus, a concentration has an EFTA dimension where:

(1) the combined worldwide turnover of all the undertakings concerned is more than € 5000 million; and

(2) the aggregate EFTA-wide turnover of each of at least two of the undertakings concerned is more than € 250 million, and

(3) each of the undertakings concerned does not achieve more than two-thirds of its aggregate EFTA-wide turnover within one and the same EFTA State.[36]

or where:[37]

---

the picture it may be noted that, on the face of it, in *ICI/Unilever*, Case IV/M933, decision of 23 June 1997, in *Credit Suisse First Boston/Barclays*, Case IV/M1068, decision of 19 December 1997 and in *AOL/Time Warner*, Case COMP/M1845, decision of 11 October 2000, the Commission apparently has established a Community dimension on the basis of turnover generated in the EEA area. Presumably the references to the EEA are nothing but simple written mistakes.

[36] Cf. Art. 57 EEA and Annex XIV EEA, Point A(1)(a) and (b).

[37] Apparently the Council adopted the amendment of the Merger Regulation (Council Regulation (EC) No 1310/97) without considering the consequences for the EEA Agreement. Hence, the EFTA States were left with the choice of either copying the amendments into the EEA Agreement or keeping the original rules of the EEA Agreement. The first solution would mean surrendering even more competence to the Commission while the second solution was likely to create very complicated problems in respect of the division of jurisdiction. Fortunately the EFTA States agreed to the first solution albeit the amendment of the EEA Agreement only entered into force on 1 April 1998 whilst the Merger Regulation was amended with effect from 1 March 1998. The amendments were introduced by EEA Joint Committee Decision No 27/98, OJ L310/9 of 19.11.1998. Formally speaking the amendment (*i.e.* the introduction of the second set of thresholds into the EEA Agreement) not only means that the Commission has exclusive jurisdiction in the whole EEA where a concentration meets the second set of thresholds in the Community. In theory at least, it also means that where a concentration meets the new set of turnover thresholds in the EFTA States without at the same time having a Community dimension, the ESA has jurisdiction to vet this concentration. In reality the new set of thresholds is unlikely to bring any concentration within ESA's jurisdiction, however. This is particularly so as it is very difficult to conceive of a concentration where all the undertakings concerned generate a combined aggregate turnover of more

(1) the combined aggregate worldwide turnover of all the undertakings concerned is more than € 2500 million; and

(2) in each of at least three EFTA States, the combined aggregate turnover of all the undertakings concerned is more than € 100 million; and

(3) in each of the three EFTA States included for the purpose of the preceding threshold, the aggregate turnover of each of at least two of the undertakings concerned is more than € 25 million; and

(4) the aggregate EFTA-wide turnover of each of at least two of the undertakings concerned is more than € 100 million; and

(5) each of the undertakings concerned do not achieve more than two-thirds of its aggregate EFTA-wide turnover within one and the same EFTA State.

Two things are worthy of note. First, a concentration may well concurrently have a Community and an EFTA dimension. In such a situation, a question as to the allocation of jurisdiction arises. Secondly, in relative terms, the EFTA dimension thresholds are higher than are the Community dimension thresholds.[38] This has become particularly clear after Austria, Finland and Sweden left EFTA to join the Community. Not surprisingly, pure EFTA cases, *i.e.* cases coming within the ESA's

---

than € 100 million in each of Iceland, Liechtenstein and Norway (*see* Art. 1(3)(b) of the Merger Regulation) without at the same time also meeting at least one of the two sets of turnover thresholds in the Community (*i.e.* without having a Community dimension). *See* likewise Asle Aarbakke and Helge Stemshaug, 'Norway – Cross Border Mergers in Company Law and Competition Law: Removing the Final Barriers' in *FIDE – XX Congress – London – 30 October-2 November 2002 – Vol. 1 National Reports* pp. 891-916 at p. 891. *Constructor/Dexion*, Case IV/M1318, decision of 30 October 1998 is an example of an EEA cooperation case, where the Commission had jurisdiction on the basis of the second set of thresholds. To complete the picture, it may be noted that at least three cases, that only met the second set of thresholds, were notified in the time lapse between 1 March and 1 April 1998, namely *DLJ/FM Holdings*, Case IV/M1139, decision of 28 April 1998, *ICI/Williams*, Case IV/M1167, decision of 29 april 1998 and *UPM-Kymmene/April*, Case IV/M1006, decision of 11 June 1998 (the last-mentioned case was declared incomplete and renotified on 3 April 1998). Hence, these cases came within the scope of the Merger Regulation but were not covered by the EEA Agreement.

38 *See* A. Haagsma, *supra* note 1, at p. 257 and Jens Drolshammer, 'Die Zusammenschluß-kontrolle im EWR-Vertrag aus schweizerischer Sicht', in *Festschrift Alfred-Carl Gaedertz*, Beck, München 1992, pp. 111-140, at p. 123, footnote 28.

jurisdiction, have been referred to as 'hypothetical'.[39] At the time of writing (December 2002), there have been no pure EFTA cases.

The workings and the consequences of this concept of having both a Community dimension and an EFTA dimension will be explained below.

3.4. Allocation of jurisdiction

3.4.1. The main rule

Article 57(2)(a) explicitly provides that where a concentration has a Community dimension 'the EC Commission shall ... have sole competence to take decisions ...' In effect this means that the one-stop-shop principle has been extended so that not only Member State competition authorities of the Community are precluded from investigating the concentration, also *both* the ESA *and* the national EFTA State competition authorities are restrained from examining these concentrations.

Obviously, this constitutes a major concession on the part of the EFTA States since these countries have left what might be viewed as a central instrument in the competition as well as the industrial policy to a body which, in principle, they have no power over.[40]

Where the ESA has jurisdiction to examine a concentration, in principle, this means that the Commission does not have concurrent jurisdiction since the

---

[39] Cf. Claude Rouam, 'L'Espace économique européen: un horizon nouveau pour la politique de concurrence?', *Revue du Marché Commun et de l'Union Européenne*, January 1992, No. 354, pp. 53-57 at p. 56. Indeed, ESA has observed that '[p]ure EFTA cases are viewed as unlikely to occur in practice' and has called the delimitation of authority competence a '*de facto* one-sided allocation of jurisdiction in favour of the Commission' cf. *EFTA Surveillance Authority comments on the European Commission's Merger Review Green Paper*, *supra* note 34, p. 4

[40] Thus, C. Federlin, *supra* note 29 claims that '[t]he merger control by ESA is ... subsidiary in character'. A telling example of how the EEA merger scheme in reality precluded the Norwegian State from intervening when a foreign insurance company made a bid for Norwegian insurance company Storebrand may be found in *Sampo/Storebrand*, Case COMP/M2491, decision of 27 July 2001. *See* paras. 38 and 39 of the decision.

concentration does not have a Community dimension.[41] It clearly follows from Article 57(2)(b) EEA, however, that '[t]his is without prejudice to the competence of EC Member States'. In other words, where a concentration has an EFTA dimension but no Community dimension, this concentration might be examined by the ESA and one or more national Community competition authorities concurrently. In these cases, then, there is no one-stop-shop principle which applies. Consequently, in the unlikely situation that a concentration has an EFTA dimension but no Community dimension, the parties to the concentration should check whether, in addition to notifying the ESA, the concentration must also be notified to the competition authorities of one or more Community Member States.[42] On the other hand, in cases where the ESA has jurisdiction, the national competition authorities of the EFTA States are, as a main rule, precluded from applying their national legislation on competition to any such concentration.[43]

3.4.2. Referral from the Commission to a Member State

Under Article 9 of the Merger Regulation, the Commission may under certain specific circumstances, refer a notified concentration to the competent authority of a Member State.[44] This gives rise to two questions. First, how does it affect the competence of the ESA and the EFTA States' competition authorities? And second, does the Commission have competence to refer a notified concentration to the competent authority of an EFTA State?

Where the Commission refers a case to the competition authority of a Member State, this means that that particular Member State competition authority acquires exclusive jurisdiction to vet the concentration regarding the geographic market

---

[41] This follows from Art. 57(2)(b) EEA read in conjunction with Art. 57(2)(a) EEA and Art. 21 of the Merger Regulation *a contrario*. The Commission might, however, still have competence to examine a concentration under Arts. 81 and 82 of the EC Treaty in accordance with the residual powers of enforcement derived from Art. 85 of the Treaty.

[42] *See* also C. Federlin, *supra* note 29 at p. 60 and Elisabeth Czachay, 'Division of Competences between the EFTA Surveillance Authority and the EC Commission in the handling of Individual Antitrust and Merger Cases' in *EEA Competition Law*, (Vassili Christianos and Steen Treumer, eds.), European Institute of Public Administration, Maastricht 1994 at p. 70.

[43] Cf. The EFTA Surveillance Agreement, Protocol 4, Chapter XIII, Art. 21.

[44] *See* chapter 1, section 3.2.

and the product market in respect of which the concentration has been referred.[45] Thus, the competition authorities of the other Member States are still precluded from vetting the concentration. Moreover, the referral to a Member State does not as such affect the Community dimension of the concentration, meaning that the EFTA Member States' competition authorities as well as the ESA remain precluded from vetting the transaction.

Nonetheless, it is easy to imagine examples where it would be contrary to the interests of the EFTA States if the Commission referred a concentration for examination by a national competition authority of a Community Member State.

Example

A Norwegian and a British undertaking enter into a concentration. The concentration has a Community dimension, but it threatens to create a dominant position in both Britain and Norway, as a result of which effective competition would be significantly impeded in these two markets, both of which present all the characteristics of a distinct market.

If, upon a request from the British competition authorities, the Commission refers the above-described concentration to the British authorities, this may well be in perfect harmony with the Merger Regulation and it seems not to be in clear contravention of the EEA Agreement. It seems fairly obvious, however, that such a referral is likely to be inconsistent with the interests of Norway since it is unlikely that the British authorities will take the consequences of the concentration in the Norwegian market into account.[46]

Fortunately, the EEA Agreement does provide an indication of the solution to this problem. Article 2(2)(a) of Protocol 24 EEA lays down that where a concentration threatens to create or strengthen a dominant position as a result of which effective competition will be impeded in a distinct market in an EFTA State, the Commission and the ESA shall co-operate. Clearly this seems only to be possible

---

[45] Cf. Christopher Jones and Enrique González-Díaz, *The EEC Merger Regulation*, Sweet & Maxwell, London 1992, pp. 38-46, in particular p. 45.

[46] Under British law a merger can only be blocked where it has been found that it might operate against the public interest. Though it seems that the Monopolies and Mergers Commission is not completely precluded from taking consequences in foreign markets into account when examining whether a merger will be against the public interest, it seems highly unlikely that the Monopolies and Mergers Commission will do this. *See* further Richard Whish, *Competition Law*, 4th edition, Butterworths, London 2001, pp. 816-817 and 374-375.

where the Commission has not referred the case to a national competition authority or where it has only referred the part of the case concerning the distinct market in the Member State.[47] Thus, the EEA Agreement indicates that the Commission shall either refuse to refer or make only a partial referral in the situation outlined here. In addition, the Commission shall take the situation in the territory of the EFTA States into account when examining the concentration and the Commission has the power to prohibit a concentration even where the concentration only strengthens or creates a dominant position within the territory of the EFTA States.[48]

The second question outlined above is whether the Commission has the competence to refer a concentration having a Community dimension to the national competition authority of an EFTA State. Article 6 of Protocol 24 EEA clearly provides that the Commission does have the power to refer a notified concentration to an EFTA State where the distinct market requirement has been fulfilled.[49] However, whereas Article 9 of the Merger Regulation was amended in 1997[50] these amendments were not replicated in Article 6 of Protocol 24 EEA. This has created 'discrepancies between the rights of the EFTA States and EU Member States as regards the possibilities of having mergers referred to them by the Commission'.[51]

---

[47] Concerning the latter possibility, *see Compass/Restorama/Rail Gourmet/Gourmet Nova*, Case COMP/M2639, decision of 26 February 2002 (Art. 9(3) decision).

[48] This follows from the fact that in accordance with the EEA Agreement, Art. 2 of the Merger Regulation shall be adapted so that the term 'common market' is replaced by the term 'functioning of the EEA Agreement', cf. Point A(1)(d)-(f) of Annex XIV EEA. *See* also Joos Stragier, 'The Competition Rules of the EEA Agreement and their Implementation', *European Competition Law Review*, 1993, no. 1, pp. 30-38, at pp. 31-32. Until now it appears that the Commission has only made referrals to the competition authorities of the Member States where this would not contravene the EEA Agreement.

[49] Until now there has been only one such example, namely *Aker Maritime/Kvaerner (II)*, Case COMP/M2683, decision of 23 January 2002, where the Commission made a partial referral to Norway.

[50] *See* further *supra* note 37.

[51] Cf. *EFTA Surveillance Authority comments on the European Commission's Merger Review Green Paper*, *supra* note 34, at p. 6. ESA also makes a number of other comments on the interaction between Art. 9 of the Regulation and Art. 6 of Protocol 24 EEA. In particular the Authority observes that:

'• Article 6 applies in respect of EEA co-operation cases handled by the Commission (i.e. those cases that are covered by the provisions of Protocol 24 EEA);

• It reflects the criteria set out in Article 9(1) and (2) of the EC Merger Regulation *before* these provisions were amended by Article 8 of Council Regulation (EC) No. 1310/97;

3.4.3. Referral from a Member State to the Commission

Where a concentration has neither a Community nor an EFTA dimension, a referral from one or more Member States to the Commission, in accordance with Article 22(3) of the Merger Regulation,[52] does not appear to create any problems. Where a concentration has an EFTA dimension but no Community dimension, however, one or more Member States might refer the concentration to the Commission in accordance with Article 22(3) of the Merger Regulation.

> *Example*
>
> A Norwegian, an Icelandic and a Danish undertaking enter into a concentration which has an EFTA dimension but no Community dimension so the ESA has competence to examine the concentration. According to Article 57(2)(b), however, this is without prejudice to the Danish competition authority and it decides to refer the case to the Commission in Brussels.

There seems to be nothing in the EEA Agreement or in the Merger Regulation which prevents such a referral. Furthermore, such a referral seems not to constitute an infringement on the competence of the ESA since, in Article 22(3) referrals, the Commission should be viewed as a 'substitute' for the Member State competition authority and Article 57(2)(b) of the EEA Agreement explicitly reserves competence for the Community Member States in the field of concentration control. In other words, both the Commission and the ESA would have jurisdiction to examine the concentration.[53]

- The provisions at Articles 9(3)-(8) and 9(10) of the EC Merger Regulation are not replicated in Protocol 24 EEA and thus Article 6 is silent on procedures;
- Article 6 does not require that an EFTA State make a referral request: although the Commission waited for such a request in the *Aker/Kvaerner (II)* case the text as it currently stands does not bar the Commission from referring a case on its own initiative where the established criteria are met; and
- At present Article 6 does not expressly refer to partial referrals.'

52 *See* chapter 1, section 3.2.

53 So far it appears that none of those cases that have been referred from a Member State to the Commission have had an EFTA dimension or otherwise have been of particular importance to one or more of the EFTA States. Today the possibility of referring cases to the Commission under Art. 22(3) is only used to a limited extent and so problems are not very likely to arise. The proposed amendments to the Merger Regulation may however change this. If so, it is to be hoped that the present problems relating to referrals from the EFTA States and

3.4.4. Consequences of splitting the EEA into two separate areas

As explained above, it was decided that concentration control under the EEA Agreement should be based on either a Community dimension or an EFTA dimension while an EEA dimension could not be applied. The consequences of this might be illustrated through three examples.

Example

Undertakings A and B have decided to merge. The aggregate worldwide turnover of A and B is more than € 5 billion and neither of the undertakings achieve more than two-thirds of the 'relevant' turnover in a single State in the territory of the EEA. While A has a turnover of more than € 250 million in the Community, but less than € 250 million in turnover in the EFTA Area, however, undertaking B has a turnover of less than € 250 million in the Community while B's turnover in the EFTA Area exceeds this figure. Both A and B are only active in two EFTA States and in two EC Member States.

Example

The situation is identical to the one set out in the preceeding example with only one material difference: Undertaking B neither achieves a turnover of more than € 250 million in the EFTA Area nor in the Community. If the EEA were to be viewed as a whole, however, B's turnover would exceed the € 250 million threshold.

Example

Again we have undertakings A and B which intend to merge. The € 5 billion threshold has been met and both A and B have a Community-wide turnover of more than € 250 million. However, both A and B derive more than two-thirds of their Community-wide turnover in one and the same Member State. If, however, the two-thirds rule were to be based on the turnover in the EEA Area, rather than the turnover derived within the Community only, this threshold would not have been met in the case of both undertakings concerned.

EU Member States identified by the ESA in *EFTA Surveillance Authority comments on the European Commission's Merger Review Green Paper*, *supra* note 34, at p. 7 are duly considered and remedied.

In all three examples, the Commission is precluded from examining the concentrations since they do not have a Community dimension.[54] Likewise, the ESA is precluded from examining the concentrations described in the two first examples while it might be that the concentration described in the last example possesses an EFTA dimension, in which case, the ESA has jurisdiction over the concentration.[55]

The EEA Agreement has only brought with it one change to the definition of Community dimension: 'In the last subparagraph the term "Member State" shall be replaced by "State"'.[56] In other words, one shall no longer read the two-thirds rule as a reference to the turnover generated in a 'Member State', but as a reference to turnover generated in a 'State' thus encompassing both Community and EFTA States. The question therefore is whether the Commission or the ESA must relinquish jurisdiction where two-thirds of the Community-wide or EFTA-wide turnover is derived within one and the same State *regardless* of whether this State is an EFTA or a Member State.

Example

Two Norwegian undertakings decide to merge. The undertakings have a world-wide turnover of more than € 5 billion and each of the two undertakings concerned has a turnover of more than € 250 million within the Community. While the two undertakings do not derive more than two-thirds of their Community-wide turnover within one and the same *Member State,* however, they each derive more than two-thirds of their worldwide turnover within Norway and thus clearly derive more than two-thirds of their Community-wide (and of their EFTA-wide) turnover within one and the same *State.*

The question is whether the Commission has jurisdiction to vet the concentration set out in the above example. It seems that the drafters of the EEA Agreement did not intend to bring about any change in the definition of Community dimension. Furthermore, it would seem somewhat strange if the turnover in, say, Norway should be compared with the Community-wide turnover or if the turnover in, for example,

---

[54] A Member State might, however, refer the concentration to the Commission under Art. 22(3) of the Merger Regulation, *see* further section 3.4.3 above.

[55] Since the EEA Agreement entered into force on 1 January 1994 several concentrations have had an EEA dimension, but neither a Community dimension nor an EFTA-dimension. For an example, *see Telenor/Canal+/Nethold*, Case 97/251 before the Norwegian competition authority (not publicly available).

[56] Cf. Point A(1)(c) of Annex XIV EEA.

Germany should be compared with the EFTA-wide turnover since the Community-wide and the EFTA-wide turnovers do not include the turnovers derived in Norway or Germany respectively. Hence, it is submitted that the two-thirds rule only apply with regard to Member States in the case of the Community dimension – and with regard to EFTA States in the case of the EFTA dimension.[57]

3.5. Co-operation in the field of concentrations

Detailed provisions on co-operation between the European Commission and the ESA in the field of concentrations are contained in Protocol 24 EEA.[58] The main elements concerning when co-operation is to take place are:

(1) The ESA and the European Commission shall exchange information and shall consult each other on general policy issues at the request of either of the surveillance authorities.[59]

(2) In cases where the Commission has sole competence, the European Commission and the ESA shall co-operate[60] in the handling of concentrations where:

(a) the combined turnover of the undertakings concerned in the territory of the EFTA States equals 25% or more of their total turnover within the EEA territory;[61] or

---

[57] *See* in support of this interpretation *Bellamy & Child – European Commmunity Law of Competition*, (P.M. Roth, ed.), 5th edition, Sweet & Maxwell, London 2001, p. 360 and 380 and Frank L. Fine, *Mergers and joint ventures in Europe: the law and policy of the EEC*, 2nd. edition, Graham & Trotman Ltd., London 1994, p. 23. Concerning this point, *see* also Olivier Mach, 'Le contrôle des concentrations (art. 57. EEE)' in *Accord EEE – Commentaires et réflexions*' (Olivier Jacot-Guillarmod (ed.)), Zürich 1992, pp. 355-375 at p. 372.

[58] For an exposition of the substantive rules regarding such co-operation, *see* J. Bourgeois, *supra* note 28, and Dr. T. Jakob-Siebert, 'EEA and Eastern European Agreements with the European Community', *1992 Fordham Corp. L. Inst.* (B. Hawk, ed. 1993), pp. 403-436.

[59] Cf. Art. 1(1) of Protocol 24 EEA.

[60] Provided, of course, that the product in question is covered by the EEA Agreement. *See* for example *Masterfoods/Royal Canin*, *supra* note 7 and *Nestlé/Ralston Purina*, *supra* note 7.

[61] Cf. Art. 2(1)(a) of Protocol 24 EEA. *See* for example *Voith/Sulzer*, Case IV/M478, decision of 29 July 1994, *Ericsson/Raychem*, Case IV/M519, decision of 21 November 1994, *Scandinavian Project*, Case IV/M522, decision of 28 November 1994, *Telia/Telenor*, Case IV/M1439, decision of 13 October 1999, [2001] OJ L40/1 and *Sampo/Storebrand*, *supra* note 40.

(b) each of at least two of the undertakings concerned has a turnover exceeding € 250 million in the territory of the EFTA States;[62] or

(c) the concentration is liable to create or strengthen a dominant position as a result of which effective competition would be significantly impeded in the territories of the EFTA States or a substantial part thereof;[63] or

(d) the concentration threatens to create or strengthen a dominant position as a result of which effective competition would be significantly impeded in a market within an EFTA State which presents all the characteristics of a distinct market, be it a substantial part of the territory covered by the EEA Agreement or not;[64] or

---

[62] Cf. Art. 2(1)(b) of Protocol 24 EEA. *See* for example *Thomson CSF/Deutsche Aerospace*, Case IV/M527, decision of 2 December 1994, *Shell Chimie/ELF Atochem*, Case IV/M475, decision of 22 December 1994, *Orkla/Volvo*, Case IV/M582, decision of 20 September 1995, *Telia/Telenor/Schibsted*, Case IV/JV1, decision of 27 May 1998 (the transaction also qualified under Art. 2(1)(a)), *Norsk Hydro/Saga*, *supra* note 32, *Siemens/E.ON/Shell/SSG*, Case COMP/M2367, decision of 27 March 2001, *The Airline Group/NATS*, Case COMP/M2315, decision of 14 May 2001 and *Sampo/Varma Sampo/If Holding/JV*, Case COMP/M2676, decision of 18 December 2001. Presumably *Skanska/Scancem*, Case IV/M1157, decision of 11 November 1998, [1999] OJ L183/1, also came within this category.

[63] Cf. Art. 2(1)(c) of Protocol 24 EEA. *See* for example *British Steel/Svensk Stål/NSD*, Case IV/M503, decision of 7 November 1994, *Electrolux/AEG*, Case IV/M458, decision of 21 June 1994, *Schneider/Lexel*, Case IV/M1434, decision of 3 June 1999, *Sanitec/Sphinx*, Case IV/M1578, decision of 1 December 1999, [2000] OJ L294/1, *Volvo/Scania*, Case IV/M1672, decision of 14 March 2000, [2001] OJ L143/74, *Industri Kapital (Nordkem/Dyno)*, Case COMP/M1813, decision of 12 July 2000, *SCA/Metsä Tissue*, Case COMP/M2097, decision of 31 January 2001, [2002] OJ L57/1 and *Pernod Ricard/Diageo/Seagram Spirits*, Case COMP/M2268, decision of 8 May 2001. *Astra/Zeneca*, Case COMP/M1403, decision of 26 February 1999 (cf. para. 63) as well as *Skandia/Storebrand/Pohjola*, Case IV/JV21, decision of 17 August 1999 (cf. paras. 20 and 31) presumably also fall into this category.

[64] Cf. Art. 2(2)(a) of Protocol 24 EEA. Compare this with Art. 9 of the Merger Regulation. Note that according to the wording of Art. 2(2)(a) of Protocol 24 EEA the Commission is under obligation to co-operate in the 'distinct-market' situations regardless of whether or not the ESA has made any request to this effect. In *Aker Maritime/Kvaerner (II)*, *supra* note 49, a market presenting all the characteristics of a distinct market within Norway was identified in Norway. At the request of the Norwegian competition authorities the case was partially referred thereto.

(e) an EFTA State wishes to adopt measures to protect legitimate interests such as public security, plurality of media and prudential rules.[65]

(3) The ESA only has sole competence where the concentration in question does not have a Community dimension. Thus, there is no Community interest with respect to such concentrations and accordingly the EEA Agreement does not provide for any formalised system for co-operation in these cases.

A large number of co-operation cases now exist. At the time of writing (December 2002), it appears that there have not been any cases where the ESA has found it necessary to formally disagree with the Commission as to whether a case is a co-operation case.[66]

4. FINAL COMMENT

The examination in this chapter has shown that the delimitation of jurisdiction under the EEA Agreement regarding the control of concentrations has created only a few lacunae and pitfalls. Presumably, the main reason for this is that, instead of creating a symmetrical system under which the ESA and the Commission will have to co-operate closely in the majority of the cases, the system is asymmetric in that the Commission alone is able to deal with the majority of the cases. While this approach is commendable from an administrative point of view, it is less satisfactory politically from the point of view of the EFTA countries.

In addition, it is submitted that the idea of dividing the EEA market into a Community market and an EFTA market is unsatisfactory. As shown above, concentrations which possess neither a Community nor an EFTA dimension might still have an EEA dimension. Thus, these concentrations take place in a market which, after the entering into force of the EEA Agreement, must be seen as one internal market and the different treatment of cases with an EEA dimension, an EFTA dimension

---

[65] Cf. Arts. 2(2)(b) and 7 of Protocol 24 EEA. *See* also Art. 21(3) of the Merger Regulation. In *Sampo/Storebrand*, *supra* note 40, Norway considered adopting such protective measures based on prudential rules. *See* further paras. 38 and 39 of the decision.

[66] ESA itself considers 'the co-operation between the Commission and the Authority in [the field of merger control] to be very effective', cf. *EFTA Surveillance Authority comments on the European Commission's Merger Review Green Paper*, *supra* note 34, at p. 4.

or a Community dimension should cause some worries as it necessarily must lead to an uneven playing field.

Put differently, the EEA has created an enormous common market in which undertakings are given ample room for manoeuvre. From this, it follows logically that the competition control of, *inter alia,* concentrations should be constructed so as to cover the full territory of the EEA. But as has been shown in this chapter, this has not been done. The consequence is that a number of concentrations which should really be dealt with at EEA level will now be dealt with at national level – if at all. Since the national authorities are not in a position to take into account the effects of these concentrations at EEA level, but only the effects at national level, this might have some adverse consequences.

A second point worthy of mention is the fact that the EFTA countries are bound by certain Community legislation and judgments by the European Court of Justice in Luxembourg while they are not bound by the Commission's own case law.

The Commission has considered a large number of difficulties in applying the Merger Regulation. This is not least the case with respect to the calculation of the Community dimension. The ESA is, however, not bound by these decisions and one might imagine that the ESA does not agree with the Commission's interpretation on every single point. Thus, situations where, for example, the ESA and the Commission disagree as to the correct interpretation and, therefore, to the correct allocation of jurisdiction may arise. Should such disagreement ever arise, this is likely to cause very considerable problems due to the tight time limits that apply with regard to the examination of concentrations.[67]

---

[67] The system for settling disputes between, on the one hand, the ESA and, on the other hand, the Commission as provided in Arts. 109(5) and 111 EEA seems to be inadequate in the present case. *See also* S. Norberg *et al, supra* note 7 pp. 268-270.

8. FORUM SHOPPING UNDER THE MERGER REGULATION

1. INTRODUCTION

This work is concerned with jurisdiction. An aspect closely related to jurisdiction is forum shopping: Is it possible to choose another forum which better meets one's needs?[1]

Lawyers working in the field of concentration control often prefer to notify the Commission rather than having to notify one or more Member State competition authorities. In particular, the fact that the Merger Regulation has introduced mutual exclusivity between, on the one hand, Community level and, on the other hand, Member State level has given rise to speculation about the possibilities of adapting a merger so that the merging parties themselves decide which authority – the Commission or Member State authorities – shall vet it.[2] Thus, for instance, having seen the planned merger between Impala Platinum of South Africa and the

---

[1] Whether forum shopping is good or bad remains an open question. *See* in this regard for instance the discussion between Friedrich K. Juenger and Brian R. Opeskin: Friedrich K. Juenger 'What's Wrong with Forum Shopping?' *Sydney Law Review*, vol. 16, 1994, pp. 5-13, Brian R. Opeskin 'The Price of Forum Shopping: A Reply to Professor Juenger', *Sydney Law Review*, vol. 16, 1994, pp. 14-27 and Friedrich K. Juenger 'Forum Shopping: A Rejoinder', *Sydney Law Review*, vol. 16, 1994, pp. 28-31.

[2] Damien Neven, Robin Nuttall and Paul Seabright, *Merger in Daylight – The Economics and Politics of European Merger Control*, Centre for Economic Policy Research, London 1993 at p. 79 observe that '[t]he prospect of alternative jurisdictions will presumably be a relatively minor consideration in the majority of deals where the commercial rationale can be expected to dominate. Still, these considerations may matter at the margin.' Simon Bishop and Mike Walker, *Economics of E.C. Competition Law: Concepts, Application and Measurement*, Sweet & Maxwell, London 1999, at p. 139 go further as they find that '[i]n general parties prefer to be investigated under the Merger Regulation and joint ventures are often structured so as to fall under the jurisdiction of the Merger Regulation'. The two authors at p. 140 continue by observing that '[i]t should be noted that some firms deliberately engaged in complex merger plans solely to raise their turnovers above the thresholds in order to avoid what are seen as particularly difficult competition authorities'.

platinum division of Lonrho of the UK be prohibited by the European Commission, Mr Michael McMahon, chairman of Impala Platinum, was quoted as saying: '… I can structure this transaction such that it falls outside [the European Commission's] rules.'[3]

In this chapter, I shall examine the possibilities which are open to the parties with regard to influencing the jurisdictional issue. Part of this examination is based upon a number of questionnaire answers from leading lawyers working in the field of merger control. Furthermore, information obtained from the Merger Task Force of the European Commission in Brussels and from national competition authorities of the Member States has played a significant role.

Before proceeding to the examination, it is probably advisable to briefly reiterate the Merger Regulation's rules on the allocation of jurisdiction.

2. A BRIEF OUTLINE OF THE JURISDICTIONAL RULES

Before the introduction of the Merger Regulation, a concentration could be examined under two different sets of competition rules in Europe: Under Articles 81 and 82 of the EC Treaty, the Commission had powers to examine certain concentrations and, at the same time, the concentration could come under the Member State competition authorities' scrutiny where the Member States had introduced concentration controls.

The introduction of the Merger Regulation meant that a system of reciprocal exclusivity was introduced. Thus, in principle, if a transaction comes within the scope of the Regulation, neither Articles 81 and 82 nor Member State competition rules apply.

The Regulation applies where an operation constitutes a 'concentration' and where this concentration has a 'Community dimension'. If an operation does not constitute a concentration, it might fall within the scope of Articles 81-82 and/or the Member States' competition rules. As a clear main rule, an operation which does constitute a concentration will not be examined under Articles 81-82 regardless of whether it has a Community dimension.[4] Thus, in principle, a concentration

---

3 Cf. *Financial Times*, Thursday 2 May 1996, p. 21. In the end the transaction was not restructured, however.

4 Cf. Sir Leon Brittan, *European Competition Policy – Keeping the Playing-Field Level*, Brassey London and CEPS Brussels, 1992 at p. 94.

without a Community dimension will not be examined under Articles 81-82 nor can it be examined under the Merger Regulation. Such an operation therefore falls within the exclusive ambit of the Member State competition authorities. The main principles may be illustrated in the following way:

Table 1: The Division of Jurisdiction

	+ Concentration	– Concentration
+ Community dimension	Merger Regulation	Articles 81 + 82 National Competition Authorities
– Community dimension	National Competition Authorities	Articles 81 + 82 National Competition Authorities

A concentration is a durable change of control. Thus, to find a concentration, it must first be found that the control over some economic entity has changed and, second, it must be ascertained that this change is durable. Whether a concentration is constituted is a question concerned with the substance of the transaction in question.

The Community dimension is not really concerned with substance as it is simply found on the basis of two sets of turnover thresholds as has been explained in the preceding chapters.[5]

From the above, it will be clear that where a lawyer believes that an intended operation will fare significantly better under the Regulation than under the alternative system, he or she should consider the possibilities of turning this operation into a concentration with a Community dimension, (or *vice versa*).

There may be many valid reasons for wanting to change an operation in this way. The most obvious and important is that the lawyer expects that the change

---

[5] In chapter 9 below I argue, however, that the Commission is precluded from taking jurisdiction over a concentration where this will constitute an infringement of public international law, irrespective of whether the concentration in question meets the thresholds.

will make it easier to obtain the necessary clearance.[6] It is, therefore, of interest to the parties to the concentration to find ways to decide themselves whether the intended operation shall fall within or outside the scope of the Merger Regulation. There are two ways of achieving this. Firstly, by deciding whether the operation shall constitute a concentration[7] and, secondly, by deciding whether it shall have a Community dimension. Since this work is only concerned with the Community dimension, in this chapter, I shall restrict myself to looking only at the latter of these two ways.[8]

3. GIVING THE CONCENTRATION A COMMUNITY DIMENSION

3.1. Introduction

In principle, it should not be possible for the undertakings to tinker with the Community dimension since it is based on the (audited) turnover figures of the undertakings concerned.

Nevertheless, there are, in fact, two main ways of influencing the Community dimension. The first involves the determination of which undertakings must be either included or excluded when the Community dimension is being calculated. Thus, by putting forward convincing arguments that certain undertakings must be either included in (or excluded from) the group of the undertaking concerned when

---

6 *See* also my article 'Merger Control in the European Community – A Summary of the Five Years since the Introduction of the Merger Regulation', *World Competition – Law and Economics Review*, 1995, vol. 19, pp. 5-24 at pp. 23-24 concerning the possibility of using the Merger Regulation for making an operation so to speak 'immune' to Arts. 81-82.

7 Richard Whish, *Competition Law*, fourth edition, Butterworths London 2001 at p. 749 explains that 'legal advisers would often deliberately design joint ventures to fall on the concentrative side of the divide – an example of legal formalism affecting substance'.

8 In my article 'Forum Shopping and the European Merger Control Regulation', *The Columbia Journal of European Law*, Vol. 3, No. 1, Fall/Winter 1996/97, pp. 109-123 at pp. 112-116 I have examined the possibilities of changing a transaction from constituting a concentration to constituting a co-operation agreement and *vice versa*. This examination relates to the Merger Regulation before the 1997 amendment however. In the same article at p. 121-122 I examine to what extent the provisions relating to ancillary restraints may be used for the purposes of forum shopping.

calculating the Community dimension, it may be possible to bring the group turn-overs above (or below) the thresholds. Indeed, in *Accor/Wagons-Lits*,[9] this appears to be exactly the approach taken by Accor.[10] Whether this way of influencing the Community dimension in a concentration case is open entirely depends on the actual facts of the individual case. In particular, the second set of thresholds in Article 1(3) is likely to make this option worth contemplating in an increasing number of cases, however.

The second way of affecting the Community dimension implies a careful structuring of the deal whereby the final outcome is more or less unaffected while, at the same time, the undertakings concerned have themselves decided which authority shall have jurisdiction. I will examine this latter method below.[11]

It is, however, important to observe that the ways of deciding which jurisdiction a concentration shall fall within as outlined below are only open to a minority of the cases.

3.2. Making an acquisition through a joint venture

Where two undertakings make a joint bid through a joint venture, *i.e.,* the joint venture is a pure bid vehicle, the Commission will consider the two parent under-takings to be the undertakings concerned. If, however, the two parent undertakings together have an already existing full-function joint venture,[12] it may be possible to arrange the acquisition to be made through this joint venture instead.[13] In the

---

9 Case IV/M126, [1992] OJ L204/1.

10 *See* chapter 3, section 2.5.5.

11 A third way exists since the undertakings may base their choice of partners for a concentra-tion on which authority will have jurisdiction to vet the concentration. Thus, Timothy Portwood, *Mergers under EEC Competition Law*, Athlone Press Ltd., London 1994 at p. 18 writes that '[t]o avoid EC control large companies may be tempted [to] choose less efficient mergers with smaller firms, thereby reducing the competitive potential of Community in-dustries.' It is my impression that Timothy Portwood's fears have proved to be rather un-founded.

12 The distinction between full-function joint ventures and joint ventures which are bid vehi-cles is explained above in chapter 2, section 3.3.

13 This possibility appear to have been available in *GKN/Brambles/SKP*, Case IV/M1160, de-cision of 26 May 1998. For obvious reasons it does not appear from the decision whether the parties actually considered the possibility.

latter case, it may be possible to convince the Commission that the joint venture should be considered to be the undertaking concerned rather than the two parents.[14] Obviously, this opens some possibilities for deciding whether an acquisition shall have a Community dimension. Four examples may illustrate this possibility.[15]

Example 1

Undertaking C wishes to acquire undertaking X. Undertaking C is a full-function joint venture between undertakings A and B which both belong to the group of C as defined in Article 5(4) of the Regulation. X has a Community-wide turnover of € 90 million. A and B each have € 4 billion in Community-wide turnover. If C acquires X, C and X will be the undertakings concerned. C will have an aggregate Community-wide turnover of € 8 billion, but X will only have a turnover in the Community of € 90 million. Thus, the requirement that at least two of the undertakings concerned achieve a Community-wide turnover of more than € 250 million has not been met[16] and the concentration does not possess a Community dimension.[17]

---

14 It is, however, important to add that even though the Commission makes the presumption that a full-function joint venture is the undertaking concerned this presumption will be rebutted where the Commission finds 'elements which demonstrate that the parent companies are in fact the real players behind the operation.' Thus 'where the acquisition leads to a substantial diversification in the nature of the joint venture's activities, this may … indicate that the parent companies are the real players in the operation. This will normally be the case when the joint venture acquires a target company operating on a different product market.' Cf. Commission Notice on the Concept of Undertakings Concerned, OJ 2.3.1998 C66/14 at paras. 27 and 28 (Undertaking Concerned Notice).

15 The introduction of the second set of thresholds in 1997 means that the number of conceivable situations which must be distinguished has grown considerably. In particular it is worth noting that although it may be possible to avoid one set of thresholds, it is still possible that the second set will catch the transaction.

16 Moreover, the requirement in the second set of thresholds that at least two of the undertakings each generate € 100 million in the Community has not been met either.

17 According to Heinz F. Löffler in *Langen/Bunte Kommentar zum deutschen und europäischen Kartellrecht*, 7th ed., Luchterhand, Neuwied 1994 at p. 1955, in the Commission's first prohibition decision *Aérospatiale-Alenia/De Haviland*, Case IV/M053, decision of 2 October 1991, [1991] OJ L334/42, the acquiring parties Aérospatiale and Alenia could have avoided the prohibition simply by avoiding coming within the scope of the Merger Regulation. According to Löffler the target, De Haviland, was to be acquired by Aérospatiale and Alenia whereupon it would be transferred to the two acquirers' longstanding joint venture ATR active in the same market as De Haviland. If instead ATR had made the acquisition

Example II

In example II, we might take the same facts as in example I. Now, however, undertaking C 'persuades' its parent undertakings to set up a joint venture, D, with the sole purpose of acquiring undertaking X. By doing this, the joint venture D must be considered to be a bid vehicle and the Commission must consider undertakings A and B to be the undertakings concerned. In this way, there are three undertakings concerned: A, B and X and since A and B each achieve more than € 250 million in the Community, this threshold has now been met.

Example III

In examples III and IV, the same exercise is done as in examples I and II, only this time we will be concerned with the two-thirds rule. Again we have undertaking C which wants to acquire undertaking X. C is a full-function joint venture between undertakings A and B which both belong to the group of C as defined in Article 5(4) of the Regulation. A has a Community-wide turnover of € 400 million while B has a Community-wide turnover of only € 250 million. Together A and B have a worldwide turnover exceeding € 5 billion. X achieves more than two-thirds of its € 300 million Community-wide turnover in Germany. A achieves almost all of its Community-wide turnover in Germany, while B achieves slightly less than two-thirds of its Community-wide turnover in Germany. Assume that C is considered to be the undertaking concerned (together with X). This means that the turnovers of A and B are attributed to C. In this way, C must be considered to achieve more than two-thirds of its Community-wide turnover in Germany. Thus, since X and C are the undertakings concerned and since they both achieve more than two-thirds of their Community-wide turnover in Germany, the concentration does not have a Community dimension.

Example IV

In example IV, we will take the same facts as in example III. Now, however, undertakings A and B decide to 'help' C by setting up a joint venture, D, to carry out the acquisition. In this situation, A, B and X will be the undertakings concerned. As B achieves less than two-thirds of its Community-wide turn-

---

itself, the joint venture would be the undertaking concerned and the transaction would not meet the thresholds.

over in Germany 'each of the undertakings concerned' does not achieve more than two-thirds of its Community-wide turnover in 'one and the same Member State'. Thus, the concentration has a Community dimension.

Subsequent to the acquisition, the acquirers may decide to carry out an organisational reshuffle in which the newly acquired X is transferred between the full-function joint venture C and the new joint venture set up between A and B.

The above approach will rarely be very costly and may be a good alternative in a number of cases. One problem is that the subsequent 'reshuffling' may be considered to constitute a new concentration which is notifiable. This, however, seems unlikely since the transfer takes place between the same parties.[18] The transfer to/from a full-function joint venture to/from a non-full-function joint venture does not constitute a real qualitative change of control. If this were so, any such organisational reshuffling would mean that the parties should consider whether they transferred business between a non-full function entity and a full-function entity. Where such a transfer took place the parties would have made a concentration and would have to notify this if it had a Community dimension. It appears to be unlikely that such internal reshuffling would need to be notified with the Commission.[19]

A second problem is that the transaction may be considered to constitute a circumvention and that the 'real transaction' should be the one to form the basis for allocating jurisdiction. On this point, the problem will be, firstly, that the authority claiming circumvention must normally bear the burden of proof, and secondly that the authority (if any) which originally did take jurisdiction is likely to argue in favour of the (circumventing) parties. One may, therefore, reasonably assume that this will not normally present a major obstacle.

---

[18] *See Lufthansa/Menzies/LSG/JV*, Case COMP/M1913, decision of 29 August 2000, paras. 6-9.

[19] Perhaps *Shell/Monteshell*, Case IV/M505, decision of 16 December 1994 at para. 6 may be taken to support this view. Nevertheless, Evelyn Egger, 'Um welche Fusionen kümmert sich die EU?', *Die Versicherungs Rundschau*, 1995, no. 4, pp. 6-7 at p. 6 indicates that in special cases purely intragroup reorganisations may come within the scope of the Merger Regulation. Unfortunately she does not elaborate on this interesting view point, but perhaps *Airbus*, Case COMP/M2061, decision of 18 October 2000 is one such example.

3.3. Escaping the two-thirds rule by including an extra undertaking concerned

As noted above in chapter 2, section 2.2, the two-thirds rule is not completely clear. The question is whether it applies to all the undertakings concerned or only to those undertakings with a Community-wide turnover of more than € 250 million respectively € 100 million. The difference may be important as the following example illustrates.

Example

Undertakings A, B and C have set up a joint venture with the sole purpose of acquiring undertaking X. Undertakings A, B and X all achieve more than two-thirds of their Community-wide turnover in Spain while undertaking C achieves most of its Community-wide turnover in France. The Community-wide turnover of A and B is more than € 250 million while it is less than € 100 million for C and X. Hence, not all of the undertakings concerned achieve more than two-thirds of their aggregate Community-wide turnover in one and the same Member State. *But* all of the undertakings concerned with a Community-wide turnover of more than € 250 million (and indeed of more than € 100 million) do achieve more than two-thirds of it within one and the same Member State, namely Spain.

As shown in chapter 2 at section 2.2, the Commission (rightly, it is submitted) considers that the two-thirds threshold has been met (*i.e.,* that not all the undertakings concerned achieve more than two-thirds of their turnover in one and the same Member State) if just one of the undertakings concerned does not achieve more than two-thirds of its Community-wide turnover in the same Member State as do(es) the other undertaking(s) concerned, regardless of the actual size of the Community-wide turnover.

Provided the interpretation proves to be correct, this means that in some cases, where all the undertakings concerned derive more than two-thirds of their Community-wide turnover within one and the same Member State, it might be desirable to 'add' to the transaction an (insignificant) 'undertaking concerned' deriving less than two-thirds of its Community-wide turnover in that Member State in order to give the transaction a Community dimension.

3.4. Acquisition of sole control over previously reduced or enlarged companies

In chapter 2, section 4.10, I have provided an account of the *Dan Air* case.[20] As I shall show below, the ruling in this case provides undertakings with the possibility of deciding for themselves which authority shall have jurisdiction.

The central facts in the *Dan Air* case were the following. In 1992, British Airways took over Dan Air, but did not want to use Dan Air's charter activities. These activities were therefore closed down before the formal acquisition. It appears, however, that British Airways took over the liabilities – and possibly also some of the rights – linked to the Dan Air charter activities. The problem was that in order to calculate the thresholds the Merger Regulation in Article 5(1) explicitly provides that the turnover of 'the preceding financial year' must be used. As Dan Air's charter activities had been operating in the preceding financial year, this would mean that the turnover derived from these would have to be included. The consequence would be that Dan Air would have a Community-wide turnover of more than € 250 million, which would give the concentration a Community dimension. In contrast, if the turnover derived from the charter activities were excluded, Dan Air's turnover would be less than € 250 million, meaning that the concentration would not have a Community dimension and would therefore be outside the reach of the Commission.[21]

The Court of First Instance decided that the Dan Air charter activities should not be included when deciding whether the British Airways acquisition had a Community dimension. Consequently, the concentration did not have a Community dimension and therefore the Commission had been right in abstaining from examining the transaction under the Merger Regulation.

The rule applied in the *Dan Air* case shows that where 'the target company has divested an entity or closed a business prior to the date of the event triggering notification or where such a divestment or closure is a pre-condition for the operation, then sales of the divested entity or closed business are not to be included when calculating turnover. Conversely, if the target company has acquired an entity prior to the date of the event triggering notification, the sales of the latter are to be added.'[22]

---

[20] Case T-3/93, *Air France* v. *Commission*, 1994 E.C.R. II-121.

[21] It is recalled that in 1992 only the first set of thresholds applied.

[22] Undertaking Concerned Notice, para. 17. *See* also Commission Notice on Calculation of Turnover, OJ C66/25 of 2.3.1998, at para. 27.

The consequence of the *Dan Air* rule is that the undertakings may now be able to decide which jurisdiction to fall within, simply by deciding the order in which to make (i) the event triggering notification and (ii) the closure of some unwanted business.

Three examples may illustrate this:

Example I

Undertaking A has a worldwide turnover of € 1.9 billion. A intends to take over the ailing undertaking X which has a worldwide turnover of € 600 million. Thus, the aggregate worldwide turnover is € 2.6 billion. A, however, intends to close down a part of X's business, generating a turnover of € 150 million. If this closure is made before the event triggering notification, the concentration is outside the scope of the Regulation, if it is made after this event, it may be within the scope of the Regulation.

Example II

If undertaking A from example I had a turnover of more than € 5 billion in the Community, but the target X only had a turnover in the Community of € 300 million (all of which is generated in one Member State only), the closure of the business activities of X, generating more than € 50 million, would mean that the Community-wide turnover of X would be less than € 250 million. Thus, if this closure is made before the decisive event triggering notification, only one of the undertakings concerned will have a Community-wide turnover of more than € 250 million and the concentration will be outside the jurisdiction of the Commission. If the order is reversed so that the closure is only made after the decisive event triggering notification, then both undertakings have a Community-wide turnover of more than € 250 million and the Commission may have jurisdiction.

Example III

The last example concerns undertaking A with a turnover of more than € 5 billion in the Community. More than two-thirds of undertaking A's Community-wide turnover is derived in Germany. A wants to acquire undertaking X with a Community-wide turnover of € 1 billion, of which € 610 million is derived in Germany. However, A intends to close down the activities of B outside Germany, generating more than € 100 million. If this is done before the event triggering notification, both undertakings derive more than two-thirds of their Community-wide turnover in Germany and the concentration falls outside the scope of the Regulation. If the closure is made after this event, the concentration has a Community dimension.[23]

What is striking here is that situations which are completely identical from an economic viewpoint may be dealt with at either Community or Member State level depending on the order in which, so to speak, the relevant papers are signed.[24]

3.5. Splitting one transaction or joining more transactions

When the drafters to the Merger Regulation created the first set of thresholds, they were aware that the 'parts rule' in Article 5(2)(1)[25] could be used for circumventing the Regulation if the parties split the transaction into more separate transactions. Consequently, they included a special provision to prevent this in Article 5(2)(2).[26]

Nonetheless, the second set of thresholds, included in 1997, may be circumvented by splitting up the transaction.

Example

Three undertakings, A, B and C, decide to merge. Their combined aggregate worldwide turnover is more than € 2.5 billion. All three undertakings are present in the Community. A generates € 200 million in Member States X and Y, B generates € 200 million in Member States X and Z, and C generates € 200 million in Member States Y and Z. If the three undertakings merge, they meet the second set of thresholds. Thus, the combined aggregate worldwide turnover is more than € 2.5 billion, the aggregate Community-wide turnover of each of at least two of the undertakings concerned is more than € 100 million, the combined aggregate turnover of all the undertakings concerned is more than € 100 million in each of at least three Member States (Member States X, Y and Z) and, in each of these three Member States, the aggregate turnover of

---

[23] In *Allianz/Vereinte*, Case IV/M812, decision of 11 November 1996 the Commission applied the *Dan Air* rule to the two-thirds threshold. *See* in connection to this case also *Allianz/Hermes*, Case IV/M813, decision of 27 September 1996.

[24] For further references on this point, *see* above chapter 2, section 4.10.

[25] *See* chapter 2, part 4.

[26] *See* chapter 2, section 4.11.

each of at least two of the undertakings concerned is more than € 25 million (A and B in Member State X, A and C in Member State Y, B and C in Member State Z). Lastly, the undertakings concerned do not all generate more than two-thirds of their Community-wide turnover in one and the same Member State.

If, however, the three undertakings agree that first two of them will merge to become one entity and then the third undertaking will join the merged entity, it will be impossible to have at least two undertakings with a turnover of at least € 25 million in at least three Member States.

Presumably, this possibility of circumvention will only rarely be available. Moreover, the parties still run the risk that the Commission finds that the arrangement amounts to circumvention. Still, in a limited number of cases, it may prove to constitute an interesting option.

An example of how it may be possible to circumvent the Merger Regulation's present jurisdictional rules by 'joining more transactions' into one is presented by the Commission in the *2001 Green Paper on the review of the Merger Regulation.*[27] This example I will reproduce *in extenso:*

Example

'Consider a situation where Company A intends to sell the following assets (which, for the sake of the argument, may be active in the same relevant market and have been run as a single entity by A) to company B:

- – 100% of its subsidiary A1,
- – its 50% stake in A2 (a jointly controlled company), and
- – its 25% stake in A3 (not a controlling stake).

… Under the current rules the acquisitions of A1 and A2 would be considered as separate concentrations, whereas the acquisition of the stake in A3 would not be characterised as a concentration at all. The two first-mentioned would, depending on the turnovers involved in each of those two transactions, be subject to assessment under the Merger Regulation or by (multiple) Member State(s). The result would be completely different if A, prior to the sale, would put A1-A3 in a holding company (for example, for tax reasons) that subsequently was transferred to B. In this case there would only be one

---

27 *2001 Green Paper on the review of Council Regulation (EEC) No 4064/89,* COM(2001) 745 final, Brussels 11.12.2001, paras. 131-132.

concentration under which B would acquire sole control over the holding company. Moreover, all turnover related to the assets held by that company would be taken into account for the decision on jurisdiction, which as a result would mean that the entire transfer of assets would be subject to an assessment at either Community or Member State level …'

The combination of both an acquisition of sole control and an acquisition of joint control (setting up a joint venture) may also provide other possibilities of forum shopping. Consider the following situation:

Example

The Japanese undertaking A has an aggregate worldwide turnover of € 6 billion. A generates sales of € 500 million in the Community through its two subsidiaries X and Y. X generates € 450 million while Y generates € 50 million. B is a Belgian undertaking generating a turnover of € 2 billion (all in the Community, but less than two-thirds in any one Member State). A and B agree that B shall acquire sole control of X and joint control of Y. Although the two transactions take place within a short period of time they must be viewed as independent.[28] If A and B agree that B shall acquire joint control over Y before acquiring X, both transaction will have a Community dimension. If, however, A and B decide to make the two transactions in reverse order, only B's acquisition of sole control over X will have a Community dimension. This is so since A will only generate a Community wide turnover of € 50 million after the sale of X.

3.6. Other possibilities

It is likely that other possibilities of getting around the Community dimension jurisdiction rules exist.[29] It is, though, important to be aware that there is always a

---

[28] Since only one of the two transactions concern an acquisition of sole control the two transactions are not caught by Art. 5(2)(2). *See* further above, chapter 2, section 4.11.2 and *Bank of New York/Royal Bank of Scotland Trust Bank*, Case IV/M1618, decision of 25 August 1999 and *Bank of New York/Royal Bank of Scotland/RBSI Security Services*, Case IV/M1660, decision of 26 August 1999.

[29] European Commission, 'Competition and Integration – Community merger control policy', *European Economy* no. 57 1994 at p. 41 suggests that some transactions have been changed

risk that the interpretation applied by the undertakings will not be accepted by the relevant authorities, making it imperative to take the necessary precautions. In particular, it is advisable to obtain the Commission's prior acceptance of the interpretation of the rules with regard to the specific case before bringing about the operation.

---

from being partial acquisitions to being joint ventures in order to give the transaction a Community dimension. Changing the transaction in this way, however, has a material impact on the final outcome (joint control instead of sole control).

9. THE REAL COMMUNITY DIMENSION

1. INTRODUCTION

When the Merger Regulation was adopted Sir Leon Brittan, then commissioner responsible for competition policy, explained that the turnover thresholds delimiting the Regulation's scope constituted nothing but 'a blunt and even arbitrary instrument'.[1] My examination of the turnover thresholds in the preceding chapters supports this assertion.

In this concluding chapter I will first consider the turnover thresholds' suitability as a means for defining the 'real Community dimension' whereupon I will consider the possibility of improving the Regulation's current jurisdictional delimitation.

2. THE TURNOVER THRESHOLDS AND REAL COMMUNITY DIMENSION

2.1. 'Real Community dimension'

In the first edition of this work, I introduced the concept of 'real Community dimension'[2] which I defined as 'matters falling within the Treaty'.[3] Since the Community is founded upon the principle of attributed powers, the Community's ambit cannot be wider than the scope of the Treaty. This definition of the Community dimension I still consider to be correct.[4]

---

[1] Sir Leon Brittan, *Competition Policy and Merger Control in the Single European Market*, Grotius Publications Ltd., Cambridge 1991, p. 53.

[2] At least, to my knowledge, the notion had not been used earlier.

[3] Page 249 of the first edition.

[4] In the *Green Paper on the Review of Council Regulation (EEC) No. 4064/89*, Brussels 11 December 2001, COM(2001) 745/6 final (hereinafter '*2001 Green Paper*') the Commission

To what extent the turnover thresholds provide a precise reflection of the real Community dimension concerns two questions. First, whether the thresholds catch transactions that do not possess a real Community dimension. Secondly, whether transactions that arguably should be controlled at Community level fail to meet the thresholds. The former of these two questions may be divided into one concerning the Regulation's external reach, *i.e. vis-à-vis* third states, and one concerning its internal scope, *i.e. vis-à-vis* the Member States.[5]

In what follows, I first consider to what extent the turnover thresholds, as interpreted by the Commission, catch concentrations that do not possess a real Community dimension. I then consider whether transactions that arguably should be vetted by the Commission may, in some instances, fail to meet the thresholds. On that basis, I answer the question of whether the Regulation's turnover thresholds properly reflect the 'real Community dimension'.

2.2. The external limit of the Merger Regulation

2.2.1. *Before the* Gencor *judgment*

Being a creature of public international law, the Community is *a fortiori* also bound by this law. This necessarily means that the Treaty, as well as any legislation that

---

has defined 'real Community dimension' as 'opposed to a national dimension' (Annex I, para. 32, *see* likewise *Report from the Commission to the Council on the application of the Merger Regulation thresholds*, Brussels 28 June 2000, COM(2000) 399 final (hereinafter '*Commission's 2000 Report*') at para. 19). This is not a fitting definition. For example, an insignificant concentration between foreign undertakings taking place outside the Community and producing no effects in the Community whatsoever, *neither* has a national (*i.e.* Member State) dimension *nor* a Community dimension. Richard Burnley, 'An Appropriate Jurisdictional Trigger for the EC Merger Regulation and the Question of Decentralisation', *World Competition*, 2002 pp. 263-277 at p. 264 refers to 'true 'Community dimension''. At p. 269 he seems to define this as concentrations that fulfil the 'interstate trade criterion' (*i.e.* concentrations that have an appreciable effect on trade between the Member States). *See* likewise my article 'The Delimitation of Jurisdiction with regard to Concentration Control under the EEA Agreement', *European Competition Law Review* 1995 pp. 30-39 at p. 33.

5 The scope is equally limited as to the substantive issues it covers cf. Art. 2 of the Treaty. Exceptional cases apart, it is unlikely that concentrations between business undertakings will not fall within the Treaty's substantive coverage.

derives its authority therefrom, must be interpreted, and its scope limited, in the light of applicable public international law.[6]

In respect of the delimitation of jurisdiction under public international law a distinction is often drawn between, on the one hand, what is known as prescriptive or legislative jurisdiction and, on the other hand, what is known as enforcement jurisdiction. Prescriptive jurisdiction concerns the question of what a State may regulate, whereas enforcement jurisdiction concerns the executive action in pursuance of or consequent to these provisions to the specific case. The question of whether the turnover thresholds are in conformity with public international law must be examined in the light of the rules on prescriptive jurisdiction.

International law provides several bases from which a State may draw legislative authority; some of these bases are more controversial than others.[7] The two generally recognised bases for legislative jurisdiction, and the only ones that will normally be relevant in respect of the Merger Regulation, are those of territoriality and nationality.[8] There is a general consensus that a State has the competence to prescribe the laws that are to apply to its own nationals and to resources and persons within its own territory. Jurisdiction based on territoriality covers both acts which originated within the territory of the State (so-called subjective territoriality) and acts which originated abroad, but which were completed, at least in part, within the State's territory (so-called objective territoriality). The limits of objective territoriality have been (and continue to be) the cause of much dispute, however. In particular, it has been disputed whether the so-called effects doctrine is consistent with the territoriality principle.[9] This doctrine was primarily developed in American competition law.

---

[6] The European Court of Justice made this clear in Case C-286/90, *Anklagemyndigheden* v. *Peter Michael Poulsen and Diva Navigation Corp.* 1992 ECR I-6019. *See* also Case T-115/94, *Opel Austria* v. *Council*, 1997 ECR II-39 at para. 90.

[7] Indeed, in *The Lotus Case (France* v. *Turkey)* (1927) P.C.I.J. Series A, no. 10, (pp. 18-21) the Permanent Court of International Justice took the view that jurisdiction may be assumed in the absence of contrary prohibitive rules. This view has been criticised by a substantial number of authorities and has also been contradicted by the views of the International Court in later cases, cf. Ian Brownlie, *Principles of Public International Law*, fifth ed., Oxford University Press, Oxford 1998, pp. 305-306.

[8] Other bases include the passive personality principle, the protective or security principle, and the universality principle.

[9] In particular British lawyers have been very sceptical towards the effects doctrine and have taken the view that it goes further than what is allowed under public international law. A

Under the effects doctrine a State may take jurisdiction over persons outside its territory if the conduct of those persons has produced effects within its territory. Within the field of competition law this doctrine is normally traced back to the *American Alcoa* judgment of 1945[10] in which judge Learned Hand argued that 'it is settled law ... that any state may impose liabilities, even upon persons not within its allegiance, for conduct outside its borders that has consequences within its borders which the state reprehends; and these liabilities other states will ordinarily recognize'.[11] Since the Alcoa judgment was delivered, American courts have developed and refined the doctrine and today it forms an integral part of US competition law.[12]

The European Commission itself asserts that it has submitted to the effects doctrine since 1964.[13] In contrast, until today the European Court of Justice has refrained from endorsing the doctrine. In 1988, the Court pronounced the well-known *Wood Pulp* judgment.[14] The case concerned an alleged collusion between foreign wood pulp producers on prices charged to customers in the Community. The Commission fined the involved undertakings which in turn challenged the fines before the Court. According to the undertakings engaged in the price fixing, the Commission did not have the requisite jurisdiction under the territoriality principle. Advocate General Darmon rejected this argument and advised the Court

---

telling example of this may be found in the British *Aide-Mémoire* to the Commission of the European Communities of 20 October 1969, reproduced in I. Brownlie, *supra* note 7 at pp. 314-317. This scepticism seems to have been mitigated over the years, however.

10 *United States* v. *Aluminium Co. of America* (Alcoa), United States Circuit Court of Appeals, Second Circuit, 148 F.2d 416; 1945 U.S. App.

11 *United States* v. *Aluminium Co. of America* (Alcoa), *supra* note 10, at p. 443.

12 A fine account of this development can be found in Joseph P. Griffin, 'Extraterritoriality in U.S. and EU Antitrust Enforcement', *Antitrust Law Journal* 1999 pp. 159-199.

13 *See* the Commission's *XIth Report on Competition Policy – 1981*, Luxembourg 1982 at points 34-37. *See* also its XIV*th Report on Competition Policy – 1984*, Luxembourg 1985 at point 60. Note, however, that according to C.S. Kerse, *E.C. Antitrust Procedure*, fourth edition, London 1998 at p. 338 '[t]he Community has itself recognised the controversial nature of the effects doctrine, classifying it as one of the bases of jurisdiction which have found less than general acceptance under international law'.

14 Joined Cases 89, 104, 114, 116, 117 and 125-129/85, *A. Ahlström Osakeyhtiö and others* v. *Commission*, ECR 1988 5193. The judgment is generally referred to as Wood Pulp or Wood Pulp I.

to adopt the effects doctrine.[15] The Court, importantly, did not follow its Advocate General and thus did not adopt the effects doctrine.[16] It nevertheless found that the Commission had had the requisite jurisdiction under the territoriality principle since 'an infringement of Article [81], such as the conclusion of an agreement which has had the effect of restricting competition within the common market, consists of conduct made up of two elements, the formation of the agreement, decision or concerted practice and the implementation thereof. If the applicability of prohibitions laid down under competition law were made to depend on the place where the agreement, decision or concerted practice was formed, the result would obviously be to give undertakings an easy means of evading those provisions. The decisive factor is therefore the place where it is implemented.'[17] The Court continued to observe that '[t]he producers in this case implemented their pricing agreement within the common market'.[18]

The *Wood Pulp* ruling has given rise to much discussion.[19] It introduces the notion of 'implementation', but fails to provide a definition thereof. Some observ-

---

[15] Or, to be more precise, the 'criterion of qualified effect' as he termed it.

[16] *See* likewise Sir Leon Brittan, *supra* note 1, at p. 10-11 and 13, I. Brownlie, *supra* note 7 at p. 312 with note 68 and Aidan Robertson and Marie Demetriou, ''But that was in another country …': The extraterritorial application of US antitrust laws in the US Supreme Court', *International and Comparative Law Quarterly* 1994, pp. 417-425 at p. 423. It is worth of note that the Court simply refrained from pronouncing itself upon the effects doctrine. In other words, it did not rule out adopting it in future. In the Dyestuffs cases (*see* in particular Case 48/69, *ICI*, ECR 1972 619, Case 52/69, *Geigy*, ECR 1972 787 and Case 53/69, *Sandoz*, ECR 1972 845), Advocate General Mayras had equally advised the Court to adopt the effects doctrine. In these cases also the Court chose not to follow the advice of its Advocate General. Instead it held that jurisdiction could be based upon the single economic entity doctrine.

[17] Para. 16 of the judgment.

[18] Para. 17 of the judgment.

[19] *See* for example Dieter G.F. Lange and John Byron Sandage, 'The *Wood Pulp* Decision and its Implications for the Scope of EC Competition Law', *Common Market Law Review* 1989, pp. 137-165, Laurence Idot, 'Jurisprudence – Arrêt du 27 septembre 1988 (Cour plénière) Entreprises de 'pâte de bois' C. Commission des Commautés européennes', *Revue trimestrielle de droit européen*, 1989 pp. 341-359, Vaughan Lowe, 'International Law and the Effects Doctrine in the European Court of Justice', *The Cambridge Law Journal* 1989, pp. 9-11, Mark Friend, 'The Long Arm of Community Law', *European Law Review*, 1989, pp. 169-172, Theofanis Christoforou and David B. Rockwell, 'European Economic Community Law: The Territorial Scope of Application of EEC Antitrust Law', *Harvard International Law Journal*, Volume 30, 1989 pp. 195-206, F.A. Mann, 'The Public International Law of

ers have taken the view that the Court of Justice simply endorsed the effects doctrine.[20] This is not correct. Instead the Court introduced the (less far-reaching[21]) notion of implementation, thereby avoiding to take a position on the effects doctrine.[22] It therefore based the Community's jurisdiction on the fact that not only did the anticompetitive agreement produce effects in the Community but, indeed, it was consummated ('implemented') there. In other words, jurisdiction was founded upon the fact that the illicit price fixing agreement was specifically aimed at the Community's market for wood pulp.[23]

In my view the Court's creation of the implementation criterion was an elegant way of avoiding – or deferring, to be more precise – the sensitive question of whether Community law should fully adopt the effects doctrine. However, whereas the implementation criterion is likely to catch most of the situations where purely foreign undertakings engage in anticompetitive *behaviour* (such as price fixing) that severely affects competition in the Community, it is much more difficult – not to say impossible – to argue that *concentrations* between only foreign undertakings that produce such effects in the Community are implemented

---

Restrictive Practices in the European Court of Justice', *International and Comparative Law Quarterly*, 1989, pp. 375-377, Bernhard Beck, 'Extraterritoriale Anwendung des EG-Kartellrechts Rechtsvergleichende Anmerkungen zum "Zellstoff"-Urteil des Europäischen Gerichtshof', *Recht der internationalen Wirtschaft*, 1990, pp. 91-95 and Clive Schmitthoff, 'Jurisdiction of EEC over non-EEC enterprises infringing EEC competition law', *Journal of Business Law*, 1988, pp. 455-456.

20   *See* for example F.A. Mann, *supra* note 19, B. Beck, *supra* note 19, C. Schmitthoff, *supra* note 19.

21   This may be illustrated by an example: London has a large market for both insurance and reinsurance. If British reinsurance companies decide to boycott a specific type of insurance (or a specific insurance company) on the London insurance market, this may have appreciable effects in, for instance, the USA. Hence, although the anticompetitive arrangement is both formed and implemented in Britain it may nevertheless have effects in *e.g.* the USA. For another example, *see* V. Lowe, *supra* note 19, p. 11.

22   *See* likewise Alison Jones and Brenda Sufrin, *EC Competition Law – Text, Cases and Materials*, Oxford University Press, Oxford 2001 at p. 1055. It is worth noting that at the time when the judgment in *Wood Pulp* was rendered, some of the Member States (in particular the British Government) were opposing the American authorities' reliance upon the effects doctrine.

23   Likewise, Sir Leon Brittan, *supra* note 1 at p. 12. *See* also D.G.F. Lange and J.B. Sandage, *supra* note 19, at pp. 161-162.

there.[24] Put differently, the implementation criterion is not suited for delimiting jurisdiction *vis-à-vis* concentrations.[25]

To sum up, there is a strong argument that under public international law the effects doctrine provides an acceptable basis for prescriptive jurisdiction. Going beyond the limits of this doctrine, and not having any other generally accepted jurisdictional basis, is widely considered to be against public international law. Nevertheless, before the Court of First Instance rendered judgment in *Gencor*[26] the Community's judiciary had only accepted the implementation criterion as a basis for the extra-territorial reach of the Community's competition laws. Essentially, the implementation criterion was a restricted version of the effects doctrine as it has been developed in American competition law.

In what follows I will base my examination on the assumption that under public international law the effects doctrine generally forms the widest jurisdictional basis for vetting concentrations.

2.2.2. The Gencor *judgment by the Court of First Instance*

The question of the limits to the Community's jurisdiction to vet foreign concentrations under the Merger Regulation was put to the Court of First Instance in the *Gencor* case.[27] Below I briefly explain the relevant facts of the case followed by an

---

[24] Contrast with Sir Leon Brittan, *supra* note 1, who at p. 43 observes that 'to use the jurisdictional language of our Court of Justice, there can be no doubt that mergers which are liable to have a significant impact on the competitive structure of our market are *implemented* in our territory' (italics in the original).

[25] The *Wood Pulp* judgment was rendered in 1988, *i.e.* before the Merger Regulation was adopted. Although Arts. 81 and 82 could be applied to concentrations in exceptional cases, one may reasonably assume that the judges deciding *Wood Pulp* only had anticompetitive behaviour – not structural concentrations – in mind when they introduced the notion of implementation. And it would be unjust to criticise them for this.

[26] Case T-102/96, *Gencor Ltd. v. Commission*, ECR 1999 II-753 (not appealed).

[27] *Supra* note 26. The case has generated a considerable number of commentaries. *See* in particular Morten P. Broberg, 'The European Commission's Extraterritorial Powers in Merger Control – The Court of First Instance's Judgment in *Gencor v. Commission*', *International and Comparative Law Quarterly*, 2000, pp. 172-182, Yves van Gerven and Lorelien Hoet, '*Gencor*: Some Notes on Transnational Competition Law Issues *European Court of First Instance 25 March 1999, T-102/96, Gencor Ltd. v. Commission*', *Legal Issues of Economic Integration*, 2001 pp. 195-210, Piet Jan Slot, 'Case T-102/96, *Gencor Ltd v. Commission*,

analysis of its treatment of the prescriptive jurisdiction question. As a preliminary remark it should be noted that although the *Gencor* ruling does clarify certain matters with regard to the Community's extraterritorial jurisdiction, it also leaves a number of questions unanswered.

The *Gencor* case concerned the creation of a joint venture whereby the South African company Gencor and the British company Lonrho would combine their respective South African platinum activities. The South African Competition Board considered that the concentration did not give rise to concerns under South African competition law. The European Commission, however, took the view that the transaction would lead to the creation of a dominant duopoly position in the world platinum market and the concentration was therefore prohibited. Gencor challenged this prohibition claiming *inter alia* that under public international law the Commission lacked jurisdiction over the concentration.

The Court of First Instance rejected Gencor's argument. It first observed that '[t]he applicant cannot, by reference to the judgment in Wood pulp, rely on the criterion as to the implementation of an agreement to support its interpretation of the territorial scope of the Regulation … According to Wood pulp, the criterion as to the implementation of an agreement is satisfied by mere sale within the Community, irrespective of the location of the sources of supply and the production plant'.[28] The Court went on to examine whether the contested decision was consistent with the effects doctrine.[29] It found that this was the case.

The Court thus recognised two different bases upon which the Commission may found its jurisdiction under the Merger Regulation. Firstly, the implementation criterion and, secondly, the effects doctrine.[30] I will examine these in turn.

Judgment of 25 March 1999 of the Court of First Instance, Fifth Chamber, extended composition, [1999] ECR II-753', *Common Market Law Review* 2001 pp. 1573-1586 and Francisco Enrique González-Díaz, 'Recent Developments in EC Merger Control Law – '*The Gencor Judgment*' ', *World Competition* 1999 pp. 3-28.

28 *Supra* note 26 at para. 87.

29 The Court referred to 'public international law', not to the 'effects doctrine'. However, it is apparent from the criteria laid down in para. 90 of the judgment that the examination concerned the effects doctrine.

30 It is worth noting that the Court of First Instance very clearly distinguished between the implementation criterion and the effects doctrine. Hence, the Court did not consider the implementation criterion to be just another name for the effects doctrine.

According to the Court of First Instance the implementation criterion is satisfied 'by mere sale within the Community'. To my mind this is not a convincing construction of the Court of Justice's implementation criterion. As explained above, in the *Wood Pulp* judgment the Court of Justice basically abstained from taking a position on the effects doctrine and instead created the less far-reaching implementation criterion. The *Wood Pulp* case concerned a price fixing agreement. Such agreement is 'consummated' or 'implemented' where the parties are selling at the agreed prices. Hence, if the parties had been selling into the Community at prices that had not been fixed in advance, the implementation criterion would not have been met. Mere sales within the Community were not enough. Only because the sales were made at fixed prices in the Community was the criterion met.

It is respectfully submitted that the Court of First Instance overlooks the fact that when the Court of Justice created the implementation criterion the judges had anticompetitive *behaviour* in mind. It is not difficult to conceive of an agreement between foreign undertakings that is consummated (implemented) in the Community. In contrast, concentrations concern the creation of (possibly) anticompetitive *structures* and it is therefore very difficult to imagine a concentration between purely foreign undertakings that is implemented in the Community.[31] Unless, that is, one accepts the Court of First Instance's view that pure sales amount to implementation.

It is worth noting that in a number of situations the Court of First Instance's construction of the implementation criterion would go even further than the effects doctrine; thereby in itself indicating that the construction is at odds with the criterion laid down in the *Wood Pulp* judgment. This is so where the parties are selling into the Community but the actual transaction does not produce effects there.[32]

---

[31] P.J. Slot, *supra* note 27, at p. 1580 likewise observes that 'it can be questioned whether in the case of mergers, the *Wood Pulp* test is appropriate. In the case of mergers of companies with global presence the criterion of implementation of the agreement does not really make sense'. Contrast with André Fiebig, 'The Extraterritorial Application of the European Merger Control Regulation', *Columbia Journal of European Law*, 1998, pp. 79-100 at pp. 88-89.

[32] Examples of this are provided below in section 2.2.3. One commentator appears to take the view that mere sales into the Community means that both the implementation criterion and the effects doctrine automatically have been fulfilled, cf. Antonio F. Bavasso, '*Gencor: A Judicial Review of the Commission's Policy and Practice – Many Lights and Some Shadows*', World Competition 1999, pp. 45-65 at p. 50. *See* equally the same author in 'Boeing/ McDonnell Douglas: Did the Commission Fly Too High?', *European Competition Law Review*, 1998, 243-248 at pp. 245-246 and Evelyne Tichadou, 'Internationalrechtliche Aspekte des Wettbewerbsrechts am Beispiel des Boeing-Falles', *Zeitschrift für europarechtliche*

Moreover, a concentration only has a Community dimension as defined in Article 1 of the Merger Regulation where at least two of the undertakings concerned have sales in the Community. This means that any concentration with a Community dimension fulfils the Court of First Instance's construction of the implementation criterion. Hence, the Court construed the criterion in such a way that potentially it would be more – rather than less – far-reaching than the effects doctrine.

Having found that the concentration in the *Gencor* case fulfilled the implementation criterion, the Court of First Instance went on to consider the case in the light of the effects doctrine and in so doing it ruled that '[a]pplication of the Regulation is justified under public international law when it is *foreseeable* that a proposed concentration will have an *immediate* and *substantial* effect in the Community'.[33] The Court found that these three criteria were met[34] and therefore concluded that 'the application of the Regulation … was consistent with public international law'.[35] It thus rather unambiguously endorsed the effects doctrine as an appropriate jurisdictional basis of EC competition law.[36]

The endorsement of the effects doctrine by the Court of First Instance is not without ambiguities, however. The doctrine is examined under the headline 'Compatibility of the contested decision with public international law', but in principle such compatibility had already been established as part of the examination of the

---

Studien, 2000, pp. 61-77 at p. 68. Obviously, this view is not correct. Hence, it was with good reason that in section V of Case IV/M877, *Boeing/McDonnell Douglas*, decision of 30 July 1997, [1997] OJ L336/16, the Commission found it necessary to observe that '[n]ot only does the operation have a Community dimension within the legal sense of the Merger Regulation …, it also has an important economic impact on the large commercial jet aircraft market within the EEA …'.

[33] *Supra* note 26 at para. 90, italics added.

[34] In order for a concentration to be prohibited it must create or strengthen 'a dominant position as a result of which effective competition would be significantly impeded in the common market or in a substantial part of it …' cf. Art. 2(3). Hence it seems that one may reasonably assume that if a concentration fulfils the criterion in Art. 2(3), then it also fulfils the effects doctrine.

[35] *Supra* note 26 at para. 101.

[36] The Court's definition of the effects doctrine draws heavily upon American law, *see* in particular the Foreign Trade Antitrust Improvements Act (FTAIA) of 1982, Public LA 97-290-Oct. 8, 1982 96 STAT. 1233, title IV, section 402. Advocate General Darmon in his opinion in the *Wood Pulp* case also proposed that the Court of Justice should adopt a 'criterion of the direct, substantial and foreseeable effect'. (para. 57) In so doing, he explicitly referred to American law.

implementation criterion. A possible explanation might be that the Court was of the view that prescriptive jurisdiction should be examined in the light of the implementation criterion whereas enforcement jurisdiction should be examined in the light of the effects doctrine. Indeed at para. 90 of the judgment, the Court explains that '[a]pplication of the Regulation is justified under public international law when it is foreseeable that a proposed concentration will have an immediate and substantial effect in the Community'. The term 'application' indicates that the Court was considering enforcement jurisdiction.[37] Nevertheless, as observed by P.J. Slot, when examining the effects doctrine the Court of First Instance first of all discusses the criteria of foreseeable, immediate and substantial effect in the Community. These three criteria are generally considered to form part of prescriptive jurisdiction,[38] and Slot therefore takes the view that the Court asserts to be examining enforcement jurisdiction but does so on the basis of criteria that concern prescriptive jurisdiction. In the words of Slot 'the approach of the CFI is erroneous'.[39] Slot's analysis is solid and stringent. Upon reflection, however, the hypothesis that the Court of First Instance has confused prescriptive jurisdiction with that of enforcement fails to convince.[40] In my view it is more likely that the Court purposely examined prescriptive jurisdiction both in the light of the implementation criterion and in the light of the effects doctrine.[41] The upshot is that the Court's endorsement

---

[37] Moreover, as part of the examination of the applicability of the effects doctrine the Court of First Instance also considered the principles of non-interference and of proportionality, both of which concern enforcement jurisdiction.

[38] *See* P.J. Slot, *supra* note 27, in particular at pp. 1579 and 1581.

[39] P.J. Slot, *supra* note 27 at p. 1581.

[40] *See* in support of this Bo Vesterdorf, 'Recent developments in European Competition case-law, the CFI' in *Neueste Entwicklungen im europäischen und internationalen Kartellrecht – sechstes St. Galler Internationales Kartellrechtsforum 1999*, Helbing & Lichtenhahn, Basel 2000, pp. 131-151. President Vesterdorf, one of the judges deciding the *Gencor* case, at pp. 147-148 rather clearly draws a distinction between prescriptive jurisdiction and enforcement jurisdiction. The effects doctrine he deals with as part of the former of the two. In Case T-8/98, *Siderca* v. *Commission* the question arose whether in the *Gencor* judgment the Court of First Instance was referring to prescriptive or to enforcement jurisdiction. In the view of the applicant (supported by the British Government) *Gencor* concerned prescriptive jurisdiction. The case was later withdrawn and the question thus left unanswered by the Court.

[41] This could be due to disagreement between the five judges deciding the case. Another possibility is that the judges included the endorsement of the effects doctrine as an *obiter dictum* that may be relied upon in future cases.

of the effects doctrine was an *obiter dictum*. Indeed, the '*obiter* hallmark' is reinforced by the fact that the Court – for no apparent reason – refrained from considering whether the Commission had had jurisdiction on the basis of nationality (it is recalled that Lonrho – one of the two parties involved in the concentration – is a British undertaking).[42] If jurisdiction could be based on nationality, it would not seem to be necessary to consider whether it could also be based upon the much more disputed effects doctrine.

Whilst the judgment in *Gencor* may leave the reader somewhat puzzled, it cannot seriously be doubted that it implies the adoption of the effects doctrine by the Court of First Instance.[43] Even though it is within the power of the Court of Justice to reverse the finding of the Court of First Instance in a future judgment, I am personally convinced that this will not happen. Hence, if, in the future, the Court of Justice were faced with a situation where the alternative to adopting the effects doctrine would be to completely relinquish jurisdiction within the sphere of competition law I am confident that it would adopt the doctrine.

2.2.3. Has the Commission duly observed the Regulation's limits?

The mechanical application of the turnover thresholds as laid down in Article 1 of the Merger Regulation may catch concentrations that have no real links to the

---

[42] Before the Court the Commission had argued that there were two bases underlying its competence. The first was the principle of nationality since Lonrho was incorporated under the laws of a Member State. Only second was the principle of territoriality. *See* para. 64 of the judgment. F.E. González-Díaz, *supra* note 27, at p. 10 also seems to indicate that the Court's pronouncement on the effects doctrine is really *obiter*.

[43] *See* likewise for example C. Paul Rogers III, 'Cross-Border Mergers and Antitrust: Jurtisdiction, Enforcement and Cooperation Issues' in *Cross-Border Mergers and Acquisitions and the Law* (Norbert Horn, ed), Kluwer Law International, the Hague 2001 at p. 365. There are certain indications in the Regulation's preamble that the drafting fathers had the effects doctrine in mind with regard to its jurisdictional reach. Thus recital 5 provides that the Regulation shall apply to 'concentrations which may significantly impede effective competition in the common market or in a substantial part of it', recital 7 provides that the Regulation is created to 'permit effective control of all concentrations from the point of view of their effect on the structure of competition in the Community' and recital 9 provides that 'the provisions to be adopted in this Regulation should apply to significant structural changes the impact of which on the market goes beyond the national borders of any one Member State'.

Community and that do not produce any effects within the territory of the Community. Indeed, the Commission itself has explicitly acknowledged that a number of concentrations meet the turnover thresholds without producing appreciable effects at Community level.[44] This is, first of all, the case *vis-à-vis* full-function joint ventures since even insignificant joint ventures may meet the turnover thresholds.[45] Nevertheless, the Commission has required the parties to these concentrations to notify and has thereby gone beyond the effects doctrine.[46]

The *JCSAT/SAJAC* case[47] provides a striking example of the Commission disregarding the effects doctrine. The case involved the concentration between some

---

[44] Thus, the Commission has observed that 'a number of JVs have been notified which either, were of insignificant economic importance or, engaged in activities outside the Community having no or minimal impact within the Community.' European Commission, *Community Merger Control – Review of the Application of Council Regulation (EEC) No. 4064/89 of 21 December 1989 on the Control of Concentrations between Undertakings – Working Paper of the Services of the Commission*, Revised version: 17.5.1993 (B), at p. 28. Likewise, Opinion of the Economic and Social Committee on the Review of the Community Merger Regulation, OJ C18/21 of 22.1.1996 at point 2.4.1. *See* also Sir Leon Brittan, *The Future of EC Competition Policy*, speech given at the Centre of European Policy Studies, Brussels, Monday 7 December 1992 at p. 10.

[45] Contrast with Reyaz A. Kassamali, 'From Fiction to Fallacy: Reviewing the E.C. Merger Regulation's Community-Dimension Thresholds in the Light of Economics and Experience in Merger Control', (1996) 21 *European Law Review – Checklist*, No. 2, pp. CC89-CC114 at p. CC107 who strangely finds that the turnover thresholds only catch large transactions.

[46] *See Bellamy & Child – European Community Law of Competition*, 5th ed., (P.M. Roth, ed.), Sweet & Maxwell, London 2001 at pp. 379-380 where it is observed that '[t]he jurisdictional tests … do not depend on whether the effects of the concentration will be felt mainly, or at all, within the Community.' The fourth edition of the work (Vivien Rose, ed., Sweet & Maxwell, London 1993) was more explicit since at p. 329 it was noted that 'the extraterritorial effects of the notification requirements of the Merger Regulation appear to go beyond the "effects doctrine"'. Likewise, Rainer Bechtold, *1992 Fordham Corp. L. Inst.* (B. Hawk ed. 1993) at p. 609 criticises the Commission for not following the effects doctrine in merger control. He particularly points to joint ventures as an area where this problem arises. *See* also Colin Overbury, *id.*, at pp. 617-618, Barry E. Hawk and Henry L. Huser, *European Community Merger Control: A Practitioner's Guide*, Kluwer Law International, The Hague 1996, at p. 94, Gerwin Van Gerven, 'Case Note: Gambogi/Cogei', *EC Merger Control Reporter*, Kluwer Law International, The Hague 1991 and later (looseleaf), pp. 620.1-620.4 at p. 620.3, Andre Fiebig, 'International Law Limits on the Extraterritorial Application of the European Merger Control Regulation and Suggestions for Reform', *European Competition Law Review* 1998 pp. 323-331 at 329 and A. Jones and B. Sufrin, *supra* note 22 at p. 727.

[47] Case IV/M346, decision of 30 June 1993.

Japanese satellite operators belonging to large Japanese conglomerates. There was no doubt that the transaction constituted a concentration and that this concentration met the turnover thresholds. It was equally clear that the concentration would not produce any appreciable effects on competition in the Community. Nevertheless, the Commission examined the case and found that 'the concentration has presently no effect in the Community'[48] and '[t]his situation is not likely to change …'.[49] The Commission cleared the transaction.[50] Article 6(1)(a) of the Regulation however provides that: 'Where [the Commission] concludes that the concentration notified does not fall within the scope of this Regulation, [the Commission] shall record that by means of a decision'. In other words, where a concentration falls outside the scope of the Regulation, the Commission must cede jurisdiction and it must do so by a (legally binding) decision. In my view, the Commission should have ceded jurisdiction when finding that the transaction in the *JCSAT/SAJAC* case involved foreign companies, that it took place in a foreign country and that it did not produce any present or future effects inside the Community.[51]

The adoption of the effects doctrine in the *Gencor* judgment is widely perceived as a major victory for the Commission, expanding (or confirming) its wide jurisdictional reach. Nevertheless, it is probably more correct to regard it as a two-edged sword. Thus, the increased focus upon whether a concentration produces effects in the Community may mean that the Commission will increasingly cease jurisdiction where a concentration does not produce any foreseeable, direct and

---

48 Para. 11 of the decision.

49 Para. 12 of the decision.

50 A so-called Art. 6(1)(b) decision.

51 F.E. González-Díaz, *supra* note 27, at p. 8 equally suggests that the Commission should adopt an Art. 6(1)(a) decision where it lacks international jurisdiction. Contrast however with A.F. Bavasso, *supra* note 32, at p. 51. The latter author generally appears to take the rather surprising view that public international law does not affect the Commission's jurisdiction under the Merger Regulation. Another example where it is arguable that the Commission has acted *ultra vires* by taking jurisdiction beyond what is generally considered permissible under public international law is *Nestlé/Pillsbury/Häagen-Dazs US*, Case IV/M1689, decision of 6 October 1999, where the Commission at para. 7 observed that '[t]here are no affected markets in the EEA' and at para. 8 went on to observe that 'it appears that the notified operation will have no impact on competition in the EEA'. *See* also *BHP/Mitsubishi/QCT*, Case COMP/M2153, decision of 28 September 2000 concerning a transaction whereby 'the undertakings Broken Hill Property Company Ltd … [Australia] and Mitsubishi Corporation … [Japan] acquire joint control of QCT Resources Ltd [Australia] …'.

substantial effects on competition in the Community; something that was very unlikely to happen before the *Gencor* judgment.[52] An indication that the *Gencor* ruling has already made the Commission aware of the limits provided by the effects doctrine may be found in the decision *MCI WorldCom/Sprint*.[53] In that decision the Commission, in respect of a specific market, examined whether the concentration would have 'immediate, substantial and foreseeable effects on the European Community'.[54] It found that it could not be 'concluded that the effects on [the market in question by the merger] would be immediate and foreseeable'[55] and it therefore concluded that '[f]or these reasons, the Commission had no jurisdiction under the Merger Regulation to examine the effects of the merger on the [market in question]'.[56]

The approach of the Commission taken in the *MCI WorldCom/Sprint* case is to be welcomed.[57]

---

[52] At present, the resources of the Merger Task Force appear to be strained to their limits. This is likely to make the Commission more willing to cease jurisdiction in such cases.

[53] *MCI WorldCom/Sprint*, Case COMP/M1741, decision of 28 June 2000.

[54] Para. 304 of the decision.

[55] Para. 314 of the decision.

[56] Para. 315 of the decision. It should be noted that the Commission seems to refer to prescriptive jurisdiction, not to enforcement jurisdiction. *See* also *Telia/Sonera/Motorola/Omnitel*, Case IV/JV9, decision of 18 August 1998, in particular para. 35 (together with press release IP/98/772 of 20 August 1998).

[57] Actually as early as in 1991 the present head of the Merger Task Force, Götz Drauz, held that the Commission would only claim jurisdiction over 'mergers and joint ventures which take place outside the EC or to which non-EC companies are a party' if 'they are likely to have a direct and substantial effect on competition <u>within</u> the common market' (underlining from the original), cf. 'EEC Merger Control – The First year' in *Papers of Antitrust Keynote Speakers – Section on Business Law, 10th Biennial Conference, Hong Kong, Committee C, Antitrust and Trade Law, October 1991*, p. 36. This view appears to be echoed in *Community Merger Control – Green Paper on the Review of the Merger Regulation*, Brussels 31.1.1996, COM(96) 19 final at paras. 23-26, where the Commission seems to require 'significant cross-border effects' in order for the Regulation to apply. Unfortunately the case law of the Commission does not really mirror the approach advocated by Mr. Drauz.

2.2.4. Conclusion on the extraterritorial reach

The definition of Community dimension in Article 1 of the Merger Regulation has been worded in such a way that in reality it has almost universal application. The Court of Justice has made it very clear, however, that the scope of the Treaty as well as of any secondary legislation must be limited in the light of applicable public international law. Within the field of competition law, the effects doctrine today is widely (though not universally) recognised as forming the widest (lawful) jurisdiction over concentrations between foreign undertakings. In the *Gencor* judgment the Court of First Instance has adopted the effects doctrine. Even though this adoption is not in line with the case law of the Court of Justice and even though it bears the hallmark of an *obiter*, I consider it unlikely that the Court of Justice will reverse this adoption.

The consequence is that the Merger Regulation applies to foreign concentrations fulfilling the turnover thresholds laid down in Article 1 thereof *provided* that it is foreseeable that the concentration will produce immediate and substantial effects upon competition in the Community. Applying the Regulation to foreign concentrations that do not fulfil the effects doctrine (*i.e.* they do not possess a real Community dimension) will therefore be *ultra vires*. If a concentration does not fall within the scope of the Merger Regulation, the Commission cannot oblige the parties to notify the concentration or suspend the transaction until it has been declared compatible with the common market.[58] Consequently, in my opinion, failure to notify such transactions neither means that the Commission may hold the concentration invalid nor that the Commission may fine the parties. Obviously, if the parties should choose to notify on a fail-safe basis, the Commission may consider the notification,[59] but as soon as it is apparent that the concentration falls

---

[58] Art. 7(1) of the Regulation. The Court of First Instance in the *Gencor* judgment apparently took a different view since it held that '[i]n order for the Commission to assess whether a concentration is within its purview, it must first be in a position to examine that concentration, a fact which justifies requiring the parties to the concentration to notify the agreement', cf. para. 76. The Court does not explain on what legal basis the Commission may oblige foreign undertakings to notify a transaction that does not come within its jurisdiction.

[59] Voluntary submission to the Community's jurisdiction cannot be inferred from the parties notification of a concentration, cf. the Court of First Instance in the *Gencor* judgment at para. 76.

outside the scope of the Merger Regulation the Commission 'shall record that finding by means of a decision' and close the case.[60]

2.3. The internal limit of the Merger Regulation

2.3.1. Member State control or Community control?

As explained in chapter 1 above, the Merger Regulation was only adopted following a protracted discussion about the delimitation between the Member States and the Community of its scope. After the adoption of the Regulation in 1989, this discussion continued, albeit in a more temperate form. At the heart of the discussion lies the basic question of who is to have the power to allow or prohibit concentrations in Europe – Member States or the Commission. This is first of all a political question, but it also has a legal dimension. When the Community takes action, it must duly observe the principles of subsidiarity and of proportionality.[61] Either principle only comes into play when the Community exercises its powers. Hence, the two principles do not define the Community's *vires*, but rather they constitute important principles for the exercise of its powers.[62] Consequently, where

---

[60] Art. 6(1)(a). Helge Schäfer, *Internationaler Anwendungsbereich der präventiven Zusammenschlußkontrolle im deutschen und europäischen Recht*, Peter Lang, Frankfurt a.M. 1993 at p. 222 also finds that where the Commission cannot prohibit a concentration due to international law, Art. 6 requires that the examination is quickly ended.

[61] Whilst I consider the two principles to be more than mere guidelines, I must admit that I am somewhat uncertain as to the precise legal value of the principle of subsidiarity. For example I am far from certain that the Court of Justice would be prepared to annul a Community act solely on the ground that it infringes that principle. *See* likewise John Temple Lang, 'What Powers Should the European Community Have', *European Public Law*, 1995, pp. 97-116 at p. 106. It may be noted that an authority such as Alan Dashwood in *Wyatt & Dashwood's European Union Law* (A.M. Arnull, A.A. Dashwood, M.G. Ross and D.A. Wyatt, eds.), fourth ed., Sweet & Maxwell, London 2000, at p. 161 appears to be of the view that the principle is none the less justiciable. So far the Court of Justice has not delivered a definitive ruling on this point, although its pronouncement in Case C-491/01, *British American Tobacco*, judgment of 10 December 2002 (not yet reported) at para. 185 lends support to the viewpoint advanced by Professor Dashwood.

[62] For example, if the Community issues a regulation in contravention of the principle of attributed powers, it would not make much sense to also consider whether the regulation infringes the principle of subsidiarity or of proportionality, it is submitted.

the Community breaches either of the two principles by an act, the act will not be void (or 'non-existent'), but it may be invalid.[63]

Article 5(2)-(3) of the Treaty set out the principles of subsidiarity and proportionality in the following way:

'(2) In areas which do not fall within its exclusive competence, the Community shall take action, in accordance with the principle of subsidiarity, only if and insofar as the objectives of the proposed action cannot be sufficiently achieved by the Member States and can therefore, by reason of the scale or effects of the proposed action, be better achieved by the Community.

(3) Any action by the Community shall not go beyond what is necessary to achieve the objectives of this Treaty'.

It is reasonable to ask whether the competition field falls within the exclusive competence of the Community, which would mean that the principle of subsidiarity does not apply. In my opinion the answer is far from clear[64] although several observers[65]

---

63 In contrast, in accordance with the principle of attributed powers in Art. 5(1) of the Treaty the Community may only act within the limits of the powers that have been conferred upon it. If the Community goes beyond these powers, it has acted *ultra vires* and the act is void – or 'non-existent' as the European Court of Justice would put it. Above in section 2.2.4 I assert that the Commission acts *ultra vires* if it takes jurisdiction over concentrations that under public international law fall outside its jurisdiction.

64 *See* likewise P.J.G. Kapteyn and P. Verloren van Themaat, *Introduction to the Law of the European Communities – From Maastricht to Amsterdam*, 3rd edition (edited and further revised by Laurence W. Gormley), Kluwer Law International, The Hague 1998 who at p. 139 find that 'in the field of Community competition policy ... it is not always clear to what extent the undeniable powers conferred on the Community have a real exclusive effect, and to what extent they merely lead to the primacy of primary and secondary Community law over national laws which are incompatible with such Community law'. In the same vein Trevor C. Hartley, *The Foundations of European Community Law*, fourth edition, OUP, Oxford 1998 at p. 112 more generally observes that 'the principle of subsidiarity applies only in areas which do not fall within the exclusive jurisdiction of the Community, and it is far from clear which areas should be so regarded'.

65 *See* for example A. Dashwood, *supra* note 61 at p. 158 (referring to the implementation of the rules on competition laid down by Arts. 81 and 82), A.G. Toth, 'The Principle of Subsidiarity in the Maastricht Treaty', *Common Market Law Review* 1992 pp. 1079-1105 at pp. 1091-1092, Tim Jeppesen, *Subsidiarity: A Janus Head?*, European Studies Discussion Paper, Odense Universitet, Odense 1995, p. 28 and Nicolas Bernard, 'The Future of European Economic Law in the Light of the Principle of Subsidiarity', *Common Market Law Review* 1996 pp. 633-666 at pp. 656-659 (finding at p. 656 that 'there is clearly exclusive

as well as the Commission[66] take the stance that the answer to the question is affirmative,[67] whilst others support the view that subsidiarity does apply in the field of competition.[68] So far no authoritative ruling has clarified this. It is not necessary to answer the question here since the principle of subsidiarity does not apply to the calculation of turnover in any event, as I will show below.[69]

When the Merger Regulation was unanimously adopted by the Member States it was clear that the thresholds had been fixed at a rather high – but arbitrary – level. It was also clear that a number of concentrations that arguably ought to be controlled by the Commission would escape the thresholds and equally that some concentrations that were best handled at Member State level would be caught by

---

competence in relation to concentrations with a Community dimension' while being some-what more doubtful in respect of the Community rules under Arts. 81 and 82).

66   Cf. *The Principle of Subsidiarity – Communication of the Commission to the Council and the European Parliament,* SEC(92) 1990 Final, at p. 7. Strangely, however, in more instances the Commission has made reference to the subsidiarity principle in connection to the Merger Regulation. *See* for example the *2001 Green Paper* at paras. 4, 16, 19, 23, 29, 65, 66, 69, 81, 84 and *Commission's 2000 Report* at paras. 2.

67   Of course the Commission has exclusive jurisdiction in the field covered by the Merger Regulation, but this exclusivity may be inferred from the Merger Regulation, not from the Treaties as such. P.J.G. Kapteyn and P. Verloren van Themaat, *supra* note 64 at p. 139 with note 106 equally observe that 'Community competence in the field of merger control is at least in part clearly exclusive in nature ...'.

68   *See* for example Eleanor J. Morgan, 'Subsidiarity and the division of jurisdiction in EU merger control', *The Antitrust Bulletin,* 2000 pp. 153-193 at pp. 178 and 187, Michael Reynolds and Colin Overbury, 'Should the Merger Task Force be given more power?', *International Financial Law Review,* Vol. 12, No. 7, July 1993, pp. 31-33, Gráinne de Búrca and Bruno de Witte, *The Delimitation of Powers between the EU and its Member States,* European University Institute – Robert Schuman Centre of Advanced Studies at p. 9, Rein Wesseling, 'Subsidiarity in Community Antitrust Law: Setting the Right Agenda', *European Law Review* 1997 pp. 35-54 at p. 37.

69   Sir Leon Brittan,' Subsidiarity in the Constitution of the European Community' in *Collected Courses of the Academy of European Law – Recueil des cours de l'Academie de droit européen – 1992 – European Community Law, Vol. III Book 1*, Martinus Nijhoff Publishers, Dordrecht 1994, at p. 27 found that '[t]he Merger Regulation provides an excellent example of how subsidiarity can be put into practice'. David Begg *et al* in *Making Sense of Subsidiarity: How Much Centralization for Europe?*, Centre for Economic Policy Research (CEPR), London 1993 at pp. 135-137 examine the application of the principle of subsidiarity in the area of merger control. The authors at p. 137 conclude that – from an economic point of view – 'merger control is a good illustration of a case where the gains from centralization are high'.

the thresholds. Indeed, the drafting fathers included provisions to remedy these defects.[70] The amendment of the thresholds in 1997 (which was also unanimously agreed) did not materially change this. In these circumstances I consider it entirely improbable that the Court of Justice would be prepared to *generally* hold the thresholds (and thus the Merger Regulation as such) to infringe the two principles.[71] It may be added that most observers seem to take the view that the thresholds are too high; not that they are too low as one would probably expect them to be if they were contravening the principle of subsidiarity.[72]

Whilst it is fairly obvious that the thresholds as such do not infringe the principles of proportionality and subsidiarity, it is equally clear that in a number of situations one may reasonably ask whether it is really in conformity with these two principles to require a *specific* concentration to be notified to the Commission. An example may illustrate this:

---

[70] Arts. 9 (the German clause) and 22(3) (the Dutch clause).

[71] With regard to the principle of subsidiarity it may be added that in Joined Cases C-36-37/97, *Kellinghusen* v. *Amt für Land- und Wasserwirtschaft Kiel* and *Ketelsen* v. *Amt für Wasserwirtschaft Husum*, ECR 1998 I-6337, the Court at para. 35 held that 'as to the breach of the principle of subsidiarity, it should be stated that the second paragraph of Article [5] of the Treaty was not yet in force when [two regulations] were adopted and that provision cannot have retroactive effect'. *See* likewise the judgment of the Court of First Instance in Case T-29/92, *SPO and others* v. *Commission*, ECR 1995 II-289, who at para. 331 held that 'the principle of subsidiarity did not, before the entry into force of the Treaty on European Union, constitute a general principle of law by reference to which the legality of Community acts should be reviewed'. Subsidiarity was only inserted into the Treaty in 1993 so it follows from the two rulings that this principle would only apply to the amendment of the Merger Regulation introduced in 1997.

Perhaps it could also be argued that the invariable and arbitrary turnover thresholds, defining Community dimension, put an excessive limit on the Commission's margin of appreciation to such extent that it infringes the principle of proportionality. This argument is not persuasive, however, since the Commission had no express power to examine concentrations before the entry into force of the Merger Regulation. The thresholds thus do not limit the Commission's discretion in any way.

[72] One could ask, however, whether it is not out of proportion to require a very considerable number of undertakings to fulfil the onerous task of notifying their concentrations when taking into account that only a clear minority thereof give rise to real concerns. I personally find the requirement to be disproportionate because I believe that it is possible to create a system that is better at weeding out a great number of *de minimis* cases. Nevertheless, I am convinced that the Court would not take the same stance.

Example

Two small companies belonging to large international groups (that together fulfil the turnover thresholds) are both based in a remote village in the eastern part of Germany. The region and the village are undergoing a deep recession and the local garage, the only one in the village, is therefore about to close. However, the two companies are dependent upon the services of the garage. They therefore decide to make a joint acquisition and to let it carry on in exactly the same way as it used to.

Most would probably agree that to require the acquisition in the example to be notified under the Merger Regulation (whether on a short form or not) and to have the Commission examine it, would be disproportionate because the time and money the parties will have to put into such notification is out of proportion with the (un)likelihood that the concentration may endanger competition in the Community.[73] Moreover, there would seem to be a strong argument that even if there were any danger to competition, this is best dealt with at Member State level. Are these objections not just another expression of the principles of proportionality and of subsidiarity?

The answer is no. Neither of the two principles apply in respect of the calculation of the turnover thresholds. This is so since the turnover thresholds do not leave anything to the Commission's discretion. Or put differently, the Regulation does not vest in the Commission discretion to decide whether a given concentration shall be considered to have a Community dimension or not. To the extent that the two principles come into play,[74] they only do so where a provision is capable of

---

[73] The problem is also known in the United States, cf. International Competition Policy Advisory Committee, Antitrust Division, *International Competition Policy Advisory Committee – To the Attorney General and Assistant Attorney General for Antitrust – Final Report 2000* (available at www.usdoj.gov/atr/icpac/finalreport.htm), at pp. 13-14 who observe: 'A final area that deserves attention concerns ensuring that the notification thresholds are only as broad as necessary to identify transactions that have the potential to generate appreciable anticompetitive effects within the United States ... While recognizing that small transactions are not necessarily competitively benign, the Advisory Committee finds that the notification thresholds currently employed in the United States are too low and capture too many lawful transactions'.

[74] It is not clear whether the principle of subsidiarity applies in respect of the *interpretation* of secondary Community legislation, such as directives and regulations, or whether it only applies to the *adoption* of such legislation. Advocate General Jacobs in his opinion in Case C-188/95, *Fantask*, ECR 1997 I-6783 at para. 28 appears to support the view that the

more than one interpretation, *i.e.* where the Commission is given a certain margin of discretion.[75] The calculation of the Community dimension only leaves the Commission with discretion in matters of a purely technical nature such as what undertakings must be included in the groups of the undertakings concerned and what is the correct definition of 'ordinary activities'. Such discretion does not concern the question of whether a concentration possesses a Community dimension. This means that the principles of subsidiarity and proportionality do not apply with regard to the calculation of the Community dimension.[76]

In conclusion it is unlikely that the Court of Justice will strike down a merger decision on the basis of proportionality or subsidiarity in a case where the Commission has taken jurisdiction within the competence conferred upon it by the Merger Regulation.[77]

---

principle of subsidiarity cannot be used to guide the interpretation of a provision. But contrast with Advocate General Alber in his opinion in Case C-318/96, *SPAR Österreichische Warenhandels* v. *Finanzlandesdirektion für Salzburg*, ECR 1998 I-785 at para. 59.

[75] Or in the words of Nicholas Emiliou, 'when there is a choice between several appropriate measures recourse should be made to the least onerous ...', cf. *The Principle of Proportionality in European Law – A Comparative Study*, Kluwer Law International, The Hague 1996 at p. 2.

[76] Other provisions of the Merger Regulation do vest a wide discretion in the Commission, however. For example in respect of a request from a Member State that the Commission refer a case in accordance with Art. 9.

[77] In contrast, if a concentration like the one in the example above is either prohibited or cleared with strict conditions, I consider it likely that the Court of Justice will accept an argument that is (also) based upon proportionality in respect of the prohibition or the conditions. Note that according to Art. 2, the Commission may only prohibit a concentration if it significantly impedes competition 'in the common market or in a substantial part of it'. Apparently, the Commission has found that where the geographic market that might be affected by a proposed transaction is limited to a small area relative to the Member State as a whole, this does not constitute a substantial part of the common market and so the Commission is not 'in a position to review the effects of the operation on competition' in the affected market, cf. *RMC/UMA/JV*, Case COMP/M2596, decision of 12 March 2003 and IP/03/368. Hence, according to this wording, the Commission is precluded not only from prohibiting but also from reviewing the concentration if it does not concern 'a substantial part' of the common market. This approach to some extent resembles subsidiarity (although it should be noted that in the actual case the Commission did not renounce jurisdiction completely).

2.4. Concentrations with a real Community dimension that escape the thresholds

Even the drafters of the Merger Regulation were aware that the arithmetical de-limitation of jurisdiction established by the Regulation's turnover thresholds by its very nature was unlikely to fully reflect the real Community dimension. This has been recognised in Article 22(3) referring to concentrations which, while falling below the turnover thresholds, still have a real Community dimension as they affect trade between Member States.[78]

It is remarkable that although the Commission has not been too keen to acknowledge that in certain respects the Regulation catches concentrations without a real Community dimension, it has been very eager to show that a number of important concentrations that clearly possessed a real Community dimension have fallen below the thresholds. This was, for instance, the case in the concentration between Fried Krupp AG and Hoesch whereby one of the largest steel producers in the world was formed. Each of the parties achieved more than two-thirds of their Community-wide turnover within Germany, however, and the concentration therefore failed to meet the turnover thresholds.[79]

The 1997 revision of the Regulation has expanded its scope somewhat. As the Regulation continues to define Community dimension on the basis of the turnover of the undertakings concerned, however, the possibility that a concentration possesses a real Community dimension, but does not meet the turnover thresholds,

---

[78] *See* also *British Airways/Dan Air*, Case IV/M278, decision of 17 February 1993 at para. 7.

[79] *See* European Commission, *supra* note 44, at pp. 16-17 which also provides other like examples. For further examples, *see* Lothar Dressel, *Handelsblatt* 10 November 1992, Mario Siragusa and Romano Subiotto, 'The EEC Merger Control Regulation: The Commission's Evolving Case Law', *Common Market Law Review*, 1991, pp. 877-934 at p. 898, European Commission, 'Competition and Integration – Community merger control policy', *European Economy*, No. 57 1994, pp. 38-39, M. Reynolds and C. Overbury, *supra* note 68 at p. 32 and Rainer Kögel, *Die Angleichung der deutschen an die europäische Fusionskontrolle*, Nomos Verlagsgesellschaft, Baden-Baden 1996 at p. 303 with further references. The Commission in its *2001 Green Paper*, Annex 1, para. 74 with note 16, provides another illustrative example, namely 'the concentration between the Chase Manhattan Corporation and Robert Flemmings Holdings Limited. Both of these international financial companies manage assets that are measured in hundreds of billions USD and are active in 40-50 countries worldwide. Still, for both companies more than 2/3 of [each of] their combined [EU-wide] turnover is attributable to the United Kingdom.'

remains. This is particularly the case where the parties do not generate a world-wide turnover of € 2.5 billion or where the two-thirds rule is not met.[80]

It is thus clear that the turnover thresholds still fail to catch a number of concentrations with a real Community dimension.[81]

2.5. Conclusion on whether the turnover thresholds provide a suitable definition of 'real Community dimension'?

The above examination shows that the turnover thresholds may catch transactions that arguably fall outside the scope of the Treaty. Applying the Regulation to such transactions would be *ultra vires*. To the extent that the Commission takes due account of the *vires* when applying the Regulation's definition of Community dimension, this will not create a problem. However, the Commission does not pay due attention to the *vires* which means that transactions without a real Community dimension are vetted by the Commission if they meet the thresholds.[82]

Moreover, it is recalled that in chapter 8, I show that it is possible to change an operation from having a Community dimension to having no such dimension (or *vice versa*), without materially altering the operation. If the Regulation's definition

---

[80] Paul Malric-Smith (who is head of unit in the Merger Task Force), 'Commission's 2000 Report to the Council on the Functioning of the Merger Regulation' in *EC Merger Control: Ten Years On*, International Bar Association, London 2000, pp. 353-359 at p. 358 has pointed out that the Regulation has failed to catch in particular concentrations in the new economy since even undertakings occupying important positions in 'new economy' markets frequently generate comparatively low levels of turnover.

[81] The question has been raised whether this accords with the requirement in Article 3(g) of the EC Treaty that the Community shall institute a system ensuring that competition in the common market is not distorted. For a discussion of this question, *see* Jacques H.J. Bourgeois, 'EEC Control over International Mergers', *Yearbook of European Law 1990*, (A. Barav and D.A. Wyatt eds.), Clarendon Press, Oxford 1991, pp. 103-132 at p. 109, R.A. Kassamali, *supra* note 45 at p. CC100 and the first edition of this work at pp. 256-257.

[82] During the negotiations leading up to what eventually became the Merger Regulation, the Council Working Group drafting the Regulation apparently considered the jurisdictional issue, but decided not to enter this discussion to any significant extent, cf. C.J. Cook and C.S. Kerse, *E.C. Merger Control*, 3rd ed., Sweet & Maxwell, London 2000 at p. 11-12. Perhaps an explicit inclusion in the Regulation's substantive provisions of a clause requiring the transaction to produce transborder effects inside the Community could have avoided the present problems. *See* also R. Kögel, *supra* note 79 at p. 302.

of Community dimension were a true reflection of the real Community dimension, a material change of the transaction would be required in order to change it from/ to having a Community dimension as defined in the Regulation. Chapter 8 therefore supports the conclusion that the Regulation's definition of Community dimension differs from the real Community dimension.

Lastly, it must be pointed out that the cause of the discrepancy between the real Community dimension and the turnover thresholds is that the latter, by their very nature, are primarily quantitative; only the geographic allocation of turnover implies a (somewhat vague) qualitative element. Moreover, the thresholds relate to the size of the parties, not to the transaction itself giving rise to the concentration. In contrast, the focus of the real Community dimension is upon the actual transaction and the (actual or potential) consequences flowing therefrom. These differences mean that the turnover thresholds inadequately reflect the real Community dimension.[83]

Hence, in my view the turnover thresholds laid down in Article 1 of the Merger Regulation provide only a poor reflection of the real Community dimension.[84]

---

[83] Likewise Alexis P. Jacquemin, 'Mergers and European Policy' in *Merger and Competition Policy in the European Community*, (P.H. Admiral, ed.), Basil Blackwell, Oxford 1990, pp. 3-38 at p. 33, Ken George and Alexis Jacquemin, 'Competition Policy in the European Community' in *Competition Policy in Europe and North America: Economic Issues and Institutions*, (Alexis Jacquemin, ed.), Harwood Academic Publishers, Chur (Switzerland) 1990, pp. 206-245 at p. 240, Peter D. Camesasca, *European Merger Control: Getting the Efficiencies Right*, Intersentia-Hart, Antwerpen 2000, pp. 218 and 274-275 and R. Kögel, *supra* note 79 at p. 302 who at p. 303 furthermore points out that the Merger Regulation's definition of Community dimension holds an element of arbitrariness. For the same view, *see* also Dirk Dirksen, 'Praktische Erfahrungen im ersten Jahr der europäischen Fusionskontrolle' in *Schwerpunkte des Kartellrechts 1990/91*, Carl Heymanns Verlag KG, Köln 1992, pp. 119-133 at p. 125 and Dieter Wolf, 'The Drive Towards Political and Economic Integration', *International Business Lawyer*, Vol. 26, No 3, 1997, pp. 110-111 at 111. For a similar view – albeit *vis-à-vis* the turnover thresholds delimiting the scope of the German merger control scheme – *see* Hans-Jürgen Ruppelt, *Kommentar zum deutschen und europäischen Kartellrecht*, 9th edition, Luchterhand, Berlin 2001, p. 995.

[84] Contrast with the finding at para. 19 in the *Commission's 2000 Report* on the thresholds that 'the criteria in Article 1(2) remain effective in identifying mergers that have a real Community dimension as opposed to a national dimension'. The finding has been reiterated in *2001 Green Paper*, Annex 1, para. 32.

3. IS IT POSSIBLE TO IMPROVE THE REGULATION'S DEFINITION OF COMMUNITY DIMENSION?

3.1. Introduction

Having found that the Merger Regulation's definition of Community dimension is not a good reflection of the real Community dimension, one may reasonably ask whether it would not be possible to construct a delimitation that is better at weeding out concentrations that are very unlikely to impede competition in the Community. This question concerns the (technical) delimitation of the scope of the Merger Regulation and the possibilities of improving this delimitation.

In order to answer this question, I will first try to identify the causes of the problems in the present definition of Community dimension (section 3.2). Then, I will consider the most obvious methods of remedying these problems (section 3.3) and finally, I will make some recommendations for improving the delimitation (section 3.4).

3.2. The problem in the present definition

In section 2.5, above, I conclude that the discrepancy between the real Community dimension and the turnover thresholds is first of all due to two facts. Firstly, turnover thresholds are primarily quantitative, whereas the real Community dimension is a qualitative measure. Secondly, the real Community dimension is concerned with the actual transaction, while the turnover thresholds measure the size of the parties, not the importance of the actual transaction *vis-à-vis* the market in question.[85]

The differences between the real Community dimension and the turnover thresholds mean that, instead of catching concentrations likely to impede competition, the Merger Regulation catches concentrations involving undertakings generating significant turnovers. The consequence is that a merger creating a virtual monopoly in the Community might escape the Regulation if the parties do not meet the thresh-

---

[85] Indeed, in Case 85/76, *Hoffmann-La Roche & Co. AG* v. *EC Commission (the vitamins case)*, [1976] ECR 461, the Court of Justice at paras. 42 and 47 rejected the Commission's submission that overall turnover is relevant in establishing a dominant position under Art. 82.

olds while a joint venture between large conglomerates must be notified if it meets the thresholds regardless of whether it presents any competition problems.[86] As pointed out by the ABA Section of Antitrust Law,[87] by focusing on the turnover of the parties, the Regulation 'creates a substantial bias in favour of control of transactions involving high turnover, low margin businesses (e.g., food retailing) and against control of transactions involving low turnover, high margin businesses. Such a bias would be understandable if there were some reason to believe that mergers in high turnover, low margin businesses are more likely to produce anticompetitive effects.' The Section of Antitrust Law point out that they 'are not aware, however, of any reason to suppose this is true, and the bias relating to high turnover businesses may be an unintended consequence of the Regulation.'[88]

Even though the *vires* of the Merger Regulation (*i.e.,* that the concentration must possess a real Community dimension) in principle excludes a fair number of concentrations having only insignificant effects at Community level, the fact that this only seems to carry little weight with the Commission in itself makes a change of Article 1 (defining the Regulation's scope) desirable.

In other words, the problem is that the class of concentrations, which the turnover thresholds single out for a substantive examination under the Merger Regulation, does not correspond to the class of concentrations which is most likely to create competition problems at Community level and which therefore should be subjected to a substantive review.[89] Of course, there is an overlap between these two classes, but this overlap is rather arbitrary.[90]

---

[86] Raising the present turnover thresholds is likely to mean that fewer *de minimis* concentrations are likely to be notifiable, but this is simply due to the fact that such an increase will reduce the total number of notifiable concentrations. Put differently, raising the turnover thresholds does not go to the heart of the problem. For a different view, *see* P.J. Slot, *supra* note 27 at p. 1581 with note 19.

[87] 'Comments of the American Bar Association Section of Antitrust Law with Respect to the Amended Proposal for a Council Regulation (EEC) on the Control of Concentrations between Undertakings', *Antitrust Law Journal* 1990, vol. 59, pp. 245-261 at p. 252.

[88] *See* also European Commission, *supra* note 79, at p. 35.

[89] Likewise R.A. Kassamali, *supra* note 45 at p. CC99 and Rein Wesseling, *The Modernisation of EC Antitrust Law*, Hart Publishing, Oxford 2000, pp. 136-137.

[90] Likewise, R. Kögel, *supra* note 79 at p. 303 and Wayne D. Collins, 'Review Essay – The Coming of Age of EC Competition Policy', *Yale Journal of International Law*, 1992, Vol. 17, pp. 249-296 at p. 280.

3.3. Solutions

3.3.1. Introduction

Having identified the problem, the question is how to solve it. Three solutions deserve closer scrutiny:

> First, the system could be completely changed to one based on market shares instead of turnover, so that concentrations creating market shares above a given level must be notified.[91]

> Secondly, one could use thresholds based on the size of the transaction (instead of the present ones based on the size of the parties).

> Thirdly, one could retain the system of thresholds based on the size of the undertakings, but refine the allocation of jurisdiction through the use of a *de minimis* rule based on the size of the transaction.

The question thus is whether (technically) the present delimitation of jurisdiction can be improved. Below, I will examine the three possible solutions. Three points are important in this examination. First of all, it is necessary to assess whether the solution may be better at catching only those concentrations possessing a real Community dimension.

Secondly, it is important that the solution provides a clear-cut dividing line.[92] This follows from the fact that merger control continues to be a very contentious

---

[91] Indeed, when the Merger Regulation was adopted the Council and the Commission stated 'their readiness to consider taking other factors into account in addition to turnover when the thresholds are revised', cf. 'Notes on Council Regulation (EEC) 4064/89' published in *Bulletin of the European Communities, Supplement 2/90*.

[92] Likewise, Damien Neven, Robin Nutall and Paul Seabright, *Merger in Daylight – The Economics and Politics of European Merger Control*, Centre for Economic Policy Research, London 1993, who at p. 237 note that 'the precision of the procedure used to sort mergers with a European dimension from the others matters a great deal'. *See* also Thomas Lampert, *Die Anwendbarkeit der EG-Fusionskontrollverordnung im Verhältnis zum Fusionskontrollrecht der Mitgliedstaaten – rechtsvergleichen zum Verhältnis zwischen dem US-Antitrustrecht des Bundes und der Einzelstaaten*, Carl Heymanns Verlag KG, Köln 1995 at p. 184, but contrast with Matthew Bishop, 'European or National? The Community's New Merger Regulation' in *European Mergers and Merger Policy*, (Matthew Bishop and John Kay, eds.), Oxford University Press, Oxford 1993, pp. 294-317 at p. 316 who finds that '[t]he need is not for a clear demarcation between Community and national merger policies but for greater integration between them'. *See* further my final comments below in part 4.

area so that an ambiguous dividing line is likely to incite discussion between the Member States and the Commission concerning who is to have jurisdiction, and it is likely to encourage forum shopping. The legal uncertainty flowing from such ambiguity is especially unfortunate in the field of merger control where particular emphasis is placed on the ability to swiftly reach a final decision.[93]

Lastly, since we are only dealing with the allocation of jurisdiction, not with substantive appraisal, the solution must not be excessively costly and time consuming. It is untenable if the parties must defray substantial costs with the sole purpose of ascertaining whether a concentration must be notified.

3.3.2. Market shares

The essential question in merger control is whether the concentration provides the parties with the ability of setting their prices significantly above the competitive level. This ability presupposes that the parties have market power, *i.e.,* that to a significant degree they are able to behave independently of their competitors and customers.[94] In other words, an essential part of merger control is to find out whether a concentration creates market power.

Market power and market shares are not synonymous. A high market share is at most an indication of market power, not a proof.[95] Market shares are, nevertheless, much more closely related to market power than is the size of the parties,[96] and it therefore appears relevant to consider the use of market shares as a solution to the problem.

The very fact that market shares are more closely related to market power than is the size of the parties in itself means that they will be better at weeding out

---

[93] For example if both the Commission and a Member State consider that a concentration comes within their respective jurisdictions and this question is brought before the Court of Justice, the long time which the undertakings may have to wait before a final decision in the case (even if the so-called 'fast track procedure' is used) is likely to have adverse consequences on the performance of the concentration.

[94] *See* for example Case 27/76, *United Brands Company and United Brands Continental B.V.* v. *Commission of the European Communities*, [1978] ECR 207 at point 65.

[95] Cf. Philip Areeda and Louis Kaplow, *Antitrust Analysis – Problems, Text, Cases*, 5th ed., Aspen Law & Business, New York 1997, p. 554, pp. 562-565 and pp. 571-572.

[96] The European Commission, *supra* note 57 at point 131 in respect of *de minimis* concentrations notes that '[m]arket share thresholds would be more appropriate', (but adds that they 'would reduce legal certainty').

unproblematic cases already at the notification stage.[97] Thus one could imagine that concentrations involving market shares of less than, say 25%, of a substantial part of the common market would not be notifiable.

That market shares are better at weeding out insignificant concentrations does not mean that they do not create problems. The most important problem is that market shares are not an unambiguous concept. In order to calculate a market share, it is necessary to define the product market, the geographic market and the temporal market. Even slight differences in the definition of just one of these may lead to significant changes in the final market share figure. The consequence necessarily is that to calculate an incontestable market share figure on the basis of general guidelines is impossible in the majority of cases.[98] As Phillip Areeda and Louis Kaplow note: 'The boundaries of any product and geographic market are necessarily imprecise.'[99] Indeed it seems that there is almost consensus that market shares are not a suitable alternative on which to base the Commission's exclusive jurisdiction to vet certain concentrations.[100]

---

[97] Cf. Alexis Jacquemin, 'Horizontal Concentration and European Merger Policy', *European Economic Review*, 34 (1990), pp. 539-550 at p. 547. *See* also R. Kögel, *supra* note 79 at p. 310.

[98] The situation might be different, if the calculation is made on the basis of guidelines that have been drafted in respect of a very specific market. In my article 'The De Minimis Notice', *European Law Review*, Vol. 20, No. 4, August 1995, pp. 371-387 I have advanced a similar view regarding the creation of a legally binding *de minimis* rule in the field of Art. 81. However, to make different guidelines for all the various products (and services) would be an insurmountable task.

[99] *Supra* note 95 at p. 581.

[100] Cf. C.J. Cook and C.S. Kerse, *supra* note 82 at pp. 58, Alec Burnside, 'Comment – European Merger Control: Department Shopping?', *In Competition*, 1996, issue 2, pp. 1-2 at p. 2, R. Kögel, *supra* note 79 at pp. 309-310, R. Burnley, *supra* note 4 at p. 271, European Commission, *supra* note 79 at p. 53 and *see* also the Economic and Social Committee, *supra* note 44 at point 2.4.3. The Commission, *supra* note 44 at p. 22 concludes: 'Whilst other criteria, such as market share data, can be useful to help determine jurisdiction they are often unavailable or imprecise. Usually they can only be accurately established after extensive analysis and in critical cases are frequently a subject of contention.' Contrast however with R.A. Kassamali, *supra* note 45 at pp. CC108-CC114. *See* also J. William Rowley, Omar K. Wakil and A. Neil Campbell, 'Streamlining International Merger Control' in *EC Merger Control: Ten Years On*, International Bar Association, London 2000, pp. 15-37 at p. 17 and John Bridgeman, 'Commission and National Competence – a Debate', *International Business Lawyer*, 1998, pp. 102-103 at 103. E.J. Morgan, *supra* note 68 at p. 166 seems to take the view that it is inconsistent to reject the use of market shares for establishing jurisdiction

Moreover, even if one accepted the ambiguities inherent in market shares, one should be acutely aware that in order to establish a precise market definition, it will often be necessary to 'contact the main customers and the main companies in the industry to enquire into their views about the boundaries of product and geographic markets and to obtain the necessary factual evidence to reach a conclusion.'[101] Undertakings often treat their specific sales figures as confidential and it therefore seems unlikely that under normal circumstances an undertaking which is about to enter a concentration would be able to obtain the sales figures of its competitors in order to calculate its exact market share.

The fact that market shares constitute an ambiguous concept together with the fact that it may be difficult to obtain the necessary information to calculate the figures is likely to mean that fail-safe notification will become the order of the day. Thus, instead of weeding out a number of insignificant concentrations and saving the parties to these concentrations the trouble of going through a laborious notification, one may foresee that the parties will continue to notify the Commission. In addition, the parties will have to notify Member State competition authorities if the concentration may fall within the jurisdiction of one or more of these, in case it is found that it does not meet the market share threshold.

I therefore find that market shares do not[102] provide a solution.[103]

---

whilst at the same time the Merger Regulation makes reference to precisely market shares with regard to the possibility of being exempt from providing market data in the notification form, and with regard to the presumption that where a concentration leads to a market share that does not exceed 25%, competition problems do not arise. In my opinion the three situations are not comparable since the consequences are likely to be considerably less adverse if a party to a concentration makes a slight miscalculation in the two last-mentioned situations than if the party miscalculates its market share in respect of the duty to notify. In any event, at p. 167 also E.J. Morgan apparently finds that the use of market shares is not possible until '[f]urther steps toward more predictable and consistent' market definitions have been established.

[101] Quotation taken from 'Commission Notice on the definition of the relevant market for the purposes of Community competition law', OJ 9.12.1997, C3/25.

[102] Likewise the Commission, *2001 Green Paper*, Annex 1, paras. 24-26, but contrast with Frédéric Jenny, 'National Authorities and the Commission', *International Business Lawyer*, 1998, pp. 105-111. In order to provide a complete picture it should be noted, however, that the Commission is using markets shares in its *de minimis* notice (Commission Notice on agreements of minor importance which do not appreciably restrict competition under Article 81(1) of the Treaty establishing the European Community (*de minimis*), OJ 22.12.2001 C368/13).

3.3.3. Size of transaction

Even before the adoption of the Merger Regulation, the American Bar Association Section of Antitrust Law expressed the view that jurisdiction based on the size of the transaction would be superior to thresholds based on the size of the parties.[104]

The present thresholds do reflect the size of the transaction *vis-à-vis* true mergers and *vis-à-vis* acquisitions of parts by only one acquirer to a fair extent.[105] The main difference between the present thresholds and thresholds based on the size of the transaction, therefore, is in the field of joint ventures (and joint acquisitions);[106] the area where the present thresholds exhibit the most significant problems.

The certified accounting figures may measure the size of the transaction in three different ways. Either it may relate to the turnover of the business involved in the transaction or it may relate to the assets of the business or it may be based on both.[107]

---

103 The Belgian merger control scheme has been closely modelled over the Merger Regulation. One of the few differences originally was that the scope was defined both according to turnover thresholds and according to a market share figure (20%). As noted by Frank K. Wohlgemuth, 'Das Belgische Kartellrecht', *Wirtschaft und Wettbewerb*, Vol. 44, 1994, No. 11, pp. 901-915 at p. 914 the use of marketshares created considerable problems in practice. Likewise Johan Ysewyn, 'When to Notify a Merger in Belgium', *European Legal Developments Bulletin*, (Baker & McKenzie), January 1996, Vol. 8, No. 1, pp. 16-18 at p. 17. For good reasons, the Belgian market share based threshold was abandoned in July 1999.

104 *Supra* note 87 at p. 247 and pp. 252-253. *See* also International Competition Policy Advisory Committee, Antitrust Division, *supra* note 73, p. 10 of the executive summary.

105 In the case of a true merger, the transaction involves all of the undertakings to the concentration. There is consequently no difference between measuring the size of the transaction and the size of the parties in such cases. (In the case of a 'true merger' between two subsidiaries the situation really concerns the creation of a joint venture between the parent undertakings). Where only one undertaking acquires part of another undertaking the present sets of thresholds require that the part acquired generates minimum € 250 million (first set of thresholds) or minimum € 100 million (second set of thresholds). In this way the present thresholds to a fair extent relate to the size of the transaction regarding the more straightforward acquisitions of parts.

106 Likewise, European Commission, *supra* note 79 at pp. 37-38.

107 Both the British Fair Trading Act 1973, section 64 and the American Hart-Scott-Rodino Antitrust Improvements Act 1976, which added section 7A to the Clayton Act, refer to the size of the assets involved in the transaction. (The British assets test will, however, be replaced by a turnover test). *See* also European Commission, *supra* note 79 at p. 53. C.J. Cook and C.S. Kerse, *supra* note 82 at p. 58 apparently find that using only a test based on assets would not be adequate.

Basing jurisdiction on the turnover and/or the asset size of the transaction presumably will exclude a fair number of those *de minimis* transactions which are caught by the present thresholds. Moreover, using the certified accounts essentially makes the system as precise and clear-cut as the present one.

The proposal is not without problems, however. First, it may be possible to circumvent the system; for instance, by splitting the transactions into parts. Anti-circumvention provisions similar to the one presently found in Article 5(2)(2) may remedy this. Secondly, the proposed system may lose some important concentrations which are caught by the present system, *i.e.*, those transactions which are small but nevertheless have adverse effects on competition.[108] The main cause is that the proposed system is still a purely quantitative one. Thus, like the present thresholds, the proposal does not pay due account to the actual size and structure of the market of the concentration in question.[109] In other words, there is a kind of trade-off between, on the one hand, how clear-cut and easy to apply the delimitation is, and, on the other hand, how accurately the delimitation may cream off the problematic concentrations.[110] The problems identified here do not, to my mind, weigh up the advantages of a system based on the size of the transaction.

In conclusion, I consider a system which measures the size of the business being subject to the transaction to constitute a delimitation which is better than the existing one at weeding out concentrations that are very unlikely to impede competition. The main problem in changing the system is that it necessarily leads to a different allocation of competence between the Commission and the Member States. Thus, one may presume that the Commission will be in favour of this system if it brings more important concentrations within the Commission's jurisdiction, and that the Member States are likely to be against the system, precisely if it vests increased jurisdiction in the Commission.

---

[108] Likewise the Commission, *supra* note 44 at p. 29.

[109] In contrast market shares take account of the size of the market, but in themselves pure market shares do not reflect the structure of the market. R. Burnley, *supra* note 4, at p. 271 equally observes that thresholds based on the value of the transaction are 'entirely arbitrary with regard to the potential effect on Community competition structures' and for this reason dismisses this as a solution.

[110] It is worth noting, however, that in the Commission's past practice only a few minor joint ventures, caught by the present thresholds, have given rise to competition problems. One may therefore fairly presume that the problems issuing from the proposal will be limited.

3.3.4. Refining the present system

At the time of writing it is almost certain that the Merger Regulation's referral mechanisms (the so-called German and Dutch clauses) will undergo important amendments.[111] The underlying idea is that these provisions shall compensate for the imprecision of the rough turnover thresholds.[112] Whether or not a concentration has a Community dimension, so that the undertakings are obliged to notify, is not affected by the referral mechanisms.[113] Put differently, the flaws of the present thresholds remain. As this work is only concerned with the delimitation of the Commission's competence, I will not engage upon an examination of the possible application of the referral mechanisms.

One possible way of improving the delimitation of jurisdiction is by adding a *de minimis* rule to the present thresholds.[114] In that way, the advantages of basing the calculation on turnover will be retained and, at the same time, the concentrations lacking a real Community dimension could be weeded out.[115] This *de minimis* rule should be based on the effects issuing from the actual transaction since this is the

---

[111] During the work on the 2003 revision, the Germans in particular advocated a 'fine-tuning' of the referral mechanisms as a means for compensating for the imprecision of the turnover thresholds. *See* for example Ulf Böge, 'Dovetailing Cooperation, Dividing Competence – a Member State's View of Merger Control in Europe' in *EC Merger Control: Ten Years On*, International Bar Association, London 2000, pp. 363-372 at pp. 368-370. In contrast the Commission originally was less enthusiastic about the idea, cf. for instance P. Malric-Smith, *supra* note 80 at p. 355.

[112] Note though that the referral mechanisms concern the relations between the Community and the Member States. The referral mechanisms will therefore not provide a remedy in respect of those concentrations that meet the thresholds but fall outside the Community's extraterritorial competence.

[113] *See* also chapter 1 at section 3.2.

[114] Cf. R. Kögel, *supra* note 79 at p. 302 and p. 310 and Dominique Berlin and Hugues Calvet, 'Concentrations – 1er janvier 1995 – 31 décembre 1996', *Revue trimestrielle de droit européen*, 1997, pp. 521-627 at pp. 556-557. The latter point to *Mitsubishi Bank/Tokyo Bank*, Case IV/M596, decision of 17 July 1995 and *McDermott/ETPM*, Case IV/M648, decision of 27 November 1995 as examples of cases that should have been caught by a *de minimis* rule.

[115] The Commission in its *2001 Green Paper*, para. 34, *in fine* observes that 'there is wide agreement that turnover is the best proxy for establishing which concentrations have a Community interest'.

only way to measure whether the transaction is *de minimis*.[116] In order to ensure that this *de minimis* rule would be both easy to apply and relate to the transaction rather than to the parties, it would have to be based on the size of the transaction. In other words, this refined system would combine the present 'size of the undertakings' thresholds with a 'size of transaction' threshold.

Indeed, in 1994 the Commission introduced such rule *vis-à-vis* minor joint ventures,[117] although this is not a true *de minimis* rule since it does not exclude these minor joint ventures from the scope of the Regulation. Instead, it eases the notification requirements by only requiring the parties to submit a so-called short form (*i.e.*, a reduced) notification.

It seems that introducing a true *de minimis* rule along the lines provided in the Commission's short form notification rule, *i.e.*, one based on the size of the transaction, would be able to prevent a fair number of superfluous notifications.[118] It is, however, likely that such a rule would also exclude some concentrations deserving closer scrutiny. This could be 'compensated' for by lowering the present thresholds. Although this would not bring these 'lost' concentrations back within the scope of the Regulation, it would 'compensate' for the loss by catching some of those concentrations with a real Community dimension which presently fall below the thresholds.[119]

Moreover, further refinement of the present thresholds could be attained by replacing the present two-thirds threshold with one requiring that the entity which is the subject of the transaction should generate a minimum turnover (or hold a

---

[116] An essentially identical view is put forward by the Economic and Social Committee, *supra* note 44 at point 2.4.4.

[117] According to point C of Form CO a reduced notification is sufficient where the turnover of the joint venture and/or the turnover of the contributed activities is less than € 100 million in the EEA territory and the total value of assets transferred to the joint venture is less than € 100 million in the EEA territory.

[118] In the *2001 Green Paper* at para. 177 the Commission has tabled the idea of a block exemption regulation based upon the experience gained in respect of the short form notification rules.

[119] It is worth of note that the scope of the American Hart-Scott-Rodino Antitrust Improvements Act of 1976 (with later amendments) is principally delimited by a size-of-transaction test. If the transaction does not meet this size-of-transaction test, it may still be notifiable if it meets a second – lower – size-of-transaction *and* at the same time also meets a size-of-the-parties test. It is moreover worth noting that recently the American authorities have given the size-of-transaction test a more prominent role at the cost of the size-of-the-parties test.

minimum of assets if assets were included as an alternative) in at least two Member States. This rule would be better at capturing the international spillovers flowing from the mergers.[120]

A *de minimis* rule based on turnover, like the one set forth here, will provide both a clear-cut delimitation and will not be excessively costly while being better at weeding out insignificant concentrations. It therefore fulfils the criteria set out above in section 3.3.1.[121]

3.4. Recommendations for improving the delimitation of jurisdiction

In my opinion, the above examination shows that it is possible to construct a delimitation which is better at weeding out the *de minimis* cases without at the same time losing too many of the real Community dimension cases. This may be done by introducing a real *de minimis* threshold into the present system, for instance,

---

[120] This rule has been proposed by D. Neven *et al*, *supra* note 92, at p. 198 and pp. 237-238. These authors base their 'absolute international spillover rule' on the size of the parties, not the size of the transaction and it therefore suffers from the same deficiencies as does the present system. By instead relating the rule to the transaction itself I believe that this weakness can be remedied.

[121] R. Burnley, *supra* note 4, at p. 272 puts forward another proposal for refining the present system. He observes that 'Commission data provides that all of the undertakings involved in transactions that were notified in three or more Member States had an aggregate turnover of more than 1 billion euro. Meanwhile the aggregate Community-wide turnover of each of most of the undertakings involved in such transactions is above 100 million.' He therefore proposes to base the Community dimension upon the thresholds found in Art. 1(2), but to lower these to € 1 billion and € 100 million respectively, to dispense with the two-thirds rule and to improve the referral clause (German clause) in Art. 9. The proposal is interesting, but it also begs a number of questions. Why, for example, refer to the turnover of undertakings involved in concentrations that were notified in three or more Member States? Also concentrations that have only been notified in two Member States are likely to have had an effect on interstate trade. Indeed, a concentration that is not notifiable at all might produce such effects. In contrast, in the case of joint ventures, a concentration that does not produce any effects on interstate trade may be notifiable in several Member States. Moreover, Burnley's proposal is likely to lead to a considerable increase in the number of notifiable *de minimis* transactions (setting up of joint ventures). Another problem is that instead of reducing the problem caused by the thresholds excessive extraterritorial reach, the proposal is likely to exacerbate this problem. In my view Burnley's proposal is interesting, but does not solve the problems inherent in the present system.

along the lines provided by the Commission for short form notifications. This *de minimis* threshold is based on the size of the transaction, so it should rightly be categorised as a combination of the 'size of parties' and 'size of transaction' measures.

Another solution consists of a more fundamental change of the thresholds from the present ones, based on the size of the undertakings, to thresholds relating only to the size of the transaction itself. This also appears to provide a workable solution.

4. FINAL COMMENTS

One of the most important aims underlying the Merger Regulation is to create a level playing field. In other words, in a single market, the undertakings must be treated in an equal fashion regardless of whether they are based in Italy or Germany. The Merger Regulation achieves this aim only to a limited extent since the turnover thresholds only catch a limited number of those concentrations which do produce a significant impact across the borders inside the Community. Moreover, a fair number of those concentrations which actually do meet the turnover thresholds do not produce such an impact.

The inbuilt inadequacy in the turnover thresholds was clearly pointed out by Alexis Jacquemin, Pierre Buigues and Fabienne Ilzkovitz even before the Regulation was adopted.[122] These authors showed that, in a number of industries, the total turnover in the Community did not even reach the threshold level, meaning that in theory all the Community undertakings in these industries could merge without coming within the scope of the Regulation.[123] These three authors simultaneously

---

[122] European Commission, 'Horizontal mergers and competition policy in the European Community', *European Economy*, No. 40, May 1989, at p. 50.

[123] Indeed, these authors reached their conclusions on the basis of a preliminary proposal for a Merger Regulation which set the worldwide turnover threshold at € 1 billion and the Community-wide turnover at € 100 million. Today, however, the first set of turnover thresholds requires a worldwide turnover of € 5 billion (and a Community-wide turnover of € 250 million) and the second set of turnover thresholds requires a worldwide turnover of € 2.5 billion (and a Community-wide turnover of € 100 million) so that the total turnover in even more industries is likely not to meet these thresholds. Moreover, at the time when the Regulation entered into force Valentine Korah, *An Introductory Guide to EEC Competition Law and Practice*, 4th ed., ESC Publishing Ltd., Oxford 1990 at p. 213 observed that 'some half

found that the total turnover in other industries was so high that concentrations which reached the thresholds would not necessarily have any significant impact on competition. The inclusion of the second set of turnover thresholds (with lower worldwide and Community-wide turnover requirements) together with the expansion of the Community, inflation and the restructuring of European industry imply some changes to the situation. Nevertheless, many concentrations which are likely to produce adverse effects on the competition structure in the Community still fail to meet the turnover thresholds.

In my opinion, if the intention is to achieve a true level playing field, the road ahead must be harmonisation of the Member States' competition rules regarding concentrations.[124] If all Member States had merger control schemes and if these schemes and the Community scheme (*i.e.*, the Merger Regulation) only differed in respect of minor details, we would be able to create a level playing field.[125] The question is whether such a solution, which is akin to a limitation of the Member States' sovereignty, is desirable, not to mention politically feasible.[126] The winds

---

of the gross Community product consists of industries in which there are no two firms with aggregate turnover of five billion [EUROs].' *See* also European Commission, *supra* note 79 at p. 35 and pp. 51-52 and *European Economy – Supplement A*, No. 7, July 1996 at p. 2 as well as European Commission, *supra* note 57, paras. 35-45.

124 A fairly drastic proposal for such harmonisation has been provided by Christian Zschocke, 'Harmonisierung der Fusionskontrolle aus der Sicht des Praktikers', *Wirtschaft und Wettbewerb*, Vol. 46, 1996 No. 2, pp. 85-91. See also J. Bridgeman, *supra* note 100, at p. 103.

125 *See* for example M. Bishop, *supra* note 92 at p. 316. Indeed after the problems experienced between the Americans and the Europeans regarding the merger between Boeing and McDonnell Douglas, the European trade Commissioner, Sir Leon Brittan (formerly Commissioner for competition), called for an international agreement on competition rules. Failing such an agreement he feared that the future would bring 'more and more clashes when powerful competition authorities seek to deal with the same case, applying different rules', cf. Emma Tucker, 'Competition rules: WTO urged to act', *Financial Times*, Friday 25 July 1997 at p. 4. Note though that F. Jenny, *supra* note 102 at p. 106 observes that harmonisation does not solve the problem.

126 The question of adopting a more uniform approach between national merger control laws and the Merger Regulation arose in the German case *Großbacköfen* (decision by BGH of 24 October 1995, KVR 17/94, reported in *Wirtschaft und Wettbewerb*, vol. 46, issue 4, 1996, pp. 318-327) in which the German Federal Supreme Court held that a decision under German merger control law must not be influenced by the way a case would have been decided had it been within the scope of the Merger Regulation.

which presently sweep through the European political landscape are not exactly encouraging to proponents of such radical harmonisation being initiated by the Community. A slow but steady harmonisation process is, however, taking place as yet more Member States adopt competition rules which mirror those of the Community.[127] Thus, slowly, we may be able to obtain a true level playing field in respect of concentrations in the common market.

---

[127] Likewise, Christopher Jones, 'The European Dimension in Competition Policy', speech given in London on 21 January 1997.

ANNEX 1

Council Regulation (EEC) No 4064/89 of 21 December 1989[1] on the control of concentrations between undertakings – as amended by Council Regulation (EC) No 1310/97 of 30 June 1997 and by the Act concerning the conditions of accession of the Kingdom of Norway, the Republic of Austria, the Republic of Finland and the Kingdom of Sweden and the adjustments to the Treaties on which the European Union is founded.[2]

THE COUNCIL OF THE EUROPEAN COMMUNITIES,

Having regard to the Treaty establishing the European Economic Community, and in particular Articles [83] and [308] thereof,

Having regard to the proposal from the Commission,[3]

Having regard to the opinion of the European Parliament,[4]

Having regard to the opinion of the Economic and Social Committee,[5]

(1) Whereas, for the achievement of the aims of the Treaty establishing the European Economic Community, Article [3(g)] gives the Community the objective of instituting' a system ensuring that competition in the common market is not distorted';

(2) Whereas this system is essential for the achievement of the internal market by 1992 and its further development;

---

[1] This is the consolidated text of the Merger Regulation with later amendments. Only texts published in the Official Journal of the European Union are authentic.

[2] ANNEX I – List referred to in Article 29 of the Act of Accession – III. COMPETITION – B. PROCEDURAL REGULATIONS; OJ No. C241, 29/8/94 p. 57.

[3] OJ No C 130, 19.5.1988, p. 4.

[4] OJ No C 309, 5.12.1988, p. 55.

[5] OJ No C 208, 8.8.1988, p. 11.

(3) Whereas the dismantling of internal frontiers is resulting and will continue to result in major corporate re-organizations in the Community, particularly in the form of concentrations;

(4) Whereas such a development must be welcomed as being in line with the requirements of dynamic competition and capable of increasing the competitiveness of European industry, improving the conditions of growth and raising the standard of living in the Community;

(5) Whereas, however, it must be ensured that the process of re-organization does not result in lasting damage to competition; whereas Community law must therefore include provisions governing those concentrations which may significantly impede effective competition in the common market or in a substantial part of it;

(6) Whereas Articles [81] and [82], while applicable, according to the case-law of the Court of Justice, to certain concentrations, are not, however, sufficient to cover all operations which may prove to be incompatible with the system of undistorted competition envisaged in the Treaty;

(7) Whereas a new legal instrument should therefore be created in the form of a Regulation to permit effective monitoring of all concentrations from the point of view of their effect on the structure of competition in the Community and to be the only instrument applicable to such concentrations;

(8) Whereas this Regulation should therefore be based not only on Article [83] but, principally, on Article [308] of the Treaty, under which the Community may give itself the additional powers of action necessary for the attainment of its objectives, and also with regard to concentrations on the markets for agricultural products listed in Annex II to the Treaty;

(9) Whereas the provisions to be adopted in this Regulation should apply to significant structural changes the impact of which on the market goes beyond the national borders of any one Member State;

(10) Whereas the scope of application of this Regulation should therefore be defined according to the geographical area of activity of the undertakings concerned and be limited by quantitative thresholds in order to cover those concentrations which have a Community dimension; whereas, at the end of an initial phase of the implementation of this Regulation, these thresholds should be reviewed in the light of the experience gained;

(11) Whereas a concentration with a Community dimension exists where the aggregate turnover of the undertakings concerned exceeds given levels worldwide and throughout the Community and where at least two of the

undertakings concerned have their sole or main fields of activities in different Member States or where, although the undertakings in question act mainly in one and the same Member State, at least one of them has substantial operations in at least one other Member State; whereas that is also the case where the concentrations are effected by undertakings which do not have their principal fields of activities in the Community but which have substantial operations there;

(12) Whereas the arrangements to be introduced for the control of concentrations should, without prejudice to Article [86] (2) of the Treaty, respect the principle of non-discrimination between the public and the private sectors; whereas, in the public sector, calculation of the turnover of an undertaking concerned in a concentration needs, therefore, to take account of undertakings making up an economic unit with an independent power of decision, irrespective of the way in which their capital is held or of the rules of administrative supervision applicable to them;

(13) Whereas it is necessary to establish whether concentrations with a Community dimension are compatible or not with the common market from the point of view of the need to preserve and develop effective competition in the common market; whereas, in so doing, the Commission must place its appraisal within the general framework of the achievement of the fundamental objectives referred to in Article 2 of the Treaty, including that of strengthening the Community's economic and social cohesion, referred to in Article [158];

(14) Whereas this Regulation should establish the principle that a concentration with a Community dimension which creates or strengthens a position as result of which effective competition in the common market or in a substantial part of it is significantly impeded is to be declared incompatible with the common market;

(15) Whereas concentrations which, by reason of the limited market share of the undertakings concerned, are not liable to impede effective competition may be presumed to be compatible with the common market; whereas, without prejudice to Articles [81] and [82] of the Treaty, an indication to this effect exists, in particular, where the market share of the undertakings concerned does not exceed 25 % either in the common market or in a substantial part of it;

(16) Whereas the Commission should have the task of taking all the decisions necessary to establish whether or not concentrations of a Community

dimension are compatible with the common market, as well as decisions designed to restore effective competition;

(17) Whereas to ensure effective control undertakings should be obliged to give prior notification of concentrations with a Community dimension and provision should be made for the suspension of concentrations for a limited period, and for the possibility of extending or waiving a suspension where necessary; whereas in the interests of legal certainty the validity of transactions must nevertheless be protected as much as necessary;

(18) Whereas a period within which the Commission must initiate a proceeding in respect of a notified concentration and a period within which it must give a final decision on the compatibility or incompatibility with the common market of a notified concentration should be laid down;

(19) Whereas the undertakings concerned must be accorded the right to be heard by the Commission as soon as a proceeding has been initiated; whereas the members of management and supervisory organs and recognized workers' representatives in the undertakings concerned, together with third parties showing a legitimate interest, must also be given the opportunity to be heard;

(20) Whereas the Commission should act in close and constant liaison with the competent authorities of the Member States from which it obtains comments and information;

(21) Whereas, for the purposes of this Regulation, and in accordance with the case-law of the Court of Justice, the Commission must be afforded the assistance of the Member States and must also be empowered to require information to be given and to carry out the necessary investigations in order to appraise concentrations;

(22) Whereas compliance with this Regulation must be enforceable by means of fines and periodic penalty payments; whereas the Court of Justice should be given unlimited jurisdiction in that regard pursuant to Article [229] of the Treaty;

(23) Whereas it is appropriate to define the concept of concentration in such a manner as to cover only operations bringing about a durable change in the structure of the undertakings concerned; whereas it is therefore necessary to exclude from the scope of this Regulation those operations which have as their object or effect the coordination of the competitive behaviour of independent undertakings, since such operations fall to be examined under the appropriate provisions of Regulations implementing Article [81] or

Article [82] of the Treaty; whereas it is appropriate to make this distinction specifically in the case of the creation of joint ventures;

(24) Whereas there is no coordination of competitive behaviour within the meaning of this Regulation where two or more undertakings agree to acquire jointly control of one or more other undertakings with the object and effect of sharing amongst themselves such undertakings or their assets;

(25) Whereas the application of this Regulation is not excluded where the undertakings concerned accept restrictions directly related and necessary to the implementation of the concentration;

(26) Whereas the Commission should be given exclusive competence to apply this Regulation, subject to review by the Court of Justice;

(27) Whereas the Member States may not apply their national legislation on competition to concentrations with a Community dimension, unless the Regulation makes provision therefor; whereas the relevant powers of national authorities should be limited to cases where, failing intervention by the Commission, effective competition is likely to be significantly impeded within the territory of a Member State and where the competition interests of that Member State cannot be sufficiently protected otherwise than by this Regulation; whereas the Member States concerned must act promptly in such cases; whereas this Regulation cannot, because of the diversity of national law, fix a single deadline for the adoption of remedies;

(28) Whereas, furthermore, the exclusive application of this Regulation to concentrations with a Community dimension is without prejudice to Article [296] of the Treaty, and does not prevent the Member States' taking appropriate measures to protect legitimate interests other than those pursued by this Regulation, provided that such measures are compatible with the general principles and other provisions of Community law;

(29) Whereas concentrations not referred to in this Regulation come, in principle, within the jurisdiction of the Member States; whereas, however, the Commission should have the power to act, at the request of a Member State concerned, in cases where effective competition would be significantly impeded within that Member State's territory;

(30) Whereas the conditions in which concentrations involving Community undertakings are carried out in non-member countries should be observed, and provision should be made for the possibility of the Council's giving the Commission an appropriate mandate for negotiation with a view to obtaining non-discriminatory treatment for Community undertakings;

(31) Whereas this Regulation in no way detracts from the collective rights of workers as recognized in the undertakings concerned,

HAS ADOPTED THIS REGULATION:

Article 1

Scope

1. Without prejudice to Article 22, this Regulation shall apply to all concentrations with a Community dimension as defined in paragraphs 2 and 3.

2. For the purposes of this Regulation, a concentration has a Community dimension where;

(a) the aggregate worldwide turnover of all the undertakings concerned is more than [€] 5 000 million, and

(b) the aggregate Community-wide turnover of each of at least two of the undertakings concerned is more than [€] 250 million,

unless each of the undertakings concerned achieves more than two-thirds of its aggregate Community-wide turnover within one and the same Member State.

3. For the purposes of this Regulation, a concentration that does not meet the thresholds laid down in paragraph 2 has a Community dimension where:

(a) the combined aggregate worldwide turnover of all the undertakings concerned is more than [€] 2 500 million;

(b) in each of at least three Member States, the combined aggregate turnover of all the undertakings concerned is more than [€] 100 million;

(c) in each of the three Member States included for the purpose of (b), the aggregate turnover of each of at least two of the undertakings concerned is more than [€] 25 million; and

(d) the aggregate Community-wide turnover of each of at least two of the undertakings concerned is more than [€] 100 million;

unless each of the undertakings concerned achieves more than two-thirds of its aggregate Community-wide turnover within one and the same Member State.

4. Before 1 July 2000 the Commission shall report to the Council on the operation of the thresholds and criteria set out in paragraphs 2 and 3.

5. Following the report referred to in paragraph 4 and on a proposal from the Commission, the Council, acting by a qualified majority, may revise the thresholds and criteria mentioned in paragraph 3.

Article 2

Appraisal of concentrations

1. Concentrations within the scope of this Regulation shall be appraised in accordance with the following provisions with a view to establishing whether or not they are compatible with the common market.

In making this appraisal, the Commission shall take into account:

    (a) the need to preserve and develop effective competition within the common market in view of, among other things, the structure of all the markets concerned and the actual or potential competition from undertakings located either within or without the Community;

    (b) the market position of the undertakings concerned and their economic and financial power, the opportunities available to suppliers and users, their access to supplies or markets, any legal or other barriers to entry, supply and demand trends for the relevant goods and services, the interests of the intermediate and ultimate consumers, and the development of technical and economic progress provided that it is to consumers' advantage and does not form an obstacle to competition.

2. A concentration which does not create or strengthen a dominant position as a result of which effective competition would be significantly impeded in the common market or in a substantial part of it shall be declared compatible with the common market.

3. A concentration which creates or strengthens a dominant position as a result of which effective competition would be significantly impeded in the common market or in a substantial part of it shall be declared incompatible with the common market.

4. To the extent that the creation of a joint venture constituting a concentration pursuant to Article 3 has as its object or effect the co-ordination of the competitive behaviour of undertakings that remain independent, such co-ordination shall be appraised in accordance with the criteria of Article [81](1) and (3) of the Treaty, with a view to establishing whether or not the operation is compatible with the common market.

In making this appraisal, the Commission shall take into account in particular:

- whether two or more parent companies retain to a significant extent activities in the same market as the joint venture or in a market which is downstream or upstream from that of the joint venture or in a neighbouring market closely related to this market;

- whether the co-ordination which is the direct consequence of the creation of the joint venture affords the undertakings concerned the possibility of eliminating competition in respect of a substantial part of the products or services in question.

Article 3

Definition of concentration

1. A concentration shall be deemed to arise where:

   (a) two or more previously independent undertakings merge, or

   (b) – one or more persons already controlling at least one undertaking, or

      – one or more undertakings

acquire, whether by purchase of securities or assets, by contract or by any other means, direct or indirect control of the whole or parts of one or more other undertakings.

2. The creation of a joint venture performing on a lasting basis all the functions of an autonomous economic entity shall constitute a concentration within the meaning of paragraph 1 (b).

3. For the purposes of this Regulation, control shall be constituted by rights, contracts or any other means which, either separately or jointly and having regard to the considerations of fact or law involved, confer the possibility of exercising decisive influence on an undertaking, in particular by:

   (a) ownership or the right to use all or part of the assets of an undertaking;

   (b) rights or contracts which confer decisive influence on the composition, voting or decisions of the organs of an undertaking.

4. Control is acquired by persons or undertakings which:

   (a) are holders of the rights or entitled to rights under the contracts concerned, or

   (b) while not being holders of such rights or entitled to rights under such contracts, have the power to exercise the rights deriving therefrom.

5. A concentration shall not be deemed to arise where:

(a) credit institutions or other financial institutions or insurance companies, the normal activities of which include transactions and dealing in securities for their own account or for the account of others, hold on a temporary basis securities which they have acquired in an undertaking with a view to reselling them, provided that they do not exercise voting rights in respect of those securities with a view to determining the competitive behaviour of that undertaking or provided that they exercise such voting rights only with a view to preparing the sale of all or part of that undertaking or of its assets or the sale of those securities and that any such sale takes place within one year of the date of acquisition; that period may be extended by the Commission on request where such institutions or companies justify the fact that the sale was not reasonably possible within the period set;

(b) control is acquired by an office holder according to the law of a Member State relating to liquidation, winding up, insolvency, cessation of payments, compositions or analogous proceedings;

(c) the operations referred to in paragraph 1 (b) are carried out by the financial holding companies referred to in Article 5 (3) of the Fourth Council Directive 78/660/EEC of 25 July 1978 on the annual accounts of certain types of companies,[6] as last amended by Directive 84/569/EEC,[7] provided however that the voting rights in respect of the holding are exercised, in particular in relation to the appointment of members of the management and supervisory bodies of the undertakings in which they have holdings, only to maintain the full value of those investments and not to determine directly or indirectly the competitive conduct of those undertakings.

Article 4
Prior notification of concentrations

1. Concentrations with a Community dimension as referred to by this Regulation shall be notified to the Commission not more than one week after the conclusion of the agreement, or the announcement of the public bid, or the acquisition of a controlling interest. That week shall begin when the first of those events occurs.

---

6   OJ No L 222, 14.8.1978, p. 11.

7   OJ No L 314, 4.12.1984, p. 28.

2. A concentration which consists of a merger within the meaning of Article 3 (1) (a) or in the acquisition of joint control within the meaning of Article 3 (1) (b) shall be notified jointly by the parties to the merger or by those acquiring joint control as the case may be. In all other cases, the notification shall be effected by the person or undertaking acquiring control of the whole or parts of one or more undertakings.

3. Where the Commission finds that a notified concentration falls within the scope of this Regulation, it shall publish the fact of the notification, at the same time indicating the names of the parties, the nature of the concentration and the economic sectors involved. The Commission shall take account of the legitimate interest of undertakings in the protection of their business secrets.

Article 5

Calculation of turnover

1. Aggregate turnover within the meaning of Article 1 (2) shall comprise the amounts derived by the undertakings concerned in the preceding financial year from the sale of products and the provision of services falling within the undertakings' ordinary activities after deduction of sales rebates and of value added tax and other taxes directly related to turnover. The aggregate turnover of an undertaking concerned shall not include the sale of products or the provision of services between any of the undertakings referred to in paragraph 4.

Turnover, in the Community or in a Member State, shall comprise products sold and services provided to undertakings or consumers, in the Community or in that Member State as the case may be.

2. By way of derogation from paragraph 1, where the concentration consists in the acquisition of parts, whether or not constituted as legal entities, of one or more undertakings, only the turnover relating to the parts which are the subject of the transaction shall be taken into account with regard to the seller or sellers.

However, two or more transactions within the meaning of the first subparagraph which take place within a two-year period between the same persons or undertakings shall be treated as one and the same concentration arising on the date of the last transaction.

3. In place of turnover the following shall be used:
   (a) for credit institutions and other financial institutions, as regards Articles 1(2) and (3) the sum of the following income items as defined in Directive

86/635/EEC of 8 December 1986 on the annual accounts and consolidated accounts of banks and other financial institutions[8], after deduction of value added tax and other taxes directly related to those items, where appropriate:

(i) interest income and similar income;

(ii) income from securities:

- income from shares and other variable yield securities;
- income from participating interests;
- income from shares in affiliated undertakings;

(iii) commissions receivable;

(iv) net profit on financial operations;

(v) other operating income.

The turnover of a credit or financial institution in the Community or in a Member State shall comprise the income items, as defined above, which are received by the branch or division of that institution established in the Community or in the Member State in question, as the case may be;

(b) for insurance undertakings, the value of gross premiums written which shall comprise all amounts received and receivable in respect of insurance contracts issued by or on behalf of the insurance undertakings, including also outgoing reinsurance premiums, and after deduction of taxes and parafiscal contributions or levies charged by reference to the amounts of individual premiums or the total volume of premiums; as regards Article 1 (2) (b) and (3) (b), (c) and (d) and the final part of Article 1 (2) and (3), gross premiums received from Community residents and from residents of one Member State respectively shall be taken into account.

4. Without prejudice to paragraph 2, the aggregate turnover of an undertaking concerned within the meaning of Article 1 (2) and (3) shall be calculated by adding together the respective turnover of the following:

(a) the undertaking concerned;

(b) those undertakings in which the undertaking concerned, directly or indirectly;

- owns more than half the capital or business assets, or
- has the power to exercise more than half the voting rights, or

---

8   OJ No L 372, 31.12.1986, p. 1.

- has the power to appoint more than half the members of the supervisory board, the administrative board or bodies legally representing the undertakings, or

- has the right to manage the undertakings' affairs;

(c) those undertakings which have in an undertaking concerned the rights or powers listed in (b);

(d) those undertakings in which an undertaking as referred to in (c) has the rights or powers listed in (b);

(e) those undertakings in which two or more undertakings as referred to in (a) to (d) jointly have the rights or powers listed in (b).

5. Where undertakings concerned by the concentration jointly have the rights or powers listed in paragraph 4 (b), in calculating the turnover of the undertakings concerned for the purposes of Article 1 (2) and (3);

(a) no account shall be taken of the turnover resulting from the sale of products or the provision of services between the joint undertaking and each of the undertakings concerned or any other undertaking connected with any one of them, as set out in paragraph 4 (b) to (e);

(b) account shall be taken of the turnover resulting from the sale of products and the provision of services between the joint undertaking and any third undertakings. This turnover shall be apportioned equally amongst the undertakings concerned.

Article 6

Examination of the notification and initiation of proceedings

1. The Commission shall examine the notification as soon as it is received.

(a) Where it concludes that the concentration notified does not fall within the scope of this Regulation, it shall record that finding by means of a decision.

(b) Where it finds that the concentration notified, although falling within the scope of this Regulation, does not raise serious doubts as to its compatibility with the common market, it shall decide not to oppose it and shall declare that it is compatible with the common market.

The decision declaring the concentration compatible shall also cover restrictions directly related and necessary to the implementation of the concentration

(c) Without prejudice to paragraph 2, where the Commission finds that the concentration notified falls within the scope of this Regulation and raises serious doubts as to its compatibility with the common market, it shall decide to initiate proceedings.

2. Where the Commission finds that, following modification by the undertakings concerned, a notified concentration no longer raises serious doubts within the meaning of paragraph 1(c), it may decide to declare the concentration compatible with the common market pursuant to paragraph 1(b).

The Commission may attach to its decision under paragraph 1(b) conditions and obligations intended to ensure that the undertakings concerned comply with the commitments they have entered into vis-à-vis the Commission with a view to rendering the concentration compatible with the common market.

3. The Commission may revoke the decision it has taken pursuant to paragraph 1(a) or (b) where:

(a) the decision is based on incorrect information for which one of the undertakings is responsible or where it has been obtained by deceit, or

(b) the undertakings concerned commit a breach of an obligation attached to the decision.

4. In the cases referred to in paragraph 3, the Commission may take a decision under paragraph 1, without being bound by the deadlines referred to in Article 10(1).

5. The Commission shall notify its decision to the undertakings concerned and the competent authorities of the Member States without delay.

Article 7

Suspension of concentrations

1. A concentration as defined in Article 1 shall not be put into effect either before its notification or until it has been declared compatible with the common market pursuant to a decision under Article 6(1)(b) or Article 8(2) or on the basis of a presumption according to Article 10(6).

2. *deleted.*

3. Paragraph 1 shall not prevent the implementation of a public bid which has been notified to the Commission in accordance with Article 4 (1), provided that the acquirer does not exercise the voting rights attached to the securities in question or

does so only to maintain the full value of those investments and on the basis of a derogation granted by the Commission under paragraph 4.

4. The Commission may, on request, grant a derogation from the obligations imposed in paragraphs 1 or 3. The request to grant a derogation must be reasoned. In deciding on the request, the Commission shall take into account inter alia the effects of the suspension on one or more undertakings concerned by a concentration or to a third party and the threat to competition posed by the concentration. That derogation may be made subject to conditions and obligations in order to ensure conditions of effective competition. A derogation may be applied for and granted at any time, even before notification or after the transaction.

5. The validity of any transaction carried out in contravention of paragraph 1 shall be dependent on a decision pursuant to Article 6 (1) (b) or 8 (2) or (3) or by virtue of the presumption established by Article 10 (6).

This Article shall, however, have no effect on the validity of transactions in securities including those convertible into other securities admitted to trading on a market which is regulated and supervised by authorities recognized by public bodies, operates regularly and is accessible directly or indirectly to the public, unless the buyer and seller knew or ought to have known that the transaction was carried out in contravention of paragraph 1.

Article 8

Powers of decision of the Commission

1. Without prejudice to Article 9, each proceeding initiated pursuant to Article 6 (1) (c) shall be closed by means of a decision as provided for in paragraphs 2 to 5.

2. Where the Commission finds that, following modification by the undertakings concerned if necessary, a notified concentration fulfils the criterion laid down in Article 2(2) and, in the cases referred to in Article 2(4), the criteria laid down in Article [81](3) of the Treaty, it shall issue a decision declaring the concentration compatible with the common market.

It may attach to its decision conditions and obligations intended to ensure that the undertakings concerned comply with the commitments they have entered into vis-à-vis the Commission with a view to rendering the concentration compatible with the common market. The decision declaring the concentration compatible with the common market shall also cover restrictions directly related and necessary to the implementation of the concentration.

3. Where the Commission finds that a concentration fulfils the criterion defined in Article 2(3) or, in the cases referred to in Article 2(4), does not fulfil the criteria laid down in Article [81](3) of the Treaty, it shall issue a decision declaring that the concentration is incompatible with the common market.

4. Where a concentration has already been implemented, the Commission may, in a decision pursuant to paragraph 3 or by a separate decision, require the undertakings or assets brought together to be separated or the cessation of joint control or any other action that may be appropriate in order to restore conditions of effective competition.

5. The Commission may revoke the decision it has taken pursuant to paragraph 2 where:

(a) the declaration of compatibility is based on incorrect information for which one of the undertakings concerned is responsible or where it has been obtained by deceit, or

(b) the undertakings concerned commit a breach of an obligation attached to the decision.

6. In the case referred to in paragraph 5, the Commission may take a decision pursuant to paragraph 3, without being bound by the deadline referred to in Article 10 (3).

Article 9

Referral to the competent authorities of the Member States

1. The Commission may, by means of a decision notified without delay to the undertakings concerned and the competent authorities of the other Member States, refer a notified concentration to the competent authorities of the Member State concerned in the following circumstances.

2. Within three weeks of the date of receipt of the copy of the notification a Member State may inform the Commission, which shall inform the undertakings concerned, that:

(a) a concentration threatens to create or to strengthen a dominant position as a result of which effective competition will be significantly impeded on a market within that Member State, which presents all the characteristics of a distinct market, or

(b) a concentration affects competition on a market within that Member State, which presents all the characteristics of a distinct market and which does not constitute a substantial part of the common market.

3. If the Commission considers that, having regard to the market for the products or services in question and the geographical reference market within the meaning of paragraph 7, there is such a distinct market and that such a threat exists either:

(a) it shall itself deal with the case in order to maintain or restore effective competition on the market concerned, or

(b) it shall refer the whole or part of the case to the competent authorities of the Member State concerned with a view to the application of that State's national competition law.

If, however, the Commission considers that such a distinct market or threat does not exist it shall adopt a decision to that effect which it shall address to the Member State concerned.

In cases where a Member State informs the Commission that a concentration affects competition in a distinct market within its territory that does not form a substantial part of the common market, the Commission shall refer the whole or part of the case relating to the distinct market concerned, if it considers that such a distinct market is affected.

4. A decision to refer or not to refer pursuant to paragraph 3 shall be taken where:

(a) as a general rule within the six-week period provided for in Article 10 (1), second subparagraph, where the Commission has not initiated proceedings pursuant to Article 6 (1) (b), or

(b) within three months at most of the notification of the concentration concerned where the Commission has initiated proceedings under Article 6 (1) (c), without taking the preparatory steps in order to adopt the necessary measures pursuant to Article 8 (2), second subparagraph, (3) or (4) to maintain or restore effective competition on the market concerned.

5. If within the three months referred to in paragraph 4 (b) the Commission, despite a reminder from the Member State concerned, has taken no decision on referral in accordance with paragraph 3 or taken the preparatory steps referred to in paragraph 4 (b), it shall be deemed to have taken a decision to refer the case to the Member State concerned in accordance with paragraph 3 (b).

6. The publication of any report or the announcement of the findings of the examination of the concentration by the competent authority of the Member State

concerned shall be effected not more than four months after the Commission's referral.

7. The geographical reference market shall consist of the area in which the undertakings concerned are involved in the supply of products or services, in which the conditions of competition are sufficiently homogeneous and which can be distinguished from neighbouring areas because, in particular, conditions of competition are appreciably different in those areas. This assessment should take account in particular of the nature and characteristics of the products or services concerned, of the existence of entry barriers or of consumer preferences, of appreciable differences of the undertakings' market shares between neighbouring areas or of substantial price differences.

8. In applying the provisions of this Article, the Member State concerned may take only the measures strictly necessary to safeguard or restore effective competition on the market concerned.

9. In accordance with the relevant provisions of the Treaty, any Member State may appeal to the Court of Justice, and in particular request the application of Article [243], for the purpose of applying its national competition law.

10. This Article may be re-examined at the same time as the thresholds referred to in Article 1.

Article 10

Time limits for initiating proceedings and for decisions

1. The decisions referred to in Article 6 (1) must be taken within one month at most. That period shall begin on the day following the receipt of a notification or, if the information to be supplied with the notification is incomplete, on the day following the receipt of the complete information.

That period shall be increased to six weeks if the Commission receives a request from a Member State in accordance with Article 9 (2), or where, after notification of a concentration, the undertakings concerned submit commitments pursuant to Article 6(2), which are intended by the parties to form the basis for a decision pursuant to Article 6(1)(b).

2. Decisions taken pursuant to Article 8 (2) concerning notified concentrations must be taken as soon as it appears that the serious doubts referred to in Article 6 (1) (c) have been removed, particularly as a result of modifications made by the undertakings concerned, and at the latest by the deadline laid down in paragraph 3.

3. Without prejudice to Article 8 (6), decisions taken pursuant to Article 8 (3) concerning notified concentrations must be taken within not more than four months of the date on which the proceeding is initiated.

4. The periods set by paragraphs 1 and 3 shall exceptionally be suspended where, owing to circumstances for which one of the undertakings involved in the concentration is responsible, the Commission has had to request information by decision pursuant to Article 11 or to order an investigation by decision pursuant to Article 13.

5. Where the Court of Justice gives a judgment which annuls the whole or part of a Commission decision taken under this Regulation, the periods laid down in this Regulation shall start again from the date of the judgment.

6. Where the Commission has not taken a decision in accordance with Article 6 (1) (b) or (c) or Article 8 (2) or (3) within the deadlines set in paragraphs 1 and 3 respectively, the concentration shall be deemed declared compatible with the common market, without prejudice to Article 9.

Article 11

Requests for information

1. In carrying out the duties assigned to it by this Regulation, the Commission may obtain all necessary information from the Governments and competent authorities of the Member States, from the persons referred to in Article 3 (1) (b), and from undertakings and associations of undertakings.

2. When sending a request for information to a person, an undertaking or an association of undertakings, the Commission shall at the same time send a copy of the request to the competent authority of the Member State within the territory of which the residence of the person or the seat of the undertaking or association of undertakings is situated.

3. In its request the Commission shall state the legal basis and the purpose of the request and also the penalties provided for in Article 14 (1) (b) for supplying incorrect information.

4. The information requested shall be provided, in the case of undertakings, by their owners or their representatives and, in the case of legal persons, companies or firms, or of associations having no legal personality, by the persons authorized to represent them by law or by their statutes.

5. Where a person, an undertaking or an association of undertakings does not provide the information requested within the period fixed by the Commission or provides incomplete information, the Commission shall by decision require the information to be provided. The decision shall specify what information is required, fix an appropriate period within which it is to be supplied and state the penalties provided for in Articles 14 (1) (b) and 15 (1) (a) and the right to have the decision reviewed by the Court of Justice.

6. The Commission shall at the same time send a copy of its decision to the competent authority of the Member State within the territory of which the residence of the person or the seat of the undertaking or association of undertakings is situated.

Article 12

Investigations by the authorities of the Member States

1. At the request of the Commission, the competent authorities of the Member States shall undertake the investigations which the Commission considers to be necessary pursuant to Article 13 (1), or which it has ordered by decision pursuant to Article 13 (3). The officials of the competent authorities of the Member States responsible for conducting those investigations shall exercise their powers upon production of an authorization in writing issued by the competent authority of the Member State within the territory of which the investigation is to be carried out. Such authorization shall specify the subject matter and purpose of the investigation.

2. If so requested by the Commission or by the competent authority of the Member State within the territory of which the investigation is to be carried out, officials of the Commission may assist the officials of that authority in carrying out their duties.

Article 13

Investigative powers of the Commission

1. In carrying out the duties assigned to it by this Regulation, the Commission may undertake all necessary investigations into undertakings and associations of undertakings. To that end the officials authorized by the Commission shall be empowered:

(a) to examine the books and other business records;

(b) to take or demand copies of or extracts from the books and business records;

(c) to ask for oral explanations on the spot;

(d) to enter any premises, land and means of transport of undertakings.

2. The officials of the Commission authorized to carry out the investigations shall exercise their powers on production of an authorization in writing specifying the subject matter and purpose of the investigation and the penalties provided for in Article 14 (1) (c) in cases where production of the required books or other business records is incomplete. In good time before the investigation, the Commission shall inform, in writing, the competent authority of the Member State within the territory of which the investigation is to be carried out of the investigation and of the identities of the authorized officials.

3. Undertakings and associations of undertakings shall submit to investigations ordered by decision of the Commission. The decision shall specify the subject matter and purpose of the investigation, appoint the date on which it shall begin and state the penalties provided for in Articles 14 (1) (c) and 15 (1) (b) and the right to have the decision reviewed by the Court of Justice.

4. The Commission shall in good time and in writing inform the competent authority of the Member State within the territory of which the investigation is to be carried out of its intention of taking a decision pursuant to paragraph 3. It shall hear the competent authority before taking its decision.

5. Officials of the competent authority of the Member State within the territory of which the investigation is to be carried out may, at the request of that authority or of the Commission, assist the officials of the Commission in carrying out their duties.

6. Where an undertaking or association of undertakings opposes an investigation ordered pursuant to this Article, the Member State concerned shall afford the necessary assistance to the officials authorized by the Commission to enable them to carry out their investigation. To this end the Member States shall, after consulting the Commission, take the necessary measures within one year of the entry into force of this Regulation.

Article 14

Fines

1. The Commission may by decision impose on the persons referred to in Article 3 (1) (b), undertakings or associations of undertakings fines of from [€] 1 000 to 50 000 where intentionally or negligently:

(a) they omit to notify a concentration in accordance with Article 4;

(b) they supply incorrect or misleading information in a notification pursuant to Article 4;

(c) they supply incorrect information in response to a request made pursuant to Article 11 or fail to supply information within the period fixed by a decision taken pursuant to Article 11;

(d) they produce the required books or other business records in incomplete form during investigations pursuant to Article 12 or 13, or refuse to submit to an investigation ordered by decision taken pursuant to Article 13.

2. The Commission may by decision impose fines not exceeding 10 % of the aggregate turnover of the undertakings concerned within the meaning of Article 5 on the persons or undertakings concerned where, either intentionally or negligently, they:

(a) fail to comply with an obligation imposed by decision pursuant to Article 7 (4) or 8 (2), second subparagraph;

(b) put into effect a concentration in breach of Article 7 (1) or disregard a decision taken pursuant to Article 7 (2);

(c) put into effect a concentration declared incompatible with the common market by decision pursuant to Article 8 (3) or do not take the measures ordered by decision pursuant to Article 8 (4).

3. In setting the amount of a fine, regard shall be had to the nature and gravity of the infringement.

4. Decisions taken pursuant to paragraphs 1 and 2 shall not be of a criminal law nature.

Article 15

Periodic penalty payments

1. The Commission may by decision impose on the persons referred to in Article 3 (1) (b), undertakings or associations of undertakings concerned periodic penalty payments of up to [€] 25 000 for each day of the delay calculated from the date set in the decision, in order to compel them:

(a) to supply complete and correct information which it has requested by decision pursuant to Article 11;

(b) to submit to an investigation which it has ordered by decision pursuant to Article 13.

2. The Commission may by decision impose on the persons referred to in Article 3 (1) (b) or on undertakings periodic penalty payments of up to [€] 100 000 for each day of the delay calculated from the date set in the decision, in order to compel them:

(a) to comply with an obligation imposed by decision pursuant to Article 7 (4) or 8 (2), second subparagraph, or

(b) to apply the measures ordered by decision pursuant to Article 8 (4).

3. Where the persons referred to in Article 3 (1) (b), undertakings or associations of undertakings have satisfied the obligation which it was the purpose of the periodic penalty payment to enforce, the Commission may set the total amount of the periodic penalty payments at a lower figure than that which would arise under the original decision.

Article 16

Review by the Court of Justice

The Court of Justice shall have unlimited jurisdiction within the meaning of Article [229] of the Treaty to review decisions whereby the Commission has fixed a fine or periodic penalty payments; it may cancel, reduce or increase the fine or periodic penalty payment imposed.

Article 17

Professional secrecy

1. Information acquired as a result of the application of Articles 11, 12, 13 and 18 shall be used only for the purposes of the relevant request, investigation or hearing.

2. Without prejudice to Articles 4 (3), 18 and 20, the Commission and the competent authorities of the Member States, their officials and other servants shall not disclose information they have acquired through the application of this Regulation of the kind covered by the obligation of professional secrecy.

3. Paragraphs 1 and 2 shall not prevent publication of general information or of surveys which do not contain information relating to particular undertakings or associations of undertakings.

Article 18

Hearing of the parties and of third persons

1. Before taking any decision provided for in Article 7 (4), 8 (2), second sub-paragraph, and (3) to (5), 14 and 15, the Commission shall give the persons, undertakings and associations of undertakings concerned the opportunity, at every stage of the procedure up to the consultation of the Advisory Committee, of making known their views on the objections against them.

2. By way of derogation from paragraph 1, a decision to grant a derogation from suspension as referred to in Article 7 (4) may be taken provisionally, without the persons, undertakings or associations of undertakings concerned being given the opportunity to make known their views beforehand, provided that the Commission gives them that opportunity as soon as possible after having taken its decision.

3. The Commission shall base its decision only on objections on which the parties have been able to submit their observations. The rights of the defence shall be fully respected in the proceedings. Access to the file shall be open at least to the parties directly involved, subject to the legitimate interest of undertakings in the protection of their business secrets.

4. Insofar as the Commission and the competent authorities of the Member States deem it necessary, they may also hear other natural or legal persons. Natural or legal persons showing a legitimate interest and especially members of the administrative or management organs of the undertakings concerned or recognized workers' representatives of those undertakings shall be entitled, upon application, to be heard.

Article 19

Liaison with the authorities of the Member States

1. The Commission shall transmit to the competent authorities of the Member States copies of notifications within three working days and, as soon as possible, copies of the most important documents lodged with or issued by the Commission pursuant to this Regulation. Such documents shall include commitments which are intended by the parties to form the basis for a decision pursuant to Articles 6(1)(b) or 8(2).

2. The Commission shall carry out the procedures set out in this Regulation in close and constant liaison with the competent authorities of the Member States, which may express their views upon those procedures. For the purposes of Article

9 it shall obtain information from the competent authority of the Member State as referred to in paragraph 2 of that Article and give it the opportunity to make known its views at every stage of the procedure up to the adoption of a decision pursuant to paragraph 3 of that Article; to that end it shall give it access to the file.

3. An Advisory Committee on concentrations shall be consulted before any decision is taken pursuant to Articles 8 (2) to (5), 14 or 15, or any provisions are adopted pursuant to Article 23.

4. The Advisory Committee shall consist of representatives of the authorities of the Member States. Each Member State shall appoint one or two representatives; if unable to attend, they may be replaced by other representa-tives. At least one of the representatives of a Member State shall be competent in matters of restrictive practices and dominant positions.

5. Consultation shall take place at a joint meeting convened at the invitation of and chaired by the Commission. A summary of the facts, together with the most important documents and a preliminary draft of the decision to be taken for each case considered, shall be sent with the invitation. The meeting shall take place not less than 14 days after the invitation has been sent. The Commission may in exceptional cases shorten that period as appropriate in order to avoid serious harm to one or more of the undertakings concerned by a concentration.

6. The Advisory Committee shall deliver an opinion on the Commission's draft decision, if necessary by taking a vote. The Advisory Committee may deliver an opinion even if some members are absent and unrepresented. The opinion shall be delivered in writing and appended to the draft decision. The Commission shall take the utmost account of the opinion delivered by the Committee. It shall inform the Committee of the manner in which its opinion has been taken into account.

7. The Advisory Committee may recommend publication of the opinion. The Commission may carry out such publication. The decision to publish shall take due account of the legitimate interest of undertakings in the protection of their business secrets and of the interest of the undertakings concerned in such publication taking place.

Article 20

Publication of decisions

1. The Commission shall publish the decisions which it takes pursuant to Article 8 (2), where conditions and obligations are attached to them, and to Article 8 (2) to (5) in the Official Journal of the European Communities.

2. The publication shall state the names of the parties and the main content of the decision; it shall have regard to the legitimate interest of undertakings in the protection of their business secrets.

Article 21

Jurisdiction

1. Subject to review by the Court of Justice, the Commission shall have sole competence to take the decisions provided for in this Regulation.

2. No Member State shall apply its national legislation on competition to any concentration that has a Community dimension.

The first subparagraph shall be without prejudice to any Member State's power to carry out any enquiries necessary for the application of Article 9 (2) or after referral, pursuant to Article 9 (3), first subparagraph, indent (b), or (5), to take the measures strictly necessary for the application of Article 9 (8).

3. Notwithstanding paragraphs 1 and 2, Member States may take appropriate measures to protect legitimate interests other than those taken into consideration by this Regulation and compatible with the general principles and other provisions of Community law.

Public security, plurality of the media and prudential rules shall be regarded as legitimate interests within the meaning of the first subparagraph.

Any other public interest must be communicated to the Commission by the Member State concerned and shall be recognized by the Commission after an assessment of its compatibility with the general principles and other provisions of Community law before the measures referred to above may be taken. The Commission shall inform the Member State concerned of its decision within one month of that communication.

Article 22

Application of the Regulation

1. This Regulation alone shall apply to concentrations as defined in Article 3, and Regulations No 17, (EEC) No 1017/68, (EEC) No 4056/86 and (EEC) No 3975/87 shall not apply, except in relation to joint ventures that do not have a Community dimension and which have as their object or effect the coordination of the competitive behaviour of undertakings that remain independent.

2. *Deleted.*

3. If the Commission finds, at the request of a Member State or at the joint request of two or more Member States, that a concentration as defined in Article 3 that has no Community dimension within the meaning of Article 1 creates or strengthens a dominant position as a result of which effective competition would be significantly impeded within the territory of the Member State or States making the joint request, it may, insofar as that concentration affects trade between Member States, adopt the decisions provided for in Article 8(2), second subparagraph, (3) and (4).

4. Articles 2(1)(a) and (b), 5, 6, 8 and 10 to 20 shall apply to a request made pursuant to paragraph 2. Article 7 shall apply to the extent that the concentration has not been put into effect on the date on which the Commission informs the parties that a request has been made.

The period within which proceedings may be initiated pursuant to Article 10(1) shall begin on the day following that of the receipt of the request from the Member State or States concerned. The request must be made within one month at most of the date on which the concentration was made known to the Member State or to all Member States making a joint request or effected. This period shall begin on the date of the first of those events.

5. Pursuant to paragraph 2 the Commission shall take only the measures strictly necessary to maintain or restore effective competition within the territory of the Member State or States at the request of which it intervenes.

Article 23

Implementing provisions

The Commission shall have the power to adopt implementing provisions concerning the form, content and other details of notifications pursuant to Article 4, time limits pursuant to Articles 7, 9, 10 and 22, and hearings pursuant to Article 18. The

Commission shall have the power to lay down the procedure and time limits for the submission of commitments pursuant to Articles 6(2) and 8(2).

Article 24

Relations with non-member countries

1. The Member States shall inform the Commission of any general difficulties encountered by their undertakings with concentrations as defined in Article 3 in a non-member country.

2. Initially not more than one year after the entry into force of this Regulation and thereafter periodically the Commission shall draw up a report examining the treatment accorded to Community undertakings, in the terms referred to in paragraphs 3 and 4, as regards concentrations in non-member countries. The Commission shall submit those reports to the Council, together with any recommendations.

3. Whenever it appears to the Commission, either on the basis of the reports referred to in paragraph 2 or on the basis of other information, that a non-member country does not grant Community undertakings treatment comparable to that granted by the Community to undertakings from that non-member country, the Commission may submit proposals to the Council for the appropriate mandate for negotiation with a view to obtaining comparable treatment for Community undertakings.

4. Measures taken pursuant to this Article shall comply with the obligations of the Community or of the Member States, without prejudice to Article [307] of the Treaty, under international agreements, whether bilateral or multilateral.

Article 25

Entry into force

1. This Regulation shall enter into force on 21 September 1990.

2. This Regulation shall not apply to any concentration which was the subject of an agreement or announcement or where control was acquired within the meaning of Article 4 (1) before the date of this Regulation's entry into force and it shall not in any circumstances apply to any concentration in respect of which proceedings were initiated before that date by a Member State's authority with responsibility for competition.

1. As regards concentrations to which this Regulation applies by virtue of accession, the date of accession shal be substituted for the date of entry into force of this Regulation. The provision of paragraph 2, second alternative, applies in the same way to proceedings initiated by a competition authority of the new Member States or by the EFTA Surveillance Authority.

This Regulation shall be binding in its entirety and directly applicable in all Member States.

Done at Brussels, 21 December 1989.

For the Council

The President

E. CRESSON

ANNEX 2

Commission Regulation (EC) No 447/98 of 1 March 1998 on the notifications, time limits and hearings provided for in Council Regulation (EEC) No 4064/89 on the control of concentrations between undertakings[1]

THE COMMISSION OF THE EUROPEAN COMMUNITIES,

Having regard to the Treaty establishing the European Community,

Having regard to the Agreement on the European Economic Area,

Having regard to Council Regulation (EEC) No 4064/89 of 21 December 1989 on the control of concentrations between undertakings,[2] as last amended by Regulation (EC) No 1310/97,[3] and in particular Article 23 thereof,

Having regard to Council Regulation No 17 of 6 February 1962, First Regulation implementing Articles [81] and [82] of the Treaty,[4] as last amended by the Act of Accession of Austria, Finland and Sweden, and in particular Article 24 thereof,

Having regard to Council Regulation (EEC) No 1017/68 of 19 July 1968 applying rules of competition to transport by rail, road and inland waterway,[5] as last amended by the Act of Accession of Austria, Finland and Sweden, and in particular Article 29 thereof,

Having regard to Council Regulation (EEC) No 4056/86 of 22 December 1986 laying down detailed rules for the application of Articles [81] and [82] of the Treaty

---

[1] OJ L 61, 2.3.1998, p. 1. Only texts published in the Official Journal of the European Union are authentic.

[2] OJ L 395, 30.12.1989, p. 1; corrected version, OJ L 257, 21.9.1990, p. 13.

[3] OJ L 180, 9.7.1997, p. 1.

[4] OJ 13, 21.2.1962, p. 204/62.

[5] OJ L 175, 23.7.1968, p. 1.

to maritime transport,[6] as amended by the Act of Accession of Austria, Finland and Sweden, and in particular Article 26 thereof,

Having regard to Council Regulation (EEC) No 3975/87 of 14 December 1987 laying down the procedure for the application of the rules on competition to undertakings in the air transport sector,[7] as last amended by Regulation (EEC) No 2410/92,[8] and in particular Article 19 thereof,

Having consulted the Advisory Committee on Concentrations,

(1) Whereas Regulation (EEC) No 4064/89 and in particular Article 23 thereof has been amended by Regulation (EC) No 1310/97;

(2) Whereas Commission Regulation (EC) No 3384/94,[9] implementing Regulation (EEC) No 4064/89, must be modified in order to take account of those amendments; whereas experience in the application of Regulation (EC) No 3384/94 has revealed the need to improve certain procedural aspects thereof; whereas for the sake of clarity it should therefore be replaced by a new regulation;

(3) Whereas the Commission has adopted Decision 94/810/ECSC, EC of 12 December 1994 on the terms of reference of hearing officers in competition procedures before the Commission;[10]

(4) Whereas Regulation (EEC) No 4064/89 is based on the principle of compulsory notification of concentrations before they are put into effect; whereas, on the one hand, a notification has important legal consequences which are favourable to the parties to the concentration plan, while, on the other hand, failure to comply with the obligation to notify renders the parties liable to a fine and may also entail civil law disadvantages for them; whereas it is therefore necessary in the interests of legal certainty to define precisely the subject matter and content of the information to be provided in the notification;

(5) Whereas it is for the notifying parties to make full and honest disclosure to the Commission of the facts and circumstances which are relevant for taking a decision on the notified concentration;

---

6   OJ L 378, 31.12.1986, p. 4.

7   OJ L 374, 31.12.1987, p. 1.

8   OJ L 240, 24.8.1992, p. 18.

9   OJ L 377, 31.12.1994, p. 1.

10   OJ L 330, 21.12.1994, p. 67.

(6) Whereas in order to simplify and expedite examination of the notification, it is desirable to prescribe that a form be used;

(7) Whereas since notification sets in motion legal time limits pursuant to Regulation (EEC) No 4064/89, the conditions governing such time-limits and the time when they become effective must also be determined;

(8) Whereas rules must be laid down in the interests of legal certainty for calculating the time limits provided for in Regulation (EEC) No 4064/89; whereas in particular, the beginning and end of the period and the circumstances suspending the running of the period must be determined, with due regard to the requirements resulting from the exceptionally short legal time-limits referred to above; whereas in the absence of specific provisions the determination of rules applicable to periods, dates and time-limits should be based on the principles of Council Regulation (EEC, Euratom) No 1182/71;[11]

(9) Whereas the provisions relating to the Commission's procedure must be framed in such a way as to safeguard fully the right to be heard and the rights of defence; whereas for these purposes the Commission should distinguish between the parties who notify the concentration, other parties involved in the concentration plan, third parties and parties regarding whom the Commission intends to take a decision imposing a fine or periodic penalty payments;

(10) Whereas the Commission should give the notifying parties and other parties involved, if they so request, an opportunity before notification to discuss the intended concentration informally and in strict confidence; whereas in addition it should, after notification, maintain close contact with those parties to the extent necessary to discuss with them any practical or legal problems which it discovers on a first examination of the case and if possible to remove such problems by mutual agreement;

(11) Whereas in accordance with the principle of the rights of defence, the notifying parties must be given the opportunity to submit their comments on all the objections which the Commission proposes to take into account in its decisions; whereas the other parties involved should also be informed of the Commission's objections and granted the opportunity to express their views;

(12) Whereas third parties having sufficient interest must also be given the opportunity of expressing their views where they make a written application;

---

[11] OJ L 124, 8.6.1971, p. 1.

(13) Whereas the various persons entitled to submit comments should do so in writing, both in their own interest and in the interest of good administration, without prejudice to their right to request a formal oral hearing where appropriate to supplement the written procedure; whereas in urgent cases, however, the Commission must be able to proceed immediately to formal oral hearings of the notifying parties, other parties involved or third parties;

(14) Whereas it is necessary to define the rights of persons who are to be heard, to what extent they should be granted access to the Commission's file and on what conditions they may be represented or assisted;

(15) Whereas the Commission must respect the legitimate interest of undertakings in the protection of their business secrets and other confidential information;

(16) Whereas, in order to enable the Commission to carry out a proper assessment of commitments that have the purpose of rendering the concentration compatible with the common market, and to ensure due consultation with other parties involved, third parties and the authorities of the Member States as provided for in Regulation (EEC) No 4064/89, in particular Article 18(1) and (4) thereof, the procedure and time-limits for submitting such commitments as provided for in Article 6(2) and Article 8(2) of Regulation (EEC) No 4064/89 must be laid down;

(17) Whereas it is also necessary to define the rules for fixing and calculating the time limits for reply fixed by the Commission;

(18) Whereas the Advisory Committee on Concentrations must deliver its opinion on the basis of a preliminary draft decision; whereas it must therefore be consulted on a case after the inquiry into that case has been completed; whereas such consultation does not, however, prevent the Commission from reopening an inquiry if need be,

HAS ADOPTED THIS REGULATION:

CHAPTER I – NOTIFICATIONS

Article 1

Persons entitled to submit notifications

1. Notifications shall be submitted by the persons or undertakings referred to in Article 4(2) of Regulation (EEC) No 4064/89.

2. Where notifications are signed by representatives of persons or of undertakings, such representatives shall produce written proof that they are authorised to act.

3. Joint notifications should be submitted by a joint representative who is authorised to transmit and to receive documents on behalf of all notifying parties.

Article 2

Submission of notifications

1. Notifications shall be submitted in the manner prescribed by form CO as shown in the Annex. Joint notifications shall be submitted on a single form.

2. One original and 23 copies of the form CO and the supporting documents shall be submitted to the Commission at the address indicated in form CO.

3. The supporting documents shall be either originals or copies of the originals; in the latter case the notifying parties shall confirm that they are true and complete.

4. Notifications shall be in one of the official languages of the Community. This language shall also be the language of the proceeding for the notifying parties. Supporting documents shall be submitted in their original language. Where the original language is not one of the official languages of the Community, a translation into the language of the proceeding shall be attached.

5. Where notifications are made pursuant to Article 57 of the EEA Agreement, they may also be in one of the official languages of the EFTA States or the working language of the EFTA Surveillance Authority. If the language chosen for the notifications is not an official language of the Community, the notifying parties shall simultaneously supplement all documentation with a translation into an official language of the Community. The language which is chosen for the translation shall determine the language used by the Commission as the language of the proceedings for the notifying parties.

Article 3

Information and documents to be provided

1. Notifications shall contain the information, including documents, requested by form CO. The information must be correct and complete.

2. The Commission may dispense with the obligation to provide any particular information, including documents, requested by form CO where the Commission considers that such information is not necessary for the examination of the case.

3. The Commission shall without delay acknowledge in writing to the notifying parties or their representatives receipt of the notification and of any reply to a letter sent by the Commission pursuant to Article 4(2) and (4).

Article 4

Effective date of notification

1. Subject to paragraphs 2, 3 and 4, notifications shall become effective on the date on which they are received by the Commission.

2. Where the information, including documents, contained in the notification is incomplete in a material respect, the Commission shall inform the notifying parties or their representatives in writing without delay and shall set an appropriate time-limit for the completion of the information. In such cases, the notification shall become effective on the date on which the complete information is received by the Commission.

3. Material changes in the facts contained in the notification which the notifying parties know or ought to have known must be communicated to the Commission without delay. In such cases, when these material changes could have a significant effect on the appraisal of the concentration, the notification may be considered by the Commission as becoming effective on the date on which the information on the material changes is received by the Commission; the Commission shall inform the notifying parties or their representatives of this in writing and without delay.

4. Incorrect or misleading information shall be considered to be incomplete information.

5. When the Commission publishes the fact of the notification pursuant to Article 4(3) of Regulation (EEC) No 4064/89, it shall specify the date upon which the notification has been received. Where, further to the application of paragraphs 2, 3 and 4, the effective date of notification is later than the date specified in this publi-

cation, the Commission shall issue a further publication in which it will state the later date.

Article 5

Conversion of notifications

1. Where the Commission finds that the operation notified does not constitute a concentration within the meaning of Article 3 of Regulation (EEC) No 4064/89, it shall inform the notifying parties or their representatives in writing. In such a case, the Commission shall, if requested by the notifying parties, as appropriate and subject to paragraph 2 of this Article, treat the notification as an application within the meaning of Article 2 or a notification within the meaning of Article 4 of Regulation No 17, as an application within the meaning of Article 12 or a notification within the meaning of Article 14 of Regulation (EEC) No 1017/68, as an application within the meaning of Article 12 of Regulation (EEC) No 4056/86 or as an application within the meaning of Article 3(2) or of Article 5 of Regulation (EEC) No 3975/87.

2. In cases referred to in paragraph 1, second sentence, the Commission may require that the information given in the notification be supplemented within an appropriate time-limit fixed by it in so far as this is necessary for assessing the operation on the basis of the Regulations referred to in that sentence. The application or notification shall be deemed to fulfil the requirements of such Regulations from the date of the original notification where the additional information is received by the Commission within the time-limit fixed.

CHAPTER II – TIME-LIMITS

Article 6

Beginning of periods

1. The period referred to in Article 9(2) of Regulation (EEC) No 4064/89 shall start at the beginning of the working day following the date of the receipt of the copy of the notification by the Member State.

2. The period referred to in Article 9(4)(b) of Regulation (EEC) No 4064/89 shall start at the beginning of the working day following the effective date of the notification, within the meaning of Article 4 of this Regulation.

3. The period referred to in Article 9(6) of Regulation (EEC) No 4064/89 shall start at the beginning of the working day following the date of the Commission's referral.

4. The periods referred to in Article 10(1) of Regulation (EEC) No 4064/89 shall start at the beginning of the working day following the effective date of the notification, within the meaning of Article 4 of this Regulation.

5. The period referred to in Article 10(3) of Regulation (EEC) No 4064/89 shall start at the beginning of the working day following the day on which proceedings were initiated.

6. The period referred to in Article 22(4), second subparagraph, second sentence, of Regulation (EEC) No 4064/89 shall start at the beginning of the working day following the date of the first of the events referred to.

Article 7

End of periods

1. The period referred to in Article 9(2) of Regulation (EEC) No 4064/89 shall end with the expiry of the day which in the third week following that in which the period began is the same day of the week as the day from which the period runs.

2. The period referred to in Article 9(4)(b) of Regulation (EEC) No 4064/89 shall end with the expiry of the day which in the third month following that in which the period began falls on the same date as the day from which the period runs. Where such a day does not occur in that month, the period shall end with the expiry of the last day of that month.

3. The period referred to in Article 9(6) of Regulation (EEC) No 4064/89 shall end with the expiry of the day which in the fourth month following that in which the period began falls on the same date as the day from which the period runs. Where such a day does not occur in that month, the period shall end with the expiry of the last day of that month.

4. The period referred to in Article 10(1), first subparagraph, of Regulation (EEC) No 4064/89 shall end with the expiry of the day which in the month following that in which the period began falls on the same date as the day from which the period

runs. Where such a day does not occur in that month, the period shall end with the expiry of the last day of that month.

5. The period referred to in Article 10(1), second subparagraph, of Regulation (EEC) No 4064/89 shall end with the expiry of the day which in the sixth week following that in which the period began is the same day of the week as the day from which the period runs.

6. The period referred to in Article 10(3) of Regulation (EEC) No 4064/89 shall end with the expiry of the day which in the fourth month following that in which the period began falls on the same date as the day from which the period runs. Where such a day does not occur in that month, the period shall end with the expiry of the last day of that month.

7. The period referred to in Article 22(4), second subparagraph, second sentence, of Regulation (EEC) No 4064/89 shall end with the expiry of the day which in the month following that in which the period began falls on the same date as the day from which the period runs. Where such a day does not occur in that month, the period shall end with the expiry of the last day of that month.

8. Where the last day of the period is not a working day, the period shall end with the expiry of the following working day.

Article 8

Recovery of holidays

Once the end of the period has been determined in accordance with Article 7, if public holidays or other holidays of the Commission referred to in Article 23 fall within the periods referred to in Articles 9, 10 and 22 of Regulation (EEC) No 4064/89, a corresponding number of working days shall be added to those periods.

Article 9

Suspension of time limit

1. The periods referred to in Article 10(1) and (3) of Regulation (EEC) No 4064/89 shall be suspended where the Commission, pursuant to Article 11(5) and Article 13(3) of that Regulation, has to take a decision because:

(a) information which the Commission has requested pursuant to Article 11(1) of Regulation (EEC) No 4064/89 from one of the notifying parties or another involved party, as defined in Article 11 of this Regulation, is not provided or not provided in full within the time limit fixed by the Commission;

(b) information which the Commission has requested pursuant to Article 11(1) of Regulation (EEC) No 4064/89 from a third party, as defined in Article 11 of this Regulation, is not provided or not provided in full within the time limit fixed by the Commission owing to circumstances for which one of the notifying parties or another involved party, as defined in Article 11 of this Regulation, is responsible;

(c) one of the notifying parties or another involved party, as defined in Article 11 of this Regulation, has refused to submit to an investigation deemed necessary by the Commission on the basis of Article 13(1) of Regulation (EEC) No 4064/89 or to cooperate in the carrying out of such an investigation in accordance with that provision;

(d) the notifying parties have failed to inform the Commission of material changes in the facts contained in the notification.

2. The periods referred to in Article 10(1) and (3) of Regulation (EEC) No 4064/89 shall be suspended:

(a) in the cases referred to in paragraph 1(a) and (b), for the period between the end of the time limit fixed in the request for information and the receipt of the complete and correct information required by decision;

(b) in the cases referred to in paragraph 1(c), for the period between the unsuccessful attempt to carry out the investigation and the completion of the investigation ordered by decision;

(c) in the cases referred to in paragraph 1(d), for the period between the occurrence of the change in the facts referred to therein and the receipt of the complete and correct information requested by decision or the completion of the investigation ordered by decision.

3. The suspension of the time limit shall begin on the day following that on which the event causing the suspension occurred. It shall end with the expiry of the day on which the reason for suspension is removed. Where such a day is not a working day, the suspension of the time-limit shall end with the expiry of the following working day.

Article 10

Compliance with the time-limits

1. The time limits referred to in Article 9(4) and (5), and Article 10(1) and (3) of Regulation (EEC) No 4064/89 shall be met where the Commission has taken the relevant decision before the end of the period.

2. The time limit referred to in Article 9(2) of Regulation (EEC) No 4064/89 shall be met where a Member State informs the Commission before the end of the period in writing.

3. The time limit referred to in Article 9(6) of Regulation (EEC) No 4064/89 shall be met where the competent authority of the Member State concerned publishes any report or announces the findings of the examination of the concentration before the end of the period.

4. The time limit referred to in Article 22(4), second subparagraph, second sentence, of Regulation (EEC) No 4064/89 shall be met where the request made by the Member State or the Member States is received by the Commission before the end of the period.

CHAPTER III – HEARING OF THE PARTIES AND OF THIRD PARTIES

Article 11

Parties to be heard

For the purposes of the rights to be heard pursuant to Article 18 of Regulation (EEC) No 4064/89, the following parties are distinguished:

(a) notifying parties, that is, persons or undertakings submitting a notification pursuant to Article 4(2) of Regulation (EEC) No 4064/89;

(b) other involved parties, that is, parties to the concentration plan other than the notifying parties, such as the seller and the undertaking which is the target of the concentration;

(c) third parties, that is, natural or legal persons showing a sufficient interest, including customers, suppliers and competitors, and especially members of the administration or management organs of the undertakings concerned or recognised workers' representatives of those undertakings;

(d) parties regarding whom the Commission intends to take a decision pursuant to Article 14 or 15 of Regulation (EEC) No 4064/89.

Article 12

Decisions on the suspension of concentrations

1. Where the Commission intends to take a decision pursuant to Article 7(4) of Regulation (EEC) No 4064/89 which adversely affects one or more of the parties, it shall, pursuant to Article 18(1) of that Regulation, inform the notifying parties and other involved parties in writing of its objections and shall fix a time limit within which they may make known their views.

2. Where the Commission, pursuant to Article 18(2) of Regulation (EEC) No 4064/89, has taken a decision referred to in paragraph 1 of this Article provisionally without having given the notifying parties and other involved parties the opportunity to make known their views, it shall without delay send them the text of the provisional decision and shall fix a time limit within which they may make known their views.

Once the notifying parties and other involved parties have made known their views, the Commission shall take a final decision annulling, amending or confirming the provisional decision. Where they have not made known their views within the time limit fixed, the Commission's provisional decision shall become final with the expiry of that period.

3. The notifying parties and other involved parties shall make known their views in writing or orally within the time limit fixed. They may confirm their oral statements in writing.

Article 13

Decisions on the substance of the case

1. Where the Commission intends to take a decision pursuant to Article 8(2), second subparagraph, or Article 8(3), (4) or (5) of Regulation (EEC) No 4064/89, it shall, before consulting the Advisory Committee on Concentrations, hear the parties pursuant to Article 18(1) and (3) of that Regulation.

2. The Commission shall address its objections in writing to the notifying parties.

The Commission shall, when giving notice of objections, set a time limit within which the notifying parties may inform the Commission of their views in writing.

The Commission shall inform other involved parties in writing of these objections.

The Commission shall also set a time limit within which those other involved parties may inform the Commission of their views in writing.

3. After having addressed its objections to the notifying parties, the Commission shall, upon request, give them access to the file for the purpose of enabling them to exercise their rights of defence.

The Commission shall, upon request, also give the other involved parties who have been informed of the objections access to the file in so far as this is necessary for the purposes of preparing their observations.

4. The parties to whom the Commission's objections have been addressed or who have been informed of those objections shall, within the time limit fixed, make known in writing their views on the objections. In their written comments, they may set out all matters relevant to the case and may attach any relevant documents in proof of the facts set out. They may also propose that the Commission hear persons who may corroborate those facts. They shall submit one original and 29 copies of their response to the Commission at the address indicated in form CO.

5. Where the Commission intends to take a decision pursuant to Article 14 or 15 of Regulation (EEC) No 4064/89 it shall, before consulting the Advisory Committee on Concentrations, hear pursuant to Article 18(1) and (3) of that Regulation the parties regarding whom the Commission intends to take such a decision.

The procedure provided for in paragraph 2, first and second subparagraphs, paragraph 3, first subparagraph, and paragraph 4 is applicable, mutatis mutandis.

Article 14

Oral hearings

1. The Commission shall afford the notifying parties who have so requested in their written comments the opportunity to put forward their arguments orally in a formal hearing if such parties show a sufficient interest. It may also in other cases afford such parties the opportunity of expressing their views orally.

2. The Commission shall afford other involved parties who have so requested in their written comments the opportunity to express their views orally in a formal hearing if they show a sufficient interest. It may also in other cases afford such parties the opportunity of expressing their views orally.

3. The Commission shall afford parties on whom it proposes to impose a fine or periodic penalty payment who have so requested in their written comments the opportunity to put forward their arguments orally in a formal hearing. It may also in other cases afford such parties the opportunity of expressing their views orally.

4. The Commission shall invite the persons to be heard to attend on such date as it shall appoint.

5. The Commission shall invite the competent authorities of the Member States, to take part in the hearing.

Article 15

Conduct of formal oral hearings

1. Hearings shall be conducted by the Hearing Officer.

2. Persons invited to attend shall either appear in person or be represented by legal representatives or by representatives authorised by their constitution as appropriate. Undertakings and associations of undertakings may be represented by a duly authorised agent appointed from among their permanent staff.

3. Persons heard by the Commission may be assisted by their legal adviser or other qualified persons admitted by the Hearing Officer.

4. Hearings shall not be public. Each person shall be heard separately or in the presence of other persons invited to attend. In the latter case, regard shall be had to the legitimate interest of the undertakings in the protection of their business secrets and other confidential information.

5. The statements made by each person heard shall be recorded.

Article 16

Hearing of third parties

1. If third parties apply in writing to be heard pursuant to Article 18(4), second sentence, of Regulation (EEC) No 4064/89, the Commission shall inform them in writing of the nature and subject matter of the procedure and shall fix a time limit within which they may make known their views.

2. The third parties referred to in paragraph 1 shall make known their views in writing within the time limit fixed. The Commission may, where appropriate, afford the parties who have so requested in their written comments the opportunity to participate in a formal hearing. It may also in other cases afford such parties the opportunity of expressing their views orally.

3. The Commission may likewise afford to any other third parties the opportunity of expressing their views.

Article 17

Confidential information

1. Information, including documents, shall not be communicated or made accessible in so far as it contains business secrets of any person or undertaking, including the notifying parties, other involved parties or of third parties, or other confidential information the disclosure of which is not considered necessary by the Commission for the purpose of the procedure, or where internal documents of the authorities are concerned.

2. Any party which makes known its views under the provisions of this Chapter shall clearly identify any material which it considers to be confidential, giving reasons, and provide a separate non-confidential version within the time limit fixed by the Commission.

CHAPTER IV – COMMITMENTS RENDERING THE CONCENTRATION COMPATIBLE

Article 18

Time limits for commitments

1. Commitments proposed to the Commission by the undertakings concerned pursuant to Article 6(2) of Regulation (EEC) No 4064/89 which are intended by the parties to form the basis for a decision pursuant to Article 6(1)(b) of that Regulation shall be submitted to the Commission within not more than three weeks from the date of receipt of the notification.

2. Commitments proposed to the Commission by the undertakings concerned pursuant to Article 8(2) of Regulation (EEC) No 4064/89 which are intended by the parties to form the basis for a decision pursuant to that Article shall be submitted to the Commission within not more than three months from the date on which proceedings were initiated. The Commission may in exceptional circumstances extend this period.

3. Articles 6 to 9 shall apply mutatis mutandis to paragraphs 1 and 2 of this Article.

Article 19

Procedure for commitments

1. One original and 29 copies of commitments proposed to the Commission by the undertakings concerned pursuant to Article 6(2) or Article 8(2) of Regulation (EEC) No 4064/89 shall be submitted to the Commission at the address indicated in form CO.

2. Any party proposing commitments to the Commission pursuant to Articles 6(2) or Article 8(2) of Regulation (EEC) No 4064/89 shall clearly identify any material which it considers to be confidential, giving reasons, and provide a separate non-confidential version within the time limit fixed by the Commission.

CHAPTER V – MISCELLANEOUS PROVISIONS

Article 20

Transmission of documents

1. Transmission of documents and invitations from the Commission to the addressees may be effected in any of the following ways:

   (a) delivery by hand against receipt;

   (b) registered letter with acknowledgement of receipt;

   (c) fax with a request for acknowledgement of receipt;

   (d) telex;

   (e) electronic mail with a request for acknowledgement of receipt.

2. Unless otherwise provided in this Regulation, paragraph 1 also applies to the transmission of documents from the notifying parties, from other involved parties or from third parties to the Commission.

3. Where a document is sent by telex, by fax or by electronic mail, it shall be presumed that it has been received by the addressee on the day on which it was sent.

Article 21

Setting of time limits

In fixing the time limits provided for pursuant to Article 4(2), Article 5(2), Article12(1) and (2), Article 13(2) and Article 16(1), the Commission shall have regard to the time required for preparation of statements and to the urgency of the case. It shall also take account of working days as well as public holidays in the country of receipt of the Commission's communication.

These time limits shall be set in terms of a precise calendar date.

Article 22

Receipt of documents by the Commission

1. In accordance with the provisions of Article 4(1) of this Regulation, notifications must be delivered to the Commission at the address indicated in form CO or have been dispatched by registered letter to the address indicated in form CO before the expiry of the period referred to in Article 4(1) of Regulation (EEC) No 4064/89.

Additional information requested to complete notifications pursuant to Article 4(2) and (4) or to supplement notifications pursuant to Article 5(2) must reach the Commission at the aforesaid address or have been dispatched by registered letter before the expiry of the time limit fixed in each case.

Written comments on Commission communications pursuant to Article 12(1) and (2), Article 13(2) and Article 16(1) must have reached the Commission at the aforesaid address before the expiry of the time limit fixed in each case.

2. Time limits referred to in subparagraphs two and three of paragraph 1 shall be determined in accordance with Article 21.

3. Should the last day of a time limit fall on a day which is not a working day or which is a public holiday in the country of dispatch, the time limit shall expire on the following working day.

Article 23

Definition of working days

The expression 'working days` in this Regulation means all days other than Saturdays, Sundays, public holidays and other holidays as determined by the Commission and published in the Official Journal of the European Communities before the beginning of each year.

Article 24

Repeal

Regulation (EEC) No 3384/94 is repealed.

Article 25

Entry into force

This Regulation shall enter into force on 21 March 1998.

This Regulation shall be binding in its entirety and directly applicable in all Member States.

Done at Brussels, 1 March 1998.

For the Commission

Karel VAN MIERT

Member of the Commission

ANNEX

FORM CO RELATING TO THE NOTIFICATION OF A CONCENTRATION
PURSUANT TO REGULATION (EEC) No 4064/89[12]

GUIDANCE NOTE I

Calculation of turnover for insurance undertakings

(Article 5(3)(a))

For the calculation of turnover for insurance undertakings, we give the following
example (proposed concentration between insurance A and B):

I. Consolidated profit and loss account

Income	Insurance A	Insurance B
Gross premiums written	5 000	300
– gross premiums received from Community residents	(4 500)	(300)
– gross premiums received residents of one (and the same) Member State X	(3 600)	(270)
Other income	500	50
Total income	**5 500**	**350**

---

[12] Only the guidance notes attached to Form CO are reproduced here. Form CO as such has
been left out.

II. Calculation of turnover

1. Aggregate worldwide turnover is replaced by the value of gross premiums written worldwide, the sum of which is [€] 5 300 million.

2. Community-wide turnover is replaced, for each insurance undertakings, by the value of gross premiums written with Community residents. For each of the insurance undertakings, this amount is more than [€] 250 million.

3. Turnover within one (and the same) Member State X is replaced, for insurance undertakings, by the value of gross premiums written with residents of one (and the same) Member State X. For insurance A, it achieves 80 % of its gross premiums written with Community residents within Member State X, whereas for insurance B, it achieves 90 % of its gross premiums written with Community residents in that Member State X.

III. Conclusion

Since

(a) the aggregate worldwide turnover of insurances A and B, as replaced by the value of gross premiums written worldwide, is more than [€] 5 000 million;

(b) for each of the insurance undertakings, the value of gross premiums written with Community residents is more than [€] 250 million; but

(c) each of the insurance undertakings achieves more than two thirds of its gross premiums written with Community residents in one (and the same) Member State X,the proposed concentration would not fall under the scope of the Regulation.

GUIDANCE NOTE II

Calculation of turnover for joint undertakings

A. Creation of a joint undertaking (Article 3(2))

In a case where two (or more) undertakings create a joint undertaking that constitutes a concentration, turnover is calculated for the undertakings concerned.

B. Existence of a joint undertaking (Article 5(5))

For the calculation of turnover in case of the existence of a joint undertaking C between two undertakings A and B concerned in a concentration, we give the following example:

I. Profit and loss accounts ([€] million)

Turnover	Undertaking A	Undertaking B
Sales revenues world-wide	10 000	2 000
– Community	(8 000)	(1 500)
– Member State Y	(4 000)	(900)

Turnover	Joint undertaking C
Sales revenue world-wide	100
– with undertaking A	(20)
– with undertaking B	(10)
Turnover with third undertakings	70
– Community-wide	(60)
– in Member State Y	(50)

II. Consideration of the joint undertaking

(a) The undertaking C is jointly controlled (in the meaning of Article 3(3) and (4)) by the undertakings A and B concerned by the concentration, irrespective of any third undertaking participating in that undertaking C.

(b) The undertaking C is not consolidated A and B in their profit and loss accounts.

(c) The turnover of C resulting from operations with A and B shall not be taken into account.

(d) The turnover of C resulting from operations with any third undertaking shall be apportioned equally amongst the undertakings A and B, irrespective of their individual shareholdings in C.

III. Calculation of turnover

(a) Undertaking A's aggregate worldwide turnover shall be calculated as follows: [€] 10 000 million and 50 % of C's worldwide turnover with third undertakings (i.e. [€] 35 million), the sum of which is € 10 035 million.

Undertaking B's aggregate worldwide turnover shall be calculated as follows: [€] 2 000 million and 50 % of C's world-wide turnover with third undertakings (i.e. [€] 35 million), the sum of which is € 2 035 million.

(b) The aggregate worldwide turnover of the undertakings concerned is [€] 12 070 million.

(c) Undertaking A achieves [€] 4 025 million within Member State Y (50 % of C's turnover in this Member State taken into account), and a Community-wide turnover of [€] 8 030 million (including 50 % of C's Community-wide turnover).

Undertaking B achieves [€] 925 million within Member State Y (50 % of C's turnover in this Member State taken into account), and a Community-wide turnover of [€] 1 530 million (including 50 % of C's Community-wide turnover).

IV. Conclusion

Since

(a) the aggregate worldwide turnover of undertakings A and B is more than [€] 5 000 million;

(b) each of the undertakings concerned by the concentration achieves more than [€] 250 million within the Community;

(c) each of the undertakings concerned (undertaking A 50.1 % and undertaking B 60.5 %) achieves less than two thirds of its Community-wide turnover in one (and the same) Member State Y;

the proposed concentration would fall under the scope of the Regulation.

GUIDANCE NOTE III

Application of the two-thirds rule

(Article 1)

For the application of the two thirds rule for undertakings, we give the following examples (proposed concentration between undertakings A and B):

I. Consolidated profit and loss accounts

Example 1 ([€] million)

Turnover	Undertaking A	Undertaking B
Sales revenues world-wide	10 000	500
– within the Community	(8 000)	(400)
– in Member State X	(6 000)	(200)

Example 2 (a) ([€] million)

Turnover	Undertaking A	Undertaking B
Sales revenues world-wide	4 800	500
– within the Community	(2 400)	(400)
– in Member State X	(2 100)	(300)

Example 2 (b)

Same figures as in example 2 (a) BUT undertaking B achieves [€] 300 million in Member State Y.

II. Application of the two-thirds rule

Example 1

1. Community-wide turnover is, for undertaking A, [€] 8 000 million and for undertaking B [€] 400 million.

2. Turnover in one (and the same) Member State X is, for undertaking A ([€] 6 000 million), 75% of its Community-wide turnover and is, for undertaking B ([€] 200 million), 50% of its Community-wide turnover.

3. Conclusion: In this case, although undertaking A achieves more than two-thirds of its Community-wide turnover in Member State X, the proposed concentration would fall under the scope of the Regulation due to the fact that undertaking B achieves less than two-thirds of its Community-wide turnover in Member State X.

Example 2 a)

1. Community-wide turnover of undertaking A is [€] 2 400 million and of undertaking B, [€] 400 million.

2. Turnover in one (and the same) Member State X is, for undertaking A, [€] 2 100 million (ie. 87.5% of its Community-wide turnover); and, for undertaking B, [€] 300 million (ie. 75% of its Community-wide turnover).

3. Conclusion: In this case, each of the undertakings concerned achieves more than two-thirds of its Community-wide turnover in one (and the same) Member State X; the proposed concentration would not fall under the scope of the Regulation.

Example 2 b)

Conclusion: In this case, the two-thirds rule would not apply due to the fact that undertakings A and B achieve more than two-thirds of their Community-wide turnover in different Member States X and Y. Therefore, the proposed concentration would fall under the scope of the Regulation.

ANNEX 3

Commission Notice on calculation of turnover under Council Regulation (EEC) No 4064/89 on the control of concentrations between undertakings[1]

I. 'ACCOUNTING' DETERMINATION OF TURNOVER

I.1. Turnover as a reflection of business activity
    I.1.1. The concept of turnover
    I.1.2. Ordinary activities
I.2. 'Net' turnover
    I.2.1. The deduction of rebates and taxes
    I.2.2. The deduction of 'internal' turnover
I.3. Adjustment of turnover calculation rules for the different types of operations
    I.3.1. The general rule
    I.3.2. Acquisition of parts of companies
    I.3.3. Staggered operations
    I.3.4. Turnover of groups
    I.3.5. Turnover of State-owned companies

II. GEOGRAPHICAL ALLOCATION OF TURNOVER

II.1. General rule
II.2. Conversion of turnover into [Euro]

III. CREDIT AND OTHER FINANCIAL INSTITUTIONS AND INSURANCE UNDERTAKINGS

III.1. Definitions
III.2. Calculation of turnover
    III.2.1. Credit and financial institutions (other than financial holding companies)
        III.2.1.1. General

---

[1] OJ C 66, 2.3.1998, p. 25. Only texts published in the Official Journal of the European Union are authentic.

III.2.1.2. Turnover of leasing companies
III.2.2. Insurance undertakings
    III.2.2.1. Gross premiums written
    III.2.2.2. Investments of insurance undertakings
III.2.3. Financial holding companies

1. The purpose of this Notice is to expand upon the text of Articles 1 and 5 of Council Regulation (EEC) No 4064/89[2] as last amended by Council Regulation (EC) No 1310/97[3] (hereinafter referred to as 'the Merger Regulation') and in so doing to elucidate certain procedural and practical questions which have caused doubt or difficulty.

2. This Notice is based on the experience gained by the Commission in applying the Merger Regulation to date. The principles it sets out will be followed and further developed by the Commission's practice in individual cases.

    This Notice replaces the Notice on calculation of turnover.[4]

3. The Merger Regulation has a two fold test for Commission jurisdiction. One test is that the transaction must be a concentration within the meaning of Article 3.[5] The second comprises the turnover thresholds contained in Article 1 and designed to identify those transactions which have an impact upon the Community and can be deemed to be of 'Community interest'. Turnover is used as a proxy for the economic resources being combined in a concentration, and is allocated geographically in order to reflect the geographic distribution of those resources.

    Two sets of thresholds are set out in Article 1, in paragraph 2 and paragraph 3 respectively. Article 1(2) sets out the thresholds which must first be checked in order to establish whether the transaction has a Community dimension. In this respect, the worldwide turnover threshold is intended to measure the overall dimension of the undertakings concerned; the Community turnover threshold seek to determine whether the concentration involves a minimum level of

---

[2]   OJ L 395, 30.12.1989, p. 1; corrected version OJ L 257, 21.9.1990, p. 13.

[3]   OJ L 180, 9.7.1997, p. 1.

[4]   OJ C 385, 31.12.1994, p. 21.

[5]   See the Notice on the concept of concentration.

activities in the Community; and the two-thirds rule aims to exclude purely domestic transactions from Community jurisdiction.

Article 1(3) must only be applied in the event that the thresholds set out in Article 1(2) are not met. This second set of thresholds is designed to tackle those transactions which fall short of achieving Community dimension under Article 1(2), but would need to be notified under national competition rules in at least three Member States (so called 'multiple notifications'). For this purpose, Article 1(3) provides for lower turnover thresholds, both worldwide and Community-wide, to be achieved by the undertakings concerned. A concentration has a Community dimension if these lower thresholds are fulfilled and the undertakings concerned achieve jointly and individually a minimum level of activities in at least three Member States. Article 1(3) also contains a two-thirds rule similar to that of Article 1(2), which aims to identify purely domestic transactions.

4. The thresholds as such are designed to establish jurisdiction and not to assess the market position of the parties to the concentration nor the impact of the operation. In so doing they include turnover derived from, and thus the resources devoted to, all areas of activity of the parties, and not just those directly involved in the concentration. Article 1 of the Merger Regulation sets out the thresholds to be used to determine a concentration with a 'Community dimension' while Article 5 explains how turnover should be calculated.

5. The fact that the thresholds of Article 1 of the Merger Regulation are purely quantitative, since they are only based on turnover calculation instead of market share or other criteria, shows that their aim is to provide a simple and objective mechanism that can be easily handled by the companies involved in a merger in order to determine if their transaction has a Community dimension and is therefore notifiable.

6. The decisive issue for Article 1 of the Merger Regulation is to measure the economic strength of the undertakings concerned as reflected in their respective turnover figures, regardless of the sector where such turnover was achieved and of whether those sectors will be at all affected by the transaction in question. The Merger Regulation has thereby given priority to the determination of the overall economic and financial resources that are being combined through the merger in order to decide whether the latter is of Community interest.

7. In this context, it is clear that turnover should reflect as accurately as possible the economic strength of the undertakings involved in a transaction. This is the purpose of the set of rules contained in Article 5 of the Merger Regulation

which are designed to ensure that the resulting figures are a true representation of economic reality.

8. The Commission's interpretation of Articles 1 and 5 with respect to calculation of turnover is without prejudice to the interpretation which may be given by the Court of Justice or the Court of First Instance of the European Communities.

I. 'ACCOUNTING' CALCULATION OF TURNOVER

I.1. Turnover as a reflection of activity

I.1.1. The concept of turnover

9. The concept of turnover as used in Article 5 of the Merger Regulation refers explicitly to 'the amounts derived from the sale of products and the provision of services'. Sale, as a reflection of the undertaking's activity, is thus the essential criterion for calculating turnover, whether for products or the provision of services. 'Amounts derived from sale' generally appear in company accounts under the heading 'sales'.

10. In the case of products, turnover can be determined without difficulty, namely by identifying each commercial act involving a transfer of ownership.

11. In the case of services, the factors to be taken into account in calculating turnover are much more complex, since the commercial act involves a transfer of 'value'.

12. Generally speaking, the method of calculating turnover in the case of services does not differ from that used in the case of products: the Commission takes into consideration the total amount of sales. Where the service provided is sold directly by the provider to the customer, the turnover of the undertaking concerned consists of the total amount of sales for the provision of services in the last financial year.

13. Because of the complexity of the service sector, this general principle may have to be adapted to the specific conditions of the service provided. Thus, in certain sectors of activity (such as tourism and advertising), the service may be sold through the intermediary of other suppliers. Because of the diversity of such sectors, many different situations may arise. For example, the turnover of

a service undertaking which acts as an intermediary may consist solely of the amount of commissions which it receives.

14. Similarly, in a number of areas such as credit, financial services and insurance, technical problems in calculating turnover arise which will be dealt with in Section III.

I.1.2. Ordinary activities

15. Article 5(1) states that the amounts to be included in the calculation of turnover must correspond to the 'ordinary activities' of the undertakings concerned.

16. With regard to aid granted to undertakings by public bodies, any aid relating to one of the ordinary activities of an undertaking concerned is liable to be included in the calculation of turnover if the undertaking is itself the recipient of the aid and if the aid is directly linked to the sale of products and the provision of services by the undertaking and is therefore reflected in the price.[6] For example, aid towards the consumption of a product allows the manufacturer to sell at a higher price than that actually paid by consumers.

17. With regard to services, the Commission looks at the undertaking's ordinary activities involved in establishing the resources required for providing the service. In its Decision in the Accor/Wagons-Lits case,[7] the Commission decided to take into account the item 'other operating proceeds' included in Wagons-Lits's profit and loss account. The Commission considered that the components of this item which included certain income from its car-hire activities were derived from the sale of products and the provision of services by Wagons-Lits and were part of its ordinary activities.

---

6 See Case IV/M.156 – Cereol/Continentale Italiana of 27 November 1991. In this case, the Commission excluded Community aid from the calculation of turnover because the aid was not intended to support the sale of products manufactured by one of the undertakings involved in the merger, but the producers of the raw materials (grain) used by the undertaking, which specialized in the crushing of grain.

7 Case IV/M.126 – Accor/Wagons-Lits, of 28 April 1992.

I.2. 'Net' turnover

18. The turnover to be taken into account is 'net' turnover, after deduction of a number of components specified in the Regulation. The Commission's aim is to adjust turnover in such a way as to enable it to decide on the real economic weight of the undertaking.

I.2.1. The deduction of rebates and taxes

19. Article 5(1) provides for the 'deduction of sales rebates and of value added tax and other taxes directly related to turnover'. The deductions thus relate to business components (sales rebates) and tax components (value added tax and other taxes directly related to turnover).

20. 'Sales rebates' should be taken to mean all rebates or discounts which are granted by the undertakings during their business negotiations with their customers and which have a direct influence on the amounts of sales.

21. As regards the deduction of taxes, the Merger Regulation refers to VAT and 'other taxes directly related to turnover'. As far as VAT is concerned, its deduction does not in general pose any problem. The concept of 'taxes directly related to turnover' is a clear reference to indirect taxation since it is directly linked to turnover, such as, for example, taxes on alcoholic beverages.

I.2.2. The deduction of 'internal' turnover

22. The first subparagraph of Article 5(1) states that 'the aggregate turnover of an undertaking concerned shall not include the sale of products or the provision of services between any of the undertakings referred to in paragraph 4', i.e. those which have links with the undertaking concerned (essentially parent companies or subsidiaries).

23. The aim is to exclude the proceeds of business dealings within a group so as to take account of the real economic weight of each entity. Thus, the 'amounts' taken into account by the Merger Regulation reflect only the transactions which take place between the group of undertakings on the one hand and third parties on the other.

I.3. Adjustment of turnover calculation rules for the different types of operations

I.3.1. The general rule

24. According to Article 5(1) of the Merger Regulation, aggregate turnover comprises the amounts derived by the undertakings concerned in the preceding financial year from the sale of products and the provision of services. The basic principle is thus that for each undertaking concerned the turnover to be taken into account is the turnover of the closest financial year to the date of the transaction.

25. This provision shows that since there are usually no audited accounts of the year ending the day before the transaction, the closest representation of a whole year of activity of the company in question is the one given by the turnover figures of the most recent financial year.

26. The Commission seeks to base itself upon the most accurate and reliable figures available. As a general rule therefore, the Commission will refer to audited or other definitive accounts. However, in cases where major differences between the Community's accounting standards and those of a non-member country are observed, the Commission may consider it necessary to restate these accounts in accordance with Community standards in respect of turnover. The Commission is, in any case, reluctant to rely on management or any other form of provisional accounts in any but exceptional circumstances (see the next paragraph). Where a concentration takes place within the first months of the year and audited accounts are not yet available for the most recent financial year, the figures to be taken into account are those relating to the previous year. Where there is a major divergence between the two sets of accounts, and in particular, when the final draft figures for the most recent years are available, the Commission may decide to take those draft figures into account.

27. Notwithstanding paragraph 26, an adjustment must always be made to account for acquisitions or divestments subsequent to the date of the audited accounts. This is necessary if the true resources being concentrated are to be identified. Thus if a company disposes of part of its business at any time before the signature of the final agreement or the announcement of the public bid or the acquisition of a controlling interest bringing about a concentration, or where

such a divestment or closure is a pre-condition for the operation[8] the part of the turnover to be attributed to that part of the business must be subtracted from the turnover of the notifying party as shown in its last audited accounts. Conversely, the turnover to be attributed to assets of which control has been acquired subsequent to the preparation of the most recent audited accounts must be added to a company's turnover for notification purposes.

28. Other factors that may affect turnover on a temporary basis such as a decrease in orders for the product or a slow-down in the production process within the period prior to the transaction will be ignored for the purposes of calculating turnover. No adjustment to the definitive accounts will be made to incorporate them.

29. Regarding the geographical allocation of turnover, since audited accounts often do not provide a geographical breakdown of the sort required by the Merger Regulation, the Commission will rely on the best figures available provided by the companies in accordance with the rule laid down in Article 5(1) of the Merger Regulation (see Section II.1).

I.3.2. Acquisitions of parts of companies

30. Article 5(2) of the Merger Regulation provides that 'where the concentration consists in the acquisition of parts, whether or not constituted as legal entities, of one or more undertakings, only the turnover relating to the parts which are the subject of the transaction shall be taken into account with regard to the seller or sellers'.

31. This provision states that when the acquirer does not purchase an entire group, but only one, or part, of its businesses, whether or not constituted as a subsidiary, only the turnover of the part acquired should be included in the turnover calculation. In fact, although in legal terms the seller as a whole (with all its subsidiaries) is an essential party to the transaction, since the sale-purchase agreement cannot be concluded without him, he plays no role once the agreement has been implemented. The possible impact of the transaction on the market will depend only on the combination of the economic and financial resources that are the subject of a property transfer with those of the acquirer and not on the remaining business of the seller who remains independent.

---

[8] See Judgment of the Court of First Instance in Case T-3/93, Air France v Commission, [1994] ECR II-21.

I.3.3. Staggered operations

32. Sometimes certain successive transactions are only individual steps within a wider strategy between the same parties. Considering each transaction alone, even if only for determining jurisdiction, would imply ignoring economic reality. At the same time, whereas some of these staggered operations may be designed in this fashion because they will better meet the needs of the parties, others could be structured like this in order to circumvent the application of the Merger Regulation.

33. The Merger Regulation has foreseen these scenarios in Article 5(2), second subparagraph, which provides that 'two or more transactions within the meaning of the first subparagraph which take place within a two-year period between the same persons or undertakings shall be treated as one and the same concentration arising on the date of the last transaction'.

34. In practical terms, this provision means that if company A buys a subsidiary of company B that represents 50 % of the overall activity of B and one year later it acquires the other subsidiary (the remaining 50 % of B), both transactions will be taken as one. Assuming that each of the subsidiaries attained a turnover in the Community of only [€] 200 million, the first transaction would not be notifiable unless the operation fulfilled the conditions set out in Article 1(3). However, since the second transaction takes place within the two-year period, both have to be notified as a single transaction when the second occurs.

35. The importance of the provision is that previous transactions (within two years) become notifiable with the most recent transaction once the thresholds are cumulatively met.

I.3.4. Turnover of groups

36. When an undertaking concerned in a concentration within the meaning of Article 1 of the Merger Regulation[9] belongs to a group, the turnover of the group as a whole is to be taken into account in order to determine whether the thresholds are met. The aim is again to capture the total volume of the economic resources that are being combined through the operation.

---

[9]   See the Commission Notice on the concept of undertakings concerned.

37. The Merger Regulation does not define the concept of group in abstract terms but focuses on whether the companies have the right to manage the undertaking's affairs as the yardstick to determine which of the companies that have some direct or indirect links with an undertaking concerned should be regarded as part of its group.

38. Article 5(4) of the Merger Regulation provides the following:

'Without prejudice to paragraph 2 [acquisitions of parts], the aggregate turnover of an undertaking concerned within the meaning of Article 1(2) and (3) shall be calculated by adding together the respective turnovers of the following:

(a) the undertaking concerned;

(b) those undertakings in which the undertaking concerned directly or indirectly:

    – owns more than half the capital or business assets, or

    – has the power to exercise more than half the voting rights, or

    – has the power to appoint more than half the members of the supervisory board, the administrative board or bodies legally representing the undertakings, or

    – has the right to manage the undertaking's affairs;

(c) those undertakings which have in an undertaking concerned the rights or powers listed in (b);

(d) those undertakings in which an undertaking as referred to in (c) has the rights or powers listed in (b);

(e) those undertakings in which two or more undertakings as referred to in (a) to (d) jointly have the rights or powers listed in (b).'

This means that the turnover of the company directly involved in the transaction (point (a)) should include its subsidiaries (point (b)), its parent companies (point (c)), the other subsidiaries of its parent companies (point (d)) and any other undertaking jointly controlled by two or more of the companies belonging to the group (point (e)). A graphic example is as follows:

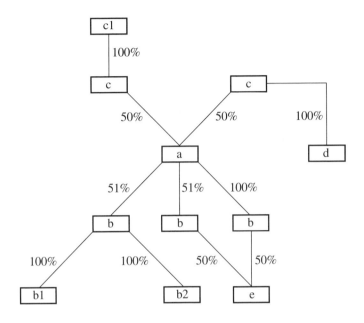

The undertaking concerned and its group:

a: The undertaking concerned

b: Its subsidiaries and their own subsidiaries (b1 and b2)

c: Its parent companies and their own parent companies (c1)

d: Other subsidiaries of the parent companies of the undertaking concerned

e: Companies jointly controlled by two (or more) companies of the group

Note: these letters correspond to the relevant points of Article 5(4).

Several remarks can be made from this chart:

1. As long as the test of control of point (b) is fulfilled, the whole turnover of the subsidiary in question will be taken into account regardless of the actual shareholding of the controlling company. In the example, the whole turnover of the three subsidiaries (called b) of the undertaking concerned (a) will be included.

2. When any of the companies identified as belonging to the group also controls others, these should also be incorporated into the calculation. In the example, one of the subsidiaries of a (called b) has in turn its own subsidiaries b1 and b2.

3. When two or more companies jointly control the undertaking concerned (a) in the sense that the agreement of each and all of them is needed in order to manage the undertaking's affairs, the turnover of all of them should be included.[10] In the example, the two parent companies (c) of the undertaking concerned (a) would be taken into account as well as their own parent companies (c1 in the example). Although the Merger Regulation does not explicitly mention this rule for those cases where the undertaking concerned is in fact a joint venture, it is inferred from the text of Article 5(4)(c), which uses the plural when referring to the parent companies. This interpretation has been consistently applied by the Commission.

4. Any intra-group sale should be subtracted from the turnover of the group (see paragraph 22).

39. The Merger Regulation also deals with the specific scenario that arises when two or more undertakings concerned in a transaction exercise joint control of another company. Pursuant to point (a) of Article 5(5), the turnover resulting from the sale of products or the provision of services between the joint venture and each of the undertakings concerned or any other company connected with any one of them in the sense of Article 5(4) should be excluded. The purpose of such a rule is to avoid double counting. With regard to the turnover of the joint venture generated from activities with third parties, point (b) of Article 5(5) provides that it should be apportioned equally amongst the undertakings concerned, to reflect the joint control.[11]

40. Following the principle of point (b) of Article 5(5) by analogy, in the case of joint ventures between undertakings concerned and third parties, the Commis-

---

[10] See Commission Notice on the concept of undertakings concerned (paragraphs 26-29).

[11] For example, company A and company B set up a joint venture C. These two parent companies exercise at the same time joint control of company D, although A has 60 % and B 40 % of the capital. When calculating the turnover of A and B at the time they set up the new joint venture C, the turnover of D with third parties is attributed in equal parts to A and B.

sion's practice has been to allocate to each of the undertakings concerned the turnover shared equally by all the controlling companies in the joint venture. In all these cases, however, joint control has to be demonstrated.

The practice shows that it is impossible to cover in the present Notice the whole range of scenarios which could arise in respect of turnover calculation of joint venture companies or joint control cases. Whenever ambiguities arise, an assessment should always give priority to the general principles of avoiding double counting and of reflecting as accurately as possible the economic strength of the undertakings involved in the transaction.[12]

41. It should be noted that Article 5(4) refers only to the groups that already exist at the time of the transaction, i.e. the group of each of the undertakings concerned in an operation, and not to the new structures created as a result of the concentration. For example, if companies A and B, together with their respective subsidiaries, are going to merge, it is A and B, and not the new entity, that qualify as undertakings concerned, which implies that the turnover of each of the two groups should be calculated independently.

42. Since the aim of this provision is simply to identify the companies belonging to the existing groups for the purposes of turnover calculation, the test of having the right to manage the undertaking's affairs in Article 5(4)[13] is somewhat different from the test of control set out in Article 3(3), which refers to the acquisition of control carried out by means of the transaction subject to examination. Whereas the former is simpler and easier to prove on the basis of factual evidence, the latter is more demanding because in the absence of an acquisition of control no concentration arises.

I.3.5. Turnover of State-owned companies

43. While Article 5(4) sets out the method for determining the economic grouping to which an undertaking concerned belongs for the purpose of calculating turnover, it should be read in conjunction with recital 12 to Regulation (EEC) No 4064/89 in respect of State-owned enterprises. This recital states that in order

---

12 See for example Case IV/M.806 – BA/TAT, of 26 August 1996.

13 See for example Case IV/M.126 – Accor/Wagons-Lits, of 28 April 1992, and Case IV/M.940 – UBS/Mister Minit, of 9 July 1997.

to avoid discrimination between the public and private sector, account should be taken 'of undertakings making up an economic unit with an independent power of decision, irrespective of the way in which their capital is held or of the rules of administrative supervision applicable to them'. Thus the mere fact that two companies are both State-owned should not automatically lead to the conclusion that they are part of a group for the purposes of Article 5. Rather, it should be considered whether there are grounds to consider that each company constitutes an independent economic unit.

44. Thus where a State-owned company is not part of an overall industrial holding company and is not subject to any coordination with other State-controlled holdings, it should be treated as an independent group for the purposes of Article 5, and the turnover of other companies owned by that State should not be taken into account. Where, however, a Member State's interests are grouped together in holding companies, or are managed together, or where for other reasons it is clear that State-owned companies form part of an 'economic unit with an independent power of decision', then the turnover of those businesses should be considered part of the group of the undertaking concerned's for the purposes of Article 5.

II. GEOGRAPHICAL ALLOCATION OF TURNOVER

II.1. General rule

45. The thresholds other than those set by Article 1(2)(a) and Article 1(3)(a) select cases which have sufficient turnover within the Community in order to be of Community interest and which are primarily cross-border in nature. They require turnover to be allocated geographically to achieve this. The second subparagraph of Article 5(1) provides that the location of turnover is determined by the location of the customer at the time of the transaction:

'Turnover, in the Community or in a Member State, shall comprise products sold and services provided to undertakings or consumers, in the Community or in that Member State as the case may be.'

46. The reference to 'products sold' and 'services provided' is not intended to discriminate between goods and services by focusing on where the sale takes place in the case of goods but the place where a service is provided (which might be different from where the service was sold) in the case of services. In

both cases, turnover should be attributed to the place where the customer is located because that is, in most circumstances, where a deal was made, where the turnover for the supplier in question was generated and where competition with alternative suppliers took place.[14] The second subparagraph of Article 5(1) does not focus on where a good or service is enjoyed or the benefit of the good or service derived. In the case of a mobile good, a motor car may well be driven across Europe by its purchaser but it was purchased at only one place – Paris, Berlin or Madrid say. This is also true in the case of those services where it is possible to separate the purchase of a service from its delivery. Thus in the case of package holidays, competition for the sale of holidays through travel agents takes place locally, as with retail shopping, even though the service may be provided in a number of distant locations. This turnover is, however, earned locally and not at the site of an eventual holiday.

47. This applies even where a multinational corporation has a Community buying strategy and sources all its requirements for a good or service from one location. The fact that the components are subsequently used in ten different plants in a variety of Member States does not alter the fact that the transaction with a company outside the group occurred in only one country. The subsequent distribution to other sites is purely an internal question for the company concerned.

48. Certain sectors do, however, pose very particular problems with regard to the geographical allocation of turnover (see Section III).

II.2. Conversion of turnover into [Euro]

49. When converting turnover figures into [Euro] great care should be taken with the exchange rate used. The annual turnover of a company should be converted at the average rate for the twelve months concerned. This average can be obtained from the Commission. The audited annual turnover figures should not be broken down into component quarterly, monthly, or weekly sales figures which are converted individually at the corresponding average quarterly,

---

[14] If the place where the customer was located when purchasing the goods or service and the place where the billing was subsequently made are different, turnover should be allocated to the former.

monthly or weekly rates, with the [Euro] figures then added to give a total for the year.

50. When a company has sales in a range of currencies, the procedure is no different. The total turnover given in the consolidated audited accounts and in that company's reporting currency is converted into [Euro] at the average rate for the twelve months. Local currency sales should not be converted directly into [Euro] since these figures are not from the consolidated audited accounts of the company.

III. CREDIT AND OTHER FINANCIAL INSTITUTIONS AND INSURANCE UNDERTAKINGS

III.1. Definitions

51. The specific nature of banking and insurance activities is formally recognized by the Merger Regulation which includes specific provisions dealing with the calculation of turnover for these sectors.[15] Although the Merger Regulation does not provide a definition of the terms, 'credit institutions and other financial institutions' within the meaning of point (a) of Article 5(3), the Commission in its practice has consistently adopted the definitions provided in the First and Second Banking Directives:
    – 'Credit institution means an undertaking whose business is to receive deposits or other repayable funds from the public and to grant credits for its own account[16]
    – 'Financial institution shall mean an undertaking other than a credit institution, the principal activity of which is to acquire holdings or to carry one or more of the activities listed in points 2 to 12 in the Annex[17]

---

[15] See Article 5(3) of the Merger Regulation.

[16] Article 1 of First Council Directive 77/780/EEC of 12 December 1977 on the coordination of laws, regulations and administrative provisions relating to the taking up and pursuit of the business of credit institutions (OJ L 322, 17.12.1977, p. 30).

[17] Article 1(6) of Second Council Directive 89/646/EEC of 15 December 1989 on the coordination of laws, regulations and administrative provisions relating to the taking up and pursuit of the business of credit institutions (OJ L 386, 30.12.1989, p. 1).

52. From the definition of 'financial institution' given above, it is clear that on the one hand holding companies must be regarded as financial institutions and, on the other hand, that undertakings which perform on a regular basis as a principal activity one or more activities expressly mentioned in points 2 to 12 of the above-mentioned Annex must also be regarded as financial institutions within the meaning of point (a) of Article 5(3) of the Merger Regulation. These activities include:

    – lending (*inter alia*, consumer credit, mortgage credit, factoring, …),

    – financial leasing,

    – money transmission services,

    – issuing and managing instruments of payment (credit cards, travellers' cheques and bankers' drafts),

    – guarantees and commitments,

    – trading on own account or on account of customers in money market instruments, foreign exchange, financial futures and options, exchange and interest rate instruments, and transferable securities,

    – participation in share issues and the provision of services related to such issues,

    – advice to undertakings on capital structure, industrial strategy and related questions and advice and services relating to mergers and the purchase of undertakings,

    – money broking,

    – portfolio management and advice,

    – safekeeping and administration of securities.

III.2. Calculation of turnover

53. The methods of calculation of turnover for credit and other financial institutions and for insurance undertakings are described in Article 5(3) of the Merger Regulation. The purpose of this Section is to provide an answer to supplementary questions related to turnover calculation for the above-mentioned types of undertakings which were raised during the first years of the application of the Merger Regulation.

III.2.1. Credit and financial institutions (other than financial holding companies)

III.2.1.1. General

54. There are normally no particular difficulties in applying the banking income criterion for the definition of the worldwide turnover to credit institutions and other kinds of financial institutions. Difficulties may arise for determining turnover within the Community and also within individual Member States. For this purpose, the appropriate criterion is that of the residence of the branch or division, as provided by Article 5(3)(a)(v), second subparagraph, of the Merger Regulation.

III.2.1.2. Turnover of leasing companies

55. There is a fundamental distinction to be made between financial leases and operating leases. Basically, financial leases are made for longer periods than operating leases and ownership is generally transferred to the lessee at the end of the lease term by means of a purchase option included in the lease contract. Under an operating lease, on the contrary, ownership is not transferred to the lessee at the end of the lease term and the costs of maintenance, repair and insurance of the leased equipment are included in the lease payments. A financial lease therefore functions as a loan by the lessor to enable the lessee to purchase a given asset. A financial leasing company is thus a financial institution within the meaning of point (a) of Article 5(3) and its turnover has to be calculated by applying the specific rules related to the calculation of turnover for credit and other financial institutions. Given that operational leasing activities do not have this lending function, they are not considered as carried out by financial institutions, at least as primary activities, and therefore the general turnover calculation rules of Article 5(1) should apply.[18]

---

[18] See Case IV/M.234 – GECC/Avis Lease, 15 July 1992.

III.2.2. Insurance undertakings

III.2.2.1. Gross premiums written

56. The application of the concept of gross premiums written as a measure of turnover for insurance undertakings has raised supplementary questions notwithstanding the definition provided in point (b) of Article 5(3) of the Merger Regulation. The following clarifications are appropriate:

   – 'gross' premiums written are the sum of received premiums (which may include received reinsurance premiums if the undertaking concerned has activities in the field of reinsurance). Outgoing or outward reinsurance premiums, i.e. all amounts paid and payable by the undertaking concerned to get reinsurance cover, are already included in the gross premiums written within the meaning of the Merger Regulation,

   – wherever the word 'premiums' is used (gross premiums, net (earned) premiums, outgoing reinsurance premiums, etc.), these premiums are related not only to new insurance contracts made during the accounting year being considered but also to all premiums related to contracts made in previous years which remain in force during the period taken into consideration.

III.2.2.2. Investments of insurance undertakings

57. In order to constitute appropriate reserves allowing for the payment of claims, insurance undertakings, which are also considered as institutional investors, usually hold a huge portfolio of investments in shares, interest-bearing securities, land and property and other assets which provide an annual revenue which is not considered as turnover for insurance undertakings.

58. With regard to the application of the Merger Regulation, a major distinction should be made between pure financial investments, in which the insurance undertaking is not involved in the management of the undertakings where the investments have been made, and those investments leading to the acquisition of an interest giving control in a given undertaking thus allowing the insurance undertaking to exert a decisive influence on the business conduct of the subsidiary or affiliated company concerned. In such cases Article 5(4) of the Merger Regulation would apply, and the turnover of the subsidiary or affiliated com-

pany should be added to the turnover of the insurance undertaking for the determination of the thresholds laid down in the Merger Regulation.[19]

III.2.3. Financial holding companies[20]

59. A financial holding company is a financial institution and therefore the calculation of its turnover should follow the criteria established in point (a) of Article 5(3) for the calculation of turnover for credit and other financial institutions. However, since the main purpose of a financial holding is to acquire and manage participation in other undertakings, Article 5(4) also applies, (as for insurance undertakings), with regard to those participations allowing the financial holding company to exercise a decisive influence on the business conduct of the undertakings in question. Thus, the turnover of a financial holding is basically to be calculated according to Article 5(3), but it may be necessary to add turnover of undertakings falling within the categories set out in Article 5(4) ('Article 5(4) companies').

In practice, the turnover of the financial holding company (non-consolidated) must first be taken into account. Then the turnover of the Article 5(4) companies must be added, whilst taking care to deduct dividends and other income distributed by those companies to the financial holdings. The following provides an example for this kind of calculation:

	[€] million
1. Turnover related to financial activities (from non-consolidated P&L)	3 000
2. Turnover related to insurance Article 5(4) companies (gross premiums written)	300
3. Turnover of industrial Article 5(4) companies	2 000
4. Deduct dividends and other income derived from Article 5(4) companies 2 and 3	–200
5. Total turnover financial holding and its group	**5 100**

---

[19] See Case IV/M.018 – AG/AMEV, of 21 November 1990.

[20] The principles set out in this paragraph for financial holdings may to a certain extent be applied to fund management companies.

60. In such calculations different accounting rules, in particular those related to the preparation of consolidated accounts, which are to some extent harmonised but not identical within the Community, may need to be taken into consideration. Whilst this consideration applies to any type of undertaking concerned by the Merger Regulation, it is particularly important in the case of financial holding companies[21] where the number and the diversity of enterprises controlled and the degree of control the holding holds on its subsidiaries, affiliated companies and other companies in which it has shareholding requires careful examination.

61. Turnover calculation for financial holding companies as described above may in practice prove onerous. Therefore a strict and detailed application of this method will be necessary only in cases where it seems that the turnover of a financial holding company is likely to be close to the Merger Regulation thresholds; in other cases it may well be obvious that the turnover is far from the thresholds of the Merger Regulation, and therefore the published accounts are adequate for the establishment of jurisdiction.

---

[21] See for example Case IV/M.166 – Torras/Sarrió, of 24 February 1992, Case IV/M.213 – Hong Kong and Shanghai Bank/Midland, of 21 May 1992, IV/M.192 – Banesto/Totta, of 14 April 1992.

ANNEX 4

Commission Notice on the concept of undertakings concerned under Council Regulation (EEC) No 4064/89 on the control of concentrations between undertakings[1]

I. INTRODUCTION

II. THE CONCEPT OF UNDERTAKING CONCERNED

III. IDENTIFYING THE UNDERTAKINGS CONCERNED IN DIFFERENT TYPES OF OPERATIONS

III.1. Mergers
III.2. Acquisition of sole control
    III.2.1. Acquisition of sole control of the whole company
    III.2.2. Acquisition of sole control of part of a company
    III.2.3. Acquisition of sole control after reduction or enlargement of the target
        company
    III.2.4. Acquisition of sole control through a subsidiary of a group
III.3. Acquisition of joint control
    III.3.1. Acquisition of joint control of a newly-created company
    III.3.2. Acquisition of joint control of a pre-existing company
    III.3.3. Acquisition of joint control with a view to immediate partition of
        assets
III.4. Acquisition of control by a joint venture
III.5. Change from joint control to sole control
III.6. Change in the shareholding in cases of joint control of an existing joint
        venture
    III.6.1. Reduction in the number of shareholders leading to a change from
        joint to sole control

---

[1] OJ C 66, 2.3.1998, p. 14. Only texts published in the Official Journal of the European Union are authentic.

III.6.2. Reduction in the number of shareholders not leading to a change from joint to sole control

III.6.3. Any other changes in the composition of the shareholding

III.7. 'Demergers' and the break-up of companies

III.8. Exchange of assets

III.9. Acquisitions of control by individual persons

III.10. Management buy-outs

III.11. Acquisition of control by a state-owned company

I. INTRODUCTION

1. The purpose of this notice is to clarify the Commission's interpretation of the term 'undertakings concerned' used in Articles 1 and 5 of Council Regulation (EEC) No 4064/89[2] as last amended by Regulation (EC) No 1310/97[3] (hereinafter referred to as 'the Merger Regulation') and to help identify the undertakings concerned in the most typical situations which have arisen in cases dealt with by the Commission to date. The principles set out in this notice will be followed and further developed by the Commission's practice in individual cases.

    This Notice replaces the Notice on the notion of undertakings concerned.[4]

2. According to Article 1 of the Merger Regulation, the Regulation only applies to operations that satisfy two conditions. First, several undertakings must merge, or one or more undertakings must acquire control of the whole or part of other undertakings through the proposed operation, which must qualify as a concentration within the meaning of Article 3 of the Regulation. Secondly, those undertakings must meet the turnover thresholds set out in Article 1.

3. From the point of view of determining jurisdiction, the undertakings concerned are, broadly speaking, the actors in the transaction in so far as they are the merging, or acquiring and acquired parties; in addition, their total aggregate economic size in terms of turnover will be decisive in determining whether the thresholds are met.

---

[2] OJ L 395, 30.12.1989, p. 1; corrected version L 257, 21.9.1990, p. 13.

[3] OJ L 180, 9.7.1997, p. 1.

[4] OJ C 385, 31.12.1994, p. 12.

4. The Commission's interpretation of Articles 1 and 5 with respect to the concept of undertakings concerned is without prejudice to the interpretation which may be given by the Court of Justice or by the Court of First Instance of the European Communities.

II. THE CONCEPT OF UNDERTAKING CONCERNED

5. Undertakings concerned are the direct participants in a merger or acquisition of control. In this respect, Article 3(1) of the Merger Regulation provides that: 'A concentration shall be deemed to arise where:

    (a) two or more previously independent undertakings merge, or

    (b) – one or more persons already controlling at least one undertaking, or

        – one or more undertakings

    acquire, whether by purchase of securities or assets, by contract or by any other means, direct or indirect control of the whole or parts of one or more other undertakings'.

6. In the case of a merger, the undertakings concerned will be the undertakings that are merging.

7. In the remaining cases, it is the concept of 'acquiring control' that will determine which are the undertakings concerned. On the acquiring side, there can be one or more companies acquiring sole or joint control. On the acquired side, there can be one or more companies as a whole or parts thereof, when only one of their subsidiaries or some of their assets are the subject of the transaction. As a general rule, each of these companies will be an undertaking concerned within the meaning of the Merger Regulation. However, the particular features of specific transactions require some refinement of this principle, as will be seen below when analysing different possible scenarios.

8. In concentrations other than mergers or the setting-up of new joint ventures, i.e. in cases of sole or joint acquisition of pre-existing companies or parts of them, there is an important party to the agreement that gives rise to the operation who is to be ignored when identifying the undertakings concerned: the seller. Although it is clear that the operation cannot proceed without his consent, his role ends when the transaction is completed since, by definition, from the moment the seller has relinquished all control over the company, his links with it disappear. Where the seller retains joint control with the acquiring

company (or companies), it will be considered to be one of the undertakings concerned.

9. Once the undertakings concerned have been identified in a given transaction, their turnover for the purposes of determining jurisdiction should be calculated according to the rules set out in Article 5 of the Merger Regulation.[5] One of the main provisions of Article 5 is that where the undertaking concerned belongs to a group, the turnover of the whole group should be included in the calculation. All references to the turnover of the undertakings concerned in Article 1 should therefore be understood as the turnover of their entire respective groups.

10. The same can be said with respect to the substantive appraisal of the impact of a concentration in the market place. When Article 2 of the Merger Regulation provides that the Commission is to take into account 'the market position of the undertakings concerned and their economic and financial power', that includes the groups to which they belong.

11. It is important, when referring to the various undertakings which may be involved in a procedure, not to confuse the concept of 'undertakings concerned' under Articles 1 and 5 with the terminology used in the Merger Regulation and in Commission Regulation (EC) No 447/98 of 1 March 1998 on the notifications, time-limits and hearings provided for in Council Regulation (EEC) No 4064/89 (hereinafter referred to as the 'Implementing Regulation')[6] referring to the various undertakings which may be involved in a procedure. This terminology refers to the notifying parties, other involved parties, third parties and parties who may be subject to fines or periodic penalty payments, and they are defined in Chapter III of the Implementing Regulation, along with their respective rights and duties.

---

[5] The rules for calculating turnover in accordance with Article 5 are detailed in the Commission Notice on calculation of turnover.

[6] OJ L 61, 2.3.1998, p. 1.

III. IDENTIFYING THE UNDERTAKINGS CONCERNED IN DIFFERENT TYPES OF OPERATIONS

III.1. Mergers

12. In a merger, several previously independent companies come together to create a new company or, while remaining separate legal entities, to create a single economic unit. As mentioned earlier, the undertakings concerned are each of the merging entities.

III.2. Acquisition of sole control

III.2.1. Acquisition of sole control of the whole company

13. Acquisition of sole control of the whole company is the most straightforward case of acquisition of control; the undertakings concerned will be the acquiring company and the acquired or target company.

III.2.2. Acquisition of sole control of part of a company

14. The first subparagraph of Article 5(2) of the Merger Regulation provides that when the operation concerns the acquisition of parts of one or more undertakings, only those parts which are the subject of the transaction shall be taken into account with regard to the seller. The concept of 'parts' is to be understood as one or more separate legal entities (such as subsidiaries), internal subdivisions within the seller (such as a division or unit), or specific assets which in themselves could constitute a business (e.g. in certain cases brands or licences) to which a market turnover can be clearly attributed. In this case, the undertakings concerned will be the acquirer and the acquired part(s) of the target company.

15. The second subparagraph of Article 5(2) includes a special provision on staggered operations or follow-up deals, whereby if several acquisitions of parts by the same purchaser from the same seller occur within a two-year period, these transactions are to be treated as one and the same operation arising on the date of the last transaction. In this case, the undertakings concerned are the acquirer and the different acquired part(s) of the target company taken as a whole.

III.2.3. Acquisition of sole control after reduction or enlargement of the target company

16. The undertakings concerned are the acquiring company and the target company or companies, in their configuration at the date of the operation.

17. The Commission bases itself on the configuration of the undertakings concerned at the date of the event triggering the obligation to notify under Article 4(1) of the Merger Regulation, namely the conclusion of the agreement, the announcement of the public bid or the acquisition of a controlling interest. If the target company has divested an entity or closed a business prior to the date of the event triggering notification or where such a divestment or closure is a pre-condition for the operation,[7] then sales of the divested entity or closed business are not to be included when calculating turnover. Conversely, if the target company has acquired an entity prior to the date of the event triggering notification, the sales of the latter are to be added.[8]

III.2.4. Acquisition of sole control through a subsidiary of a group

18. Where the target company is acquired by a group through one of its subsidiaries, the undertakings concerned for the purpose of calculating turnover are the target company and the acquiring subsidiary. However, regarding the actual notification, this can be made by the subsidiary concerned or by its parent company.

19. All the companies within a group (parent companies, subsidiaries, etc.) constitute a single economic entity, and therefore there can only be one undertaking concerned within the one group – i.e. the subsidiary and the parent company cannot each be considered as separate undertakings concerned, either for the purposes of ensuring that the threshold requirements are fulfilled (for example, if the target company does not meet the [€] 250 million Community-turnover threshold), or that they are not (for example, if a group was split into two companies each with a Community turnover below [€] 250 million).

---

7   See judgment of the Court of First Instance of 24 March 1994 in Case T-3/93 – Air France v Commission [1994] ECR II-21.

8   The calculation of turnover in the case of acquisitions or divestments subsequent to the date of the last audited accounts is dealt with in the Commission Notice on calculation of turnover, paragraph 27.

20. However, even though there can only be one undertaking concerned within a group, Article 5(4) of the Merger Regulation provides that it is the turnover of the whole group to which the undertaking concerned belongs that shall be included in the threshold calculations.[9]

III.3. Acquisition of joint control

III.3.1. Acquisition of joint control of a newly-created company

21. In the case of acquisition of joint control of a newly-created company, the undertakings concerned are each of the companies acquiring control of the newly set-up joint venture (which, as it does not yet exist, cannot be considered to be an undertaking concerned and moreover, as yet, has no turnover of its own).

III.3.2. Acquisition of joint control of a pre-existing company

22. In the case of acquisition of joint control of a pre-existing company or business,[10] the undertakings concerned are each of the companies acquiring joint control on the one hand, and the pre-existing acquired company or business on the other.

23. However, where the pre-existing company was under the sole control of one company and one or several new shareholders acquire joint control while the initial parent company remains, the undertakings concerned are each of the jointly-controlling companies (including this initial shareholder). The target company in this case is not an undertaking concerned, and its turnover is part of the turnover of the initial parent company.

---

9 The calculation of turnover in the case of company groups is dealt with in the Commission Notice on calculation of turnover, paragraphs 36 to 42.

10 I.e. two or more companies (companies A, B, etc.) acquire a pre-existing company (company X). For changes in the shareholding in cases of joint control of an existing joint venture, see Section III.6.

III.3.3. Acquisition of joint control with a view to immediate partition of assets

24. Where several undertakings come together solely for the purpose of acquiring another company and agree to divide up the acquired assets according to a pre-existing plan immediately upon completion of the transaction, there is no effective concentration of economic power between the acquirers and the target company since the assets acquired are jointly held and controlled for only a 'legal instant'. This type of acquisition with a view to immediate partition of assets will in fact be considered to be several operations, whereby each of the acquiring companies acquires its relevant part of the target company. For each of these operations, the undertakings concerned will therefore be the acquiring company and that part of the target which it is acquiring (just as if there was an acquisition of sole control of part of a company).

25. This scenario is referred to in recital 24 of Regulation (EEC) No 4064/89, which states that the Regulation applies to agreements whose sole object is to divide up the assets acquired immediately after the acquisition.

III.4. Acquisition of control by a joint venture

26. In transactions where a joint venture acquires control of another company, the question arises whether or not, from the point of view of the acquiring party, the joint venture should be regarded as a single undertaking concerned (the turnover of which would include the turnover of its parent companies), or whether each of its parent companies should individually be regarded as undertakings concerned. In other words, the issue is whether or not to 'lift the corporate veil' of the intermediate undertaking (the vehicle). In principle, the undertaking concerned is the direct participant in the acquisition of control. However, there may be circumstances where companies set up 'shell' companies, which have little or no turnover of their own, or use an existing joint venture which is operating on a different market from that of the target company in order to carry out acquisitions on behalf of the parent companies. Where the acquired or target company has a Community turnover of less than [€] 250 million, the question of determining the undertakings concerned may be decisive for jurisdictional purposes.[11] In this type of situation, the Commis-

---

11 The target company hypothetically has an aggregate Community turnover of less than [€] 250 million, and the acquiring parties are two (or more) undertakings, each with a Com-

sion will look at the economic reality of the operation to determine which are the undertakings concerned.

27. Where the acquisition is carried out by a full-function joint venture, i.e. a joint venture which has sufficient financial and other resources to operate a business activity on a lasting basis[12] and is already operating on a market, the Commission will normally consider the joint venture itself and the target company to be the undertakings concerned (and not the joint venture's parent companies).

28. Conversely, where the joint venture can be regarded as a vehicle for an acquisition by the parent companies, the Commission will consider each of the parent companies themselves to be the undertakings concerned, rather than the joint venture, together with the target company. This is the case in particular where the joint venture is set up especially for the purpose of acquiring the target company, where the joint venture has not yet started to operate, where an existing joint venture has no legal personality or full-function character as referred to above or where the joint venture is an association of undertakings. The same applies where there are elements which demonstrate that the parent companies are in fact the real players behind the operation. These elements may include a significant involvement by the parent companies themselves in the initiation, organisation and financing of the operation. Moreover, where the acquisition leads to a substantial diversification in the nature of the joint venture's activities, this may also indicate that the parent companies are the real players in the operation. This will normally be the case when the joint venture acquires a target company operating on a different product market. In those cases, the parent companies are regarded as undertakings concerned.

---

munity turnover exceeding [€] 250 million. If the target is acquired by a 'shell' company set up between the acquiring undertakings, there would only be one company (the 'shell' company) with a Community turnover exceeding [€] 250 million, and thus one of the cumulative threshold conditions for Community jurisdiction would not be fulfilled (namely, the existence of at least two undertakings with a Community turnover exceeding [€] 250 million). Conversely, if instead of acting through a 'shell' company, the acquiring undertakings acquire the target company themselves, then the turnover threshold would be met and the Merger Regulation would apply to this transaction. The same considerations apply to the national turnover thresholds referred to in Article 1(3).

12 The criteria determining the full-function nature of a joint venture are contained in the Commission Notice on the concept of full-function joint ventures.

29. In the TNT case,[13] joint control over a joint venture (JVC) was to be acquired by a joint venture (GD NET BV) between five postal administrations and another acquiring company (TNT Ltd). In this case, the Commission considered that the joint venture GD NET BV was simply a vehicle set up to enable the parent companies (the five postal administrations) to participate in the resulting JVC joint venture in order to facilitate decision-making amongst themselves and to ensure that the parent companies spoke and acted as one; this configuration would ensure that the parent companies could exercise a decisive influence with the other acquiring company, TNT, over the resulting joint venture JVC and would avoid the situation where that other acquirer could exercise sole control because of the postal administrations' inability to reach a unified position on any decision.

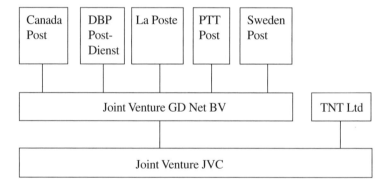

---

13 Case IV/M.102 – TNT/Canada Post, DBP Postdienst, La Poste, PTT Post and Sweden Post, of 2 December 1991.

III.5. Change from joint control to sole control

30. In the case of a change from joint control to sole control, one shareholder acquires the stake previously held by the other shareholder(s). In the case of two shareholders, each of them has joint control over the entire joint venture, and not sole control over 50 % of it; hence the sale of all of his shares by one shareholder to the other does not lead the sole remaining shareholder to move from sole control over 50 % to sole control over 100 % of the joint venture, but rather to move from joint control to sole control of the entire company (which, subsequent to the operation, ceases to be a 'joint' venture).

31. In this situation, the undertakings concerned are the remaining (acquiring) shareholder and the joint venture. As is the case for any other seller, the 'exiting' shareholder is not an undertaking concerned.

32. The ICI/Tioxide case[14] involved such a change from joint (50/50) control to sole control. The Commission considered that '… decisive influence exercised solely is substantially different to decisive influence exercised jointly, since the latter has to take into account the potentially different interests of the other party or parties concerned … By changing the quality of decisive influence exercised by ICI on Tioxide, the transaction will bring about a durable change of the structure of the concerned parties …'. In this case, the undertakings concerned were held to be ICI (as acquirer) and Tioxide as a whole (as acquiree), but not the seller Cookson.

III.6. Change in the shareholding in cases of joint control of an existing joint venture

33. The decisive element in assessing changes in the shareholding of a company is whether the operation leads to a change in the quality of control. The Commission assesses each operation on a case-by-case basis, but under certain hypotheses, there will be a presumption that the given operation leads, or does not lead, to such a change in the quality of control, and thus constitutes, or does not constitute, a notifiable concentration.

---

[14] Case IV/M.023 – ICI/Tioxide, of 28 November 1990.

34. A distinction must be made according to the circumstances of the change in the shareholding; firstly, one or more existing shareholders can exit; secondly, one or more new additional shareholders can enter; and thirdly, one or more existing shareholders can be replaced by one or more new shareholders.

III.6.1. Reduction in the number of shareholders leading to a change from joint to sole control

35. It is not the reduction in the number of shareholders per se which is important, but rather the fact that if some shareholders sell their stakes in a given joint venture, these stakes are then acquired by other (new or existing) shareholders, and thus the acquisition of these stakes or additional contractual rights may lead to the acquisition of control or may strengthen an already existing position of control (e.g. additional voting rights or veto rights, additional board members, etc.).

36. Where the number of shareholders is reduced, there may be a change from joint control to sole control (see also Section III.5.), in which case the remaining shareholder acquires sole control of the company. The undertakings concerned will be the remaining (acquiring) shareholder and the acquired company (previously the joint venture).

37. In addition to the shareholder with sole control of the company, there may be other shareholders, for example with minority stakes, but who do not have a controlling interest in the company; these shareholders are not undertakings concerned as they do not exercise control.

III.6.2. Reduction in the number of shareholders not leading to a change from joint to sole control

38. Where the operation involves a reduction in the number of shareholders having joint control, without leading to a change from joint to sole control and without any new entry or substitution of shareholders acquiring control (see Section III.6.3.), the proposed transaction will normally be presumed not to lead to a change in the quality of control and will therefore not be a notifiable concentration. This would be the case where, for example, five shareholders initially have equal stakes of 20 % each and where, after the operation, one shareholder exits and the remaining four shareholders each have equal stakes of 25 %.

39. However, this situation would be different where there is a significant change in the quality of control, notably where the reduction in the number of shareholders gives the remaining shareholders additional veto rights or additional board members, resulting in a new acquisition of control by at least one of the shareholders, through the application of either the existing or a new shareholders' agreement. In this case, the undertakings concerned will be each of the remaining shareholders which exercise joint control and the joint venture. In Avesta II,[15] the fact that the number of major shareholders decreased from four to three led to one of the remaining shareholders acquiring negative veto rights (which it had not previously enjoyed) because of the provisions of the shareholders' agreement which remained in force.[16] This acquisition of full veto rights was considered by the Commission to represent a change in the quality of control.

III.6.3. Any other changes in the composition of the shareholding

40. Finally, in the case where, following changes in the shareholding, one or more shareholders acquire control, the operation will constitute a notifiable operation as there is a presumption that it will normally lead to a change in the quality of control.

41. Irrespective of whether the number of shareholders decreases, increases or remains the same subsequent to the operation, this acquisition of control can take any of the following forms:
   – entry of one or more new shareholders (change from sole to joint control, or situation of joint control both before and after the operation),
   – acquisition of a controlling interest by one or more minority shareholders (change from sole to joint control, or situation of joint control both before and after the operation),
   – substitution of one or more shareholders (situation of joint control both before and after the operation).

---

15 Case IV/M.452 – Avesta II, of 9 June 1994.

16 In this case, a shareholder who was a party to the shareholders' agreement sold its stake of approximately 7 %. As the exiting shareholder had shared veto rights with another shareholder who remained, and as the shareholders' agreement remained unchanged, the remaining shareholder now acquired full veto rights.

42. The question is whether the undertakings concerned are the joint venture and the new shareholder(s) who would together acquire control of a pre-existing company, or whether all of the shareholders (existing and new) are to be regarded as undertakings concerned acquiring control of a new joint venture. This question is particularly relevant when there is no express agreement between one (or more) of the existing shareholders and the new shareholder(s), who might only have had an agreement with the 'exiting' shareholder(s), i.e. the seller(s).

43. A change in the shareholding through the entry or substitution of shareholders is considered to lead to a change in the quality of control. This is because the entry of a new parent company, or the substitution of one parent company for another, is not comparable to the simple acquisition of part of a business as it implies a change in the nature and quality of control of the whole joint venture, even when, both before and after the operation, joint control is exercised by a given number of shareholders.

44. The Commission therefore considers that the undertakings concerned in cases where there are changes in the shareholding are the shareholders (both existing and new) who exercise joint control and the joint venture itself. As mentioned earlier, non-controlling shareholders are not undertakings concerned.

45. An example of such a change in the shareholding is the Synthomer/Yule Catto case,[17] in which one of two parent companies with joint control over the pre-existing joint venture was replaced by a new parent company. Both parent companies with joint control (the existing one and the new one) and the joint venture were considered to be undertakings concerned.

III.7. 'Demergers' and the break-up of companies

46. When two undertakings merge or set up a joint venture, then subsequently demerge or break up their joint venture, and in particular the assets[18] are split between the 'demerging' parties, particularly in a configuration different from

---

[17] Case IV/M.376 – Synthomer/Yule Catto, of 22 October 1993.

[18] The term 'assets' as used here means specific assets which in themselves could constitute a business (e.g. a subsidiary, a division of a company or, in some cases, brands or licences) to which a market turnover can be clearly attributed.

the original, there will normally be more than one acquisition of control (see the Annex).

47. For example, undertakings A and B merge and then subsequently demerge with a new asset configuration. There will be the acquisition by undertaking A of various assets (assets which may previously have been owned by itself or by undertaking B and assets jointly acquired by the entity resulting from the merger), with similar acquisitions by undertaking B. Similarly, a break-up of a joint venture can be deemed to involve a change from joint control over the joint venture's entire assets to sole control over the divided assets.[19]

48. A break-up of a company in this way is 'asymmetrical'. For such a demerger, the undertakings concerned (for each break-up operation) will be, on the one hand, the original parties to the merger and, on the other, the assets that each original party is acquiring. For the break-up of a joint venture, the undertakings concerned (for each break-up operation) will be, on the one hand, the original parties to the joint venture, each as acquirer, and, on the other, that part of the joint venture that each original party is acquiring.

III.8. Exchange of assets

49. In those transactions where two (or more) companies exchange assets, regardless of whether these constitute legal entities or not, each acquisition of control constitutes an independent concentration. Although it is true that both transfers of assets in a swap are usually considered by the parties to be interdependent, that they are often agreed in a single document and that they may even take place simultaneously, the purpose of the Merger Regulation is to assess the impact of the operation resulting from the acquisition of control by each of the companies. The legal or even economic link between those operations is not sufficient for them to qualify as a single concentration.

50. Hence the undertakings concerned will be, for each property transfer, the acquiring companies and the acquired companies or assets.

---

[19] Case IV/M.197 – Solvay-Laporte/Interox, of 30 April 1997.

III.9. Acquisitions of control by individual persons

51. Article 3(1) of the Merger Regulation specifically provides that a concentration is deemed to arise, inter alia, where 'one or more persons already controlling at least one undertaking' acquire control of the whole or parts of one or more undertakings. This provision indicates that acquisitions of control by individuals will bring about a lasting change in the structure of the companies concerned only if those individuals carry out economic activities of their own. The Commission considers that the undertakings concerned are the target company and the individual acquirer (with the turnover of the undertaking(s) controlled by that individual being included in the calculation of the individual's turnover).

52. This was the view taken in the Commission decision in the Asko/Jacobs/Adia case,[20] where Asko, a German holding company with substantial retailing assets, and Mr Jacobs, a private Swiss investor, acquired joint control of Adia, a Swiss company active mainly in personnel services. Mr Jacobs was considered to be an undertaking concerned because of the economic interests he held in the chocolate, confectionery and coffee sectors.

III.10. Management buy-outs

53. An acquisition of control of a company by its own managers is also an acquisition by individuals, and what has been said above is therefore also applicable here. However, the management of the company may pool its interests through a 'vehicle company', so that it acts with a single voice and also to facilitate decision-making. Such a vehicle company may be, but is not necessarily, an undertaking concerned. The general rule on acquisitions of control by a joint venture applies here (see Section III.4.).

54. With or without a vehicle company, the management may also look for investors in order to finance the operation. Very often, the rights granted to these investors according to their shareholding may be such that control within the meaning of Article 3 of the Merger Regulation will be conferred on them and not on the management itself, which may simply enjoy minority rights. In the

---

[20] Case IV/M.082 – Asko/Jacobs/Adia, of 16 May 1991.

CWB/Goldman Sachs/Tarkett decision,[21] the two companies managing the investment funds taking part in the transaction were those acquiring joint control, and not the managers.

III.11. Acquisition of control by a State-owned company

55. In those situations where a State-owned company merges with or acquires control of another company controlled by the same State,[22] the question arises as to whether these transactions really constitute concentrations within the meaning of Article 3 of the Merger Regulation or rather internal restructuring operations of the 'public sector group of companies'.[23] In this respect, recital 12 of Regulation (EEC) No 4064/89 sets out the principle of non-discrimination between public and private sectors and declares that 'in the public sector, calculation of the turnover of an undertaking concerned in a concentration needs, therefore, to take account of undertakings making up an economic unit with an independent power of decision, irrespective of the way in which their capital is held or of the rules of administrative supervision applicable to them'.

56. A merger or acquisition of control arising between two companies owned by the same State may constitute a concentration and, if so, both of them will qualify as undertakings concerned, since the mere fact that two companies are both owned by the same State does not necessarily mean that they belong to the same 'group'. Indeed, the decisive issue will be whether or not these companies are both part of the same industrial holding and are subject to a coordinated strategy. This was the approach taken in the SGS/Thomson decision.[24]

---

21 Case IV/M.395 – CWB/Goldman Sachs/Tarkett, of 21 February 1994.

22 The term 'State' as used here means any legal public entity, i.e. not only Member States, but also regional or local public entities such as provinces, departments, Länder, etc.

23 See also Commission Notice on the concept of concentration, paragraph 8.

24 Case IV/M.216 – CEA Industrie/France Telecom/Finmeccanica/SGS-Thomson, of 22 February 1993.

ANNEX

'DEMERGERS' AND BREAK-UP OF COMPANIES[25]

Merger scenario

Before merger

| Company A |

| Company B |

After merger

| Merged Company |
| Combined Assets |

After breaking up the merger

Company A:	Company B:
Divided Assets of merged company:	Divided Assets of merged company:
– some (initial) assets of A	– some (initial) assets of A
– some (initial) assets of B	– some (initial) assets of B
– some (subsequent) assets of the merged company	– some (subsequent) assets of the merged company

---

[25] By 'assets', reference is made to specific assets which in themselves could constitute a business (e.g. a subsidiary, a division of a company, in certain cases brands or licences) to which a market turnover can clearly be attributed.

Joint venture scenario

Before JV

After JV

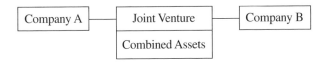

After breaking up the JV

Company A:
Divided Assets of joint venture:
– some (initial) assets of A
– some (initial) assets of B
– some (subsequent) assets of the JV

Company B:
Divided Assets of joint venture:
– some (initial) assets of A
– some (initial) assets of B
– some (subsequent) assets of the JV

BIBLIOGRAPHY

Aarbakke, Asle and Helge Stemshaug, 'Norway – Cross Border Mergers in Company Law and Competition Law: Removing the Final Barriers' in *FIDE – XX Congress – London – 30 October-2 November 2002 – Vol. 1 National Reports* pp. 891-916.

Agence Europe, 'CE/concurrence: La prise de contrôle de Dan Air par la British Airways ne relève pas des compétences de la Commission en matière de fusions', 31 October 1992.

Allan, Bill and Christopher Bright, 'Restrictive Agreements and Dominant Positions: Opening New Markets' in *Business Law in the European Economic Area* (C. Bright, ed.), Clarendon Press, Oxford 1994.

American Bar Association, 'Comments of the American Bar Association Section of Antitrust Law with Respect to the Amended Proposal for a Council Regulation (EEC) on the Control of Concentrations between Undertakings', *Antitrust Law Journal* 1990, vol. 59, pp. 245-261.

Areeda, Philip and Louis Kaplow, *Antitrust Analysis – Problems, Text, Cases*, 5th ed., Aspen Law & Business, New York 1997.

Ashurst, Mark, 'Impala intent on leaping European fences', *Financial Times*, Thursday 2 May 1996, p. 21.

Bader, Udo-Olaf, 'Inhalt und Bedeutung der 2. Bankrechtskoordinerungsrichtlinie – ein EG-Grundgesetz für die Banken?', *Europäische Zeitschrift für Wirtschaftsrecht*, issue 4, 1990, pp. 117-122.

Baker & McKenzie, *European Legal Developments Bulletin*, January 2002, Vol. 14, issue 1.

Bavasso, Antonio F., '*Gencor*: A Judicial Review of the Commission's Policy and Practice -*Many Lights and Some Shadows*', World Competition 1999, pp. 45-65.

Bavasso, Antonio F., 'Boeing/McDonnell Douglas: Did the Commission Fly Too High?', *European Competition Law Review*, 1998, 243-248.

Bechtold, Rainer, 'EEC Merger Regulation – Panel Discussion', *1992 Fordham Corp. L. Inst.* 607 (B. Hawk ed. 1993).

Beck, Bernhard, 'Extraterritoriale Anwendung des EG-Kartellrechts Rechtsvergleichende Anmerkungen zum "Zellstoff"-Urteil des Europäischen Gerichtshof', *Recht der internationalen Wirtschaft*, 1990, pp. 91-95.

Begg, David, *et al* in *Making Sense of Subsidiarity: How Much Centralization for Europe?*, Centre for Economic Policy Research (CEPR), London 1993 at pp. 135-137.

Begg, P.F.C., *Corporate Acquisitions and Mergers – A Practical Guide to the Legal, Financial and Administrative Implications*, 3rd ed., Graham & Trotman, London 1991.

Bellamy & Child – Common Market Law of Competition, 4th ed., (V. Rose, ed.), Sweet & Maxwell, London 1993.

Bellamy & Child – European Community Law of Competition, 5th ed., (P.M. Roth, ed.), Sweet & Maxwell, London 2001.

Benson, Peter Suppli, 'EU lurer videre på Carlsberg', *Politiken* 5 June 2000.

Berlin, Dominique, *Contrôle communautaire des concentrations*, Editions A. Pedone, Paris 1992.

Berlin, Dominique, 'Concentrations – (1er janvier 1998 – 31 décembre 1998)', *Revue trimestrielle de droit européen*, No. 1, 2000, pp. 139-237.

Berlin, Dominique, and Hugues Calvet, 'Concentrations – 1er janvier 1995 – 31 décembre 1996', *Revue trimestrielle de droit européen*, 1997, pp. 521-627.

Bernard, Nicolas, 'The Future of European Economic Law in the Light of the Principle of Subsidiarity', *Common Market Law Review* 1996, pp. 633-666.

Bird & Bird, *Internet Law and Regulation* (G.J.H. Smith, ed.), 3rd ed., Sweet & Maxwell, London 2002.

Bishop, Matthew, 'European or National? The Community's New Merger Regulation' in *European Mergers and Merger Policy*, (Matthew Bishop and John Kay, eds.), Oxford University Press, Oxford 1993, pp. 294-317.

Bishop, Simon and Mike Walker, *Economics of E.C. Competition Law: Concepts, Application and Measurement*, Sweet & Maxwell, London 1999.

Blanchet, Thérèse, Risto Piipponen, Maria Westman-Clément, *The Agreement on the European Economic Area (EEA) – A Guide to the Free Movement of Goods and Competition Rules*, Clarendon Press, Oxford 1994.

Bos, Pierre, Jules Stuyck, and Peter Wytinck, *Concentration Control in the European Economic Community*, Graham & Trotman Ltd., London 1992.

Bos, Pierre-Vincent, 'Towards a Clear Distribution of Competence between EC and National Competition Authorities', *European Competition Law Review*, Vol. 16, No. 7, 1995, pp. 410-416.

Boulouis, Jean, 'Les avis de la Cour de justice des Communautés sur la compatibilité avec le Traité CEE du projet d'accord créant l'Espace économique européen', *Revue trimestrielle de droit européen*, no. 3, 1992, pp. 457-463.

Bourgeois, Jacques H.J., 'EEC Control Over International Mergers', *Yearbook of European Law 1990*, (A. Barav and D.A. Wyatt, eds.), Clarendon Press, Oxford 1991, pp. 103-132.

Bourgeois, Jacques H.J., 'Case Note: Aerospatiale/MBB', *EC Merger Control Reporter*, Kluwer Law International, The Hague 1991 and later (looseleaf), pp. 100.1-100.3.

Bourgeois, Jacques, *Competition Rules and their Enforcement in the Enlarged Free Trading Area*, Paper delivered at European Study Conferences' competition conference, Brussels, November 1992.

Brandtner, Barbara, 'The 'Drama' of the EEA – Comments on Opinions 1/91 and 1/92', *European Journal of International Law*, no. 3, 1992, pp. 300-328.

Bridgeman, John, 'Commission and National Competence – a Debate', *International Business Lawyer*, March 1998, vol. 26, no. 3, pp. 102-103

Brittan, Sir Leon, *Competition Policy and Merger Control in the Single European Market*, Grotius Publications Ltd., Cambridge 1991.

Brittan, Sir Leon, *European Competition Policy – Keeping the Playing-Field Level*, Brassey London and CEPS Brussels, 1992.

Brittan, Sir Leon, speech to the Friedrich-Ebert-Stiftung, entitled *European Policy on Competition*, Bonn, 25 June 1992.

Brittan, Sir Leon, speech to the Centre of European Policy Studies in Brussels on 7 December 1992, entitled *The Future of EC Competition Policy*. (A summary of the speech may be found in press release IP(92)1009 of 8 December 1992. This press release has been reproduced in [1993] 4 C.M.L.R. 7 pp. 14-17).

Brittan, Sir Leon, 'The Early Days of EC Merger Control' in *EC Merger Control: Ten Years On*, International Bar Association, London 2000, p. 2.

Brittan, Sir Leon, '*The Future of EC Competition Policy*', speech given at the Centre of European Policy Studies, Brussels, Monday 7 December 1992 at p. 10.

Brittan, Sir Leon 'Subsidiarity in the Constitution of the European Community' in *Collected Courses of the Academy of European Law – Recueil des cours de l'Academie de droit européen – 1992 – European Community Law, Vol. III, Book 1*, Martinus Nijhoff Publishers, Dordrecht 1994.

Broberg, Morten P., 'A Comment on the Geographic Allocation of Turnover under the Merger Regulation', *European Competition Law Review*, Vol. 18, issue 2, 1997, pp. 29-35.

Broberg, Morten P., 'The Commission's Jurisdiction over Mergers in the Financial Sector', *Legal Issues of European Integration*, 1996, no. 2, pp. 35-92.

Broberg, Morten P., 'The De Minimis Notice', *European Law Review*, vol. 20, 1995, pp. 371-387.

Broberg, Morten P., 'The Delimitation of Jurisdiction with regard to Concentration Control under the EEA Agreement', *European Competition Law Review*, vol. 16, no. 1, 1995, pp. 30-39.

Broberg, Morten P., 'The European Commission's Extraterritorial Powers in Merger Control – The Court of First Instance's Judgment in *Gencor v. Commission*', *International and Comparative Law Quarterly*, 2000, pp. 172-182.

Broberg, Morten P., 'The EC Commission's Green Paper on the Review of the Merger Regulation', *European Competition Law Review*, Vol. 17, issue 5, 1996 at pp.

Broberg, Morten P., 'The European Commission's Jurisdiction under the Merger Control Regulation', *Nordic Journal of International Law*, Vol. 63, 1994, pp. 17-108.

Broberg, Morten P., 'Forum Shopping and the European Merger Control Regulation', *The Columbia Journal of European Law*, Vol. 3, No. 1, Fall/Winter 1996/97, pp. 109-123.

Broberg, Morten P.; 'Fusionskontrolforordningens kontrolbegreb' in *Festskrift til Mogens Koktvedgaard*, (Mads Bryde Andersen, Caroline Heide-Jørgensen and Jens Schovsbo, eds.), Jurist- og Økonomforbundets Forlag, Copenhagen 2003.

Broberg, Morten P., 'Geographic Allocation of Turnover under the Merger Regulation', *World Competition – Law and Economics Review*, Vol. 20, issue 2, 1996, pp. 23-43.

Broberg, Morten P., 'Merger Control in the European Community – A Summary of the Five Years since the Introduction of the Merger Regulation', *World Competition – Law and Economics Review*, 1995, Vol. 19, pp. 5-24.

Broberg, Morten P., 'Muddying the Clear Waters: On the Commission's Proposal for a New Delimitation of Jurisdiction in the Field of Merger Control', *European Competition Law Review* Vol. 23, no. 9, 2002.

Brown, Adrian, 'Case Note: Siemens/Italtel', *EC Merger Control Reporter*, Kluwer Law International, The Hague 1991 and later (looseleaf), pp. 1826.25-1826.27.

Brownlie, Ian, *Principles of Public International Law*, fifth ed., Oxford University Press, Oxford 1998.

Búrca, Gráinne de and Bruno de Witte, *The Delimitation of Powers between the EU and its Member States*, European University Institute – Robert Schuman Centre of Advanced, Policy Papers (Series on Constitutional Reform of the EU), CR 2001/03.

Burnley, Richard, 'An Appropriate Jurisdictional Trigger for the EC Merger Regulation and the Question of Decentralisation', *World Competition*, 2002 pp. 263-277.

Burnside, Alec, 'Comment – European Merger Control: Department Shopping?', *In Competition*, 1996, issue 2, pp. 1-2.

Burnside, Alec, 'Preventing Structural Impediments to Competition: Merger Control in the European Economic Area' in *Business Law in the European Economic Area* (Christopher Bright, ed.), Clarendon Press, Oxford 1994.

Burnside, Alec and Carl Meyntjens, 'The EEC Merger Regulation and its Impact on Non-EEC Business', *Brigham Young University Law Review*, Vol. 1990, No. 4, pp. 1373-1411.

Butterworths Merger Control Review, Vol. 6, No 3, June 1997.

Böge, Ulf, 'Dovetailing Cooperation, Dividing Competence – a Member State's View of Merger Control in Europe' in *EC Merger Control: Ten Years On*, International Bar Association, London 2000, pp. 363-372.

Camesasca, Peter D., *European Merger Control: Getting the Efficiencies Right*, Intersentia-Hart, Antwerpen 2000.

Christoforou, Theofanis and David B. Rockwell, 'European Economic Community Law: The Territorial Scope of Application of EEC Antitrust Law', *Harvard International Law Journal*, Volume 30, 1989 pp. 195-206,

Chronas, Athanassios D., *Legal Constraints in the Liberalisation of the European Air Transport Sector: With special reference to the external aviation relations of the Community and the extraterritorial application of EEC Competition Law to foreign-based airlines*, LL.M. dissertation, European University Institute, Florence, 1991.

Clarotti, Paolo, 'The Harmonization of Legislation Relating to Credit Institutions', *Common Market Law Review*, no. 2, 1982, pp. 245-267.

Clifford Chance, *Insurance in the EEC – The European Community's Programme for a New Regime*, 2nd edition, Lloyd's of London Press Ltd., London 1991.

Clough, Mark, *EC Merger Regulation – A practical guide to the EC merger and acquisition rules*, Financial Times Management Report, London 1994.

Collins, Wayne D. 'Review Essay – The Coming of Age of EC Competition Policy', *Yale Journal of International Law*, 1992, Vol. 17, pp. 249-296.

Cook, C.J. and C.S. Kerse, *EEC Merger Control Regulation 4064/89*, 1st ed., Sweet & Maxwell, London 1991.

Cook, C.J. and C.S. Kerse, *E.C. Merger Control*, 3rd ed., Sweet & Maxwell, London 2000.

Criscione, Paolo, 'The Italian Anti-trust Act: Three Years Later', *European Competition Law Review*, issue 2, 1994, pp. 108-112.

Cuziat, Eric, 'La revision du règlement sur le contrôle des concentrations – La proposition de la Commission', *Competition Policy Newsletter*, Vol. 2, No. 2, Summer 1996, pp. 9-11.

Czachay, Elisabeth, 'Division of Competences between the EFTA Surveillance Authority and the EC Commission in the handling of Individual Antitrust and Merger Cases' in *EEA Competition Law*, (Vassili Christianos and Steen Treumer, eds.), European Institute of Public Administration, Maastricht 1994.

Dashwood, Alan, 'Control of Concentrations in the EEC: The New Council Regulation' in *Le contrôle des concentrations d'entreprises*, F.I.D.E., 14e Congrès, Madrid 1990, Vol. III, pp. 21-44.

Dashwood, Alan, in *Wyatt & Dashwood's European Union Law* (A.M. Arnull, A.A. Dashwood, M.G. Ross and D.A. Wyatt, eds.), fourth ed., Sweet & Maxwell, London 2000.

Davies, Lars and Chris Reed, 'The Trouble with Bits – first steps in internet law', *Journal of Business Law*, July 1996, pp. 416-430.

Dickinson, Gerard, 'Insurance' in *European Economy – Market services and European integration – The challenges for the 1990s*, 1993, no. 3 (Pierre Buigues, Fabienne Ilzkovitz, J.-F. Lebrun and André Sapir, eds.), pp. 183-210.

Dirksen, Dirk, 'Praktische Erfahrungen im ersten Jahr der europäischen Fusions-kontrolle' in *Schwerpunkte des Kartellrechts 1990/91*, Carl Heymanns Verlag KG, Köln 1992, pp. 119-133.

Downes, T. Antony and Julian Ellison, *The Legal Control of Mergers in the EC*, Blackstone Press Ltd., London 1991.

Drauz, Götz, 'EEC Merger Control – The First Year' in *Papers of Antitrust Keynote Speakers – Section on Business Law, 10th Biennal Conference, Hong Kong, Committee C, Antitrust and Trade Law, October 1991*, IBA, London 1991.

Drauz, Götz and Dirk Schroeder, *Praxis der europäischen Fusionskontrolle*, 3rd ed., RWS Verlag, Köln 1995.

Dressel, Lothar, *Handelsblatt* 10 November 1992.

Drolshammer, Jens, 'Die Zusammenschlußkontrolle im EWR-Vertrag aus schweizerischer Sicht', in *Festschrift Alfred-Carl Gaedertz*, Beck, München 1992, pp. 111-140.

Dutheil de la Rochère, Jacqueline, 'L'Espace économique européen sous le regard des juges de la Cour de justice des Communautés européennes', *Revue du Marché et de l'Union Européenne*, July/August 1992, No 360, pp. 603-612.

Economic and Social Committee, *Opinion on the Review of the Merger Regulation*, ECOSOC 1157/95.

Economic and Social Committee, *Review of the Community Merger Regulation*, OJ C18/21 of 22 January 1996.

Edwards, Vanessa, *EC Company Law*, Clarendon Press, Oxford 1999.

EFTA Surveillance Authority, *EFTA Surveillance Authority comments on the European Commission's Merger Review Green Paper*, available at www.eftasurv. int/fieldsofwork/fieldcompetition/otherpublications/, 3 April 2002.

Egger, Evelyn, 'Um welche Fusionen kümmert sich die EU?', *Die Versicherungs Rundschau*, 1995, no. 4, pp. 6-7.

Ehlermann, Claus-Dieter, 'Anwendung des Gemeinschaftsrechts durch Behörden und Gerichte der Mitgliedstaaten' in *Gedächtnisschrift für Eberhard Grabitz*, (Albrecht Randelzhofer, Rupert Scholz and Dieter Wilke, eds.), C.H. Beck'sche Verlagsbuchhandlung, München 1995.

Ehlermann, Claus-Dieter, 'In Brüssel gibt es keine industripolitischen Intrigen, sondern nur andere Auffassungen vom Wettbewerb', *Handelsblatt* 25 November 1992.

Ehlermann, Claus-Dieter, *Submission of Mr. Claus Dieter Ehlermann to the House of Lords Select Committee on the European Communities*, given on 16 June 1993 in London (available in DG COMP's library).

Emiliou, Nicholas, '*The Principle of Proportionality in European Law – A Comparative Study*, Kluwer Law International, The Hague 1996.

European Commission, *XIV Report on Competition Policy 1984*, Luxembourg 1985.

European Commission, *XXth Report on Competition Policy 1990*, Luxembourg 1991.

European Commission, *XXIst Report on Competition Policy 1991*, Luxembourg 1992.

European Commission, *XXIIIrd Report on Competition Policy 1993*, Luxembourg 1994.

European Commission, *XXIVth Report on Competition Policy 1994*, Luxembourg 1995.

European Commission, *XXVth Report on Competition Policy 1995*, Luxembourg 1996.

European Commission, *XXVIth Report on Competition Policy 1996*, Luxembourg 1997.

European Commission, *XXVIIth Report on Competition Policy 1997*, Luxembourg 1998.

European Commission, *XXVIIIth Report on Competition Policy 1998,* Luxembourg 1999.

European Commission, *XXIXth Report on Competition Policy 1999*, Luxembourg 2000.

European Commission, *2001 Green Paper on the review of Council Regulation (EEC) No 4064/89,* COM(2001) 745 final, Brussels 11.12.2001.

European Commission, *The Accounting Harmonization in the European Communities – Problems of applying the fourth directive on the annual accounts of limited companies*, Luxembourg 1990.

European Commission, *Communication from the Commission to the Council and to the European Parliament Regarding the Revision of the Merger Regulation*, COM (96) 313 final, Brussels 12.9.1996.

European Commission, *Community Merger Control – Green Paper on the Review of the Merger Regulation*, COM(96) 19 final, Brussels 31.1.1996.

European Commission, 'Competition and Integration – Community merger control policy', *European Economy*, no. 57, 1994.

European Commission, *Directorate-General for Competition – Merger Task Force, Revision of the EEC Merger Regulation, Article 5(3)(a), Turnover of credit institutions and other financial institutions*, Undated (from before March 1993), (not publicly available).

European Commission, 'Horizontal mergers and competition policy in the European Community', *European Economy*, No 40, May 1989.

European Commission, *European Economy – Supplement A*, No. 7, July 1996.

European Commission, *Pluralism and Media Concentration in the Internal Market – An assessment of the need for Community action*, COM(92) 480 final, Brussels, 23 December 1992.

European Commission, *The Principle of Subsidiarity – Communication of the Commission to the Council and the European Parliament*, SEC(92) 1990 Final.

European Commission, *Report from the Commission to the Council on the application of the Merger Regulation thresholds*, Brussels 28 June 2000, COM(2000) 399 final.

European Commission *Review of the Application of Council Regulation (EEC) No. 4064/89 of 21 December 1989 on the Control of Concentrations between Undertakings*, Working Paper of the Services of the Commission, Revised version of 17 May 1993 (B).

Farmer, Paul and Richard Lyal (eds.), *EC Tax Law*, Clarendon Press, Oxford 1994.

Faull, Jonathan & Ali Nikpay, *The EC Law of Competition*, Oxford University Press, Oxford 1999.

Federlin, Christine, 'Division of Competences between the EFTA Surveillance Authority and the EC Commission in the handling of Individual Antitrust and Merger Cases' in *EEA Competition Law* (Vassili Christianos and Steen Treumer, eds.), European Institute of Public Administration, Maastricht 1994.

Fiebig, André, 'Outsourcing under the EC Merger Control Regulation', *European Competition Law Review*, 1996, issue 2, pp. 123-133.

Fiebig, André, 'The Extraterritorial Application of the European Merger Control Regulation', *Columbia Journal of European Law*, 1998, pp. 79-100.

Fiebig, Andre, 'International Law Limits on the Extraterritorial Application of the European Merger Control Regulation and Suggestions for Reform', *European Competition Law Review* 1998 pp. 323-331.

Fine, Frank L., *Mergers and Joint Ventures in Europe – The Law and Policy of the EEC*, 2nd ed., Graham & Trotman Ltd, London 1994.

Friend, Mark, 'The Long Arm of Community Law', *European Law Review*, 1989, pp. 169-172.

George, Ken and Alexis Jacquemin, 'Competition Policy in the European Community' in *Competition Policy in Europe and North America: Economic Issues and Institutions*, (Alexis Jacquemin, ed.), Harwood Academic Publishers, Chur (Switzerland) 1990, pp. 206-245.

Gerber, David J. *Law and Competition in Twentieth Century Europe – Protecting Prometheus*, Clarendon Press, Oxford 1998.

González-Díaz, F. Enrique, 'Case Note: Air France/Sabena', *EEC Merger Control Reporter*, Kluwer Law International, The Hague 1991 and later (looseleaf), p. 932.18.

González díaz, Enrique, 'Case Note: TNT/GD Net', *EC Merger Control Reporter*, Kluwer Law International, The Hague 1991 and later (looseleaf), p. 516.

González-Díaz, F. Enrique, 'Tenth Anniversary of the Merger Regulation: the Way Forward' in *EC Merger Control: Ten Years On*, International Bar Association, London 2000.

González-Díaz, Francisco Enrique, 'Recent Developments in EC Merger Control Law – 'The Gencor Judgment'', *World Competition* 1999 pp. 3-28.

Goyder, D.G., *EC Competition Law*, 3rd ed., Oxford University Press, Oxford 1998.

Griffin, Joseph P., 'Extraterritoriality in U.S. and EU Antitrust Enforcement', *Antitrust Law Journal* 1999 pp. 159-199.

Gugerbauer, Norbert, *Handbuch der Fusionskontrolle – Kommentar zur Verordnung Nr. 4064/89 des Rates über die Kontrolle von Unternehmenszusammenschlüssen und zu den §§ 41ff KartG*, Verlag Orac, Wien 1995.

Haagsma, Auke, 'The Competition Rules of the EEA and the Europe Agreements: Lawyer's Paradise or User's Safe Harbour', in *Procedure and Enforcement in EC and US Competition Law*, (Piet Jan Slot and Alison McDonnel, eds.), Sweet & Maxwell, London 1993, pp. 241-266.

Hansen, Søren Friis, 'The 'Takeover' of Corporate Group Law – Examples from a Scandinavian Perspective', in *The Internationalisation of Companies and Company Law* (Mette Neville and Karsten Engsig Sørensen, eds.), DJØF Publishing, Copenhagen 2001.

Harder, Charlotte and Bent Højgaard Sørensen, 'Ølgigant slipper for fusionskontrol', *Berlingske Tidende*, 10 June 2000.

Harhoff, Frederik, 'Greenland's Withdrawal from the European Communities', *Common Market Law Review*, Vol. 20, 1983, pp. 13-33.

Hartley, Trevor C., *Civil Jurisdiction and Judgments*, Sweet & Maxwell, London 1984.

Hartley, Trevor C., 'The European Court and the EEA', *International and Comparative Law Quarterly* 1992, Vol. 41, pp. 841-848.

Hartley, Trevor C., *The Foundations of European Community Law*, fourth edition, OUP, Oxford 1998.

Hawk Barry E. and Henry L. Huser, *European Community Merger Control: A Practitioner's Guide*, Kluwer Law International, the Hague 1996.

Hirsbrunner, Simon, 'Referral of Mergers in E.C. Merger Control', *European Competition Law Review*, 1999, pp. 372-378.

Idot, Laurence, 'Jurisprudence – Arrêt du 27 septembre 1988 (Cour plénière) Entreprises de 'pâte de bois' C. Commission des Commautés européennes', *Revue trimestrielle de droit européen*, 1989 pp. 341-359.

Immenga, Ulrich, 'Zur Umsatzberechnung öffentlicher Unternehmen im Rahmen der europäischen Fusionskontrolle' in *Festschrift für Ulrich Everling* (Ole Due, Marcus Lutter and Jürgen Schwarze, eds.), Nomos Verlagsgesellschaft, Baden-Baden 1995.

International Competition Policy Advisory Committee, Antitrust Division, *International Competition Policy Advisory Committee – To the Attorney General and Assistant Attorney General for Antitrust – Final Report 2000* (available at www.usdoj.gov/atr/icpac/finalreport.htm)

Jacot-Guillarmod, Olivier, (ed.), *Accord EEE – Commentaires et réflexions*, Schulthess Polygraphischer Verlag, Zürich 1992.

Jacquemin, Alexis, 'Horizontal Concentration and European Merger Policy', *European Economic Review*, 34 1990, pp. 539-550.

Jacquemin, Alexis P., 'Mergers and European Policy' in *Merger and Competition Policy in the European Community*, (P.H. Admiral, ed.), Basil Blackwell, Oxford 1990, pp. 3-38.

Jakob-Siebert, Thinam, 'EEA and Eastern European Agreements with the European Community', *1992 Fordham Corp. L. Inst.* (B. Hawk, ed. 1993), pp. 403-436.

Jakob-Siebert, Thinam, 'Wettbewerbspolitik im europäischen Wirtschaftsraum (EWR) – Das Zwei-Pfeiler-System', *Wirtschaft und Wettbewerb*, Mai 1992, Heft 5, pp. 387-400.

Jenny, Frédéric, 'Competition and Competition Policy', in *Singular Europe – Economy and Polity of the European Community after 1992*, (Willam James Adams, ed.), The University of Michigan Press, Ann Arbor 1992.

Jenny, Frederic, 'National Authorities and the Commission', *International Business Lawyer*, Vol. 26, no. 3, 1998, pp. 105-111.

Jeppesen, Tim, *Subsidiarity: A Janus Head?*, European Studies Discussion Paper, Odense Universitet, Odense 1995.

Jones, Alison and Brenda Sufrin, *EC Competition Law – Text, Cases and Materials*, Oxford University Press, Oxford 2001.

Jones, Christopher, 'Case Note: AG/Amev', *EC Merger Control Reporter*, Kluwer Law International, The Hague 1991 and later (looseleaf), p. 16.1.

Jones, Christopher, 'Case Note: Alcatel/STC', *EC Merger Control Reporter*, Kluwer Law International, The Hague 1991 and later (looseleaf), p. 1180.1.

Jones, Christopher and Enrique González-Díaz, *The EEC Merger Regulation*, Sweet & Maxwell, London 1992.

Jones, Christopher, 'The European dimension in Competition Policy', speech given in London on 21 January 1997.

Jones, Christopher, and F. Enrique González-Díaz, *The EEC Merger Regulation*, Sweet & Maxwell, London 1992.

Jonquières, Guy de, 'Storm over the Atlantic – The challenge by the EU competition commissioner to Boeing's merger plans may spark a row with the US', *Financial Times*, Thursday 22 May 1997, p. 13.

Jordan, Margaret, 'European Community', *International Financial Law Review* – Special supplement, March 1991 pp. 13-18.

Juenger, Friedrich K., 'Forum Shopping: A Rejoinder', *Sydney Law Review*, Vol. 16, 1994, pp. 28-31.

Juenger, Friedrich K., 'What's Wrong with Forum Shopping?' *Sydney Law Review*, Vol. 16, 1994, pp. 5-13.

Kapteyn, P.J.G. and P. Verloren van Themaat, *Introduction to the Law of the European Communities – From Maastricht to Amsterdam*, 3rd edition (edited and further revised by Laurence W. Gormley), Kluwer Law International, The Hague 1998.

Kassamali, Reyaz A., 'From Fiction to Fallacy: Reviewing the E.C. Merger Regulation's Community-Dimension Thresholds in the Light of Economics and Experience in Merger Control', (1996) 21 *European Law Review Checklist* No. 2, pp. CC89-CC114.

Kerse, C.S., *E.C. Antitrust Procedure*, fourth edition, London 1998.

Kleinmann, Werner, 'Die Umsatzschwellen für Zusammenschlüsse von gemein-schaftsweiter Bedeutung in der Europäischen Fusionskontrolle und ihre Revision', *Wirtschaftsrecht und Wirtschaftspolitik*, vol. 150, Wettbewerbspolitik im Spannungsfeld nationaler und internationaler Kartellrechtsordnungen, 1997, pp. 131-141

Kögel, Rainer, *Die Angleichung der deutschen an die europäische Fusionskontrolle*, Nomos Verlagsgesellschaft, Baden-Baden 1996.

Korah, Valentine, *Exclusive Dealing Agreements in the E.E.C. – Regulation 67/67 replaced*, European Law Centre Ltd., 1984.

Korah, Valentine, *An Introductory Guide to EEC Competition Law and Practice*, 4th ed., ESC Publishing Ltd., Oxford 1990.

Krause, Hartmut, 'E.C. Merger Control: An Outside View from Inside the Merger Taskforce', *Journal of Business Law*, November 1995, pp. 627-637.

Lampert, Thomas, *Die Anwendbarkeit der EG-Fusionskontrollverordnung im Verhältnis zum Fusionskontrollrecht der Mitgliedstaaten – rechtsvergleichen zum Verhältnis zwischen dem US-Antitrustrecht des Bundes und der Einzelstaaten*, Carl Heymanns Verlag KG, Köln 1995.

Lang, John Temple, 'What Powers Should the European Community Have', *European Public Law*, 1995, pp. 97-116.

Lange, Dieter G.F. and John Byron Sandage, 'The *Wood Pulp* Decision and its Implications for the Scope of EC Competition Law', *Common Market Law Review* 1989, pp. 137-165.

Lanzke, Gert Uwe, 'Umsetzung und Anwendung der europäischen Bankrichtlinien durch die Mitgliedstaaten', *Wertpapier Mitteilungen – Zeitschrift für Wirtschafts- und Bankrecht*, Vol. 48, 1994, pp. 2001-2010.

Linklaters & Paines, *Competition Law Bulletin*, Spring 1991.

Livingston, Dorothy, *Competition Law and Practice*, FT Law & Tax, London 1995.

Löffler, Heinz F. in *Langen/Bunte – Kommentar zum deutschen und europäischen Kartellrecht*, 7th ed., Luchterhand, Neuwied 1994.

Löffler, Heinz F. in *Langen/Bunte – Kommentar zum deutschen und europäischen Kartellrecht*, 9th ed., Luchterhand, Neuwied 2001

Lovell White Durrant, *EU and Competition Law Newsletter*, July 1996.

Lovells, *EU and Competition Newsletter*, August/September 2002, Issue no. 44, pp. 3-4.

Lovergne, J. and A. Maillé, 'Réflexions sur le fonctionnement du contrôle communautaire des concentrations', *Revue de la concurrence et de la consommation*, No. 72, March-April 1993, pp. 5-27.

Lowe, Philip, *Telecommunication Services and Competition Law in Europe*, speech given at the 5th Annual Seminar on 'Telecommunication Services and Competition Law in Europe', Amsterdam 15 April 1994.

Lowe, Vaughan, 'International Law and the Effects Doctrine in the European Court of Justice', *The Cambridge Law Journal* 1989, pp. 9-11.

Maccarthy, Clare, 'Carlsberg in Dkr 10bn deal with Orkla', Financial Times, 1 June 2000.

Mach, Olivier, 'Le contrôle des concentrations (art. 57. EEE)' in *Accord EEE – Commentaires et réflexions* (Olivier Jacot-Guillarmod, ed.), Zürich 1992, pp. 355-375.

Maciver, Angus K., 'The First Year of Enforcement under the EEC Merger Regulation – A View from the Trenches', *1991 Fordham Corp. L. Inst.*, (B. Hawk, ed. 1992), pp. 751-765.

Mahon, Barry, 'Barry Mahon looks at the background to the Dialog-Data-Star linkup – What did you expect?', *Information World Review*, May 1993, pp. 5-6.

Maitland-Walker, Julian, *EC Insurance Directives*, Lloyd's of London Press Ltd., 1992.

Malric-Smith, Paul, 'Commission's 2000 Report to the Council on the Functioning of the Merger Regulation' in *EC Merger Control: Ten Years On*, International Bar Association, London 2000, pp. 353-359.

Mann, F.A., 'The Public International Law of Restrictive Practices in the European Court of Justice', *International and Comparative Law Quarterly*, 1989, pp. 375-377.

Merkin, Robert (ed.), *Encyclopedia of Competition Law*, Sweet & Maxwell, London 1987 and later (looseleaf).

Mohamed, Sideek, 'National Interests Limiting E.U. Cross-Border Bank Mergers', *European Competition Law Review*, 2000 pp. 248-257.

Monopolkommission, *Die Wettbewerbsordnung erweitern: Hauptgutachten 1986/87*, Monopolkommission, Nomos Verlagsgesellschaft, Baden-Baden 1988.

Morgan, Eleanor J., 'European Community Merger Control in the Service Industries', *Service Industries Journal*, Vol. 14, no. 1, 1994.

Morgan, Eleanor J., 'Subsidiarity and the division of jurisdiction in EU merger control', *The Antitrust Bulletin*, Spring 2000, pp. 153-193.

Navarro Varona, Edurne, 'Case Note: Deutsche Bank/Banco de Madrid', *EC Merger Control Reporter*, Kluwer Law International, The Hague 1992 and later (looseleaf), p. 1102.7.

Neale, Alan D. and Mel L. Stephens, *International Business and National Jurisdiction*, Clarendon Press, Oxford 1988.

Neven, Damian, Robin Nuttall and Paul Seabright, *Merger in Daylight – The Economics and Politics of European Merger Control*, Centre for Economic Policy Research, London 1993.

Niederleithinger, Ernst, 'Vier Prognosen zur europäischen Fusionskontrolle' in *Festschrift für Karlheinz Quack zum 65. Geburtstag am 3. Januar 1991*, (Harm Peter Westermann and Wolfgang Rosener, eds.), Walter de Gruyter, Berlin 1991.

Nitsche, Ingrid, *Broadcasting in the European Union: The Role of Public Interest in Competition Analysis*, T.M.C. Asser Press, The Hague, 2001.

Nobes, Christopher, *Interpreting European Financial Statements*, 2nd ed., Butterworths, London 1994.

Norberg, Sven, 'The Agreement on a European Economic Area', *Common Market Law Review*, 1992, pp. 1171-1198.

Norberg, Sven, 'EES-avtalet – De institutionella lösningarna för ett dynamiskt och homogent EES', *Svensk Juristtidning*, 1992, pp. 337-348.

Norberg, Sven, Karin Hökborg, Martin Johansson, Dan Eliasson and Lucien Dedichen, *The European Economic Area – EEA Law – A Commentary on the EEA Agreement*, CE Fritzes AB, Stockholm 1993.

O'Keeffe, Siún, 'Merger Regulation Thresholds: An Analysis of the Community-dimension Thresholds in Regulation 4064/89', *European Competition Law Review*, 1994, No. 1, pp. 21-31.

Opeskin, Brian R., 'The Price of Forum Shopping: A Reply to Professor Juenger', *Sydney Law Review*, Vol. 16, 1994, pp. 14-27.

Overbury, Colin, 'Case Note: Solvay-Laporte/Interox', *EC Merger Control Reporter*, Kluwer Law International, The Hague 1991 and later (looseleaf), pp. 772.1-772.2.

Overbury, Colin, 'EEC Merger Regulation – Panel Discussion', *1992 Fordham Corp. L. Inst.* 607 (B. Hawk ed. 1993).

Overbury, H. Colin, 'Politics or Policy? The Demystification of EC Merger Control', *1992 Fordham Corp. L. Inst.* 557-589 (B. Hawk, ed. 1993).

Pathak, Anand S., 'Case Note: Ifint/Exor', *EC Merger Control Reporter*, Kluwer Law International, The Hague 1991 and later (looseleaf), pp. 702.3-702.5.

Picat, Marc and Eric Resler, 'Between Commercial Agency and Distributorship', *International Business Lawyer*, May 2002, Vol. 30, no. 5.

Platteau, K., 'EC Merger Control in the Banking and Financial Sector', *Revue de la Banque*, No. 4, 1996, pp. 223-229.

Pool, Bill, *The creation of the internal market in insurance*, Office for Official Publications of the European Communities, Luxembourg 1990.

Portwood, Timothy G., *Mergers under EEC Competition Law*, The Athlone Press, London 1994.

Price, Charles, 'Case Note: Accor/Wagons-Lits', *EC Merger Control Reporter*, Kluwer Law International, The Hague 1991 and later (looseleaf), pp. 752.23-752.24.

Price, Charles and Paul Maeyaert, 'Case Note: ASKO/Omni', *EC Merger Control Reporter*, Kluwer Law International, The Hague 1991 and later (looseleaf), pp. 88.1.

RB-Børsen, *Frygt for EU-stop for Carlsberg-fusion*, 31 May 2000.

Reynolds, Michael J., *Procedural Elements of the Regulation on the Control of Concentrations*, Paper delivered at European Study Conferences' competition conference, Brussels, November 1992.

Reynolds, Michael and Colin Overbury, 'Should the Merger Task Force be given more power?', *International Financial Law Review*, Vol. 12, No. 7, July 1993, pp. 31-33.

Riesenkampff, Alexander, 'Perspektiven und Probleme der europäischen Fusions-kontrolle', *Beiträge zum Handels- und Wirtschaftsrecht – Festschrift für Fritz Rittner zum 70. Geburtstag*, (Manfred Löwisch, Christian Schmidt-Leithoff and Burkhard Schmeidel, eds.), CH. Beck, München 1991, pp. 491-507.

Ritter, Lennart, W. David Braun and Francis Rawlinson, *EEC Competition Law – A Practitioner's Guide*, 1st edition, Kluwer Law and Taxation Publishers, Deventer 1991.

Ritter, Lennart, W. David Braun and Francis Rawlinson, *EEC Competition Law – A Practitioner's Guide*, 2nd edition, Kluwer Law International, The Hague 2000.

Robertson, Aidan, and Marie Demetriou, ''But that was in another country ...': The extraterritorial application of US antitrust laws in the US Supreme Court', *International and Comparative Law Quarterly* 1994, pp. 417-425.

Rogers III, C. Paul, 'Cross-Border Mergers and Antitrust: Jurtisdiction, Enforcement and Cooperation Issues' in *Cross-Border Mergers and Acquisitions and the Law* (Norbert Horn, ed), Kluwer Law International, the Hague 2001.

Rouam, Claude, 'L'Espace économique européen: un horizon nouveau pour la politique de concurrence?', *Revue du Marché Commun et de l'Union Européenne*, January 1992, No 354, pp. 53-57.

Rowley, J. William, Omar K. Wakil and A. Neil Campbell, 'Streamlining International Merger Control' in *EC Merger Control: Ten Years On*, International Bar Association, London 2000, pp. 15-37.

Rudo, Joachim, 'Die Behandlung mehrerer Erwerbsvorgänge als einheitlicher Zusammenschluß im Rahmen der Umsatzberechnung nach Art. 5 Abs. 2 Fusionskontrollverordnung', *Recht der Internationalen Wirtschaft – Betriebs-Berater International*, Vol. 43, August 1997, pp. 641-648

Ruppelt, Hans-Jürgen, *Kommentar zum deutschen und europäischen Kartellrecht*, 9th edition, Luchterhand, Berlin 2001.

Schäfer, Helge, *Internationaler Anwendungsbereich der präventiven Zusammenschlußkontrolle im deutschen und europäischen Recht*, Peter Lang, Frankfurt a.M. 1993.

Schellenberg, Martin, 'Europäische Konzentrationskontrolle im Medienbereich', *Deutsche Zeitschrift für Wirtschaftsrecht*, 1994, No. 10, pp. 410-415.

Schermers, Henry G., 'Opinion 1/91 of the Court of Justice, 14 December 1991; Opinion 1/92 of the Court of Justice, 10 April 1992', 29 *Common Market Law Review* 1992, 991-1009.

Schmitthoff, Clive, 'Jurisdiction of EEC over non-EEC enterprises infringing EEC competition law', *Journal of Business Law*, 1988, pp. 455-456.

Schroeder, Dirk, 'Case Note: Paribas/MTH/MBH', *EC Merger Control Reporter*, Kluwer Law International, The Hague 1991 and later (looseleaf), p. 460.2.

Scott, Jonathan, 'Case Note: Arjomari-Prioux/Wiggins Teape Appleton', *EC Merger Control Reporter*, Kluwer Law International, The Hague 1991 and later (looseleaf), pp. 24.1-24.2.

Scott, Jonathan, 'Case Note: Hong Kong and Shanghai Bank/Midland', *EC Merger Control Reporter*, Kluwer Law International, The Hague 1991 and later (looseleaf), p. 786.1.

Siragusa Mario and Romano Subiotto, 'The EEC merger control regulation: The Commission's evolving case law', *Common Market Law Review*, Vol. 28, 1991, pp. 877-934.

Skapinker, Michael, 'Boeing merger: EU sets out objections', *Financial Times*, Friday 23 May 1997, p. 6.

Slot, Piet Jan, 'Case T-102/96, *Gencor Ltd* v. *Commission*, Judgment of 25 March 1999 of the Court of First Instance, Fifth Chamber, extended composition, [1999] ECR II-753', *Common Market Law Review* 2001 pp. 1573-1586.

Snelders, Robbert, 'Developments in E.C. Merger Control in 1995', *European Law Review, Competition Law Survey 1996*, pp. CC66-CC88.

Soames, Trevor, 'The 'Community Dimension' in the EEC Merger Regulation: The Calculation of the Turnover Criteria', *European Competition Law Review*, 1990, no. 5, pp. 213-225.

Sousi-Roubi, Blanche, and Jacques Zachmann, 'Le contrôle communautaire des concentrations bancaires – La spécifité en question', *Revue de Droit Bancaire et de la Bourse*, No. 36, March/April 1993, pp. 77-85.

Spies, *Published accounts for the Spies Group for the year 1 May 1982 to 30 April 1983.*

Stockenhuber, Peter, *Die Europäische Fusionskontrolle – Das materielle Recht*, Nomos Verlagsgesellschaft, Baden-Baden 1995.

Stockmann, Kurt and Klaus-Peter Schultz, *Kartellrechtspraxis und Kartellrechtssprechung 1995/96*, RWS Verlag, Köln 1996.

Stragier, Joos, 'The Competition Rules of the EEA Agreement and their Implementation', *European Competition Law Review*, 1993, no. 1, pp. 30-38.

Strivens, Robert, 'Competition Law under the EEA Agreement', *International Business Lawyer*, December 1993, Vol. 21, No 11, pp. 512-517.

Struijlaart, Robin A., 'Minority Share Acquisitions Below the Control Thresholds of the EC Merger Control Regulation: An Economic and Legal Analysis', *World Competition* 2002, pp. 173-204.

Thompson, Anthony, *The Second Banking Directive*, Butterworths & Co. (Publishers) Ltd., London 1991.

Tichadou, Evelyne, 'Internationalrechtliche Aspekte des Wettbewerbsrechts am Beispiel des Boeing-Falles', *Zeitschrift für europarechtliche Studien*, 2000, pp. 61-77.

Toth, A.G., 'The Principle of Subsidiarity in the Maastricht Treaty', *Common Market Law Review* 1992 pp. 1079-1105.

Tucker, Emma, 'Competition rules: WTO urged to act', *Financial Times*, Friday 25 July 1997, p. 4.

Van Bael Ivo and Jean-François Bellis, *Competition Law of the European Community*, 3rd ed., CCH Europe, Bicester (UK) 1994.

Van Gerven, Gerwin, 'Case Note: Gambogi/Cogei', *EC Merger Control Reporter*, Kluwer Law International, The Hague 1991 and later (looseleaf), pp. 620.1-620.4.

Van Gerven, Gerwin, 'Case Note: Kelt/American Express', *EC Merger Control Reporter*, Kluwer Law International, The Hague 1991 and later (looseleaf), pp. 345-346.

Van Gerven, Gerwin, 'Case Note: RVI/VBC/Heuliez', *EC Merger Control Reporter*, Kluwer Law International, The Hague 1991 and later (looseleaf), pp. 176.1-176.2.

Van Gerven, Yves and Lorelien Hoet, '*Gencor*: Some Notes on Transnational Competition Law Issues *European Court of First Instance 25 March 1999, T-102/96, Gencor Ltd. v. Commission*', *Legal Issues of Economic Integration*, 2001 pp. 195-210.

Vesterdorf, Bo, 'Recent developments in European Competition case-law, the CFI' in *Neueste Entwicklungen im europäischen und internationalen Kartellrecht – sechstes St. Galler Internationales Kartellrechtsforum 1999*, Helbing & Lichtenhahn, Basel 2000, pp. 131-151.

Weatherill, Stephen, 'The Changing Law and Practice of UK and EEC Merger Control', *Oxford Journal of Legal Studies*, Vol. 11, Winter 1991, pp. 520-544.

Wesseling, Rein 'Subsidiarity in Community Antitrust Law: Setting the Right Agenda', *European Law Review* 1997 pp. 35-54.

Wesseling, Rein, *The Modernisation of EC Antitrust Law*, Hart Publishing, Oxford 2000.

Whish, Richard, *Competition Law*, 4th edition, Butterworths, London 2001.

Wohlgemuth, Frank K., 'Das belgische Kartellrecht', *Wirtschaft und Wettbewerb*, Vol. 44, Issue 11, 1994, pp. 901-915.

Wolf, Dieter, 'The Drive Towards Political and Economic Integration', *International Business Lawyer*, Vol. 26, No 3, 1997, pp. 110-111.

Woolcock, Stephen, *European Mergers: National or Community Controls?*, Royal Institute of International Affairs, Discussion Paper No. 15, London 1989.

Ysewyn, Johan, 'When to Notify a Merger in Belgium', *European Legal Developments Bulletin*, (Baker & McKenzie), January 1996, Vol. 8, No. 1, pp. 16-18.

Zachmann, Jacques, *Le contrôle communautaire des concentrations*, Librairie Générale de Droit et de Jurisprudence, Paris 1994.

Zavvos, George S., 'Banking Integration and 1992: Legal Issues and Policy Implications', *Harvard International Law Journal*, vol. 31, no. 2, 1990, pp. 463-506.

Zschocke, Christian, 'Harmonisierung der Fusionskontrolle aus der Sicht des Praktikers', *Wirtschaft und Wettbewerb*, Vol. 46, 1996 No. 2, pp. 85-91.

TABLE OF CASES

COMMISSION DECISIONS IN MERGER CASES

@Home Benelux B.V., Case IV/JV11, decision of 15 September 1998.   27, 90

A&C/Grossfarma, Case COMP/M2573, decision of 30 August 2001.   71

A.P. Møller, Case IV/M969, decision of 10 February 1999, [1999]
OJ L183/29.   30, 89

ABB/BREL, Case IV/M221, decision of 26 May 1992.   47

ABB/Daimler-Benz, Case IV/M580, decision of 18 October 1995,
[1997] OJ L11/1.   9

ABB/Renault Automation, Case IV/M409, decision of 9 March 1994.   70, 130

ABC/Générale des Eaux/Canal+/W.H.Smith TV, Case IV/M110,
decision of 10 September 1991.   27

Accor/Ebertz/Dorint, Case COMP/M2997, decision of 23 December
2002.   30, 32

Accor/Wagons-Lits, Case IV/M126, decision of 28 April 1992,
[1992] OJ L204/1 of 21 July 1992.   103-105, 124, 139,
147-148, 249

Adeg/Edeka, Case IV/M1303, decision of 9 November 1998.   95, 109, 122

AEGON/Scottish Equitable, Case IV/M349, decision of 25 June 1993.   203

Aérospatiale-Alenia/De Haviland, Case IV/M053, decision of 2
October 1991, [1991] OJ L334/42.   250

AG/Amev, Case IV/M018, decision of 21 November 1990.   32, 217-219, 221-222

AGF/LA UNION Y EL FENIX, Case IV/M403, decision of 25
April 1994.   219

AGF/Royal, Case IV/M1131, decision of 23 April 1998.   55

Air France/Sabena, Case IV/M157, decision of 5 October 1992.   132, 180

Airbus, Case COMP/M2061, decision of 18 October 2000.   252

Aker Maritime/Kvaerner (II), Case COMP/M2683, decision of 23
January 2002.   237, 238, 242

Akzo/Nobel Industries, Case IV/M390, decision of 10 January 1994.   65, 69, 70

Alcan/Alusuisse, Case COMP/M1663, decision of 14 March 2000.   24

Alcan/Inespal/Palco, Case IV/M322, decision of 14 April 1993.   130

Alcan/Pechiney, Case COMP/M1715, aborted.   25

Alcatel/AEG Kabel Case IV/M165, decision of 18 December 1991.   9

Alcatel/STC, Case IV/M366, decision of 13 September 1993.   65, 184-185

Alcatel/Telettra, Case IV/M042, decision of 12 April 1991, [1991] OJ L122/48.   43

Alcoa/British Aluminium, Case COMP/M2111, decision of 27 October 2000.   66

Alliance Unichem/Unifarma, Case IV/M1220, decision of 23 July 1998.   8

Allianz/AGF, Case IV/M1082, decision of 8 May 1998.   55

Allianz/DKV, Case IV/M252, decision of 10 September 1992.   208-209

Allianz/Elvia/Lloyd Adriatico, Case IV/M539, decision of 3 April 1995.   65, 66

Allianz/Hermes, Case IV/M813, decision of 27 September 1996.   64, 141, 256

Allianz/Vereinte, Case IV/M812, decision of 11 November 1996.   64, 256

Ameritech/TeleDanmark, Case IV/M1046, decision of 5 December 1997.   122

Andersen Consulting/BT/JV, Case COMP/M1994, decision of 28 July 2000.   109

Anglo American/Tarmac, Case COMP/M1779, decision of 13 January 2000.   8

Anglo American Corporation/Lonrho, Case IV/M754, decision of 23 April 1997, [1998] OJ L149/21.   66

AOL/Time Warner, Case COMP/M1845, decision of 11 October 2000.   232

Arjomari-Prioux/Wiggins Teape Appleton, Case IV/M025, decision of 10 December 1990.   84, 91, 100-103, 138

Asahi Glass/Mitsubishi/F2 Chemicals, Case COMP/JV42, decision of 21 March 2000.   27

ASKO/Jacobs/Adia, Case IV/M082, decision of 16 May 1991.   28

ASKO/Omni, Case IV/M065, decision of 21 February 1991.   203

Astra/Zeneca, Case COMP/M1403, decision of 26 February 1999.   242

AT&T/IBM Global Network, Case IV/M1396, decision of 22 April 1999.   45

Auchan/Leroy Merlin/IFIL/La Rinascente, Case IV/M934, decision of 16 June 1997.   30

Avesta/British Steel/NCC, Case IV/M239, decision of 4 September 1992.   27, 32-33

Avesta (II), Case IV/M452, decision of 9 June 1994. 49-50

AXA-UAP/Royale Belge, Case IV/M1193, decision of 12 June 1998. 47

Avnet/Veba Electronics, Case COMP/M2134, decision of 18 October 2000. 41

Babcock Borsig/AE Energietechnik, Case IV/M1552, decision of
30 June 1999. 85

Bain/Hoechst-Dade Behring, Case IV/M954, decision of 2 September
1997. 27, 32

Balli/Klockner, Case COMP/M2481, decision of 31 September 2001. 11

Banco Santander Central Hispanico/AKB, Case COMP/M2578,
decision of 12 November 2001. 98

Banesto/Totta, Case IV/M192, decision of 14 April 1992. 84, 219

Bank Austria/Creditanstalt, Case IV/M873, decision of 11 March 1997. 137

Bank of New York/Royal Bank of Scotland/RBSI Security Services,
Case IV/M1660, decision of 26 August 1999. 70, 258

Bank of New York/Royal Bank of Scotland Trust Bank, Case IV/M1618,
decision of 25 August 1999. 70, 258

BASF/Shell, Case IV/M1041, decision of 23 December 1997. 38

BASF/Svalöf Weibull, Case IV/M1420, decision of 3 March 1999. 32

Bass Plc/Saison Holdings BV, Case IV/M1133, decision of 23 March
1998. 105

Bayer/Röhm/Makroform, Case COMP/M1814, decision of 17 April 2000. 32

Bayernwerk/Isarwerk, Case IV/M808, decision of 25 November 1996. 8

BC Funds/Sanitec, Case COMP/M2397, decision of 6 June 2001. 105

Bell Cable Media/Cable & Wireless/Videotron, Case IV/M853,
decision of 11 December 1996. 66

Bertelsmann/Kirch/Premiere, Case IV/M993, decision of 27 May 1998,
OJ L53/1 of 27.2.1999. 9

BHF/Billiton, Case COMP/M2413, decision of 14 June 2001. 11

BHP/Mitsubishi/QCT, Case COMP/M2153, decision of 28 September
2000. 273

Blokker/Toys 'R' Us, Case IV/M890, decision of 26 June 1997,
[1998] OJ L316. 45, 105

Boeing/McDonnel Douglas, Case IV/M877, decision of 30 July 1997,
[1997] OJ L336/16. 269

Bombardier/ADtranz, Case COMP/M2139, decision of 3 April 2001,
[2002] OJ L69/50.   135

Bosch/Allied Signal, Case IV/M726, decision of 9 April 1996.   25

Bosch/Rexroth, Case COMP/M2060, decision of 4 December 2000.   41

BP Chemicals/Solvay/HDPE JV, Case COMP/M2299, decision of
29 October 2001.   71

BP Chemicals/Solvay (PP), Case COMP/M2297, decision of
29 October 2001.   54, 71

BP/E.ON, Case COMP/M2533, decision of 6 September 2001.   8

BP/JV Dissolution, Case COMP/M1820, decision of 2 February 2000.   54

BP/PETROMED, Case IV/M111, decision of 29 July 1991.   84

Bravida/Semco/Prenad/Totalinstallatören/Backlunds, Case
COMP/M3004, decision of 13 December 2002.   67

British Aerospace/GEC Marconi, Case IV/M1438, decision of 25 June 1999.   11

British Aerospace/Lagardère, Case IV/M820, decision of 23 September 1996.   11

British Aerospace/VSEL, Case IV/M528, decision of 24 November 1994.   11

British Airways/Air Liberté, Case IV/M857, decision of 28 February
1997.   65, 142, 181

British Airways/Dan Air, Case IV/M278, decision of 17 February 1993.   9-10, 282

British Airways/TAT, Case IV/M259, decision of 27 November 1992.   180

British Airways/TAT (II), Case IV/M806, decision of 26 August 1996.   158

British Steel/Europipe, Case IV/M1014, decision of 26 February 1998.   130

British Steel/Hoogovens, Case IV/M1595, decision of 15 July 1999.   11

British Steel/Svensk Stål/NSD, Case IV/M503, decision of 7 November
1994.   11, 242

British Telecom/MCI(II), Case IV/M856, decision of 14 May 1997,
[1997] OJ L336/1.   185

BSCH/A. Champalimaud, Case IV/M1616, decisions of 20 July 1999 and
20 October 1999.   13

BT/Concert, Case COMP/M2642, decision of 17 December 2001.   54

Campsa, Case IV/M138, decision of 19 December 1991.   53-54

Canal+/Lagardère, Case COMP/JV47, decision of 22 June 2000.   25, 98

Canal+/Lagardère/Liberty Media, Case COMP/JV40, decision of 22
June 2000.   25, 98

Cap Gemini/Ernst & Young, Case COMP/M1901, decision of 17 May 2000.   108-109

Cargill/Vandemoortele, Case IV/M1126, decision of 20 July 1998.   86

Cargill/Vandemoortele – JV, Case IV/M1227, decision of 20 July 1998.   86

Carlyle/Gruppo Riello, Case COMP/M2003, decision of 27 June 2000.   28

Carnival Corporation/P&O Princess, Case COMP/M2706, decision of 24 July 2002.   9, 182

Castle Tower/TDF/Candover/Berkshire, Case IV/M887, decision of 27 February 1997.   27

CCIE/GTE, Case IV/M258, decision of 25 September 1992.   54

CD & R Fund VI Limited/Brake Bros Plc, Case COMP/M2891, decision of 25 July 2002.   105

CEA Industrie/France Télécom/Finmeccanica/SGS-Thomson, Case IV/M216, decision of 22 February 1993.   49, 129, 130

Celestica/IBM (EMS), Case COMP/M1841, decision of 25 February 2000.   45

Cereol/Aceprosa, Case IV/M720, decision of 7 June 1996.   43

Cereol/Continentale Italiana, Case IV/M156, decision of 27 November 1991.   149-150

Cereol/Sofiproteol-Saipol, Case IV/M1125, decision of 10 March 1998.   85

CGEA/South Eastern Train Company Limited, Case IV/M816, decision of 7 October 1996.   65

CNH/FHE, Case COMP/M2369, decision of 26 June 2001.   25

Coca-Cola/Amalgamated Beverages GB, Case IV/M794, decision of 22 January 1997, [1997] OJ L218/15.   98

Compagnie Nationale de Navigation/Sogelfa-CIM, Case IV/M1021, decision of 1 December 1997.   8

Compass/Restorama/Rail Gourmet/Gourmet Nova, Case COMP/M2639, decision of 26 February 2002.   237

Constructor/Dexion, Case IV/M1318, decision of 30 October 1998.   233

Courtaulds/SNIA, Case IV/M113, decision of 19 December 1991.   102

Credit Suisse/Nikko/MSA, Case IV/M1273, decision of 14 August 1998.   32

Credit Suisse First Boston/Barclays, Case IV/M1068, decision of 19 December 1997.   193, 232

Cruzcampo/Heineken, Case IV/M1555, decision of 17 August 1999.   8

CSME/MSCA/ROCK, Case IV/M1522, decision of 11 June 1999.   8

Daimler Benz/Deutsche Telekom – Telematik, Case IV/M962, decision
of 31 July 1997.   145

Dana/GKN, Case COMP/M1587, decision of 4 November 1999.   71

Danish Crown/Vestjyske Slagterier, Case IV/M1313, decision of 9
March 1999, [2000] OJ L20/1.   25, 117

Degussa/Laporte, Case COMP/M2277, decision of 12 March 2001.   139

Deloitte & Touche/Andersen (UK), Case COMP/M2810, decision of 1
July 2002.   107, 109

Delta Air Lines/Pan Am, Case IV/M130, decision of 13 September 1991.   45, 180

Deutsche Bank/Banco de Madrid, Case IV/M341, decision of 28 May 1993.   64, 141

Deutsche Bank/Commerzbank/J.M. Voith, Case IV/M891, decision of
23 April 1997.   40, 216

Deutsche BP/Erdölchemie, Case COMP/M2345, decision of 26 April
2001.   136

Deutsche Post/Securicor, Case IV/M1347, decision of 23 February 1999.   155

Deutsche Telekom/BetaResearch, Case IV/M1027, decision of 27 May 1998,
OJ [1999] L53/31.   9

Deutsche Telekom/SAP-S, Case IV/M705, decision of 29 March 1996.   137

DFO/Scandlines, Case IV/M1045, decision of 29 January 1998.   130

DIA/VEBA Immobilien/Deutschbau, Case IV/M929, decision of 23 June
1997.   27

Digital/Kienzle, Case IV/M057, decision of 22 February 1991.   43

DLJ/FM Holdings, Case IV/M1139, decision of 28 April 1998.   233

Dresdner Bank/Banque Nationale de Paris, Case IV/M021, decision
of 4 February 1991.   31

Du Pont/ICI, Case IV/M214, decision of 30 September 1992, [1993]
OJ L7/13.   24, 54

EADS, Case COMP/M1745, decision of 11 May 2000.   131

EDF/London Electricity, Case IV/M1346, decision of 27 January 1999.   9, 13

EDF/South Western Electricity, Case IV/M1606, decision of 19 July
1999.   12, 45

EDF/TXU Europe/24 Seven, Case COMP/M2679, decision of 20
December 2001.   71

EDF/TXU Europe/West Burton Power Station, Case COMP/M2675,
   decision of 20 December 2001.   71

EDFI/ESTAG, Case IV/M1107, decision of 17 May 1998.   130

EDS/Lufthansa, Case IV/M560, decision of 11 May 1995.   181

Electrabel/Epon, Case IV/M1803, decision of 7 February 2000.   12

Electrolux/AEG, Case IV/M458, decision of 21 June 1994.   242

Elektrowatt/Landis & Gyr, Case IV/M692, decision of 12 February 1996. 102

Elenac/Hoechst, Case IV/M1287, decision of 24 November 1998.   38

Elf/Occidental, Case IV/M085, decision of 13 June 1991.   84

ELG Haniel/Jewometaal, Case IV/M849, decision of 25 November 1996.   11

Elkem/Sapa, Case COMP/M2404, decision of 26 June 2001.   84

Employers Reinsurance Corporation/Aachener Rückversicherungs-
   Gesellschaft AG, Case IV/M601, decision of 30 June 1995.   203

Enderly/S.B.E., Case IV/M789, decision of 15 July 1996.   27

Endesa/CDF/SNET, Case COMP/M2281, decision of 17 April 2001.   11

Enel/FT/Wind/Infostrada, Case COMP/M2216, decision of 19 January 2001.   8

Enron/MG, Case COMP/M2006, decision of 4 July 2000.   45, 85-86

ERC/NRG Victory, Case IV/M433, decision of 27 May 1994.   203

Ericsson/Raychem, Case IV/M519, decision of 21 November 1994.   241

Eridania/ISI, Case IV/M062, decision of 20 July 1991.   113

Ernst & Young/Andersen Germany, Case COMP/M2824, decision of 27 August
   2002.   109

Ernst & Young France/Andersen France, Case COMP/M2816, decision of 5
   September 2002.   109

Eucom/Digital, Case IV/M218, decision of 18 May 1992.   36

Eureko, Case IV/M207, decision of 27 April 1992.   27

Eurocom/RSCG, Case IV/M147, decision of 18 December 1991.   90

Exxon/Mobil, Case IV/M1383, decision of 29 September 1999.   9

Ferruzi Finanziaria/Fondiaria, Case IV/M576, decision of 9 June 1995.   47

Fletcher Challenge/Methanex, Case IV/M331, decision of 31 March 1993.   27

Flextronics/Italdata, Case COMP/M2116, decision of 25 September 2000.   45

Ford/Jardine, Case IV/M1435, decision of 23 February 1999.   38

Fortis/CGER, Case IV/M342, decision of 15 November 1993.   70, 133

Fortis/La Caixa, Case IV/M254, decision of 5 November 1992.   38

France Telecom/EDITEL/LINCE, Case IV/M1553, decision of 30 July 1999.   36

Frantschach/B+K/Volfin, Case IV/M733, decision of 8 May 1996.   123

Frantschach/Bischof+Klein/F+B Verpackungen, Case IV/M961, decision of
    26 September 1997.   25

GE/Power Controls B.V., Case IV/M577, decision of 28 April 1995.   47

GEAL/CREA/CGE, Case IV/M1186, decision of 18 June 1998.   128, 131

GEC/Thomson-CSF (II), Case IV/M724, decision of 15 May 1996.   11

GEC/VSEL, Case IV/M529, decision of 7 December 1994.   11

GEC Alsthom NV/AEG, Case IV/M706, decision of 3 September 1996.   38

GEC Marconi/Alenia, Case IV/M1258, decision of 28 August 1998.   11

GECC/AVIS LEASE, Case IV/M234, decision of 15 July 1992.   196

GEES/Unison, Case COMP/M2738, decision of 17 April 2002.   10

Gehe/Lloyds Chemists, Case IV/M716, decision of 22 March 1996.   8

Gencor/Shell, Case IV/M470, decision of 29 August 1994.   81, 122

General Re/Kölnische Re, Case IV/M491, decision of 24 October 1994.   203

Generali/AMB/Athena, Case IV/M1098, decision of 23 April 1998.   55

GKN/Brambles/SKP, Case IV/M1160, decision of 26 May 1998.   249

Go-Ahead/VIA/Thameslink, Case IV/M901, decision of 24 April 1997.   27, 139

Govia/Connex South Central, Case COMP/M2446, decision of 20 July 2001.   8

Granaria/Ûltje/Intersnack/May-Holding, Case COMP/JV32, decision of 28
    February 2000.   26, 123

Grand Metropolitan/Cinzano, Case IV/M184, decision of 7 February 1992.   47

GTS Hermes Inc./HIT Rail BV, Case IV/M683, decision of 5 March 1996.   35

Haniel/Fels, Case COMP/M2495, decision of 17 October 2001.   8

Haniel/Ytong, Case COMP/M2568, decision of 30 November 2001.   8

Henkel/Schwarzkopf, Case IV/M630, decision of 31 October 1995.   156

Hicks/Bear Stearns/Johns Manville, Case COMP/M2133, decision of
    25 September 2000.   28

Hitachi/IBM Harddisk Business, Case COMP/M2821, decision of 2
    August 2002.   43

Hochtief/Aer Rianta/Düsseldorf Airport, Case IV/M1035, decision of
    22 December 1997.   27, 130-131

Hoechst/Wacker, Case IV/M284, decision of 10 May 1993.   31

Holdercim/Cedest, Case IV/M460, decision of 6 July 1994.   8

Hong Kong and Shanghai Bank/Midland, Case IV/M213, decision
of 21 May 1992.   166, 219-220, 222

IBM/PWC Consulting, Case COMP/M2946, decision of 23
September 2002.   109

IBM France/CGI, Case IV/M336, decision of 19 May 1993.   12

ICI/Tioxide, Case IV/M023, decision of 28 November 1990.   47

ICI/Unilever, Case IV/M933, decision of 23 June 1997.   232

ICI/Williams, Case IV/M1167, decision of 29 april 1998 .   233

ICL/Nokia Data, Case IV/M105, decision of 17 July 1991.   43

IFINT/EXOR, Case IV/M187, decision of 2 March 1992.   83, 84, 92-95, 102, 125

INA/LuK, Case COMP/M1789, decision of 22 December 1999.   47

Inchcape plc/Gestetner Holding PLC, Case IV/M583, decision of
1 June 1995.   143

Industri Kapital (Nordkem/Dyno), Case COMP/M1813, decision of
12 July 2000.   242

Ingersoll-Rand/Clark Equipment, Case IV/M588, decision of 15
May 1995.   64, 141

Ingersoll-Rand/MAN, Case IV/479, decision of 28 July 1994.   70

Interbrew/Bass, Case COMP/M2044, decision of 22 August 2000.   8

Ispat/Unimetal, Case IV/M1509, decision of 22 June 1999.   30

IVO/Stockholm Energi, Case IV/M1231, decision of 5 August 1998. 132

James River/Rayne, Case IV/M162, decision of 13 February 1992. 51

JCSAT/SAJAC, Case IV/M346, decision of 30 June 1993.   272-273

Jefferson Smurfit Group Plc/Munksjo AB, Case IV/M613, decision of
31 July 1995.   81, 102

Kali + Salz/MdK/Treuhand, Case IV/M308, decison of 14 December 1993,
[1994] OJ L186/38.   131

Kali+Salz/Mdk/Treuhand, Case IV/M308, decision of 9 July 1998. 87

Kelt/American Express, Case IV/M116, decision of 20 August 1991. 45

Kesko/Tuko, Case IV/M784, decision of 20 November 1996, OJ L110/53,
26.4.1997.   10

Kingfisher/BUT, Case IV/M1248, decision of 21 August 1998.   105

Kingfisher/Grosslabor, Case IV/M1482, decision of 12 April 1999. 52-53, 65

Kirch/Richemont/Multichoice/Telepiù, Case IV/M584, decision of 5 May
1995.   33

Klöckner/Comercial de Laminados, Case IV/M971, decision of 26
    August 1997.   11, 77

Klöckner/ODS, Case IV/M918, decision of 5 August 1997.   11, 47, 77

Knorr-Bremse/Robert Bosch, Case IV/M1342, decision of 14
    December 1998.   51

KNP/BT/VRG, Case IV/M291, decision of 4 May 1993, [1993]
    OJ L217/35.   88

Kohlberg Kravis Roberts/Wassall/Zumtobel, Case COMP/M1876,
    decision of 13 April 2000.   32

Koipe-Tabacalerea/Elosua, Case IV/M117, decision of 28 July 1992.   130

Krauss-Maffei/Wegmann, Case IV/M1153, decision of 19 June 1998.   8

Krupp/Thyssen/Riva/Falck/Tadfin/AST, Case IV/M484, decision of
    21 December 1994, [1995] OJ L251/18.   27

Krupp (II), Case IV/M740, decision of 2 May 1996.   11

Krupp Hoesch/Thyssen, Case IV/M925, decision of 11 August 1997.   11

L'Oréal/Procasa/Cosmétique Iberica/Albesa, Case IV/M957, decision
    of 19 September 1997.   24

La Redoute/Empire, Case IV/M080, decision of 25 April 1991.   81, 89

La Roche/Syntex, Case IV/M457, decision of 20 June 1994.   202

Lafarge/Redland, Case IV/M1030, decision of 16 December 1997.   8

Leroy Merlin/Brico, Case COMP/M2898, decisions of 11, 12 and
    13 December 2002.   9

Lufthansa/Menzies/LSG/JV, Case COMP/M1913, decision of 29
    August 2000.   252

Lyonnaise des Eaux/Northumbrian Water, Case IV/M567, decision
    of 21 December 1995.   12

Lyonnaise des Eaux Dumez/Brochier, Case IV/M076, decision of
    11 July 1991.   30

Maersk Air/LFV Holding, Case IV/M1124, decision of 6 July 1998.   132

Magnetti Marelli/CEAC, Case IV/M043, decision of 24 May 1991,
    [1991] OJ L222/38.   43

MAN Roland/Omnigraph (II), Case IV/M1448, decision of 5 May 1999.   47

Mannesmann/Hoesch, Case IV/M222, decision of 12 November 1992,
    [1993] OJ L114/34.   9, 71

Mannesmann/Vallourec, Case IV/M906, decision of 3 June 1997.   11, 86, 91, 98

Mannesmann Demag/Delaval Stork, Case IV/M535, decision of
    21 December 1994.   70

Marconi/Finmeccanica, Case IV/M496, decision of 5 September 1994.   130

Marine-Wendel/SAirGroup/AOM, Case IV/M1494, decision of
    3 August 1999.   181

Masterfoods/Royal Canin, Case COMP/M2544, decision of 15 February
    2002.   224, 241

Matra/Aérospatiale, Case IV/M1309, decision of 28 April 1999.   11, 32

McCormick/CPC/Rabobank/Ostmann, Case IV/M330, decision of
    29 October 1993.   8, 24, 25

McDermott/ETPM, Case IV/M648, decision of 27 November 1995.   117, 125, 293

McDermott/ETPM (Deconcentration), Case IV/M1154, decision of
    4 June 1998.   54

MCI WorldCom/Sprint, Case COMP/M1741, decision of 28 June 2000.   86, 274

Médèric/ORRPIMMEC/CRI/Munich Re, Case IV/M949, decision of
    2 July 1997.   27

Metallgesellschaft/Safic-Alcan (II), Case IV/M834, decision of
    21 November 1996.   47

Metronet/Infraco, Case COMP/M2694, decision of 21 June 2002.   20

Metsäliitto Osuuskunta/Vapo Oy/JV, Case COMP/M2234, decision
    of 8 February 2001.   8

Michel Mineralölhandel/Thyssen-Elf Oil, Case COMP/M2335,
    decision of 28 February 2001.   45

Midland Bank, see Hong Kong and Shanghai Bank/Midland.

Mitsubishi Bank/Tokyo Bank, Case IV/M596, decision of 17 July
    1995.   293

Mobil/JV Dissolution, Case IV/M1822, decision of 2 February 2000.   54

Mondi/Frantschach, Case IV/M210, decision of 12 May 1992.   30

Montedison/Groupe Vernes/SCI, Case IV/M639, decision of 8
    December 1995.   27

MRW/MHP, Case IV/M886, decision of 22 April 1997.   158

MSG Media Service, Case IV/M469, decision of 9 November 1994,
    [1994] OJ L364/1.   9

Nabisco/United Biscuits, Case COMP/M1920, decision of 5 May 2000.   9

NAW/SALTANO/CONTRAC, Case IV/M698, decision of 26 February
    1996.   27

Nehlsen/Rethmann/SWB/Bremerhavener Entsorgungsgesellschaft, Case COMP/M2760, decision of 30 May 2002.   9

Neste/IVO, Case IV/M931, decision of 2 June 1998.   129

Nestlé/Pillsbury/Häagen-Dazs US, Case IV/M1689, decision of 6 October 1999.   273

Nestlé/Ralston Purina, Case COMP/M2337, decision of 27 July 2001.   224, 241

Newspaper Publishing, Case IV/M423, decision of 14 March 1994.   12

Nomura/Blueslate, Case IV/M1037, decision of 17 November 1997.   98, 99, 176

Noranda Forest/Glunz, Case IV/M599, decision of 8 September 1995.   102

Nordic Capital/Transpool, Case IV/M625, decision of 23 August 1995.   203

Norsk Hydro/Enichem Agricoltura-Terni (II), Case IV/M832, decision of 25 October 1996.   65

Norsk Hydro/Saga, Case IV/M1573, decision of 5 July 1999.   41, 230, 242

Norske Skog/ABITIBI/PAPCO, Case COMP/M2493, decision of 3 July 2001.   49

Northern Telecom/Matra, Case IV/M249, decision of 10 August 1992.   30

OK Ekonomisk Förening/Kuwait Petroleum Sverige AB, Case IV/M1256, decision of 21 December 1998.   109

Orkla/Volvo, Case IV/M582, decision of 20 September 1995.   242

Paribas/MBH, Case IV/M122, decision of 17 October 1991.   84, 190-191

Particitel International/Cableuropa, Case IV/M1251, decision of 30 July 1998.   49

Pechiney/Usinor, Case IV/M097, decision of 24 June 1991.   129

Péchiney World Trade/Minemet Case IV/M473, decision of 20 July 1994.   128

Pepsico/KAS, Case IV/M289, decision of 21 December 1992.   65

Pernod Ricard/Diageo/Seagram Spirits, Case COMP/M2268, decision of 8 May 2001.   242

Philips/Lucent Technologies (II), Case IV/M1358, decision of 6 January 1999.   54

PowerGen/NRG Energy/Morrison Knudsen/Mibrag, Case IV/M402, decision of 27 June 1994.   11

Preussag/Babcock Borsig, Case IV/M1594, decision of 17 August 1999.   85, 139

Preussag/ELCO Looser, Case IV/M714, decision of 14 March 1996.   137

Price Waterhouse/Coopers & Lybrand, Case IV/M1016, decision of
20 May 1998, [1999] OJ L50/27.   106-109

Promatech/Sulzer Textil, Case COMP/M2698, decision of 24 July 2002.   10

Promodes/Casino, Case IV/M991, decision of 30 October 1997.   8

Promodes/S21/Gruppo GS, Case IV/M1086, decision of 10 March 1998.   8

Prudential/HSBC/Finnish Chemicals Case IV/M883, decision of
13 February 1997.   26-27

PTT Post/TNT/GD Express Worldwide, Case IV/M843, decision of
8 November 1996.   124

PTT Post/TNT-GD Net, Case IV/M787, decision of 22 July 1996.   50

Publicis/BCOM3, Case COMP/M2785, decision of 18 June 2002.   20

Rabobank/Beeck/Homann, Case IV/M1461, 6 April 1999.   8

Reckitt & Colman plc/Benckiser NV., Case IV/M1632, decision of
3 September 1999.   15

Renault/Volvo, Case IV/M004, decision of 7 November 1990.   81

Rheinmetall/British Aerospace/STN Atlas, Case IV/M894, decision
of 24 April 1997.   8, 136

Rhodia/Donau Chemie/Albright & Wilson, Case IV/M1517, decision
of 13 July 1999.   25

Rhône-Poulenc/Novalis/Nyltech, Case IV/M1083, decision of 15 April
1998.   66

Rhône-Poulenc/SNIA, Case IV/M206, decision of 10 August 1992.   102, 130

Rhône Poulenc/SNIA II, Case IV/M355, decision of 8 September 1993.   102

Rhône Poulenc Rorer/Fisons, Case IV/M632, decision of 21 September
1995.   64, 85, 141

Rhône Poulenc-SNIA/Nordfaser, Case IV/M399, decision of 3 February
1994.   102

Ricoh/Gestetner Case, Case IV/M622, decision of 12 September 1995.   143

RMC/UMA/JV, Case COMP/M2596, decision of 12 March 2003.   281

Royal & Sun Alliance/Trygg Hansa, Case IV/M1617, decision of
26 August 1999.   54

RTL/Veronica/Endemol, Case IV/M553, decision of 20 September 1995,
[1996] OJ L134/32.   10

RVI/VBC/Heuliez, Case IV/M092, decision of 3 June 1991.   51, 81

RWE/Kärtner Energie Holding, Case COMP/M2513, decision of
2 August 2001.   131

RWE/Thyssengas, Case IV/M713, decision of 25 November 1996.   8

RWE/Vivendi/Berliner Wasserbetriebe, Case IV/M1633, decision of
13 September 1999.   131

Saab/Celsius, Case COMP/M1797, decision of 4 February 2000.   11

Saab Ericsson Space, Case IV/M178, decision of 13 January 1992.   33, 230

Saint Gobain/Wacker Chemie/NOM, Case IV/M774, decision of
4 December 1996.   27, 45

Salzgitter/Mannesmann-Röhrenwerke, Case COMP/M2045, decision
of 5 September 2000.   11

Sampo/Storebrand, Case COMP/M2491, decision of 27 July 2001.   234, 241, 243

Sampo/Varma Sampo/If Holding/JV, Case COMP/M2676, decision of
18 December 2001.   242

Sanitec/Sphinx, Case IV/M1578, decision of 1 December 1999,
[2000] OJ L294/1.   242

Sanmina-SCI/Hewlett Packard, Case COMP/M2815, decision of
28 May 2002.   45

Sanofi/Kodak, Case IV/M480, decision of 12 July 1994.   47

Sara Lee/BP Food Division, Case IV/M299, decision of 8 February
1993.   72

Saudi Aramco/MOH, Case IV/M574, decision of 23 May 1995.   30

SCA/Graninge/Scaninge Timber, Case COMP/M1996, decision of
5 July 2000.   122

SCA/Metsä Tissue, Case COMP/M2097, decision of 31 January 2001,
[2002] OJ L57/1.   242

Scandinavian Project, Case IV/M522, decision of 28 November
1994.   24, 27, 65, 70, 241

Schneider/Lexel, Case IV/M1434, decision of 3 June 1999.   242

Schroders/Liberty International Pensions Limited, Case COMP/M1997,
decision of 28 June 2000.   109

SEB/Moulinex, Case COMP/M2621, decisions of 8 January 2002.   8, 164

Secil/Holderbank/Cimpor(Art. 21), Case COMP/M2171, decision of
22 November 2000.   13

Sehb/Viag/PE/BEWAG, Case IV/M932, decision of 25 July 1997.   8

Sextant/BGT-VDO, Case IV/M290, decision of 21 December 1992.   27

Shell/DEA, Case COMP/M2389, decision of 23 August 2001.　　8

Shell/Monteshell, Case IV/M505, decision of 16 December 1994.　　252

Shell Chimie/ELF Atochem, Case IV/M475, decision of 22 December 1994.　　242

Shell UK/Gulf Oil (Great Britain), Case IV/M1013, decision of 28 November 1997.　　139

Sidmar/Klöckner Stahl, Case IV/M444, decision of 30 May 1994.　　27

Siebe/APV, Case IV/M936, decision of 16 June 1997.　　138

Siebe/BTR, Case IV/M1380, decision of 13 January 1999.　　138

Siemens/Dematic/Sachs/VDO, Case COMP/M2059, decision of 29 August 2000.　　41, 66

Siemens/E.ON/Shell/SSG, Case COMP/M2367, decision of 27 March 2001.　　242

Siemens/HUF, Case IV/M912, decision of 29 April 1997.　　145

Siemens/Italtel, Case IV/M468, decision of 17 February 1995, [1995] OJ L161/27.　　130

Siemens/Italtel, Case IV/M1717, decision of 15 December 1999.　　54, 130, 133

Siemens/Philips Kabel, Case IV/M238, decision of 8 January 1993.　　9

Siemens/Sommer Alibert, Case IV/M800, decision of 14 August 1996.　　145

Skandia/Storebrand/Pohjola, Case IV/JV21, decision of 17 August 1999.　　242

Skanska/Scancem, Case IV/M1157, decision of 11 November 1998, [1999] OJ L183/1.　　242

SLDE/NTL/MSCP/NOOS, Case COMP/M2137, decision of 16 October 2000.　　109

Société Générale de Belgique/Générale de Banque, Case IV/M343, decision of 3 August 1993.　　219

Sogecable/Canalsatélite Digital/Vìa Digital, Case COMP/M2845, decision of 14 August 2002.　　9

Solectron/Ericsson, Case COMP/M1849, decision of 29 February 2000.　　45

Solvay-Laporte/Interox, Case IV/M197, decision of 30 April 1992.　　12, 53-54

Spar/Dansk Supermarked, Case IV/M179, decision of 3 February 1992.　　84

Starck/Wienerberger, Case IV/M702, decision of 1 March 1996.　　189

Steetley/Tarmac, Case IV/M180, decision of 12 February 1992.　　8

Stinnes/BTL, Case IV/M1056, decision of 4 February 1998.   54

Stinnes/HCI, Case COMP/M2202, decision of 4 December 2000.   139

STRABAG/Bank Austria/STUAG, Case IV/M661, decision of 15 January 1996.   102

Sun Alliance/Royal Insurance, Case IV/M759, decision of 18 June 1996.   12

Swiss Life/I.N.C.A., Case IV/M644, decision of 25 October 1995.   106

Swissair/Allders International, Case IV/M782, decision of 17 July 1996.   125

Swissair/Sabena, Case IV/M616, decision of 20 July 1995.   131-132, 181

Synthomer/Yule Catto, Case IV/M376, decision of 22 October 1993.   51

Telecom Eireann, Case IV/M802, decision of 18 December 1996.   131

Telia/Sonera/Motorola/Omnitel, Case IV/JV9, decision of 18 August 1998.   274

Telia/Telenor, Case IV/M1439, decision of 13 October 1999, [2001] OJ L40/1.   241

Telia/Telenor/Schibsted, Case IV/JV1, decision of 27 May 1998.   242

Tetra Pak/Alfa-Laval, Case IV/M069, decision of 19 July 1991.   230

Texaco/Norsk Hydro, Case IV/M511, decision of 9 January 1995.   133

The Airline Group/NATS, Case COMP/M2315, decision of 14 May 2001.   242

Thomas Cook/Sunworld, Case IV/M785, decision of 7 August 1996.   177

Thomson/Daimler-Benz, Case IV/M744, decision of 21 May 1996, [1996] OJ C179/3.   116

Thomson CSF/Deutsche Aerospace, Case IV/M527, decision of 2 December 1994.   242

Thomson-CSF/Eurocopter, Case IV/M1516, decision of 10 June 1999.   38

Thomson-CSF/Finmeccanica/Elettronica, Case IV/M767, decision of 29 July 1996.   130

Thyssen/Krupp, Case IV/M1080, decision of 2 June 1998.   11

TNT/GD Net, Case IV/M102, decision of 2 December 1991.   35-36, 178

Torras/Sarrio, Case IV/M166, decision of 24 February 1992.   86, 130, 139, 198, 219

Totalfina/Elf Aquitaine, Case IV/M1628, decision of 5 October 1999.   8

Toyota Motor/Toyota Denmark, Case IV/M1592, decision of 23 July 1999.   152

Toys 'R' Us/Blokker, Case IV/M890, decision of 26 June 1997, [1998] OJ L316/1.   10

Tractebel/Distrigaz II, Case IV/M493, decision of 1 September 1994.   102

Tractebel/Synatom, Case IV/M466, decision of 30 June 1994. 102

TWD/Akzo Nobel-Kuagtextil, Case IV/M533, decision of 10 February 1995. 189

UBS/Mister Minit, Case IV/M940, decision of 9 July 1997. 105

Unilever/Diversey, Case IV/M704, decision of 20 March 1996. 25

Unilever France/Amora-Maille, Case COMP/M1802, decision of 8 March 2000. 85

UPM-Kymmene/April, Case IV/M1006, decision of 11 June 1998. 233

Usinor/Arbed/Aceralia, Case COMP/M2382, decision of 19 July 2001. 11

Usinor/ASD, Case IV/M073, decision of 29 April 1991. 11

Usinor/Cockerill Sambre, Case IV/M1329, decision of 4 February 1999. 11

USINOR/FINARVEDI, Case IV/M1203, decision of 29 September 1998. 11

Valinox/Timet, Case IV/M917, decision of 12 June 1997. 86, 90, 95-98

Varta/Bosch Case IV/M012, decision of 31 July 1991, [1991] OJ L320/26. 9

Vendex/KBB, Case IV/M1060, decision of 26 May 1998. 8

Viag/Bayernwerk, Case IV/M417, decision of 5 May 1994. 77

VIAG/EB BRÜHL, Case IV/M139, decision of 19 December 1991. 54

Vivendi Universal/Hachette (Lagardère)/Multithématique, Case COMP/M2766, decision of 3 May 2002. 98

Voith/Sulzer, Case IV/M478, decision of 29 July 1994. 241

Volkswagen/Rolls-Royce/Cosworth, Case IV/M1283, decision of 24 August 1998. 65

Volkswagen/VAG (UK), Case IV/M304, decision of 4 February 1993. 47

Volvo/Atlas, Case IV/M152, decision of 14 January 1992. 230

Volvo/Lex (2), Case IV/M261, decision of 3 September 1992. 65, 68, 72

Volvo/Procordia, Case IV/M196, decision of 11 October 1993. 230

Volvo/Scania, Case IV/M1672, decision of 14 March 2000, [2001] OJ L143/74. 242

Volvo/VME, Case IV/M575, decision of 11 April 1995. 47

Wacker/Air Products, Case IV/M1097, decision of 4 August 1998. 38, 68

Warner Bros./Lusomundo/Sogecable, Case IV/M902, decision of 12 May 1997. 35

Watt AG II, Case IV/M958, decision of 4 December 1997. 77

Winterthur/Schweizer Rück, Case IV/M518, decision of 14 March 1995.   65

WorldCom/MCI, Case IV/M1069, decision of 8 July 1998, [1999]
    OJ L116/1.   139, 183

Worms/Saint-Louis, Case IV/M909, decision of 4 June 1997.   56

WPP/Young Rubicam, Case COMP/m2000, decision of 24 August 2000.   15

WSI/Webseek, Case IV/JV8, decision of 28 September 1998.   27

Zürich/MMI, Case IV/M286, decision of 2 April 1993.   44

COMMISSION DECISIONS IN ANTITRUST CASES

RAI/Unitel, Case IV/29453, [1978] OJ L157/39.   28

Reuter/BASF, Case IV/28996, [1976] OJ L254/40.   28

DECISIONS BY THE EUROPEAN COURT OF JUSTICE AND BY THE COURT OF FIRST INSTANCE

48/69 — *ICI*, [1972] ECR 619.   264

52/69 — *Geigy*, [1972] ECR 787.   264

53/69 — *Sandoz*, [1972] ECR 845.   264

22/71 — *Béguelin Import Co.* v. *S.A.G.L. Import Export*, [1971]
    ECR 949.   78

6/72 — *Europemballage and Continental Can Co.* v. *Commission*,
    [1973] ECR 215.   2

40-48, 50, 54-56, 111, 113 and 114/73 — *Coöperatieve vereniging
'Suiker Unie' UA and others* v. *Commission of the European
Communities*, [1975] ECR 1663.   128

27/76 — *United Brands Company and United Brands Continental
B.V.* v. *Commission of the European Communities*, [1978] ECR 207.   288

85/76 — *Hoffmann-La Roche & Co. AG* v. *EC Commission
(the vitamins case)*, [1976] ECR 461.   285

35/83 — *BAT Cigaretten Fabriken GmbH* v. *Commission of the
European Communities*, [1985] ECR 363.   2, 28

170/83 — *Hydrotherm Gerätebau GmbH* v. *Firma Compact del dott.*
Ing. Mario Andreoli & C. sas, [1984] ECR 2999.   78

142 and 156/84 — *B.A.T. and R.J. Reynolds* v. *Commission*, [1987]
ECR 4487.   2

89, 104, 116, 117 and 125-129/85 — *A. Åhlström Osakeyhtiö and*
others v. *Commission of the European Communities*, [1988]
ECR 5193. ('*Wood Pulp*')   263-266, 267-268, 269

C-200/90 — *Dansk Denkavit aps and P. Poulsen Trading aps, supported*
by Monsanto-Searle A/S v. *Skatteministeriet*, [1992] ECR I-2217.   153

C-286/90 — *Anklagemyndigheden* v. *Peter Michael Poulsen and Diva*
Navigation Corp., [1992] ECR I-6019.   262

Opinion 1/91 — *Opinion of the Court of 14 December 1991. Opinion*
delivered pursuant to the second subparagraph of Article 228(1)
of the Treaty. Draft agreement between the Community, on the one
hand, and the countries of the European Free Trade Association,
on the other, relating to the creation of the European Economic Area.
[1991] ECR I-6079.   228

Opinion 1/92 — *Opinion of the Court of 10 April 1992. Opinion delivered*
pursuant to the second subparagraph of Article 228(1) of the Treaty.
Draft agreement between the Community, on the one hand, and the
countries of the European Free Trade Association, on the other,
relating to the creation of the European Economic Area.[1992]
ECR I-2821.   228

T-29/92 — *SPO and others* v. *Commission*, [1995] ECR II-289.   279

T-3/93 — *Société Anonyme à Participation Ouvrière Compagnie*
Nationale Air France v. *Commission of the European Communities*,
[1994] ECR II-121. ('*Dan Air*')   43, 58-65, 85, 137,
                                                    139, 141, 254-256

T-115/94 — *Opel Austria* v. *Council*, [1997] ECR II-39.   262

C-188/95 — *Fantask*, [1997] ECR I-6783.   280-281

C-190/95 — *ARO Lease* v. *Inspecteur van de Belastingdienst Grote*
Ondernemingen te Amsterdam, [1997] ECR I-4383.   176

T-52/96R — *Sogecable SA* v. *Commission of the European*
Communities, [1996] ECR II-797.   58, 105, 111, 121

T-102/96 — *Gencor Ltd.* v. *Commission*, [1999] ECR II-753.   266-271, 273-274,
                                                                      275

C-318/96 — *SPAR Österreichische Warenhandels* v. *Finanzlandesdirektion*
für Salzburg, [1998] ECR I-785.   281

C-36-37/97 — *Kellinghusen* v. *Amt für Land- und Wasserwirtschaft Kiel* and *Ketelsen* v. *Amt für Wasserwirtschaft Husum*, [1998] ECR I-6337. 279

T-125/97 and 127/97 — *The Coca-Cola Company and Coca-Cola Enterprises* v. *Commission,* [2000] ECR II-1733. 99

T-8/98 — *Siderca* v. *Commission*, (*see* notice in [1998] Official Journal C72/24, subsequently withdrawn). 270

C-86/99 — *Freemans* v. *Commissioners of Customs Excise*, [2001] ECR I-4167. 151

C-191/99 — *Kvaerner plc* v. *Staatssecretaris van Financiën*, [2001] ECR I-4447. 212

T-342/99 — *Airtours* v. *Commission*, [2002] ECR II-2585. 3

C-42/01 — *Portugal* v. *Commission* (pending). 13

T-310/01 (and Case T-77/02) — *Schneider Electric* v. *Commission*, judgment of 22 October 2002, (not yet reported). 3

C-491/01 — *British American Tobacco*, judgment of 10 December 2002 (not yet reported). 276

T-5/02 (and Case T-80/02) — *Tetra Laval* v. *Commission*, judgment of 25 October 2002, (not yet reported). 3

T-119/02 — *Royal Philips Electronics* v. *Commission*, judgment of 3 April 2003. 8-9

T-346/02 — *Cableuropa and others* v. *Commission* (pending). 9

T-347/02 — *Aunacable and others* v. *Commission* (pending). 9

JUDGMENTS AND DECISIONS BY NATIONAL COURTS AND AUTHORITIES AND BY THE PERMANENT COURT OF INTERNATIONAL JUSTICE

Eon/Ruhrgas, German decision that was first dealt with by the Bundes-kartellamt as E.on/Gelsenberg (Case B8-109-01neu) and E.on/Bergemann (Case B8-149-01). The two cases were joined in the Ministry of Economics (Case Gesch.-Z.:IB1-22 08 40/129). The ministerial decision was appealed to Oberlandesgericht Düsseldorf, but the complaints against the ministerial decision were subsequently withdrawn so that no judgment was rendered. (The case is reported in *Lovells EU and Competition Newsletter*, August/September 2002, Issue No. 44, pp. 3-4.) 87

Großbacköfen, decision by BGH of 24 October 1995, KVR 17/94.
(Reported in *Wirtschaft und Wettbewerb*, vol. 46, issue 4, 1996,
pp. 318-327).   297

Telenor/Canal+/Nethold, Case 97/251 before the Norwegian competition
authority (not publicly available).   240

United States v. *Aluminium Co. of America* (Alcoa), United States
Circuit Court of Appeals, Second Circuit, 148 F.2d 416; 1945 U.S. App.   263

The Lotus Case (France v. Turkey) (1927) P.C.I.J. Series A, no. 10.   262

INDEX

Accor/Wagons-Lits, 103-105, 139,
147-148, 249

accounts
    see financial year
    conversion into EURO, 154-155
    extraordinary items, 147-148
    intragroup sales, 156-164
    non-EC standards, 144-145
    operating income, 148
    ordinary activities, 146-151
    sales rebates, 151-154
    taxes, 143, 151-154
    unaudited figures, 136-138, 142-
      144
    unreliable accounts, 145-146

acquis communautaire, 226

affect trade between Member States,
4-6, 17, 48, 238, 261, 281, 282-283,
286
    see also real Community
      dimension

AG/Amev, 32, 217-219, 221-222

agent, 127-128, 168-169
    commercial agent, 127
    commission agent, 127
    commissionaire structure, 127
    del credere guarantee, 127
    economic unit, single, 127-128
    insurance underwriting through,
      203, 205
    undisclosed agency, 127

air carrier services
    geographic allocation of turnover,
      179-182

allocation of turnover
    see financial year
    see geographic allocation of
      turnover

American Alcoa 263

anti avoidance
    see circumvention

approach
    (this work), 20-21

*Arjomari-Prioux/Wiggins Teape
Appleton*, 84, 91, 100-103, 138

armament industry, 11
    see also legitimate interests

arms
    see armament industry

asset swap, 54-55

assets, acquisition of
    see part

attributed powers, principle of, 260,
276-277

audit and accounting firms, 106-109
    see also networks of undertakings

banks
    see financial services

see mixed groups

banking directives, 192-193, 194-195, 196-200, 202, 213, 221

banking income, 192-195, 199-200

definition of 'credit institutions and other financial insitutions', 196-198

geographic allocation of turnover, 186, 200-201

mixed groups, 138-139, 213-222

basic rules, 135-164

bid vehicles, 34-40, 249-252

British Airways/Dan Air
    see Dan Air

bus-transport, 182

Campsa, 53-54

Cargill/Vandemoortele, 86

Cargill/Vandemoortele - JV, 86

Carlsberg, 18

Cereol/Continentale Italiana, 149-150

charter flights, 59, 60, 62-63, 176-177

circumvention, 11-12, 43, 65-76, 245-259, 292
    see also veil, lifting the

clarity (aim of the thresholds), 5-6, 287-288

Community territory
    see also effects doctrine
    changes in, 138, 189-191
    geographic allocation of turnover, 138, 189-191

international law, 261-262, 266, 267, 269-270, 273, 275-276

concentration, 4, 7, 46, 246-247, 248

control, 79-109
    see also group
    see also joint control
    see also sole control
    Accor/Wagons-Lits, 103-105
    actual or formal (*de facto* or *de jure*), 80-83, 89-98, 101, 128-133, 215-217
    appoint board, 99-102
    Arjomari-Prioux/Wiggins Teape Appleton, 100-102
    board majority, 99-102
    business assets, 88-89
    capital, 88-89
    change in the quality of, 50-52
    consolidation in accounts, 102
    direct/indirect, 83-84, 110-115
    directors, right to nominate, 97-98, 99-102
    forum shopping, 247-248
    franchising, 105-106
    general meeting, majority in, 84, 91-92, 93-94, 96-98, 99-102
    IFINT/EXOR, 92-95
    management right, 103-105
    mixed groups, 213-220
    network of undertakings, 106-109
    option, 97-98
    personal link, 30, 80-81, 83, 89, 93-95, 97-98
    point in time when control must exist, 84-87
    public undertakings, 128-133
    voting rights, 89-98

conversion into EURO, 21, 154-155
  exchange rates, 154-155

credit institution
  see banks
  see financial services

creeping acquisitions, 73-74

cruises, 182

cut-off date
  (this work), 21
  Community territory, 189
  control, 84-87
  EEA, 243

Dan Air, 9-10, 43, 58-65, 85, 137,
  139, 141, 254-255, 282
  background, 59-60
  discontinuance of activities, 61-63
  interim closure, 62
  judgment, 60-61
  parts-rule, 61-63

demergers, 55-57

de minimis, 279, 286, 287, 288, 289,
  290, 292, 293-295, 295-296
  notice, 289

direct participant
  see undertaking concerned

discontinuance of activities, 61-63
  see also *Dan Air*

Dutch clause
  see referral from Member State to
    Commission

duties
  see taxes

economic unit, single, 106-108, 128,
  128-133, 264

ECSC-Treaty, 11, 146-147

ECU
  see EURO

EEA, 172, 223-224, 294
  see also revision of the Merger
    Regulation
  allocation of jurisdiction, 234-241
  amendment of the Merger
    Regulation, 232-233, 237
  background, 223-225, 228
  basic rules in the EEA
    competition enforcing system,
    225-229
  competition enforcement bodies,
    225-227
  co-operation between ESA and
    the Commission, 227, 236-237,
    241-243
  cut-off date, 243
  EEA dimension, 231, 243-244
  EFTA dimension, 232-234, 243-
    244
  ESA, 225-227, 228, 230, 231,
    232, 233, 234-238, 240, 241-
    243, 243-244
  judicial review, 227-229
  one-stop-shop, 229-231
  referral from Commission to
    Member State, 235-237
  referral from Member State to
    Commission, 238
  splitting the EEA Area, 239-241,
    243-244
  substantive coverage, 224, 241

effects doctrine, 262-266, 267-271,
  272-274, 275

EFTA
  see EEA

enforcement jurisdiction, 262, 270, 274

ESA, 225-227, 228, 230, 231, 232, 233, 234-238, 240, 241-243, 243-244

EURO
  conversion into, 21, 154-155
  exchange rates, 154-155
  references to ECU, vi, 154

European Economic Area
  see EEA

European Surveillance Authority
  see ESA

excise duties
  see taxes

exclusive jurisdiction
  see one-stop-shop

external limit of the Merger Regulation, 261-276

families
  undertaking concerned, 28-30, 32

family foundations
  undertakings concerned, 30, 89

ferry transport, 182

financial holding companies, 198

financial services, 192-222
  see also banks
  see also insurance undertakings
  banking income, 199-200, 200-201

definition of 'credit institutions and other financial institutions', 196-198
definition of insurance undertaking, 202-203
factoring, 197
financial leasing, 197
geographic allocation of turnover, 186, 200-201, 209-212
mixed groups, 138, 213-222
mortgage institutions, 197
venture capital investments, 216

financial year (preceding), 135-146
  see also accounts
  see also *Dan Air*
  acquisitions/divestitures completed since, 138-142
  calendar year, 136
  closure of activities since, 58-65, 254-256
  main rule, 135-136
  more/less than 12 months, 142-144
  new activities since, 58-65, 254-256
  unaudited figures, 136-138, 143
  unreliable accounts, 145-146

fines, 89, 275

forum shopping, 245-259, 283-284
  see also *Dan Air*
  acquisition of sole control through previously reduced or enlarged companies, 58, 254-256
  acquisition through joint venture, 36-37, 249-252
  bid vehicle, 249-252
  escaping two-thirds rule, 253

full-function joint venture, 249-252

group, 248-249

including an extra undertaking concerned, 253

joining more transactions, 257-258

splitting a transaction, 256-257, 292

franchising, 105-106

Gencor, 266-271, 273-274, 275

geographic allocation of turnover, 165-191, 200-201, 209-212

agents (sales through), 168-169

air carriers, 179-182

banking services, 186, 200-201

bus transport, 182

Community territory, 138, 189-191

courier services, 177-178

cruises, 182

direct export, 172-173

ferry transport, 182

financial services, 186, 200-201, 209-212

guiding rules, 172-174

incidence on competition, 170

indirect export, 173-174

insurance services, 186, 209-212

international transport, 177-182

internet, 187-188

long distance cables, 184-185

package holidays, 176-177

place of delivery, 169-171

place of purchaser, 169-171

place where product is used, 171

point of sale criterion, 180-182

postal services, 178-179

products, 169-175

radio, 186-187

railway transport, 182

relevant sale, 167-169, 171

residence of purchaser, 176-177

rights to tangible products, 174-175

sale out of the group, 167-168

sales area, 172

satellite transmission, 184-185

services, 175-188

sourcing purchases through central office, 173

telecom, 183-185

television, 186-187

train transport, 182

transport of persons, 179-182

transport of products, 177-179

German clause

see referral from Commission to Member State

gross premiums, 201-202, 204-209

see also insurance undertakings

amounts received and receivable, 204-205

contracts issued by or on behalf of the insurance undertaking, 205

outgoing reinsurance premiums, 205-206

premiums from the reserves for reimbursement in life insurance, 207-209

taxes, 206-207

group, 23, 77-134

see also control

see also intragroup sales

see also joint control
  agent, 127-128
  antitrust definition of, 78
  control, 79-109
  directive, 78
  economic unit, single, 107-108,
    128, 128-133
  forum shopping, 248-249
  geographic allocation of turnover,
    167-168
  joint control, 117-127, 159-163
  network of undertakings, 106-109
  parent undertaking, 111-114
  public undertaking, 128-133
  related undertakings, 110-134
  sister-undertaking, 114-115
  subsidiary, 110
  undertaking concerned, 110
group directive (9th Company
  Directive), 78

historical background to the Merger
  Regulation, 1-8
holding companies, 198

IFINT/EXOR, 83, 84, 92-95, 102, 125
implementation criterion, 264-266,
  267-270
improving the Regulation's definition
  of Community dimension, 285-296
  market shares, 287, 288-290
  problem in the present definition,
    285-286
  refining present system, 287, 293-
    295
  size of transaction, 287, 291-292

individuals
  undertaking concerned, 28-30, 32
industrial policy, 1-3
insurance undertakings, 201-212
  see also financial services
  amounts received and receivable,
    204-205
  contracts issued by or on behalf
    of, 205
  definition of insurance
    undertaking, 202-203
  geographic allocation of turnover,
    186, 209-212
  gross premiums, 201-202, 204-
    209
  insurance accounts directive, 201-
    209
  insurance brokering, 203, 205
  life insurance, 207-209
  mixed groups, 138, 213-222
  outgoing reinsurance premiums,
    205-206
  premiums from the reserves for
    reimbursement in life insurance,
    207-209
  proposal directive, 201-207
  reinsurance, 202-203, 205-206
  residence, 209-212
  taxes, 206-207
intergroup sales
  see intragroup sales
interim closure, 62
  see also *Dan Air*
international law, public, 144, 247,
  261-262, 266, 267, 269-270, 273,
  275-276, 277
  non-interference, 270

proportionality, 270

international transport
geographic allocation of turnover, 177-182

internet
geographic allocation of turnover, 187-188

intragroup sales, 156-164
joint venture consolidated in the accounts, 159-161
joint venture is not part of the group, 159
joint venture is part of the group, 159-161
joint venture with third party, 161-163
sales between undertakings concerned, 156-158
selling off a part, 163-164

introduction, 1-21

joint acquisition of control
see undertaking concerned
direct and indirect, 34-37
splitting assets, 40-42, 52-54

joint bidding
undertaking concerned, 30-42

joint control, 30-42, 115-127
see also sole control
Commission's approach to, 120-127
going from joint to sole control, 46-48
group members have, 115-116
together with third undertaking, 124-126, 161-163

undertaking concerned is under, 30-42, 120-122
undertakings concerned have (over third undertaking), 117-119, 122-123, 124-127, 159-161

joint venture, 30-42
see also joint control
acquisition by, 23, 34-42
bid vehicles, 34-40, 249-252
change in number of parents, 48-50
consolidation, proportional, 159
creation of, 30-33, 57-58
de minimis, 293-296
dividing assets, 52-54
forum shopping, 249-252
full-function, 30-40
independent, 37-40
reduction in number of parents, 48-50
replacing parent, 50-52
setting up of, 31-33, 57-58
splitting assets, 52-54
undertaking concerned, 30-42
with third party, 124-126, 161-163

jurisdiction
see legislative jurisdiction
see prescriptive jurisdiction
nationality, 262, 271
objective territoriality, 262
subjective territoriality, 262
territoriality, 262, 271

leasing, 196, 197
'legal entity by legal entity'
see mixed groups

legislative jurisdiction
    see prescriptive jurisdiction
legitimate interests (exception), 12, 187
lifting the veil
    see veil
Lonrho
    see Gencor

market shares, 287, 288-290
media, 186-187
Midland Bank, 219-220
mixed groups, 138, 213-222
    see also banks
    see also financial services
    see also insurance undertakings
    AG/Amev, 217-219
    control, 213-220
    evaluation of the mixed group rule, 221-222
    Midland Bank, 219-220
    venture capital investments, 216
mortgageinstitution, 197
multiple notifications, 17-18
munition
    see armament industry

national dimension, 261
national security, 11
network of undertakings, 106-109
    audit and accounting firms, 106-109
    brand, common usage of, 109

Cap Gemini/Ernst & Young, 108-109
Price Waterhouse/Coopers & Lybrand, 106-109
    representation to suppliers and customers, 95, 109
notification
    burden of, 19-20, 140-141, 272, 280, 293-294
    fail safe, 275, 290
    fine for failure to, 89
    short-form, 294
    time limit, 19, 139, 226

one-stop-shop, 6-13
    Community dimension, 13
    EEA, 229-231
    EEA dimension, 231, 243-244
    EFTA dimension, 232-234, 243-244
    exceptions to, 8-12
    explanation of, 6-8
    main rule, 6-8
operating income, 148
    see also accounts
ordinary activities
    see accounts
Orkla, 18

package holidays, 176-177
parent undertaking
    see group
part
    acquisition of, 42-76
    asset swap, 54-55

change in number of parents of a
joint venture, 48-50
client lists, 45
creating a joint venture, 57-58
creeping acquisition, 73-74
Dan Air, 58-65, 141-142
definition, 44-46
demergers, 55-57
dividing jointly controlled assets,
52-54
Hungarian merger control, 44
intra-group sale, 163-164
joint to sole control, 46-48, 254-
256
partial discontinuance of
activities, 60-65, 138-142
partial transfer of activities, 60-65
physical inventory, 45
replacing a shareholder in a joint
venture, 50-52
setting up a joint venture, 57-58
warrants, 45
person
natural persons, 28-30
place of transaction, 33
prescriptive jurisdiction, 262, 270, 274
procedure
basic overview of (Commission),
19-20
proportionality, 270, 276-281
secondary legislation, 280-281
public international law
see international law, public
public undertakings, 128-133
guiding principles, 129-130, 132-
133

qualified effects, criterion of
see effects doctrine

radio
geograhic allocation of turnover,
186-187
railway transport, 182
real Community dimension, 20-21,
260-284, 285-296
affect trade between Member
States, 261
national dimension, 260-261
referral from Commission to Member
State (German clause)
background, 8
EEA, 235-237
examples, 8-9
referral from Member State to
Commission (Dutch clause)
background, 8-9
EEA, 238
examples, 9-10
related undertakings, 110-134
see also group
joint control, 117-127
parent, 111-114
sister undertaking, 114-115
subsidiary, 110
relevant sale, 167-169
see also intragroup sales
see also geographic allocation of
turnover
sale by agent, 168-169
sale out of the group, 167-168

residence
    geographic allocation of turnover,
      176-177, 209-212
    insurance, 209-212
    legal persons (insurance), 210-
      212
    natural persons (insurance), 210-
      212
revision of the Merger Regulation, v,
    2-3, 14, 15-17, 192-193, 194-195,
    232-233, 237, 282

sales rebates, 151-154

satellite systems, 184-185, 272-273

security, national
    see armament industry

semi-fund management companies,
    221-222
    see also mixed groups

services
    geographic allocation of turnover
      derived from, 175-188

single economic unit, 107-108, 128,
    128-133, 264

sister undertaking
    see group

sole control, 46-48, 52-54
    see also joint control
    acquisition of (forum shopping),
      58, 254-256

Solvay-Laporte/Interox, 12, 53-54

Spies Rejser, 221-222

staggered transactions, 65-76, 292
    calculating time limit, 74-75

circumvention, 65-71
creeping acquisitions, 73-74
what transactions, 68-71
when are the parties 'the same',
    71-73
when must the transaction be
    examined, 75-76

state aid, 149-151

state-owned undertakings
    see public undertakings

structure
    (this work), 21

subsidiarity, 276-281

subsidiary
    see group

substantive scope of the EC Treaty,
    261

swapping assets
    see asset swap

taxes, 143, 151-154, 206-207
    insurance premiums, 206-207

television
    geographic allocation of turnover,
      186-187

territoriality principle
    see effects doctrine

territory
    see Community territory

third undertaking
    control together with, 124-126,
      161-163

thresholds, 14-18

time, point in when control must exist, 84-87, 138
 date of notification, 84-86
 date when transaction is to take place, 84-87
 event triggering notification, 84-87
 late notification, 86
 re-examination following annulment judgment, 87
 re-examination by Member State competition authority, 87

time limit
 calculation of two-year (staggered transactions), 74-75
 notification, 19, 139, 226

transport services
 geographic allocation of turnover, 177-182

turnover thresholds
 see thresholds

ultra vires
 see vires

unaudited accounts, 136-138, 141

undertaking concerned, 22-76
 see also group
 bid vehicles, 38-40
 definition, 24-30
 direct participant, 24-26
 families, 28-30, 32
 family foundations, 30, 89
 full function joint venture, 30-42
 inclusion in group, 110
 individuals, 28-30, 32
 joint bidding, 30-42
 joint to sole control, 46-48
 part, 42-76
 sole to joint control, 32-33
 two-thirds threshold, 26-28, 145, 253

unreliable accounts, 145-146

Valinox/Timet, 86, 90, 95-98

VAT
 see taxes

veil, lifting the, 29-30, 34, 35-36, 38-40, 113
 see also circumvention

venture capital investments, 216

vertical integration
 see intragroup sales

vires, 261-262, 275-276, 276-277, 283, 286

voting rights
 control, 89-98

war material
 see armament industry

Wood Pulp, 263-266, 267-268, 269

EUROPEAN MONOGRAPHS

1. Lammy Betten (ed.), *The Future of European Social Policy* (second and revised edition, 1991).
2. J.M.E. Loman, K.J.M. Mortelmans, H.H.G. Post, J.S. Watson, *Culture and Community Law: Before and after Maastricht* (1992).
3. Prof. Dr. J.A.E. Vervaele, *Fraud Against the Community: The Need for European Fraud Legislation* (1992).
4. P. Rawortli, *The Legislative Process in the European Community* (1993).
5. J. Stuyck, *Financial and Monetary Integration in the European Economic Community* (1993).
6. J.H.V. Stuyck, A.J. Vossestein (eds.), *State Entrepreneurship, National Monopolies and European Community Law* (1993).
7. J. Stuyck, A. Looijestijn-Clearie (eds.), *The European Economic Area EC-EFTA* (1994).
8. R.B. Bouterse, *Competition and Integration – What Goals Count?* (1994).
9. R. Barents, *The Agricultural Law of the EC* (1994).
10. Nicholas Emiliou, *The Principle of Proportionality in European Law: A Comparative Study* (1996).
11. Eivind Smith, *National Parliaments as Cornerstones of European Integration* (1996).
12. Jan H. Jans, *European Environmental Law* (1996).
13. Siofra O'Leary, *The Evolving Concept of Community Citizenship: From the Free Movement of Persons to Union Citizenship* (1996).
14. Laurence Gormley (ed.), *Current and Future Perspectives on EC Competition Law* (1997).
15. Simone White, *Protection of the Financial Interests of the European Communities: The Fight against Fraud and Corruption* (1998).
16. Morten P. Broberg, *The European Commission's Jurisdiction to Scrutinise Mergers*, second edition (2003).
17. Doris Hildebrand, *The Role of Economic Analysis in the EC Competition Rules*, second edition (2002).
18. Christof R.A. Swaak, *European Community Law and the Automobile Industry* (1999).
19. Dorthe Dahlgaard Dingel, *Public Procurement. A Harmonization of the National Judicial Review of the Application of European Community Law* (1999).
20. J.A.E. Vervaele (ed.) *Compliance and Enforcement of European Community Law* (1999).
21. Martin Trybus, *European Defence Procurement Law: International and National Procurement Systems as Models for a Liberalised Defence Procurement Market in Europe* (1999).
22. Helen Staples, *The Legal Status of Third Country Nationals Resident in the European Union* (1999).
23. Damien Geradin (ed.) *The Liberalization of State Monopolies in the European Union and Beyond* (2000).
24. Katja Heede, *European Ombudsman: Redress and Control at Union Level* (2000).
25. Ulf Bernitz, Joakim Nergelius (eds.) *General Principles of European Community Law* (2000).
26. Michaela Drahos, *Convergence of Competition Laws and Policies in the European Community* (2001).

27. Damien Geradin (ed.), *The Liberalization of Electricity and Natural Gas in the European Union* (2001).
28. Gisella Gori, *Towards an EU Right to Education* (2001).
29. Brendan P.G. Smith, *Constitution Building in the European Union* (2002).
30. Friedl Weiss, Frank Wooldridge, *Free Movement of Persons within the European Community* (2002).
31. Ingrid Boccardi, *Europe and Refugees: Towards an EU Asylum Policy* (2002).
32. John Vervaele, André Klip (eds.), *European Cooperation between Tax, Customs and Judicial Authorities* (2002).
33. Wouter P.J. Wils, *The Optimal Enforcement of EC Antitrust Law: Essays in Law and Economics* (2002).
34. Damien Geradin (ed.), *The Liberalization of Postal Services in the European Union* (2002).
35. Nick Bernard, *Multilevel Governance in the European Union* (2002).
36. Jill Wakefield, *Judicial Protection through the Use of Article 288(2)EC* (2002).
37. Sebastiaan Princen, *EU Regulation and Transatlantic Trade* (2002).
38. Amaryllis Verhoeven, *The European Union in Search of a Democratic and Constitutional Theory* (2002).
39. Paul Torremans, *Cross Border Insolvencies in EU, English and Belgian Law* (2002).
40. Malcolm Anderson, Joanna Apap (eds.), *Police and Justice Co-operation and the New European Borders* (2002).
41. Christin M. Forstinger, *Takeover Law in the EU and the USA: A Comparative Analysis* (2002).
42. Antonio Bavasso, *Communications in EU Antitrust Law: Market Power and Public Interest* (2003).
43. Fiona Wishlade, *Regional State Aid and Competition Policy* (2003).
44. Gareth Davies, *Nationality Discrimination in the European Internal Market* (2003).